中国社会科学院—格鲁吉亚理工大学：中国研究中心
CASS-GTU: RESEARCH INSTITUTE OF CHINA STUDIES

中国社会科学院—乌克兰国立敖德萨海事大学：中国研究中心
CASS-ONMU: CENTER OF CHINA STUDIES

中国社会科学院—乌克兰基辅格里琴科大学：中国研究中心
CHINESE ACADEMY OF SOCIAL SCIENCES–BORYS GRINCHENKO KYIV UNIVERSITY: CENTER OF CHINA STUDIES

丝路发展与美美与共

The Development of Silk Road and a Diversified and Harmonious World

张翼　马峰　等著
Zhang Yi　Ma Feng　et al.

中国社会科学出版社

图书在版编目（CIP）数据

丝路发展与美美与共 / 张翼等著 . —北京：中国社会科学出版社，2022.7
ISBN 978 – 7 – 5227 – 0197 – 4

Ⅰ.①丝⋯　Ⅱ.①张⋯　Ⅲ.①社会发展—研究—中国　Ⅳ.①D668

中国版本图书馆 CIP 数据核字（2022）第 080421 号

出 版 人	赵剑英
责任编辑	刘凯琳　侯聪睿
责任校对	芦　苇
责任印制	王　超

出　　版	中国社会科学出版社
社　　址	北京鼓楼西大街甲 158 号
邮　　编	100720
网　　址	http://www.csspw.cn
发 行 部	010 – 84083685
门 市 部	010 – 84029450
经　　销	新华书店及其他书店
印刷装订	北京君升印刷有限公司
版　　次	2022 年 7 月第 1 版
印　　次	2022 年 7 月第 1 次印刷
开　　本	710×1000　1/16
印　　张	36.25
字　　数	585 千字
定　　价	198.00 元

凡购买中国社会科学出版社图书，如有质量问题请与本社营销中心联系调换
电话：010 – 84083683
版权所有　侵权必究

前　　言

《丝路发展与美美与共》是在中国社会科学院系列海外中国研究中心框架下，由中国社会科学院学者与白俄罗斯、乌克兰、格鲁吉亚有关科研机构学者共同完成的一部高质量的合作研究成果。中国研究中心的合作机制为成果的完成提供了高质量的保障。全书聚焦中国社会发展经验、中国经济发展经验、读懂中国社会发展、"一带一路"倡议与全球发展倡议，是中外学者合作研究的重要成果载体和体现，彰显了中国与有关国家共建丝绸之路，美美与共，共享发展繁荣与进步的主旨。

在全面建成小康社会，开启全面建设社会主义现代化国家新征程的关键时刻，今年下半年，我们将召开中国共产党第二十次全国代表大会，描绘下一个阶段中国发展蓝图。我们党领导人民不仅创造了世所罕见的经济快速发展和社会长期稳定两大奇迹，而且成功走出了中国式现代化道路，创造了人类文明新形态。这些前无古人的创举，破解了人类社会发展的诸多难题，拓展了发展中国家走向现代化的途径，为人类对更好社会制度的探索提供了中国方案。

本书的出版有利于进一步提高海外中国学研究和发展，有利于增进有关国家学界进一步理解中国、读懂中国，有利于进一步增强"一带一路"民心相通、学术交流与合作，实现"丝路发展与美美与共"的思想境界，为沿线国家和人民更好地感知中国、读懂中国、理解中国提供权威信息来源，这本书也是以中国为关照、以时代为关照，建构中国自主的知识体系为鞭策的体现。

著者

二零二二年六月

Preface

The Development of Silk Road and a Diversified and Harmonious World is a high-quality cooperative research achievement jointly completed by scholars of the Chinese Academy of Social Sciences and scholars of relevant scientific research institutions in Belarus, Ukraine and Georgia under the framework of a series of overseas Center of China Studies of the Chinese Academy of Social Sciences.

The cooperation mechanism of Center of China Studies provides a high-quality guarantee for the research result. The book focuses on experiences of social development of China, experiences of economic development of China, understanding China's social development, Belt and Road Initiative and global development initiatives. It is an important carrier and embodiment of the cooperative research of Chinese and foreign scholars, and highlights the theme that China and relevant countries together build the Silk Road, as well as a diversified and harmonious world, and sharing development, prosperity and progress.

At the critical moment of building a moderately prosperous society in all respects and starting a new journey of building a modern socialist country in an all-round way, in the second half of this year, we will hold the 20th National Congress of the Communist Party of China to draw a blueprint for China's development in the next stage.

Under the leadership of CPC, the people have not only created the two miracles of rapid economic development and long-term social stability that are rare in the world, but also successfully walked out of the Chinese path of modernization and created a new form of human civilization. These unprecedented initiatives have solved many problems in the development of human society, expanded the ways for developing countries to move towards modernization, and provided a Chinese plan for mankind to explore a better social system.

The publication of this book is conducive to further improving the research and development of overseas China studies, promoting the academic circles of relevant countries to further understand China, further enhancing the people to people connection, academic exchanges and cooperation of the Belt and Road, realizing the ideological realm of "The Development of Silk Road and a Diversified and Harmonious World", and providing authoritative information sources for countries and people along the Belt and Road to better perceive and understand China. This book is also a reflection of the construction of China's independent knowledge system with the care of China and the times.

Authors
June, 2022

目 录

第一篇 中国社会发展经验

全面建成小康社会视野下的社区转型与社区治理效能
　改进 …………………………………………………… 张　翼（3）
中国发展理念的演化与社会变迁 ………………… 欧阳向英（24）
中国居家养老服务供给对老年人满意度影响 ……… 孙兆阳（37）
"十四五"时期中国青年社会融入与社会参与 ……… 马　峰（54）

第二篇 中国经济发展经验

新发展理念与中国经济增长 …………………………… 娄　峰（69）
中国数字贸易发展的经济效应、制约因素与推进方略 …… 刘洪愧（81）
中国人口老龄化背景下医保基金的可持续发展 …… 戈艳霞（107）

第三篇 读懂中国社会发展

中国保险业发展与社会
　变迁…… Sergii Rudenko　Svitlana Glovatska　Olga Shukovilova（125）
中国社会变革的里程碑：高等教育大众化与
　国际化 ……………………………… Dzmitry Smaliakou（132）
中国中产阶层的发展及其对可持续发展的影响 …… Ivan Semenist（146）

中国社会发展与知识产权保护

意义 …… Svitlana Glovatska Alina Litvinenko Viktoria Baderko（154）

第四篇 "一带一路"倡议与全球发展倡议

全球发展倡议：社会现代化的意义和目标 …… Anatoly Lazarevich（167）
"一带一路"倡议与欧亚经济联盟对接合作 ………………… 高 媛（178）
"一带一路"倡议与中乌人文

交流 ………………… Olena Shypotilova Svitlana Glovatska（193）
"一带一路"倡议：中格教育交往三十年回顾及深化 …… 卢雨菁（203）
"一带一路"倡议：深化中格经济合作 ………… Tamar Patashuri（219）

Content

Chapter 1 China's Social Development Experience

Community Transformation and Improvement of Community Governance
　Efficiency from the Perspective of Building a Moderately Prosperous
　Society in All Respects ………………………………………… Zhang Yi（245）
Evolution of Development Concepts and Social Changes in
　China ……………………………………………… Ouyang Xiangying（277）
The Influence of China's Home-Based Old-Age Care Service
　Supply on the Elderly's Satisfaction ………………… Sun Zhaoyang（296）
Chinese Youth's Social Integration and Social Participation
　During the 14th Five-Year Plan Period …………………… Ma Feng（320）

Chapter 2 China's Economic Development Experience

New Development Philosophy and China's Economic
　Growth ……………………………………………………… Lou Feng（343）
The Economic Benefits, Constraints and Promoting Strategies
　of China's Digital Trade Development ………………… Liu Hongkui（360）
Study on Sustainable Development of the Medical and Health
　Care Insurance Fund under the Background of China's Population
　Aging ……………………………………………………… Ge Yanxia（395）

Chapter 3 Understanding China's Social Development

Insurance and Social Changes in
  China ...... Sergii Rudenko, Svitlana Glovatska, Olga Shukovilova (419)
Milestones of China's Social Change: Massification and
  Internationalization of Higher Education .... Dzmitry Smaliakou (428)
Middle-Class Development in China and Its Influence for
  Sustainable Development .... Ivan Semenist (445)
Social Development of China and the Significance of Intellectual
  Property ...... Svitlana Glovatska, Alina Litvinenko, Viktoria Baderko (455)

Chapter 4 Belt and Road Initiative and Global Development Initiatives

Global Development Initiatives: The Significance and Objectives
  of Social Modernization .... Anatoly Lazarevich (469)
Cooperation Between Belt and Road Initiative and Eurasian
  Economic Union .... Gao Yuan (485)
Belt and Road Initiative and Humanistic Exchange Between
  China and Ukraine .... Olena Shypotilova, Svitlana Glovatska (508)
Belt and Road Initiative: The Retrospect of the Past 30 Years and
  Deepening of Education Cooperation Between China
  and Georgia .... Lu Yujing (521)
Belt and Road Initiative: Deepening Economic Collaboration
  Between Georgia and China .... Tamar Patashuri (544)

第一篇

中国社会发展经验

全面建成小康社会视野下的社区转型与社区治理效能改进[*]

张 翼[**]

全面建成小康社会的过程，既是定居化社会向迁居化社会的转型过程，也是熟人社区向陌生人社区转型和社区治理结构从"单位办社会"向"居委会办社会"转型的过程。社区的实体结构与治理结构发生了重大变化，在政府以组织建设从供给侧自上而下形塑社区"理想型"的同时，居民也通过需求侧的"民主协商"建构其预期的"理想型"。社区以居委会为主体，通过与环境互动形成自身的利益结构。这些因素的动态博弈不断形塑社区的"营造"动力，使之呈现出治理方式的科层化、社区类型的多元化、社区居民的异质化、治理经费的财政化等特征，形成了"强他治"与"弱自治"。为平衡各方需求，就需要在强调组织化和秩序化的同时，较好地平衡"他治"与"自治"力量，培植"社会协同"和"民主协商"参与渠道，尽快建成"社区办社会"的治理格局，建设与新发展阶段相适应的共建共治共享治理体系。

社区作为人类生活的基层单元，是一个不断被理论与实践所建构的对象。在滕尼斯那里，社区是农业社会的产物，指一定地域范围内相对固定的居民形成的、深受其文化规范宗教影响的、与某种生产和社会交

---

[*] 本文原发表于《社会学研究》2020 年第 6 期，内容略有改动。
[**] 张翼，研究员，中国社会科学院社会发展战略研究院院长。

往方式密切联系的、具有大致相同的社会心理基础的人类生活共同体。① 在工业化过程中，其特征在与社会的比较中得到凸显。在定居化社会，社区居民会经由长期互动而形成以情感和道德规范为调节手段的、具有高度认同感的、服从于传统权威的人际交往关系。社会是工商业时代的产物，在社会中形成的是阶段性的、理性的、以契约为基础的、服从于法律契约的、以正式组织为团体的人际关系。

美国社会学的芝加哥学派在帕克的带领下发扬光大了社区研究，将农业社会的社区推进到工业社会，并在城市化的意义上完善了社区理论，区别了不同社区的空间分布特征，论证了都市结构、空间距离、种族歧视、文化同化、社会隔离与区位生态形成之间的复杂关系。吴文藻强化了中国的本土化社区研究。作为吴文藻的学生，费孝通等人在翻译帕克的论文时，将英文的"community"第一次翻译为"社区"。这个概念既可以泛指工业社区、农业社区、商业社区，也可以专指村落社区。其虽然含有或明确或相对模糊的地域范围意义，却体现着不同的生产生活方式，形塑着居民对社区的认同感。因此，来自于学术研究意义的社区概念，是一个以熟人社会和亲缘关系为纽带的情感性社会共同体，这个共同体既具有地缘关系的互助共同体特征，也具有血缘关系的互助共同体特征②。当然，费孝通之所以对社区如此挂怀，其中最主要的原因是，社区研究是认识中国社会的最理想和合适的方式③。作为学术概念的社区，在改革开放之后，经由社会学恢复重建而突破理论研究视域，逐步转变为城市的各个区级政府或街道办事处"指导"之下的基层自治组织，并取代了计划经济时期的居民区概念，将居民委员会改造为社区居民委员会，形成了管理与服务意义的科层特征，实现了社区的实体性与社区居

---

① 在前农业社会即狩猎社会或牧业社会中，人类逐水草而居，处于不断迁移的状态，很难形成社区，也不可能划定社区与社区之间的边界。
② 费孝通：《中国现代化对城市社区建设的再思考》，《江苏社会科学》2001 年第 1 期。
③ 张浩：《从"各美其美"到"美美与共"——费孝通看梁漱溟乡村建设主张》，《社会学研究》2019 年第 5 期。

委会的科层性的密切结合。① 在社区之下，又依照道路、街巷、物业楼宇等小区分布，划分出一定数量的网格，构建出网格化管理或网格化治理的基层社会格局。② 因此，类行政区域意义的社区或由"居委会"治理的社区就在"社区建设"中被赋予了双重属性，既包含了社会学经典定义的社区意义，也体现着行政管理取向的社区内涵，在发展其自治能力的同时，也生成了具有清晰边界的他治特征。③ 正如费孝通所说，"城市社区管理的这种行政体制完全是中国式的"④。

因此，城市基层社会的治理越来越依托社区居委会来进行。⑤ 在"全面建设小康社会"和"全面建成小康社会"的过程中，在社会管理逐渐转型为社会治理的过程中，为顺应基层社会构成的结构变迁，社区管理也随之转型为社区治理，并在基层发挥秩序化与服务供给的双重职能。中国城市社会居民区意义的社区概念，与基于西方背景形成和演化的社

---

① 在社区研究中，学界也有人提出过社区的"脱域化"问题，认为基于一定区域并具有文化或价值认同感的社区在历史上并不普遍，仅有的也在工业化影响下消失殆尽。

② 虽然学术研究将认同分类为地域性社区（locality-based community）认同和关系性社区（relational community）认同，但这两者经常交织在一起。地域给定的是社区的边界，关系关注的是基于地域而形成的交往结构。

③ 滕尼斯所说的"社区"，更具有共同体的意义，所以很多人直接将其翻译为共同体，指的是通过血缘关系、邻里关系和朋友关系建立的为社会记忆、习惯、家族制度等规范、生活于一定地域之上的相对固定的有机人群组合。学术意义上的"社区"的基本定义就是费孝通所说的熟人社会和礼俗社会意义的社区。这种社区在企业家院、党政机关单位大院、事业单位居住区大院中仍然存在。但在商品房形成的"社区"或是房改房"社区"中，此类社区的特征部分消失，为滕尼斯所定义的社会转变为现实社会中的社区，为涂尔干所说的机械团结社区转变为有机团结社区。所以，传统社区正在为工业化社会的社区所改造，并使其显示出市场化社区和行政化社区的特征。即使是那些典型的机关家属院与企业家属院，也在市场化的作用下，通过住房买卖与住房出租等各种交易形成了陌生人社会对熟人社会的嵌入式解构特征。

④ 费孝通：《中国现代化对城市社区建设的再思考》，《江苏社会科学》2001年第1期。

⑤ "基层社会的治理"与"基层的社会治理"是两个含义不同的概念，虽然在很多情况下学者们不加区分地解读"基层社会治理"的含义，但"基层社会"仍然处于理论建构之中，而"基层的社会治理"则有相对明确的含义。党的十七大以来，"基层群众自治制度"成为中国的一项基本政治制度，特指行政村居民和社区居民这两个基层"群众"的自治。因此，"基层社会治理"所说的自治德治法治等针对的是"基层的社会治理"。党的十九届四中全会"决定"所指的"构建基层社会治理新格局"的本意，也应该是"构建基层的社会治理新格局"，而不应该是"构建基层社会的治理新格局"。因为其中涉及的"自治"的表述只能在行政村与城市社区层面自治。

区概念存在重大区别。在这种情况下,不能简单以学术传统中的社区理论去指导行政治理意义上的社区建设,而应以社会发展与社会变迁的客观现实为基础,重新认识城市居民区的现代化过程,赋予社区居民参与社区自治的法治渠道。新冠肺炎疫情的防控中,一个重要经验就是社区的组织化有效承担了防控任务,监测了人口流动轨迹,阻断了传染源,隔离了疑似病例,输入了心理辅导渠道,减少了各种损失,迅速恢复了生活秩序,推进了复产复工复学进度,迎来了积极向好的发展局面,显示了应急化时期中国式社区治理的巨大优势,并在全面建成小康社会之后的新征程中继续加快推进市域社会治理的制度创新与顶层设计,推进社会治理和服务重心继续向基层下移,使社区成为国家治理与社会治理的重要基础。唯有如此,才能在"十四五"时期更好地释放治理效能,与时俱进地提高社区治理的现代化水平。

一 从"单位办社会"到"居委会办社会":传统"社区"转型为"社会社区"

在改革开放以来整个小康社会的建成过程中,随着中国从计划经济向市场经济的转型,原来依靠户籍制度建立的定居化社会也迅速转变为迁居化社会,这使人口流动成为常态并呼唤形成新型城镇化过程的常住人口治理模式。在这种历时变化中,城市的基层社会——社区的结构发生了重大转型,具体表现为以下几点。

第一,基层社会组织方式从单位制下的"街居制"和"家属院制"转变为"社区制","单位办社会"转型为"居委会办社会"。中国在20世纪50年代初期实施的街道—居委会管理模式,在20世纪90年代以后转型为街道—社区制管理模式。社区居委会既是基层社会的自治组织,也是体现政府和街道意志的他治组织。居委会下的各个居民小组及其楼宇成为城市生活的基本单元。在单位制逐步解体过程中,"单位办社会"现象通过国有企业的改制逐渐让位于市场,使"单位人"转变为"社会人"和"市场人"。又因市场缺少类似组织而不能完全承接企业所办社会之职能,而不得不寻找新的代理机构。在改革过程中,街道与居委会逐渐被赋予承接管理区域内"单位办社会"的职能,转变为集管理与服务为一体的多功能组织,形成了中国特色的基层"居委会办社会"现象。[①] 在城市社会的不平衡发展中,因不同小区居民的收入不同、物业环境不同、居民对其生活质量的预期不同,其对社区服务的要求也不同,因而在回应居民需求中成长起来的各个社区的管理方式与能力也不同。即使在同一社区,不同物业小区的服务质量与能力也存在重大区别。

与此同时,有些城市撤销了街道这个政府的派出机构,而将社区工作直接归属于区级政府的"指导"之下,将街居制转变为"区政府—社区制"。还有些城市在党建引领下,直接将社区发展与社区治理职能划归各级党委,并在党委部门专门成立"社区发展治理委员会",以"党委—社区制"应对日益变化的治理要求。在这个意义上,社区的自治功能和他治功能都具有强化趋势。"居委会办社会"的背后,体现着"政府办社会"或者"党委办社会"的特征——没有党政相关部门的组织支持与财政支持,社区难以完成当前所承担的许多重要职责[②]。在政府履行社会管理职能过程中,城市的各个社区应不同部门的渠道性要求而建立了相应的承接机构,形成"一站式"的"办事大厅",将少则20多个、多则60多个承接组织齐集于居委会主任或支部书记的领导之下。为加强组织效力,居委会及其所属机构的科层化成为必然。有些街道为其社区党支部/党委书记或居委会主任或其他服务机构负责人赋予了科级或类似行政级别,使其"能够名正言顺"地领导"居委会办社会"的各项工作。虽然社区也登记了很多自发生成的社会组织,但因其缺少必要的资金支持,也缺少成熟的组织管理经验而无力发挥应有的治理作用。社会组织越弱,"居委会办社会"的特征就越强。如果说"街道办事处"是政府的派出机

[①] 国有企业改制与非盈利职能剥离、大批职工下岗失业、农民工向城市流动、非公经济崛起、居民生活区重建、城市房地产市场向周边地区开拓等都在"单位办社会"消解之后呼唤新的功能替代实体。

[②] 张翼:《社会转型与社会治理格局的创新》,《中国社会科学评价》2019年第1期。

构,那么,社区居委会则更像是政府的基层延伸。① 社区居委会的科层化,更多体现的是其行政化②。正因如此,费孝通才说,"居委会作为街道办事处的工作基础,在法律上是一种自治性群众组织,但在实践中执行街道行政机构下达的各项具体任务,人们称它为一种半官方的群众组织"③。

第二,在社区类型多元化的同时,社区内部居民也从同质化向异质化转型。在城市扩张过程中,社区居委会由原居委会、新建居民小区社区居委会、机关事业单位家属区、大型企业家属区、城中村等物业小区、棚户区小区组成。④ 社区由此可以分为城市社区、工矿社区、农村社区和城乡结合部社区。⑤ 在社区类型多元化的同时,社区内部居民构成也日益多元化。土地开发的碎片化、住房的金融化与住房市场的级差地租构成将不同支付能力的居民住房选择结构化为高档商品房小区、一般商品房小区、工矿小区和老旧小区等,并以消费等级将居民"小区化"为不同的阶层——社会阶层被明确地标签化和地域化了。小区的围墙形成了社区内的隔离,这种隔离既是市场配置的结果,也是社区内部不同小区居民选择的结果。同一社区内部小区之间的阶层差距越大,较高阶层小区居民的围墙需求与安全意识就越强烈。高档小区对中低档小区的隔离需要感越高,社区内部不同小区居民的融合难度就越大。于是,原有社区

---

① 社区的科层性和行政性,由其组建的基本原则所决定。《中华人民共和国城市居民委员会组织法》明确规定,"不设区的市、市辖区的人民政府或者它的派出机关对居民委员会的工作给予指导、支持和帮助。居民委员会协助不设区的市、市辖区的人民政府或者它的派出机关开展工作"。

② 李友梅:《基层社区组织的实际生活方式——对上海康健社区实地调查的初步认识》,《社会学研究》2002 年第 4 期。

③ 费孝通:《中国现代化对城市社区建设的再思考》,《江苏社会科学》2001 年第 1 期。

④ 李国庆:《棚户区改造与新型社区建设——四种低收入者住区的比较研究》,《社会学研究》2019 年第 5 期。

⑤ 中国农村的巨大变化,也解构了原有传统农村社区形态。非农化扩大了社区的地域边界,改变了社区居民的生产与交往方式,同时,也通过外来农业企业的进入改变了农村居民的同质结构。

生活的同类化转变为社区内部异质性居民的互嵌化。[①] 与此同时，社区人口的户籍化转变为流动过程的户籍人口与非户籍人口的混居化，社区人口的熟人化、亲缘化转变为业缘化和陌生人化，社区的居民化转化为社区的职业化和市场化。传统社区经常发生的面对面的、具有情感联系的街坊邻居型人际交往随之转变为缺少互动的、通过市场购买服务关系的市场交换性交往。在很大程度上，契约关系代替了伦理关系成为治理的重要基础，具有行政区划意义的社区更多表现为滕尼斯所说的"社会"特征。[②] 在社区行政化过程中，城中村的村民，因为路径依赖的利益配置关系而分化为"一社两治"一个社区两种治理模式和"一家两制"一个家庭两种成员归属——部分家庭成员选择城市居民制，部分家庭成员选择农村居民制的身份结构。依照土地城镇化过程中居民的自愿选择，愿意转变为城市户口的居民被划归社区居委会，而愿意保留农村户籍的居民仍然置于村民委员会。为节约治理成本，有些城中村形成了"一套人马两块牌子"的建制模式，有些城中村则干脆"双轨并行"，还有一些城中村形成了"社区制"和"经济组织制"两个不同类型的治理主体——以居委会管理流动人口，以经济组织管理本村或本居委会人口。在个人与家庭的利益偏好选择中，城市政府设计出结构化整合渠道，诱引个人和家庭适应政府、社会与市场。因此，"社区"转型为"社会"的过程与"单位办社会"转型为"居委会办社会"的过程是同步发生的。

第三，社区生活的同质化转型为多样化和个性化。城镇化与城镇常住人口的增加提升了社区的人口密度，造成高楼大厦内居民文化需求、宗教信仰、阶层归属以及其他生活方式的多元化。在日常生活中，居民对市场的依赖程度远远大于其对社区居委会和小区物业管理公司的依赖程度。市场化需求的发育及其细分的类型化服务，打破了社区的区划边

---

① 即使是农村社区，也在工业化过程中日渐异质化，比如费孝通在《江村经济》中就论述过乡土中国的农工商混合经济模式，详见费孝通《江村经济》，上海世纪出版集团、上海人民出版社2007年版。

② 李友梅曾经指出，"城市基层社区生活越来越显露出它的社会性"，参见李友梅《基层社区组织的实际生活方式——对上海康健社区实地调查的初步认识》，《社会学研究》2002年第4期。

界。各个物业小区为维护环境、安保以及确保幼儿园、体育活动设施等集体物品的安全性，都在日益强化边界的隔离性和管理的封闭性。互联网、大数据、人脸识别的使用不是冲破物业小区的围墙，而是为小区的身份管理提供了强有力的"全景式"技术支持。社区居民在物业小区内部，易于形成基于业主而进行的利益互动。在居民的陌生人化过程中，居民对小区的认同强于对社区的认同。在高档小区、中档小区和低档小区等分类逐渐细化、封闭性管理日益强化的背景下，社区工作人员只能靠政府的权力配置才能进入小区。小区的封闭性与社区的进入性之间产生了一定程度的张力，即使在同一开发商开发的小区中，也经常将商品房小区和回迁房小区隔离开来。尽管只有一墙之隔，但居民的阶层归属及其获得的物业服务质量差别较大。

第四，社区的"在地化"获益权转型为"在地化"与"非在地化"并存的获益权。在城镇化过程中，社区的集体资产或集体所有制改制过程中遗留的村委会和居委会所属产权资产均转型为新的社区经济组织，其收入的很大一部分具有利益获致的再分配性质。分配不当会影响社区居民的认同感。原社区成员以社区户籍身份为资格形成的剩余索取权只能由原居民继承。为保证剩余索取权的延续，相当一部分城市基层社区以及绝大多数经由城镇土地扩张而形成的城中村社区既建立了社区经济组织比如公司，也设立了社区居委会，形成治理的"双轨并行"格局。但社区经济组织的权力与财力远远大于社区居委会。

在市场化过程中，城市政府以户籍为基础建立的社区治理体系已不能适应高度迁居化社会的需要。为更好地实现"居委会办社会"职能，国家通过对居民委员会的一系列法治化改造，建构了当前社区组织的自治性科层化模式，以适应社区变迁后新结构的治理需要。不管是1954—1989年的《城市居民委员会组织条例》，还是自1990年之后实施的《中华人民共和国城市居民委员会组织法》，都规定"居委会"或"社区居委会"属于基层自治组织，组成人员包括主任、副主任和委员由本居住地区全体有选举权的居民或每户派代表选举产生，1954—1989年任期1年，

1990—2017 年任期 3 年，2018 年后每届任期 5 年并可连选连任。① 但在实际执行过程中，很多社区组成人员属区政府或街道办事处的聘任人员，个别社区书记或主任可在工作一定期限后经合规程序转型为事业编制人员。这些聘任人员可能是本城市户籍居民，但却不是本社区户籍居民。绝大多数地区不允许流动人口参与应聘。在特大城市和超大城市的很多社区，流动人口居民数量大大超过本地户籍居民数量，但流动人口既无权参与社区管理工作，也无权应聘社区管理人员。因此，社区治理就变相表现为本城市户籍居民对流动人口居民的治理、表现为少数本地户籍居民对多数非本地户籍居民的治理。这与《中华人民共和国城市居民委员会组织法》的规定不完全一致。与实际操作矛盾的是，绝大多数物业管理公司的组成人员主要是来自外地的流动人口，而非本地户籍人口。他们既不熟悉区域内的社区治理结构，也不熟悉小区的居民组成状况，形成了典型的"陌生人治理"。

上面千条线，下面一根针。地方政府各个部门的社会建设任务都要通过社区居委会来落实。在政府以其对社区建构的"理想型"指导社区改造其"现实型"的过程中，社区居委会逐步转型为集行政、自治和市场职能为一体的综合体。社区居委会既需要自上而下地完成党委、政府等经由街道安排的行政工作，也需要满足区域内的居民诉求。在行政职能与服务职能的不断扩充中，居委会组成人员的有限性与其所承担职能的无限性之间的矛盾，迫使其逐渐将服务职能与行政职能加以分化，以行政性的社区居委会对接街道，以服务化的各种"站""所"对接居民服务需求，形成名称多样的党群服务中心、社区服务中心、家政服务中心、社工服务站、社区服务站等，并通过各种标准化建设扩充了社区公共活

---

① 关于社区居委会的组织建构，在 1989 年颁布的《中华人民共和国城市居民委员会组织法》（2018 年颁布了新的修正版）、2000 年 11 月《中共中央办公厅、国务院办公厅关于转发〈民政部关于在全国推进城市社区建设的意见〉的通知》、2010 年 11 月中共中央办公厅、国务院办公厅印发的《关于加强和改进城市社区居民委员会建设工作的意见》中都有明确规定：第一，社区区域内机关、团体、部队、企事业组织不参加所在地的社区居委会。第二，社区居委会主任、副主任和委员，由本居住地区全体有选举权的居民或者由每户派代表选举产生。第三，一个社区原则上设置一个社区居民委员会。

动中心、计划生育服务中心、日间照料中心、养老订餐送餐服务中心、少儿幼儿照看服务中心、矛盾调解中心等。① 社区的扩大与网格化单元的增加使社区的管理成本上升，居委会行政职能的扩充和服务职能的扩延增加了其内设机构的科层化层级。② 与此同时，居委会也通过市场购买了类型多样的基本公共服务。为加强社区设施的管理，各地开始推行社区党支部/党委书记通过合法选举兼任居委会主任的做法，进一步集中了居委会的权力结构，使来自科层结构的他治主体——"书记"和社区自治的民选主体——"主任"结合为一体，以便将自上而下的科层意志与来自居民的服务诉求融会贯通，达到党建引领意义的多方共治。

  这个看起来能够满足多元需求的改革，在复杂的现实中产生了千差万别的结果，使各个社区都具有其自身独具的特征。差别中的共性是治理成本的迅速攀升。社区居委会及其各种服务机构以及类型多样的活动中心既增加了治理所需的用人需求，也增大了社区建设或社区营造的项目经费压力，还增加了日常营运成本，从而加大了地方财政负担。在各省及自治区的省会城市、东部沿海地区及财政经费支持力度较大的街道所属地区，居委会及其附属机构具有可持续发展意义的示范效应。但在中西部地区、偏远地区、财政收入较低的贫困地区，社区居委会的工作力度小、组成"标准化"社区成员的数量少，活动中心场所比较简陋，社区的"三社联动"流于形式。在类似社区，专业社工的活动也微乎其微，社区的发展不具有可持续性。虽然在人员的归口上，社区党支部/党委书记归于党的部门管理、居委会主任归于民政部门指导，社区网格员归于政法部门选派，办事大厅的雇员也都有其渠道支持，但其活动经费和工作人员的工资或生活补贴等都来自财政经费。各个小区楼长与单元长的补贴更需要政府出资。没有地方财政的支持，各种类型的社区营造项目就难以顺利推进。因此，在经济上行过程中社区治理成本易于解决，在经济下行过程中社区治理效果就难以高质量地维持。

---

  ① 在探索创新过程中，上海市成立的社区卫生服务中心、社区文化活动中心、社区事务受理服务中心等具有示范意义，类似的中心全部为全额拨款事业单位。
  ② 为强化居委会及其附属机构的职能，政府建构的社区理想型只能向有人办事、有钱办事和有场地办事方向发展。

全面建成小康社会的过程是宏大社会的转型过程，也是社会转型推动下基层社会结构的转型过程。这个转型过程配合了单位制的解体与后单位制的形成，也以"居委会办社会"的方式部分解决了社会成员从"单位人"转变为"社会人"过程的归属与治理需求，在一定程度上弥补了改革所造成的"原结构之原功能损失"，达到了以下治理目标：其一，通过便捷的服务供给建构起新的社会稳定机制，解决了居民与民生相关的办事难问题，提供了具有中国特色的基层社会矛盾化解渠道，形成了以社区居委会为中心的组织网络。其二，社区的运行，在自上而下的意义上延长了政府之手，通过各种"办社会"的项目制配置，搭建起政府治理与社会治理的融通机制。其三，通过社区党支部/党委会书记兼任居委会主任与集体经济组织负责人的方式，强化了党的领导，在基层社会建构起一元多方的领导体系。其四，通过党组织的日常活动，加强了党员与社区居民之间的联系，以"网格长""楼栋长"和"单元长"等科层安排，形成信息供给的上传下达渠道，在"政社联动""警社联动"等制度配置中组建起治理体系，提升了治理能力，供给了全面建成小康社会的社区治理需求，为中国的改革稳定发展作出了重大贡献。但也衍生出很多不尽如人意的结构性负功能。

二 "强他治"与"弱自治"制度：规约与治理短板

前已述及，在全面建成小康社会过程中，社区结构发生了重大转型，这种转型要求社区在功能建设上形成升级态势，使社区结构与社区功能进一步和谐适配，在提升"硬件"的同时加强"软件"的升级。这要求社区尽快补足短板，发挥其应有的基层统筹协调作用，解决社区建设不平衡不充分的问题，更好地满足居民不断增加的差异化需求。

第一，社区居委会作为最主要的治理主体，具有很强的"他治"代理性，而社区社会组织等其他治理主体发育不足，主动自治性较弱。社区治理能力的强弱往往取决于地方党委或政府的重视和支持程度。但党政领导越重视，社区居委会就越易于表现出"居委会办社会"的"强他治"特征，同时也越难以开发治理所需的其他主体力量①，进而表现出较强的行政特征。在政府、社会和市场三种资源配置手段中，"社会"的潜在作用力尚未完全挖掘出来，使社区治理中表现出典型的"对社会进行治理"与"利用社会自治"的假说疏离。毋庸置疑，《中华人民共和国城市居民委员会组织法》规定社区居委会属于自治组织，但该法同时也规定"不设区的市、市辖区的人民政府或者它的派出机关对居委会的工作给予指导、支持和帮助。居委会协助不设区的市、市辖区的人民政府或者它的派出机关开展工作"。因此，社区居委会有义务完成街道或街道撤销后区级政府安排的工作，正如村委会和村民小组需要完成乡镇政府安排的工作一样。在当前社会形势下，应该肯定社区的他治性质，也应该健全其自治功能。② 只有行政职能和自治职能协作互补，才能满足社区良性发展与有序善治需要。政府通过市场购买服务、社会通过社区参与多主体的合作治理、市场竞争实现各方资源的有效配置。唯有如此，才能"实现政府治理、社会调节和居民自治良性互动"，尊崇"人人参与、人人尽责、人人享有"的"共建共治共享"原则。在社会力量较弱、难以形成治理能力时，就需要培育社会组织、社会企业、社工机构、居民等参与治理。如果社区内部除居委会外别无其他主体，就是单方治理而不是多方共治，也就难以开展"良性互动"。因此，社区建设或社区营造的重点一方面应该放在建设基础公共设施与组织机构上，另一方面需重视对其自治组织和自治能力的培养。

第二，社区居委会与物业管理公司和业主委员会的关系还不协调，常住流动人口与城市人户分离人口不能有效参与治理过程。对社区居民而言，经常与之发生关系的主体是其居住的小区。代表物业小区供给服务的是物业管理公司。业主委员会通过对物业管理公司的市场化选择来满足自己的

---

① 对于社区的"自治"与"他治"问题，学界长期处于争论状态。但强调自治的学者也不完全否定政府介入的可能性，强调他治的学者也经常论及自治组织的重要性。客观而言，纯粹自治的理想型并不存在。在传统中国社会，虽然存在宗法关系与乡绅等，但保甲制一直沿续到了民国时期。在保甲制之前，三老、里长和亭长的产生过程均在政府部门的控制之下。因此，所谓"皇国权不下县、县下唯宗亲"等也只是相对意义上的说法。

② 田毅鹏：《治理视域下城市社区抗击疫情体系构建》，《社会科学辑刊》2020年第1期。

日常服务需求。从形式上说，小区内部的商品与服务本质上属于业主购买的"私人物品"或"准私人物品"，业主委员会承担购买与督办职责。因此，即使在基层，社区仍然具有中层的性质，真正进行日常管理与服务的是"小区"。在业主人户分离较少的小区，业主委员会易于组建起来。在人户分离多发小区，业主委员会很难组建或经常形同虚设。换句话说，在现有格局下，业主难以依法监督物业管理公司，既不能形成购买其服务的议价权，也不能形成监督其保障服务质量的议事权。只要不发生重大冲突，小区居民均按最初物业管理公司的定价缴纳物业费，并接受与之相关的服务。但问题是，在只有物业或房屋产权人才有权参加业主委员会的情况下，其他租住居民只能"作壁上观"。外地流动人口租户是实际的社区居民，但他们却没有对社区居委会的选举权和被选举权，也没有管理小区的参与权，而只能通过出租人——业主提出建议。同样，如果从居民的实际居住权上考虑问题，则人户分离的业主与小区和社区没有建构起常态化治理关系。在社区居民与物业管理公司的争议中，社区居委会根本起不到实质干预作用，也难以发挥治理作用。这会消解居民对社区的认同感。但是社区内部产生的绝大多数矛盾恰恰来源于单个业主或部分业主与物业管理公司的冲突。要么是业主长期拖欠物业费，要么是物业管理公司不能按合同提供服务，要么是社区公共收益被少数人侵占。

第三，社区居委会的功能补足能力参差不齐。社区居委会作为基层群众自治组织，除维护自身建设外，应将工作重点放在维护社会秩序与补足物业小区所不能提供的基本公共服务上，从供给侧满足居民的多元化需求。但在某些老旧小区，物业费征缴困难且缺少自组织自治力量，因而无法购买专业物业管理公司的服务，出现"业主管理缺位现象"，形成事实上的脏乱差问题。在100—200户的小型社区，这种问题相对容易解决。在1000—2000户的中型社区或在3000—5000户及以上的大型社区，类似问题就需要各部门齐抓共管，才能维护正常社区生态系统的良性运行。[①] 另外，一旦发生社会风险，出现应急化治理之需，仅靠7—10人的社区工作人员很难完成管控任务。在常态化治理时期，如果能力欠

---

① 美国的社区规模较小，一般设计在2500—8000人。

佳，则很难整合各个小区以提升治理效能。有些社区居委会在缺少物业管理公司的情况下连废水排放与垃圾堆积问题都解决不了，严重影响居民的正常生活。

第四，社区工作人员待遇偏低，除社区党支部/党委书记和居委会主任等有望转变为事业编制外，其他人员很难长期安心工作，且学历偏低、年龄偏大，以中老年女性或退休返聘人员为主。[①] 整个网格员队伍的流失率较高。再加上很多招聘来的工作人员非本社区居民，对社区内部情况不熟。一旦发生危机事件，当地政府就不得不"下沉"干部以支持社区工作，这反过来强化了社区的"他治"特征。长此以往，居委会就形成类似于政府的工作方式，居委会成员也就越来越渴望进入体制内，以获得与事业编制人员或公务员等类似的编制，解决"身份"问题。当前，在实际工作中能不能解决编制、能够解决多少编制、能首先为谁解决编制，对这几个问题的不同回答，在很大程度上决定着社区居委会的稳定性和工作绩效的释放性。这些问题已经成为社区居委会与街道或其他党政部门讨价还价的主要内容。换句话说，社区工作人员更希望将社区居委会打造为"基层政府"，更希望将自己转变为"公务员"或"事业编制"人员，更希望具有自上而下的"行政性管理权力"，而不希望将社区建设成为自治组织，不希望将自己长期定位为社区服务人员。

社区的治理，在自治的意义上是依靠多元主体进行的共治治理。但在现有格局下，来自于政府支持的"强他治"特征主要凸显了居委会的官方作用，却没有完全调动居民群众参与的积极性。这种"弱自治"局面的产生，发挥不出"社会协同"与"公众参与"的效力，降低了治理过程的社会认同意义。党的十九届四中全会之后，因为治理格局中加入了"科技支撑"的表述，很多城市也在社区治理中增加了"智慧社区"元素，并以此回应"智慧城市"建设。但治理在技术意义上的快速改善，仍未释放"民主协商"的时代意义。社区治理的设计者更加看重居委会

---

① 2011年，国务院办公厅印发了《社区服务体系建设规划（2011—2015年）》，指出要积极推进社区服务人员的专业化、职业化，落实"一社区一名大学生"政策，实施50万名大学生服务社区计划。

的科层建设，更加重视技术的监控作用，但却忽视了"人"与"人"之间和谐关系这个意义上的价值再造。

事实上，在现代城市社会，不管是常态化治理还是应急化治理，单纯依靠社区居委会都很难满足结构复杂而又日益庞大的人群治理之需。现代社会组织与志愿服务的区域介入既可降低治理成本，也可达到协调冲突的目的。不管是社会组织还是志愿团体，都必须熟悉社区事务和服务需求，才能有针对性地将运动式治理或仪式性示范式治理真正转变为与居民的多元需求密切结合的治理。在居民的阶层和收入结构提升的同时，居民也增加了治理的参与需求，这需要社区与社会组织和志愿团体建立日常化的治理平台接口，形成共建共治共享的治理共同体，达到人人参与、人人尽责、人人享有的目的。在社区力量有限的情况下，社会组织与志愿服务参与的质量在一定程度上决定着社区治理的质量。但社区还没有建立较高质量的志愿服务接口，没有形成志愿服务供给与需求之间的联系纽带。尽管制度建设已经解决了社会组织与志愿服务的属地化管理问题，但在现实社会中还没有达到制度设计的目标。

另外，在居委会难以与社区内部居民各个主体有效融通的情况下，群众对社区的认同易于"碎片化"，难以在集体记忆中形成集体意识。社区居民经常以自我为中心，形成"家户"—"楼层"—"单元门洞"—"楼宇"—"物业小区"—"周边政治环境和商业环境"的差序格局式的认同结构，然后再外推到"学校""医院""公园""超市""理发馆""饭馆""派出所与片警"等，形成与己相关的关系网络。在这种认知取向下，居民甚至对街巷附近的自行车修理店、配钥匙的摊贩等也很关注，因为其与基本公共服务的配置密切相关。但只有极少数居民知道谁是居委会主任，也只有少数人知道那个叫作居委会的机构"整天在忙活什么"。所以，社区居委会的日常活动如果不与社区居民建立密切的日常关系，则其存在只对政府有意义，而对居民失去了主观建构意义。因为对于政府来说，其考虑的是与城市规划相关的社区区划、社区科层结构、社区管辖资源、社区完成任务的多少与质量等。因此，在社区研究中，学者们经常发出的问题是谁的社区，谁在社区，谁在管理，谁在建设，谁分享了建设成果，谁在评价社区建设成果，谁应该承担社区衰落的责任，等等。在这里，认同社区与居委会的差距越大，社区建设的成果就越难共享。

总之，在社区的不断转型过程中，伴随社区居民需求结构的升级，单纯依靠"居委会办社会"的治理结构，在全面建成小康社会过程中供给了服务之需，却难以满足现代化多元结构社会的治理要求。

三 从"居委会办社会"到"社区办社会"：在自治与共治中改进治理效能

在社区中，居委会只是其中的一个主体，只有与其他治理主体共同建构起治理体系，形成治理的民主协商机制，才能最终解决"依靠谁""服务谁"等问题，也才能从"为居民治理"阶段过渡到"依靠居民治理"阶段。在当前治理格局下，在继续维持"强他治"特征的同时建构"自治"的社会组织基础，才能在"共治"中形成"强自治"体系，逐步将"强他治"模式改造为"强自治"模式。但路径依赖决定了当前"居委会办社会"的单方治理特征。截至 2019 年年底，全国登记注册的社会组织数量只有 86.6 万个，而且其增长趋势处于降低态势。① 在社会组织发育不力的情况下，依靠社区内部的社会组织参与治理以提升治理能力的假设只在部分地区有效。因此，为推进"居委会办社会"向"社区办社会"② 转型，就必须在新发展阶段进行新的顶层设计，并将基层社会的社区治理创新从实践层面提升到理论指引层面。

第一，完善党建引领的社区治理体系，理顺社区的行政、自治和市

---

① 民政部，《2019 年民政事业发展统计公报》，http//www.mca.gov.cn/article/sj/tjgb/。
② 在社会治理意义上，或者在依靠社会进行社会治理的"自治"逻辑中，居委会作为治理主体发挥其作为组织的治理作用。在促进社会发育过程中，社区内部的各个治理主体，即社会组织、社会企业、社区治理基金会或社区发展基金会、物业管理公司、业主委员会、志愿团体以及居民代表等应该在"社区议事会"或类似平台中发挥治理作用。本文所指的"社区办社会"，是从治理主体多元化、治理资金来源多渠道化、治理需求多样化、"治理的去管理化"意义上建构的治理模式。其基本假设是"社区是开放系统而不是封闭系统"，"居委会只在治理中负有限责任而不是无限责任"，"居委会承担的是治理职能而非管理职能"，"治理结果为居民共享但治理过程并不必然获得全体居民支持"，"治理的主要依靠力量逐渐从居委会过渡到社会组织"，"治理的主要资金需求逐渐从财政转向社区基金会"，"志愿组织是服务供给的必要补充力量"。

场职能，根据不同治理需求，顺应发展趋势，推进新社区建设的制度设计。按照2018年修订的《中华人民共和国城市居民委员会组织法》，通过党的领导建构"一元多方"的治理结构：一元是党的领导，多方包括属地政府方、社会组织方、志愿服务团体方、居民自治组织方、属地企业方等，建立健全常态化治理体系和应急化治理体系。为此应该重点补足社会组织与社会企业的短板，培育与孵化居民自治力量，激发社会活力。没有社区居民的参与，治理就得不到普遍认同，治理也就难以达到秩序化社会的目的。在当前"社会协同"能力较弱的客观情况下，被行政科层扶持的"强治理"模式是必要的。但自治的"弱治理"状况需要逐渐改变。没有"强治理"的介入，"居委会办社会"的资金来源就无法保障。但在"强治理"模式中，既要防止居委会治理责任的无限化、防止治理成本的无限上涨，也要防止社区居委会的"政府化"和"衙门化"，更要扶持社会组织在"社会协同"中提升治理能力。

第二，社会治理的重心要下沉到社区，社区治理的重心要下沉到小区，小区治理改革的方向在于非本地户籍人口包括流动人口有权参与治理，在于吸纳租户居民参与民主协商的各个过程，防止社会隔离现象的发生。迁居化社会的本质就是劳动力处于不断流动之中。绝大多数人不会一辈子只居住在一个固定的社区，而会在城市与城市之间、城市内部的社区与社区之间搬迁。因此，应将物业小区纳入社区组织建设，强化业主委员会的管理功能，赋予实际物业使用者以使用权意义的议事权，吸纳流动常住人口参与基层自治，使社区居民委员会体现出"居民意义"的治理参与权，达到谁是社区居民谁就有权参与治理的目的。[①] 因此，在社区居委会人员组成中，不应以户籍限定选举权和被选举权，而应结合物业所有权和常住居民的物业租有权成比例地分配选举权和被选举权，而不能简单地将人口区别为户籍人口和非户籍人口进行制度安排。在新型城镇化背景下，原有的管理制度应适应新时代的要求，尽快进行改革。

[①] 有些国家以居民居住本社区时间的长短赋予其参与治理权限的大小，也赋予其享受基本公共服务的多少。其实，在中国的绝大多数城市，在"划片入学"这种政策的配置上也体现了这一原则。

那种依据户籍制度设计的社区治理与社区服务的合理性建立在传统社区的封闭性理论假设之上。在社区市场化程度逐步加深的现代化大背景中，吸纳居住在本社区的流动人口参与社区治理，既是大势所趋，也是现实需要，小区内部的隔离不利于居民之间的团结。如果动摇了社会团结的基础，形成某些人"认同"与某些人"不认同"意义的社会撕裂，则不但社区的有序治理难以为继，就是在社区所属小区内部，也难以保护本地户籍人口的全部利益。房东与租户属于利益共同体，社区的人口和社会组织处于动态变化之中。只有以常住人口为基础建立"开放性"和"常住型"动态治理体系，才能适应现代化引领的社会变迁之所需。

第三，促进社区基本公共服务均等化，扶持各类社区平衡发展。根据财政实力有计划地安排老旧小区改造项目，加强城乡结合部小区建设，加强新建物业小区社区建设，强化社区内机关家属院、企业大院与各类物业小区的综合协调治理能力。在社区人口规模趋于增长的态势下，不管是社区治理体系的建设还是社区治理能力的提升，都有赖于社区内部各个物业小区的治理体系和治理能力建设。对那些治理能力较弱、治理体系尚不健全、留有历史问题的社区和物业小区，当地财政部门或主管单位应予适当支持，通过购买社会服务的方式培育小区治理能力，夯实基层治理基础，建立社区与区域内党政机关和企事业单位之间的协调机制，形成治理成本分摊机制。为控制社区治理成本，还需将业主委员会组织起来，以之平衡与物业管理公司之间的失衡现状。与此同时，应继续打造社会组织和志愿服务组织参与社区治理的属地化接口，形成"多方共治"的参与局面，体现出治理的专业化、法治化效能，从而降低社区业务经费的高度财政依赖性。结合"他治"任务要求与"自治"体系建设，搭建业主委员会和物业管理公司之间的矛盾化解平台，通过供给侧结构性改革满足社区服务需要，避免社区内部资源竞争中的人群分裂。当然，对于某些在城镇化中直接从农村社区转变为城镇社区的小区来说，应扶持物业自持自管力量。社会的现代化程度越高，社区居民对组织化服务的质量要求就越高。社区居民的社会分化特征越突出，其异质性就越强，其对服务需求的差异化要求就越严格。

第四，根据城市经济增速与物价变化提升职业化社区工作人员的收入水平,根据社区实际常住人口规模确定社区工作人员数量,建立和稳定常态化社区工作队伍。应该看到,在中西部地区和东北地区,社区工作人员收入水平的低下会导致人员流失现象。在这些地方,即使毕业于社工专业的本科生和硕士生,也很少有人愿意到社区工作。要满足社区的自治需要,就必须建构与其需要相一致的工作队伍,提升社区工作人员的服务水平,与时俱进地培训其专业能力。在稳定小型社区和中型社区工作人员队伍的同时,要实事求是地扩大5000户以上特大型社区工作人员数量。应通过社区居民调查,削减街道安排的一些居民需求较少或根本没有必要的业务,将有限的人力用于民生保障与秩序化社区等基本公共服务上。与此同时,应完善社区的独立法人资格,在推荐社区党支部/党委书记兼任社区居委会主任和社区经济组织管理人员时,有意识地整合社区资源,健全社区治理的财务体系,形成透明公开的财务制度,规范财务管理,厘清政府购买服务、社区自治服务和市场化生成服务的关系,有效化解业主委员会、物业管理公司、房屋实际租户等矛盾冲突。在有条件的地方,还需要扶持社区发展基金会,吸收社会资金参与社区治理。只有发展壮大社区发展基金,才能降低社区治理对地方财政的强依赖关系,厚植社区自治的经济基础。

第五,需要建立社区服务的第三方牵头评估制度,吸纳社区、业主委员会、物业管理公司、租户代表、志愿团体等多方参与,健全监督机制。尤其是对反映强烈的物业服务质量问题和社区公共服务质量问题,更要通过事前评估、事中评估和事后评估,建立制度性、自治性监督体系。要走出运动式治理的"整治—反复—再整治—再反复"怪圈,通过建立物业管理公司黑名单制度,加强市场监管,淘汰缺少现代管理能力与难以提升服务质量的物业管理公司。在"政府—市场—社会"良性互动中达到自我管理、自我服务、自我发展的目的。

总之,在全面建成小康社会之后,中国的城镇化水平将会更高,城市的结构也将更为复杂,城市内部各个社区之间发展的不平衡不充分问题将更为凸显,社区居民构成的老龄化和迁居化特征也将同时并存,社区也会在不断转型中释放出更多结构与功能的适配性治理问题。

在这种情况下,随着新发展阶段现代化水平的不断提升,社区治理缺陷所显示的短板效应会被多元化的媒体放大。因此，未来社区仍将面临新的治理难题。在"居委会办社会"模式中，随着居民消费水平的提升以及居民对社区治理质量的升级诉求，作为政府代理人的居委会将继续增加服务供给，继续扩大居委会工作人员的规模，继续要求为其增加福利待遇与生活补贴，继续期望居委会工作人员有机会转变为事业编制人员，或继续谋求建构其转变为公务员的行政运转机制。这种在"无限责任"假设指导下的"居委会办社会"的质量，将主要依赖财政经费的支持力度。居民对社区治理的服务需求是刚性增长的，但财政增速却完全取决于经济增速。在经济增速减缓的理论研判中，"无限责任"社区治理的项目制的可持续性正在经受转型考验。因此，在全面建成小康社会过程中，将"单位办社会"的管理模式升级为"居委会办社会"的治理模式，不但必要而且还具有路径依赖意义的实践创新性。但在全面建成小康社会之后的新征程中，还需要在治理体系建设中继续将"居委会办社会"升级为"社区办社会"，只有这样，才能利用社区内外部社会力量建构"多元主体共治模式"。

社区内外部社会组织的发育程度决定了"社区办社会"的能力。"以社会力量去治理社会"的理论假设与"以政府力量治理社会"的理论假设都具有现实合理性。的确，社会组织的成长与强大有时会挑战居委会的权力，也会产生不同社会组织之间的治理取向的差异性。但在居民阶层多元化的背景下，要使居民不将矛盾的对象针对居委会背后的政府力量，就必须在"民主协商"中尊重不同社会组织的意见分殊。只要建立起社区的议事会平台，意见领袖就会在平台内谋求达成一致的可能性，而不会将治理失效的责任单方面归之于居委会。居民参与的社会组织越多，就越易于利用社会组织之间的多元协商与平衡能力解决争端，就越可能借助社区认同意识化解矛盾。

正因如此，必须系统总结现存各种问题，补足短板，建设共建共治共享的治理体系，提升社区治理的自治德治法治能力、激发社会活力、扩大居民民主协商参与治理的合法渠道，通过自治和共治化解日益高升的他治成本，以高质量服务供给满足居民需求，不断提升社区居民的幸福感、获得感和安全感。

参考文献：

费孝通：《中国现代化对城市社区建设的再思考》，《江苏社会科学》2001年第1期。

费孝通：《江村经济》，上海世纪出版集团、上海人民出版社2007年版。

李国庆：《棚户区改造与新型社区建设——四种低收入者住区的比较研究》，《社会学研究》2019年第5期。

李友梅：《基层社区组织的实际生活方式——对上海康健社区实地调查的初步认识》，《社会学研究》2002年第4期。

田毅鹏：《治理视域下城市社区抗击疫情体系构建》，《社会科学辑刊》2020年第1期。

张浩：《从"各美其美"到"美美与共"——费孝通看梁漱溟乡村建设主张》，《社会学研究》2019年第5期。

张翼：《社会转型与社会治理格局的创新》，《中国社会科学评价》2019年第1期。

中国发展理念的演化与社会变迁

欧阳向英[*]

2021年是中国共产党成立100周年。这一百年间，中国社会发生了翻天覆地的变化，从逐渐瓦解的半殖民地半封建社会走进繁荣富强的中国特色社会主义新时代。中国人民从"站起来"到"富起来"再到"强起来"，历史三部曲波澜壮阔。中国社会实现了跨越性的历史进步，但过程并不是一帆风顺的。自诞生之日起，中国共产党就一直在探索解放中国和建设中国的道路，根据不同时期主要矛盾的变化和生产力水平的不同提出过不尽相同的发展理念和措施，在某些阶段发现问题也做出过调整。如今，中国成为世界第二大经济体，很多国家在羡慕中国成就的同时并不了解中国发展道路的艰巨性和曲折性。因此，在建党百年之际，系统梳理中国共产党在发展理念上的探索与成绩是必要的，也可以为其他发展中国家执政党提供借鉴和参考。

一 问题提出

从理论上看，社会发展到底是一个"自然历史过程"，还是"理性"或"绝对精神"引导下的过程？对这个问题的回答在不同思想家那里是不一样的。马克思的答案是前者，黑格尔的回答是后者。然而，马克思

[*] 欧阳向英，研究员，中国社会科学院世界经济与政治研究所马克思主义世界政治经济理论研究室主任。

的自然是"人化自然",并不排斥人的因素以及观念因素。马克思讲,历史常常是跳跃式发展的。要实现"跳跃式发展",有两个关键因素:一是人及其实践活动,通过人来实现历史选择;二是科学技术,也依靠人来发展进步。这说明,没有排除了人的因素的纯粹自然,而社会作为人的集合一定是在某种观念的指引下前行的。问题在于主观如何见之于客观,也就是人对社会发展规律认识和探索的过程。

从现实来看,以"一带一路"建设为例,一些发展尚处落后的国家和地区,希望引进高新技术、发展数字经济,而对本国原有的农业、畜牧业、矿业和加工业等缺乏改造计划。一方面,当地政府希望中国就高新技术和数字经济提供支持,但对与其配套的基础设施和产业环境考虑较少,导致项目无法谈成或谈成也不能落实;另一方面,一些中国企业对当地的优势产业,如矿产和能源开发感兴趣,而当地政府将其视为战略物资,不向中国企业发放许可证,导致企业无法正常运营。

"一带一路"某些沿线国家的愿望和顾虑不是不可以理解。只是,面对现实问题,双方要把行动调整到同一频率,才可能促成合作,而调到同一频率的前提是形成共识。从中国的实践经验来看,中国的发展也不是一蹴而就的,发展理念和产业政策经过了多轮调整。按照什么模式,优先发展什么,怎么发展,需要根据实际情况,既有坚定目标又能灵活调整,作出决定。举个例子,中国是世界能源进口大国,继2017年成为全球最大原油进口国后,2018年成为全球最大天然气进口国。很多人不了解,20世纪七八十年代中国也曾是重要的石油输出国。1985年中国石油出口约3600万吨,达到中国石油出口历史最高点,带来67亿美元的外汇,占当年外贸出口总额的24.5%,这就是"石油换外汇"战略,为的是买回国家发展需要的设备和材料。1985年后,随着中国经济持续高速发展,出口逐渐下降,进口逐渐增加(见表1)。2020年中国原油进口量5.42亿吨,价值1.22万亿元。可见,产业的发展轨迹既有其自身逻辑,也要服务于国家发展的大局。

表1　　　　1972—1993年中国原油生产和石油进出口数据

年份	原油产量/百万吨	年增长率(%)	石油进口量/百万吨	石油出口量/百万吨	净进口(+)或净出口量(-)
1972	45.672	15.87	0.652	0.806	-0.154
1973	53.614	17.39	0.138	1.819	-1.681
1974	64.850	20.96	0.113	5.180	-5.067
1975	77.059	18.83	0.203	10.579	-10.376
1976	87.156	13.10	0.201	9.300	-9.097
1977	93.638	7.44	0.301	10.691	-10.390
1978	104.049	11.22	0.001	11.333	-11.332
1979	106.149	2.02	—	—	—
1980	105.942	-0.20	0.827	18.062	-17.235
1981	101.219	-4.46	0.710	18.842	-18.132
1982	102.205	0.97	1.572	20.897	-19.325
1983	106.066	3.78	1.349	20.926	-19.577
1984	114.601	8.05	1.125	28.687	-27.562
1985	124.887	8.89	0.900	36.304	-35.404
1986	130.670	4.63	3.501	34.620	-31.119
1987	134.125	2.64	3.234	32.938	-29.704
1988	137.028	2.16	5.084	31.423	-26.339
1989	137.651	0.45	10.651	31.064	-20.413
1990	138.284	0.46	7.556	31.104	-23.548
1991	139.791	1.09	12.495	29.307	-16.812
1992	142.037	1.61	21.247	28.956	-7.709
1993	144.004	1.38	32.960	23.150	+9.810

资料来源：李昕：《1949年以来中国石油进出口地位演变》，《西南石油大学学报》（社会科学版）2014年第1期。

二　百年中国发展理念与成就

回顾百年中国发展历程，对发展道路的探索、对现代化的追求贯穿始终。"实现现代化是近代以来世界各国特别是发展中国家孜孜以求的目标。……中国的巨大成功，拓展了发展中国家走向现代化的途径，给世界上那些既希望加快发展又希望保持自身独立性的国家和民族提供了全新选择，为解决人类问题贡献了新方案。"①

从1840年起，中国逐渐沦为半殖民地半封建国家，反帝反封建成为

---

①　中共中央宣传部理论局：《新中国发展面对面》，学习出版社、人民出版社2019年版，第17—18页。

近代中国革命的一个根本任务。洋务运动和维新变法先后失败,证明地主阶级内部的改良运动不会成功;辛亥革命的成果被袁世凯窃取,继之以北洋军阀混战,证明资产阶级的试验也不会成功。1917 年"十月革命"一声炮响,为中国送来了马克思主义。正是在这种背景下,1921 年中国共产党诞生于上海。"新文化运动"为共产党的成立奠定了思想基础,而新文化的基本口号是要民主、要科学。要不要现代化?当时是有争议的。"因为近几年中国的粗放养蚕业受到现代化大工厂廉价生产的排挤,妇女便常常到这些工厂去打短工。"① 这是张太雷于 1921 年 6 月 10 日致共产国际报告中的内容,也是中国共产党人第一次使用"现代化"一词。到 20 世纪 20 年代中期,中国共产党人已普遍知晓"现代化"的概念。1926 年第 5 号《新青年》刊载了瞿秋白的译著,批驳了社会民主党和改良派工会领袖所谓中国应当实行"经济上的现代化"的虚伪性。这里的"现代化"指资本主义的商业经营方式,带有批判的性质。由于《新青年》此时已经改版为中共中央正式的理论性机关刊物,可以认为对"现代化"的质疑和批评是早期共产党人的普遍态度。可贵的是,早期共产党人就认识到,中国将来实现社会主义时,必是共性与特性相结合。社会主义的理想,"因各地、各时之情形不同,务求其适合者行之,遂发生共性与特性结合的一种新制度(共性是普遍者,特性是随时随地不同者),故中国将来发生之时,必与英、德、俄……有异"②。

1931 年"九一八"事变爆发,日寇悍然侵华,举国震惊。面对全民族的强敌,中国人对"现代化"的认识有所改变。1931 年秋,瞿秋白在探讨"苏维埃的文化革命"时,主张要发动新文字革命直到"实现中国现代化的罗马化"③。1933 年《申报月刊》组织"中国现代化问题"讨论。1937 年,谢觉哉作为中共中央代表派驻八路军兰州办事处时,多次致信国民党西北行辕主任贺耀祖,提出"购进并学习使用现代化武器,

---

① 《张太雷文集》,人民出版社 2013 年版,第 21 页。
② 李大钊:《社会主义与社会运动》(1923 年 9 月—1924 年 4 月),载《李大钊全集》(第 4 卷),人民出版社 2013 年版,第 248 页。
③ 《瞿秋白文集》(第 7 卷),人民出版社 2013 年版,第 229 页。

是西北后方一件极重要的事"①。

1938年,毛泽东第一次使用了"现代化"一词,"革新军制离不了现代化"②。周恩来也在《怎样进行持久战?》中多次使用"现代化"的说法。至此,中国共产党人已明确赋予"现代化"正面内涵。

1931—1945年,日寇侵华给我国带来了极大伤害。1945年4月23日至6月11日,中共七大在延安召开,提出政治路线:打败日本侵略者,建立一个新民主主义的中国。这时中共还不是执政党,但已拥有陕甘宁、晋察冀、晋冀鲁豫、晋绥、山东等敌后抗日根据地,在国民党统治区的工作也如火如荼。在社会生产力遭到极大破坏的背景下,党的七大和七届二中全会报告明确提出,中国要实现"工业化和农业近代化",并"使中国稳步地由农业国转变为工业国"。也就是说,尽管现代化是共产党领导下的新中国发展愿景和奋斗目标,但在整个社会生产力还很落后的情况下,第一步要实现的是近代化,而不是现代化。1949年10月,中国人民政治协商会议通过《共同纲领》,在一个时期起着临时宪法的作用。其中,关于经济建设,《共同纲领》规定,国家应多方面"调剂国营经济、合作社经济、农民和手工业者的个体经济、私人资本主义经济和国家资本主义经济,使各种社会经济成分在国营经济领导之下,分工合作,各得其所,以促进整个社会经济的发展"③。这也充分反映了过渡时期新民主主义的性质,没有急于提出跑步进入社会主义现代化强国。

中华人民共和国成立初期,人民焕发了当家做主的劳动热情,国民经济得到全面恢复。1952年,工农业总产值810亿元,比1949年增长77.6%。其中,工业总产值比1949年增长145.1%,农业总产值增长48.4%,朝着从农业国变为工业国的目标迈出了坚实的一步。④ 1954年,

---

① 《谢觉哉日记》(上册),人民出版社1984年版,第189页。
② 《毛泽东选集》(第2卷),人民出版社1991年版,第511页。
③ 中共中央党史研究室:《中国共产党的九十年》,中共党史出版社、党建读物出版社2016年版,第344页。
④ 中共中央党史研究室:《中国共产党的九十年》,中共党史出版社、党建读物出版社2016年版,第414页。

在第一届全国人民代表大会上，第一次明确提出要实现工业、农业、交通运输业和国防的四个现代化任务。可是究竟什么是现代化，是"楼上楼下，电灯电话"，还是另有一个模板，暂时说不清。1956年，毛泽东在中央政治局扩大会议上作《论十大关系》的讲话。他指出："一切民族、一切国家的长处都要学。"① 将建设社会主义的道路从一切向苏联看齐转到探索适合中国的发展道路上来。1964年，第三届全国人民代表大会上，周恩来做政府工作报告，将现代化调整为现代农业、现代工业、现代国防和现代科学技术的"四个现代化"②。具体目标是分"两步走"，用15年建立一个独立的比较完整的工业体系和国民经济体系，到20世纪末全面实现四个现代化。到1965年年底，调整国民经济的任务全面完成。工农业生产总值超过历史最高水平；农轻重的比例关系得到改善；积累与消费的比例关系基本恢复正常；财政收支平衡，市场稳定，人民生活水平有所提高。然而出于多种原因，1966年5月中国爆发了史无前例的"文化大革命"，社会陷入动乱。其间虽然在粮食生产、工业交通、基本建设和科学技术乃至外交等方面取得了一批重要成就，但总体而言，中国与世界发达国家和周边主要国家（含地区）的差距拉大了。1965—1975年，中国GDP年均增长4.7%，而日本、韩国和中国台湾地区则分别为8.0%、11.6%和9.1%。这也表明，现代化不仅仅是经济和社会领域的事，政治和思想领域也需要现代化。

改革开放前夕，无论从GDP总量，还是从人均GDP来说，中国都属于较为落后的发展中国家。1978年，农村居民家庭人均纯收入仅为133.6元，农村家庭恩格尔系数67.7%，而城镇居民人均纯收入为343.4元，恩格尔系数57.5%。③ 1979年，邓小平在与日本首相大平正芳会谈时，提出把四个现代化量化为到20世纪末国民生产总值达到人均1000美元，

---

① 《毛泽东著作选读》（下册），人民出版社1986年版，第740页。
② 中共中央党史研究室：《中国共产党的九十年》，中共党史出版社、党建读物出版社2016年版，第536页。
③ 曾国安、胡晶晶：《论20世纪70年代末以来中国城乡居民收入差距的变化及其对城乡居民消费水平的影响》，《经济评论》2008年第1期。

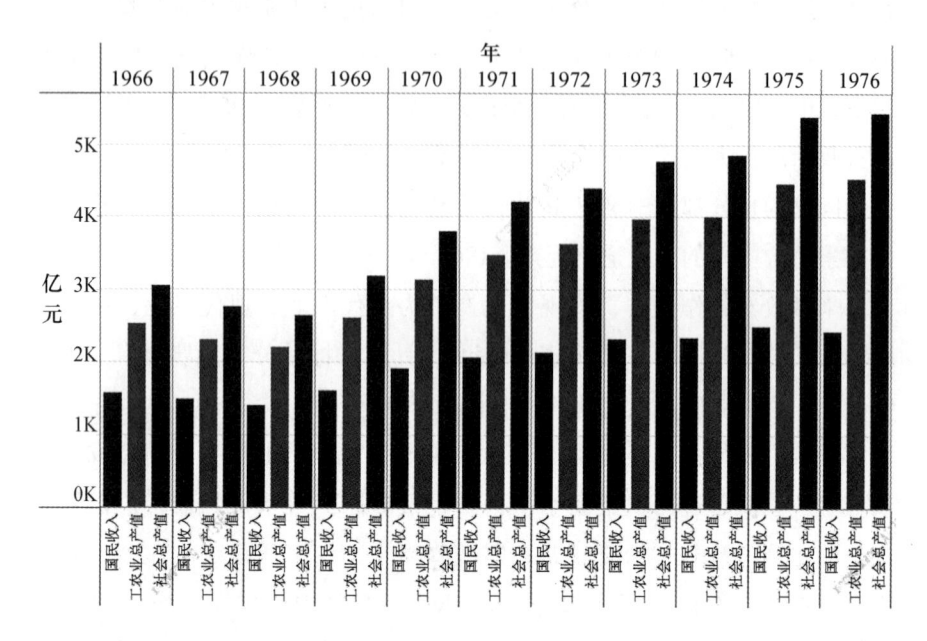

图1　1966—1976年社会总产值、工农业总产值和国民收入

资料来源：国家统计局编：《中国统计年鉴（1984）》，中国统计出版社1984年版，第20—21页。

实现小康水平。① 措施就是改革开放，从建立经济特区开始，探索有中国特色的社会主义道路。从经济特区到沿海开放，再到内陆开放，引进的外资越来越多，随之而来的先进技术和管理经验改变着人们的思维，民营经济规模迅速扩大，为国民经济注入了活力。党的十三大提出中国经济"三步走"的总体战略部署：第一步，解决人民的温饱问题，这个任务已经基本实现；第二步，到20世纪末，人民生活达到小康水平；第三步，到21世纪中叶，人均国民生产总值达到中等发达国家水平，人民过上比较富裕的生活。② 1987年，发展目标的第一步还是解决温饱问题，应该说是实事求是的。"七五"计划胜利完成后，1990年12月，党的十三

---

①　《邓小平文选》第2卷，人民出版社1994年版，第237页。
②　中共中央党史研究室：《中国共产党的九十年》，中共党史出版社、党建读物出版社2016年版，第745页。

届七中全会提出,今后十年,要实现现代化建设的第二步战略目标,把国民经济的整体素质提高到一个新水平。① 全会报告概括了中国特色社会主义基本理论和基本实践,总结出 12 条原则,标志着党对中国特色社会主义道路在认识上的进一步深化。1992 年,邓小平南方谈话指出:"社会主义的本质,是解放生产力,发展生产力,消灭剥削,消除两极分化,最终达到共同富裕。"② 社会主义要最终战胜资本主义,就必须大胆吸收和借鉴人类社会创造的一切文明成果,包括资本主义发达国家的一切反映现代社会化生产规律的先进经营方式、管理方法。

20 世纪 90 年代,中央对经济体制进行了全面配套改革,包括财税体制改革、金融体制改革、外贸体制改革、投资体制改革、计划体制改革、价格体制改革、分房制度改革、国有企业改革等,为保证经济发展创造了有利条件。1993 年中国经济首次突破 3 万亿元大关,扣除物价上涨因素,全国城镇居民人均可支配收入比上年增加 9.5%,农村居民人均收入增长 3.2%,城乡居民存款总额年末达到 15204 亿元,比上年增长 29%。党在复杂和严峻的国际环境中,毫不动摇地坚持对外开放的基本国策,推动形成了多层次、多渠道、全方位对外开放的新格局。2001 年 12 月 11 日,中国正式成为世贸组织的第 143 名成员。随着经济建设速度的加快,粗放增长所带来的人口—资源—环境协调问题日益凸显。2003 年 10 月,党的十六届三中全会通过《关于完善社会主义市场经济体制若干问题的决定》,第一次在党的正式文件中完整地提出了科学发展观,要求"坚持以人为本,树立全面、协调、可持续的发展观,促进经济社会和人的全面发展",按照"统筹城乡发展、统筹区域发展、统筹经济社会发展、统筹人与自然和谐发展、统筹国内发展和对外开放"的要求推进各项事业的发展与进步。③ 2003—2007 年,中国国内生产总值增速连续五年达到或超过 10%,大大高于同期世界经济平均增长率,经济总量从第六位上升

---

① 中共中央党史研究室:《中国共产党的九十年》,中共党史出版社、党建读物出版社 2016 年版,第 785 页。

② 《邓小平文选》第 3 卷,人民出版社 1993 年版,第 373 页。

③ 中共中央党史研究室:《中国共产党的九十年》,中共党史出版社、党建读物出版社 2016 年版,第 898 页。

到第四位，进出口总额从世界第六位上升到世界第三位。党的十七大强调要坚持走中国特色新兴工业化道路，其中电子信息产业发展尤为迅猛，到 2011 年中国已成为世界第一电子信息制造大国。

党的十八次全国代表大会上，习近平当选为中共中央总书记。2015 年，党的十八届五中全会确立创新、协调、绿色、开放、共享的新发展理念。2017 年，习近平总书记在党的十九大报告中指出"中国特色社会主义进入了新时代"，标志着中国发展进入了新的历史方位。新时代的中国要决胜全面建成小康社会、开启全面建设社会主义现代化国家新征程，为此在经济建设、政治建设、文化建设、社会建设、生态文明建设等方面做出"五位一体"的全面部署，"一带一路"、亚投行、金砖银行、RCEP 等顶层设计逐步实施。中国的迅猛发展令西方发达国家感到"威胁"。2018 年，美国挑起对华经贸摩擦和科技"脱钩"，中国的外部形势更加严峻。

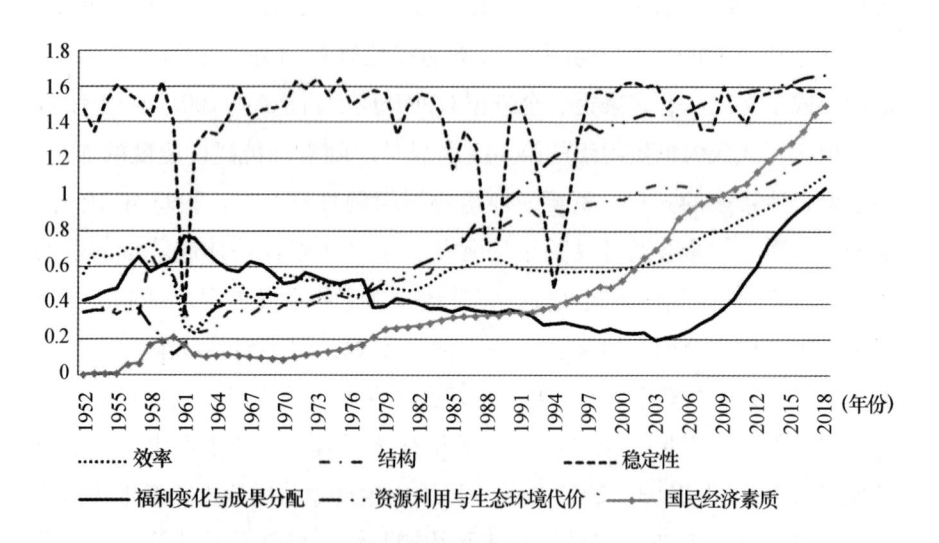

图 2 1952—2018 年中国经济增长质量六大维度指数数值变化

资料来源：任保平、刘戈非：《新中国成立以来经济增长质量的历史演变和评价考察》，《求索》2020 年第 5 期。

党的十五大报告首次提出"两个一百年"奋斗目标：到建党一百年

时,使国民经济更加发展,各项制度更加完善;到 21 世纪中叶新中国成立一百年时,基本实现现代化,建成富强民主文明的社会主义国家。党的十九大报告描绘了全面建成社会主义现代化强国的时间表、路线图,即 2020 年全面建成小康社会、实现第一个百年奋斗目标的基础上,再奋斗 15 年,在 2035 年基本实现社会主义现代化。从 2035 年到 21 世纪中叶,在基本实现现代化的基础上,再奋斗 15 年,把我国建成富强民主文明和谐美丽的社会主义现代化强国。盘点第一个时间节点 2020 年:经历了新冠肺炎疫情的洗礼,2020 年中国成为全球唯一实现经济正增长的主要经济体,经济总量迈上百万亿元的新台阶。这个成就来之不易,首要的原因是党中央坚持把人民生命安全和身体健康放在第一位,第一时间实施集中统一领导,为抗击疫情取得胜利和经济发展稳定转好提供了保障。2020 年 5 月 14 日,中共中央政治局常委会会议首次提出"深化供给侧结构改革,充分发挥我国超大规模市场优势和内需潜力,构建国内国际双循环相互促进的新发展格局"①。此后,习近平总书记多次强调,要"逐步形成以国内大循环为主体、国内国际双循环相互促进的新发展格局"②,重塑我国国际合作和竞争新优势。2021 年中国共产党迎来百年诞辰,中央对全面建成小康社会进行系统评估和总结后,正式宣布中国已全面建成小康社会。坚守正道、锐意创新,百年大党展现出风华正茂的雄姿,在更高起点上进一步推进改革开放,领导中国走向新胜利。

三 总结

回顾中国百年发展史,全部历史经验归结为一点,坚强有力的党的领导是中国革命和建设成功的关键。党的力量从哪里来? 一是从正确的理论指导中来。在中国人民艰苦探索独立和发展道路的过程中,中国共

---

① 《中共中央政治局常务委员会召开会议 习近平主持会议》,人民网,2020 年 5 月 15 日。

② 《中共中央关于制定国民经济和社会发展第十四个五年规划和二〇三五年远景目标的建议》,国务院网站,http://www.gov.cn/zhengce/2020－11/03/content_5556991.htm,2020 年 11 月 3 日。

产党率先找到了马克思列宁主义毛泽东思想，才得以战胜帝国主义、封建主义和官僚资本主义，战胜党内各种"左"倾和右倾错误路线，指导中国革命走向胜利。二是从实践的探索中来。社会主义没有成熟的模式，建设一个大国穷国不能只靠书本。中国共产党从创立伊始就将理论与实践相结合，探索有中国特色的发展道路。党的十一届三中全会后，中国共产党人逐步确立了邓小平理论、"三个代表"重要思想和科学发展观一道作为党必须长期坚持的指导思想，而习近平新时代中国特色社会主义思想是马克思主义中国化的最新成果，是指导中国实现"两个一百年"奋斗目标的指南。三是从群众中来。群众路线是党的根本工作路线，一切为了群众，一切依靠群众，从群众中来，到群众中去。人民当家作主是社会主义民主政治的本质和核心。习近平总书记在讲话中用"8个能否"来评价一个国家政治制度是不是民主的、有效的：国家领导层能否依法有序更替；全体人民能否依法管理国家事务和社会事务、管理经济和文化事业；人民群众能否畅通表达利益要求；社会各方面能否有效参与国家政治生活；国家决策能否实现科学化、民主化；各方面人才能否通过公平竞争进入国家领导和管理体系；执政党能否依照宪法法律规定实现对国家事务的领导；权力运用能否得到有效制约和监督。① 事实证明，只要我们党永葆为人民谋幸福、为民族谋复兴、为世界谋大同的初心，就能统筹好国际国内两个大局，发展与安全并重，推动国家发展与世界和平。

国家发展战略是筹划和指导发展国家实力和潜力，以实现国家发展目标的方略。经济发展战略服务于国家发展战略，与制度制定者对国情、对发展路径和未来愿景的认识有关，不同时期、不同发展阶段应该有不同的策略。中国的发展战略绝大多数时期都是符合现实、贴近国情的，但也有个别时候急于求成，给党和国家的事业带来损失。从党的发展历程来看，对何谓现代化和如何进行现代化建设，经历了一个探索过程。共产党刚创立之初，对现代化是怀疑的，但抗日战争爆发后这个观念就

---

① 崔清新、陈菲：《习近平用"8个能否"评价制度是否民主有效》，新华网，http：//politics.people.com.cn/n/2014/0909/c1001-25622836.html，2021年6月30日。

转变了。新中国成立将工业化视为现代化的主要指标，后来又发展为"四个现代化"目标。党的十八大提出了全面现代化思想，党的十八届三中全会指出全面深化改革的总目标是推进国家治理体系和治理能力现代化。党的十九大提出了以新发展理念为指导的现代化理念，并进一步提出了"两步走"的现代化建设路线图，推动了现代化的理论创新。只有立足实践，理论之树才能常青。

回首百年，中国经历了学习西方—学习苏联—学习一切先进文明成果—走自己的路的探索过程。实事求是是中国共产党历来经验的科学总结，同时党也非常重视理论创新和实践创新。中国也走过弯路，遇到过挫折，但最终乘风破浪，不断前行。回顾中国发展观的演化，或许对发展中国家制订发展策略有所启发。要善于抓社会主要矛盾，改革一切不适应生产力发展的体制，也要以开放的胸怀拥抱世界，这样才能学习人类一切优秀成果，但最终是要为我所用，走自己的路，促进国家和社会的发展与繁荣。

参考文献：

崔清新、陈菲：《习近平用"8个能否"评价制度是否民主有效》，新华网，http://politics.people.com.cn/n/2014/0909/c1001-25622836.html，2021年6月30日。

《邓小平文选》第2卷，人民出版社1994年版。

《邓小平文选》第3卷，人民出版社1993年版。

《瞿秋白文集》（第7卷），人民出版社2013年版。

《李大钊全集》（第4卷），人民出版社2013年版。

《毛泽东选集》（第2卷），人民出版社1991年版。

《毛泽东著作选读》（下册），人民出版社1986年版。

《谢觉哉日记》（上册），人民出版社1984年版。

曾国安、胡晶晶：《论20世纪70年代末以来中国城乡居民收入差距的变化及其对城乡居民消费水平的影响》，《经济评论》2008年第1期。

《张太雷文集》，人民出版社2013年版。

中共中央党史研究室：《中国共产党的九十年》，中共党史出版社、党建读物出版社2016年版。

《中共中央关于制定国民经济和社会发展第十四个五年规划和二〇三五年远景目标的建议》，国务院网站，http：//www.gov.cn/zhengce/2020-11/03/content_5556991.htm，2020年11月3日。

中共中央宣传部理论局：《新中国发展面对面》，学习出版社、人民出版社2019年版。

《中共中央政治局常务委员会召开会议　习近平主持会议》，人民网，2020年5月15日。

中国居家养老服务供给对老年人满意度影响*

孙兆阳**

一 问题提出

自2000年进入老龄化社会以来,中国老龄化呈现加速发展的趋势,养老服务需求迅速增加,养老工作面临巨大压力。如图1所示,2010年中国65岁以上老年人数有1.19亿,是1982年4940万的2.4倍,占比从4.9%增加到8.9%,平均每年增长0.14个百分点。而2020年,老年人数达到1.91亿,人口占比也迅速提高到13.5%,10年间平均每年提高0.46个百分点。党的十八大以来,以习近平同志为核心的党中央坚持以人民为中心的发展思想,高度重视老龄化事业和养老工作发展,注重提高老年人生活幸福感、获得感和安全感,我国养老工作和养老服务事业高速发展,养老服务内容和范围迅速扩大。但是,关于养老服务供给结构变化效果的实证研究还比较少,服务供给的丰富对老年人满意度影响程度还不清楚,所以本文从服务供给角度研究居家养老服务对老年人满意度的影响。

---

* 本文原题为《居家养老服务供给对老年人满意度影响研究——基于8省市调查数据的分析》,原发表于《中共中央党校(国家行政学院)学报》2021年第1期,内容略有改动。

** 孙兆阳,中国社会科学院大学副教授。

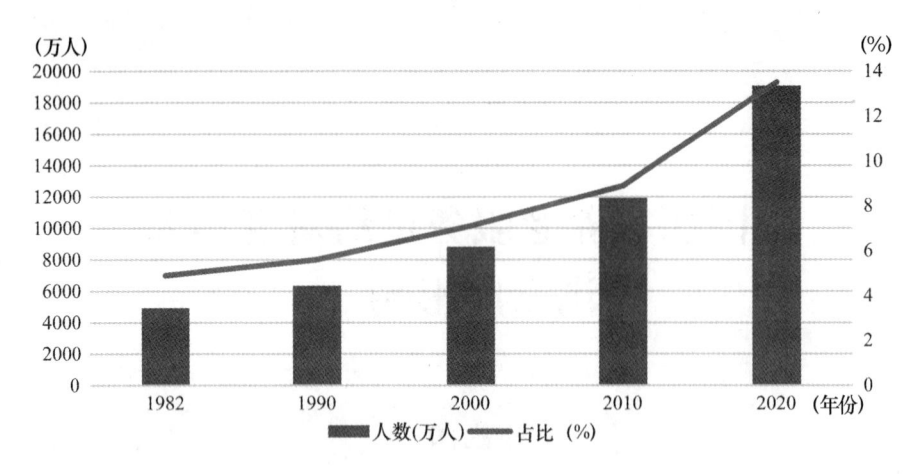

```
(万人)                                                              (%)
20000                                                               14
18000
16000                                                               12
14000                                                               10
12000                                                               8
10000
 8000                                                               6
 6000                                                               4
 4000
 2000                                                               2
    0                                                               0
      1982      1990      2000      2010      2020  (年份)
              ■ 人数(万人)  —— 占比 (%)
```

图1　中国65岁以上老年人数量和占比

资料来源：国家统计局网站（https://data.stats.gov.cn）。

（一）居家养老服务体系的确立

习近平总书记准确把握我国老龄化趋势和老龄工作重要性。2016年5月，习近平总书记在中央政治局第三十二次集体学习上指出，"我国是世界上人口老龄化程度比较高的国家之一，老年人口数量最多，老龄化速度最快，应对人口老龄化任务最重"[①]。截至2019年年底，中国65岁及以上老年人口约1.76亿人，占全体人口的12.6%，是世界上老年人群体最大的国家。进一步来看，受到生育政策调整的影响，中国在20世纪60—70年代中期出现"婴儿潮"，现在他们大部分在45岁至59岁之间，约3.28亿人，人口占比23.5%，并将在接下来15年间陆续进入退休年龄。到21世纪中叶，预计中国老年人口将达到3.66亿人，人口占比为26.1%，老年人口抚养比将达到43.7%[②]，给中国尚未完备的养老体系带来巨大压力。

习近平总书记强调发挥党对老龄工作的统筹领导作用。老龄化社会

[①] 《习近平在中共中央政治局第三十二次集体学习时强调　党委领导政府主导社会参与全民行动　推动老龄事业全面协调可持续发展》，《人民日报》2016年5月29日第1版。

[②] Department of Economic and Social Affairs, Population Division, "World Population Prospects 2019, Volume II: Demographic Profiles – China", New York: United Nations, 2019.

的到来是一种客观事实和社会趋势，做好养老工作不仅是为老年人提供经济赡养和公共服务，更要从国家法律政策到社会意识的全面性、整体性、系统性的变革。社会政策要想发挥持久有效的作用，需要将社会看成一个整体，形成促进和协调不同系统共同发挥作用的整体制度框架，而不是仅仅依靠某一项目、某一部门或某一社会系统承担责任。① 为此，习近平总书记强调，要坚持党委领导、政府主导、社会参与、全民行动相结合，坚持应对人口老龄化和促进经济社会发展相结合，坚持满足老年人需求和解决人口老龄化问题相结合，从增强积极的老龄化思想观念、完善老龄政策制度、发展养老服务产业和老龄产业、发挥老年人积极作用、健全老龄工作体制机制等方面提出战略方向。② 全国人大常委会两次修订《老年人权益保障法》，国务院先后颁布《关于加快养老服务业的若干意见》《关于推进养老服务发展的意见》等一系列重要文件，财政部、民政部、发展和改革委等国家部委从法律法规、资金支持、市场建设、体系制度、人才培养等多方面为养老事业的发展提供配套政策支持，构成了中国特色养老工作政策体系的四梁八柱。

习近平总书记提出并确立居家养老体系建设战略布局。在强调积极应对人口老龄化的基础上，养老服务体系建设被纳入"十三五"规划，实现了养老战略国家层面的统筹。习近平总书记在党的十九大报告中指出，要"积极应对人口老龄化，构建养老、孝老、敬老政策体系和社会环境，推进医养结合，加快老龄事业和产业发展"③。养老工作的战略目标在党的十九届四中全会中进一步明确，"积极应对人口老龄化，加快建设居家社区机构相协调、医养康养相结合的养老服务体系"④。习近平总书记的战略论述为推进多层次养老保障体系建设，保障民众老有所养，

---

① 张秀兰、徐月宾：《构建中国的发展型家庭政策》，《中国社会科学》2003 年第 6 期。
② 《习近平在中共中央政治局第三十二次集体学习时强调　党委领导政府主导社会参与全民行动　推动老龄事业全面协调可持续发展》，《人民日报》2016 年 5 月 29 日第 1 版。
③ 习近平：《决胜全面建成小康社会　夺取新时代中国特色社会主义伟大胜利——在中国共产党第十九次全国代表大会上的报告》，人民出版社 2017 年版，第 48、46 页。
④ 习近平：《中共中央关于坚持和完善中国特色社会主义制度　推进国家治理体系和治理能力现代化若干重大问题的决定》，人民出版社 2019 年版，第 28 页。

为建设新时代中国特色养老事业指明了方向。中国在人均 GDP 只有 1 万美元的情况下，建成世界上最大的社保网络，充分体现了党中央"以人民为中心"的执政理念。经过中央和地方各级政府努力，中国基本建立了以居家为基础、社区为依托、机构为补充、医养相结合的养老服务体系，老年人优待项目更加丰富、范围大幅拓宽，敬老养老助老社会氛围日益浓厚，多元化养老服务供给体系初步形成。

（二）养老服务与老年人满意度

随着国家政策正式确立建设居家养老服务体系，一些研究开始关注其对老年人满意度的影响。有的研究分析了老年人对不同社区环境建设内容的满意程度，以及这些主观感受对他们总体生活满意度的影响。[①] 还有的从可靠性、响应性等 5 个维度评估了上海市社区养老服务质量。[②] 从农村的经验看，家庭收入、健康状况、养老保险和医疗保险、子女婚配费用、子女孝顺程度、代际合作等个人家庭因素，以及政策支持、政府和社会关心程度、社会舆论等家庭外部因素，对老年人养老满意度有较强正向影响。[③] 从城市经验看，经济独立度、服务可及度、自身健康度、居住舒适度、社区服务优度、子女看望、住房条件、居住宜居环境等因素对提升老年人居家养老满意度有较强积极作用。[④] 从全国情况看，女性、居住在农村、有配偶、高龄、健康、社会参与多、子女见面多、收

[①] 钱雪飞:《影响城乡老年人生活满意度的社区养老社会环境建设现状——基于 1440 份问卷调查》,《西北人口》2011 年第 3 期。

[②] 章晓懿、刘帮成:《社区居家养老服务质量模型研究——以上海市为例》,《中国人口科学》2011 年第 3 期。

[③] 胡仕勇、李洋:《农村老年人家庭养老满意度的影响因素分析》,《中国农村经济》2012 年第 12 期；王彦方、王旭涛:《影响农村老人生活满意度和养老模式选择的多因素分析》,《中国经济问题》2014 年第 5 期。

[④] 颜秉秋、高晓路:《城市老年人居家养老满意度的影响因子与社区差异》,《地理研究》2013 年第 7 期；余杰、Mark Rosenberg、程杨:《北京市老年人居家养老满意度与机构养老意愿研究》,《地理科学进展》2015 年第 12 期；唐迪、余运江、孙旭、高向东:《政府购买社区养老服务的满意度研究——基于上海调查数据的实证分析》,《西北人口》2017 年第 3 期。

入高的老年人有更高的生活满意度。①

整体来看，虽然各研究对影响老年人生活满意度因素采用的变量名称和口径不尽一致，但主要包括了个人、家庭和社区三个层面的因素。上述研究有两个方面的问题：一是大多使用地方性数据或区域性数据，而且数据采集的时间也比较早（大部分在2013年之前），已经不足以分析党的十八大以来养老工作的新变化。二是主要关注个体和家庭因素的影响，缺乏对养老服务供给效果的分析，而这正是党的十八大以来养老工作的主要特点。鉴于此，本文利用一套2019年全国8省市社区—老年人匹配调查数据，重点分析居家养老服务体系建设下养老服务供给对老年人养老满意度的影响。

二 研究假设

为了解决养老服务"低水平均衡陷阱"②、养老服务供求失衡等问题③，党的十八大以来，我国居家养老服务体系建设重要抓手是鼓励养老服务供给多元化，即充分发挥政府、社区、家庭主要供给者力量④，同时鼓励企业、志愿者、社会组织等市场和社会力量全面深入参与服务供给⑤，以扩大养老服务供给内容和范围，更好地满足老年人需求。那么，居家养老服务体系建设和养老服务供给的丰富提高了老年人养老满意度吗？

满意度是一种心理状态，是对客观事物的主观评价，养老满意度是老年人对自身养老生活状态的评价。如果养老服务供给对老年人养老工

---

① 刘吉：《我国老年人生活满意度及其影响因素研究——基于2011年"中国健康与养老追踪调查"（CHARLS）全国基线数据的分析》，《老龄科学研究》2015年第1期。

② 林宝：《养老服务业"低水平均衡陷阱"与政策支持》，《新疆师范大学学报》（哲学社会科学版）2017年第1期。

③ 倪东升、张艳芳：《养老服务供求失衡背景下中国政府购买养老服务政策研究》，《中央财经大学学报》2015年第11期。

④ 同春芬、汪连杰：《福利多元主义视角下我国居家养老服务的政府责任体系构建》，《西北人口》2015年第1期。

⑤ 彭华民：《福利三角：一个社会政策分析的范式》，《社会学研究》2006年第4期。

作满意度有影响,那么就可以把老年人满意度看作是养老服务供给的函数。因为市场和社会提供的养老服务对家庭养老功能有替代效应,所以市场上服务项目提供得越多,就越能弥补家庭养老功能缺失后老年人的需求,使老年人的生活更加幸福愉快,从而他们对养老的满意度也会得到提升。为此,本文提出:

假设1:增量效应假设,即老年人居住附近供给的养老服务项目越多,老人年满意度越高。

根据已有研究经验[①],本文采用定序逻辑回归方法进行验证。假设1将养老服务数量作为老年人满意度的自变量,模型如下所示:

$$Y_i^* = \beta N_i + \gamma X_i + \varepsilon_i \tag{1}$$

其中,N_i 表示老年人居家附近提供的养老服务数量,是连续变量;X_i 表示影响满意度的控制变量;ε_i 为误差项,且服从逻辑分布;i 表示观测值。Y_i^* 是无法观察到的连续的潜变量,可观察的是老年人满意度的有序离散变量 Y_i,两者有如下关系:

$$Y_i = j(j = 1, 2, 3), \; 若 c_{j-1} < Y_i^* \leq c_j \tag{2}$$

其中 c_0、c_1、c_2、c_3 是阈值,为待估参数,且 $c_0 = -\infty$,$c_3 = +\infty$。

同时,本文认为因为老年人人口特征和家庭条件不同,他们对养老服务需求的程度也不一样,在这种条件下,服务的供给对老年人的满足感也会不同,这就意味着养老服务项目对老年人满意度的影响存在异质性。为此,本文提出:

假设2:异质效应假设,即养老服务项目对老年人满意度提升效果存在差别,有的服务能提升老年人满意度,有的则不能。

根据公式(1),该假设模型设定如下:

$$Y_i^* = \beta S_i + \gamma X_i + \varepsilon_i \tag{3}$$

其中,S_i 表示附近提供的养老服务项目,即主要解释变量;X_i 表示影响满意度的控制变量;ε_i 为误差项,且服从逻辑分布;i 表示观测值。Y_i^* 与 Y_i 满足公式(2)设定。

---

① 张淼:《我国农村老年人养老状况及满意度分析》,《调研世界》2016年第6期。

三 数据来源和变量选取

(一) 数据

为了深入研究中国养老服务体系建设情况和老年人养老需求,中国社会科学院社会发展战略研究院于 2019 年 5 月至 7 月,开展了"中国老龄化与养老工作调查"。调查采用多阶段、多层次与人口规模成比例的概率抽样方法,从全国范围内抽取 8 个省市、80 个县、800 个社区、每个社区 10—15 名老年人。这 8 个省市为辽宁、河北、山东、上海、河南、广东、四川和陕西,分别代表全国东北、华北、华东、华南、西南、西北六大地理区域。实际收到有效社区问卷 693 份、老年人问卷 7261 份,回收率分别为 86.6%、90.8%。

(二) 变量选取

本文的因变量是老年人满意度,由两部分组成:一是老年人对本社区养老工作满意度,包括医疗卫生服务质量、为老年人生活提供帮助、基础设施和生活环境三个方面;二是生活满意度,包括幸福感、获得感、安全感三个方面,由问题"总体来讲,我是一个幸福的人""跟 5 年前相比,您觉得自己生活状况如何""即使生活从头再来,我也没有什么想要改变的了"得到。选项取值为:不满意 =1、一般 =2、满意 =3。虽然这几个维度不能涵盖老年人满意度的所有方面,但所涉及的内容都是居家养老服务体系建设过程中老年人关心的重点问题,也是衡量老年人居家养老工作实践效果的主要方面。老年人总体及分类满意度情况如表 1 所示。

表 1　　　　　　　调查老年人生活满意度情况　　　　　　单位:%

	城乡区划		年龄段			性别		合计
	乡村	城镇	60—69 岁	70—79 岁	80 岁以上	男性	女性	
医疗卫生服务质量	58.2	48.6	50.3	54.3	55.9	54.1	50.2	52.1
生活提供的帮助	59.4	60	59	60.5	62.1	60.6	59	59.8

续表

	城乡区划		年龄段			性别		合计
	乡村	城镇	60—69岁	70—79岁	80岁以上	男性	女性	
基础设施和生活环境	62.5	61.8	61.8	62.6	62.1	62.5	61.7	62.1
幸福感	63.5	65.9	64.9	64.6	66.8	64.9	65.2	65.1
获得感	85.5	75.3	79	78.2	80.7	79.8	78.3	79
安全感	49.8	49.6	48.7	50.2	53.6	50.6	48.8	49.7

资料来源：根据笔者计算所得。已加权。

本文自变量是养老服务供给。根据已有研究经验①，本文将养老服务分为四个方面：生活辅助，包括送餐服务、帮忙洗澡、家庭保洁；健康护理，包括上门看病、社区照料、老年用品购买/租赁；精神文化，包括疾病预防知识讲座、心理咨询/聊天、文体娱乐活动；权益保障，指法律维权服务。该变量操作为"附近是否有某项服务"，有＝1，无＝0。同时，根据老年人选择结果，可以知道附近养老服务供给的数量，没有为0，全有为10，为连续变量。老年人附近养老服务供需情况如表2所示。

表2　　　　老年人附近养老服务供需情况　　　　单位：%

	供给	需求	供给缺口
送餐服务	28.5	10.5	18.0
帮忙洗澡	12.8	9.1	3.7
家庭保洁	24.0	15.3	8.7
上门看病	49.7	40.4	9.3
社区照料	22.6	20.1	2.5
老年用品购买/租赁	19.0	18.0	1.0
疾病预防知识讲座	41.4	54.2	-12.8
文体娱乐活动	64.6	61.5	3.1
心理咨询/聊天	21.4	31.2	-9.8
法律维权服务	41.2	41.6	-0.4

注：供给缺口＝供给－需求。

资料来源：根据笔者计算所得。

---

① 章晓懿、刘帮成：《社区居家养老服务质量模型研究——以上海市为例》，《中国人口科学》2011年第3期；丁志宏、王莉莉：《我国社区居家养老服务均等化研究》，《人口学刊》2011年第5期；王琼：《城市社区居家养老服务需求及其影响因素——基于全国性的城市老年人口调查数据》，《人口研究》2016年第1期。

本文将控制变量分为三大类：个人特征、家庭支持、社区养老环境。个人特征变量包括：性别，年龄，受教育程度，月收入，自评健康，失能情况，户口类型。家庭支持变量包括：配偶，存活子女个数，赡养情况。社区养老环境：地区分类，免费使用活动场所，社区卫生服务中心，日间照料中心/养老驿站，省份。变量统计性特征如表3所示。

表3　　　　　　　　变量统计性描述

变量	变量定义	数量	平均值	标准差
性别	女性=1，男性=0	7261	0.334	0.472
年龄	老年人年龄	7261	71.502	8.109
受教育程度	未上过学=1，小学（私塾）=2，初中=3，高中/中专/职高=4，大学及以上=5	7248	2.362	0.981
月收入	每月总收入	7261	1387.005	1776.246
健康状况	健康=1，不健康=0	7229	0.368	0.482
失能情况	失能=1，自理=0	7261	0.122	0.328
户口	非农业=1，农业=0	7240	0.243	0.429
是否有配偶	是=1，否=0	7261	0.797	0.402
孩子数量	存活子女数量	7261	2.76	1.534
赡养情况	由儿子赡养=1，由女儿赡养=2，儿子女儿轮流赡养=3，不由子女赡养=4	7215	2.526	1.312
地区分类	城镇=1，农村=0	7261	0.374	0.484
免费活动场所	是=1，否=0	7231	0.801	0.399
社区卫生服务中心	是=1，否=0	7220	0.881	0.324
日间照料中心/养老驿站	是=1，否=0	7246	0.271	0.444
省份	行政区划编码	7261	35.164	13.539
医疗卫生服务质量	不满意=1，一般=2，满意=3	7236	2.477	0.597
为老年人生活提供的帮助	不满意=1，一般=2，满意=3	7227	2.527	0.604
基础设施和生活环境	不满意=1，一般=2，满意=3	7246	2.561	0.577
幸福感	不满意=1，一般=2，满意=3	7236	2.613	0.56

续表

变量	变量定义	数量	平均值	标准差
获得感	不满意=1，一般=2，满意=3	7171	2.774	0.477
安全感	不满意=1，一般=2，满意=3	7212	2.47	0.631
服务数量	养老服务数量加总	7125	3.089	2.755
送餐服务	是=1，否=0	7229	0.223	0.416
帮忙洗澡	是=1，否=0	7221	0.112	0.316
家庭保洁	是=1，否=0	7224	0.193	0.394
上门看病	是=1，否=0	7245	0.552	0.497
社区照料	是=1，否=0	7209	0.204	0.403
老年用品购买或租赁	是=1，否=0	7215	0.173	0.378
疾病预防知识讲座	是=1，否=0	7229	0.403	0.491
法律维权服务	是=1，否=0	7211	0.41	0.492
心理咨询/聊天	是=1，否=0	7210	0.204	0.403
文体娱乐活动	是=1，否=0	7234	0.625	0.484

资料来源：根据笔者计算所得。

四 研究发现

居家养老是指老年人居住在家中，主要从社区获取养老服务，社区是养老服务供给的运转平台，企业和社会组织提供服务内容，养老机构为高龄失能老人提供服务补充，政府为弱势老年人群体托底的养老服务体系。在居家养老服务体系下，老年人从社区获取大部分养老服务，社区可以是服务的提供者，更主要是服务平台的组织者。如果养老服务能够满足老年人的需求，让他们的生活更加合意舒适，那么老年人附近的服务项目越多，他们的满意度就应该越高。根据公式（1），表3-4模型（1）—（6）汇总了回归结果。整体上看，养老服务数量对老年人所有类别满意度都有较强正向影响，且显著性都在1%水平以上。这说明增加养老服务项目能够有效提高老年人满意度，假设1得到验证。从影响程度看，养老服务对老年人环境满意度提升效果高于生活满意度，其中对社区基础设施和生活环境影响效果最大；在生活满意度中，对老年人幸福感影响效果最大，对安全感影响不显著。这说明养老服务供给能够整体提高老年人满意度，但对老年人不同方面的满意度影响效果不一样。所以各地在发展养老服务产业时，不能一拥而上，要根据本地老年人需求和满意度特点，重点推进更能提高老年人满意度的项目。

养老服务项目从不同的角度满足老年人需求，需求程度不同，服务项目对老年人满足程度也不一样，对他们满意度影响效果也就有差异。根据公式（3），表4模型（7）—（12）汇报了回归结果。结果显示，生活辅助类服务对老年人满意度提升影响最小，对所有类别满意度都没有显著正向影响，甚至大多数为负向影响，且部分显著性在5%水平以上，说明这类服务不是老年人的主要需求，其项目供给对老年人影响不大。健康护理、精神文化和权益保障对老年人满意度提升总体上有正向影响，且显著性大部分在1%水平以上。对社区养老环境满意度影响显著性高于生活满意度，其中对为老年人提供生活帮助影响最大，对老年人安全感影响最小。健康护理类中上门看病对所有满意度都有显著正向影响，精神文化类的疾病预防知识讲座也都有正向影响，且几乎都在1%水平上显著。而其中的社区照料和文体娱乐活动只对环境满意度有显著正向影响。不同养老服务类别和项目对老年人满意度影响方向、范围和显著性都有差异，这说明养老服务具有显著的异质性，假设2得到检验。

表4　　　　　养老服务供给对老年人满意度影响回归结果

因变量	环境满意度			生活满意度		
	医疗卫生服务质量	为老年人提供生活帮助	社区基础设施和生活环境	幸福感	获得感	安全感
	(1)	(2)	(3)	(4)	(5)	(6)
养老服务数量	0.138***	0.148***	0.163***	0.102***	0.068***	0.023
	(0.018)	(0.019)	(0.018)	(0.017)	(0.015)	(0.016)
控制变量	是	是	是	是	是	是
观测值	6,746	6,739	6,756	6,747	6,689	6,737
伪 R^2	0.0728	0.0627	0.0674	0.0671	0.0730	0.0315

续表

因变量		环境满意度			生活满意度		
		医疗卫生服务质量	为老年人提供生活帮助	社区基础设施和生活环境	幸福感	获得感	安全感
		(7)	(8)	(9)	(10)	(11)	(12)
生活辅助	送餐服务	-0.409***	-0.208***	-0.037	-0.238***	-0.258***	-0.292***
		(0.078)	(0.080)	(0.081)	(0.083)	(0.094)	(0.075)
	帮忙洗澡	-0.082	-0.235**	-0.047	0.008	-0.108	0.231**
		(0.103)	(0.109)	(0.107)	(0.113)	(0.120)	(0.100)
	家庭保洁	-0.230***	-0.130	-0.092	-0.135	-0.053	-0.012
		(0.088)	(0.093)	(0.094)	(0.096)	(0.109)	(0.083)
健康护理	上门看病	0.444***	0.213***	0.261***	0.168**	0.215***	0.027
		(0.067)	(0.068)	(0.069)	(0.069)	(0.083)	(0.062)
	社区照料	0.373***	0.506***	0.404***	-0.060	0.003	0.056
		(0.086)	(0.092)	(0.091)	(0.089)	(0.108)	(0.085)
	老年用品购买或租赁	0.294***	0.163*	0.175*	0.352***	0.126	0.190**
		(0.086)	(0.095)	(0.093)	(0.095)	(0.106)	(0.087)
精神文化	疾病预防知识讲座	0.351***	0.239***	0.038	0.326***	0.296***	0.273***
		(0.075)	(0.078)	(0.079)	(0.083)	(0.099)	(0.073)
	心理咨询/聊天	0.339***	0.484***	0.399***	0.139	-0.299***	0.189**
		(0.089)	(0.098)	(0.094)	(0.094)	(0.112)	(0.080)
	文体娱乐活动	0.269***	0.352***	0.449***	-0.001	-0.012	-0.056
		(0.070)	(0.069)	(0.069)	(0.071)	(0.089)	(0.065)
权益保护	法律维权服务	0.006	0.227***	0.128*	0.204***	0.401***	-0.055
		(0.074)	(0.075)	(0.074)	(0.077)	(0.090)	(0.069)
	控制变量	是	是	是	是	是	是
	观测值	6,746	6,739	6,756	6,747	6,689	6,737
	伪 R^2	0.0970	0.0844	0.0769	0.0669	0.0883	0.0355

注：括号内是稳健性标准误；***、**、* 分别表示在1%、5%、10%水平上显著。限于文章篇幅，没有显示所有变量回归结果，如有需求可以向笔者索取。

资料来源：根据笔者计算所得。

为什么不同的服务项目对老年人满意度影响效果不同呢？这主要受老年人年龄结构和服务需求偏好影响。生活辅助类服务长期以来由家庭成员提供，老年人和社会认识中容易形成路径依赖和传统习惯，而且调查中老年人月均收入为1387元，在有家庭成员服务替代的情况下，老年人不愿长期支付这类服务。虽然调查显示空巢老人比例已经达到57.4%，但是中国老年人现在仍然以低龄群体为主，截至2019年底，60—69岁老年人占比达60%，他们健康状况和自理能力较好，所以对这类服务需求还比较低。这类服务属于老年人日常需求，如果价格定得过高，老年人难以购买，如果服务价格过低，企业没有利润，也无法持续发展。因为这类服务目前还不是老年人群体的主要需求，短期内不具备大范围普及的需求基础，需要着重于长期的市场建设。但对于高龄、失能老人来说，他们因自理能力和条件限制，对此类需求弹性很小，为了满足他们需求和提高生活质量，政府应该加强对这类老年人的专项补助，或对服务企业减租、减税，以充分调动市场的力量。

健康护理、精神文化和权益保护类服务需要较高的专业知识和技能，在传统养老模式下也无法由家庭成员提供，而需要专门机构和专业人员来提供。特别是上门看病、疾病预防知识讲座和法律维权服务需要职业医师、护士、律师、法官等专业人员的服务，对老年人来说必不可少，且又不具备可替代性，所以这些服务的供给最能提升老年人的满意度。随着中国全面进入小康社会，老年人对生活质量也提出了更高的要求，2018年中国人均预期寿命已达77岁[1]，健康已经成为老年人最重视的需要，没有健康的生理和心理条件，老年人不可能享受幸福、惬意的晚年生活。上门看病和健康知识不仅能够满足老年人治疗病痛的需求，更能减少他们就医交通、看病等待等时间和精力的消耗，还能够加强预防疾病，这些服务对于有慢性病或身体机能受限的老年人就更加重要。近年来，涉及老年人的财产、赡养、婚姻、诈骗和非法集资等侵权案件时有发生，老年人的财产和身心都受到威胁，所以此项服务供给能够满足老

---

[1] 国家卫生和健康委员会：《中国卫生和健康统计年鉴2019》，中国协和医科大学出版社2020年版。

年人的迫切需求，也就能提高他们的满意度。在专业服务价格较高的情况下，可以鼓励从业人员、相关专业大学生等群体提供志愿服务，完善养老服务社会多元供给体系。

中国居家养老服务体系建设和养老服务产业发展要实现由"扶弱型"向"普及型"、从"补充型"向"提高型"转变。在居家养老服务建设初期，养老服务供给重点以高龄、失能、独居、空巢老年人为主，所以着重发展助餐、助洁、助行、助浴等生活辅助服务，具有显著的"扶弱型"特征。但是，这类老年人数量比例较小，绝大多数低龄老年人自理能力较强，对此类服务支付意愿不强，所以前几年火爆的"老年餐桌""老年食堂"近期遇到可持续经营困难，对老年人群体整体满意度提升影响不大。所以，在服务对象上，中国居家养老体系建设应该由"扶弱型"向"普及型"转变，即在重点关注特别困难群体的同时，更加关注主体老年人的需求。在服务内容上，应该由"补充型"向"提高型"转变，即由助餐、助洁、助浴等家庭服务转向更能提高老年人生活质量的上门看病、健康知识、心理辅导、法律咨询等内容。由于中国目前医疗卫生体制和医护人员数量的限制，为老年人的完全免费上门看病、护理等服务还难以实现，那么"互联网+医疗"和智慧养老的功能发挥就更加重要。但是，本次调查显示只有38.2%的社区提供免费上网，使用手机或电脑上网的老年人比例仅为21.5%，而且仅有29.7%的老年人愿意通过互联网购买养老服务，这些基础设施和服务建设还需要进一步加强。

五　结论

本文利用2019年"中国老龄化和养老工作调查"数据，采用定序逻辑回归方法，从养老服务供给角度，从环境满意度和生活满意度两大类，对社区的医疗卫生服务、生活帮助、基础环境、幸福感、获得感和安全感6个方面，分析了居家养老服务体系建设对老年人满意度的影响。结果显示，党的十八大以来，以习近平同志为核心的党中央高度重视养老工作，逐步确立并推动居家养老服务体系建设，养老服务产业高速发展，养老服务内容和范围迅速增长，呈现出较强的增量效应，即养老服务项目越多，老年人满意度越高；呈现出异质效应，即养老服务项目对老年人影响程度不同，健康护理对老年人满意度影响最大，精神文化和权益保护影响较大，生活辅助没有显著正向影响。

因此，随着老龄化加速发展，中国"十四五"期间要继续加强居家养老服务体系建设，以满足老年人多元化需求，提高他们的养老满意度。在发展方向上，要注重由"扶弱型"向"普及型"、从"补充型"向"提高型"转变，在保证少数特别困难老年人生活辅助类服务的同时，更大程度地发展健康辅助、精神文化和权益保障类服务，提高老年人生理和心理健康程度，保证老年人合法权益不受侵犯。在发展的方式上，要推广"互联网＋医疗"、智慧养老、人工智能、大数据的运用，线上服务和线下智能装备结合，以精准医疗、精准服务更好地提高老年人生活质量。在供给主体上，要鼓励服务供给主体多元化，在充分发挥政府、社区、家庭等传统主体作用的同时，调动企业、社会组织的积极性，鼓励医生、律师、相关专业学生进入社区的志愿服务，以弥补政府和市场供给的不足，满足老年人对健康、法律、文化等多方面的需求，提高老年人养老满意度。

参考文献：

丁志宏、王莉莉：《我国社区居家养老服务均等化研究》，《人口学刊》2011年第5期。

国家卫生和健康委员会：《中国卫生和健康统计年鉴2019》，中国协和医科大学出版社2020年版。

胡仕勇、李洋：《农村老年人家庭养老满意度的影响因素分析》，《中国农村经济》2012年第12期。

林宝：《养老服务业"低水平均衡陷阱"与政策支持》，《新疆师范大学学报》（哲学社会科学版）2017年第1期。

刘吉：《我国老年人生活满意度及其影响因素研究——基于2011年"中国健康与养老追踪调查"（CHARLS）全国基线数据的分析》，《老龄科学研究》2015年第1期。

倪东升、张艳芳：《养老服务供求失衡背景下中国政府购买养老服务政策研究》,《中央财经大学学报》2015 年第 11 期。

彭华民:《福利三角:一个社会政策分析的范式》,《社会学研究》2006 年第 4 期。

钱雪飞:《影响城乡老年人生活满意度的社区养老社会环境建设现状——基于 1440 份问卷调查》,《西北人口》2011 年第 3 期。

唐迪、余运江、孙旭、高向东:《政府购买社区养老服务的满意度研究——基于上海调查数据的实证分析》,《西北人口》2017 年第 3 期。

同春芬、汪连杰:《福利多元主义视角下我国居家养老服务的政府责任体系构建》,《西北人口》2015 年第 1 期。

王琼:《城市社区居家养老服务需求及其影响因素——基于全国性的城市老年人口调查数据》,《人口研究》2016 年第 1 期。

王彦方、王旭涛:《影响农村老人生活满意度和养老模式选择的多因素分析》,《中国经济问题》2014 年第 5 期。

习近平:《决胜全面建成小康社会 夺取新时代中国特色社会主义伟大胜利——在中国共产党第十九次全国代表大会上的报告》,人民出版社 2017 年版。

《习近平在中共中央政治局第三十二次集体学习时强调 党委领导政府主导社会参与全民行动 推动老龄事业全面协调可持续发展》,《人民日报》2016 年 5 月 29 日第 1 版。

习近平:《中共中央关于坚持和完善中国特色社会主义制度 推进国家治理体系和治理能力现代化若干重大问题的决定》,人民出版社 2019 年版。

颜秉秋、高晓路:《城市老年人居家养老满意度的影响因子与社区差异》,《地理研究》2013 年第 7 期。

余杰,Mark Rosenberg,程杨:《北京市老年人居家养老满意度与机构养老意愿研究》,《地理科学进展》2015 年第 12 期。

张淼:《我国农村老年人养老状况及满意度分析》,《调研世界》2016 年第 6 期。

张秀兰、徐月宾:《构建中国的发展型家庭政策》,《中国社会科学》2003 年第 6 期。

章晓懿、刘帮成:《社区居家养老服务质量模型研究——以上海市为例》,《中国人口科学》2011年第3期。

Department of Economic and Social Affairs, Population Division, "World Population Prospects 2019, Volume Ⅱ: Demographic Profiles – China", New York: United Nations, 2019.

"十四五"时期中国青年社会融入与社会参与

马 峰[*]

"十四五"时期中国进入新发展阶段,开启全面建设社会主义现代化国家新征程。长期繁荣、稳定的社会发展环境为青年发展提供了全新的选择,中国青年社会参与的广度与深度将发生根本性变化。同时,中国社会发展环境面临深刻变化,新发展阶段形成更为安全、更高质量、更可持续的青年社会参与环境,需要厚植青年发展动力,形成与新发展阶段发展要求相适应的青年发展环境。

一 引言

"青年是国家经济社会发展的生力军和中坚力量。党和国家事业要发展,青年首先要发展。"[①] 为促进青年发展,为青年发展搭建人生出彩的舞台,党中央先后印发了《中长期青年发展规划(2016—2025年)》(以下简称"《规划》")、《关于促进劳动力和人才社会性流动体制机制改革的意见》(以下简称"《意见》")。《规划》和《意见》的出台,体现了国家从顶层设计、全面深化改革的制度层面,立足中华民族伟大复兴战

---

[*] 马峰,中国社会科学院社会发展战略研究院副研究员。
[①] 《中共中央 国务院印发〈中长期青年发展规划(2016—2025年)〉》,中华人民共和国中央人民政府网,2017年4月13日,http://www.gov.cn/zhengce/2017-04/13/content_5185555.htm#1。

略全局,定位青年成长和发展的现实需求、当代中国经济社会发展的阶段性特征,努力为青年发展塑造全面、系统化的制度环境、发展环境,"全党要关心和爱护青年,为他们实现人生出彩搭建舞台"①。

青年发展与社会发展之间是互动的关系,良好的社会发展可以更好地促进青年发展。同样,良好的青年发展也会为社会发展、社会环境的持续优化,提供不竭的青春活力与青年红利。当今世界正在经历百年未有之大变局,世纪疫情催动这一变局加速演化,国内外环境正在发生深度调整,变局与新局交替出现,深刻影响中国社会发展。"我国发展环境面临深刻复杂变化。当前和今后一个时期,我国发展仍然处于重要战略机遇期,但机遇和挑战都有新的发展变化。"②

"十四五"时期中国将进入新发展阶段,新发展阶段社会发展对于青年发展必然产生深刻影响。因此,在执行《规划》和《意见》的同时,要针对新发展阶段发生的环境、条件变化特征,"深刻认识我国社会主要矛盾变化带来的新特征新要求,深刻认识错综复杂的国际环境带来的新矛盾新挑战"③,既要及时有针对性地判断青年发展的新动态与新特征,紧贴时代脉动提高青年社会参与力度。同时,聚集新发展阶段全面建设社会主义现代化国家的时代要求,立足中华民族伟大复兴战略全局,形成与新发展阶段发展要求相适应的青年发展环境。

二 中国青年社会参与的广度与深度发生根本性变化

"十三五"时期先后迎来改革开放四十周年和新中国成立七十周

---

① 习近平:《决胜全面建成小康社会 夺取新时代中国特色社会主义伟大胜利——在中国共产党第十九次全国代表大会上的报告》,《光明日报》2017年10月28日第1版。
② 《中共中央关于制定国民经济和社会发展第十四个五年规划和二〇三五年远景目标的建议》,《人民日报》2020年11月4日第1版。
③ 《中共中央关于制定国民经济和社会发展第十四个五年规划和二〇三五年远景目标的建议》,《人民日报》2020年11月4日第1版。

年，站在改革开放四十周年和新中国成立七十周年的历史维度来看，国家的发展和人民的生活发生了翻天覆地的变化。经济实力、科技实力、综合国力跃上新的大台阶，"预计二〇二〇年国内生产总值突破一百万亿元；脱贫攻坚成果举世瞩目，五千五百七十五万农村贫困人口实现脱贫；粮食年产量连续五年稳定在一万三千亿斤以上；污染防治力度加大，生态环境明显改善；对外开放持续扩大，共建'一带一路'成果丰硕；人民生活水平显著提高，高等教育进入普及化阶段，城镇新增就业超过六千万人，建成世界上规模最大的社会保障体系，基本医疗保险覆盖超过十三亿人，基本养老保险覆盖近十亿人"①。今天中国社会发展的历史性成就，为新时代青年成长提供了历史上最好的发展环境。与百年前的青年一代相比，今日之青年处于历史上最好的发展时期。

第一，教育发展为青年参与社会发展提供了起点的平台。

习近平总书记指出："抓好教育是扶贫的根本大计，要让贫困家庭的孩子都能接受公平的有质量的教育，起码学会一项有用的技能，不要让孩子输在起跑线上，尽力阻断贫困代际传递。"② "十三五"时期国家经济社会发展迈上新的发展台阶。家庭生活的殷实、富足，也为青年的成长提供了稳定的家庭生活环境，使得家庭可以为孩子的成长、成才提供更稳定的物质基础，可以使孩子的发展朝着更多元、更具个性，更符合自身特质的方向发展。发展的质量、水平，较之其他历史时期也更高。从家庭寄予期望最高的子女教育来看，教育发展为青年发展，为青年在社会立足，促进起点的公平，带动机会的公平发挥了难以替代的作用，更有利于塑造青年发展向上的社会环境，有利于形成青年发展奋斗成功的社会氛围。

---

① 《中共中央关于制定国民经济和社会发展第十四个五年规划和二〇三五年远景目标的建议》，《人民日报》2020年11月4日第1版。
② 《习近平关于社会主义社会建设论述摘编》，中央文献出版社2017年版，第52页。

表1　　　　中国各类学校招生人数变化趋势（2010—2019年）　　单位：万人

年份	中等职业学校（机构）招生数	普通高等学校招生数	普通高等学校本科招生数	普通高等学校专科招生数	普通高中招生数
2010	711.3957	661.8	351.2563	310.5	836.2
2011	649.9626	681.5	356.6411	324.9	850.8
2012	597.0785	688.8	374.0574	314.8	844.6
2013	541.2624	699.8	381.4331	318.4	822.7
2014	495.3553	721.4	383.4152	338	796.6
2015	479.8174	737.8	389.4184	348.4	796.6
2016	466.1428	748.6	405.4007	343.2	802.9
2017	451.5235	761.5	410.7534	350.7	800.1
2018	428.5024	790.9931	422.159	368.8341	792.7063
2019	600.4	914.9026	431.3	483.6146	839.4949

资料来源：国家统计局。

从表1的趋势来看，中等职业教育、高等教育聚集着中国主要的青年群体。"十三五"时期，各级各类中等职业和高等教育机构招生人数总体上呈现上升的趋势，但是在个别学历层次上也有分化。高等学校本专科招生人数与规模基本稳定，中等职业院校（机构）招生人数下降幅度较大，普通高中招生人数基本稳定，普通高中与普通高校依然是招生的"大户"，可见家庭在子女受教育的倾向、去向、观念上倾斜是明显的，家长希望女子受更好教育的愿望强烈，社会环境的变迁为青年接受更好的教育提供了坚实的物质基础。从2018年数据来看，与之前相比，表4-1中所示的5个方面的指标均出现转折性增长，2019年普通高校招生突破914.9万人，同样，中等职业学校（机构）招生经历多年下滑后，出现大幅反弹，突破600.4万人。青年受教育的机会、可能，特别是接受高等教育的机会越来越多，职业教育在经济高质量发展转型的时代背景下，也成为一些年轻人实现人生转折的重要"杠杆"和"拐点"。"2019年，全国学前教育毛入园率达83.4%，比2000年提高37个百分点；义务教育巩固率94.8%；高中阶段毛入学率89.5%，是2000年的2倍；高等教育毛入学率51.6%，是2000年的4倍，迈入普及化发展阶段。2019年，新增劳动力平均受教育年限13.7年，比2010年增加1.29年，其中受过高等教育的比例达 50.9%。"①

第二，就业发展为青年社会参与提供广阔空间。

习近平总书记在 2019 年的新年贺词中说道："我注意到，今年，恢复高考后的第一批大学生大多已经退休，大批'00 后'进入高校校园。1 亿多非户籍人口在城市落户的行动正在继续，1300 万人在城镇找到了工作，解决棚户区问题的住房开工了 580 万套，新市民有了温暖的家。"②恢复高考后的第一批大学生大多已经退休，他们在韶华之年经历了改革开放四十多年的社会环境变迁，正安享退休生活，而新一代的大学生"00 后"正步入校园，享受青年的时光，一代代的青年发展构成了国家发展的主基调，如表 2 所示，截止到 2019 年中国高等学校毕（结）业学生人数达到 758.5298 万人，这与十年前相比、与改革开放之初相比，发展是跨越性的。新时代的青年有更多的机会和可能，实现人生的梦想，也有更多实现跨阶层流动的可能。

表 2　　中国劳动力及普通高等学校、中等职业学校（机构）毕业生数　　单位：万人

年份	劳动力	普通高等学校毕（结）业生数	中等职业学校（机构）毕业生数
2010	78388	575.4	543.6524
2011	78579	608.2	541.1252
2012	78894	624.7	554.384
2013	79300	638.7	557.5587
2014	79690	659.4	516.1519
2015	80091	680.9	473.2654
2016	80694	704.2	440.5572
2017	80686	735.8	406.3981
2018	80567	753.3087	396.977
2019	89640	758.5298	493.4

资料来源：国家统计局。

---

① 万东华：《从社会发展看全面建成小康社会成就》，《人民日报》2020 年 8 月 4 日第 11 版。
② 《国家主席习近平发表二〇一九年新年贺词》，《光明日报》2019 年 1 月 1 日第 1 版。

青年发展是社会发展的重要组成部分,社会既安定有序,又充满活力,要积极推动青年融入社会环境变迁之中,进而带动整体的社会创造。"防止社会阶层固化,关键是深化改革、促进机会公平。事实上,当一个人在社会中能够靠自己努力获得成功时,就证明这个社会是具有流动性的,机会是公平的。"① 青年处在人生的起始阶段,在最需要资源的阶段,应该赋予其发展的资源,在最需要支持阶段,应该赋予其发展的平台。机会的公平、持续的社会流动环境和可持续的上升通道是涉及青年发展的重要方面。党的十一届三中全会后,中国人口的空间分布较之前发生剧烈变动。从乡村到城市,从内地到沿海,从西部到东部,中国人口的空间流动随着改革开放政策的深入推进,工业化、城镇化的发展,形成了规模庞大流动的人口大潮。而在此期间,无论是早期走出来的青年,还是今天成长起来的青年,他们参与到这样的流动大潮中,接受着社会环境的变迁,反过来又推动着社会环境发生更深刻的变革。"十三五"时期,这一变革更加明显。实际上,"任何人都脱离不了时代的发展,时代发展的多重因素促使人完成社会化进程,进而对社会的发展施加影响"②。

今日之中国,"拥有 1 亿多市场主体和 1.7 亿多受过高等教育或拥有各类专业技能的人才,还有包括 4 亿多中等收入群体"③。一个流动的中国,凝聚了青春的力量。改革开放以来,中国人口流动的变化在与中国发展变化同步的同时,也带来了人民生活的改善和进一步社会流动的变化。

"就业是社会稳定的重要保障。一个人没有就业,就无法融入社会,也难以增强对国家和社会的认同。失业的人多了,社会稳定就面临很大危险。"④ 从就业发展情况来看,中华人民共和国成立之初,经济凋敝,

---

① 马峰:《用全面深化改革激发社会活力正确看待社会流动问题》,《人民日报》2017 年 7 月 20 日第 7 版。

② 李春玲、马峰:《"空巢青年":游走在"生存"与"梦想"间的群体》,《人民论坛》2017 年第 4 期。

③ 《坚持用全面辩证长远眼光分析经济形势 努力在危机中育新机于变局中开新局》,《人民日报》2020 年 5 月 24 日第 1 版。

④ 《习近平关于社会主义社会建设论述摘编》,中央文献出版社 2017 年版,第 68 页。

就业形势不理想。改革开放以来，持续的就业增长，以及从就业规模到就业结构的深刻变化，为青年既增加了广阔的就业机会，更增加了各种就业可能和就业选择。就业是民生之本，也是青年迈入社会，安身立命的第一步，就业也涉及人的尊严。"一个健康向上的民族，就应该鼓励劳动、鼓励就业、鼓励靠自己的努力养活家庭，服务社会，贡献国家。"① 充分就业的实现，高质量就业的发展，为中国青年个人的成长和发展，提供了更广阔的发展空间。全面深化改革，以更大的勇气，破除体制机制障碍，发挥了进一步做大、做厚中等收入群体，畅通青年向上流动通道的关键作用。"现在在高校学习的大学生都是20岁左右，到2020年全面建成小康社会时，很多人还不到30岁；到本世纪中叶基本实现现代化时，很多人还不到60岁。"② 因此，"要全面深化改革，营造公平公正的社会环境，促进社会流动，不断激发广大青年的活力和创造力"③。教育与就业涉及青年发展重要方面，教育代表着起点的公平，而就业代表着机会的公平，也是实现社会阶层跃升，促进青年实现纵向流动的重要方式和凭借的媒介。

三 新发展阶段青年社会参与态势分析

习近平总书记在经济社会领域专家座谈会上指出："'十四五'时期是我国全面建成小康社会、实现第一个百年奋斗目标之后，乘势而上开启全面建设社会主义现代化国家新征程、向第二个百年奋斗目标进军的第一个五年，我国将进入新发展阶段。"④ 新发展阶段不断满足人民对美好生活的向往，实现更高质量、更有效率、更加公平、更可持续、更为

---

① 《习近平关于社会主义社会建设论述摘编》，中央文献出版社2017年版，第68页。
② 习近平：《青年要自觉践行社会主义核心价值观——在北京大学师生座谈会上的讲话》，《光明日报》2014年5月5日第2版。
③ 习近平：《青年要自觉践行社会主义核心价值观——在北京大学师生座谈会上的讲话》，《光明日报》2014年5月5日第2版。
④ 习近平：《在经济社会领域专家座谈会上的讲话》，《光明日报》2020年8月25日第2版。

安全的发展是社会发展的主要方面。

当前,"国内发展环境也经历着深刻变化。我国已进入高质量发展阶段,社会主要矛盾已经转化为人民日益增长的美好生活需要和不平衡不充分的发展之间的矛盾,人均国内生产总值达到 1 万美元,城镇化率超过 60%,中等收入群体超过 4 亿人,人民对美好生活的要求不断提高"[①]。面对世界大变局,国内新发展格局,需要将青年社会发展参与与新发展阶段发展要求紧密结合,进一步扩大青年发展空间,拓展青年社会流动渠道,不断满足青年美好生活发展需求。

人民美好生活需要日益广泛,不仅对物质文化生活提出了更高要求,而且在民主、法治、公平、正义、安全、环境等方面的要求日益增长。这也是青年十分关心的领域,每一项都涉及青年的切身利益、成长利益、发展利益。

一项长期预测研究表明:"未来四十年里,中国经济将一直保持高速增长的态势;到 2052 年,中国经济总量将达到 2012 年的五倍,这相当于 3.5% 的年平均增长率。"[②] "到 2052 年,中国 GDP 总量将相当于所有 33 个经济合作发展组织(OECD)国家 GDP 的总和。"[③] 新发展阶段要从统筹中华民族伟大复兴战略全局与世界百年未有之大变局出发,努力促进青年的全面发展和社会发展参与的全面进步,厚植青年发展动力,形成与新发展阶段发展要求相适应的青年发展环境。

第一,促进青年社会参与,形成更安全的青年发展环境。

首先,要建立与新发展格局相适配的社会发展环境。格局转换是全局性的、全面性的,主要矛盾的转移其影响是全方面的。建立与新发展格局相适配的社会发展格局,一方面,需要提高社会治理的能力与水平,聚焦现代化的发展目标和步骤,将新发展格局转换与新社会发展格局的

---

① 习近平:《在经济社会领域专家座谈会上的讲话》,《光明日报》2020 年 8 月 25 日第 2 版。

② [挪威] 乔根·兰德斯:《2052:未来四十年的中国与世界》,秦雪征、谭静、叶硕译,译林出版社 2019 年版,第 261 页。

③ [挪威] 乔根·兰德斯:《2052:未来四十年的中国与世界》,秦雪征、谭静、叶硕译,译林出版社 2019 年版,第 261 页。

转换统筹到国家治理体系与治理能力现代化的轨道上来，以治理现代化牵引格局转换，形成青年社会发展参与的制度优势与共享发展成果的运作机制，更多体现发展的同步性。另一方面，促进青年群体更充分、更高质量的就业缔造和转移，健全全覆盖、可持续的社保体系，强化公共卫生和疾控体系，更广领域的实现经济发展与社会发展的协同，拓宽青年社会流动的广度和深度。

其次，以全面深化改革破除影响青年社会参与的不平衡、不充分问题。在收入分配、社会流动、社会保障、社会风险防范与化解、社会利益格局调整等方面，需要最大限度地凝聚社会发展共识，必须在全面深化改革向纵深方向发展的进程中加以解决和破解。一方面，拓宽青年群体在基层治理现代化中的参与途径和渠道，形成公共利益与青年发展共享发展新机制。另一方面，进一步优化收入分配结构，做大、做强、做厚中等收入群体，加大相对贫困问题的解决力度，使"人民生活更加美好，人的全面发展、全体人民共同富裕取得更为明显的实质性进展"[1]。

最后，实现发展的均衡性，缩小数字鸿沟、智能鸿沟，增强青年参与社会发展的资源共享性，以职业教育为突破口，厚植社会青年的发展后劲和能力，提高其在劳动力市场中的竞争力，助力青年融入社会发展大局之中，成为社会发展的共享者、共建者。

第二，厚植青年发展动力，形成更高质量的青年发展环境。

首先，畅通青年参与社会发展的"四业"[2]。"从世界青年发展角度来看：一方面要关注影响青年发展的经济增长、社会流动、收入分配、社会安全等深层次社会发展问题；另一方面要关注青年在'四业'即：就业、学业、置业、创业等涉及个人未来发展方面的需求。社会发展与青年发展需求构成了一个整体的两个方面，既要不断地解决影响青年发展的深层次社会发展问题，塑造良好的经济社会发展环境，又要引导青

---

[1] 《中共中央关于制定国民经济和社会发展第十四个五年规划和二〇三五年远景目标的建议》，《人民日报》2020年11月4日第1版。

[2] "四业"主要包括学业、就业、置业、创业。学业涉及起点的公平，就业涉及机会的公平。

年融入社会发展、参与社会发展,让青年在参与分享中促进社会发展。"①夯实青年参与社会发展的基础。做好涉及青年的"四业"工作。"四业"是青年参与社会发展的主要路径,不但要保证其畅通,而且要提供更强有力的制度环境。

其次,立足新发展阶段畅通青年流动通道,促进教育、就业高质量发展。新发展阶段要努力改善人民生活品质,提高社会建设水平。根据新发展阶段的新特征,一方面,注重形成更高质量的就业结构,提高人才培养、人才教育与就业岗位需求的适配度,加大就业供给侧改革力度,改善就业供给结构性矛盾,畅通就业循环体系。另一方面,着力改善教育空间布局,实现优质教育均衡发展,筑牢教育公平底线,通过教育赋予技能,通过教育赋予希望,通过教育赋予青年人生发展的升腾动力,努力实现更可持续的教育与就业发展环境,促进社会建设现代化,为青年融入国家发展和社会建设提供更高水平的融入环境。

最后,全面贯彻落实《中长期青年发展规划(2016—2025年)》。制度的生命力在于执行,规划要发挥作用,关键在于执行力。进一步做好规划执行与政策配套,完善支持青年发展的政策体系,充分发挥从中央到县级青年工作联席会议机制,及时研究青年发展问题、及时评估规划落实进度、及时解决困扰青年发展难题,实现与《中长期青年发展规划(2016—2025年)》与"十四五"规划的联结,形成政策合力,为青年成长、发展释放更具稳定性、预期性的政策信号,做好政策托底与青年发展舞台搭建的共建机制,促进青年发展更加公平,更多惠及各类青年群体,促进各类青年群体享有基本公共服务的可及性、均等化。

第三,加强青年社会参与制度建设,形成更可持续的青年发展环境。

用制度体系形成青年融入社会发展、社会建设的制度红利。百年来青年投身民族复兴、国家富强的征程中,释放的青年红利、青春红利,正是党和人民事业生生不息的力量源泉。新时代走好民族复兴的长征路、应对前进中的各项艰难险阻,依然要发挥好青年的主力军作用,释放好

---

① 马峰:《南非青年参与社会发展价值观研究——基于风险社会与文化转型双重语境下的价值观分析》,《西南民族大学学报》2019年第10期。

青年红利、青春红利。

发挥好青年的创新天性，在各行各业促进青年创新发展创造发展。创新创造是青年的天性，在天性使然的年纪，投入到创新创造之中，必然能产生大的成就。青年的创新创造活动是社会创新创造活动的先声和潮头，加快青年创新创造扶持计划，发挥好前海深港现代服务业合作区创新创造形成的好经验、好做法。一方面，以营造现代营商环境为突破口，推动独角兽等创新创造性企业组织竞相而出，以创新创造促动社会更高质量发展、产业更高质量演化、科技更快迈向中高端。另一方面，以解决相对贫困问题为路径，加大对各类青年群体的扶持力度。辅助青年致富、成才，辅导青年成长、进步，形成综合性的涵盖金融、教育、技能培训、职业培养系统性的辅助体系，在中西部地区，加快建立青年创新创造辅助服务中心，通过小额信贷、项目扶持、定向培养、东西青年协同发展、城乡青年互助进步，形成青年全面均衡融入社会发展与社会建设的新格局。

青年的发展与经济社会的发展是同步的，国家稳定、社会向上，就会赢得向上的青年。今天的青年，在享有历史最好的发展机遇的同时，也承担了历史赋予的新的使命和发展责任。青年的未来系于国家和民族的未来，习近平总书记充分肯定当代青年的担当和作为，指出："在新冠肺炎疫情防控斗争中，你们青年人同在一线英勇奋战的广大疫情防控人员一道，不畏艰险、冲锋在前、舍生忘死，彰显了青春的蓬勃力量，交出了合格答卷。广大青年用行动证明，新时代的中国青年是好样的，是堪当大任的！"[1]

习近平总书记的肯定是对新时代青年最好的激励。在抗击疫情总结表彰大会上，习近平总书记再次充分肯定新时代青年、点赞新时代青年，指出："青年是国家和民族的希望。在这次抗疫斗争中，青年一代的突出表现令人欣慰、令人感动。"[2] "青年一代不怕苦、不畏难、不惧牺牲，用

---

[1] 《习近平回信勉励北京大学援鄂医疗队全体"90后"党员》，《人民日报》2020年3月17日第1版。

[2] 习近平：《在全国抗击新冠肺炎疫情表彰大会上的讲话》，《人民日报》2020年9月9日第2版。

臂膀扛起如山的责任,展现出青春激昂的风采,展现出中华民族的希望!让我们一起为他们点赞!"①在新时代社会环境变迁中要统筹协调推进新时代青年融入社会环境发展中,让付出牺牲、做出奋斗的新时代青年共享创造的喜悦、共享发展的成果,为新时代青年成长进步搭建更广阔的发展舞台、事业平台。

参考文献:

《国家主席习近平发表二〇一九年新年贺词》,《光明日报》2019 年 1 月 1 日第 1 版。

《坚持用全面辩证长远眼光分析经济形势 努力在危机中育新机于变局中开新局》,《人民日报》2020 年 5 月 24 日第 1 版。

李春玲、马峰:《"空巢青年":游走在"生存"与"梦想"间的群体》,《人民论坛》2017 年第 4 期。

马峰:《南非青年参与社会发展价值观研究——基于风险社会与文化转型双重语境下的价值观分析》,《西南民族大学学报》2019 年第 10 期。

马峰:《用全面深化改革激发社会活力正确看待社会流动问题》,《人民日报》2017 年 7 月 20 日第 7 版。

万东华:《从社会发展看全面建成小康社会成就》,《人民日报》2020 年 8 月 4 日第 11 版。

习近平:《决胜全面建成小康社会 夺取新时代中国特色社会主义伟大胜利——在中国共产党第十九次全国代表大会上的报告》,《光明日报》2017 年 10 月 28 日第 1 版。

习近平:《青年要自觉践行社会主义核心价值观——在北京大学师生座谈会上的讲话》,《光明日报》2014 年 5 月 5 日第 2 版。

习近平:《在经济社会领域专家座谈会上的讲话》,《光明日报》2020 年 8 月 25 日第 2 版。

习近平:《在全国抗击新冠肺炎疫情表彰大会上的讲话》,《人民日

---

① 习近平:《在全国抗击新冠肺炎疫情表彰大会上的讲话》,《人民日报》2020 年 9 月 9 日第 2 版。

报》2020年9月9日第2版。

《习近平关于社会主义社会建设论述摘编》,中央文献出版社2017年版,第52页。

《习近平关于社会主义社会建设论述摘编》,中央文献出版社2017年版,第68页。

《习近平回信勉励北京大学援鄂医疗队全体"90后"党员》,《人民日报》2020年3月17日第1版。

《中共中央关于制定国民经济和社会发展第十四个五年规划和二〇三五年远景目标的建议》,《人民日报》2020年11月4日第1版。

《中共中央 国务院印发〈中长期青年发展规划(2016—2025年)〉》,中华人民共和国中央人民政府网,2017年4月13日,http://www.gov.cn/zhengce/2017-04/13/content_5185555.htm#1。

[挪威]乔根·兰德斯:《2052:未来四十年的中国与世界》,秦雪征、谭静、叶硕译,译林出版社2019年版。

第二篇

中国经济发展经验

新发展理念与中国经济增长

娄 峰[*]

自改革开放以来，中国经济飞速发展，取得了举世瞩目的成就：2020年国内生产总值达到14.7万亿美元，占全球比重的16.8%，连续十二年居世界第二位；中国对世界经济增长的贡献率（汇率法）连续十五年全球第一；国际进出口连续四年稳居世界第一。然而，随着经济总量的提升和改革开放的不断深入，中国经济也面临新的挑战：新增劳动力持续减少、资源环境约束日益突出、国际贸易保护主义抬头，中美贸易摩擦加剧。同时，由于新一轮科技革命和产业变革正在孕育兴起，各学科间进一步交叉融合，全球化科技竞争与合作广泛而深入，科技创新的周期在缩短，国际社会科技主导地位的竞争日趋激烈。

在如此复杂的国际国内大背景下，中国政府明确了新发展理念：创新、协调、绿色、开放和共享。这是基于国际国内发展环境变化，以及中国经济发展阶段变化做出的重大判断，以新发展理念引领中国经济社会发展，解决中国经济发展中的重大结构性问题和培育经济发展新动能，是推动经济健康可持续发展的必由之路，对确保中国经济中长期平稳较快增长具有重要的现实意义。

本文将在深入分析新发展理念本质内涵的基础上，构建中国科技—能源—环境动态经济系统模型，设置高、中、低三种情景预测和模拟测算2021—2040年中国中长期经济增长率及最优的产业升级和结构转换路

---

[*] 娄峰，中国社会科学院数量经济与技术经济研究所经济预测分析研究室主任、研究员。

径；并对中国经济发展进行国际比较，最后提出相关政策建议。

一 新发展理念的本质内涵

新发展理念蕴含着十分深刻而丰富的含义。其不仅为当下新时代发展方法、机制以及方向等问题予以了明确回答，而且将新时代发展的方向、动力等方面融结成了紧密的有机体系。新发展理念是中国政府对社会发展新形势情况更为深刻、科学的认知，也是中国在新趋势下治理国家的新理念，是具有巨大潜力的理论武器。

第一，新发展理念的创新内涵。"创新是一个民族进步的灵魂，是国家兴旺发达的不竭动力。如果自主创新能力上不去，一味靠技术引进就永远难以摆脱技术落后的局面。一个没有创新能力的民族，难以屹立于世界先进民族之林。"[1] 习近平总书记指出："创新是一个民族进步的灵魂，是一个国家兴旺发达的不竭源泉"[2]。党的十八届五中全会提出创新、协调、绿色、开放、共享五大发展理念，把创新放在首位，以创新引领发展，突出了创新的极端重要性。创新是引领发展的第一动力，坚持创新发展，就必须把创新摆在国家发展全局的核心位置，不断推进理论创新、制度创新、科技创新、文化创新等各方面的创新，让创新贯穿党和国家一切工作，让创新在全社会蔚然成风。中国改革开放的40多年，也是文化、科技、制度、理论等各方面创新的系统过程，这也是中国经济发展的源泉和动力。国家与国家间的竞争，本质上就是创新的竞争；唯有加强创新，掌握核心关键技术，才能确保中国产业链、供应链不受制于人，才能够不断提升产品质量，在竞争日益激烈的国际市场中寻求发展空间，从而推动中国的现代化进程。

第二，新发展理念的协调内涵。由于经济是一个完整的有机系统，生产、消费、投资、贸易、储蓄、分配、人口、能源、环境、货币、财

---

[1] 王伟光主编：《"三个代表"重要思想研究》，人民出版社2002年版，第547页。
[2] 习近平：《在同各界优秀青年代表座谈时的讲话》，《人民日报》2013年5月5日第2版。

政、金融等经济变量相互联系，互相影响，触一发而动全身，认识和解决任何一个具体问题，都不是仅仅面对单个问题，而必须与其他问题联系起来考虑。根据经济学中的木桶定律，最低的限制因素往往决定事物发展的高度；因此，利用协调的方式来解决发展过程中累积的失衡矛盾，只有有机结合补短板、展优势，实现二者的共同协调，才能真正推动中国社会的协调平衡发展，实现中国经济的整体发展与进步。

第三，新发展理念的绿色内涵。人与自然之间的关系具有协和共生性，经济增长固然重要，但为了实现这个目标而对自然资源进行过度消耗、对生态环境造成严重破坏，则会适得其反。习近平总书记在分析经济发展和环境保护之间的相关性时，明确提出"我们既要绿水青山，也要金山银山。宁要绿水青山，不要金山银山，而且绿水青山就是金山银山"，"要正确处理好经济发展同生态环境保护的关系，牢固树立保护生态环境就是保护生产力、改善生态环境就是发展生产力的理念"[1]，"我国生态环境矛盾有一个历史积累过程，不是一天变坏的，但不能在我们手里变得越来越坏，共产党人应该有这样的胸怀和意志"[2]，这一方面扼要阐述了环境和经济的本质关系；另一方面也说明了要注重与协调人和自然之间的共生关系，着力于保护生态环境，切不可以破坏环境为代价推动经济发展。

第四，新发展理念的开放内涵。随着经济全球化和产业链一体化的快速发展，世界开放性与多元性的不断提升，国际合作与竞争也面临越来越复杂的局面，国际力量的对比和博弈达到了从未有过的程度。开放发展，合作共赢，是中国改革开放的基本经验之一；也是中国走向未来，走向人类共同体的必然要求。"深入推进高水平制度型开放，增创国际合作和竞争新优势。对外开放是我国的基本国策，任何时候都不能动摇。当今时代，任何关起门来搞建设的想法，任何拒人于千里之外的做法，任何搞唯我独尊、赢者通吃的企图，都是逆历史潮流而动的！当前，经

---

[1] 中共中央宣传部编：《习近平总书记系列重要讲话读本》，人民出版社、学习出版社2014年版，第120、137页。

[2] 本书编写组编：《将改革进行到底》，人民出版社、学习出版社2017年版，第115页。

济全球化遇到一些回头浪，但世界决不会退回到相互封闭、彼此分割的状态，开放合作仍然是历史潮流，互利共赢依然是人心所向。要敞开大门欢迎各国分享中国发展机遇，积极参与全球经济治理。凡是愿意同我们合作的国家、地区和企业，我们都要积极开展合作。"① 中国政策明确提出，未来中国必须找到有效处理内外联动关系的方法与策略，切实提高中国的对外开放质量，形成深度融合的发展格局，同时也提高了中国在国际市场中的话语权和影响力。

第五，新发展理念的共享内涵。"坚持共享发展，必须坚持发展为了人民、发展依靠人民、发展成果由人民共享，作出更有效的制度安排，使全体人民在共建共享发展中有更多获得感，增强发展动力，增进人民团结，朝着共同富裕方向稳步前进。""十三五"规划《建议》（以下简称《建议》）的这一表述，简明扼要地指出了共享发展的内涵和目标。这是中国人民追求的发展目标之一，唯有在实现公平正义的前提下实现共同富裕，作为实践主体的人民群众的创造性、能动性和积极性才会得到提升，幸福感与获得感也会加强，才会为社会发展提供更多的动力，为美好生活的实现奠定坚实的基础。

二 2021—2040 年中国经济增长潜力的情景预测

在上述新发展理念的本质内涵基础上，本文根据经济学相关原理，构建了中国科技—能源—环境动态经济系统模型，该模型包括九大模块：生产模块、贸易模块、居民收入和需求模块、企业模块、政府收支模块、均衡闭合模块、社会福利模块、环境模块和动态模块，共 3762 个方程。基于该模型系统，设置高、中、低三种情景预测和模拟测算 2021—2040 年中国中长期经济增长率及最优的产业升级和结构转换路径，主要结论如下：

---

① 习近平：《在浦东开发开放 30 周年庆祝大会上的讲话》，人民出版社 2020 年版，第 8—9 页。

第一,在基准情景下,2021—2025 年、2026—2030 年、2031—2035 年和 2036—2040 年四个时期 GDP 年均增长率分别为 6.2%、4.8%、4.3% 和 3.8%。在增长较快情景中,如果中国稳步推进城镇化,促进制造业转型与升级,增强产品国际竞争力,并且进一步加大财政性教育经费在 GDP 中的比重,提高劳动者素质,加强研发投入,提高产品附加值,全面深化市场化改革,那么中国在 2021—2025 年、2026—2030 年、2031—2035 年和 2036—2040 年四个时期,可能保持年均 6.8%、5.4%、4.9% 和 4.4% 的较快增长率。在增长较慢情景中,2021—2025 年、2026—2030 年、2031—2035 年和 2036—2040 年四个时期的 GDP 年均增长率分别为 5.7%、4.3%、3.4% 和 2.8%(如表 1 所示)。

表1　　　　2021—2040 年中国潜在经济增长率预测　　　　（单位：%）

年份	基准情景	增长较快情景	增长较慢情景
2021	9.0	10.4	7.9
2022	5.7	6.1	5.4
2023	5.6	6.0	5.2
2024	5.5	5.9	5.0
2025	5.2	5.7	4.9
"十四五"平均	6.2	6.8	5.7
2026	5.1	5.6	4.6
2027	4.9	5.5	4.4
2028	4.8	5.4	4.2
2029	4.7	5.2	4.1
2030	4.6	5.1	3.9
"十五五"平均	4.8	5.4	4.3
2031	4.4	5.0	3.8
2032	4.4	5.0	3.5
2033	4.3	4.9	3.4
2034	4.3	4.7	3.3
2035	4.2	4.7	3.2

续表

	基准情景	增长较快情景	增长较慢情景
"十六五"平均	4.3	4.9	3.4
2036	4.1	4.6	3.0
2037	3.9	4.5	2.9
2038	3.8	4.4	2.8
2039	3.7	4.3	2.7
2040	3.6	4.2	2.6
"十七五"平均	3.8	4.4	2.8

图1显示了2020—2040年中国GDP在不同情境的增长趋势。2020年和2021年中国GDP增速大起大落的主要原因是受新冠肺炎疫情的影响，使得中国2020年GDP增速明显低于其潜在增速，而2021年GDP增速的大幅回升是因为上年的基数原因，这两年的平均增速依然在合理范围内，这一方面说明新冠肺炎疫情在中国得到迅速有效控制，其未能对我国的潜在经济增速产生实质性影响；然而值得注意的是：对比较快情景和较慢情景，两者随着时间的推移差距越来越大，到2040年，较慢情景下GDP增速低于较快情景1.6个百分点，这也从侧面说明中国全面深化市场化改革的重要性和必要性。

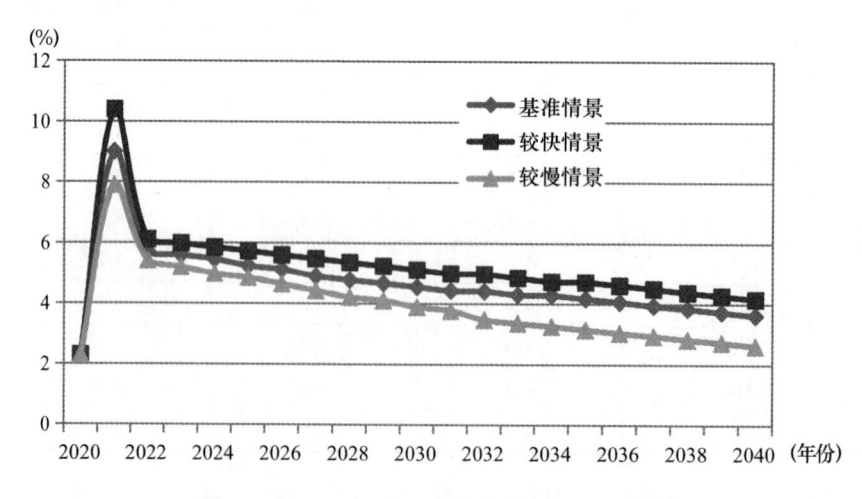

图1 2020—2040年不同情景下中国GDP增速

第二，在基准情境下，2040年中国不变价GDP规模将为2010年的13.59倍、2015年的5.38倍、2020年的2.66倍。2021—2040年，国民经济的增长不仅表现在总量的迅速增加，而且也将使得经济结构发生重大改变，这是由于三次产业的增长速度不同，经长期积累从量变到质变的结果。在未来20年中，三次产业变化趋势大致说明如下：(1) 从产业结构上看，三次产业在经济总额中的比重呈现平稳变化的发展趋势，其中，第一产业和第二产业比重逐年下降，而第三产业比重则逐年上升；(2) 2021—2040年，第一产业比重基本稳定，仅仅下降约1.8个百分点；而第二产业增加值占GDP的比重则下降近10个百分点。第三产业一直保持其在国民经济中的最大份额，并在2029年第三产业比重将超过60%，其在国民经济中处于绝对支配的地位进一步巩固和加强。2040年，三次产业增加值在国民经济中的比重分别为7.0%、27.2%和65.8%。

第三，根据中国科技—能源—环境动态经济系统模型预测结果，2021—2040年，中国的经济增长动力及其结构也将发生显著变化，其中从消费结构上看，农村居民消费和城镇居民消费在最终消费中的占比将逐年增加，尤其是城镇居民消费占比增长显著；而政府消费在总消费中的比重则逐年下降，这一方面与中国加强城镇化建设的战略决策有关，随着城镇化的大力发展，城镇人口将不断扩大，另外城镇居民的收入及社会福利也将进一步提高；另一方面也与中国政府实施"勤俭节约""扼制公款吃喝"的长期政策有关，政府消费比重下降的主要原因在于其消费增长率小于城镇居民消费增长率，从而其相对占比逐渐下降。从经济增长动力上看，自2012年起，最终消费占比超过资本形成率占比，消费已经并继续成为中国经济增长的主动力；未来20年内，投资拉动型为主的经济增长将逐步发生改变为以消费需求为主导的发展新阶段；消费增长（尤其是居民消费增长）将成为未来中国经济增长和发展的主要动力；投资增长将更多地取决于市场需求，取决于经济发展状况，这无疑有利于改善投资结构，有利于提高投资效率。

第四，预测结果显示：各部门的发展速度及其变化是各不相同的。

农业一直以比较稳定的低速发展，其增速将从 2019 年的 3.1% 缓慢下降到 2040 年的 2.3% 左右；煤炭、采掘等行业以及这些部门对应的原材料加工业如建材、冶炼等行业表现出相似的情况。石油、化工、电力等行业在 2020 年以前，在国民经济中将有重要地位，之后开始出现衰退。食品、轻纺等轻工业尽管速度一直低于 GDP，但十分稳定，与 GDP 基本保持同步变化。机械工业、电子仪器仪表行业，由于资本与技术的高度密集，在未来国民经济中将发挥重要的作用，这些行业的发展速度将始终快于 GDP 的增长；作为第三产业的交通邮电、商业服务业、金融、保险行业在未来经济中扮演着领头羊的角色，这些行业的快速发展，对带动国民经济量和质的提高，促进经济结构调整，具有十分重要的作用。由于各部门增长速度不同，它们在国民经济中的地位也随之发生变化。一些原来在国民经济中比重较高的行业，如农业、食品、纺织、建材和化学工业等传统行业，随着工业化的逐步完成和第三产业的崛起，其在国民经济中的份额逐渐下降，代之而起的是一批资本和技术高度密集的新型产业，如交通运输设备制造业、电子及通信设备制造业、金融保险业等。

三　研究结论及政策建议

　　世界经济发展史证明，当一个经济体快速持续发展达到一定水平时，经济增长速度就必然会发生转折，进入逐渐放缓下降阶段。与西方众多发达国家的发展经历类似，中国正在进入潜在经济增长逐渐下降的发展阶段，但是，我们在坦然接受这一客观发展规律的同时，仍然需要积极地从需求和供给两方面因素努力减缓潜在经济增长率的下降幅度，因为中国仍然处于发展中国家行列，中国的科技进步与创新还有很大的提升空间，制度改革红利还有进一步的释放潜力，不断升级的居民消费还有巨大的需求市场。具体建议如下：

　　第一，加强自主创新能力，促进科技创新。核心技术是现代企业竞争的基础。必须充分注重科学研究和技术创新，以关键共性技术、前沿引领技术、颠覆性技术创新为突破口，努力实现关键核心技术的自主可控，提高中国先进制造业产业链和供应链的稳定性和安全性。当前，中国经济发展正处于产业结构调整升级的关键时期，迫切需要加强和依靠科技创新。一方面，以新发展理念和"供给侧结构性改革"为发展契机，制定和完善相关规划和产业政策，促进企业自主创新、自主能力和自主意愿。此外，中国政府应建立和完善风险投资机制创新，促进风险投资机构的发展，确保企业科技研发管理制度的税收改革和优化，鼓励和引导企业加强研发投资，提高企业的创新意识。科技政策自主创新、投融资体制重组的重要性。加强知识产权保护，完善科技成果和产业支持体系、技术服务体系、技术产权交易体系，建立企业知识产权外部环境保护体系，确保企业知识产权的可持续发展。企业经济效益和社会效益的自主创新。

第二，中国应以质量和效率代替数量，提高资本利用率和劳动生产率。在加大科技创新力度，努力提高全要素生产率的同时，贯彻落实新发展理念本质内涵，提高传统生产资源的供给效率和供给质量。首先，改革是社会经济发展的动力源泉，进一步放开高端制造业、现代服务业的市场准入，促进行政审批和垄断行业改革，促进供给不足和回报率高的领域投资，加快推进投资负面清单、贸易便利化、金融改革与人民币国际化、事中事后监管等方面的改革与配套，以开放促改革；其次，适应现代经济发展的需要，必须加大人力资本投资，同时优化劳动力配置，降低劳动力成本和自由流动，促进城乡、企业、大学、科研机构、技术性体育之间的劳动力有序流动，并将退休年龄延长到老龄化人口，促进人口长期均衡发展。

第三，创新投融资模式，着力引入长期权益性社会资本，推进可持续型的基础设施和新型城镇化建设。

从短期来看，我们认为投资仍然是促进中国经济增长最为重要的因素之一。这是因为，尽管中国的人口结构已经在向着不利于经济增长的方向行进，但是在很长一段时间里中国的劳动力供给仍然较为充裕。与此同时，长期以来中国一直是一个储蓄率很高的国家，这种高储蓄在很长时间里不会改变，高储蓄为高投资提供了一种可能性，但是值得注意的是我们必须掌握好投资的效率和方向。其中，关键是促进研发、高端制造业、现代服务业、生态环保、基础设施等领域投资，优化投资结构。

世界城镇化历史表明，城镇化发展具有明显的阶段性特征，城镇化率处于30%—70%是城镇化中期阶段，发展速度较快。目前，中国城镇化建设正处于快速发展阶段，城镇人口的比重由1978年的17.9%提高到2020年的63.89%。从国际经验看，城镇化率只有达到70%左右，一个地区的城镇化进程才会稳定下来。城镇化建设不仅仅是提高"城镇化率"的问题，应该注重将"城乡一体化"寓于"新型城镇化"建设之中。随着城镇化水平持续提高，大、中、小城市建设将需要修建铁路、公路等交通设施，以及电力、燃气、自来水和污水处理等基础设施，需要提供养老保障、教育条件、医疗系统、住房保障等，户籍人口城镇化的提速势必带来巨大的投资需求。

在新型城镇化过程中，无论是交通等基础设施建设还是公共服务均等化都需要巨量资金投入。但在当前，并没有建立适应城镇化资金需求的多元化投融资机制，融资方式仍以银行贷款为主，最终还款来源仍是土地收入。随着地方政府财政收入减少、银行借贷困难以及地方债务凸显等问题日益突出，巨大的资金缺口成为新型城镇化面临的最直接难题。面对巨大的资金需求，如果不创新融资机制，基础设施和新型城镇化建设将是难以承受和难以持续的。鉴于中国高储蓄率还将维持一段时期，必须根据交通等基础设施和新型城镇化建设项目进行分类，并深入推动投融资体制机制改革，着力引入长期权益性社会资本，交通等基础设施和新型城镇化建设的巨大潜力才可转化为经济增长可持续型的重要动力。

第四，打破垄断，放松准入，积极发展混合所有制经济，大力发展具有高附加值的现代服务业和高端制造业。

当前，中国的一些行业、一些领域形成了较为严重的垄断，尽管在国内依靠垄断地位赚取较高利润，但浪费严重、服务质量差等问题突出，严重制约了现代服务业以及一些垄断性行业中竞争性业务的发展。打破垄断，放松民营资本的准入门槛，积极发展混合所有制经济，既是提高中国企业国际竞争力和服务质量的要求，又是未来提高潜在增长水平的重要增长点。从产业结构的变动来看，2013年尽管中国的第三产业增加值在 GDP 中的比重首次超过第二产业，但是中国第三产业发展仍然不足，特别是高附加值的现代服务业。

未来 20 年，全面深化改革成为时代的主旋律。2021 年政府工作报告指出，要增强各类所有制经济活力，制定非国有资本参与中央企业投资项目的办法，在金融、石油、电力、铁路、电信、资源开发、公用事业等七大领域，向非国有资本推出一批投资项目。制定非公有制企业进入特许经营领域具体办法，激活民间投资增长潜力，稳定民间投资的增长。实施铁路投融资体制改革，在更多领域放开竞争性业务，为经济增长提供新动力。除了打破垄断、放松准入之外，还应加大财政贴息及定向金融支持的力度，大力支持引导市场主体发展节能环保、新一代信息技术、生物、高端装备制造、新能源、集成电路、新材料等高端制造业，促进金融、保险、现代信息和物流、物联网、文化创意、教育培训、医疗养老等现代服务业的发展。

参考文献：

本书编写组编：《将改革进行到底》，人民出版社、学习出版社 2017 年版。

顾海良：《新发展理念的马克思主义政治经济学探讨》，《马克思主义与现实》2016 年第 1 期。

刘伟：《坚持新发展理念推动现代化经济体系建设》，《管理世界》2017 年第 12 期。

刘伟：《习近平新时代中国特色社会主义经济思想的内在逻辑》，《经济研究》2018 年第 5 期。

丘海平：《新发展理念的重大理论和实践价值》，《政治经济学评论》2019 年第 10 卷第 6 期。

任理轩：《深入贯彻新发展理念》，《人民日报》2021 年 5 月 11 日第 15 版。

王伟光主编：《"三个代表"重要思想研究》，人民出版社 2002 年版。

习近平：《在浦东开发开放 30 周年庆祝大会上的讲话》，人民出版社 2020 年版。

习近平：《在同各界优秀青年代表座谈时的讲话》，《人民日报》2013年5月5日第2版。

项久雨：《新发展理念与文化自信》，《中国社会科学》2018年第6期。

杨嘉懿、李家祥：《以"五大发展理念"把握、适应、引领经济发展新常态》，《经济纵横》2016年第4期。

张兴茂、李保民：《论经济社会的五大发展新理念》，《马克思主义研究》2015年第12期。

中共中央宣传部编：《习近平总书记系列重要讲话读本》，人民出版社、学习出版社2014年版。

中国社会科学院宏观经济研究中心课题组：《未来15年中国经济增长潜力与"十四五"时期经济社会发展主要目标及指标研究》，《中国工业经济》2020年第4期。

中国数字贸易发展的经济效应、制约因素与推进方略[*]

刘洪愧[**]

近年来,随着新一代信息通信技术和数字技术的加快发展,以数字经济为支撑的数字贸易迅速发展。根据联合国贸发会(UNCTAD)有关报告,2017 年全球电子商务规模已达到 29 万亿美元,大约 13 亿人曾有网上购物经历。[①] 世界贸易组织(WTO)2018 年的报告也预计到 2030 年,数字技术的使用有望使得全球贸易增加 34%。[②] 此外,也有研究预计到 2020 年,全球跨境 B2C 销售额将达到 1 万亿美元[③],全球将大约有 500 亿美元的设备连接到互联网中。[④] 中国的数字经济和数字贸易同样发展迅速。根据相关报告所整理的数据,中国的互联网用户从 2000 年的 2150 万人迅速增加到 2019 年的 8.29 亿人,而且中国目前的互联网使用人数仅占

---

[*] 本文原题为《数字贸易发展的经济效应与推进方略》,原发表于《改革》2020 年第 3 期,内容略有改动。

[**] 刘洪愧,中国社会科学院经济研究所副研究员。

[①] UNCTAD, "Global e-commerce sales surged to \$29 trillion", March 29, 2019, https://unctad.org/en/pages/newsdetails.aspx? OriginalVersionID=2034.

[②] WTO, *World Trade Report 2018*: *The Future of World Trade*: *How Digital Technologies Are Transforming Global Commerce*, World Trade Organization publication, 2018.

[③] McKinsey Global Institute (MGI), "Globalization in Transition: The Future of Trade and Value Chains", 2019.

[④] CISCO, "The Internet of Things, At-A-Glance", https://www.cisco.com/c/dam/en_us/solutions/trends/iot/docs/iot-aag.pdf.

总人口的 58%，未来有望继续增加，中国 2018 年的互联网零售额已经达到 1.1 万亿美元，居全球第一位，大约为美国的 2 倍。① E – Marketer 预计中国 2019 年的电子商务零售额将突破 1.99 万亿美元，可占中国零售总额的 35.3%，占全球网上销售额的 55.8%。②

数字化是正在进行的第四次工业革命的主要特征，而数字技术的使用催生出数字贸易，它极大减少了贸易成本和时间，不仅使得新的贸易产品不断涌现，而且将改变几乎所有行业的贸易方式和贸易规模，最终成为国际贸易新的发展动力。然而，数字贸易新的特征也使得已有国际贸易规则体系越发不再适用，从而面临诸多制约因素，特别是 WTO 框架下的多边贸易规则已经落后于数字贸易发展实践，无法支撑其发展需要。基于此，各国都在双边或区域贸易协定层面商谈和制定数字贸易规则，探讨未来的国际贸易新规则体系。

一 数字贸易的内涵界定及其与传统贸易的比较

数字贸易（Digital Trade）是脱胎于数字经济的一种新型贸易模式，是经济全球化、信息通信技术和数字技术发展到一定阶段的产物，具有诸多新的内涵。它摆脱了有形产品的交换所需要的运输、仓储等约束，极大拓展了可贸易产品的边界，具有很大的发展潜力。而且，从人类社会交换经济或贸易经济的发展历史来看，数字贸易在交换媒介和方式上显著有别于传统贸易，代表着一种全新的生产、交换和消费模式，代表未来贸易发展的方向，具有重要的经济学理论价值。

（一）数字贸易的内涵界定

数字贸易作为一种新型的贸易模式，目前还很少有国家将其从传统

---

① Congressional Research Service, "Digital Trade and U. S. Trade Policy", May 21, 2019, https://crsreports.congress.gov.

② E – Marketer, "2019：China to Surpass US in Total Retail Sales", January 23, 2019, https://www.emarketer.com/newsroom/index.php/2019 – china – to – surpass – us – in – total – retail – sales/.

贸易中分离出来单独加以统计和研究。虽然诸多国家、组织和学者从不同角度对数字贸易进行了界定，但是其在国内外学术界还尚未形成一个公认的标准定义。数字贸易最早起源于美国，因此相较于其他国家，美国学者和政府机构的相关研究最多，对数字贸易概念的阐述也相对全面。2013年7月，美国国际贸易委员会（USITC）在《美国和全球经济中的数字贸易Ⅰ》中总结认为，数字贸易是指通过网络传输而实现的产品和服务的交换活动，具体包括四个方面的内容：一是数字交付内容，如数字化的音乐、游戏、视频和书籍等；二是社交媒体，如社交网站、用户评价网站等；三是包括普通搜索引擎和专业搜索引擎在内的搜索引擎；四是其他数字化产品和服务，如应用软件、通过云计算提供的数据和计算服务以及通过互联网传递的通信服务等。[1]但该定义主要强调数字贸易产品和服务必须通过互联网实现交付，排除了大部分借助互联网实现交易的实物产品。随后，2014年USITC发布的报告《美国和全球经济中的数字贸易Ⅱ》对数字贸易的内涵进行了扩充和延伸。该报告定义："数字贸易既包括服务也涉及货物，其中互联网和基于互联网的技术在产品订购、生产和交付中发挥重要作用"，更加强调基于互联网技术的数字贸易在金融和保险、制造业等其他行业中的支撑作用。[2]美国贸易代表办公室（USTR）在2017年发布的《数字贸易的主要壁垒》中也指出，数字贸易是一个比较宽泛的概念，它既包括在互联网上的产品销售和线上服务的提供，也包括能够实现全球价值链（Global Value Chain，GVC）的数据流、实现智能制造的服务等，当今社会几乎所有商业活动都或多或少是数据驱动的或依赖数据来保持国际竞争力。[3]再之后，Deardorff在研究数字贸易中的比较优势问题时提出，国际数字贸易是一种涉及多国的贸易

---

[1] U. S. International Trade Commission, "Digital Trade in the U. S. and Global Economies, Part Ⅰ", July 2013.

[2] U. S. International Trade Commission, "Digital Trade in the U. S. and Global Economies, Part Ⅱ", August 2014.

[3] The Office of the U. S. Trade Representative, Key Barriers to Digital Trade, March 2017, https：//ustr. gov/about－us/policy－offices/press－office/fact－sheets/2017/march/key－barriers－digital－trade.

活动，其中所包含的某些贸易产品本身就是数字产品，或者贸易产品的订购、交付、支付或服务中的任何一个步骤或环节是通过互联网技术或数字技术来实现的。①

当然，其他国际组织也从不同角度对数字贸易进行了研究和界定。OECD 发表了一系列研究报告，总体也认为目前还不存在被普遍接受的关于数字贸易的标准定义，但学界和研究机构基本一致认为其既包括借助互联网及网上平台进行交易的货物和服务，也包括通过网络直接提供的数字产品和服务。② 国内方面，熊励等较早对数字贸易进行研究，认为数字贸易是指依托互联网平台、以数字技术为主要手段，为供求双方提供交易所需的数字化电子信息的创新型商业模式。③ 马述忠等对数字贸易的内涵进行了系统梳理，将其定义为：通过信息通信技术（ICT）的有效使用以实现传统有形货物、新型数字产品与服务、数字化知识与信息的高效交换，进而推动消费互联网向产业互联网转型并最终实现制造业智能化的新型贸易活动，是传统贸易在数字经济时代的拓展与延伸。④ 该定义将互联网、数字技术、产业转型以及贸易联系在一起，比较符合工业 4.0 时代中全球贸易的发展趋势。伊万·沙拉法诺夫等则从广义的角度认为，数字贸易包括信息通信技术产品和服务的交易、数字产品及服务、人员流动和数据传输四个核心因素。⑤

从以上梳理中不难看出，数字贸易的概念和经济学内涵在其发展过程中不断完善。早期的数字贸易研究主要强调数字产品和服务，未将其

---

① Deardorff A. V.,"Comparative Advantage in Digital Trade", Working Papers 664, Research Seminar in International Economics, University of Michigan, 2017.

② López González J, Jouanjeanm,"Digital Trade: Developing a Framework for Analysis", OECD Trade Policy Papers, No. 205, 2017, OECD Publishing; López González J, Ferencz J.,"Digital Trade and Market Openness", OECD Trade Policy Papers, No. 217, 2018, OECD Publishing.

③ 熊励、刘慧、刘华玲：《数字与商务：2010 年全球数字贸易与移动商务研讨会论文集》，上海社会科学院出版社 2010 年版。

④ 马述忠、房超、郭继文等：《世界与中国数字贸易发展蓝皮书（2018）》，2018 年 9 月；马述忠、房超、梁银峰：《数字贸易及其时代价值与研究展望》，《国际贸易问题》2018 年第 10 期。

⑤ 伊万·沙拉法诺夫、白树强：《WTO 视角下数字产品贸易合作机制研究——基于数字贸易发展现状及壁垒研究》，《国际贸易问题》2018 年第 2 期。

他有形货物纳入,这种定义相对来说比较狭隘,具有一定的局限性,与现实经济发展不符。而最近的研究则将所有产品和服务纳入到数字贸易的范畴当中,仅强调互联网、信息通信技术等数字技术在贸易中的应用,这极大地拓宽了数字贸易的边界,使其内涵变得更加完善且符合实际。但目前来看,国内外学界对数字贸易的理论研究仍处于初始阶段,随着数字贸易的发展,其概念还将处于演进之中。但大多数学者认为,数字贸易是显著区别于传统贸易的新一代贸易模式。

(二) 数字贸易与传统贸易的比较

从历史的角度看,本文认为国际贸易经历了三个大的发展阶段,分别是传统的最终产品贸易、全球价值链(GVC)贸易、数字贸易。[①] 每个阶段的贸易方式、贸易产品、发展动力和贸易政策的着重点都不一样。第一个阶段是20世纪70年代之前的最终产品贸易阶段,主要特征是国际运输技术的进步和运输成本的下降使得国家之间的最终品贸易得到空前发展。第二个阶段是20世纪70年代以来的GVC贸易阶段,主要特征是跨国生产分工成本的下降使得同一产品的生产可以在多个国家进行,相应的中间产品和零部件贸易占据主导地位,使得全球贸易额和增速远高于全球GDP。而未来的第三个阶段将是数字贸易阶段,其主要特征是数字技术的进步使得数字产品和服务不断涌现,如云计算、3D打印、在线支付、社交媒体、网络平台、数字音乐、电子书等。有形的产品贸易也越来越依赖电子商务来实现,产品越来越小规模化、个性化、数字化,产品和服务的界限也越来越模糊。

更具体地讲,笔者通过对已有文献的查阅和整理,从多个经济学维度对数字贸易和传统贸易的异同进行了总结与比较(见表1)。目前来看,数字贸易和传统贸易具有基本相似的贸易本质、贸易目的以及经济学理论支撑,但是两者在赖以产生的时代背景、贸易参与者、贸易对象、贸易方式、贸易的时效性以及贸易监管政策等方面,均具有显著的差异。

---

① López González J, Jouanjeanm, "Digital Trade: Developing a Framework for Analysis", OECD Trade Policy Papers, No. 205, 2017, OECD Publishing.

表1　　　　　　　　　　　数字贸易与传统贸易的比较

		传统贸易	数字贸易
不同点	产生的时代背景	以蒸汽机为代表的第一次工业革命、电力技术为代表的第二次工业革命和计算机及信息技术为代表的第三次工业革命	第三次工业革命和以人工智能、工业机器人、物联网、量子通信、虚拟现实以及生物技术为代表的第四次工业革命
	贸易参与者	以大型跨国企业为主，中小型企业通过代理商、零售商和批发商等中间机构间接交易，供给和需求方通常并不直接进行交易磋商	互联网平台企业的重要性越发凸显，中小微企业成为主力军，且平台企业的出现，互联网和数字技术的使用使得供给和需求方直接交易成为可能
	贸易对象	主要是有形的货物和生产要素，服务贸易占比较少	既包括数字产品和服务，也包括借助平台企业实现交易的传统货物，服务贸易占比将不断上升
	贸易运输方式	主要采取陆运、海运等运输方式，通关需要更多的实物文件（如证明材料、纸质单据等）	有形商品主要采取邮政和快递等方式寄送，数字产品和服务则采用数字化传递方式，整个交易过程可实现无纸化和电子化
	贸易时效性	一个完整交易的时间周期长、不确定因素多、贸易成本高、易受空间因素的制约	平台企业的出现以及信息通信技术的应用缩短了贸易周期、减小了贸易不确定性并降低交易成本，大幅弱化了地理等因素的制约
	贸易监管政策	WTO等国际组织是主要监管机构，各国的贸易政策，双边及区域层面的贸易协定等构成全球贸易监管的主要法律规范	不仅包括传统贸易下的监管机构和监管法律规范，还更加强调数字贸易中的数据监管、隐私保护等，但数字贸易国际监管政策还在形成中
相似点	贸易本质	两种贸易模式本质上都是货物、服务和生产要素在不同经济主体之间的流动和转移	
	贸易目的	都是为了追求贸易福利、发展本国经济、保护本国经济利益	
	经济理论支撑	经典古典国际贸易理论：比较优势理论、绝对优势理论等	

资料来源：根据López González & Jouanjean（2017）、《世界与中国数字贸易发展蓝皮书（2018年）》等相关资料整理而成。

例如，数字贸易不仅可以对其他产品和服务的贸易起到促进作用，而且许多数字产品自身也是可贸易品。再如，在数字贸易时代，关税可能不再是主要的贸易壁垒，而是出现了许多新形式的贸易壁垒，特别是数据和数据的自由流动将成为影响数字贸易的关键因素。相应地，贸易政策的着重点也发生了变化，除市场准入和非歧视待遇等传统贸易政策外，数据流动和存储政策、隐私保护、知识产权保护等受到越来越多的关注，也成为各国谈判的重点。当然，随着数字贸易的发展以及经济学理论探索的深入，有望形成新的经济学理论来系统研究数字贸易。

二 数字贸易发展的经济效应

互通有无的贸易可以增加所有参与者的福利，这早已被中国春秋时期的管子、亚当·斯密的绝对优势理论和李嘉图的相对优势理论所证明。数字贸易可以降低交易成本、增加贸易产品种类，自然有重要的经济学价值。具体而言，从经济学微观主体、市场效率以及全球贸易发展动力等角度，数字贸易都产生了直接的正外部效应（如表 2 所示）。

表 2　　数字贸易对消费者、生产者和市场所产生的直接效益

经济主体	数字贸易的好处	实例
消费者	·更好地接近并了解产品 ·更多的产品选择 ·通过额外渠道实现服务交付	·消费者偏爱多元化通道，采用将传统方式、线上和移动渠道相结合的方法获取产品和服务信息 ·在线搜索和评论使消费者更加易于发现和了解产品、比较价格和交易采购
生产者	·改善物流管理 ·更加高效的供应链管理 ·降低运营成本 ·更有效的商业管理 ·更多的市场准入	·基于互联网的物流服务可提高全球供应链的效率，使电子商务增长 ·云计算可以使企业外包计算机硬件和软件服务，使企业聚焦于其核心业务运营 ·云计算可以使数据密集型行业和交易密集型行业降低成本 ·网络化企业可创造更加高效的服务交付 ·机器间（M2M）交流和数据分析能使资源管理更加的高效

续表

经济主体	数字贸易的好处	实例
市场	·增加市场信息和效率 ·市场将有更多更好的互动	·生产者利用社交媒体收集消费者的反馈并进行市场调研 ·数据分析可帮助生产者根据客户偏好定制产品，进行更有效的产品定价

资料来源：根据美国国际贸易委员会（USITC）发布的《全球数字贸易Ⅰ：市场机会和关键的外国贸易约束》整理。

（一）消费者视角：贸易品种类增加与消费者福利改善

第一，数字贸易可直接增加贸易品种类和数量，从而提升消费者福利。

根据微观经济学理论，消费者偏好于产品的多样化消费；国际贸易理论也指出，贸易通过丰富一国产品种类而提高消费者福利。数字贸易不仅可以使消费者更便捷地了解更多产品和服务信息，而且直接增加了可贸易品的种类和数量，从而可提高消费者福利。一是数字产品可进行贸易，增加了可贸易产品种类。在传统贸易模式下，可贸易产品主要以有形实物产品和生产要素等为主。然而，数字贸易的产生和发展将催生出更多数字消费产品（如社交网络游戏、视频、移动应用、在线教育、电子书、在线医疗等)[1]，并将它们不断引入到国际贸易中，在原有传统可贸易产品的基础上，使原先不可贸易的产品变得可贸易，增加了可贸易产品的种类。而随着5G通信技术、虚拟现实、云计算和人工智能（AI）等数字经济的加快发展[2]，未来有望进一步丰富数字产品和服务种类，给消费者带来新的福利。甚至于在不久的将来，虚拟现实产品的贸易额将超过有形产品的贸易额。二是数字贸易推动传统贸易产品转型升级，更新并增加可贸易产品种类。随着互联网和数字技术不断与金融、保险、娱乐、教育、医疗、零售等众多行业深度融合发展，数字贸易事

---

[1] 夏杰长、肖宇：《数字娱乐消费发展趋势及其未来取向》,《改革》2019年第12期。
[2] 李晓华：《数字经济新特征与数字经济新动能的形成机制》,《改革》2019年第11期。

实上已渗入几乎所有行业的诸多部门，并推动大多数传统贸易产品转型升级，增加了贸易产品种类。例如，传统贸易中音频、视频、软件和书籍等产品需要以实物为载体进行传输和移动，而在数字贸易当中，可将这些产品转变为虚拟产品，以数据包等形式进行在线交付。这种传统贸易产品的升级，给消费者提供更多元化选择的余地，改善了消费者福利。

第二，数字贸易使得交易成本下降，间接增加贸易品种类，从而提升消费者福利。

一是交易成本降低有利于丰富可贸易品种类。网上交易平台、大数据、云计算等新型数字技术的出现和广泛应用，使贸易参与者搜集和获取信息的成本大幅降低，需求和供给成功匹配的概率更高；也更加便于贸易参与主体进行议价，从而使交易决策和行为变得更加高效。另外，新技术的应用还会使整个交易过程的跟踪、监督、顾客评价和售后服务变得更加高效、快捷和透明，监督成本也大幅降低。一系列交易成本的降低，使一些原本因成本过高而无法参与贸易活动的不可贸易产品和服务变得可贸易。

二是交易成本降低有利于贸易企业的新产品研发。对于贸易参与的生产方来说，交易成本下降会产生两方面效应：一方面，低交易成本会加剧生产商之间的竞争，进而激励那些寻求区别于竞争对手的生产者不断创新，以缓解市场竞争所产生的压力；另一方面，交易成本的下降会使企业有机会将更多的人力、财力投入到新产品研发当中。特别地，低交易成本将使得市场规模扩大，进而引发数字技术创新，促使数字产品种类不断增加。

三是交易成本降低会促使贸易品价格下降。交易成本减少将有效降低总的贸易成本，进而会促使贸易品价格降低，从而使消费者受益。一方面，从需求理论来看，交易成本的降低会减轻贸易中由生产者直接转嫁给消费者的一部分贸易成本负担，使得贸易产品价格下降。另一方面，从市场竞争角度来看，降低贸易成本会吸引更多的企业进入国际贸易市场并参与全球竞争，使国际贸易市场变得更加有效。对于同类可贸易品来说，参与贸易市场的企业数量越多，贸易竞争就愈加激烈，商品价格也会随之降低。

(二) 生产者视角：提供全球价值链发展新动力

经过将近40年的发展，有形产品的全球生产分工已经非常深入，其GVC链条越来越长、协调成本越来越高，分工所需的成本已经大于分工的收益，这也是近年来全球生产分工放缓的重要原因。而数字技术和数字贸易的广泛运用不仅可以降低已有产品GVC的组织和协调成本，而且提供了一系列新的可贸易产品及相应的新产品的GVC。所以，从生产端视角看，数字贸易有望给全球价值链提供新的动力，并推动重构新型全球价值链体系。一是数字技术（如大数据、云计算、物联网等）在国际生产分工各环节的使用将使得GVC的组织和协调变得更加高效、成本更低，从而使GVC分工的深度和广度进一步延伸，将推动已有GVC获得新的发展。二是从价值链发展路径来看，数字贸易将推动形成新的全球价值链及新的发展路径。新的数字产品和服务不断涌现，并从其产生开始就具有全球生产和消费的属性，无疑将推动形成一系列数字产品GVC分工模式的出现，这种分工和交换模式将不同于传统产品的GVC模式。三是从价值链发展形式来看，数字贸易将推动全球价值链向其高级形式转变。数字贸易将使得全球价值链分工的交易成本更低，再加上数字产品种类和服务范围的不断扩大，将会进一步延伸全球价值链长度，而数字贸易本身去中心化、无界化发展将会吸引更多国家参与到国际生产分工中来，助推GVC实现转型升级。四是从价值链治理角度来看，数字贸易规则体系的构建将为全球价值链转型发展提供保障。在全球范围内，尽管还没有出台一套完整意义的专门服务于数字贸易的法律规则体系，但全球价值链的主要贸易议题都被包含于数字贸易政策议题当中，成为各国贸易谈判的问题之一。因此，全球数字贸易规则体系也将适用并服务于全球价值链发展。

(三) 市场效率视角：降低贸易壁垒和信息不对称程度

从市场效率视角来看，数字贸易的发展以及数字技术的广泛应用所产生的直接效应是：增加市场信息，并使市场信息变得更加充分；促进市场主体间的互动，改善市场效率。数字贸易集约化、无界化和平台化发展趋势将促使贸易参与主体间的联系更加紧密，有效降低信息不对称，实现生产要素在全球范围内高效配置。一是降低贸易生产端和消费端之间的信息不对称程度。在传统贸易模式下，受时间、空间、距离的约束，贸易产品供求双方获取信息的渠道有限，存在严重的信息不对称问题，从而造成市场效率低下。而在数字贸易背景下，消费和供给数据可查询、可追溯，网络平台企业也记录了消费者的购买和评价信息。所以，消费者可便捷地获取生产者所提供产品价格、质量、数量、型号、性质和服务等多维度信息；生产者也可以利用社交媒体或交易平台所提供的消费品种类、数量、偏好以及评价等信息，更全面和精准地掌握消费者需求信息。二是降低贸易壁垒，使得更多中小微企业广泛参与到全球贸易中。在传统贸易中，受贸易成本、信息不对称等多种因素的制约，中小微企业无法有效参与到全球贸易活动中去，从而出现跨国企业垄断国际贸易市场的局面。然而，数字贸易的产生极大减少了贸易参与成本和门槛，为中小微企业参与全球贸易活动搭建了新的平台。此外，借助数字交易平台，中小微企业不仅能够了解客户的需求偏好，而且还能够掌握竞争对手的产品信息、市场占有率及发展状况等，更容易做到产品差异化生产，以此来保持市场竞争力。三是降低贸易参与企业之间和整个贸易环节中的信息不对称程度。数字贸易背景下供应链实时跟踪系统以及产品追踪溯源系统的使用，将显著提高整个供应链过程的透明度，企业对上下游产品将具有更多信息，从而提高了市场化生产的效率。

（四）贸易发展新动力视角：助推全球服务贸易快速发展

数字贸易的本质是服务的交换及其价值的实现，这不仅体现在直接的数字贸易产品中，也蕴含在电子商务和平台企业的服务中，从而决定了它将成为服务贸易发展的新动力。数据显示，在全球范围内超过50%的服务贸易已实现数字化，超过12%的商品贸易通过互联网企业所提供的数字平台进行。① 5G 通信、虚拟现实、云计算、大数据、人工智能（AI）、3D 打印等新技术的出现及应用，以及数字经济、互联网经济和平台企业等新经济模式的出现，极大丰富了服务贸易的种类，为服务贸易发展和变革提供了新动力。麦肯锡统计数据指出，受数字技术和数字贸易的推动，跨境服务增速比商品贸易增速高 60%，由此产生的经济价值远超过传统贸易统计所能涵盖的范围。如果纳入出口商品的附加值、企业输送给境外子公司的无形资产和面向全球用户的免费数字服务这三项指标所创造的经济价值，服务贸易占全球贸易比重将由原来的 23% 上升至 50% 以上。② 未来，数字技术不仅将与金融、教育、医疗、设计、咨询等各类专业服务更加深入融合，且将催生更多新的数字消费产品，共同推动数字全球价值链（Digital Global Value Chains）的形成，从而使得服务贸易占国际贸易的比重不断上升。

三 数字贸易发展的制约因素

数字贸易的生产和交换属性也使得其发展面临诸多规则约束：第一，数字贸易使得有形货物和无形服务的界限更加模糊，从而在传统国际贸易规则（如 WTO 的 GATS 协定）下，数字贸易产品的分类和界定尚不明确、不统一。第二，数字贸易严重依赖于数据的自由流动，而各国由于法律法规、文化习俗、历史传统的不同，对数据隐私保护的要求程度不同，在数据隐私保护上难以达成一致意见。第三，各国数字贸易发展程度差异较大，从而使得各国有关数字贸易的政策目标也不同，监管规则和重点自然也不同。在这种情况下，数字贸易产品的生产、交易、支付和使用等环节的法律规则体系缺失严重，国际社会还没有制定出一套完善的数字贸易国际规则体系来对其进行引导和监管。

---

① 敦煌网:《把握数字贸易机遇助力中小企业出海——敦煌网梦想合伙人项目大力推动中小企业跨境电商拓展海外市场》，2017 年 2 月 23 日，https://seller.dhgate.com/news/media/i258602.html#cms_把握数字贸易机遇助力中小企业出海 – list – 1。

② McKinsey Global Institute (MGI), "Globalization in Transition: The Future of Trade and Value Chains", 2019.

虽然WTO框架包含货物贸易、服务贸易、知识产权保护、信息技术协定等领域的一系列规则，但是对数字产品缺乏一揽子解决方案。最重要的是，关于数据流动等方面的数字贸易关键壁垒目前还没有纳入WTO相关协定中。2017年，WTO的71个成员国针对数字贸易产品进行谈判，内容涉及市场准入、数据流动、数据隐私保护、国民待遇、知识产权保护等，且在2019年共同发布了关于电子商务的倡议，但是由于美国、欧盟和中国等大型经济体在数字贸易政策上的分歧太大，短期内达成一致意见仍非常困难。①

而且，为抵御数字贸易自由化对本国发展的冲击，许多国家以保护国家安全、信息和个人隐私等为理由，纷纷采取一系列专门针对数字贸易的非关税贸易壁垒，包括数字贸易本地化措施、数据隐私保护、知识产权保护、网络审查和技术性壁垒等。这些措施的本质在于是否允许数据和信息跨境自由流动，而后者是数字贸易发展的关键。此外，与数字贸易相关的市场准入和外国投资措施也在一定程度上限制了数字贸易的发展，例如对电子支付的准入限制以及要求数字产品的硬软件达到本国的特定技术标准。数字贸易国际规则的不完善以及由此形成的各国的贸易壁垒在一定程度上限制了其发展。

（一）世界范围内的数字贸易本地化措施十分普遍

数字贸易本地化（Digital Trade Localization）措施主要包括：要求使用本地数字产品软硬件；要求特定的合伙方为本地企业；对技术转让的跨国限制等。② 总体来看，全球范围内的数字贸易本地化措施十分普遍，近年来许多国家仍在不断推出新的数字贸易本地化措施，2008年国际金融危机以来增速明显加快（如图1所示）。各国实施数字贸易本地化的方式也多种多样（如表3所示）。一些国家要求所有数字贸易企业必须接受

---

① WTO，"Work Programme on Electronic Commerce"，December 13，2017，https：//www.wto.org/english/tratop_e/ecom_e/wkprog_e.htm；WTO，"Joint Statement on Electronic Commerce"，January 25，2019，https：//trade.ec.europa.eu/doclib/docs/2019/january/tradoc_157643.pdf.

② Congressional Research Service，"Digital Trade and U.S. Trade Policy"，May 21，2019，https：//crsreports.congress.gov.

数据存储和数据服务器本地化的规定，如巴西、加拿大等国在进行贸易执法和监管时，要求企业使用一些指定的本地化数据内容。欧盟、韩国、俄罗斯、印度尼西亚、越南、巴西和印度等国则以保护信息安全和个人隐私为由，要求数据本地化。例如，巴西曾讨论是否将与本国公民有关的国内企业和外国企业的数据全部储存在国内；欧盟出台了新的法规，可以在更广泛的领域内实施数据本地化措施；德国的新商业准则（Commercial Code）要求国内企业将会计数据和文件储存在国内，2017年出台了关于通信业数据本地存储的新要求；为了满足欧盟的要求，美国公司已经在欧盟建立云计算中心；印度通信部2015年出台相关政策，建议实施数据本地化措施，并要求通信业M2M（Machine–to–Machine）服务商将印度顾客数据全部存储于印度。①

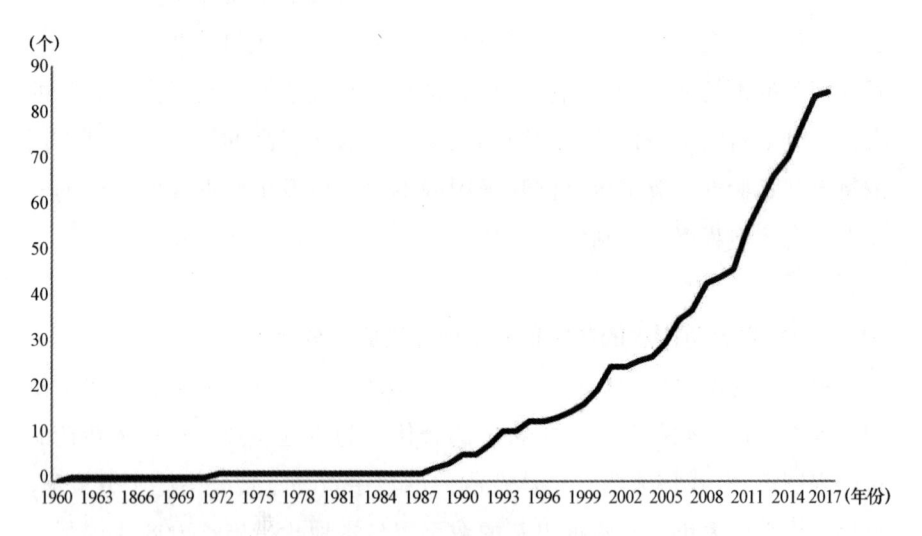

图1　全球数据本地化措施数量（1960—2017年）

注：该数据库中包含全球65个国家的数据本地化措施。
资料来源：欧洲国际政治经济研究中心（ECIPE）数字贸易评估数据库。

---

① United States International Trade Commission, "Global Digital Trade 1—Market Opportunities and Key Foreign Trade Restrictions", August 2017.

表3　　　　　　　　　数字贸易本地化措施的实例

分类	国家	来源
要求数据本地化储存	阿根廷、澳大利亚、加拿大、中国、希腊、印度尼西亚、委内瑞拉等	商业软件联盟（BSA） 企业圆桌会议（BRT） 花旗银行（Citi）
强制或鼓励数字内容本地化	澳大利亚、巴西、中国、印度和某些欧盟成员国	美国贸易代表（USTR） 商业软件联盟（BSA） 企业圆桌会议（BRT） 美国电影协会（MPAA）
提供政府采购偏好，支持本地化公司	巴西、加拿大、中国、印度、尼日利亚、巴拉圭、委内瑞拉等	美国贸易代表（USTR） 企业圆桌会议（BRT）

资料来源：根据美国国际贸易委员会（USITC）相关报告整理而成。

全球数据本地化措施数量年年攀升，究其原因在于相对有形的货物贸易，无形的数字贸易产品无法征收关税、也更难识别和监管，内含更多风险因素。然而，数字贸易本地化措施不仅会增加本国企业负担，也不利于外国投资者在本国投资，而且有可能引发国家间利益冲突，从而不利于跨境数字贸易的发展。特别地，数据本地化要求限制了许多依赖数据流动的服务贸易的发展（如云计算、大数据、金融服务等），也增加了企业数据存储的成本，造成规模不经济，特别是对中小企业非常不利，当然也不利于GVC的发展。

短期来看，因为数据本地化措施涉及原因较多，不仅包括经济因素，还包括伦理、道德、文化、风俗等诸多方面，所以难以在短期内得到妥善解决。那么，如何在数据自由流动、隐私保护和国家安全之间寻求一个平衡点，找到合适的数据本地化程度，将对数字贸易的发展至关重要。

（二）各国数据隐私保护的分歧仍然较大

各国以防止泄露个人和企业敏感数据、保护国家安全等为由，纷纷采取了一系列数据隐私保护措施。例如，欧盟2018年生效的《欧盟数据保护通用条例》（General Data Protection Regulation，GDPR）要求欧盟境内的企业按照规定保护个人数据隐私，俄罗斯和印度尼西亚等国也使用欧盟的监管标准。而美国等亚太国家则使用 APEC 的数据隐私标准（Cross-Border Privacy Rules，CBPR）。然而，各国对数据隐私相关信息的搜集、披露和保护等监管体制存在差异，不同国家对数据隐私保护的标准和文化不尽相同。国际社会也没有形成统一的标准，这导致各国在数据隐私保护中存在较大分歧，阻碍了全球数字贸易的发展。例如，欧盟到目前为止还没有接受其与美国的《服务贸易协定》（TISA）谈判中关于跨国数据流动的条款，欧盟也没有在与日本的 FTA 中加入跨境数据流动的条款，仅承诺 3 年以内可以重新考虑该问题。①

美国依赖其在信息技术方面的优势地位，更多提倡跨境数据自由流动，对隐私保护关注较少，但以欧盟为代表的大多数国家则普遍认为跨境数据自由流动不利于数据隐私保护，会对个人隐私带来威胁。尽管 2000 年美国与欧盟达成了《安全港隐私保护原则》（Safe Harbor Privacy Principles），在安全港协议框架下实现了跨境数据的自由流动，但该协议最终因美国企业对欧洲客户数据的滥用而宣告流产。2016 年，为了实现数据传输和共享，美欧再次达成新的数据共享协议——《欧美隐私盾协议》（EU-US Privacy Shield），该协议就美欧数据传输中个人隐私保护做出了新的规范。其中，就美国获取欧盟相关数据的前提做了明确界定，新协议强化了欧盟的数据主权，美国承担了更多义务，欧盟则拥有更多权利。虽然美欧在跨境数据自由流动和数据隐私保护的某些方面谈判顺利，并取得了一些共识，但从根本上来说，美国与欧盟之间的分歧仍然存在，并未完全消除。

过度的数据隐私保护既不利于企业成长，也阻碍了数字贸易发展。对于企业来说，数字贸易壁垒的存在给企业带来了较重的成本负担；对于数字贸易本身来说，由数据隐私保护问题而引发的贸易壁垒，严重阻碍了数字贸易向透明化和效率化方向发展。《美国和全球经济中的数字贸易 I》指出，欧盟不同成员国对《欧盟数据保护指导》（EU Data Protec-

---

① Meltzer J P., "Cybersecurity and Digital Trade: What Role for International Trade Rules?", Working Paper 132, Global Economy and Development Brookings Institution.

tion Directive）不同的实施方式将会对美国和欧盟企业造成不确定性并增加成本，欧盟委员会估计监管方式的不同对欧盟企业所带来的成本每年大约为 30 亿美元。① 另外，一些研究估计美国与欧盟之间的数据隐私保护机制的差异使得每年双边贸易流减少了 6500 亿美元。② 所以，全球各国应该加强谈判和合作，在数据隐私和保护机制中寻找到共同点，对原有的监管措施进行改革，形成有利于数字贸易发展的新型隐私保护措施和框架。

（三）各国关于数字产品的知识产权保护仍有较大争议

数字贸易是知识密集型产品，且容易被复制和盗版，所以相对有形货物来说，更需要知识产权的保护。欧盟 2019 年出台了新的版权法以适应数字经济和数字贸易的新需要，未来更多国家可能会跟进。但是，各国关于数字贸易相关的知识产权保护制度仍不够健全，不同国家对数字产品知识产权的保护标准存在较大差异，还没有达成共识，这些问题都已成为阻碍数字贸易发展的重要壁垒之一。例如，数字内容的盗版是数字贸易发展中较大的不利因素。相关报告指出，2008 年假冒和盗版商品的贸易额为 3600 亿美元，到 2015 年这一数值上升至 9600 亿美元，其中，各国盗版数字音乐、电影和软件的贸易价值从 2008 年的 300 亿—750 亿美元上升到 2015 年的 800 亿—2400 亿美元。③

此外，随着数字贸易发展导致的线上产品种类不断增加，与之相关的知识产权纠纷也日渐增多，而传统的知识产权保护法律无法解决数字产品的知识产权保护。为此，在 WTO 框架下，美国、欧盟等成员国纷纷以"知识产权保护"为中心议题展开讨论，虽然在某些议题上达成了一致意见，但是在很多议题上仍存在较大争议。不同国家的议案都代表本

---

① U. S. International Trade Commission, "Digital Trade in the U. S. and Global Economies, Part Ⅰ", July 2013.

② U. S. International Trade Commission, "Digital Trade in the U. S. and Global Economies, Part Ⅰ", July 2013.

③ Congressional Research Service, "Digital Trade and U. S. Trade Policy", May 2017, https://crsreports.congress.gov.

国的利益诉求,这很有可能在两国之间形成数字贸易壁垒。对此,国际谈判应将数字贸易知识产权保护纳入其中。同时,各国应该健全知识产权保护法律法规、统一标准、加强合作。

(四) 各国出于网络安全考虑普遍存在网络审查

出于秩序稳定、公众利益和国家安全等因素的考虑,各国都对互联网内容和网站平台制定有各类审查措施。例如,日本对信息和网络服务有国家安全审查要求;印度也有相关法案阻止有可能威胁其国家主权、国防、扰乱公共秩序等方面的国外网络信息进入公众视野;印度尼西亚的电子传输法案授权政府筛选和过滤网络信息;泰国则设有网络数据过滤委员会(Computer Data Filtering Committee)以筛除掉一些违反公共利益和秩序和信息,俄罗斯则人为过滤掉了上千个国外网站。[①]

影响更大的是,对于相同的内容,不同国家可能有不同的审查措施和审查标准,这种差异化的网络审查标准极易形成无形的市场准入壁垒,限制企业参与全球数字贸易活动。因为,要完成一次数字贸易活动,必须借助互联网来实现数字产品和服务的传输,网络审查标准直接决定了数字产品和服务能否进入一国市场。目前,在全球范围内,巴西、印度、印度尼西亚以及俄罗斯等国的内容审查要求相对较多。另外,为保护和支持本国数字贸易产业和企业的发展,各国政府都以网络安全为由,采用网络审查和网络执法等手段,对国外数字贸易企业进行审查,限制了跨境数字贸易的发展。

四 中国数字贸易发展的推进方略

从上文不难看出,数字贸易具有不同于传统贸易的诸多特征,甚至有望使得国际贸易进入新的发展阶段。数字贸易的发展也将给微观市场主体创造新的机遇,并提高市场效率,创造国际贸易发展新动力,从而

---

① United States International Trade Commission, "Global Digital Trade 1—Market Opportunities and Key Foreign Trade Restrictions", August 2017.

产生显著的经济效应。鉴于此，中国需要从国家层面提高数字贸易的战略定位，学术界、政策制定者和相关部门要加快研究形成数字贸易发展的新理念、新规则和新政策。

（一）国家层面要提高数字贸易的战略定位

随着 5G 通信技术、3D 打印、云计算、物联网、虚拟现实等数字技术的不断完善，数字贸易在不久的将来有望取得突破性发展，并对未来的贸易方式、贸易规则、贸易产品、贸易参与者起到深远影响。而且，货物贸易已经发展到瓶颈，未来国际贸易发展的重点是服务贸易，部分货物贸易也将服务化，而这些也都依托于数字贸易的发展。鉴于数字贸易可能产生的重大影响，许多国家已将数字贸易纳入到本国的发展战略中，出台了相应的法律法规和政策来促进数字贸易发展，同时积极参与全球数字贸易规则谈判。事实上，早在 1998 年，美国商务部关于《浮现中的数字经济》报告的出台就正式拉开了全球发展数字经济的序幕。进入 21 世纪，法国在 2008 年率先提出数字贸易发展战略，随后，日本、英国等国家和地区也相继出台了有关数字经济和数字贸易的战略报告。[①] 例如，美国国会研究服务局 2017 年发布了《数字贸易与美国的贸易政策》，强调数字贸易在全球贸易和经济发展中的地位和作用将更加突出，美国应在塑造全球数字贸易政策方面起到引领作用。[②] 欧盟 2017 年也出台了《数字贸易战略》报告。

近年来，中国也积极响应数字贸易发展趋势，出台了若干政策文件，如在 2018 年出台了《电子商务法》。2022 年政府工作报告指出，"促进数字经济发展，加强数字中国建设整体布局"。中国学术界和政策制定者要学习借鉴美国国际贸易委员会（USITC）和美国贸易代表办公室（USTR）的做法，对数字贸易进行更加系统的研究。具体来看，可以由相关部委牵头，组建包括学术界和政策制定者的联合研究团队，避免相互游离，

[①] 马述忠、房超、郭继文等：《世界与中国数字贸易发展蓝皮书（2018）》，2018 年 9 月。

[②] López González J, Jouanjeanm, "Digital Trade: Developing a Framework for Analysis", OECD Trade Policy Papers, No. 205, 2017, OECD Publishing.

从而将理论和实际相结合，更加系统地研究我国数字贸易发展现状和特征、全球范围数字贸易的未来发展方向、可能的重要性影响等，从而为制定国家层面的数字贸易发展战略提供理论指导。此外，要鼓励各省市根据国家层面的数字贸易发展战略并结合本地区比较优势，制定更加具体的发展方向和重点领域，形成各有侧重、既竞争又互补的区域发展格局。

（二）探索形成数字贸易发展理念和监管思路

从上文可知，数字贸易具有不同于传统贸易的新经济效应，也面临新的贸易壁垒，所以需要探索形成新的发展理念和监管思路。第一，总体而言，数字贸易对几乎所有行业都有重要影响，其也将使得贸易产品融数据、货物、服务三位于一体，从而使仅仅着眼于某一行业或贸易产品某一维度的政策不再有效。因此，数字贸易发展理念和监管思路要更加强调全局视野、树立整体思维并综合施策。第二，在数字贸易背景下，平台企业的作用更加凸显，所以政策制定需要考虑如何鼓励各类平台企业发展，但同时也要出台相关法律法规防止平台企业垄断而造成效率损失。第三，数字贸易政策制定要突出普惠性，确保广泛的信息进入权，防止出现数字鸿沟而造成新的不平等，特别地，要确保广大中小微企业和普通消费者能够享受到数字贸易的红利。第四，数字贸易国际规则正在形成之中，中国要加快吸收和学习数字贸易国际通行规则和标准，特别是《跨大西洋贸易投资伙伴关系协定》（TTIP）、《服务贸易协定》（TI-SA）、美加墨协定（USMCA）等区域贸易协定中的新规则，并结合中国情况大胆试点和复制推行，从而在未来的规则制定中占得先机。例如，可以在各自贸试验区、海南自贸港率先试点和推行国际通行的数字贸易规则，从而积累相关监管经验。第五，在WTO《贸易便利化协定》下，中国要进一步提高与数字贸易相关的货物和服务的贸易便利化程度，从而提高数字贸易国际竞争力。第六，数字贸易监管政策要在跨境数据自由流动、国家安全、本国经济发展、隐私保护之间寻找一个平衡点。总体上，既要确保跨境数据高效流动，从而保证中国数字贸易国际竞争力，也要确保不发生较大的威胁国家安全的数据泄露、窃取、丢失等安全事件，还要有利于本国数字产业发展，确保个人隐私得到恰当保护。

(三) 推动在 WTO 框架下完善数字贸易国际规则

数字贸易的不断发展势必将改变现有的国际贸易规则，而有效的多边国际贸易规则对全球及我国的数字贸易健康发展都具有重要意义。历史经验也表明，中国加入 WTO 后获益良多，所以推动在 WTO 框架下完善数字贸易规则对中国经济和贸易发展具有重要积极作用。但是目前来看，WTO 缺乏关于数字贸易的规则体系，相关谈判也停滞不前。目前为止，WTO 仅仅是临时性免除电子传输关税，《信息技术协定》（ITA）则只是免除部分与数字贸易密切相关的 ICT 产品的关税。而且，关于是否永久免除电子传输关税仍没有达成一致意见，ITA 也无法处理相关的非关税贸易壁垒。最重要的是，数据跨境流动等关键的数字贸易壁垒还没有纳入 WTO 相关协定中，《服务贸易总协定》（GATS）准入规则也以"正面清单"为主，无法解决新出现的数字产品准入问题，因为许多新出现的数字产品不在已有的"正面清单"中，《与贸易有关的知识产权协定》（TRIPS）则没有专门针对数字贸易的知识产权保护条款。

在此情况下，中国要积极推动在 WTO 框架下完善数字贸易国际规则的制定，为我国数字贸易发展提供良好环境。第一，可推动在 WTO 现有协定下增加若干数字贸易规则。例如，可在 GATS、ITA、TRIPS、《贸易便利化协定》等协定中改革贸易产品分类体系，并纳入跨境数据流动、隐私保护、技术转让、知识产权保护等与数字贸易相关的条款。第二，推动形成 WTO 多边框架下商讨数字贸易国际规则的常设工作小组。该工作小组可参考目前各类 FTA 和 RTA，特别是上文提及的几大区域贸易协定中被普遍使用和接受的数字贸易规则和条款，用以形成 WTO 框架下为各国所接受的条款草案，并提交 WTO 进行讨论。第三，也可尝试推动在 WTO 框架下形成一个解决数字贸易问题的专门协定。

(四) 在双边和区域贸易协定中加强数字贸易规则谈判

虽然在 WTO 框架下达成数字贸易协定是对中国来说最理想的目标，但是短期来看困难重重，可能是一个比较漫长曲折的过程。因此，各国都试图在双边和区域贸易协定中纳入数字贸易条款，逐步解决数字贸易发展壁垒。事实上，目前双边或区域贸易协定关于数字贸易的规则较多、也更深入。其中，《跨太平洋伙伴关系协定》（TPP）、TTIP、TiSA、USMCA 中的数字贸易条款代表了数字贸易规则的最新发展和可能方向。其中，TPP 因为美国的退出而夭折，但是其关于数字贸易的若干规则仍具有参考价值。例如，TPP 中禁止数字贸易关税，禁止跨境数据流动的限制措施，禁止数字本地化要求，禁止强制性源代码公布要求，禁止技术转让等[1]条款都在 USMCA 中有所体现。而 USMCA 则是第一个包含完善的数字贸易新规则的正式协定，其有可能成为未来 RTA 谈判中数字贸易规则的标准。TTIP 则是美欧在跨境数字贸易规则方面的最大合作平台，TiSA 目前有 23 个成员国，包括美国、欧盟、澳大利亚等主要的发达国家，占世界服务贸易比重大约为 70%，具有一定的代表性。TTIP 和 TiSA 都旨在解决跨境数据流动、数字本地化、知识产权保护等诸多领域的数字贸易壁垒问题。其中，TTIP 在网络的开放性、承认电子认证服务、线上消费者保护、监管合作等数字贸易议题都取得了不错的进展。

在此背景下，中国也要在双边和区域贸易协定中，加强数字贸易规则的谈判。事实上，我国已经与世界各国签订了数十个双边和区域协定，还有更多协定正在谈判中。所以，我国可以考虑先在这些双边和区域贸易协定中进行数字贸易谈判和规则构建，不断积累经验。第一，深入研究 USMCA、TPP、TIPP、TiSA 等贸易协定文本中关于数字贸易的先进和合理做法，并研究其在我国实行的可能性，可考虑将合适的措施纳入我国未来将要签订的双边和区域贸易协定中。第二，在未来的双边和区域贸易谈判中，可就数字贸易产品分类、跨境数据流动、监管合作等进行更加大胆的承诺。第三，结合我国数字贸易发展特征，也可提出一些具有引领性的数字贸易规则。

---

[1] Congressional Research Service, "Digital Trade and U. S. Trade Policy", May 21, 2019, https://crsreports.congress.gov.

(五) 加快完善数字基础设施建设

正如货物贸易依赖于交通运输技术的进步，数字贸易则高度依赖数字基础设施的完善程度。所以，世界各国正在加快完善数字基础设施建设，力求在未来的数字贸易竞争力占据优势地位，我国也不能例外。第一，数字基础设施是个比较新的概念，在数字经济时代其重要性将越来越突出。所以，需要更加科学地界定数字基础设施的范围和边界，并对我国数字基础设施进行摸底，找出其短板并妥善解决。第二，加快新一代 ICT 硬件基础设施建设，特别是要加快 5G 通信网络建设，同时要重视中西部地区的数字基础设施建设，防止出现新的基础设施鸿沟。第三，推动完善我国的网络平台企业建设，建立一批具有国际竞争力的世界一流平台企业。平台企业虽然以营利为目标，但同时具有准公共物品的性质，也可纳入数字基础设施的范畴，前提是要促使它们更具普惠性和公共性，从而帮助中国中小微企业开展数字贸易。当然，也可适当建立一批非营利性的平台企业。第四，利用我国数字基础设施领域的竞争优势，积极参与海外数字基础设施建设，并适当推动我国信息技术相关标准成为国际通用标准，从而在数字贸易竞争中占据一定优势。

(六) 探索构建数字贸易下新的产品分类体系

在数字贸易背景下，有形货物和无形服务的界限越来越模糊，传统的"二分法"产品分类体系越来越不适用，甚至起到阻碍作用。特别是，WTO 将贸易产品分为货物和服务的方法在数字贸易时代已经不适用。例如，对于 3D 打印，一方面，它可作为一种设计服务被视为服务贸易，但另一方面，这种服务贸易又可以被购买方打印成有形货物从而被视为货物贸易。事实上，许多货物贸易越来越服务化，货物与服务变得你中有我，我中有你。所以，需要探索构建数字贸易背景下新的产品分类体系。第一，要全面总结数字贸易产品的新特征，进而对现有的货物和服务分类体系进行改革，探索形成新的产品分类方法。新的分类方法可不拘泥于货物还是服务，而要更加关注产品的使用功能。第二，要对未来数字贸易背景下可能出现的新产品、新业态、新模式进行前瞻性研究，并探讨新的产品分类体系将如何嵌入不断出现的新产品。所以，总体而言要使新的产品分类体系更加具有包容性。第三，要使得在新的产品分类体系下，可以更为合理地对数字贸易进行监管，并有助于确定未来的关税标准及其影响，进而评估数字贸易对经济发展的正面和负面作用。

参考文献：

敦煌网：《把握数字贸易机遇助力中小企业出海——敦煌网梦想合伙人项目大力推动中小企业跨境电商拓展海外市场》，2017年2月23日，https：//seller. dhgate. com/news/media/i258602. html#cms_把握数字贸易机遇助力中小企业出海－list－1。

李晓华：《数字经济新特征与数字经济新动能的形成机制》，《改革》2019年第11期。

马述忠、房超、郭继文等：《世界与中国数字贸易发展蓝皮书（2018）》，2018年9月。

马述忠、房超、梁银峰：《数字贸易及其时代价值与研究展望》，《国际贸易问题》2018年第10期。

夏杰长、肖宇：《数字娱乐消费发展趋势及其未来取向》，《改革》2019年第12期。

熊励、刘慧、刘华玲：《数字与商务：2010年全球数字贸易与移动商务研讨会论文集》，上海社会科学院出版社2010年版。

伊万·沙拉法诺夫、白树强：《WTO视角下数字产品贸易合作机制研究——基于数字贸易发展现状及壁垒研究》，《国际贸易问题》2018年第2期。

CISCO, "The Internet of Things, At – A – Glance", https：//www. cisco. com/c/dam/en_us/solutions/trends/iot/docs/iot – aag. pdf.

Congressional Research Service, "Digital Trade and U. S. Trade Policy", May 2017, https：//crsreports. congress. gov.

Congressional Research Service, "Digital Trade and U. S. Trade Policy", May 21, 2019, https：//crsreports. congress. gov.

Deardorff A. V. , "Comparative Advantage in Digital Trade", Working Papers 664, Research Seminar in International Economics, University of Michigan, 2017.

E – Marketer, "2019: China to Surpass US in Total Retail Sales", January 23, 2019, https://www.emarketer.com/newsroom/index.php/2019 – china – to – surpass – us – in – total – retail – sales/.

López González J, Ferencz J. , "Digital Trade and Market Openness", OECD Trade Policy Papers, No. 217, 2018, OECD Publishing.

López González J, Jouanjeanm, Digital Trade: Developing a Framework for Analysis, OECD Trade Policy Papers, No. 205, 2017, OECD Publishing.

McKinsey Global Institute (MGI), "Globalization in Transition: The Future of Trade and Value Chains", 2019.

Meltzer J P. , "Cybersecurity and Digital Trade: What Role for International Trade Rules?", Working Paper 132, Global Economy and Development Brookings Institution.

The Office of the U. S. Trade Representative, "Key Barriers to Digital Trade", March 2017, https://ustr.gov/about – us/policy – offices/press – office/fact – sheets/2017/march/key – barriers – digital – trade.

UNCTAD, "Global e – commerce sales surged to \$29 trillion", March 29, 2019, https://unctad.org/en/pages/newsdetails.aspx? OriginalVersionID = 2034.

United States International Trade Commission, "Global Digital Trade 1—Market Opportunities and Key Foreign Trade Restrictions", August 2017.

U. S. International Trade Commission, "Digital Trade in the U. S. and Global Economies, Part Ⅱ", August 2014.

U. S. International Trade Commission, "Digital Trade in the U. S. and Global Economies, Part Ⅰ", July 2013.

WTO, "Joint Statement on Electronic Commerce", January 25, 2019, https://trade.ec.europa.eu/doclib/docs/2019/january/tradoc_157643.pdf.

WTO, "Work Programme on Electronic Commerce", December 13,

2017, https://www.wto.org/english/tratop_e/ecom_e/wkprog_e.htm.

WTO, *World Trade Report 2018: The Future of World Trade: How Digital Technologies Are Transforming Global Commerce*, World Trade Organization publication, 2018.

中国人口老龄化背景下医保基金的可持续发展[*]

戈艳霞[**]

医疗保障制度是减轻群众就医负担、增进民生福祉、维护社会和谐稳定的重大制度安排。医保制度设计需要根据社会发展、疾病结构变迁与人口老龄化程度不断调整。过去几十年中国人口结构相对年轻，经济增速较快，基本医保基金运行良好，在改革窗口期收获了改革红利。但未来十五年，伴随人口老龄化进程加速和经济常态化发展，中国医保基金在收支平衡上或将面临前所未有的风险挑战。

当前中国人口进入快速老龄化发展阶段，人口年龄结构、就业结构、城乡结构的转折性变化将对未来医保基金的收入和支出带来重要影响。在医保基金的收入方面，一是劳动年龄人口减少且就业率下降，导致职工医保缴费人数增速放缓；二是受人口城乡结构影响，农村人口减少，参加城乡居民医保缴费人数减少。综合来讲，在人口结构变化和经济下行压力的双重影响下，预计"十四五"时期全国医保缴费人数增速趋缓，医保基金缴费收入增长趋缓。在医保基金的支出方面，当前中国人口结构老龄化已进入加速发展期，对医保基金支出的冲击影响呈放大趋势。理论上讲，人口老龄化对医保基金支出的影响主要有两个方面：一是老

---

[*] 本文原题为《人口老龄化背景下医保基金可持续发展的风险分析》，原发表于《中国医疗保险》2021年第2期，内容略有改动。

[**] 戈艳霞，中国社会科学院社会发展战略研究院社会治理研究室副主任、副研究员。

年人数和比重的提高，增加居民总体的患病次数和治疗（就诊和住院）次数；二是老年人患病周期长，并发症多，次均治疗费用贵。两方作用叠加导致人口老龄化对医保基金支出的冲击更大。综合来讲，在人口老龄化快速发展的背景下，医保基金的可持续发展将面临前所未有的挑战。

合理筹资、稳健运行是医保制度可持续的基本保证。为了有效防范风险，确保基金可持续，2016年《"健康中国2030"规划纲要》明确提出要"健全基本医保稳定可持续筹资和待遇水平调整机制，实现基金中长期精算平衡"①。2020年2月印发的《中共中央 国务院关于深化医疗保障制度改革的意见》（以下简称"《意见》"）更是明确提出"要建立与社会主义初级阶段基本国情相适应、与各方承受能力相匹配、与基本健康需求相协调的医保基金筹资机制，切实加强基金运行管理，加强基金风险预警和防范，坚决守住不发生系统性风险底线"②。

围绕医保基金的中长期精算平衡及实现途径，学界开展了不少讨论。其中，李子君、封进和王贞认为延迟退休年龄能改善职工医保基金的财务运行状况③；邓大松和杨红燕、史若丁和汪兵韬认为提高缴费率的改革方案更为有效④；李亚青和申曙光、文裕慧提出退休职工参与医保缴费以缓解职工医保基金收支不平衡⑤；陈友华、王金营和戈艳霞则提出优化生育政策，增强生育政策包容性，以缓解人口老龄化及其带来的

---

① 《中共中央 国务院印发〈"健康中国2030"规划纲要〉》，中华人民共和国中央人民政府网，2016年10月25日，http://www.gov.cn/xinwen/2016-10/25/content_5124174.htm。

② 《中共中央 国务院关于深化医疗保障制度改革的意见》，中华人民共和国中央人民政府网，2020年3月5日，http://www.gov.cn/zhengce/2020-03/05/content_5487407.htm。

③ 李子君：《城镇职工医保基金收支预测及其比较分析——基于不同政策组合视角并以湖北省为例》，《湖南农业大学学报》（社会科学版）2019年第20（03）期；封进、王贞：《延迟退休年龄对城镇职工医保基金平衡的影响——基于政策模拟的研究》，《社会保障评论》2019年第3（02）期。

④ 邓大松、杨红燕：《老龄化趋势下基本医疗保险筹资费率测算》，《财经研究》2003年第12期；史若丁、汪兵韬：《人口老龄化对城镇基本医疗保险基金冲击的分析》，《改革与开放》2011年第21期。

⑤ 李亚青、申曙光：《退休人员不缴费政策与医保基金支付风险——来自广东省的证据》，《人口与经济》2011年第3期；文裕慧：《城镇职工基本医疗保险退休人员适当缴费研究》，《现代管理科学》2015年第10期。

相关问题。① 总体而言，已有研究主要集中于延迟退休政策效应和退休职工参与缴费的分析，但影响医保基金可持续发展的因素是多方面的，在当前人口老龄化加速发展的大趋势下，缴费人数占比下降和医疗需求持续增长都将对医保基金的可持续发展带来深远影响。笔者依据2019年基本医保制度，考虑多方面核心因素，构建了中国医保基金的动态收支平衡预测模型，结合未来人口规模和结构、人口健康趋势和就医需求、工资水平、参保负担结构变化，预测了2020—2035年中国医保基金的收支平衡状况，并对影响医保基金可持续发展的主要因素进行剖析，提出加快医保基金制度改革、提高基金可持续发展能力的相关建议。

一 中国医保基金收支结存的测算方法

中国现行基本医保制度包括职工医保和居民医保，在筹资机制上，职工医保是参保人和单位雇主按法定缴费基数和缴费比例共担筹集；居民医保是参保人和各级财政按法定金额共担筹资。基本医保的支出一般分解为住院报销支出和门诊报销支出两个部分。两种报销支出有各自的起付线和报销比例，职工医保和居民医保在这两种支出报销上也有着各自不同的起付线和报销比例。人口规模和结构变化也是决定医保基金收支平衡的基础性因素，特别是在当前人口转型期，人口规模和结构变化对医保基金收支平衡有着不可忽视的影响：一方面，中国劳动力规模和结构变化将对医保基金的缴费收入带来明显变化；另一方面，随着人口老龄化发展，老年人口的规模和比重不断增加，参保人的总体医疗需求将逐年增多，医保基金支出也会随之增加。

据此，在现行医保制度下，医保缴费收入的计算方法可表示为：

$$I_n = I_n^z (Z * \bar{W}_n * \omega_n^1 + Z * \bar{W}_n * \omega_n^2) \\ + I_n^j (C * a_n + C * b_n) \tag{1}$$

---

① 陈友华：《二孩政策地区经验的普适性及其相关问题——兼对"21世纪中国生育政策研究"的评价》，《人口与发展》2009年第15（01）期；王金营、戈艳霞：《全面二孩政策实施下的中国人口发展态势》，《人口研究》2016年第40（06）期。

其中，I_n 表示第 n 年医保缴费收入。$I_n^z(Z*\bar{W}_n*\omega_n^1+Z*\bar{W}_n*\omega_n^2)$ 表示第 n 年的职工医保缴费收入函数，Z 表示当年职工医保缴费人数，$\bar{W}_n$ 表示职工医保的人均缴费基数，ω_n^1 表示职工个人的缴费比例，ω_n^2 表示所在单位或雇主的缴费比例；$I_n^j(C*a_n+C*b_n)$ 表示第 n 年的居民医保缴费收入函数，C 表示当年居民医保的参保人数，a_n 表示居民人均缴费金额，b_n 表示人均各级财政筹资金额。

医保报销支出的计算方法可表示为：

$$P_n = P_n^z\left(\sum_{i=15}^{60} x_i*X_i*\alpha_i + \sum_{i=15}^{60} y_i*Y_i*\beta_i\right)$$
$$+ P_n^j\left(\sum_{k=0}^{100} x_k*X_k*\mu_k + \sum_{k=0}^{100} y_k*Y_k*\vartheta_k\right) \quad (2)$$

其中，P_n 表示第 n 年医保报销支出。$P_n^z\left(\sum_{i=15}^{60} x_i*X_i*\alpha_i + \sum_{i=15}^{60} y_i*Y_i*\beta_i\right)$ 表示第 n 年职工医保报销支出函数，x_i 表示 i 岁职工医保人口的住院次数，X_i 为 i 岁人口的次均住院费用，α_i 表示住院费用报销比例；y_i 表示 i 岁职工医保人口的门诊次数，Y_i 为 i 岁人口的次均门诊费用，β_i 表示门诊费用报销比例。

$P_n^j\left(\sum_{k=0}^{100} x_k*X_k*\mu_k + \sum_{k=0}^{100} y_k*Y_k*\vartheta_k\right)$ 表示第 n 年居民医保报销支出函数，x_k 表示 k 岁居民医保人口的住院次数；X_k 表示次均住院费用，μ_k 表示住院费用报销比例；y_k 表示 k 岁居民医保人口的门诊次数；Y_k 表示次均门诊费用；ϑ_k 表示门诊费用报销比例。

进一步地，第 n 年医保基金收支结存 t_n 可表示为：

$$t_n = I_n - P_n$$

医保基金累计结存 T_n 可表示为：

$$T_n = T_{n-1} + t_n$$

根据以上公式，将相关参数和基础数据代入，即可得到医保基金收支数据。需要说明的是，本文中使用的 2020—2035 年分年龄性别的人口数据，来自笔者前期的人口预测研究成果，详细说明参见《全面二孩政策实施下的中国人口发展态势》一文。另外，任何一个预测模型都建立在一定的假设基础上。本文在现有数据基础上，遵循各因素变化规律尽可能合理设定假设条件。笔者假设预测期内参保人年龄的就诊率和住院率延续2013—2018年国家卫生服务调查变化趋势；次均就诊费用、次均住院费用、职工工资延续2010—2019年的平均增长速度。此外，囿于数据限制，本文中的职工医保基金未包含生育险。

二 未来十五年中国医保基金的收支概况

在现行医保制度和以上假设前提下，预测结果显示，中国医保基金的收支平衡不具有可持续性。预计在2026年医保基金当年结存将首次出现缺口，到2034年累计结存将首次出现缺口。分地区看，一些劳动力人口流出较多、人口老龄化速度较快的地区将面临更加严峻的医保基金支付压力（见图1）。

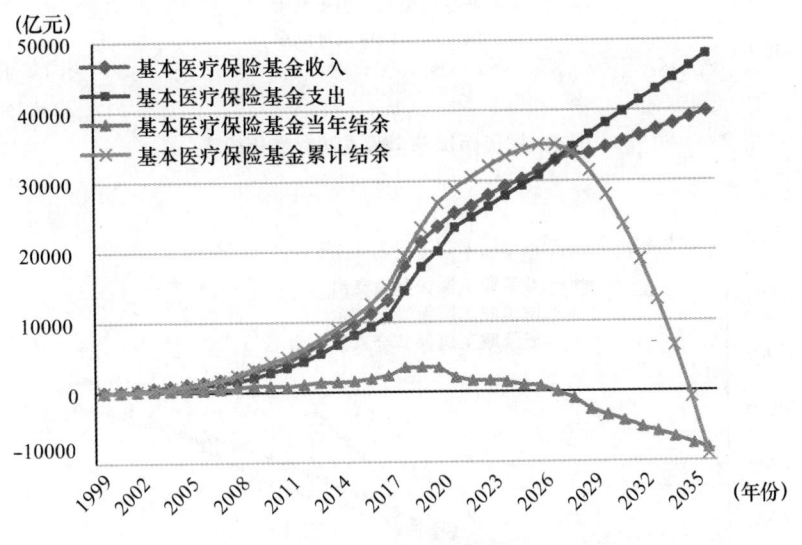

图1 中国基本医疗保险收支结存变化趋势

通过对职工医保和城乡居民医保的收支平衡预测，我们可以更加明确地看出问题的严峻性。由于居民医保参保人群的年龄结构老化速度更快，居民医保基金出现负值的时间可能会更早。预测结果显示，在现行制度下，到 2021 年左右居民医保基金当年结存即有可能出现缺口，到 2023 年左右累计结存也将首次出现缺口（见图 2）；再看职工医保，虽然目前职工医保基金尚有较多结存，但在现行制度下，职工医保基金的当年结存也将在 10 年后，即在 2030 年首次出现缺口，累计结存将在 2039 年左右出现缺口（见图 3）。

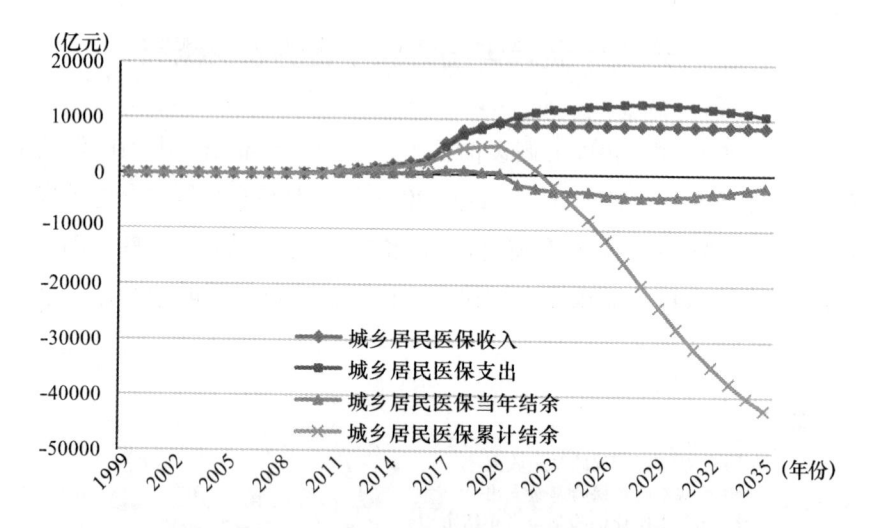

图 2　居民医保基金收支结存变化趋势

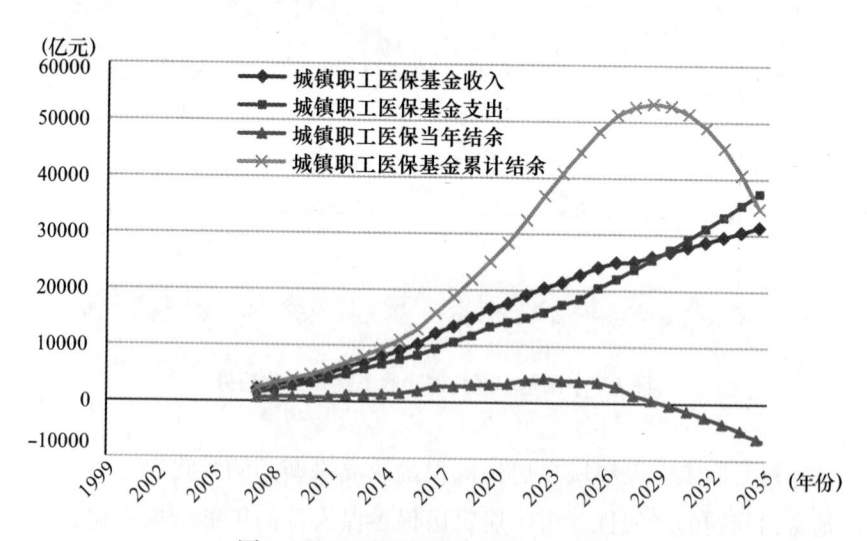

图 3　职工医保基金收支结存变化趋势

三 影响中国医保基金可持续发展的主要因素

（一）中国将进入深度老龄社会

根据国际标准，一个国家或地区 65 岁及以上的人口比例达到 7% 以上，即可被称为老龄化社会；65 岁及以上的人口比例达到 14%，即可被称为深度老龄社会；而当 65 岁及以上的人口比例超过 20% 时，则被称为进入超级老龄社会。

2020 年中国第七次人口普查数据显示，截至 2020 年 11 月 1 日零时，全国总人口为 14.43 亿人，其中 60 岁及以上人口为 2.64 亿人，占 18.70%；65 岁及以上人口为 1.91 亿人，占 13.50%。[①] 2021 年是中国人口老龄化发展历程中的重要节点。人口预测数据显示，进入 2021 年后中国 65 岁以上老年人口比重将超过 14%，中国将从老龄社会进入深度老龄社会。之后，中国 65 岁以上老年人口比重将进一步增长到 2025 年的 15%，2030 年的 19% 和 2035 年的 23%（见图 4）。需要特别注意的是，进入 2027 年以后，伴随 20 世纪 60 年代中期中国第二次生育高峰人群陆续进入老年阶段，中国老年人口数量将加速增长，预计 2027—2035 年，中国 65 岁及以上老年人口年均增长 1270 万人。届时中国人口老龄化将进入一个新的加速发展期，老龄化速度加快且老年人口规模更大。

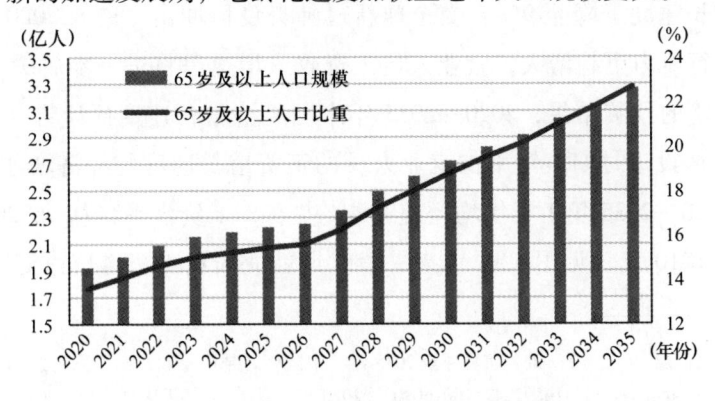

图 4　2020—2035 年老年人口变化趋势

---

① 国家统计局：《第七次全国人口普查公报》，2021 年 5 月 11 日。

（二）未富先老，政府财政负担沉重

发达国家进入老龄社会时，人均 GDP 通常会达到 10000 美元，进入深度老龄社会时，人均 GDP 平均在 20000 美元，超级老龄社会（主要指德国、日本）时的人均 GDP 通常达到 40000 美元。中国在 2000 年进入老龄社会时的人均 GDP 只有 800 美元，2021 年进入深度老龄社会时人均 GDP 水平略多于 10000 美元。发达国家在面对日益严重的人口老龄化现象时大都出现了医疗费用负担过重的情况，而中国处在相同人口老龄化阶段时的财政储备远不及发达国家，这意味着中国人口老龄化与政府财政支付能力之间的矛盾将更加突出，医保制度也将面临更大的挑战与压力。

（三）工资增长较慢，医保基金收入增速放缓

在缴费比例一定的情况下，就业人员的工资收入增速将在很大程度上决定医保基金的收入增速。2000—2015 年，中国经济高速增长，就业人员工资增长速度也很快，其间中国城镇单位就业人员年平均工资从 9333 元加速增长到 62029 元，年均增长速度 38%。2015 年以后，伴随着国内外经济社会形势变化，中国就业人员工资增长速度放缓，2015—2019 年，中国城镇单位就业人员年平均工资从 62029 元增长到 90134 元，年均增长速度下降至 9%。受全球新冠肺炎疫情冲击，进入 2020 年后，经济下行压力更趋增大，就业人员工资收入增速恐将进一步放缓。根据中国经济的预测结果，2020—2035 年中国经济增长速度预计将在 3%—5%。① 假设该时期城镇单位就业人员的工资增长速度与经济增速趋同，那么 2020—2035 年工资年均增速在 4% 左右，工资水平将从 96720 元增长到 161010 元（见图 5）。未来一段时期就业人员工资增长速度明显放

---

① 黄群慧：《保持 5% 的经济增速至 2035 年，中国将跨越中等收入陷阱》，搜狐智库，https://www.sohu.com/a/416892247_100160903，2020 年 9 月 7 日；《人大副校长：2020—2035 年中国经济潜在增速谨慎预期 3.17%》，中国新闻网，https://www.chinanews.com/cj/2020/11-22/9344776.shtml，2020 年 11 月 22 日；杨伟民：《中国到 2035 年经济总量或人均收入翻一番要求年均增长 4.73%》，中国新闻网，https://www.chinanews.com/cj/2020/11-28/9349651.shtml，2020 年 11 月 28 日。

缓，将在很大程度上导致医保基金收入增速明显放缓。

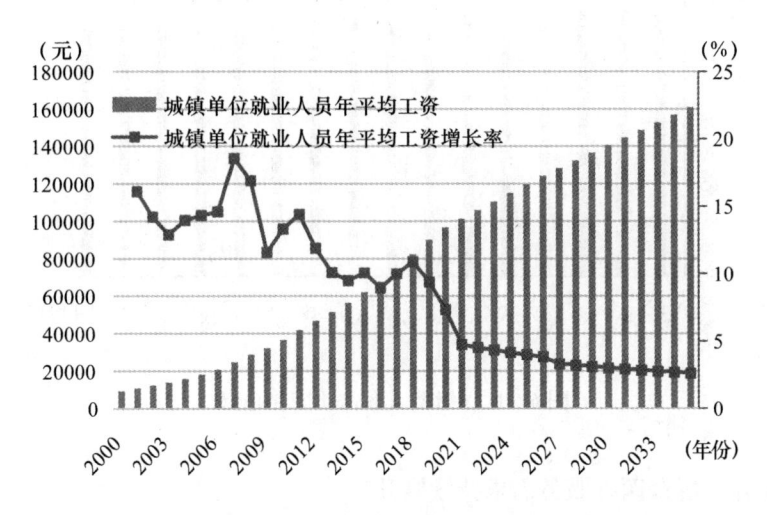

图5　城镇单位就业人员工资变化趋势

（四）缴费人数在参保人数中的比重持续下降

伴随劳动年龄人口的逐渐减少，医保缴费人数占参保人数比重将持续下降，缴费负担持续增大。根据2020—2035年中国年龄别的劳动力人数和年龄别参保率以及退休人数等预测，全国医保缴费人数占参保人数的比重将从2020年的94%下降到2025年的93%、2030年的92%和2035年的90%。其中职工医保缴费人数占比下降速度更快，预计将从2020年的75%下降到2025年的72%、2030年的70%和2035年的68%（见图6）。

如果将参保人数和缴费人数之比定义为医保基金缴费负担系数，那么2020—2035年，中国医保基金缴费负担系数将逐年增大，预计将从2020年的1.07增加到2025年的1.08，到2030年提高为1.09，2035年升至1.11；其中职工医保缴费负担增加幅度更明显，预计将从2020年的1.34增长到2025年的1.38，并在2030年和2035年升至1.43和1.47。

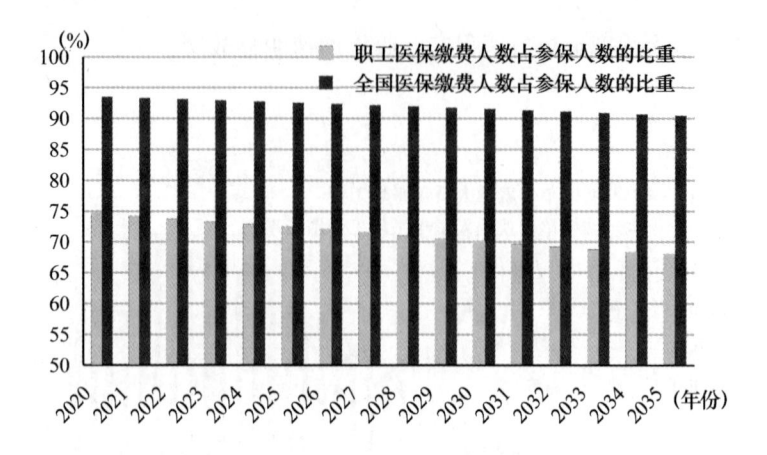

图 6　医保缴费人数占比变化趋势

（五）群众医疗服务需求持续攀升

伴随着中国群众健康意识的提升，群众对医疗服务的需求持续攀升。一是住院服务需求增幅明显。全国卫生服务调查数据显示，2018年全国中国居民全年住院人次率约为18%，比1993年增加了14个百分点；全年人均住院次数约为0.18次，比1993年增加了0.14（见图7）。二是就诊服务需求增幅明显。全国卫生服务调查数据显示，2018年全国中国居民两周就诊人次率约为23%，比1993年增加了6个百分点；全年人均就诊次数约为6次，比1993年增加了1.6次（见图8）。

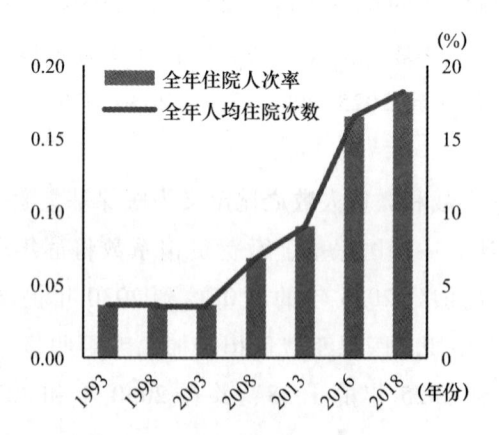

图 7　住院就诊服务需求变化趋势

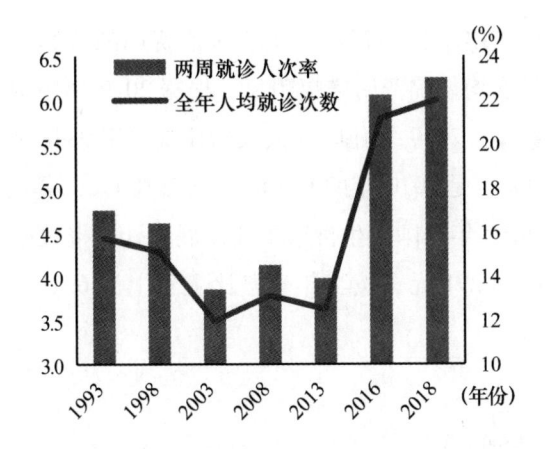

图 8　就诊人次和人均就诊次数变化趋势

（六）人均卫生支出增长速度较快

伴随医疗器械和疾病诊断技术的进步，治疗和用药费用大大提高，这也是中国医疗费用上涨和个人卫生支出增长的主要推动力量。根据国家统计局数据测算，2014—2019 年中国人均卫生费用的年均增长速度为 12.45%，人均可支配收入的年均增长速度为 9.02%。人均卫生费用的增长速度明显快于人均可支配收入的增长速度（见图 9），居民的卫生费用负担在持续加重。

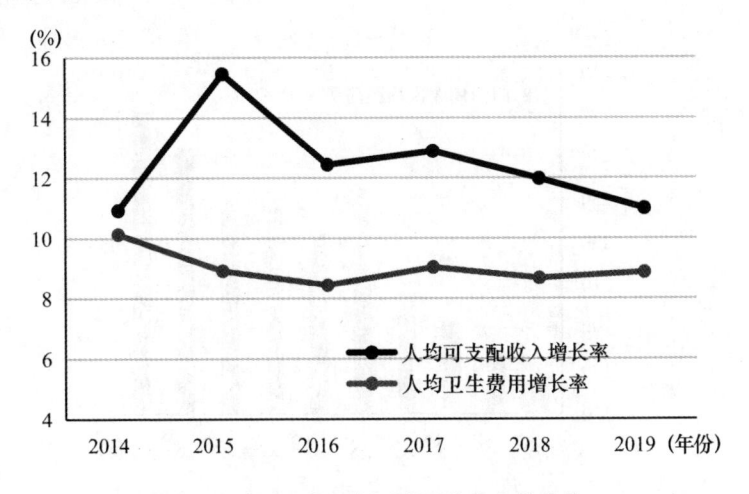

图 9　人均卫生费用与可支配收入变化趋势

在人均卫生支出增长的背后是次均医疗费用的持续增长。主要表现在两方面：一是次均住院费用增幅明显。根据2019年中国卫生健康事业发展统计公报数据，2019年住院病人人均住院费用9848元，按当年价格比上年上涨6.0%，是2010年的1.6倍（见图10）。二是次均门诊费用增幅明显。根据2019年中国卫生健康事业发展统计公报数据，2019年门诊病人次均门诊费用291元，按当年价格比上年上涨6.1%，是2010年的1.7倍（见图11）。

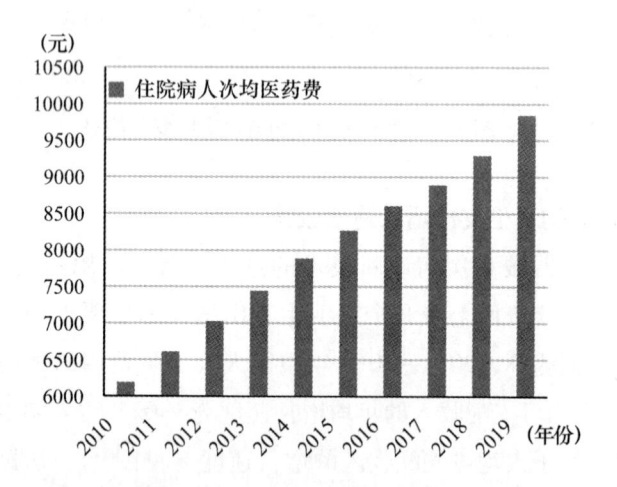

图10　次均住院费用增长趋势

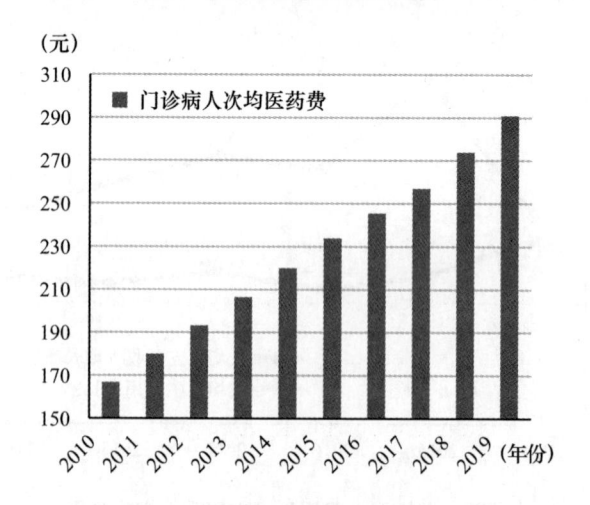

图11　次均门诊费用增长趋势

四 总结及建议

当前中国人口进入快速老龄化发展阶段，人口年龄结构、就业结构、城乡结构的转折性变化将对未来医保基金的收入和支出带来重要影响。在现行医保制度下，通过构建动态收支平衡预测模型，根据人口规模和结构、人口健康和就医、工资水平与参保缴费等数据，模拟2020—2035年中国医保基金的收支平衡状况。结果发现：现行制度下，医保基金运行不具有可持续性。预计医保基金当年结存在2026年首次出现缺口，累计结存在2034年出现缺口。其中，职工医保基金累计结存预计在2039年左右出现缺口；居民医保基金累计结存预计在2023年左右出现缺口。

以科学合理的管理达到基金收支平衡是实现基本医保制度可持续发展的重要前提。在人口老龄化背景下，建议牢牢把握"十四五"这个关键时期，加快健全稳健可持续的筹资运行机制，积极推进医保支付方式改革，加强基金运行管理和风险预警防范，坚决守住不发生系统性风险底线。

（一）健全医保筹资机制，扩大医保资金来源

坚决贯彻落实《意见》关于健全稳健可持续的筹资运行机制的具体要求。一是根据经济社会发展情况逐步提高医保缴费基数，确保基本医保基金来源稳定可持续。2018年7月，中共中央办公厅、国务院办公厅印发《国税地税征管体制改革方案》，明确从2019年1月1日起，将包括基本医疗保险在内的各项社会保险费交由税务部门统一征收。相对于社保部门，税务部门掌握职工工资数据，由税务部门统一征收社保费有利于解决长期存在的费基不实的问题，可以有效保护参保人的权益和基金的可持续发展。尽管中央已经正式出台文件，但目前还有相当一部分企业的职工医保缴费基数仍以基本工资为基础。建议尽快落实以实际工资确定缴费基数，确保医保基金收入增长与经济社会发展步伐一致。二是完善筹资分担和调整机制，均衡个人、用人单位、政府三方筹资缴费责任。中国可借鉴发达国家的经验，在应对日益增长的医保基金收支压

力上，逐步增加个人筹资缴费比重，完善筹资分担和调整机制。三是加强财政补贴力度，特别是增加对居民医保的投入。建议进一步提高烟草与酒类等影响居民健康的产业税费，并将部分税收用于弥补医疗保险基金缺口。四是巩固提高统筹层次，全面做实基本医疗保险市地级统筹，鼓励推进省级统筹，做大做强基金池，增强基金抗风险能力。

（二）改革医保支付机制，优化医保支出结构，提高医保基金使用效率

建立管用高效的医保支付机制，优化医保基金使用结构，提高医保基金使用效率。一是改革医保支付机制。逐步适度提高需方分担力度，提高个人自付比例，扩大个人费用分担的医疗服务范围，以避免过度医疗风险。二是优化医保支出结构。一方面，适度扩大门诊费用的报销范围和提高报销比例，通过加强"小病"和慢病的治疗和管理，从根本上降低重大疾病的发生风险；另一方面，优化医保报销药品结构，突出常见病、慢性病以及负担重、危害大疾病和公共卫生等方面的基本用药需求，注重儿童等特殊人群用药。此外，加快落实《关于建立健全职工基本医疗保险门诊共济保障机制的指导意见》，改革职工医保个人账户、建立健全门诊共济保障机制，提高医保基金使用效率，逐步减轻参保人员医疗费用负担，实现制度更加公平可持续。三是探索医疗服务和药品器械分开支付方式，从体制机制上弱化医院、医生与药品器械的经济联系，减少过度处方问题，控制医疗费用过快增长以及不合理的医保支出浪费问题。

（三）加强医保基金可持续发展研究

未来10—20年，伴随人口老龄化的加快和经济常态化发展，中国医保基金收支平衡面临前所未有的风险挑战，急需加强基金风险预警和防范。一是加强医保基金可持续发展研究，对影响医保基金收入和支出两侧的核心要素进行充分考虑，并建立常态化的监测和预测分析机制。在人口老龄化加速发展的背景下，特别需要加强对居民医疗服务需求结构和医疗服务价格等关系医保支出的因素分析研究。二是科学编制医疗保

障基金收支预算，加强预算执行监督，全面实施预算绩效管理，实现基金中长期精算平衡，健全基金运行风险评估、预警机制，确保基金运行稳健可持续。落实按统筹层次编制医保基金收支预算，逐级汇总；同时把医保基金预算纳入政府预算绩效管理体系，对于推动医保基金精算平衡，确保基金长期可持续运行具有十分重要的意义。

参考文献：

陈友华：《二孩政策地区经验的普适性及其相关问题——兼对"21世纪中国生育政策研究"的评价》，《人口与发展》2009年第15（01）期。

邓大松、杨红燕：《老龄化趋势下基本医疗保险筹资费率测算》，《财经研究》2003年第12期。

封进、王贞：《延迟退休年龄对城镇职工医保基金平衡的影响——基于政策模拟的研究》，《社会保障评论》2019年第3（02）期。

国家统计局：《第七次全国人口普查公报》，2021年5月11日。

黄群慧：《保持5%的经济增速至2035年，中国将跨越中等收入陷阱》，搜狐智库，https://www.sohu.com/a/416892247_100160903，2020年9月7日。

李亚青、申曙光：《退休人员不缴费政策与医保基金支付风险——来自广东省的证据》，《人口与经济》2011年第3期。

李子君：《城镇职工医保基金收支预测及其比较分析——基于不同政策组合视角并以湖北省为例》，《湖南农业大学学报》（社会科学版）2019年第20（03）期。

《人大副校长：2020—2035年中国经济潜在增速谨慎预期3.17%》，中国新闻网，https://www.chinanews.com/cj/2020/11-22/9344776.shtml，2020年11月22日。

史若丁、汪兵韬：《人口老龄化对城镇基本医疗保险基金冲击的分析》，《改革与开放》2011年第21期。

王金营、戈艳霞：《全面二孩政策实施下的中国人口发展态势》，《人口研究》2016年第40（06）期。

文裕慧：《城镇职工基本医疗保险退休人员适当缴费研究》，《现代管理科学》2015年第10期。

杨伟民：《中国到2035年经济总量或人均收入翻一番要求年均增长4.73%》，中国新闻网，https：//www.chinanews.com/cj/2020/11 - 28/9349651.shtml，2020年11月28日。

《中共中央　国务院关于深化医疗保障制度改革的意见》，中华人民共和国中央人民政府网，2020年3月5日，http：//www.gov.cn/zhengce/2020 - 03/05/content_ 5487407.htm。

《中共中央　国务院印发〈"健康中国2030"规划纲要〉》，中华人民共和国中央人民政府网，2016年10月25日，http：//www.gov.cn/xinwen/2016 - 10/25/content_ 5124174.htm。

第三篇
读懂中国社会发展

中国保险业发展与社会变迁

Sergii Rudenko,[*] Svitlana Glovatska[**],
Olga Shukovilova[***]

中国保险市场的发展是国家社会变迁的标志,是脱贫致富、全面建成小康社会的工具之一。

中国保险市场是发展中国家市场中最具发展潜力、增长最快的市场,中国保险业取得的成功得益于政府主导的各项改革措施以及国家经济形势的稳定。

根据英国经济与商业研究中心(BCEBR)的数据,目前中国按GDP排名是世界第二大经济体,并且将在2028年成为世界最领先的经济体,这相比之前的预测提前了五年。可以说,正是经济的稳定给了中国补贴保险业和发展保险业的机会。[①]

此外,中国是目前世界第二大保险市场,也被视为未来十年全球保险业增长的主要推动力。

1986年以前中国保险市场上只有"中国人民保险公司"(PICC)一家。由于缺乏竞争的推动力,中国保险行业停滞不前,在垄断被打破后,

---

[*] Sergii Rudenko,教授、博士,乌克兰国立敖德萨海事大学校长,中国社会科学院—乌克兰国立敖德萨海事大学中国研究中心理事会乌方主席。

[**] Svitlana Glovatska,乌克兰国立敖德萨海事大学副教授、博士,中国社会科学院—乌克兰国立敖德萨海事大学中国研究中心乌方主任。

[***] Olga Shukovilova,乌克兰国立敖德萨海事大学学生。

[①] Катаргин. С. Как устроен страховой рынок в Китае, www.if24.ru/strahovoj-rynok-v-kitae/.

中国的保险业才开始获得积极的发展。

(亿元)

年份	总资产	财产保险公司	人寿保险公司	再保险公司	内资保险公司	外资保险公司
2002	6320.00	948.00	5161.00	211.00		
2003	9088.00	1176.00	7657.00	255.00		
2004	11953.68	1411.38	8352.90	262.37	11540.63	413.05
2005	15286.44	1718.81	13458.27	292.70	14630.97	665.64
2006	19704.19	2340.45	17446.26	311.31	18862.60	862.66
2007	28912.78	3880.51	23249.16	877.26	27656.26	1256.51
2008	33418.83	4687.03	27138.45	994.45	31893.93	1524.91
2009	40634.75	4892.62	33655.05	1162.01	38582.37	2052.39
2010	50481.61	5833.52	42642.66	1151.79	47860.49	2621.12
2011	59828.94	7919.95	49798.19	1579.11	56822.12	3006.83
2012	73545.73	9477.47	60991.22	1845.25	70080.33	3465.40
2013	82886.95	10941.45	68250.07	2103.93	78551.67	4335.28
2014	101591.47	14061.48	82487.20	3513.56	94950.98	6640.49
2015	123597.63	18481.13	99324.83	5187.38	115057.96	6539.80
2016	153764.66	23849.82	126557.51	2765.61	144646.59	9118.07
2017	169377.32	24901.04	131885.05	3150.32	158956.86	10420.46
2018	183305.24	23502.73	146032.48	3633.48	171695.83	11609.41

图1 2002—2018年中国保险公司资产情况

资料来源：Statista 研究部。

当前的中国保险市场以两种体系为代表：强制性社会保险体系和商业保险体系。

为了规范保险活动，保护保险活动当事人的合法权益，加强对保险业的监督管理，促进保险事业的健康发展，中国政府1995年制定了《中华人民共和国保险法》。保险法的通过和监管机构的建立使中国保险市场趋于稳定。2001年加入世界贸易组织（WTO）后中国保险市场对外资保险公司开放，这使其发展更加贴近了全球保险市场。

《中华人民共和国社会保险法》于2010年通过，旨在规范社会保险

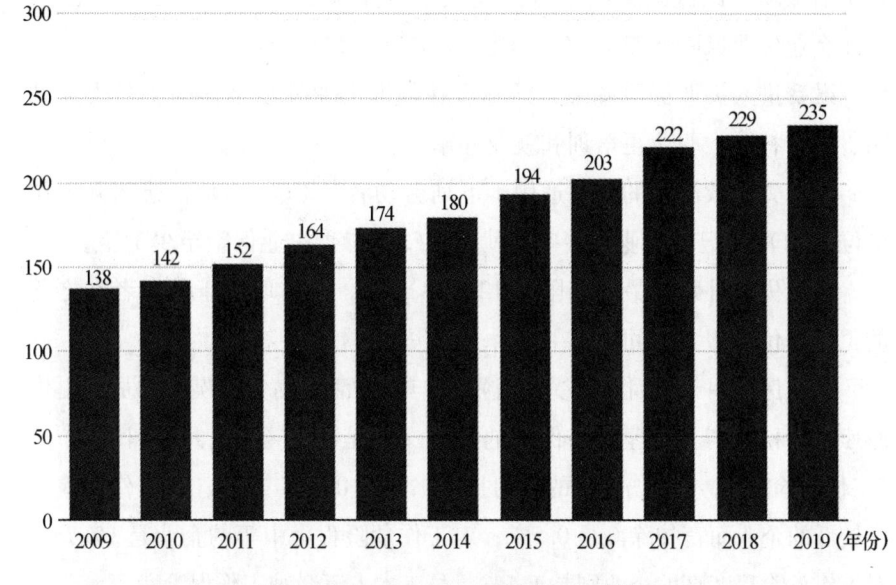

图 2　2009—2019 年中国保险公司数量

资料来源：Statista。

关系，维护公民参加社会保险和享受社会保险待遇的合法权益。

社会保险制度坚持广覆盖、保基本、多层次、可持续的方针，社会保险水平应当与经济社会发展水平相适应。

国家依法建立强制性社会保险制度，以实现公民的养老、疾病治疗、工伤治疗与休养以及生育相关的各项保障，这些险种包括：基本养老保险、基本医疗保险、工伤保险、失业保险、生育保险。

基本养老保险制度是根据《国务院关于建立统一的企业职工基本养老保险制度的决定》（国发〔1997〕26号）制定的。该制度旨在为退休后的劳动者提供基本生活工资。目前企业基本养老保险缴费比例为20%，职工或员工的扣除额为8%。

根据《国务院关于建立城镇职工基本医疗保险制度的决定》（国发〔1998〕44号），城镇所有用人单位，包括企业、机关、事业单位、社会团体、民办非企业单位及其职工，都要参加基本医疗保险。基本医疗保险的单位缴费额度为10%，员工缴费为2%。

失业保险制度建立的目的是为那些在寻找新工作时失去收入的人提

供生活保障。该保险适用于城镇地区企事业单位的所有职工。在北京，目前企业失业保险缴费为1%，职工缴费为0.2%。

缴费进入失业保险基金，该基金在领取失业补助金期间支付失业补贴、医疗补贴、职业再培训和就业补贴。

领取失业救济金的权利适用于下列劳动者：（1）不是自愿离开工作单位；（2）登记为失业者并申请就业；（3）参加失业保险至少1年。

领取失业补贴的最长期限为12—24个月，具体取决于劳动者在之前的工作单位的服务时间。

工伤保险用于为因工作受伤或罹患与职业活动相关的疾病的员工提供医疗保健和福利。管理工伤保险的主要文件是2010年12月20日颁布的《工伤保险条例》。工伤保险的平均扣除水平在0.75%左右，对工作危险程度较低的企业而言扣除额是0.5%；对工作危险程度中等的企业是1%，而对工作危险程度高的企业则是1.5%。员工本人不缴纳工伤保险费。

生育保险用于提供产假期间的医疗服务和物质福利。保险制度适用于城镇地区的劳动者，保费由企业交付并且不应超过工资总额的0.5%。保费进入生育保险基金，用于医疗、生育补贴（即产假期间的工资）、配偶产假补贴等。

住房公积金用于住房建设和员工抵押贷款。公积金的缴款由政府机关、国有企业、城镇集体所有制企业、外资企业、城镇私营企业以及城镇其他企事业单位、团体及其职工缴纳。住房公积金是职工的财产。职工可将其用于购买、建设、重建以及大修其住房。此外，如果退休、残疾、出国、用于支付抵押贷款的利息或支付超过家庭工资规模的租金，也可支取住房公积金。

根据2019年3月24日发布的《关于住房公积金管理条例》，单位和员工的缴费金额须不少于员工上一年平均月工资的5%。目前，北京市住房公基金的缴费比例为企业和职工各12%。①

为了缓解企业所面临的财务困难、劳动力成本升高、原材料价格上

---

① Обязательные отчисления на социальное страхование в КНР，www.chinawindow.ru/china/legal－information－china/business－faq/social－security－prc/.

涨等压力，中国政府下调了失业保险、工伤保险和生育保险的企业缴费额度。在经济放缓的背景下，这些措施的目标在于减轻企业负担和刺激经济增长。据中国国务院统计，此次降低保费缴纳额度将为中国企业节省 270 亿元人民币，释放的资金可用于生产现代化，例如用于完成"中国制造 2025"规划中研发高附加值的高新技术产品。①

表 1　　　　　　　　　　中国的社会保险

项目	总量				指数（%）2018年占以下各年的百分比			年均增长率（%）	
	1978	2000	2017	2018	1978	2000	2017	1979—2018	2001—2018
社会福利和保险：									
社会保险基金收入（亿元）		2644.9	67154.5	79254.8		2996.5	118.0		20.8
社会保险基金支出（亿元）		2385.6	57145.6	67792.7		2841.7	118.6		20.4
基本养老保险缴费人员（亿元）		13617.4	91548.3	94293.3		692.4	103.0		11.3
参加失业保险的雇员人数（亿元）		10408.4	18784.2	19643.5		188.7	104.6		3.6
基本医疗保险缴费人员（万人）		3786.9	117681.4	134458.6		3550.6	114.3		21.9

资料来源：Statista 研究部。

应该指出的是，世界上大多数发达国家中都有上述这些类型的保险存在。

2019 年，《国务院关于修改外资保险公司管理条例的决定》获得通过，此后公布了多项改革措施，以方便外资保险公司进入中国市场，从而为保险业的发展提供了额外的激励：允许外国保险公司和外国金融机构成为中国保险公司的股东。据新华社报道，截至 2020 年年底，外资在全国设立外资保险公司 64 家、办事处 124 家和保险代理机构 18 家，总资产达到 1.46 万亿元，2020 年保险公司总资产增加 13.3%，达到 23.3 万亿元。此外，中国"十四五"规划和 2021 年的"两会"进一步明确了放宽外资保险公司进入中国保险市场的条件。

不过，加拿大皇家银行资本市场分析师认为，外资保险公司不会达到中国大型保险公司的规模和市场份额，而是会为中国国内保险市场的

---

① Снижение отчислений в фонды социального страхования, www.chinawindow.ru/china/legal-information-china/business-faq/social-security-decrease/.

发展做出贡献，因为中国政府欢迎外资的流入。根据瑞士再保险研究院的数据，外资保险公司的规模仅占中国保险市场的 2% 左右，而最大的 5 家国有保险公司则占据了 70% 以上的市场（详见图 3）。①

内资保险公司	766 380.8 家	98.04%
外资保险公司	15 306.5 家	1.96%
总计	781 687.3 家	
前五大国有保险公司市场占比		73.50%
前十大国有保险公司市场占比		85.05%

图 3　中外保险公司的比例

瑞士再保险研究院估计，在全球范围内，新兴市场的保险公司受到新冠肺炎疫情流行的打击将是最大的，因为 2020 年和 2021 年保费收入将下降 3.6%。然而中国保险市场是一个例外：从 2020 年到 2021 年保费收入平均增长了 7%。这一增长得益于经济的快速复苏、公共政策的支持、风险意识的提高以及保险公司与客户之间的积极互动——正是这种增长将驱动全球保险业的新机会向新兴亚洲国家尤其是中国的转移②。

据中国银保监会统计，截至 2020 年四季度末，保险公司实现基本保费收入 4.5 万亿元，同比增长 6.1%。保险公司理赔金的支付额为 1.4 万亿元，比上年增长 7.9%；保单量平稳增长：截至 2020 年四季度末新增保单 526 亿张，同比增长 6.3%。截至 2020 年三季度末，银保监会统计的保险公司平均综合偿付能力系数为 242.5%，平均基本偿付能力系数为 230.5%。综合风险评级为 A 类 98 家，B 类 73 家，C 类 5 家，D 类 1 家。③

分析师们表示，当前中国和亚洲将变得比以前更加强大，因为在未

---

① Swiss Re Institute, "The Chinese Insurance Market", Switzerland, 2018, p. 39.
② Swiss Re Institute, "The Chinese Insurance Market", Switzerland, 2018, p. 39.
③ China Banking and Insurance Regulatory Commission, "Supervisory Statistics of the Banking and Insurance Sectors – – 2020 Q4", Feburary 9, 2021, www. cbirc. gov. cn/en/view/pages/ItemDetail. html? docId = 967412&itemId = 983.

来的几年内，更高的风险意识和被唤醒的社会保护需求将会刺激增长，其中中国将位居榜首。

分析师们预计，未来几年中国的保费将出现两位数的增长：到2030年中国的保费将增长7770亿欧元，与英国、法国、德国和意大利的市场总规模相当。①

"第四次工业革命"将为保险行业的发展注入新的动力，创造和拓展风险管理新需求并提供技术支持，将保险业面临的挑战转化为机遇。

参考文献：

China Banking and Insurance Regulatory Commission, "Supervisory Statistics of the Banking and Insurance Sectors – – 2020 Q4", Feburary 9, 2021, www.cbirc.gov.cn/en/view/pages/ItemDetail.html? docId = 967412&itemId = 983.

Swiss Re Institute, "The Chinese Insurance Market", Switzerland, 2018.

Allianz представил прогноз развития страхового рынка Азии и Китая до 2030 года, https：//forinsurer.com/news/20/07/13/38229.

Снижение отчислений в фонды социального страхования, www.chinawindow.ru/china/legal – information – china/business – faq/social – security – decrease/.

Катаргин. С. Как устроен страховой рынок в Китае, www.if24.ru/strahovoj – rynok – v – kitae/.

Обязательные отчисления на социальное страхование в КНР, www.chinawindow.ru/china/legal – information – china/business – faq/social – security – prc/.

---

① Allianz представил прогноз развития страхового рынка Азии и Китая до 2030 года, https：//forinsurer.com/news/20/07/13/38229.

中国社会变革的里程碑：
高等教育大众化与国际化

Dzmitry Smaliakou[*]

近 30 年来，大众化、国际化的大学已成为国家高等教育体系发展的重中之重。同时，这些领域的发展不仅是衡量国民高等教育成功与否的重要标准，也是衡量国家地位的标准，这些领域的滞后则表明整个国家的社会滞后。有鉴于此，大众化和国际化高等教育的发展可以从现代化的角度来观察，并被认为是国家更新社会、政府和经济结构能力的一个要素。从社会哲学的意义上来说，这是社会应对历史时刻不断变化带来的挑战的一种能力，或者说应对时代要求的能力。

对现代化的关注开辟了另一个重要的社会哲学视角——国家主体性，这往往与国家作为独立主体的能力相呼应，国际伙伴将其视为国际对话的平等组成部分。在这方面，高等教育的大众化和国际化可以代表一个国家主体作为国际谈判一方的能力，作为主体，能够在现代世界格局下制定和保存协议的能力。这种理解还包括假设没有其他强大的赞助方（该赞助方首先需要为任何进一步的协议提供初步许可），也没有强加和保护主体意见的大都市。在这种背景下，大众化和国际化的高等教育被视为国家"成熟"的最重要条件之一，是其主体性的一个要素。

此外，在现代环境下，知识经济为社会及其主要活动的转型提供了更有效、创伤更小的机制。科技进步极大地简化了社会经济的现代化，

---

[*] Dzmitry Smaliakou，白俄罗斯国家科学院哲学研究所中国哲学与文化研究中心高级研究员。

但同时也对国民主体的智力和创造能力以及发达的社会和教育基础设施提出了更高的要求。在这方面，可以说全球化和知识经济使高等教育的性质和功能发生了巨大转变，但与此同时高等教育也对全球交流与合作产生了深远的影响。这种影响力不仅被认为是利益相关者之间的经济竞争或影响力竞争，而且是"全球公共部门改革浪潮"[1] 的重要组成部分，社会和经济创新提供了从一个历史时期向另一个历史时期的过渡。

中国是发展中国家在社会和经济转型的艰难条件下，成功实现高等教育大众化和国际化的最突出例子之一。高等教育的快速发展不仅影响了中国经济的重建，促进了 GDP 的大幅增长，而且还彻底消除了贫困。[2] 在这方面，重点关注中国高等教育大众化和国际化的经验，有助于更好地从结构和规模上理解中国在过去 30 年经历的社会变革。本文的研究结果将有助于更好地理解现代社会进程的本质、社会现代化的结构，从而有助于把握社会经济发展时代社会变迁的意义。

一　方法框架

有许多描述高等教育国际化起源的社会哲学假设，这些假设大多数基于宏观因素，例如全球化。特别是，H. De Wit[3]和 J. Knight[4]将他们的研究指向国际化的辩证性质，作为一种反对全球化的形式。所提出的方法通常作为现代理论模型的一个共同点，而地缘政治议程，包括以不断变化的经济模式问题的形式提出的那些议程，在某种程度上与全球化现

---

[1] Mok, K. H., "Restructuring in Hong Kong, Taiwan and Mainland China", *Higher Education Research & Development*, 2003, Vol. 22, Iss. 2, pp. 117 – 129.

[2] Textor, C., "Ratio of residents living below the extreme poverty line in China 2000 – 2020", https://www.statista.com/statistics/1086836/china – poverty – ratio/

[3] De Wit, H., "The history of internationalization of higher education", in D. Deardorff et al., eds., The SAGE handbook of inter – national higher education, California, 2012, pp. 43 – 60.

[4] Knight, J., "Internationalization remodeled: definition, approaches, and rationales", *Journal of Studies in International Education*, 1997, Vol. 1, No. 8, pp. 5 – 31.

象有关。其他研究者如 J. Stier①也从全球化的概念出发，认为国际化是发达国家和发展中国家之间的持续交流。发达国家在这种交流中提供了他们的技术和创新，另外，发展中国家提供了在新兴市场工作和互动的经验。

高等教育的国际化和大众化与素质问题紧密相关。特别值得一提的是 M. Tight②、M. Giannakis、N. Bullivant③以及 Y. Yang④的文章，这些文章描述了高等教育如何在大众化大学的条件下形成了提高教育质量的要求。在社会发展方面，特别体现了大众高等教育与阶级自由化和社会解放之间的联系。⑤ 总体来说，大众高等教育、教育质量问题与社会经济发展之间的联系不仅存在于发展中国家的框架中，而且也存在于发达国家的例子中。特别是，P. J. Gumport 对美国大众化高等教育和后大众化高等教育的形成进行了广泛的研究。⑥

作者的模型也从宏观因素出发，但并不是专门以全球化为研究角度。这一变化的关键在于帝国主义的解体，这一解体到 20 世纪末完成，并仍然以后帝国主义和新帝国主义的表现形式影响着全球。世界帝国主义的传播形成了高等教育国际化发展的社会政治条件，有助于互动主体的国

---

① Stier, J., "Taking a critical stance toward internationalization ideologies in higher education: idealism, instrumentalism and educationalism", *Globalisation, Societies and Education*, 2004, Vol. 2, iss. 1, pp. 83 – 97.

② Tight M., "Mass Higher Education and Massification", *High Education Policy*, 2019, No. 32, pp. 93 – 108.

③ Giannakis M., Bullivant N., "The Massification of Higher Education in the UK: aspects of service quality", *Journal of Further and Higher Education*, 2016, Vol. 40, No. 5, pp. 630 – 648.

④ Yang Y., "Higher Education in China: Massification, Accessibility, and Quality Issues", in Collins C., Lee M., Hawkins J., Neubauer D. eds., *The Palgrave Handbook of Asia Pacific Higher Education*, New York: Palgrave Macmillan, 2016, pp. 315 – 330.

⑤ Hornsby D. J., Osman R., "Massification in higher education: large classes and student learning", *High Education*, 2014, No. 67, pp. 711 – 719; Dias D., "Has Massification of Higher Education led to more Equity? Clues to a reflection on Portu – guese education arena", *International Journal of Inclusive Education*, 2015, Vol. 19, No. 2, pp. 103 – 120; Mok K. H., Wu A., "Higher Education, Changing Labour Market and Social Mobility in the Era of Massification in China", *Journal of Education and Work*, 2016, Vol. 29, No. 1, pp. 77 – 97.

⑥ Gumport P. J., "The United States Country Report: Trends in Higher Education from Massification to Post – Massification", 1997, http://course.napla.coplacdigital.org/wp – content/uploads/2016/09/Trends – in – Higher – Education – from – Massification – to – Post – Massification.pdf.

家稳定。① 注重尊重民族特色成为不仅在教育领域，而且在国际合作和经济互动中的重要趋势，它从根本上改变了全球化的旧观念，即对众多不完善的细节进行有目的的、普遍化的改进。在这方面，高等教育国际化被理解为在国际一体化与高等教育质量提升的向量交汇处形成的过程，在每个方向都有助于相互加速发展。②

在这一概念中，大众高等教育通过形成提高教育质量的需要，并作为实施一体化议程的制度工具，是形成国际化学术需求的内在因素。从这个意义上说，大众化大学既是实施整合的工具，也是实施整合的要求之一。高等教育的大众化和国际化共同作为地方去殖民化的手段，允许民族国家发展自己的主体性，以及解决与异化劳动和生产资料垄断相关的马克思主义经典问题。③

总体来说，高等教育大众化和国际化是民族国家质量重构的要素。民族主体性、群体性和国际化大学的形成，使后殖民主体被承认为谈判的一方。在国内政策方面，高等教育大众化和国际化是利用外部资源实现社会现代化和稳定发展的契机。这两个过程共同为国家的社会和经济生活提供了质的重组，使国家主体融入国际互动结构，从而加强国家稳定，显著提高知识领域的工作质量。④ 在这些情况下，一些国家成功地将高等教育大众化和国际化，而另一些国家由于各种原因（主要是殖民）而相对落后。⑤ 因此，高等教育大众化和国际化的能力就是社会和经济现代化的能力，即国民主体社会经济快速发展的能力。

---

① Smaliakou D. A., "The genesis of higher education internationalisation", *The Education and Science Journal*, 2019, Vol. 8, No. 20, pp. 9 – 28.

② Smaliakou D. A., "Internationalization of higher education: socio – philosophical aspect", *Doklady of the National Academy of Sciences of Belarus*, 2020, Vol. 3, No. 64, pp. 371 – 378.

③ Smaliakou D., "Institutional conditions of internationalisation of higher education: Mass higher school", *The Education and Science Journal*, 2021, Vol. 23, No. 5, pp. 11 – 37.

④ Smaliakou, D. A., *Internationalisation of Higher Education: theory, practice, prospects*, Minsk: Belarusian Science, 2020, p. 223.

⑤ Smaliakou, D. A., "Internationalisation of Higher Education in light of national development problems, Proceedings of the National Academy of Sciences of Belarus", *Humanitarian Series*, 2021, Vol. 2, No. 66, pp. 135 – 141.

二 科学假设

从社会哲学的角度看,高等教育大众化是公共生活质量的重构机制,影响着经济和社会文化互动的变化。从制度上讲,高等教育的大众化是通过公共—私营合作关系实现的,这种合作关系既提供了充足的资金,又在劳动力市场和竞争力需求方面提供了灵活性。

中国是高等教育大众化和国际化有效实施的成功范例,中国高等教育体系和经济体系的并行发展使其能够在社会内部显著实现经济和社会关系的现代化,确保经济的动态增长,包括基础设施和福利的发展。

三 科学文献和统计资料

笔者试图分析中国高等教育大众化和国际化的过程,他撰写了两本专著《白俄罗斯和中国在高等教育领域的合作》[①]、《高等教育国际化:理论、实践和前景》[②] 和一系列文章(《借鉴中国经验改善白俄罗斯高等教育》[③]、《高等教育国际化的制度条件:大众高等学校》[④])。在此基础上,建立了中国大众高等学校及其国际化的理论模型,确定了这些过程实施的主要阶段,并概述了主要结果。

在本文的框架中,使用了专门的分析和统计材料,以更好地了解中

---

① Smaliakou, D. A., "Belarusian and Chinese cooperation in sphere of Higher Education", Minsk: Institute of Philosophy National Academy of Science of Belarus, 2017, p. 149.

② Smaliakou, D. A., *Internationalisation of Higher Education: theory, practice, prospects*, Minsk: Belarusian Science, 2020, p. 223.

③ Smaliakou, D. A., "Improving higher education in Belarus taking into account the Chinese experience", Herald of the Belarusian State Economic University, *Journal of Science*, 2019, No. 1, pp. 19 – 28.

④ Smaliakou D., "Institutional conditions of internationalisation of higher education: Mass higher school", *The Education and Science Journal*, 2021, Vol. 23, No. 5, pp. 11 – 37.

国的进程。[①]

四　研究结果和讨论

高等教育大众化这个术语最终于 20 世纪 60 年代在科学文献中确立，

[①] 以下作品被用作分析文献：Pan M. , Luo D. , "A comparative analysis on models of higher education massification", Front, 2008, No. 3, pp. 64 – 78；Gao Y. , "Massification of Higher Education in China: Problems and Solutions", in Wu A. , Haw – kins J. eds. , *Massification of Higher Education in Asia: Quality, Excel – lence and Governance*, Singapore: Springer, 2018. pp. 9 – 19；Wu A. , Hawkins J. , *Massification of Higher Education in Asia*, Singapore: Springer, 2018, p. 147；Mok K. H. , Chan S. J. , "After Massification and Response to Internationalization: Quality Assurance of Higher Education in Taiwan and Hong Kong", in Collins C. , Lee M. , Hawkins J. , Neubauer D. eds. , *The Palgrave Handbook of Asia Pacific Higher Education*, New York: Palgrave Macmillan, 2016, pp. 423 – 438；Mok K. , Jiang J. , "Massification of higher education and challenges for graduate employment and social mobility: East Asian experiences and sociological reflections", *International Journal of Educational Development*, 2018, pp. 44 – 51；Reddy K. S. , Xie E. , Tang Q. , "Higher education, high – impact research, and world university rankings: A case of India and comparison with China", *Pacific Science Review B: Humanities and Social Sciences*, 2016, Vol. 1, No. 2, pp. 1 – 21；Ding, X. , China's Higher Education Market, DIFID WB Collaboration on Knowledge and Skills in the New Economy, 2004, January, https: //siteresources. worldbank. org/EDUCATION/Resources/2782001126210664195/16369711126210694253/China_Higher_Education. pdf.

统计资料来自：https: //www. statista. com/；https: //tradingeconomics. com/；Roser M. , Ortiz – Ospina E. , Tertiary Education, 2013, https: //ourworldindata. org/tertiary – education；联合国教科文组织统计研究所的报告和数据：Research facilities in science and technology in Asia, Unesco, 1968, https: //gospin. unesco. org/files/his_pdfs/Research_facilities_in_S – T_in_Asia_China_en. pdf；World Science report, Unesco, 1988, https: //gospin. unesco. org/files/his_pdfs/WSR1998_China_EN. pdf；World Science report, Unesco, 2015, https: //gospin. unesco. org/files/his_pdfs/USR2015_China_RU. pdf；Facts and figures: Business and innovation from the UNESCO Science Report, Towards 2030, Unesco, https: //en. unesco. org/node/252281；World Inequality Database on Education, https: //www. education – inequalities. org/；以及特别是 Calderon, A. J. , Analytics & Insights, Massification of higher education revisited, Rmit University, 2018, http: //cdn02. pucp. education/academico/2018/08/23165810/na_mass_revis_230818. pdf；Fu – tao Huang, A Comparative Study of Massification of Higher Education in China and Japan, https: //www. researchgate. net/publication/44835451_A_Comparative_study_of_massification_of_higher_education_in_China_and_Japan? enrichId = rgreq – dadf04403177d6a39e365ac7f649f324 – XXX&enrichSource = Y292ZXJQYWdlOzQ0ODM1NDUxOOFTOjI4MTA5NzI2Mzk2MDA2NEAxNDQ0MDMwMjE4MjIy&el = 1_x_2&_esc = publicationCoverPdf 等作品的统计数据。

表示高等教育机构数量和在高等教育机构学习的学生数量的动态增长。[①]大众高等教育起源于美国,通过资助退伍军人、反对种族主义和争取妇女权利,通过其他弱势社会类别的支持,导致大学就读的学生人数的大幅增加。在这方面,以及对国家资助那些先前被排除在高等教育之外的人群接受教育,使美国的大众高等教育成为可能。学生人数的增长需要相应数量的教师,这反过来又促进了大学总数的增加。

类似的过程也发生在东南亚,韩国、日本等国家通过大幅增加对高等教育的投资,从而促进了社会和经济的密集现代化。在20世纪80年代初,这种趋势延伸到了中国,作为改革开放的一部分,大众高等教育成为国家现代化的重点之一。

值得注意的是,中国通过国际合作在高等教育现代化方面取得了经验。特别值得一提的是1872—1881年的中国教育使命(中国学生去美国留学是为了学习西方最新的知识,主要是在工程科学领域),中国第一所大学的国际渊源——按照西方模式于1898年成立的"京师大学堂",后来改名为北京大学,以及作为罗斯福奖学金项目的一部分成立的北京师范大学、清华大学,1909—1929年,有1300多名中国学生赴美国留学。在同样的背景下,还有20世纪中叶中国与苏联教育合作的经验。但以前的现代化效果有限,并没有对国家产生大规模影响。直到20世纪末,中国的社会、经济和技术发展方面仍落后于欧美,就业形势没有明显变化。

改革开放之初,中国的高等教育完全由国家预算资助:在中国学习的学生不多,但获得了少量奖学金。自20世纪80年代中期以来,中国在大学建立了付费教育制度,社会收入的不断增加导致了学生人数的增加。自1989年以来,高等教育收费已变得很普遍,但成绩较好的学生可能有资格享受学费减免优惠。在农林、教育等学科,还保留了旧的做法,学生不仅免收学费,还可以获得政府提供的奖学金。自1997年以来,中国的免费高等教育全面缩减。

[①] Gumport P. J., "The United States Country Report: Trends in Higher Education from Massification to Post-Massification", 1997, p. 50, http://course.napla.coplacdigital.org/wp-content/uploads/2016/09/Trends-in-Higher-Education-from-Massification-to-Post-Massification.pdf.

各类学生缴纳学费的可能性打开了大众高等教育的大门，这是中国经济和政治上的一个重要突破。此前，国家预算是中国高校支持精英高等教育工作的唯一资金来源，但在报考人数快速增长的背景下，这样的机制已经失效。改革后，高等教育人口的覆盖率显著提高。

同时，学生人数的增长导致学生与教师人数的比例发生变化，达到18∶1，而不太成功的大学的比例则为30∶1。因此，需要采取一些步骤来提高教学质量，这些步骤包括：取消远程教育、增加中国留学生人数、吸引外国合作伙伴准备和实施联合教育计划，以及向数量有限的先进大学投入财力和智力资源。

自20世纪80年代初以来，中国公民获得了出国接受高等教育的权利（截至1983年，就有7000名学生前往美国和日本留学），与此同时，针对留学方向的国家项目正在启动。1978年至2011年，总共有200多万中国学生出国留学。到2010年，中国在学术流动方面处于领先地位。这对于将先进经验和技术吸引到中国是必要的，包括在高等教育领域，使中国完全实现现代化，并使其经济融入世界劳工分配制度。如今，中国约有100万名学生出国留学（约占全球留学人口的18%），其中大部分在美国（333935名留学生）、澳大利亚（143323名留学生）和英国（107813名留学生）留学。①

中国一流大学的毕业生在当地雇主中非常抢手，在这方面，最好的申请者不会出国，而是进入中国的先进大学。中国一批世界一流大学的成就，得益于国家重大计划的实施："211工程"以及"985工程"，旨在增强整体机构能力，发展重点学科领域和公共服务体系建设。因此，一些中国大学有能力与世界高等教育中心抗衡。与此同时，中国通过建立联合培训项目，向外国合作伙伴迈出了更重要的一步。

目前，中国的国内学生人数不断增长：2015年的学生人数比2012年增加了40%，到2019年，学生人数又增加了50%。改革开放以来，中国的受教育水平指数翻了一番（从1980年的0.362增长到2014年的

---

① Global Flow of Tertiary-Level Students, Unesco, http://uis.unesco.org/en/uis-student-flow#slideoutmenu.

0.614),中国人口的教育水平在 2000—2010 年只增长了 10%,到 2020 年,中国接受高等教育的人口预计将超过 2 亿人。

大众教育的快速发展使中国在科学和创新领域取得了重大进展。到 2013 年,中国的科研人员人数达到 148.4 万人,而 2003 年中国发表的科学出版物仅占世界的 5%,到 2013 年这一比例上升到 20%。到 2010 年末,中国已经从一个维持生计的经济落后国家发展成为一个拥有庞大人力资源的国家,成为高等教育大国。

现代科学倾向于解释中印两国发展的差异。如果说中国成功实现了高等教育大众化,那么印度则保留了精英大学体系。与此同时,过去 20 年间中印的 GDP 和人口规模大致相同,现今中国的名义 GDP 变成了印度的 6 倍。创新不仅促成了这种状况,而且扩大了受教育人员的社会基础,尤其是以妇女和穷人为主。

2000—2020 年,按购买力平价计算,中国的 GDP 排名世界第一,2015 年中国的学生人数比 2012 年增加了 40%,到 2019 年,大学生人数增加了 50%。1994—2003 年,中国学生的增长是适度的(从 1994 年的 6% 增长到 2003 年的 17%)①,但现在,这一数字科学地增长到 32%②(平均水平)。

对于中等发展水平的国家来说,高等教育的平均水平令人印象深刻,但高等教育的社会图景更为重要。首先,值得注意的是,中国为 38% 的女性高中毕业生和 26% 的男性高中毕业生提供高等教育,最富有阶层占 31%,中产阶层占 33%,最贫困阶层为 33%,城市为 38%,农村为 26%。如果我们将这些数字与 2010 年进行比较,我们会发现社会变化非常显著(当时最贫困学生占 10%,农村学生 10%,女性 16%)③。

---

① Fu-tao Huang, "A Comparative Study of Massification of Higher Education in China and Japan", https://www.researchgate.net/publication/44835451_A_Comparative_study_of_massification_of_higher_education_in_China_and_Japan? enrichId = rgreq - dadf04403177d6a39e365ac7f649f324 - XXX&enrichSource = Y292ZXJQYWdlOzQ0ODM1NDUxO0FTOjI4MTA5NzI2Mzk2MDA2NEAxNDQ2OMD MwMjE4MjIy&el = 1_x_2&_esc = publicationCoverPdf.

② World Inequality Database on Education, https://www.education-inequalities.org/.

③ World Inequality Database on Education, https://www.education-inequalities.org/.

比较大众高等教育和 GDP 增长，我们可以发现学生人数的增长与 GPD 增长同时发生。如果说 1990 年到 1998 年 GDP 增长仅翻一番，那么在高等教育频繁大众化的时代（1998 年至今）GDP 每 4 年翻一番，从总数上看，1998 年的经济增长更为显著。①

五 未来面临的问题

未来中国高等教育面临的问题，也是社会发展的问题，可以概括为以下三点：

第一，这种"成功"（中国的大众高等教育）是以牺牲机构运营条件的公平性为代价的。不同层次的机构之间的差距越来越大，学生的学习经历也随之出现差异。②

第二，在高等教育大众化的背景下，高校毕业生，尤其是那些没有有效社会资本的大学生，可能会面临就业难的问题。③

第三，自 2000 年以来，中国在教育方面投入了大量资金，教育比例从 2000 年的不到 10% 上升到 2016 年的 48.4%。中国很有可能在未来的 5 年内达到 60%，在 10 年内达到 70%。④

第一点陈述是对教育质量的评论，这意味着中国不同大学的质量差异很大，文凭的价值也不尽相同。可以说，现在只要经济和社会有很大的发展空间，所有毕业生都能找到合适的工作，这就不那么重要了。只要这种空间被消除，高等教育系统就需要越来越高的质量。在这方面，国际事务是质量评估的最重要工具。这就是为什么即使在招生和毕业生就业问题还不那么严重的今天，发展国际关系对大学来说也如此重要。

---

① China GDP, tradingeconomics. com, https://tradingeconomics.com/china/gdp#stats.

② Qiang Zha, "CHINA: Massification has increased inequalities", University world news, 2011, https://www.universityworldnews.com/post.php?story=20110708162827633.

③ Mok, K. H., "Restructuring in Hong Kong, Taiwan and Mainland China", *Higher Education Research & Development*, 2003, Vol. 22, Iss. 2, pp. 117–129.

④ Calderon, A. J., "Analytics & Insights. Massification of higher education revisited", Rmit University, 2018, http://cdn02.pucp.education/academico/2018/08/23165810/na_mass_revis_230818.pdf.

第二点陈述也呼吁教育质量和高等教育的价值。有时候，为了未来的职业发展，毕业生需要父母或相关人员的帮助，从这点来看，教育质量就显得并不是那么重要。另外，目前中国最重要的问题是让高等教育对弱势群体（如穷人或女性）具有吸引力。在这方面，中国表现出的社会成就使中国有别于亚洲、非洲或拉丁美洲的其他发展中国家。然而，未来这个问题可能会更加严重，成为中国社会进一步发展的障碍。

第三点陈述对未来的发展持乐观态度，这将比以前的结果更难实现。要使高等教育入学率达到50%以上，需要深刻改变国家的社会状况，并为生活和工作提供新的技术和社会工具。因此，中国大学的进一步大众化和国际化更加需要对国际关系的关注，需要更快地向创新领域转变。在这种情况下，"一带一路"倡议可能会起到效果，但大学需要提高其教育质量，否则未来的学生增长将不会像以前那样有效，并可能成为隐性失业的工具。

六　结论

改革开放彻底改变了中国的经济和生活。大众化和国际化的高等教育可以被视为中国社会发展和劳动力市场变化的关键因素。由于高等教育的相互（公共和私人）资助，高等教育收费制度为大学的快速发展提供了条件。此外，学术流动也为中国受教育人数的增加做出了巨大贡献。

高等教育质量的进一步提高以及高等教育入学率达到50%的目标要求中国高校更加积极开展国际合作。在这方面，中国能否达到富裕国家的水平，还是会停留在发展中国家的水平，时间将会证明。成功的关键是创新经济，它需要越来越多的合格的创造型人才。这对中国高等教育提出了新的挑战，将会影响中国社会的进一步发展。

参考文献：

Calderon, A. J., "Analytics & Insights. Massification of higher education revisited", Rmit University, 2018, http：//cdn02. pucp. education/academico/2018/08/23165810/na_mass_revis_230818. pdf.

China GDP, tradingeconomics. com, https://tradingeconomics. com/china/gdp#stats.

De Wit, H., "The history of internationalization of higher education", in D. Deardorff et al. , eds. , *The SAGE handbook of international higher education*, California, 2012.

Dias D. , "Has Massification of Higher Education led to more Equity? Clues to a reflection on Portu – guese education arena", *International Journal of Inclusive Education*, 2015, Vol. 19, No. 2.

Fu – tao Huang, "A Comparative Study of Massification of Higher Education in China and Japan", https://www. researchgate. net/publication/44835451_A_Comparative_study_of_massification_of_higher_education_in_China_and_Japan? enrichId = rgreq – dadf04403177d6a39e365ac7f649f324 – XXX&enrichSource = Y292ZXJQYWdlOzQ0ODM1NDUxO0FTOjI4MTA5NzI2Mzk2MDA2NEAxNDQ0MDMwMjE4MjIy&el = 1_x_2&_esc = publicationCover Pdf.

Giannakis M. , Bullivant N. , "The Massification of Higher Education in the UK: aspects of service quality", *Journal of Further and Higher Education*, 2016, Vol. 40, No. 5.

Global Flow of Tertiary – Level Students, Unesco, http://uis. unesco. org/en/uis – student – flow#slideoutmenu.

Gumport P. J. , "The United States Country Report: Trends in Higher Education from Massification to Post – Massification", 1997, http://course. napla. coplacdigital. org/wp – content/uploads/2016/09/Trends – in – Higher – Education – from – Massification – to – Post – Massification. pdf.

Gumport P. J. , "The United States Country Report: Trends in Higher Education from Massification to Post – Massification", 1997, p. 50, http://course. napla. coplacdigital. org/wp – content/uploads/2016/09/Trends – in – Higher – Education – from – Massification – to – Post – Massification. pdf.

Hornsby D. J. , Osman R. , "Massification in higher education: large classes and student learning", *High Education*, 2014, No. 67.

Knight, J. , "Internationalization remodeled: definition, approaches, and rationales", *Journal of Studies in International Education*, 1997, Vol. 1, No. 8.

Mok, K. H. , "Restructuring in Hong Kong, Taiwan and Mainland China", *Higher Education Research & Development*, 2003, Vol. 22, Iss. 2.

Mok K. H. , Wu A. , "Higher Education, Changing Labour Market and Social Mobility in the Era of Massification in China", *Journal of Education and Work*, 2016, Vol. 29, No. 1.

Qiang Zha, "CHINA: Massification has increased inequalities", University world news, 2011, https://www.universityworldnews.com/post.php?story=20110708162827633.

Smaliakou, D. A. , "Belarusian and Chinese cooperation in sphere of Higher Education", Minsk: Institute of Philosophy National Academy of Science of Belarus, 2017.

Smaliakou, D. A. , *Internationalisation of Higher Education: theory, practice, prospects*, Minsk: Belarusian Science, 2020.

Smaliakou, D. A. , "Internationalisation of Higher Education in light of national development problems, Proceedings of the National Academy of Sciences of Belarus", *Humanitarian Series*, 2021, Vol. 2, No. 66.

Smaliakou, D. A. "Improving higher education in Belarus taking into account the Chinese experience", Herald of the Belarusian State Economic University, *Journal of Science*, 2019, No 1.

Smaliakou D. , "Institutional conditions of internationalisation of higher education: Mass higher school", *The Education and Science Journal*, 2021, Vol. 23, No. 5.

Smaliakou D. A. , "The genesis of higher education internationalisation", *The Education and Science Journal*, 2019, Vol. 8, No. 20.

Smaliakou D. A. , "Internationalization of higher education: socio-philosophical aspect", *Doklady of the National Academy of Sciences of Belarus*, 2020, Vol. 3, No. 64.

Stier, J. , "Taking a critical stance toward internationalization ideologies in higher education: idealism, instrumentalism and educationalism", *Globalisation, Societies and Education*, 2004, Vol. 2, iss. 1.

Textor, C., "Ratio of residents living below the extreme poverty line in China 2000 – 2020", https://www.statista.com/statistics/1086836/china-poverty-ratio/.

Tight M., "Mass Higher Education and Massification", 2019, No. 32.

World Inequality Database on Education, https://www.education-inequalities.org/.

Yang Y., "Higher Education in China: Massification, Accessibility, and Quality Issues", in Collins C., Lee M., Hawkins J., Neubauer D. eds., *The Palgrave Handbook of Asia Pacific Higher Education*, New York: Palgrave Macmillan, 2016.

中国中产阶层的发展及其对可持续发展的影响

Ivan Semenist[*]

中产阶层人数的增长及其收入水平决定了现阶段世界经济的发展，2020年消费支出增长高达41万亿美元就是证明。中国中产阶层消费占世界消费水平的17.8%，而中国人口约占世界总人口的20%。20世纪50年代，全球90%以上的中产阶层分布在欧洲和北美。而如今，全球20%以上的中产阶层分布在中国。中国正处于世界有史以来中产阶层规模扩张速度最快的阶段，在此期间，全球中产阶层已进入史无前例的扩张阶段，而这在一定程度上要归功于印度等中国的邻国。预计到2027年，中国中产阶层人数将达到12亿人，占世界总人口的四分之一。中国已成为世界上最大的中产阶层消费市场，也成为大型跨国企业的首选市场。最初，中国中产阶层消费遵循西方中产阶层的成长路径，不断追求高质量产品、大量投资房产、购置汽车等。而如今，中国正塑造自己的中产阶层潮流。中国的金融科技和电商平台正改变消费者和商家的互动方式，并将其输出至其他发展中国家。[①]

---

[*] Ivan Semenist，副教授、博士，乌克兰基辅格里琴科大学东方系主任。

[①] Homi Kharas & Meagan Dooley, "China's Influence on the Global Middle Class", https://www.brookings.edu/wp‐content/uploads/2020/10/FP_20201012_china_middle_class_kharas_dooley.pdf.

表1　　　　　　　　　2020年中产阶层消费总额排名前十国家

（单位：万亿美元，按2011年购买力平价计算）

国家	中产阶层消费总额
中国	7.3
美国	4.7
印度	2.9
日本	2.0
俄罗斯联邦	1.6
德国	1.5
印度尼西亚	1.2
英国	1.1
巴西	1.1
法国	1.0

资料来源：笔者根据卡拉斯（2010年）方法论及国际货币基金组织2020年6月GDP估计值计算得出。

研究中产阶层的形成与发展及其对主要经济指标的影响的一个积极方面在于其跨学科性。社会学家的研究有助于我们了解中产阶层这一群体的概况，经济学家将确定一个国家中产阶层与该国经济稳定性的关系，政治学家则证实中产阶层对管理决策和国家政策重点形成的影响。社会学家倾向于根据职业特征或工作状况以及相关指标划分中产阶层。中产阶层主要从事脑力劳动或基于技术的体力劳动，这一阶层通常受过良好教育，掌握了专业知识和重要的专业技能。中产阶层的这些特征有助于提升人类发展指数，提高生活水平和生活质量，促进个人职业发展，更好地规划未来。值得注意的是，中产阶层的这些特征对后代的形成和社会的发展进步非常重要，因为中产阶层群体努力为其子女争取更好的教育资源，从而构成了国家的智力资本。另外，中产阶层是确保中国繁荣和全球竞争力的前提。中国的经济实力主要取决于人力资本及其有效利用，这在一定程度上提升了收入、教育和医疗水平。当前有诸多关于中国中产阶层及其划分标准的讨论，最终形成两项主要的划分标准，即人均收入水平和家庭耐用品消费情况。中国向中产阶层国家的转型尚未完成。中产阶层人数还将继续大幅增加，预计到2027年，中国的中产阶层人数将达到 12 亿人，占世界中产阶层总数的四分之一。

需强调的是，中国中产阶层群体认为收入水平并无上限，而且收入会发生变化。他们认为收入水平是通往财富的中间环节。这体现出一种战略思维、对未来发展规划的趋势以及个人从社会最底层到最高层的逐步跨越。我们再看看有关中国中产阶层发展的跨学科研究。社会学、经济学、政治学等学科有大量研究生活和行为特征的科学著作。通过研究中国中产阶层群体在国际关系和外交政策中的行为特征，科学家们得出这样的结论：中国中产阶层群体的自由度高于其他社会阶层。[①] 换言之，中国中产阶层的存在和人数能够大大影响国际关系形成和发展的灵活度，并决定国家未来的经济走向。关于中产阶层的收入和消费水平评估方面，存在不同的观点。李培林在其著作中，谈及了中产阶层的收入标准和区分中产阶层三大标准之一的合理受益率。作者认为其他两项标准分别为职业和教育。即只要某个人口群体符合一定的收入标准、符合某种职业、符合一定的教育水平，就可以将其划分为中产阶层。这一收入标准的计算结果发表在李培林和张翼的论文《中国中产阶层的规模、认同和社会态度》中，并在中国社会学会年会"中产阶层比较国际论坛"上得到验证。过去 20 年，中国中产阶层的社会经济发展实现了稳定增长。无论以何种标准划分中产阶层，其作用和意义毋庸置疑。但评估方法的差异表明：上述三项标准（收入标准、职业和教育）作为与中产阶层相关的一个科学概念以及社会中产阶层形象（基于收入或消费等指标的中产阶层），影响着对中国中产阶层群体人数增长率的评估。学术界对按照职业划分中产阶层存在争议，还应比较工作条件，并考虑政府机构员工、主管、部门负责人、普通办事员等群体的收入水平。据国家统计局城市调查总队的调查，目前中国城镇居民的收入标准呈现阶梯状分布的特征。有一个说法，当代中国社会最富裕的 10 类人分别是：（1）私营企业主和个体户；（2）企业承包商或租赁经营人员；（3）股市参与者和成功者；

---

① Johnston, A. I., "Chinese middle class attitudes towards international affairs: Nascent liberalization?", *The China Quarterly*, 2004, No. 179, pp. 603 - 628, http://search.proquest.com/docview/229505762/fulltextPDF/131603BE30756FCFAF8/6? accountid = 35419.

(4) 外资企业首席专家；(5) 技术发明专利人员；(6) 演艺界和体育界的明星；(7) 新经济的 CEO；(8) 经验丰富的律师、经纪人和广告工作人员；(9) 海归；(10) 顶尖科学家和专家。①

该划分标准与国家统计局城市调查总队的调查基本相符。中国中产阶层主要产生于上述 10 类人群。其中，尤其值得注意的是私营企业主和外资企业的高级员工。近年来，随着民营企业的迅猛发展和部分国有企业的变相私有化，私营企业已经成为中国中产阶层的制造机。同样，诸如摩托罗拉等跨国公司也都像流水线似的为中国复制着"稀缺"的中产阶层。一些有关中产阶层发展的概念可能是中产阶层形成初期阶段所表现出的特征，这是经济快速增长、社会快速变革和多维度分化的结果。因此，可以预测的是，到 2030 年，随着经济的进一步增长、社会财富的增加以及人民生活水平的提高，中产阶层的概念将进一步深化，从而符合大众对中产阶层的看法。

关于中国中产阶层的未来，存在许多说法。美林证券公司预测，在未来 10 年内，中国的中产阶层人数将达到 3.5 亿人。中国未来需要更多的中产阶层，这一点是毫无疑问的。除上述 10 大富裕人群及一部分国家公职人员外，北大教授萧灼基认为，未来的中国中产阶层将主要来自以下五类高素质专业人才。其一，能将科技成果转化为产业的科研人员。他们将自己的研究成果以技术股的方式，投入到企业中；如果该企业上市，他们将名利双收。其二，金融证券业的中高层管理人员。这并不适用于现行体制内的从业人员，而是指民营、外资企业的工作人员。其三，中介机构的专业人员，如律师、会计师、评估师等。在中国加入世界贸易组织以后，这些人的收入将会大大提高。其四，中产阶层的另一组成群体是外资企业中的中国中高层管理人员。其五，股票市场的一些股民也有可能成为中产阶层的一员。全国政协委员、中国科学院可持续发展战略组首席研究员牛文元提出了判断一个国家是否具备适合中产阶层发展的充分条件的五项标准：(1) 城市化率是否达到七成以上；(2) "白

---

① Как живут люди в Китае － особенности и традиции Китайцев, https：//gruz－china.ru/blog/kak－zhivut－lyudi－v－kitae－osobennosti－i.

领"人数是否大于或至少持平于"蓝领";(3)恩格尔系数是否降到了平均值 0.3 或更低;(4)基尼系数是否控制并保持在 0.25—0.30;(5)人均受教育年限是否达到 12 年及以上。

同时,不同省市对于中产阶层的划分标准也存在一定差异。例如,对于北京居民而言,月收入必须至少达到 1000 美元,才能算作中产阶层,而对于农村居民来说,月收入达到 100 美元,就可算作中产阶层。①

咨询公司麦肯锡的研究显示,到 2022 年,中国 76% 的城镇人口将跻身中产阶层。对调查结果的进一步分析发现,城镇中产阶层家庭的年收入为 9000 美元至 3.4 万美元。虽然这一收入标准明显低于发达国家,但考虑到市场价格因素,位于此收入区间的中国中产阶层家庭依然能享受到同等的生活标准。② 亚洲开发银行编写的《中国中产阶层崛起》报告指出,中产阶层包括每天消费 2—20 美元的人群。③ 根据瑞士信贷银行的一项研究,在当前发展阶段,中国中产阶层人口占全国劳动年龄人口的 20%,即 1 亿人以上。在此情况下,年收入水平成为主要的划分标准,中产阶层家庭的年收入为 1 万美元至 10 万美元。值得注意的是,美国中产阶层占美国总人口的一半,韩国中产阶层占其总人口的三分之二。④ 在当前的经济发展阶段,几乎世界各国的中产阶层人数都在增加。人口的绝对数和比例均在增加,在未来 15—20 年内,他们将成为新的中产阶层。即使按照悲观预测,2019 年全球中产阶层群体总人数也将增长 10 亿,不久的将来将会超过 20 亿。根据惯性预测计算,全球中产阶层人数将达到 30 亿,亚洲将是中产阶层人数增长最快的地区。同时,在很长一段时间内,印度的中产阶层人数增长将超过中国。若中国实现其发展目标,那么到 2030 年,中国 75% 的人口将达到中产阶层的生活水平,贫困程度也将大大降低。随着中产阶层人数的增长,消费份额也随之增长。因此,

---

① Gruz – China, Kak zhivut lyudi v Kitaye – osobennosti i traditsii kitaytsev, 2019, https://gruz – china. ru/blog/kak – zhivut – lyudi – v – kitae – osobennosti – i.

② China today, Rivni zhyttya v Kytayi (serednij klas), 2019, https://prc. today.

③ Svpressa, "Podem srednego klassa v Kitae", 2019, https://svpressa. ru/world/article/45629/.

④ Gruz – China, Kak zhivut lyudi v Kitaye – osobennosti i traditsii kitaytsev, 2019, https://gruz – china. ru/blog/kak – zhivut – lyudi – v – kitae – osobennosti – i.

经济发展步伐加快，国家 GDP 随之增长。2020 年，中国成为全球中产阶层第一大消费市场，规模达 73 亿美元。美国和印度分别排名第二和第三，其消费规模分别为 47 亿美元和 29 亿美元。

中产阶层对中国经济发展的重要性正在快速增长。中产阶层人数的持续增长是中国 2020 年"内循环"战略实施的主要条件[①]，该战略主要依靠中产阶层拉动国内消费增长。中产阶层是中国经济改革的重要受益者，他们积极支持中国政府实施的经济改革政策，并希望经济改革政策保持稳定，从而确保国家的经济和自身收入的稳定增长。现阶段，为了提高世界各国的经济发展水平，必须推动中产阶层的形成和发展，这将确保提高国内消费水平，从而促进国民经济和社会发展。

通过分析中国中产阶层群体消费结构，可以看出：中国中产阶层在教育和培养后代方面投入了大量资金，而较少花费在娱乐和旅游上。中国中产阶层群体在培养孩子方面比较独特。未来一代被称为"未来小皇帝一代"，他们的消费标准远超过上一代，消费习惯也和上一代大不相同。据专家介绍，中国家庭平均 40%—50% 的收入都用来培养孩子。其中很大一部分用于支付名校的学费和辅导班学费以及购买电脑等。值得注意的是，即使到了周末，孩子也要上外语辅导班或计算机培训班。同时，这代人对快餐的需求也在增加。预计他们在即食食品行业的消费规模为 40 亿美元，中国孩子的零花钱和礼物消费达 50 亿美元。值得注意的是，中国 14 岁以下儿童人数占总人口的 25%，有望成为未来的中产阶层群体。[②] 根据以上所述，我们可以得出这样的结论：中产阶层非常重视教育。中国将提高教育水平作为促进国家整体经济进一步发展的工作重点和先决条件。今天对人力资本的投资将为提升国家未来竞争力打下基础。

总之，全球中产阶层正在快速发展。具体而言，中国中产阶层的发展将受到两方面因素的影响，其一：中国消费者偏好；其二：政治模式

---

① Bin News, "Vnutrennyaya tsirkulyatsiya – novaya ekonomicheskaya strategiya Kitaya", 2019, https: //bin. ua/news/foreign/world/254924 – vnutrennyaya – cirkulyaciya – novaya – yekonomicheskaya. html.

② Maschtenko E., "Malenkiy imperator kitayskoy semi", https: //zn. ua/SOCIUM/malenkiy_imperator_kitayskoy_semi. html.

偏好。这种政治模式有助于稳定中产阶层利益，且为中产阶层及其家人提供稳定经济增长的机会。可以说，中国的国内政策是以不断支持中产阶层扩大其规模为目的的。因为如果中产阶层成为社会主流，社会就会保持稳定、变得合理。在这种情况下，就会极大促进国家经济体系的建设和发展。国家在维护中产阶层方面发挥着越来越重要的作用，其目的不在于增加拥有平均收入的人员的数量，而是要提高生活质量，促进某种消费文化的形成，合理分配开支，养育后代。研究结果表明，中产阶层的形成和发展有利于降低贫困，促进经济增长。以增加收入来带动消费，才能实现国家的整体发展。中国中产阶层不仅拥有一定的物质财富，在分配支出方面也具有一定的特殊性。从支出结构可以看出对人力资本的投入很高，表明以人为本的经济已经形成。中国将中产阶层视为国家未来发展的"火车头"，推动"循环经济"战略的实施。

参考文献：

Bin News, "Vnutrennyaya tsirkulyatsiya – novaya ekonomicheskaya strategiya Kitaya", 2019, https：//bin.ua/news/foreign/world/254924 – vnutrennyaya – cirkulyaciya – novaya – yekonomicheskaya.html.

China today, Rivni zhyttya v Kytayi（serednij klas）, 2019, https：//prc.today.

Gruz – China, Kak zhivut lyudi v Kitaye – osobennosti i traditsii kitaytsev, 2019, https：//gruz – china.ru/blog/kak – zhivut – lyudi – v – kitae – osobennosti – i.

Homi Kharas & Meagan Dooley, "China's Influence on the Global Middle Class", https：//www.brookings.edu/wp – content/uploads/2020/10/FP_20201012_china_middle_class_kharas_dooley.pdf.

Johnston, A. I., "Chinese middle class attitudes towards international affairs：Nascent liberalization?", *The China Quarterly*, 2004, No. 179, pp. 603 – 628, http：//search.proquest.com/docview/229505762/fulltextPDF/131603BE30756FCFAF8/6？accountid = 35419.

Maschtenko E., "Malenkiy imperator kitayskoy semi", https：//zn.ua/

SOCIUM/malenkiy_imperator_kitayskoy_semi. html.

Svpressa,"Podem srednego klassa v Kitae",2019,https://svpressa.ru/world/article/45629/.

Как живут люди в Китае – особенности и традиции Китайцев, https://gruz-china.ru/blog/kak-zhivut-lyudi-v-kitae-osobennosti-i.

中国社会发展与知识产权保护意义

Svitlana Glovatska [*]
Alina Litvinenko, Viktoria Baderko [**]

知识产权制度是促进人类经济发展、社会进步、科学创新和文化繁荣的主要经济和法律制度。随着世界科学技术的飞速发展和经济全球化进程的加快,知识产权制度在经济和社会生活中的作用越来越大,知识产权保护问题正在引起国际社会的广泛关注。

中国是一个有着数千年历史的文明古国。千百年来,无数杰出的中国科学家、发明家、作家和艺术家所取得的辉煌的成就为全人类的发展和进步做出了巨大的贡献。

改革开放 40 多年来,中国政府高度重视知识产权,并以此推动了国家经济的快速发展和社会的全面进步。

自 1979 年以来,中国加入了知识产权领域的主要国际公约,现代意义上的中国知识产权客体的权利得到了承认和保护。

1980 年,中国加入了《成立世界知识产权组织公约》,成为了世界知识产权组织(WIPO)的成员。之后,中国于 1984 年 12 月 19 日加入了 1883 年通过的《保护工业产权巴黎公约》。

1989 年,中国加入了《商标国际注册马德里协定》,从而成为马德里

---

[*] Svitlana Glovatska,乌克兰国立敖德萨海事大学副教授、博士,中国社会科学院—乌克兰国立敖德萨海事大学中国研究中心乌方主任。

[**] Alina Litvinenko, Viktoria Baderko,乌克兰国立敖德萨海事大学学生。

体系的一员。由此，可以通过在任何缔约国中完成有效的国际注册，从而在多国获得商标保护。

1992 年，中国加入了 1886 年通过的《保护文学和艺术作品伯尔尼公约》和 1971 年修订的日内瓦《世界版权公约》（其前身是 1952 年通过的《世界版权公约》）。

1993 年 10 月 1 日，中国加入了《专利合作条约》（PCT）。这样，通过提交"国际"专利申请，就可以实现许多国家同时对一项发明进行专利保护。该等申请需要通过中国"世界知识产权组织申请提交和管理在线办公室"来办理。

2001 年，中国加入了世界贸易组织（WTO），成为《与贸易有关的知识产权协定》（TRIPS）的缔约国。

在过去的几十年时间里，中国的国内外专利申请数量突飞猛进。这得益于研发部门投入的增加、创新能力的提高和政府的大力支持。

1999 年，世界知识产权组织仅收到 276 件来自中国的申请，但是到了 2019 年，这一数字增加了 200 倍，并以 58990 件申请量位居《专利合作条约》（PCT）下的三大申请数量最多的国家之首——领先于美国（57840）和日本（52660），增长率为 10.6%，而美国的增长率仅为 2.8%，日本则是 5.9%。[1]

2008 年，随着《国家知识产权战略纲要》（该纲要将知识产权视为创新的主要保障和动力）的出台，标志着中国建立了统一的知识产权制度。制定这一国家战略是为了进一步挖掘国家创新潜力，建设创新型国家，提高中国企业的市场竞争力乃至国家的整体竞争力，扩大对外交往，实现互利共赢，完善社会主义市场经济体制，规范市场结构以及建设和谐社会。

2011 年 11 月，中国政府成立了由国务院副总理直接领导的"全国打击侵权假冒工作领导小组"，工作组的成员涵盖 29 个国家部委，它们的职责包括采取行政管理措施、行使刑事司法权力、维护公共秩序和处理一般法律和教育问题。

---

[1] WIPO Statistics Database，February 2021.

当时有两份文件阐明了中国在知识产权保护方面的积极努力：一份文件介绍了"全国打击侵权假冒工作领导小组"在国家层面开展的知识产权保护活动；另一份文件介绍了在地方层面，即上海市人民政府开展此类活动的经验。①

习近平在2012年当选中共中央总书记后，提出要实现"中华民族伟大复兴的中国梦"。新的"中国梦"基于两个全球化项目："一带一路"倡议（BRI）和"中国制造2025"。

中国2014年正式提出的"一带一路"倡议是其有史以来规模最大的项目，它最初包括"丝绸之路经济带"和"21世纪海上丝绸之路"②。2017年以来，在实施"一带一路"倡议的同时，也将"极地丝绸之路"和"数字丝绸之路"项目作为该倡议的补充。此外，推进"一带一路"建设工作领导小组办公室在2019年发布的报告中也提到了"绿色丝绸之路"③。

作为"一带一路"倡议的一部分，中国与乌克兰、吉尔吉斯斯坦签署了知识产权领域合作的双边协议；之后与欧美国家、日本、韩国和金砖国家在知识产权领域建立了越来越多的合作机制。此外，中国还举办了许多知识产权问题国际会议和其他的活动，以便在"一带一路"倡议框架内建立知识产权保护领域的互动机制。④

"中国制造2025"战略旨在巩固中国作为全球高科技产业领导者的地位。该战略放眼未来的10年，是国民经济10个关键部门发展的综合规划

---

① Координация защиты интеллектуальной собственности на национальном и региональном уровне, wipo/ace/12/5 rev. 2, https: // www. wipo. int/edocs/mdocs/enforcement/ru/wipo_ace_12/wipo_ace_12_5_rev_2. pdf.

② Аудит зовнішньої політики: Україна — Китай: Дискусійна записка, Інститут світової політики, 2016, http: //iwp. org. ua/ukr/public/1842. html.

③ Головацька С. М. Пройктий потенціал ініціативи "Один пояс, один шлях" / Пройктний та логістичний менеджмент: нові знання на базі двох методологій. Том 3: монографія / [авт. кол.: С. В. Руденко, І. О. Лапкіна, Т. А. Ковтун та ін.]. – Одеса: Купрійнко СВ, 2020 – 235с.

④ Чжан Чжчэн. Государственная стратегия Китая в области интеллектуальной собственности: реализация и перспективы, Государственное управление по делам интеллектуальной собственности, https: // rospatent. gov. ru/content/uploadfiles/presentations/VEFTchzendoklad. pdf.

(见图 1)，它涵盖了商品生产的所有阶段——从研发到售后服务。实现该战略所制定的目标能够确保中国"十三五"规划（2016—2020 年）的顺利实施。"中国制造 2025"战略的主要目标是在国内创新的基础上发展经济，从"模仿者"国家转变为"创造者"国家：显而易见，如果没有知识产权的保护这一战略是不可能实现的。

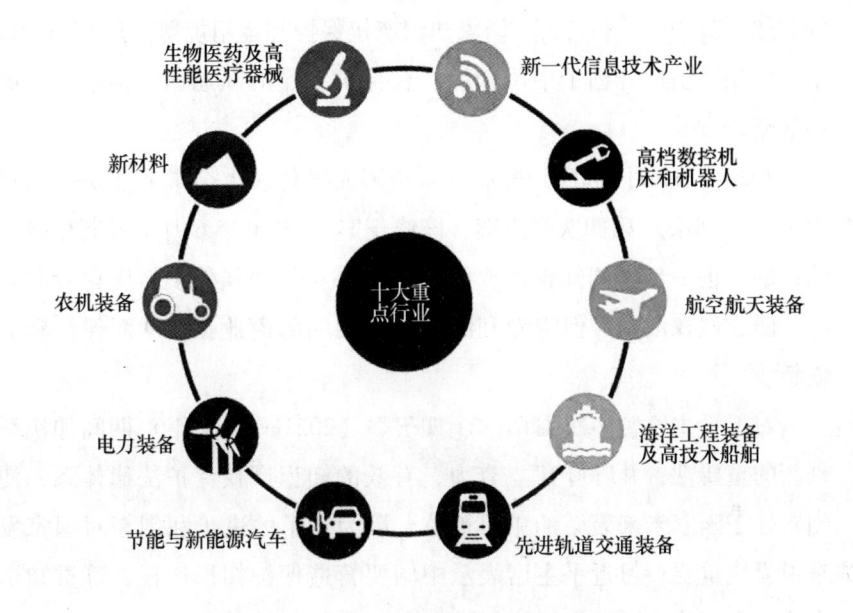

主要步骤	里程碑
2025	⟶ 迈入制造强国行列
2035	⟶ 世界制造强国阵营中等水平
2049	⟶ 世界制造强国前列

图 1　"中国制造 2025"的十大重点行业（根据国务院数据）

资料来源：笔者根据中国国务院公布数据自制。

2014 年，中国通过了《深入实施国家知识产权战略行动计划（2014—2020 年）》，以便进一步推动实施 2014—2020 年知识产权领域的国家战略。

2015 年，国务院就新形势下加快知识产权强国建设提出了若干意见；2016 年，制定了《国家创新驱动发展战略纲要》，其中明确了在知识产权领域实施的战略和加快知识产权强国建设的措施。这份文件明确了深化知识产权保护工作重点领域的改革措施，推动了知识产权的保护和运用，营造了创新创业、公平竞争的良好环境，极大地促进了创新开放和经济发展。①

2017 年，在《"十三五"国家知识产权保护和运用规划》《国家创新发展战略》等多项重要政府文件中都出现了"加快建设知识产权中心"的表述。其中《"十三五"国家知识产权保护和运用规划》还被列为国家重点规划，由此开创了中国知识产权保护工作的新局面，构建了新的发展战略。

2020 年 10 月 17 日，第十三届全国人民代表大会常务委员会通过了中国《专利法》第四次修正案，该修正案于 2021 年 6 月 1 日起生效，它的目的是进一步强调知识产权的重要性并对其加强保护，优化专利权保护，防止侵权活动，促进专利的应用和发明的商业化，从而保护和鼓励创新。②

习近平主席曾多次强调"十四五"（2021—2025 年）期间加快科技创新的重要性，并呼吁建立有力、有效的知识产权保护法律体系，使得创新处于国家未来繁荣的中心地位，因为技术的进步和创新对国家发展来说无比重要。习近平主席表示中国要营造保护知识产权、尊重知识和人才、合理奖励科学家的社会环境。③

自 2013 年以来，中国政府成功实施了 170 多项措施，严厉打击了侵犯知识产权行为，共办理涉及侵犯知识产权的案件 130 万起，追究了违法者的责任。④

---

① Shen Changyu, "China – on course to become an IP powerhouse", WIPO Magazine, https://www.wipo.int/wipo_magazine/en/2016/si/article_0002.

② Liaoteng Wang & Dr. Jian Li & Qiang Lin & Shanqiang Xiao & Xiaobin Zong & Xiaodong Li & Lulin Gao, "The Long – Awaited Fourth Amendment to the Chinese Patent Law: An In – Depth Look", https://www.ipwatchdog.com/2020/12/15/long – awaited – fourth – amendment – chinese – patent – law – depth – look/id = 128185/.

③ "Innovations in science and technology indispensable for quality development", China Daily, https://www.chinadaily.com.cn/a/202009/14/.

④ 数据来源：世界知识产权组织权利保护咨询委员会。

2019年1月，中国政府设立了最高人民法院知识产权法庭，作为最高人民法院领导下的专利和先进技术的上诉法庭。截至2020年年底，知识产权法庭共受理案件4000余件。除了该知识产权法庭外，中国还在北京、上海、广东省和海南省分别设立了4个中级法院，开展知识产权保护工作。

中国政府高度重视知识产权信息的传播和知识产权理念的教育，尊重知识产权保护工作。

中国充分认识到，只有营造一个尊重知识、崇尚创新、遵纪守法的社会文化，才能打造强大的知识产权中心并提高公众对知识产权问题的认识。近年来，中国政府组织了许多与知识产权相关的活动，如"全国知识产权宣传周""世界知识产权日"的庆祝活动，开展中小学知识产权领域试点示范教育项目等。中国政府鼓励高等教育机构设立知识产权相关专业，开发知识产权相关课程，建设公共教育平台，安排人才的专项培养并扩大知识产权管理机构与新闻媒体之间的互动。①

中国正在通过自己的实际行动建设高效的知识产权保护体系，并努力使中国的知识产权体系与欧洲和美国等国家和地区的完善体系保持一致。中国在较短的时间内走过了发达国家几十年甚至上百年走过的知识产权保护的道路。

可以肯定地说，中国正处在实现2008年制定的战略目标——在知识产权的创造、运用、保护和管理方面达到较高水平，从"模仿者"国家转变为"创造者"国家的最后完成阶段。时至今日，中国在知识产权领域的许多关键指标上都位居世界第一。

来自中国的相关数据对上述观点提供了有力的支持，这实际上表明人们对全球知识产权体系的了解正在与日俱增。随着研究经费的增加、创新能力的提高和强大的政策支持，中国的专利申请数量顺理成章地也在快速增长。

2019年，中国商标局受理的商标申请达到了780万件，国家知识产

---

① Чжан Чжчэн. Государственная стратегия Китая в области интеллектуальной собственности: реализация и перспективы, Государственное управление по делам интеллектуальной собственности, https://rospatent.gov.ru/content/uploadfiles/presentations/VEFTchzendoklad.pdf.

权局受理的各类专利申请约为 430 万件。

在国际上，中国在《马德里议定书》框架内的申请量不断增长，其在《专利合作条约》（PCT）框架内的申请量也首次超过美国。

根据世界知识产权组织的数据，自 2015 年以来中国提交的专利申请数量位居世界第一。中国的申请规模与全球总量相比涨幅惊人。

2019 年中国以 58990 件申请位居《专利合作条约》（PCT）前三大申请国家之首，就专利申请量而言，中国占全球总量的 43% 以上（如图 2）；在注册商标申请数量方面，中国超过了全球总量的 51%（图 3）；中国工业品外观设计申请量占全球总量的 52%（图 4）。①

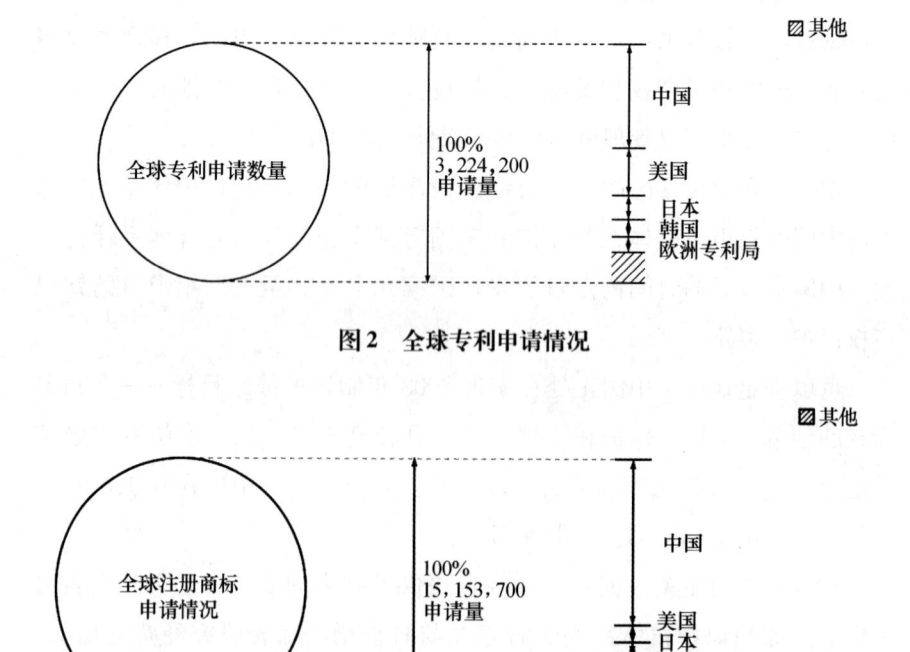

图 2　全球专利申请情况

图 3　全球注册商标申请情况

---

① WIPO Statistics Database, February 2021.

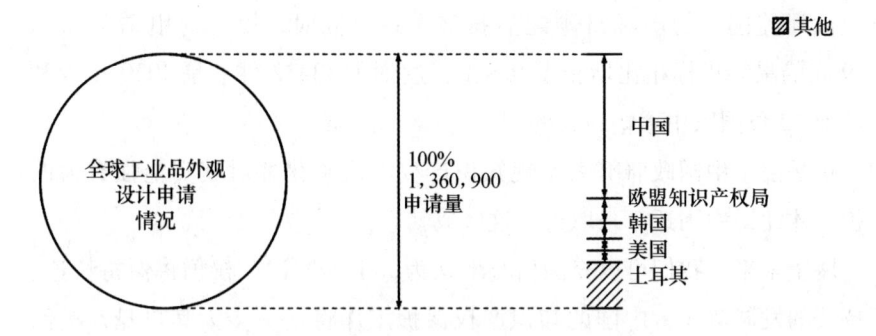

图4 全球注册工业品外观设计申请情况

2020年，尽管全球新冠肺炎疫情大流行，中国的《专利合作条约》（PCT）国际申请数量依然达到约为275900件，比2019年增加4%。中国以68720件申请量继续保持领先地位，比2019年增加了16.1%（如图5）。[①]

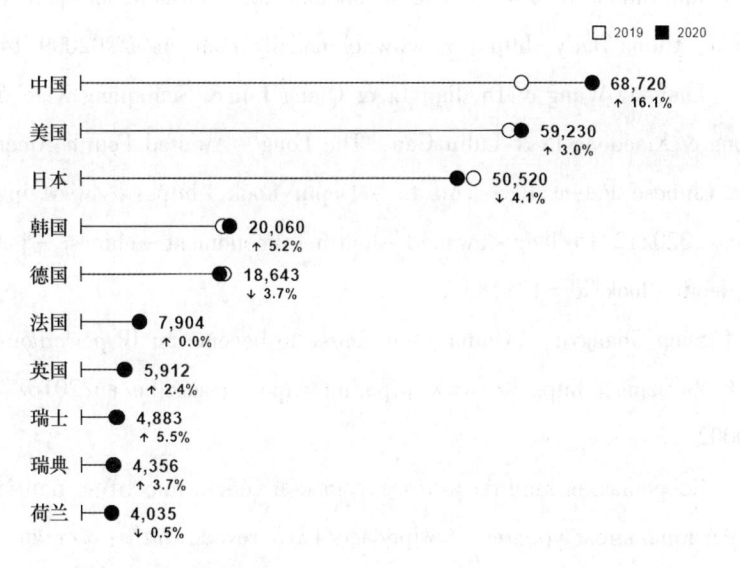

图5 2020年提交的《专利合作条约》申请数量

中国 68,720 ↑16.1%
美国 59,230 ↑3.0%
日本 50,520 ↓4.1%
韩国 20,060 ↑5.2%
德国 18,643 ↓3.7%
法国 7,904 ↑0.0%
英国 5,912 ↑2.4%
瑞士 4,883 ↑5.5%
瑞典 4,356 ↑3.7%
荷兰 4,035 ↓0.5%

中国在欧洲专利局（EPO）2020年专利指数中的排名取得了重大提

---

① WIPO Statistics Database, February 2021.

升，位列美国、德国和日本之后排名第四。同时，提交的申请数量与2019年的最终指标相比增长了9.9%，达到了13432件，是2020年专利指数前10位国家中增幅最大的。①

正是由于中国政府努力实现知识产权的民主化并对其实施强有力的保护，才使得中国近年来取得了这些成就。

展望未来，我们可以充满信心地认为，中国知识产权仍将保持快速、可持续的发展势头，中国的知识产权保护工作将进一步为其自身，进而为全球知识产权体系的发展做出贡献。

参考文献：

European Patent Office，https：//www.epo.org/about-us/annual-reports-statistics/statistics.html.

Innovations in science and technology indispensable for quality development，China Daily，https：//www.chinadaily.com.cn/a/202009/14/.

Liaoteng Wang & Dr. Jian Li & Qiang Lin & Shanqiang Xiao & Xiaobin Zong & Xiaodong Li & Lulin Gao, The Long-Awaited Fourth Amendment to the Chinese Patent Law：An In-Depth Look，https：//www.ipwatchdog.com/2020/12/15/long-awaited-fourth-amendment-chinese-patent-law-depth-look/id = 128185/.

Shen Changyu, "China-on course to become an IP powerhouse", WIPO Magazine，https：//www.wipo.int/wipo_magazine/en/2016/si/article_0002.

Координация защиты интеллектуальной собственности на национальном и региональном уровне // wipo/ace/12/5 rev. 2，https：//www.wipo.int/edocs/mdocs/enforcement/ru/wipo_ace_12/wipo_ace_12_5_rev_2.pdf.

Аудит зовнішньо ї політики：Укра ї на — Китай：Дискусійна записка // Інститут світово ї політики, 2016. http：//iwp.org.ua/ukr/

---

① European Patent Office，https：//www.epo.org/about-us/annual-reports-statistics/statistics.html.

public/1842.html.

Гловацька С. М. Проєктий потенціал ініціативи "Один пояс, один шлях" / Проєктний та логістичний менеджмент: нові знання на базі двох методологій. Том 3: монографія / [авт. кол.: С. В. Руденко, І. О. Лапкіна, Т. А. Ковтун та ін.]. – Одеса: Купрієнко СВ, 2020 – 235с.

Чжан Чжчэн. Государственная стратегия Китая в области интеллектуальной собственности: реализация и перспективы. // Государственное управление по делам интеллектуальной собственности. https://rospatent.gov.ru/content/uploadfiles/presentations/VEFTchzendoklad.pdf.

第四篇

"一带一路"倡议与全球发展倡议

全球发展倡议:社会现代化的意义和目标

Anatoly Lazarevich[*]

近年来,在公众讨论和专家讨论中,现代化——其本质、任务和实施方式——都已成为热点话题。从哲学上来说,有充分的理由把现代化归类为社会生活的要素之一,这些要素与社会文化进程有关联,并且更多的是对社会文化进程产生实际影响,而不是成为广泛讨论的主题。显然,我们不应将社会现代化简单地理解为一个孤立的历史事件或系列事件。准确地说,它代表着历史事件的特殊质量或一般目的。即使在没有被人直接谈起的情况下,现代化也在"运作";现代化可以说是文明进程上升阶段的内在标志。

现代化进程是隐性的,这相当于现代化议题并不总是很明显、但却经常"现身"于哲学历史和社会经济理论中。近代的现代化概念的前提条件形成于19—20世纪大量的社会学理论中,比如涂尔干(E. Durkheim)、马克思(K. Marx)、梅因(G. Main)、吉登斯(A. Giddens)、摩尔(W. Moore)、托夫勒(A. Toffler)、图海纳(A. Touraine)、奈斯比特(R. Nisbet)、加尔布雷斯(J. Galbraith)、哈贝马斯(J. Habermas)、茨托姆卡(P. Sztompka)、亨廷顿(S. Huntington)的理论。V. L. Inozemtsev、S. N. Gavrov[①]、V. S. Stepin、M. V. Ilyin、N. A.

---

[*] Anatoly Lazarevich,教授、博士、白俄罗斯国家科学院哲学研究所所长。

[①] Gavrov, S. N., Modernization in the name of empire. Sociocultural aspects of modernization processes in Russia, Editorial URSS, 2010; Gavrov, S. N., Modernization of Russia: post – imperial transit, МГУДТ, 2010.

Krichesvsky、V. M. Mezhuev 等俄罗斯近代科学家编制了大量关于该问题的文献；毫不夸张地说，过去5—10年来发表的关于该话题的论文和文章数量估计有几百篇。

对于社会经济现代化概念方面的讨论，白俄罗斯科学界没有置身事外。首先要说的是科学作品集《欧洲背景下的白俄罗斯与俄罗斯：现代化进程的国家管理问题》，这是在由白俄罗斯国家科学院哲学研究所组织的关于该议题的国家科学会议之后出版的。① 后来举办了多个专门讨论社会现代化问题的其他科学论坛。

同时，"科学范围内"关于社会现代化的对话通常并不能带来人们想得到的理论结果。虽然听起来有些矛盾，但专家们"太互相理解了"。人们在谈论现代化战略时，可以是指社会哲学思想所共有的一系列概念。然而，当一个在专家界讨论了很久的话题成为更广泛的公众舆论的一部分时，就会显示出一种常规现象，即科学范围内就某些概念的解释达成一致，以及公众对所讨论进程的详情、目标和价值缺乏了解。这完全适用于社会现代化的概念和现象。社会现代化有不同的解释方式，常常与其他概念（特别是与"创新发展""社会转型"）混淆，甚至被贬低为独立实体（根据"万物非新"或"任何进步的发展即为现代化"的原则）。

当然，人们不应"无条件地相信"社会现代化势在必行，也不应对其有任何怀疑。然而，同样不可否认的是，专家界对现代化概念及其使用方式产生怀疑，这种怀疑进入普通公众的意识，产生的效果是困惑甚至排斥。当现代化成为公开宣布的口号时，应具有激励作用，能够协调社会力量来实现明确的目标。然而，如果存在误解或误译，就很难谈论激励问题。此外，公众根据对变革的必要性和必然性的认识就现代化形成共识。这种共识类似于"务实"思想，也就是得到理性认可的信念，这属于美国哲学家查尔斯·皮尔斯（Charles Pierce）的思想。然而在这一点上，显然需要就现代化的目标和准则展开广泛对话，国家、科学系统、

---

① A. A. Lazarevich et al., Belarus and Russia in the European context: the problems of the state management of the modernization process: Materials of the international scientific - practical conference, Minsk, October 20 - 21, 2011; National Academy of Sciences of Belarus, Institute of philosophy. - Minsk: Pravo I ekonomika, 2012, p. 381.

教育系统、企业和公共组织应参与这种对话。

这种对话的问题领域不是推测形成的,而是来源于生活本身。下面将列出其中几个值得更加详细讨论的问题。

一 现代化是"永恒的今天"吗?

德国哲学家哈贝马斯在其著名作品《现代性——一项未竟的事业》中说,"现代的"对立于"传统的""古代的",其价值最早是在公元五世纪基都教会的修辞学中提出的。从那时起,现代性理念频繁给欧洲文化注入活力。现代性有两个互补含义:一是"革新",即克服旧的,二是"现代化建设",即使事物符合当今的迫切需要。[①] 人们可能会谈到很多不同的现代化事实:全球现代化(比如整个西方世界的农业革命和工业革命)和地方现代化(比如俄罗斯的彼得改革);浅层的现代化(比如19世纪日本的明治维新)和导致形成新的社会经济结构的深入现代化(俄罗斯帝国和其他若干国家的社会主义革命);成功的现代化(20世纪最后25年中国和东南亚国家的工业突破)和不成功的现代化(苏联的"改革"和"加速")。

20世纪50—60年代,苏联为太空探索、飞机构造、核工业、火箭科学、潜艇和许多其他类型武器生产领域的现代创新潜力奠定了基础。国际上对这些成就的反响很大,以至于有几个先进国家开始积极学习俄语,等待未来的"苏维埃奇迹"。

20世纪70年代初,苏联科学界进行了一次大范围的尝试,试图聚集全国最优秀的人才,依托巨大的科学力量,通过头脑风暴,在科技进步(STP)的基础上找到一条克服停滞的出路,开始了20年的《科技进步综合计划》相关工作。在制订这一计划的过程中,做了大量的分析工作,帮助解决了科技发展中的很多跨学科问题。

然而,上述工作得出的主要结论却令人失望:由于当时的经济体制

[①] Habermas, J., "Modern – an unfinished project", Jurgen Habermas, Political works, Praxis, 2005.

对科技进步成果没有反应，由于在冲突条件下国内生产商在国内和全球市场上缺乏竞争，所以落后是不可避免的。国家正慢慢陷入经济危机，这首先体现在20世纪80年代后半期，许多和技术无关的活动领域的产能利用率大幅下滑，很快发展成经济和政治萧条，最终以苏联解体而告终。

上述及其他很多案例的共同特点是：首先，对革新的需求是任何现代化的客观前提；其次，必须感受时代的节奏（"自发革新时代精神的相关性"——根据德国著名哲学家哈贝马斯的准则），并根据个人、主要社会团体或整个社会作为新时代文化和价值观载体的自我意识和责任，自觉形成革新需求。在这一点上，所有现代化虽然基于不同的技术基础，但在世界观、社会心理学和组织设计方面却有很多共同点。

二 现代化进程的轨迹：直线形还是波浪形

"认可"社会现代化现象是社会历史进程的一个独立因素，这存在一定难度，因为我们并不总是能够把社会现代化与社会物质和技术基础的发展区分开来。至少最近300年来，社会生产力一直在不断发展，而且发展强度不断增大。这是否意味着人类已经生活在或者现在就生活在永久现代化的条件下？也许可以这么说，但这"贬低"了以下观点：现代化是一个特殊阶段，是社会发展的一个激励因素。

另一种观点不仅认可、甚而强调现代化进程中的社会变革方面。生产流程和通信系统的改善给社会群体的形式带来进步性变化，增强了个人尊严，扩大了自我实现的可能性，总体上改善了生活质量，这种情况下现代化原则得到全面贯彻。

显然，对现代化"多余物"部分的评估标准与技术部分略有不同。通常要通过回顾、观察几十年的社会生活才能识别社会的重大变化。在这一点上，虽然现代化可以产生比较迅速的经济效应，但其社会文化影响的衡量周期要长得多。然而，这并不意味着社会文化的影响可以忽略。

结合技术进步的直线轨迹及精神文化进步的阶梯式轨迹，通过显著的稳定性"水平"面，托夫勒提出了文明浪潮的概念。这位思想家认为，人类已达到工农业浪潮的"顶峰"，很快就会以新的技术优势、新的生产和社会关系组织形式、新的生活方式和思维方式经受住后工业浪潮的考验。①

托夫勒认为,接触新浪潮的效果之一是"未来的冲击"——人们在快速变化的社会技术世界里迷失方向。②"未来的冲击"不仅丧失了人格与精神传统的"有机联系",而且还能引发对进步的排斥、社会僵化和反现代化的行为态度。这些态度以及技术落后、缺乏合格人才、缺乏投资等似乎是当今对经济结构和整个社会空间进行革新所面临的最重要风险。

三 "赶超"型现代化

人们常常(特别是在俄语文献里)可以发现,有一种现代化定义将现代化描述为改进技术性物体(机械、设备、建筑物等)、使其符合新的标准、要求和规范的过程。这种定义并不回答这些要求和规范来自何处、为什么一直在现代化进程的外部、在其外面发展。这样来理解的社会现代化"按照定义"就是赶超,其结果很有可能具有次要性属性(其任务是在比较完善的技术环境里、并且可能就在新标准已经出现的那一刻,复制已经成为标准的东西)。

在某些情况下,可能没有其他办法来克服严重的技术落后问题。然而,把赌注押在赶超型社会现代化上本身就蕴含着"永远落后"的风险。到一定阶段,有必要以这样一种方式来安排变革重点,即:从复制已知的社会和技术趋势转变为对其进行预测。换句话说,现代化进程的质量和有效性直接取决于对其战略规划的重视程度,取决于对现代化进程的"预测性反思"建立在什么样的思想基础和方法基础之上。

在我们的记忆中,另一个赶超型现代化失败的案例当然是苏联改革。苏联改革是作为一项典型的现代化事业启动的,制定的目标总体上是正确的,可以说是经典的。在1985年4月苏共中央委员会全体会议上,苏

---

① Toffler, A., *The third wave*, AST, 2002.
② Toffler, A., *Shock of the future: Translation from English*, LLC "AST Publishing house", 2002.

共中央总书记戈尔巴乔夫指出:"我们需要革命性的转变——转变到全新的技术系统,转变到能带来最高效率的最新一代技术。"① 即使现在、在过了30多年之后,也几乎不可能对技术现代化提出其他任何要求。同时,我们反复分析了这一事业的一个主要错误——侧重于发展一个主要的产业领域——重型工程。对这一领域的巨额投资挤占了可花费在科技创新活动、消费品市场增长、社会开支等方面的资金。再加上其他诸多内外部因素,很快共同导致了社会紧张局势的加剧和国家的政治解体。

在这一点上,人们应当重视以下事实:真正的现代化不只是社会某些组成部分的改善,而是社会的大规模、以演进式为主的动态转型,这种转型遵循的规律是:其子系统一致、相互依存和协同。因此,当今一个重要的科学和实践任务是创建有前途的社会和人文技术,旨在提供系统性现代化的理论基础和方法基础,建立战略规划、社会经济和文化发展预测、所有活动和教育领域的技术重组、精神教育和道德教育、数字化管理等领域基础科学与实践之间的联系。当然,没有社会和人文科学与教育领域的投资,就无法完成上述任务——在我们眼前,在这些领域的框架内,证明了利用积极融入我们日常生活的高科技的潜力以及最新科技知识来改善特定人群的生活质量、提高其道德参数和心理参数、社会参数和沟通参数是切实可行的办法。

四 "东方"和"西方"现代化

在最近几年的上述专家讨论中,人们经常提出的问题是真正现代化的源头是什么、应该是什么:"草根"运动和经济实体的自我组织,或者国家意志。这些方法的支持者的立场分别标志着西方模式现代化和东方模式现代化的原则。

第一种情况与基于有效性现象的理性务实进步理想的实现有关,这

---

① M. S. Gorbachev, "On convocation of the next XXVII congress of CPSU and tasks connected with its preparation and holding", Report of the General Secretary of the CPSU Central Committee, http://www.historyru.com/docs/rulers/gorbachev/gorbachev-doc-3.html#/overview.

在最大限度上是与科技进步相结合的。在取得经济成果的同时,也证明了社会文化空间日益去传统化和原子化。它包含在与公民社会和自治的形成、大众意识和大众文化的形成过程直接联系和反馈联系的系统中,既由这些现象产生、又产生这些现象。

第二种情况广泛基于传统、既定生活方式、首先可以通过国家机器的力量来积累管理潜力。它可以在国家倡议下、在社会文化重组框架外面按照现代时期的标准而产生,因此,它未必就是去传统化的"反面"。

第一种和第二种情况下的现代化转型主体的形象有着根本区别。在自由主义模式中,现代化转型主体首先是具有个人主动性的人、一位企业家;在保守模式中,它是一个社会群体、一个团体、一个企业的许多员工,通过非正式关系和联系联合在一起,因此这一群体称为"集体主体"。

以上情况与白俄罗斯的社会经济发展有什么关系呢?白俄罗斯地处欧洲大陆东西方文化区域的历史边境,在选择现代化战略时,显然不得不面对两种模式相互竞争的局势。这一地区的任何规划都应基于对这些备选方案的比率的平衡分析,基于并非总是得到准确预测的社会影响,因为在任何现代化进程中,这些备选方案会以某种方式结合在一起。

五 现代化及创新发展的任务

如今公众对现代化的任务和意义的认识显然并不像人们所希望的那样容易。其中一个难点在于,关于现代化的争论干扰了几年前开始的对创新发展的战略、方法和目标的讨论。现在,就连称职的对话者也会说"现代化"和"创新"是措辞,即使不是完全没有意义,至少也表示相同的过程,两者之间的区别在于修辞层面。

这种观点并不纯粹是白俄罗斯现象。让我们以 2009 年后工业发展时期著名的理论家伊诺泽姆采夫(V. L. Inozemtsev)主编出版的科学论文集《强制创新:俄罗斯的战略》为例。我们会看到以下现象:作者们提出的最重要问题之一是"对现代化和创新……的认识上的理论混乱"问题。①论文集的作者们指出"在这种情况下,多元化并不恰当——理论上的和实际实施中的现代化并不等于创新"。人们根深蒂固的观念是将现代化和创新解释为同义词,这使得现代化任务的实际实施更加复杂。

今天的"创新"概念通常是按照《弗拉斯卡蒂指南》来解释的。这份文件是1993年由经济合作与发展组织(OECD)在意大利弗拉斯卡蒂市通过的,它把创新定义为"创新的最终结果,体现为市场上引入新的或经过改进的产品,实践中使用新的或经过改进的工艺流程,或者新的社会服务方法"。这种解释允许,甚至欢迎把创新解释为创意转化成市场产品或技术、新的社会服务和沟通方式的结果。同时,俄罗斯专家库德洛夫(Kudrov)指出,广义上讲,引入创新的"结果"可以是新的生产、管理和组织流程,新的生产管理人员、甚至是新的(也就是现代化的)人——既是新产品的制造者又是新产品的消费者。②

社会的创新发展作为战略参考点假设科技潜力成为决定社会经济进程速度和质量水平、社会福利和全球竞争力的因素。在这一点上,创新堪称现代化最成熟的"表现",但现代化本身在本质上并不总是具有创新性。此外,如果现代化进程可以通过自愿决定来启动、以项目的方式来实施(如上文所述),那么创新重组就总是一个微妙的自我调节过程,不仅与创新的组织条件有关,而且与创新思维文化有关。换句话说,这一过程与经济和社会结构各个层面的创造力和创新响应能力程度的逐渐提高有关,这当然不能通过指令方式来实现。

以上所述使人能够更加清晰地明确对社会现代化的认识。说到白俄罗斯,它当然不是历史上的第一个,并不冒充"启示"。然而,白俄罗斯与以往的社会现代化仍有不同,不同之处在于:从一开始、从设定战略目标的阶段开始,就形成了关于其创新性的想法,即侧重于信息化进程、建设知识型社会。

---

① V. L. Inozemtsev ed., *Forcing to innovations: strategy for Russia*, Collection of articles and materials, Center of research of postindustrial society, 2009.

② Kudrov, V. M., "Innovative economy – imperative of time", *Modern Europe*, 2009, No. 2.

当然，这样说并不意味着要在实践中去实现。近代的社会现代化面临一项特别艰巨的任务：找到一种方法，将垂直管理的有效性、基层积极性的培养、社会经济进步的正式准则、创新创意指标、目标指标"干数字"、创业活动自由以及其他一些功能整合在一起。这是一项非常艰巨的任务，实施这项任务的责任更重。

六 现代化机制：技术、社会和文化机制

上文已经指出，创新模式下现代化的任务应满足对现代化进程主体——"现代化的"人的特殊要求。因此，除了技术部分之外，现代化的社会组织和文化部分值得最密切的关注。

一代人要对现代化的长期效果、其生产力负责——当今这一代人需要自觉接受教育。让年轻人为生活在高科技的信息社会做好系统性准备，这是教育系统最重要的任务之一，白俄罗斯科学界、主要是人文界则负责提供价值观和世界观、理论和方法支持。公民应大体了解科学的实际价值，尤其是"白俄罗斯部分"的价值，从中为专业活动和个人发展开辟新的视野，能够积累科学信息，掌握对指数级增长的信息流进行批判性分析的技能。实现人文知识的创新潜力的意义首先在于培养公民的创新意识，培养专家和管理人员的创新能力。

多年以来，在白俄罗斯国家科学院哲学研究所的支持下，创新社会化问题、创新过程的心理学问题得到了发展。创建了一种培训方法来提高管理人员、工程技术人员的创造力和创新力，实体经济部门的企业借助这种方法举办了培训研讨会。白俄罗斯国家科学院哲学研究所建立了专门的科学与实践部门——知识与能力管理中心，其专家解决理论和方法任务，营造企业的研究和创新环境，解决员工职业发展的潜在管理问题，设定预测周期，并持续改进管理和生产流程。

再强调一下现代化的一个社会文化方面。实践表明，执行得很好的现代化措施，无论以何种方式、用什么样的参数评估其有效性，最终总是会变成对现有组织和管理制度的"强度测试"。这是这些措施毋庸置疑的优势。显然，唯有那些通过现代化"压力测试"的制度、法规、行政

算法才能在未来的社会文化体系中占据一席之地。

七 那么，究竟什么是社会现代化

可不可以对这种现象给出一个明确定义呢？本文违反学术惯例，把定义问题放在文章的结尾部分，而不是放在文章的开头，这并非偶然。以上所考虑的现代化方方面面的问题给了我们回答这一问题的各种不同方法。或许，我们应该沿着这样的道路走下去：不下定义，而是对现代化的类型进行分类，首先强调内生方式（"自我激励"，源于本土文明和文化的发展逻辑）和外生方式（"赶超"，关注外来文化样本）及其种类。然而，人们可以选择另一种方式，设法通过列举社会现代化进程的准则特点，在概念上巩固对社会现代化进程的"框架"认识。

当代社会的现代化是一个复杂的社会文化过程，是在科学、工业技术和社会经济发展、社会交往和团结方式的演变、个人世界观和社会意识等层面展开的。这一过程的核心要素是社会结构的技术基础的更新，社会结构包括生产、管理、社会技术、人文技术、行为规范、生活方式。这一过程的内容是，围绕创造、组织和人员支持、强化"技术核心"的任务，持续（而不是瞬间）巩固社会的精神力量和创造力。

换句话说，社会现代化是一个对社会的所有构成部分进行革新的复杂计划，涉及科技文化教育政策、生产和管理系统的组织、公众意识和人民生活方式的系统性质变。有两个因素特别重要——创造力（创新）和需求机制及创新成果的社会化。因此，极其重要的是，利用年轻人的精力、老一辈的经验、专家的知识、科学教育和文化的潜力，在社会上营造一种富有创造力的环境。

社会现代化不应沦为独立的经济客体乃至经济部门混乱无序的转型。这是一个面向未来的综合计划，全面考虑了世界经济体系的发展前景、区域和全球合作趋势、科技进步以及保护自然、人类和人文价值的任务。换句话说，现代化与全球文明进程直接相关，其主要意识形态要素旨在实现产业发展模式的根本转型，建设创新型信息数字化社会或基于知识、专业能力和人文价值观的社会。

在实施这一现代化战略时,新的科学知识至关重要,会以特殊方式发挥基础科学的作用。未来的世界是一个高科技世界。在这个高科技世界里,没有适当的科学、人文和文化基础,就不可能建立任何现代化计划。

参考文献:

A. A. Lazarevich et al., Belarus and Russia in the European context: the problems of the state management of the modernization process: Materials of the international scientific – practical conference, Minsk, October 20 – 21, 2011.

National Academy of Sciences of Belarus, Institute of philosophy. – Minsk: Pravo I ekonomika, 2012.

Gavrov, S. N., Modernization in the name of empire. Sociocultural aspects of modernization processes in Russia, Editorial URSS, 2010.

Gavrov, S. N., Modernization of Russia: post – imperial transit, МГУДТ, 2010.

Habermas, J., "Modern – an unfinished project", Jurgen Habermas, Political works, Praxis, 2005.

Kudrov, V. M., "Innovative economy – imperative of time", *Modern Europe*, 2009, No. 2.

M. S. Gorbachev, "On convocation of the next XXVII congress of CPSU and tasks connected with its preparation and holding", Report of the General Secretary of the CPSU Central Committee, http://www.historyru.com/docs/rulers/gorbachev/gorbachev – doc – 3. html#/overview.

Toffler, A., *Shock of the future*: Translation from English, LLC "AST Publishing house", 2002.

Toffler, A., *The third wave*, AST, 2002.

V. L. Inozemtsev ed., *Forcing to innovations*: strategy for Russia, Collection of articles and materials, Center of research of postindustrial society, 2009.

"一带一路"倡议与欧亚经济联盟对接合作

高 媛*

习近平主席明确指出，发展和深化中俄关系是两国的战略选择。（两国）要加强战略协作，共同促进世界经济持续稳定增长，推动国际和地区热点问题和平解决，完善全球治理体系，为世界和平稳定注入更多正能量。① 从某种意义上讲，中俄日益成长为维护国际战略平衡与世界和平稳定不可或缺的积极因素。

2021年是《中俄睦邻友好合作条约》签署20周年，习近平主席指出，中俄双方"将在更高水平、更广领域、更深层次推进双边关系向前发展。面对世纪疫情叠加百年变局，中俄相互坚定支持，密切有效协作，生动诠释了中俄新时代全面战略协作伙伴关系的深刻内涵"②。两国"在核心利益问题上互为坚强后盾，在发展振兴道路上互为重要伙伴，在国际事务中发挥中流砥柱的作用，推动新时代中俄关系实现更大的发展，更好地造福两国，惠及世界"③。

---

* 高媛，中国社会科学院信息情报研究院副研究员。
① 杜一菲：《习近平会见俄罗斯总统普京》，《人民日报》2017年5月15日第2版。
② 《习近平同俄罗斯总统共同见证中俄核能合作项目开工仪式》，《人民日报》2021年5月20日第1版。
③ 《外交部谈中俄外长会晤成果：双方将继续在核心利益问题上互为坚强后盾》，国际在线，2021年3月23日，http://news.cri.cn/20210323/df34b8eb-7469-753c-2358-d6e456622c19.html。

一 "带盟"对接开启中俄全面战略合作新局面

世界正面临百年未有之大变局,全球正步入一个空前的大发展、大变革、大调整时期。面对逆全球化现象不断凸显、国际政治经济不确定性日趋增强等一系列新形势、新问题,能否适时提出有针对性的对策与方案,无疑是对整个世界尤其是各主要大国智慧与能力的全新考验。2013 年以来,以习近平同志为核心的党中央,在统筹国内发展与国际大势的基础上,提出了与沿线各国一道,共建"一带一路"的重大倡议。其核心内容就是"促进基础设施建设和互联互通,对接各国政策和发展战略,深化务实合作,促进协调联动发展,实现共同繁荣"①。

自 2001 年中俄两国确立战略协作伙伴关系以来,中俄在双边关系与国际事务中始终保持着平等互利、精诚合作的精神,在重大国际问题上能够以相同或相似的立场,反对霸权主义,主张世界多极化,积极维护国际社会秩序的稳定。作为联合国安理会常任理事国,中俄两国都对国际秩序的演变非常关注。在第二次世界大战结束 60 周年之际,中俄两国发表了《关于 21 世纪国际秩序的联合声明》,共同表达了对未来国际秩序的看法。与此同时,两国也相互支持各自的发展目标,在战略层面开展广泛合作。2014 年 2 月,中国国家主席习近平出席索契冬奥会开幕式,中俄两国领导人就共同推动"一带一路"倡议达成一致。2015 年,俄罗斯加入亚洲基础设施投资银行(AIIB),成为仅次于中国和印度的第三大股东。2015 年 5 月,中俄两国发表《中华人民共和国与俄罗斯联邦关于丝绸之路经济带建设和欧亚经济联盟建设对接合作的联合声明》,正式确立了"一带一盟"对接的合作方式。② 两国的合作不仅有力地维护了国际秩序的稳定,还为双边关系的进一步提升奠定了基础。2016 年,两国元

---

① 习近平:《开辟合作新起点 谋求发展新动力——在'一带一路'国际合作高峰论坛圆桌峰会上的开幕辞》,《人民日报》2017 年 5 月 16 日第 3 版。
② 《中华人民共和国与俄罗斯联邦关于丝绸之路经济带建设和欧亚经济联盟建设对接合作的联合声明》,新华社,2015 年 5 月 9 日,http://www.xinhuanet.com//world/2015-05/09/c_127780866.htm。

首共同发表了《关于加强全球战略稳定的联合声明》，旨在应对国际事务中消极力量不断增加的挑战。2017年，《中俄关于进一步深化全面战略协作伙伴关系的联合声明》的签署，进一步从政治互信、务实合作、安全合作、人文交流、国际协作等五个方面，为新时期中俄全面战略合作指明了发展方向。

2019年10月25日，国务院总理李克强与欧亚经济联盟各成员国总理共同发表了《关于2018年5月17日签署的〈中华人民共和国与欧亚经济联盟经贸合作协定〉生效的联合声明》。《联合声明》重申了中华人民共和国与欧亚经济联盟成员国（亚美尼亚共和国、白俄罗斯共和国、哈萨克斯坦共和国、吉尔吉斯共和国和俄罗斯联邦）的传统友谊和牢固的经济贸易关系，宣布《中华人民共和国与欧亚经济联盟经贸合作协定》（以下简称《协定》）正式生效。双方都认为《协定》的生效是建设共同经济发展空间、实现"一带一路"倡议与欧亚经济联盟对接，以及"一带一路"与大欧亚伙伴关系协调发展的重要举措。双方相信《协定》的签署将有助于在经贸领域开展互利合作和建设性对话，有必要尽早启动旨在促进双边贸易与合作的《协定》条款的实施工作，并保证包括《协定》联合委员会在内的合作机制应有的作用。① 以此为标志，"一带一路"倡议与欧亚经济联盟对接进入了务实合作与制度构建同步推进的新阶段。

2020年以来，尽管新冠肺炎疫情波及世界，但"一带一路"合作项目总体平稳，并没有出现大范围延期，表现出强大的韧性。② 作为一项横贯欧亚大陆的世纪伟业，顺利推进"一带一路"特别是"丝绸之路经济带"建设，离不开中俄两国战略合作的深化。俄罗斯是中国构建"一带一路"的重要合作伙伴，中国也是欧亚经济联盟的战略伙伴。双方在涉及对方核心利益的议题上相互坚定支持，积极推动包括"带盟"对接在

---

① 《关于2018年5月17日签署的〈中华人民共和国与欧亚经济联盟经贸合作协定〉生效的联合声明》，新华社，2019年10月25日，http://www.gov.cn/xinwen/2019-10/25/content_5445095.htm。

② 《"一带一路"合作韧性十足（专家解读）》，《人民日报海外版》，2020年3月16日，http://paper.people.com.cn/rmrbhwb/html/2020-03/16/content_1976481.htm。

内的发展战略协调,既顺应了当前国际政治经济新秩序调整的客观要求,也有利于不断巩固和深化两国间既有的伙伴关系,进而开启新时代中俄全面战略合作建设的新局面。①

随着"一带一路"倡议的持续推进,"带盟"对接又成为中俄全面战略合作的新抓手。中俄两国共同商定,"将继续发挥各自优势,本着互惠互利、相互理解的原则,围绕中俄发展战略对接以及'一带一路'建设与欧亚经济联盟对接,致力于深化各领域务实合作,巩固中俄关系持续发展的物质基础"②。中俄将以"带盟"对接为契机,继续在各领域全面深化战略协作与务实合作。

一方面,"一带一路"倡议思想理念的不断推广与务实政策的持续落实,有利于发掘中俄两国间巨大的合作潜力与空间,从而为新时代中俄全面战略合作关系打下坚实的物质基础。中俄两国同属欧亚大陆,山水相连、比邻而居,具备深化全方位合作的广阔空间。2017 年 7 月,习近平主席在出访俄罗斯前指出,战略性大项目是两国经贸合作的基石,其综合效益和战略效果不能用简单的数字来体现和衡量,双方要开展更多联合研制、联合生产、推广应用等合作。③ 近年来,在"带盟"对接的框架内,中俄在双边大项目方面着力推进能源领域上下游一体化合作。在互联互通层面,中国积极参与俄方提出的共同开发建设滨海国际运输走廊建议,最终促成同江铁路桥、黑河公路桥等重大跨境基础设施建设项目顺利推进并即将完工。在俄罗斯的协助下,中欧班列成为了现实。俄罗斯也积极邀请中国共同开发和利用海上通道,特别是建设北极航道,打造"冰上丝绸之路"。借助"带盟"对接的"东风",中俄两国在能源、交通、投资、重大项目等一系列领域,已经展现出全面务实合作的新局面和良好的发展前景。

另一方面,"带盟"对接还将有助于中俄继续为国际政治经济新秩序

---

① 习近平:《推动中俄全面战略协作伙伴关系再攀高峰》,《人民日报海外版》2018 年 9 月 12 日第 1 版。

② 《中华人民共和国和俄罗斯联邦关于进一步深化全面战略协作伙伴关系的联合声明》,新华社,2019 年 6 月 6 日,http://www.xinhuanet.com/2019-06/06/c_1124588552.htm。

③ 《习近平接受俄罗斯媒体采访》,《人民日报》2017 年 7 月 4 日第 1 版。

的形成发挥建设性作用。同时，后金融危机时代国际政治经济发展的现实也充分表明，西方大国主导下的"经济帝国主义、自由霸权主义、民主原教旨主义、国际金融寡头统治"，业已成为当今世界的罪恶之首、危机之源。① 面对新兴市场国家的群体性崛起，世界旧秩序的变革进入倒计时。人类命运共同体的多元共存以及多极世界的未来，为新国际秩序的到来提供了发展方向。但少数西方大国不愿自动放弃对世界政治经济秩序的垄断优势，它们仍尽力企图打造排他性的国际经贸组织与相应规则，继续以此来维护国际大资本的垄断利益。

"一带一路"倡议的开放性和包容性，为未来国际秩序的到来提供了宝贵的实践经验。如习近平主席 2018 年 4 月在博鳌亚洲论坛开幕式的演讲中所言："共建'一带一路'倡议源于中国，但机会和成果属于世界，中国不打地缘博弈小算盘，不搞封闭排他小圈子，不做凌驾于人的强买强卖。"② 中国的"一带一路"倡议，并不是西方国家那种妄图在激烈竞争条件下实现速胜的战略思维；这一倡议有别于零和博弈，其逻辑是注重迎合所有能够接受它并能以自己的视野、经验和资源对它进行丰富的一切行为体。③

2019 年，以"带盟"对接为依托，中俄两国正在加速描绘面向未来的"欧亚大陆发展路线图"。它以丝绸之路经济带和欧亚经济联盟的协同发展为基础，以共商共建共享的基本原则与开放包容的基本精神，实现"一带一路"沿线欧亚大陆各国以及域外相关国家更高程度上的互联互通与发展成果的共赢共享。因此，从某种程度上讲，以中俄两国为中心所开展的构建国际政治经济新秩序的努力与相应方案已逐步形成，中国提出的"一带一路"和俄罗斯欧亚经济联盟已经先后全面铺开，涉及的国家已经远远超越了欧亚大陆的地理界限，进而演变为国际政治经济版图

---

① 张树华：《中俄合作破世界治理之困》，《环球时报》，2016 年 9 月 27 日，https://opinion.huanqiu.com/article/9CaKrnJXO6U。
② 习近平：《开放共创繁荣 创新引领未来——在博鳌亚洲论坛 2018 年年会开幕式上的主旨演讲》，《人民日报》2018 年 4 月 11 日第 3 版。
③ ［俄］德·叶夫列缅科：《中俄战略伙伴关系和大欧亚的构建》，《国外社会科学》2017 年第 4 期。

重构中最具建设性的公共产品之一。

二 "带盟"对接助力欧亚大陆经济空间拓展

"带盟"对接不断取得新的进展,为中俄关系在新时代的发展注入了全新的动力。在"带盟"对接的宏观背景下,新时代中俄两国在经济合作及经济空间拓展等方面将迎来一系列新的机遇。

受制于各自不同的地缘政治格局、经济发展重点、国内发展状况与客观条件等多重因素的影响,中俄经济关系一直明显滞后于其他领域合作的拓展。但"一带一路"倡议的持续推进,特别是"带盟"对接进程的启动,为中俄两国补齐经济合作领域的"短板"提供了绝佳的契机。

一方面,经济合作日益成为两国关系中最具增长潜质和发展空间的领域。近年来,"一带一路"建设的不断深入推进,为中俄两国补齐经济合作领域的"短板"提供了绝佳的契机。根据中国商务部公布的最新官方数据,2018年,中俄贸易额首次突破了千亿美元大关,达到了1078亿美元。中国连续十年保持俄国第一大贸易伙伴国的地位。2017年在首届"一带一路"国际合作高峰论坛上,中方同各国政府、地方、企业等达成一系列合作共识、重要举措及务实成果,其范围涵盖政策沟通、设施联通、贸易畅通、资金融通、民心相通等5大类,共76大项、270多项具体成果。其中,中俄在投资领域的合作进展尤为突出。中国国家发展和改革委员会宣布设立中俄地区合作发展投资基金,总规模1000亿元人民币,首期100亿元人民币,推动中国东北地区与俄罗斯远东开发合作。① 可以说,在"一带一路"倡议的推动下,中俄两国已经开始逐渐打破多年来在经济合作领域的相对停滞。未来,随着两国在"一带一路"框架下务实合作的深入开展,经济合作将有望成为未来两国关系发展中最具发展潜力和增长空间的重要领域之一。

另一方面,中国"一带一路"倡议与欧亚经济联盟的对接持续取得

---

① 《"一带一路"国际合作高峰论坛成果清单》,中国外交部官方网站,2017年5月16日,http://www.fmprc.gov.cn/web/zyxw/t1461873.shtm。

重要进展。2014年,在中国政府提出"一带一路"倡议一年后,俄罗斯随之发起并成立了旨在谋求欧亚区域经济一体化的欧亚经济联盟战略。然而,随着中国"一带一路"互利共赢效应在欧亚大陆地区吸引力的不断增强,加上俄罗斯等欧亚各国出于各自加快发展的强烈意愿,中俄两国最终作出了结束"一带一路"与欧亚经济联盟之间的"平行运行"状态,积极推动两者实现对接的重大战略决定。

2015年5月,中俄签署《关于丝绸之路经济带建设和欧亚经济联盟建设对接合作的联合声明》。声明强调,中方将"支持俄方积极推进欧亚经济联盟框架内一体化进程";同时,中俄双方也将"启动与欧亚经济联盟经贸合作方面的协议谈判。双方将共同协商,确保地区经济持续稳定增长,加强区域经济一体化,维护地区和平与发展"①。近年来,在继续致力于欧亚区域一体化目标的同时,俄罗斯也逐渐选择从实际出发,在对"一带一路"倡议予以积极回应的同时,持续重视其与欧亚经济联盟的合理对接。关于"一带一路"倡议对于促进欧亚大陆一体化的重要性,俄罗斯总统普京强调指出,它不仅为"促进能源、基础设施、交通、工业和人文合作方面的一体化发展提供了一个创造性的方法",而且"为欧亚大陆在一个更广阔的范围里探讨其未来发展创造了条件"②。

2017年10月,中国与欧亚经济委员会签署了《关于实质性结束中国与欧亚经济联盟经贸合作协议谈判的联合声明》,标志着中国与欧亚经济联盟经贸合作的制度化取得了实质性进展。③ 同时也使中俄两国领导人达成的欧亚经济联盟和中国丝绸之路经济带对接合作协定,朝着制度化方向迈出了重要一步。④ 谈判取得了丰硕的成果,其中最重要的是双方经济

---

① "中华人民共和国与俄罗斯联邦关于丝绸之路经济带建设和欧亚经济联盟建设对接合作的联合声明",新华网,2015年5月9日,http://www.xinhuanet.com/world/2015-05/09/c_127780866.htm。

② [俄]弗拉基米尔·普京:《"一带一路"国际合作高峰论坛开幕式致辞》,《中国投资》2017年第11期,第33—34页。

③ 《中国与欧亚经济联盟实质性结束经贸合作协议谈判》,新华社,2017年10月1日,http://www.xinhuanet.com/2017-10/01/c_1121756577.htm。

④ 《中国与欧亚经济联盟实质性结束经贸合作协议谈判》,新华社,2017年10月1日,http://www.xinhuanet.com/2017-10/01/c_1121756577.htm。

贸易协议的签订。该《协定》范围涵盖海关合作、贸易便利化、知识产权、部门合作以及政府采购等 13 个章节，包含电子商务和市场竞争等相关条款。根据协议，中俄同意通过加强合作、信息交换、经验交流等方式，进一步简化通关手续，降低货物贸易成本。《协定》旨在进一步减少非关税贸易壁垒，提高贸易便利化水平，为产业发展营造良好的环境，促进中国与欧亚经济联盟及其成员国经贸关系深入发展，为企业和人民带来实惠，为双边经贸合作提供制度性保障。① 当然，也需要客观地认识到，从内容上看，当前的协定仍是一项框架性文件，虽然规定了未来中国与欧亚经济联盟及其成员国谈判的方向，但是并未涉及减免关税、简化报关流程、统一海关标准等实质性内容。这其中的主要原因在于，欧亚经济联盟成员国与中国在很多领域的利益安排方面尚有需要解决的重要问题，目前还未准备好取消关税壁垒并对中国商品和服务开放本国市场。短期内中国与欧亚经济联盟签署全面的自由贸易区协议（FTA）仍然面临较大困难，其根源在于欧亚经济联盟经济韧性较差，内部结构性问题仍未得到有效解决。② 未来，欧亚经济联盟与中国贸易关系的自由化还需不断克服困难，持续推进。

"带盟"对接还促进了欧亚区域内的国际经济合作制度互融，推动各方机制相互协调促进该地区的发展。通过"一带一路"倡议，中国与欧亚空间各国逐步建立起牢固的双边关系，例如"一带一路"与哈萨克斯坦"光明之路"计划的对接，在白俄罗斯设立"巨石"经济特区等成果的实现，都与"带盟"对接的顺利推进密不可分。通过"带盟"对接，中俄之间在欧亚地区有效避免了恶性竞争；在不改变双方地区经济合作方案和机制的基础上，进行相互协调。同时，欧亚地区的中小国家能够最大限度地参与到两国所倡导的地区合作方案中，获得收益的最大化。通过两大国区域层面的对接合作，丰富的双边和多边行动得以迅速开展，并形成更佳的协同效应。

---

① 《中国与欧亚经济联盟正式签署经贸合作协定》，中华人民共和国商务部，2018 年 5 月 17 日，http://www.mofcom.gov.cn/article/ae/ai/201805/20180502745041.shtml。

② 丛晓男：《中国 - 欧亚经济联盟 FTA 的经济障碍与现实选择——基于可计算一般均衡 GMR - CGE》，《俄罗斯研究》2018 年第 1 期，第 106 页。

2019年末至2020年初，在新冠肺炎疫情影响下，中国对外贸易整体呈现下滑局面，但2020年第一季度，中俄贸易额达到了253.5亿美元，同比增长3.4%，增速在中国主要贸易伙伴中排名第二。其中，中国对俄出口91.5亿美元，同比下降14.6%；自俄进口162亿美元，同比增长17.3%，进口增速在中国主要贸易伙伴中排名第一。[①] 中俄经贸关系能抵抗住疫情的冲击实现逆势上扬，主要归功于近年来中俄务实合作不断推进，提升了两国经贸合作的质量以及两国经济的相互依赖程度，使得中俄经贸承受得起外部环境变化的冲击。同时，常态化的疫情防控为两国经济发展塑造了新的动能，为区域经贸合作创造了更多的机会，中俄双方互利共赢的同时，也为世界经济复苏提供了新的增长点。

可以说，"带盟"对接带来的多孔化、多选择性的发展，不仅推动了中俄双边关系的提升，还巩固了两国在多层政治经济进程中的协调者地位。中俄两国通过共同倡建、共同推动地区合作框架，继续推动欧亚地区经济政治秩序的演进，有助于形成基于主权原则、兼顾各国发展的欧亚地区新秩序和一体化新路径。

三 "带盟"对接推动亚欧命运共同体构建

丝绸之路经济带与欧亚经济联盟对接，是欧亚空间最大的区域合作项目，不仅能够改变欧亚区域的经济景观，甚至可能为欧亚空间的秩序重构形成铺垫。"带盟"对接一方面是为欧亚经济联盟国家创造机遇，另一方面也是对欧亚各国精英在政策执行与政治成熟性方面的一次特殊考验。而"带盟"对接进程推进的结果，对亚欧地区更广泛空间内的"命运共同体"构建也具有重要意义。

2013年3月，习近平主席在莫斯科国际关系学院发表演讲时，正式提出了"命运共同体"这一概念。之后他又在多个场合对此理念进行了阐释。在博鳌亚洲论坛年会、印尼国会、巴黎联合国教科文组织总部、印尼"亚非领导人会议"、第70届联大一般性辩论、巴黎气候大会开幕

---

① 数据来源：中国海关总署官网。

式、2016年二十国集团工商峰会开幕式、瑞士日内瓦万国宫"共商共筑人类命运共同体"高级别会议、全球政党大会上，多次阐述人类命运共同体的概念与意义。

在中国共产党第十九次代表大会报告中，习近平总书记对人类命运共同体的内涵做出了明确概括，即"建设持久和平、普遍安全、共同繁荣、开放包容、清洁美丽的世界"①。构建命运共同体的主张汲取了人类历史上的宝贵思想，既传承了中国传统文化"天下为公、世界大同、天人合一"的理念，也是马克思"自由人联合体"思想的当代结晶。与西方地缘体系自我认同的原则相反，这个体系的理论基础，是自我区别原则与协同原则，将"玄同""混合"等中国传统文化观念中的"关系"范畴纳入其中。②

俄方对于欧亚地区一体化的构想，则集中反映在"大欧亚"概念上。事实上，"大欧亚"概念逐渐在区域内各国的演绎下，形成了更加宽泛的内涵。除了俄罗斯推动的大欧亚伙伴关系外，哈萨克斯坦首任总统纳扎尔巴耶夫也在2019年呼吁构建欧亚命运共同体。③"大欧亚"理念的不断丰富和扩展不仅从侧面呼应了"命运共同体"理念，也与"带盟"对接的逻辑具有内在一致性。大欧亚概念的逐步演绎，反映了欧亚地区互联互通不断增强的客观进程，同时也促进了基于理念和认同上的宏观区域建构。

一方面，交通先行是"带盟"对接的重要突破口，"一带一路"倡议的重要任务是互联、互通，发展欧亚大陆交通运输及其相应的基础设施，以保障资源的可靠供应和中国经济出口能力。这是丝绸之路经济带和欧亚经济联盟对接进程的首要任务，也是"大欧亚"概念落地的基础条件。

---

① 习近平：《决胜全面建成小康社会　夺取新时代中国特色社会主义伟大胜利——在中国共产党第十九次全国代表大会上的报告（2017年10月18日）》，《人民日报》2017年10月28日第1版。
② [俄] 马良文：《俄罗斯和中国是欧亚联合体的两个顶梁柱》，《俄罗斯研究》2018年第5期。
③ "纳扎尔巴耶夫呼吁构建欧亚命运共同体"，中国新闻网，2019年11月13日，http://www.chinanews.com/gj/2019/11-13/9006106.shtml。

只有通过对交通物流运输基础设施的根本改造，保证欧亚大陆桥实质性对接，才能把欧亚、中国和欧盟的巨大市场可靠地连接在一起。欧亚经济联盟与中国的经济贸易协议，将为基础设施建设和投资开创更为良好的条件；亚投行、金砖新开发银行等机制，是中国参与欧亚国家交通基础设施建设的制度保障。

中国力求保障交通运输线路多元化，而俄罗斯境内交通物流基础设施大项目长时间拖延，促使中国不得不寻求其他替代方向。但这并不意味着"丝绸之路经济带"会削弱俄罗斯作为欧亚大陆主要过境国的作用，目前已经开通的中欧班列均有相当的路程在俄罗斯境内。在中欧班列的推动下，俄罗斯作为欧亚大陆东西两端物流枢纽的作用将进一步强化。

当然，断言欧亚大陆在现代物流运输基础设施建设上已经取得了突破，还为时尚早。有许多情况和因素阻碍着这般大规模基础设施项目的快速启动。目前不仅在欧亚地区各国协作层面，甚至在俄罗斯一国之内都没有统一的、成体系的货物运输调节机构，只有低层次的铁路、水路、公路运输联运或协同管理体系。其结果是，所谓的"瓶颈""卡脖子"成了俄罗斯统一运输体系始终无法有效解决的慢性病，常常导致大量货物堆积在海港。这些问题不解决，启动欧亚交通物流基础设施的大型项目，将注定面临一开始经济低效，最终可能导致现有运输体系更为支离破碎的结局。因此，在欧亚经济联盟国家境内丝绸之路经济带交通运输走廊建设的过程中，必须首先解决好宏观区域的经济互联互通。不仅要实现统一运输体系管理机制现代化，而且部分国家和欧亚经济联盟一体化机构，必须实行相应的地区、产业、投资和贸易政策。总而言之，丝绸之路经济带交通运输走廊应该同时成为沟通欧亚经济空间的运输走廊。

另一方面，"带盟"对接不仅具有物质层面的内涵，在思想和理念上的"对接"也具有重要意义。大欧亚概念内涵的不断延展，在理论上为亚欧命运共同体的构建提供了更加有利的条件，而"带盟"对接则赋予了新欧亚区域主义发展的动力。大欧亚概念将欧亚地区扩充为大欧亚地区，拓展了"带盟"多边合作的内涵，提升了合作的信任层次。

这种信任必然会推动"带盟"的顺利对接与高效合作；其和谐发展符合中国、俄罗斯和欧亚经济联盟其他国家以及欧亚更大范围地区行为体的利益。

"带盟"对接既是一个促进地区发展的过程，也推动着区域规则的建构。在取得具体项目的早期收获之后，利用多边合作平台制定共同的规则与标准就变得非常重要。利用"带盟"对接框架，形成广义欧亚空间中的通用规则，利用相关规则协议的签署，形成可预期的制度化安排。共同制度的具体设计有助于对区域合作模式加以总结和提升。这也符合习近平主席和普京总统共同做出的丝绸之路经济带与欧亚经济联盟对接的历史性决定的精神。

在这样一个宏大地理空间内推动命运共同体的建构，将不可避免地受到来自内部与外部各种力量的干扰。欧亚大陆内部的各种传统与非传统安全威胁，宗教、文化、社会等方面的多元特性，都会对该进程产生不利影响。部分域外大国在欧亚内陆的很多次区域空间内都有参与地区问题的抓手，可以利用政治、经济和军事等手段，阻挠、延迟甚至破坏地区合作。

四 小结："带盟"对接塑造后疫情时代的中俄关系

经过70余年的发展，中俄关系正处于历史最好时期。两国政治互信牢固，在涉及彼此核心利益和重大关切问题上相互坚定支持。双方建立起完备的高层交往和各领域合作机制，开展了内容丰富、具有战略意义的多领域、全方位合作。

当前，新冠肺炎疫情仍在肆虐，世界各国仍然在同疫情进行斗争。特别是受到疫情的影响，正常的国际经贸关系尚未恢复。逆全球化、单边主义思潮和行径有愈演愈烈的趋势，一些西方国家为了甩锅疫情危机、维护本国的霸权地位，极力推行单边主义、孤立主义，不惜撕毁协议，损害他国利益，全球秩序受到前所未有的挑战。

面对变局，群策群力、合作共赢是世界各国的正确选择。习近平主席指出，开展国际合作离不开真诚互信、志同道合的伙伴。① 俄罗斯是中国最大邻国，也是开展各领域合作的重要优先伙伴。双方秉持可持续发展理念，积极开展天然气等清洁能源合作，将科技创新、数字经济、网络电商作为新的合作增长点，就跨界资源利用和保护、跨界自然保护区建设开展有效合作。共建"一带一路"同"大欧亚伙伴关系"理念相通，两大倡议相互支持，相互促进，并行不悖。这将有力推动区域经济融合，有利于实现共同的可持续发展。随着新时代中俄全面战略协作关系的日益巩固，两大倡议对接带来的外溢效应逐渐凸显，欧亚地区的中小国家不仅获得经济利益，而且整个地区的和平与发展都能得以维护和延续。随着国际格局转换速度不断加快，这一对接也将为建立公正合理的国际政治经济新秩序提供助力，为创建亚欧命运共同体奠定基础。

参考文献：

丛晓男：《中国-欧亚经济联盟 FTA 的经济障碍与现实选择——基于可计算一般均衡 GMR-CGE》，《俄罗斯研究》2018 年第 1 期。

杜一菲：《习近平会见俄罗斯总统普京》，《人民日报》2017 年 5 月 15 日第 2 版。

《关于 2018 年 5 月 17 日签署的〈中华人民共和国与欧亚经济联盟经贸合作协定〉生效的联合声明》，新华社，2019 年 10 月 25 日，http：//www.gov.cn/xinwen/2019-10/25/content_5445095.htm。

"纳扎尔巴耶夫呼吁构建欧亚命运共同体"，中国新闻网，2019 年 11 月 13 日，http：//www.chinanews.com/gj/2019/11-13/9006106.shtml。

"外交部谈中俄外长会晤成果：双方将继续在核心利益问题上互为坚强后盾"，国际在线，2021 年 3 月 23 日，http：//news.cri.cn/20210323/df34b8eb-7469-753c-2358-d6e456622c19.html。

习近平：《坚持可持续发展　共创繁荣美好世界——在第二十三届圣彼得堡国际经济论坛全会上的致辞》，《人民日报》2019 年 6 月 8 日第

---

① 习近平：《坚持可持续发展　共创繁荣美好世界——在第二十三届圣彼得堡国际经济论坛全会上的致辞》，《人民日报》2019 年 6 月 8 日第 2 版。

2版。

习近平:《决胜全面建成小康社会 夺取新时代中国特色社会主义伟大胜利——在中国共产党第十九次全国代表大会上的报告（2017年10月18日）》,《人民日报》2017年10月28日。

习近平:《开辟合作新起点 谋求发展新动力——在'一带一路'国际合作高峰论坛圆桌峰会上的开幕辞》,《人民日报》2017年5月16日第3版。

习近平:《开放共创繁荣 创新引领未来——在博鳌亚洲论坛2018年年会开幕式上的主旨演讲》,《人民日报》2018年4月11日第3版。

习近平:《推动中俄全面战略协作伙伴关系再攀高峰》,《人民日报海外版》,2018年9月12日第1版。

《习近平接受俄罗斯媒体采访》,《人民日报》2017年7月4日第1版。

《习近平同俄罗斯总统共同见证中俄核能合作项目开工仪式》,《人民日报》2021年5月20日第1版。

《"一带一路"国际合作高峰论坛成果清单》,中国外交部官方网站,2017年5月16日,http://www.fmprc.gov.cn/web/zyxw/t1461873.shtm。

《"一带一路"合作韧性十足（专家解读）》,《人民日报海外版》,2020年3月16日,http://paper.people.com.cn/rmrbhwb/html/2020-03/16/content_1976481.htm。

张树华:《中俄合作破世界治理之困》,《环球时报》,2016年9月27日,https://opinion.huanqiu.com/article/9CaKrnJXO6U。

《中国与欧亚经济联盟实质性结束经贸合作协议谈判》,新华社,2017年10月1日,http://www.xinhuanet.com/2017-10/01/c_1121756577.htm。

《中国与欧亚经济联盟正式签署经贸合作协定》,中华人民共和国商务部,2018年5月17日,http://www.mofcom.gov.cn/article/ae/ai/201805/20180502745041.shtml。

《中华人民共和国和俄罗斯联邦关于进一步深化全面战略协作伙伴关系的联合声明》,新华社,2019年6月6日,http://www.xinhuanet.com/2019-06/06/c_1124588552.htm。

《中华人民共和国与俄罗斯联邦关于丝绸之路经济带建设和欧亚经济联盟建设对接合作的联合声明》，新华社，2015 年 5 月 9 日，http：//www. xinhuanet. com//world/2015 – 05/09/ c_127780866. htm。

"中华人民共和国与俄罗斯联邦关于丝绸之路经济带建设和欧亚经济联盟建设对接合作的联合声明"，新华网，2015 年 5 月 9 日，http：//www. xinhuanet. com/world/2015 – 05/09/c_127780866. htm。

［俄］弗拉基米尔·普京：《"一带一路"国际合作高峰论坛开幕式致辞》，《中国投资》2017 年第 11 期。

［俄］卡拉加诺夫：《克服欧洲危机的欧亚方案——扩大解决问题的空间》，《俄罗斯研究》2017 年第 6 期。

［俄］马良文：《俄罗斯和中国是欧亚联合体的两个顶梁柱》，《俄罗斯研究》2018 年第 5 期。

［俄］德·叶夫列缅科：《中俄战略伙伴关系和大欧亚的构建》，《国外社会科学》2017 年第 4 期。

Алексей Фененко.《Транссиб》– – наиболее реалистичный вариант ЭПШП. 14 декабря 2015. https：//russiancouncil. ru/analytics – and – comments/analytics/transsib – naibolee – realistichn yy – variant – epshp/.

Большая пресс – конаференция Владимира Путина. 19 декабря, 2019，http：//www. kremlin. ru/events/president/news/62366.

Иван Тимофеев, Олег Барабанов, Тимофей Бордачев, Ярослав Лисоволик, Федор Лукьянов, Андрей Сущенцов. Не одичать в 《осыпающемся мире》. Валдай клуб. 14 мая 2020. https：//ru. valdaiclub. com/a/reports/ne – odichat – v – osypayushchemsya – mire/.

"一带一路"倡议与中乌人文交流

Olena Shypotilova[*]　　Svitlana Glovatska[**]

　　本文分析了中国和乌克兰在"一带一路"概念下的人文交流与合作。笔者认为，这一合作领域包括学生之间和大学教授之间的知识交流以及丰富乌克兰和中国的文化内涵。对乌克兰来说，该项目提供了一个利用投资、实现教育部门现代化以及创建欧亚文明统一平台的机会。

　　"一带一路"倡议是人类历史上规模最大的发展倡议，旨在创造和加强多国之间的联系，以及经济、文化和政治交流。中国的"一带一路"倡议也是世界上规模最大的宏观经济项目。中国计划为 2022 年倡议下的特定项目投资约 3500 亿美元。"一带一路"项目计划于 2049 年（即中华人民共和国成立 100 周年）完工，届时将实现广大欧亚地区和部分非洲地区共计 65 个国家的融合。

　　乌克兰作为东欧的一部分，位于各国"交通"和利益的交汇点。对乌克兰来说，中国的新欧洲政策带来了一些机遇，通过实现机遇和发展路径的多样化，"一带一路"倡议可帮助乌克兰实现经济复苏。

　　考虑欧中关系的战略意义并发展对华关系对乌克兰来说非常重要。中国在中亚开发的经济和基础设施项目将会导致未来欧中线路交通量的增长。支持中国建设连接欧洲与哈萨克斯坦和中国并穿越高加索和里海

---

[*] Olena Shypotilova，乌克兰国立敖德萨海事大学副教授、博士。
[**] Svitlana Glovatska，乌克兰国立敖德萨海事大学副教授、博士，中国社会科学院—乌克兰国立敖德萨海事大学中国研究中心乌方主任。

的"跨里海"铁路,对乌克兰来说具有重要意义。通过该路线,乌克兰可通过黑海、格鲁吉亚和阿塞拜疆运送货物。2016 年,格鲁吉亚与中国签定了自由贸易协定,且白俄罗斯获得了"16 + 1"模式下的观察员地位。这表明,"一带一路"在促进欧亚地区的市场发展、繁荣和稳定方面,潜力巨大。

乌克兰可以利用"一带一路"的经济潜力来发展本国经济,并成功实施欧洲一体化战略。乌克兰还必须为"一带一路"项目的激烈竞争做好准备,特别是来自大型公司的竞争(如全球承运人 DHL 和 UPS)。所以乌克兰需要与中国的合作伙伴建立联盟和有效关系,以便与全球公司竞争。然而,尽管媒体提到了乌克兰加入"16 + 1"模式的可能性,但实际上并没有就此开展正式谈判,仅根据相关路线图确定参与"一带一路"项目。①

乌克兰国家科学院克里姆斯基东方研究所远东部负责人、乌克兰中国研究协会会长 V. Kiktenko 强调,目前正在对乌中合作、乌克兰参与"一带一路"项目,以及互动模式等进行规划。尽管欧洲政治家对"一带一路"倡议的看法仍存在分歧,但因该倡议的经济效益源于共同利益,所以必将对跨区域合作起到推动作用。中国社会经济的强势崛起催生了"一带一路"倡议,该倡议应成为参与国家之间合作的一个重要工具。如果说欧盟一开始并没有在意北京提出的该项倡议的话,那么今天,欧洲议会和欧洲政府已认识到"一带一路"框架下经济合作的成就和前景。②

---

① Kiktenko V. O., "Ukraine in the 'One Belt, One Road project': regional and global dimension", 2018, https://sinologist.com.ua/kiktenko-v-o-ukrayina-v-proekti-odyn-poyas-odyn-shlyah-regionalnyj-ta-globalnyj-vymir/.

② Kiktenko V. O., "Ukraine in the 'One Belt, One Road project': regional and global dimension", 2018, https://sinologist.com.ua/kiktenko-v-o-ukrayina-v-proekti-odyn-poyas-odyn-shlyah-regionalnyj-ta-globalnyj-vymir/.

针对这一问题的史学研究有很多①，本文的研究目的是分析乌克兰和中国在"一带一路"概念下进行人文交流的成就和前景。

文化和人文交流关系一直是国际合作的一个特殊领域。在所有大规模国际倡议和概念中都提到了人文交流的潜在价值。中方已宣布和推出了一项大型教育项目，以促进丝绸之路经济带内的学生交流。中国政府每年向来自参与丝绸之路经济带建设的国家的学生提供1万笔助学金，其中部分奖学金通过上海合作组织大学的项目得以成功实施。②

SREB人文交流的主要方向是联合举办文化年；举办电影和电视节；组织书展；联合向联合国教科文组织提交世界文物遗产登记申请；加强旅游交流；推动体育领域的交流；扩大医疗领域的合作；加强科学合作，加大保护环境和保护生物多样性的力度；利用互联网平台和新媒体，创造良好的文化环境和积极的舆论氛围。

2010年，乌中关系进一步加强。2010—2013年，两国领导人进行了一系列正式访问，并签署了关于深化乌中合作的一系列重要文件，其中包括《乌中建立和发展战略伙伴关系联合声明》《乌中友好合作条约》《乌中关于进一步深化战略伙伴关系的联合声明》和《2014—2018年乌中发展战略伙伴关系联合声明》。

---

① Bilorus O. H., "Globalization and security of development", Kyiv: KNEU, 2001; Honcharuk A., "Ukrainian – Chinese strategic partnership at the present stage", 2014, https://sinologist.com.ua/ukrayinsko – kitajske – strategichne – pa; Glovatska S. M., "Ukraine in the global megaproject 'One Belt, One Road'", China – Ukraine: prospects for academic and business cooperation: materials International. scientific – practical conf, Odessa, Phoenix, 2019, pp. 28 – 31; Kiktenko V. O., "Reforms and openness as a basis for building socialism with Chinese characteristics", Ukraine – China, 2018, No. 14, pp. 28 – 31; Onishchenko A. V., "Ukraine and China: new realities and prospects of foreign economic cooperation in the XXI century", Scientific Bulletin of Uzhgorod University, Editors: V. P. Mikloda (ed.), M. I. Pityulych, N. M. Gapak and others, Uzhhorod: Uzhhorod National University Publishing House, 2011, Special issue. 33, Part 2, pp. 205 – 207; Popkov V. V., "China: the new format of globalization", China – Ukraine: prospects for academic and business cooperation: materials International, scientific – practical conf, Odessa, May 27 – 28, 2019, pp. 18 – 23; Liui Yenchzhao, Pekna T. V., SunVei, "The Direct investments of Chinese enterprises in Ukraine", Current economic problems, 2012. No. 8 (134), pp. 413 – 418.

② Kulyntsev Yu. V., "The Strategy of Development and Silk Road Economic Belt Concept: Integration Potential of Cultural and Humanitarian Cooperation", China in world and regional politics. History and modernity, Issue XXIV: annual edition / comp., Resp. ed. E. I. Safronova, Moscow, pp. 131 – 144.

在接下来的几年里，两国的外交部长、立法机构和公共组织进行了一系列互访。2016—2019 年乌中关系对话的中心议题是两国国际组织间的合作探讨以及"一带一路"倡议论坛中的合作对话等。此外，为发展乌克兰空间经济的高科技部门、基础设施、节能和信息技术部门，两国在业务结构级别就扩大合作和吸引投资举行了一系列会谈。

乌克兰的战略任务是加大对中国投资的吸引力，以增加高附加值商品的出口，并扩大在产业创新和科学领域的合作。对乌克兰来说，利用中国资本建立科技园区和技术开发区同样重要。向中国国内大型基础设施和农业项目提供资金（中国计划向这些项目投资 100 亿美元），对乌克兰来说也很重要。面对新冠肺炎疫情蔓延的问题，乌克兰还需从中国获得低息贷款，以稳定乌克兰经济。在当前形势下，中资银行可能成为乌克兰外部贷款的额外来源，甚至成为乌克兰 IMF 信贷收入的替代来源。

乌中战略伙伴关系的一个重要领域是两国在人文交流和文化领域的关系。众所周知，乌克兰经典文学作品出版于乌克兰苏维埃社会主义共和国时期。早在 1992 年，武汉大学就成立了首家乌克兰专门研究中心（现为乌克兰研究中心）。2002 年，中国首次举办了"乌克兰文化日"活动，这加深了中国人民对乌克兰文化的了解。此外，还在乌克兰首都基辅举行了"乌克兰与中国：合作方式"国际会议。目前，乌中文化联合委员会正在积极协调和规划乌中之间的文化合作。同时，约有 2000 名中国学生在乌克兰大学学习。乌中两国在科技和航天领域的关系蓬勃发展。两国正积极举办乌中"一带一路"论坛。两国科学院之间的关系日益紧密，在基辅设立的孔子学院也非常活跃。由于乌克兰汉学家严重不足，乌克兰应加强对中国历史、哲学、语言和文化的研究。

乌克兰教育部长 D. Tabachnyk 在 2011 年 6 月 20 日的报告中称，约有 1000 名乌克兰学生在中国学习。约有 6000 名中国学生在乌克兰学习。根据联合国教科文组织的一份报告，乌克兰的大学尤其受到中国学生的欢迎。乌克兰教育和科技部报告称，在乌克兰约有 10% 的外国留学生是中国公民。①

2016年中乌文化交流的内容也极为丰富。其中一项最重要的活动是9月23日塔拉斯·舍甫琴科（Taras Shevchenko）作品展在位于北京大兴的北京美术馆开幕。该美术馆已成为展示中国和乌克兰当代艺术家、雕塑家和摄影师作品的平台。在过去几年中，共举办了100多场中乌文化活动，以及3800多场商业展览和交流活动。近年来，在乌克兰掀起了一场"中国文化热和语言热"，而独特的乌克兰文化也引起了中国人民的浓厚兴趣。

2016年秋，由乌克兰文化部部长E. Nyschuk率领的乌克兰代表团来华访问。在与时任中国文化部部长雒树刚的会谈中，中乌双方讨论了在中国建立乌克兰文化中心、推广两国民间工艺品和文化活动等问题。中国还高度重视在教育领域向乌方提供物资和技术援助。中国为乌克兰中学购置了23500台新电脑，并为基辅东方语言中学配置了三个语言室，以帮助那里的约600名儿童学习中文。

"丝绸之路"国际贸易组织已向乌克兰拨款20万美元，用于有特殊需求的中学生的教育方案。

在乌克兰这个欧洲最大的国家独立后，中国学者开始饶有兴趣地从乌克兰的角度研究和译介乌克兰的历史和现实。据不完全统计，已出版的关于乌克兰历史的著作包括西方学者Paul Robert Magochi的《乌克兰史》译本，（中国大百科全书出版社，2009年）；刘祖熙主编的《斯拉夫文化》（浙江人民出版社，1993年，书中设有乌克兰文化专区）；赵云中的《乌克兰：沉重的历史脚步》（华东师范大学出版社，2005年）；李燕的《不忘过去着眼未来：苏联1932—1933年饥荒问题与当代乌俄两国关系研究》（社会科学文献出版社，2014年）；闻一的《乌克兰：硝烟中的雅努斯》（中信出版社，2016年）。

所发表的关于乌克兰政治、经济和外交的著作包括：库奇马（Kuch-

---

① Liu Xiangzhong, "Social – cultural exchange between China and Ukraine: history and present", 2018, https://sinologist.com.ua/lyu – syanchzhun – sotsialno – kulturnyj – obmin – mizh – kytayem – ta – ukrayinoyu – istoriya – ta – suchasnist/.

ma）的《乌克兰：政治、经济和外交》译本，（东方出版社，2001年）；宋东方的《乌克兰散记》（南京大学出版社，2016年）；沈莉华的《苏联解体后的俄罗斯与乌克兰关系研究》（黑龙江大学出版社，2017年）；任飞的《乌克兰历史与当代政治经济》（经济科学出版社，2017年）；顾志红《非常临国：乌克兰与俄罗斯》（国防大学出版社，2000年）；帕夫洛夫斯基（Pavlov）的《过渡时期的宏观经济：乌克兰的改革》译本（民主与建设出版社，2001年）；张弘的《冲突与合作：解读乌克兰与俄罗斯的经济关系（1991—2008）》（知识产权出版社，2010年）；张弘的《转型国家的政治稳定研究：对乌克兰危机的理论思考》（社会科学文献出版社，2016年）。此外，中国社会科学院俄罗斯东欧中亚研究所的黄曰炤主编了《新编乌克兰语汉语词典》（商务印书馆，2013年），该词典比以1990年版本体量更大。①

2018年9月25—27日，分别在中国的北京和敦煌举行了乌克兰文化日。在乌中文化合作小组委员会第四次会议和乌中两国政府合作委员会第三次会议召开后，两国政府随即作出了举办该活动的决定。②

9月25日，乌克兰文化部部长叶甫盖尼·尼修克（Ye. Nyschuk）和中国文化和旅游部部长雒树刚在中国北京正式启动了"乌克兰文化日"，"流金溢彩——乌克兰博物馆文物及实用与装饰艺术大展"于当日在北京故宫博物院——中国建筑和艺术博物院综合体——开幕。游客可借此了解乌克兰的珠宝和文物——从特里波耶时代（特里波耶是最古老的农业文明之一），到斯基泰人，再到基辅罗斯时代（乌克兰在中世纪最繁荣的时期）的10—12世纪的琥珀，这些琥珀从古至今一直被用来制造珠宝。

"乌克兰的文物能在这个世界上最大的博物馆——故宫博物院展出，我感到非常自豪。这真正开启了展示乌克兰文化的大门。"乌克兰文化部部长叶甫盖尼·尼修克说道，"我相信，在未来，我们两国之间的友谊和

---

① Liu Xiangzhong, "Social – cultural exchange between China and Ukraine: history and present", 2018, https://sinologist.com.ua/lyu – syanchzhun – sotsialno – kulturnyj – obmin – mizh – kytayem – ta – ukrayinoyu – istoriya – ta – suchasnist/.

② "Days of Ukrainian Culture in the People's Republic of China", https://sinologist.com.ua/dni – kultury – ukrayiny – u – kytajskij – narodnij – respublitsi/.

相互了解会进一步加深，这有利于扩大艺术空间，并提高普通公民对乌克兰和中国文化艺术作品的兴趣。我衷心祝愿'乌克兰文化日'在中国取得圆满成功，并希望乌克兰文化在中国人民心中留下难以磨灭的印象。"①

在"文化日"期间，举办了以韦廖夫卡（G. G. Veryovka）命名的乌克兰国立功勋模范民间合唱团演出、乌克兰著名摄影师弗拉基米尔·科祖克（V. Kozyuk）的作品展以及 Petrykivka 的绘画作品展等活动。作为"文化日"活动的一部分，乌克兰代表团作为主宾国参加了"丝绸之路"国际文化博览会（2018 年 9 月 27—28 日，敦煌）。

此外，中国也注重与乌克兰开展地区合作。例如，在敖德萨国立海事大学的推动下，在敖德萨举办了关于"一带一路"项目的国际科学会议。敖德萨国立海事大学校长 S. V. Rudenko 教授强调，敖德萨国立海事大学已与天津大学、西北工业大学（上海分校）、上海海事大学（上海）、中国地质大学（武汉）、武汉科技大学（武汉）、大连理工大学（大连）、中国社会科学院社会学研究所（北京）签订了直接合作协议。②

敖德萨国立海事大学与中国社会科学院社会学研究所的合作始于 2016 年。2016 年 9 月 14—18 日，双方签署了《关于首届国际科学大会——社会转型：新丝绸之路国家的家庭、婚姻、青年、中产阶级和创新管理方面的合作和组织协议》。

2017 年 4 月 24—26 日，在敖德萨总领事馆和乌克兰交通科学院南部研究中心的支持下，敖德萨国立海事大学与中国社会科学院社会学研究所举办了"第二届国际科学会议——社会转型：新丝绸之路国家的家庭、婚姻、青年、运输和创新管理"。

2017 年 4 月 25 日，敖德萨国立海事大学学术委员会举办了一次隆重

---

① "Days of Ukrainian Culture in the People's Republic of China", https：//sinologist. com. ua/dni – kultury – ukrayiny – u – kytajskij – narodnij – respublitsi/.

② Shypotilova O. P, Kozhanov A. V., "Pages of the history of cooperation of Odessa National Maritime University with the People's Republic of China", Chinese civilization：traditions and modernity：materials of the XIV International Scientific Conference, November 5, 2020, Kyiv：Helvetica Publishing House, pp. 136 – 139.

的会议，在此次会议上，敖德萨国立海事大学与中国社会科学院社会学研究所签署了一份关于共建"一带一路"社会发展研究科学中心的协议。在社会学研究所副所长赵克斌先生和中国驻敖德萨总领事赵向荣女士的带领下，中国社会科学院社会学研究所代表出席了该科学中心的隆重开幕仪式。①

2018年10月30日，在第三届科学大会"一带一路国家的社会发展：新丝绸之路在乌克兰的发展"的框架内，敖德萨国立海事大学成立了"一带一路"社会发展研究中心办公室，并在两国科学家的参与下，开设了相关课程，并备有关于中国历史、经济、传统和发展战略方面的中国文献。

2017年12月5—8日，"一带一路"社会发展研究科学中心在中国北京组织了首届中乌科技与学术对话——"中国为乌克兰带来的机遇"。敖德萨国立海事大学代表团共有8名成员参会，由该校校长S. V. Rudenko带队。与会各方都作了报告，并就扩大敖德萨国立海事大学与中国社会科学院的合作提出了建议。

2019年，敖德萨国立海事大学举办了中华人民共和国成立70周年摄影展。本次展览为学生、学者和相关人士提供了一个深入了解中国发展历史和成功经验的机会。本次展览由中国驻敖德萨总领馆和中国社会科学院联合举办，旨在展示中国所取得的成就。2019年3月，敖德萨国立海事大学举办了"中国改革开放40周年主题展"。

2019年10月16日，为纪念中华人民共和国成立70周年而举办的"关于中国研究的学生作品大赛"获奖学生名单揭晓。比赛的获胜者被授予敖德萨国立海事大学和KASN证书。获奖证书由敖德萨国立海事大学校长S. V. Rudenko教授、中国社会科学院国际合作局局长王镭教授以及中国社会科学院社会发展战略研究院院长张翼教授颁发。

因此，在"一带一路"框架内的人文交流方面，中国和乌克兰已建

---

① Shypotilova O. P, Kozhanov A. V., "Pages of the history of cooperation of Odessa National Maritime University with the People's Republic of China", Chinese civilization: traditions and modernity: materials of the XIV International Scientific Conference, November 5, 2020, Kyiv: Helvetica Publishing House, pp. 136 – 139.

立了富有成果、成效和前景的合作。所开展的活动包括学生交流、教师实习、举办科学论坛、研讨会和会议，文化日和艺术展等。可以说，乌中两国已建立了友谊的桥梁，从而确保跨文化交流和全球化进程的深化。

参考文献：

Bilorus O. H. , "Globalization and security of development", 2001, Kyiv: KNEU.

"Days of Ukrainian Culture in the People's Republic of China", https://sinologist.com.ua/dni – kultury – ukrayiny – u – kytajskij – narodnij – respublitsi/.

Glovatska S. M. , "Ukraine in the global megaproject 'One Belt, One Road'", China – Ukraine: prospects for academic and business cooperation: materials International, scientific – practical conf, （Odessa, May 27 – 28, 2019）, Odessa, Phoenix, 2019.

Honcharuk A. , "Ukrainian – Chinese strategic partnership at the present stage", 2014, https://sinologist.com.ua/ukrayinsko – kitajske – strategichne – pa.

Kiktenko V. O. , "Reforms and openness as a basis for building socialism with Chinese characteristics", Ukraine – China, 2018, No. 14.

Kiktenko V. O. , "Ukraine in the "One Belt, One Road project": regional and global dimension", 2018, https://sinologist.com.ua/kiktenko – v – o – ukrayina – v – proekti – odyn – poyas – odyn – shlyah – regionalnyj – ta – globalnyj – vymir/.

Kulyntsev Yu. V. , "The Strategy of Development and Silk Road Economic Belt Concept: Integration Potential of Cultural and Humanitarian Cooperation", China in world and regional politics, History and modernity, Issue XXIV: annual edition / comp. , Resp. ed. E. I. Safronova, Moscow.

Liui Yenchzhao, Pekna T. V. , SunVei. , "The Direct investments of Chinese enterprises in Ukraine", *Current economic problems*, 2012, No. 8.

Liu Xiangzhong. , "Social – cultural exchange between China and Ukraine: history and present", 2018, https://sinologist.com.ua/lyu – syanchzhun – sotsialno – kulturnyj – obmin – mizh – kytayem – ta – ukrayinoyu – istoriya – ta – suchasnist/.

Onishchenko A. V., "Ukraine and China: new realities and prospects of foreign economic cooperation in the XXI century", Scientific Bulletin of Uzhgorod University: Series: Economics, Editors: V. P. Mikloda (ed.), M. I. Pityulych, N. M. Gapak and others, Uzhhorod: Uzhhorod National University Publishing House, 2011, Special issue. 33. Part 2.

Popkov V. V., "China: the new format of globalization", China – Ukraine: prospects for academic and business cooperation: materials International, scientific – practical conf (Odessa, May 27 – 28, 2019), Odessa, Phoenix, 2019.

Shypotilova O. P, Kozhanov A. V., "Pages of the history of cooperation of Odessa National Maritime University with the People's Republic of China", Chinese civilization: traditions and modernity: materials of the XIV International Scientific Conference, November 5, 2020, Kyiv: Helvetica Publishing House.

"The G7 will announce an infrastructure project as opposed to China", 2021, https://www.ukrinform.ua/rubric – world/3263705 – g7 – ogolosit – pro – infrastrukturnij – proekt – na – protivagu – kitau – zmi.html.

"一带一路"倡议：中格教育交往三十年回顾及深化

卢雨菁[*]

同样是历史悠久的国家，同样地重视教育，中国和格鲁吉亚在教育领域合作大有潜力可挖。格鲁吉亚的中文教育已经走过了近30年历程，中文学习给格鲁吉亚青少年带来奖学金、留学机会、就业机会等实惠，尤其是孔子学院的建立和发展，为教育交流提供了一个平台。而中文进入格鲁吉亚教育体系，给中小学生提供了选择中文为第二外语的机会，这是两国高层所期盼的教育文化科学等方面通力合作的结果。中国的格鲁吉亚语教育和格鲁吉亚研究也已经在发展。未来教育往来合作应更加深入。

格鲁吉亚虽然国家不大，却有着悠久的历史文化。和中国一样，格鲁吉亚政府和民众也非常重视教育，全国接受教育的人口比例很高。教育方面的政府投资也比较高，如2016年度，格鲁吉亚教育和科学部预算为9.05亿拉里（4.104亿美元），而"格鲁吉亚的教育从6岁到18岁免费。宪法规定教育是免费的。国家免费提供包括教科书和笔记本电脑在内的相关费用"[①]。"格鲁吉亚独立后，教育和科技发展受到政治经济局势的严重干扰，处于非常困难的境地，但改革的进程仍比较快。俄罗斯在

---

[*] 卢雨菁，兰州大学教授，格鲁吉亚第比利斯开放大学孔子学院院长。

[①] Bureau of International Labor Affairs, U. S. Department of Labor, *Findings on the Worst Forms of Child Labor* (2001), 2002.

格鲁吉亚科教领域影响不断缩小，而西方的作用日益扩大。"① 格鲁吉亚人大多都会讲多种语言，除了英语是第一外语，中小学第二外语课程有俄语、土耳其语、德语等，如今还有了 2019 年初计划纳入中小学教育体系的汉语。学生们从幼儿园到高中都在同一所学校；本科普及率很高，像服务员、出租车司机等职业的都上过大学。

中国和格鲁吉亚自 1992 年建交以来，教育文化领域往来从无到有越来越频繁。但是截至目前，教育交流的最大部分还是体现在语言教育方面，尤其是中方在格鲁吉亚的汉语教学，以及由以孔子学院为代表的非营利单位向格鲁吉亚学生提供的各种免费课程还有渠道的奖学金。其他的合作才暂露头角，往来合作有很大潜力可挖掘。

一　格鲁吉亚中文教育的三个阶段

中国和格鲁吉亚的教育往来是在两国建立友好关系，双方不断探索加深合作的前提下。

2011 年 3 月，时任驻格鲁吉亚大使陈建福拜会时任格总统谢瓦尔德纳泽，后者回忆到苏联解体后，格鲁吉亚和中国建立了良好关系。执政期间，他积极推动恢复古丝绸之路的计划。根据这一计划，连接亚洲和欧洲大陆的公路将经过中亚和高加索地区，从而大大减少亚欧大陆间陆路运输的时间。② 正是因为这样的两国关系以及经济发展的需要，两国政治、经济、文化交流频繁，而交流需要语言的支撑，格鲁吉亚政府一直支持汉语教学。早在 2006 年 4 月，时任格鲁吉亚总统米哈伊尔·萨卡什维利应时任中国国家主席胡锦涛的邀请访华时谈道："中国青年是中国的未来，是聪明、杰出而有教养的爱国主义者。中文是 21 世纪的语言，他希望有更多的格鲁吉亚青年人学习中文，加强同中国的交流。"③

---

① 杨恕：《格鲁吉亚教育科技现状》，《东欧中亚研究》1997 年第 5 期。
② "格鲁吉亚前总统'老谢'与中国的那些事儿"，澎湃新闻，2014 年 7 月 7 日，https: //www.thepaper.cn/newsDetail_forward_1254682。
③ 中华人民共和国中央人民政府网，"格鲁吉亚总统访华前夕表示非常重视同中国的关系"，2006 年 4 月 9 日，http: //www.gov.cn/zwjw/2006 - 04/09/content_249291.htm。

中格教育往来要从汉语教学说起。格鲁吉亚的汉语教学与学习开始于世纪更替之际,历经20多年,为格鲁吉亚培养了一批懂汉语、了解中国文化的人才,活跃于格鲁吉亚的教育、旅游、商贸等不同行业,为两国文化、经济出力。

格鲁吉亚的中文教学经历了三个阶段:中文教育在格鲁吉亚的起始;孔子学院的成立扩大了中文教育面;中文进入格鲁吉亚中小学教育体系后的新发展。

(一)亚非学院中文系:中文教育与研究的起始(1992—2007年)

最早在格鲁吉亚教授汉语做汉语研究的机构是第比利斯亚非学院(Tbilisi Institute of Asia and Africa),学院1992年设立中文系,每年招生60—70人,由旅居格鲁吉亚的刘光文老师授课,后来的汉学家大都出自她门下[①],该学院的汉语教学从一开始就得到了中国驻格鲁吉亚大使馆的帮助,使馆联系国内院校每年派口语教师前往亚非学院任教;从1995年起,中文专业的学生有很多机会前往中国留学一年,也有些品学兼优的学生得到资助,在中国攻读硕士学位或者博士学位,这些学生成为格鲁吉亚中文教学和中国文化研究的中坚,曾经的汉语学习者,后来走上汉语教学的讲台,或者从事与汉语与中国人相关的工作,在企业、政府部门、旅游业从事着他们喜爱的工作。

(二)孔子学院的建立:助力语言文化交流(2008—2018年)

从2008年酝酿到2010年正式挂牌,在孔子学院总部的支持下,兰州大学与第比利斯自由大学通力合作建立自由大学孔子学院,格鲁吉亚的中文教育走向新阶段。孔子学院在第比利斯多所大学和中小学开始了中文课程,以满足学生中文学习的需求。随着时间的推移,越来越多的学生加入到中文学习的行列。

2017年11月,第比利斯开放大学孔子课堂挂牌。孔子课堂一如既往

---

① 玛琳娜·吉布拉泽:《格鲁吉亚汉学发展与汉语教学》,《世界汉语教学》2004年第4期。

致力于帮助愿意学习中文的学生学好汉语，了解中国文化，到2019年12月升级为孔子学院①时，孔院在30所中小学教学点以及4所大学教授中文。

中文教学的同时，孔子学院通过丰富多彩的文化活动帮助格鲁吉亚民众了解中国、了解中国文化。一年一度的孔子学院春节联欢会和诸如中秋、端午节文化活动，以及每周六的"相约星期六"，不定期走进不同中小学的"中国文化进校园"活动，都让格鲁吉亚民众零距离接触了中国文化的不同层面。

两所孔子学院各有所长，为格鲁吉亚学生和各行各业学中文，喜欢了解中国文化的各年龄段各阶层人士带去了学习了解的便利。

2020年6月，新疆医科大学和库塔伊西大学合作筹建第三家孔院，相信会和前两所孔院一样，为中格教育、文化交流起到重要作用。

孔子学院志愿者和教师参与教学和文化活动之外，每年都参与或独立研究格鲁吉亚中文教学相关内容，比如"格鲁吉亚汉语教学调查研究""格鲁吉亚中学生汉语学习动机研究""格鲁吉亚中小学汉语课堂管理案例分析"等，这些尝试一方面可以深入了解格鲁吉亚教育情况，另一方面为那里的汉语教学提供可参考借鉴的内容，以研究促进教育。

同样，通过中国奖学金渠道获得机会来中国学习的格鲁吉亚学生，也关注研究两国关系中的某个层面，比如：2016年华东师范大学陆雅晴（Nino Tetunashvili）博士论文《中国与格鲁吉亚关系的现状分析与未来展望》就是其中一例。

（三）中文进入格鲁吉亚教育体系：新机遇　新挑战（2019年至今）

2019年2月，中文纳入格鲁吉亚教育体系，格鲁吉亚教育部宣布，从新学年开始，在格鲁吉亚的中小学校中，中文成为必修的第二外语。家长们现在可以在选修中文和俄语之间做出选择。英文现在是格鲁吉亚的第一外语。俄语则是这个原苏联加盟共和国的第二外语。俄语之后，

---

① 中国一带一路网，"格鲁吉亚第比利斯开放大学孔子学院正式挂牌"，2019年12月22日，https://www.yidaiyilu.gov.cn/xwzx/hwxw/113409.htm。

格鲁吉亚的一些学校也选择教学意大利语、法语和德语。当地的小学生们从一年级开始必须学习英文。从五年级起，开始选择学习第二外语。家长们通常都会选择非欧洲语言的俄语作为第二外语。但最近几年来，非欧洲语言的中文在格鲁吉亚日益受到欢迎。越来越多的家长们呼吁在学校中开设中文课。① 格鲁吉亚政治学者齐塔泽说："孔子学院早就在格鲁吉亚活动，人们过去可以通过孔子学院获得中文教育。格鲁吉亚的一些高等院校也开设了东方学课程研究中国。"之前格鲁吉亚教育部长巴基阿什维利在第比利斯与中国驻格鲁吉亚大使签署了一份备忘录，其中提到在中文教育领域，中国将向格鲁吉亚提供帮助，包括为格鲁吉亚培训中文教师人才。

中文进入教育体系后，依然有很多事情要做，汉语教学之路任重道远。有些格鲁吉亚民众以及小部分从事高等教育或中等教育的教育工作者，对汉语进校园有或多或少的抵触，他们只看到问题的表面，显然不理解中国人民对他们的帮助。

2020 年 1 月，中国涉外教育集团麾下的（格鲁吉亚）中国涉外教育学院隆重举行该学院的开业庆典和剪彩仪式②，广州涉外学院派汉语教师融入到中国涉外教育学院工作，这个学院的成立和运行，标志着除了孔子学院，又多了一种教育合作的模式。

新形势下，当中文教育走进体制内，走进更多校园的时候，一套本土教材被呼唤而出。2020 年 12 月，由第比利斯开放大学孔子学院全体在岗教师编写的《轻松学中文》格汉教材上、下册出版，为广大中小学学生以及初学汉语者带来方便，统一教材、统一教学进度等变为可能，而这套教材的出版，让只懂得格鲁吉亚语的中小学生以及部分格鲁吉亚教师轻松地加入学习汉语的行列。

---

① 观察者网，"中文成格鲁吉亚第二必修外语"，2019 年 2 月 23 日，https://www.guancha.cn/internation/2019_02_23_491150.shtml。

② 搜狐网，"中国涉外教育集团在格鲁吉亚建校 引起该国国会议长和驻华大使的高度关注"，2020 年 1 月 13 日，https://www.sohu.com/a/366439914_100195858。

二 中国的格鲁吉亚语教学和格鲁吉亚研究

相比于格鲁吉亚的中文教育，中国的格鲁吉亚语教育和格鲁吉亚研究要略晚几年，是"一带一路"倡议和中格两国合作协议大背景下才逐步开始的。

2013年9月和10月，中国国家主席习近平在出访中亚和东南亚国家期间，先后提出共建"丝绸之路经济带"和"21世纪海上丝绸之路"的重大倡议，得到国际社会高度关注。各地成功举办了一系列以"一带一路"为主题的国际峰会、论坛、研讨会、博览会，对增进理解、凝聚共识、深化合作发挥了重要作用。截至2021年1月30日，中国与171个国家和国际组织，签署了205份共建"一带一路"合作文件。① 中国与格鲁吉亚相对较早就签署了合作备忘录。

2015年3月9日，中国商务部和格鲁吉亚经济与可持续发展部在京签署关于启动中国—格鲁吉亚自由贸易协定谈判可行性研究的联合声明，商定尽快成立联合专家组，启动该项目。双方同时签署关于加强共建"丝绸之路经济带"合作的备忘录，意在中格经贸合作委员会框架内，共同推进"丝绸之路经济带"建设的经贸合作，全面提升贸易、投资、经济技术合作和基础设施互联互通水平。②

值得一提的是新丝绸之路大学联盟的成立。2015年5月22日，由西安交通大学发起，来自22个国家和地区的近百所大学先后加入成立新丝绸之路大学联盟。该联盟是海内外大学结成的非政府、非营利性的开放性、国际化高等教育合作平台，以"共建教育合作平台，推进区域开放发展"为主题，推动"新丝绸之路经济带"沿线国家和地区大学之间在校际交流、人才培养、科研合作、文化沟通、政策研究、医疗服务等方面的交流与合作，增进青少年之间的了解和友谊，培养具有国际视野的

---

① 中国一带一路网，"已同中国签订共建'一带一路'合作文件的国家一览"，https：//www.yidaiyilu.gov.cn/xwzx/roll/77298.htm。
② 中国一带一路网，"中国与格鲁吉亚签署共建'丝绸之路经济带'合作文件"，2015年3月10日，https：//www.yidaiyilu.gov.cn/xwzx/hwxw/77005.htm。

高素质、复合型人才，服务"新丝绸之路经济带"沿线及欧亚地区的发展建设。截至2018年12月，已有38个国家和地区的151所高校成为新丝绸之路大学联盟成员，形成了遍布世界五大洲的高等教育合作平台，并开展了多元交流合作。①

丝绸之路（敦煌）国际文化博览会2015年10月在敦煌举行又是一个教育合作的范例。来自复旦大学、北京师范大学、兰州大学和俄罗斯乌拉尔国立经济大学、韩国釜庆大学等46所中外高校在甘肃敦煌成立了"一带一路"高校战略联盟，以探索跨国培养与跨境流动的人才培养新机制，培养具有国际视野的高素质人才。46所高校当日达成《敦煌共识》，联合建设"一带一路"高校国际联盟智库。联盟将共同打造"一带一路"高等教育共同体，推动"一带一路"沿线国家和地区大学之间在教育、科技、文化等领域的全面交流与合作，服务"一带一路"沿线国家和地区的经济社会发展。②

在这样的大背景下，格鲁吉亚研究中心的成立以及格鲁吉亚语专业的筹建便水到渠成。2017年6月兰州大学成立了格鲁吉亚研究中心，"组建有教育学、经济学、文学、文化学、语言学、法学等学科领域的专家和学者参加的学术团队"③。其中研究人员发表多篇研究论文，比如车如山、徐旭的《"一带一路"背景下中国与格鲁吉亚高等教育合作的基础与潜力》。

而在遥远的格鲁吉亚，2019年10月，格鲁吉亚理工大学成立了"中国研究中心"，致力于中国方方面面的研究。中心已经召开两次国际会议，探讨中格教育、文化、经济交流中的各种问题。

2016年前，北京大学给俄语专业的学生开设格鲁吉亚语课，那达丽（Natalia Maisuradze）的《速成格鲁吉亚语》教材2016年由北京大学出

---

① 西安交通大学网，丝绸之路大学联盟，2018年12月28日，http://www.xjtu.edu.cn/gjjl/sczldxlm.htm。
② 新浪网，"47所中外高校达成《敦煌共识》成立'一带一路'高校联盟"，2015年10月17日，http://news.sina.com.cn/c/2015-10-17/doc-ifxivsee8519127.shtml。
③ 兰州大学格鲁吉亚研究中心（简介），2018年8月19日，http://grc.lzu.edu.cn/jianjie/info-5000.shtml。

版,成为中国人学习格鲁吉亚语的第一本教材。此前的 2015 年格鲁吉亚语专业获批在北京外国语大学建立①,学制 4 年。

以上机构的成立,专业的筹建,教材的出版,都成为格鲁吉亚语学习和格鲁吉亚研究的垫脚石,逐渐形成一支懂格鲁吉亚语言,了解格鲁吉亚经济和文化的队伍指日可待。

此外,有了孔子学院以后的几年里,在格鲁吉亚的教师、志愿者以及中企员工,都开课学习格鲁吉亚语,在当时当地学习是为了能在生活中使用,部分离开格鲁吉亚回国的还在坚持学习则是出于喜爱。

截至目前,中国懂得格鲁吉亚语、了解格鲁吉亚文化的人太少,用英语或者俄语交流在某种程度上制约甚至妨碍交流的深度,入门级的格鲁吉亚语水平不能助力教育文化交流,也不能为企业提供可用人才,而依赖格鲁吉亚的汉语学生也总是造成力不从心的结果,毕竟文化不同,懂汉语的格鲁吉亚人和懂格鲁吉亚语的中国人思维方式及做事风格迥异。期望不久的将来,格鲁吉亚语专业的学生能够填补这个不足。

三 中格教育交流的多重层面

中国和格鲁吉亚的教育交流呈现多层面多种形式体现。高层互访会谈中提及加强合作是对语言文化交流的引导;两国教育机构、研究机构、文化团体的合作是在探索教育文化的合作共赢模式;前往对方国家读书学习深造的留学生则作为个体呈现教育合作的红利。

首先是从驻在国大使到国家高层对教育往来方面的关注和参与。

2012 年 5 月,由中国驻格鲁吉亚使馆主办,格鲁吉亚孔子学院协办的面向格教育部、2 所大学及 17 所中学校长师生的"汉字的故事"公开课正式开讲。格教育与科技部副部长恰赫纳什维利、格第比利斯自由大学、国际关系大学及格 17 所中学的校领导及师生、中格主流媒体等约

---

① 北京外国语大学网,"我校 8 个非通用语种专业获批成立",2016 年 3 月 2 日,https://news.bfsu.edu.cn/archives/253759。

100人参加。①

"2013年,中格两国关系稳定增长,各领域合作交流势头良好……两国文化和人文交流十分活跃。第比利斯自由大学孔子学院运作良好。5月,成功举办了第十二届'汉语桥'决赛—格鲁吉亚大学生汉语能力竞赛。6月,在格鲁吉亚举行了'格鲁吉亚人眼中的中国'征集文集的颁奖典礼。8月,格鲁吉亚文化日的活动在中国成功举行。此外,中国还在格鲁吉亚举行了杂技表演和'中国格鲁吉亚武术交流'等活动"②。这段文字描述活动,是近年来格中文化交流的一个缩影,而且各项活动常规化越办越好。

2014年2月,时任驻格鲁吉亚大使岳斌应邀前往第比利斯第98公立学校,为该校六年级(1)班40余名学生讲授中国历史文化课。该校校长和近10名老师一同听讲。在45分钟的标准课时里,岳大使通过"博大精深"四个字,讲述了中国古代哲学思想、建筑工艺、诗歌文学、音乐美术、四大发明等丰厚的文化遗产,深刻阐述了中华文化规模宏大、品质精美、内涵丰富、兼容并包的特性,解读了中国历史传统与当代内外政策的联系,宣介了中国倡导的和谐社会和和平外交理念。岳大使还以翔实的数据,介绍了中国改革开放35年来经济社会的腾飞,抒发了对实现中华民族伟大复兴的"中国梦"的憧憬。同年5月14日,驻格鲁吉亚大使岳斌应邀再赴第比利斯第98公立学校,观摩该校举办的中国历史文化公开课。大使说"随着中格关系不断深化,格学生学习汉语必将大有用武之地"。岳大使鼓励学生们增强对中国历史文化和当代发展的兴趣,努力学好汉语,成为中格友好事业接班人。③

2016年5月,格鲁吉亚时任驻华大使大卫·阿普恰乌利接受人民日报记者采访,谈到2017年,中格两国将迎来建交25周年。他表示,"自

---

① 中国新闻网,"格鲁吉亚科大中学校长师生爱上'汉字的故事'",2012年5月17日,https://www.chinanews.com.cn/hwjy/2012/05-17/3896797.shtml.

② 中华人民共和国外交部,https://www.fmprc.gov.cn/mfa_eng/wjb_663304/zzjg_663340/dozys_664276/gjlb_664280/3170_664312/.

③ 中华人民共和国驻格鲁吉亚大使馆,"驻格鲁吉亚大使岳斌赴第比利斯中学授课",2014年2月12日,https://www.fmprc.gov.cn/ce/cege/chn/kxjy/t1127842.htm.

建交以来，格中两国政治互信不断增强，经贸、文化、教育等各领域合作日益深化"。"为了更好地推进'一带一路'实施，他希望，未来格中两国能够继续增进相互了解和加强人文交流，为经贸合作提供支撑和保障。"①

2016年6月，应邀访问格鲁吉亚的时任国务院副总理张高丽在第比利斯会见格鲁吉亚总统马尔格韦拉什维利。他谈到"要扩大人文交流，充分挖掘双方在旅游、文化、教育、科技等领域和地方合作潜力，夯实中格友好的社会民意基础。要在国际和地区事务中继续保持密切沟通与合作"②。

2019年5月，中华人民共和国国务委员兼外交部长王毅访问格鲁吉亚。巴赫塔泽总理表示，"格方高度重视同中国的伙伴关系，中国是格鲁吉亚外交的重要方向，近年来，中格友好合作关系平稳发展，对双边关系特别是格中签署自贸协定后两国合作取得的发展感到满意。格方愿在格大力推广中文，欢迎更多中国企业来格投资兴业，吸引更多中国游客来格旅游。"③

2019年10月，格鲁吉亚驻华大使阿尔赤·卡岚第亚（Archil Kalandia）一行访问北京大学，北京大学副校长田刚表示，北京大学欢迎格鲁吉亚学者、学生来访，北大也开设有格鲁吉亚语公共选修课，有越来越多的中国学生开始对格鲁吉亚这个国家及其古老的语言感兴趣。他期待外国语言与文化、国际关系、公共政策等相关专业能有更多同学前往格鲁吉亚学习，也期待更多的格鲁吉亚学生、学者来北大学习、访问，希望今后可以利用北京大学的学科优势，进一步推进我校与格鲁吉亚高校的广泛交流。卡岚第亚大使表示，"格中两国都是具有悠久历史和独特文化的国家，在人文、教育、医疗等方面有着良好的合作前景，希望在未来能全面深化格鲁吉亚一流高校与北京大学的合作与交流"。他乐意为

---

① 新华网，"建设'一带一路'挖掘合作潜力——访格鲁吉亚驻华大使大卫·阿普恰乌利"，2016年5月16日，http：//www.xinhuanet.com/world/2016-05/16/c_128984637.htm。

② 中国教育信息化网，http：//www.ict.edu.cn/news/gddt/jydt/n20191204_63997.shtml。

③ "王毅部长访问格鲁吉亚，格酒助力'一带一路'"，2019年6月14日，https：//www.winesou.com/news/china_news/140413.html。

北大学生访问格鲁吉亚提供机会，赴格鲁吉亚交流不仅意味着学习语言、文化，还能增强对中欧地区政策、环境等方面的理解，促进学生的全面发展。①

2019年11月，甘肃省教育厅厅长王海燕访问格鲁吉亚，走访了第比利斯公立第21学校和高加索大学，也参观了当时的孔子课堂，她鼓励孔子课堂的中方教师和志愿者要"立足岗位，从生活中的点点滴滴着手，善于发现生活中的美，共同想办法解决一些翻译问题，既要善于讲好中国故事，也要善于讲好格鲁吉亚故事，双向交流，寓教于乐，教学相长，重在培养和保护学生主动交流的积极性，在交流活动中激发学生学习汉语的兴趣"②。

2019年2月19日晚，时任驻格鲁吉亚大使季雁池及夫人在第比利斯为格鲁吉亚汉学家举行的元宵节招待会。"格教育、科学、文化、体育部副部长阿布拉泽，工商会主席齐科瓦尼，前教育部长纳卡希泽，格议会格中议员友好小组主席达涅利亚，'丝绸之路'格中文化中心主席刘光文，格汉学家协会主席吉布拉泽等格政府、议会、教育、媒体等社会各界代表共300余人出席"。这一年度活动几年前已成为传统，新冠肺炎疫情暴发前最近一次汉学家招待会是在2020年1月，由李岩大使主持。招待会给汉学家及汉语教学、格中友好人士提供了非常好的交流机会。

2020年1月13日，时任驻格鲁吉亚大使李岩在使馆会见格新任教育、科学、文化、体育部长齐亨克利，就中格双边关系及教育、科学、文化、体育等领域合作交换意见。李大使表示中方高度重视中格关系发展，愿同格方保持密切沟通与合作，一道推动两国教育、科学、文化、体育领域合作再上新台阶。齐高度评价当前格中教育、人文领域合作成果，表示愿继续支持汉语教学在格发展壮大，推动两国在教育、科学、

---

① 北京大学网，"格鲁吉亚驻华大使访问北京大学"，2019年10月10日，http://www.oir.pku.edu.cn/info/1035/4768.htm。

② 中华人民共和国驻奥地利共和国大使馆，"张高丽访问格鲁吉亚"，2016年6月3日，https://www.mfa.gov.cn/ce/ceat//chn/zgyw/t1371387.htm。

文化、体育等领域深入开展互学互鉴，为双边关系发展增添更多成果。①

其次是两国教学科研人员在对方机构任教或任职。

近年来，中国和格鲁吉亚两国教育机构之间的来往逐渐增多。

2018年11月29日，经山东理工大学校长办公会研究，学校聘任格鲁吉亚国家科学院院士、院长格奥尔基·科维谢塔兹教授，格鲁吉亚国家科学院院士缇娜婷·萨都尼什维里教授为名誉教授。②

2019年12月5日下午，在南京市人民政府外事办公室的大力支持下，南京市第五高级中学迎来了格鲁吉亚中学校长访问团来校交流访问，校党委书记和部门负责人代表热情接待了来访嘉宾。第比利斯公立第98学校和南京五中之间建立了友好关系。③ 而大学之间的友好往来就更多更频繁，如兰州大学与第比利斯开放大学，郑州大学与第比利斯自由大学等。

2020年12月1日，经过一天的大会议程，中国学者、塞浦路斯欧洲大学校长助理、国际工程技术协会（IETI）会士、巴基斯坦工程院院士岳晓光获得多数票通过，于当天晚上收到格鲁吉亚自然科学院院长 Paata J. Kervalishvli 院士的贺信，恭喜他当选格鲁吉亚自然科学院计算机与信息科学学部外籍院士。④

最后是两国留学生，尤其是大量格鲁吉亚青年获得中国方面的奖学金前往中国学习。

一直以来，格鲁吉亚学生学习汉语的热情有增无减。在学习汉语达到一定水平之后，部分学生通过参加汉语考试检验学习成绩。两所孔子学院都设有汉语考试考点，每年举行多场次 HSK、HSKK、YCT 等考试，每次考试平均有30名考生参加。考生中大部分除了检验汉语水平，还为了申请中国（政府、中文教师）奖学金。

---

① 中华人民共和国驻格鲁吉亚大使馆，"驻格鲁吉亚大使李岩会见格教育、科学、文化、体育部长"，2020年1月14日，https：//www.mfa.gov.cn/ce/cege//chn/whjl/t1732201.htm。

② 山东理工大学网，"格鲁吉亚国家科学院两院士受聘学校名誉教授"，2018年11月29日，https：//www.sdut.edu.cn/2018/1130/c4264a254539/page.htm。

③ 南京魅力校园，"交流互动 共促发展—南京市第五高级中学开展外事接待活动"，2019年12月6日，https：//baijiahao.baidu.com/s？id=1652144081922952918&wfr=spider&for=pc。

④ 天津在线，"中国学者岳晓光当选格鲁吉亚自然科学院外籍院士"，2020年12月4日，https：//baijiahao.baidu.com/s？id=1685119974941838459&wfr=spider&for=pc。

近年来，多种奖学金让汉语学习者圆梦中国。2015 年前，中国政府奖学金每年 10 个名额，2016 年起每年 25 名。近五年就有近百名学生得到机会在中国的大学里学习。2020 年起原"孔子学院奖学金"更名为"中文教师奖学金"，并欢迎众多格鲁吉亚学生申请，仅开放孔院在过去 4 年就推荐 40 名学员走进中国大学。还有大学校长奖学金、企业奖学金等，可供格学生选择。

获得资格的学生在中国不同高校学习，或只是一年中文学习，或完成本科或研究生学历。很多学生从中国回去后，从事着与中国、中文相关的事业。无论返回格鲁吉亚还是暂时留在中国，他们成为两国文化教育交流的桥梁。

除了以上的奖学金项目帮助格鲁吉亚学生外，在格中资企业也以支持教育的方式回馈当地。

2019 年 11 月，中国化学向第比利斯公立第 64 学校的师生赠送了电脑、打印机、书包、文具等。同年 12 月，中国电建格鲁吉亚志愿者服务队到访格鲁吉亚第比利斯市 No.202 盲人学校，举行了爱心捐助和志愿者服务活动。校方代表、老师，以及水电十六局环黑海分公司相关代表参加。志愿者服务队将捐赠的盲童专用教具和玩具带到学校，并同老师和孩子们进行了真诚友善的交谈。这次捐赠是之前志愿者活动的后续，校方代表和孩子们对服务队的再次到访表示了热烈的欢迎。中国电建国别代表贺鹏表示：格鲁吉亚是中国"一带一路"倡议沿线国家，中国电建愿意助力格鲁吉亚的发展，以多种形式通过对孩子们力所能及的帮助带给孩子们温暖，在孩子们心中种下爱和希望的种子。[①] 这两个例子是中国企业对格鲁吉亚教育的支持，也体现中国人民对格鲁吉亚学生的关爱。

从留学中国的奖学金支持，到回馈当地的中企赞助，中方对格鲁吉亚的教育提供着帮助，为"一带一路"民心相通助力。

除了教育教学考察和访问，中文教学，民间文化教育往来也日渐频繁。2019 年，"'ERISIONI'歌舞剧团赴华巡演并登上中央电视台中秋节

---

① "中国电建格鲁吉亚代表处举行第比利斯盲校捐赠活动"，2019 年 12 月 16 日，http://www.sinohydro.com/index.php/shzr/1400.html。

晚会舞台,中国徽剧《惊魂记》在格4个城市演出,进一步增进了中格两国人民的相互了解和友谊"①。两国合作往来的潜力从经济到教育、文化,每一次合作都是造福两国和两国人民。

四 结语

30年来,中国和格鲁吉亚高层都努力推动两国教育、科学、文化、体育领域合作。落实到实际,中方为教育、文化交流做出了不懈努力,无论从人力、资金还是从政策(奖学金)方面都对格方提供了极大的帮助。同时,中方也积极筹建格鲁吉亚语专业,建立格鲁吉亚研究中心,实施格鲁吉亚研究。

期待未来几年,两国的教育往来拓展层面,加强学校与学校的合作,商谈师资短期(一学期或一年)交流,探讨互派留学生项目的可行性,而不仅限于单向依靠中方奖学金项目。期待学校之间建立关系之后的相互取经学习一定会给各自带来不一样的收获,期待大学之间学科与学科间的合作给双方带来切实成果。

参考文献:

北京大学网,"格鲁吉亚驻华大使访问北京大学",2019年10月10日,http://www.oir.pku.edu.cn/info/1035/4768.htm。

北京外国语大学网,"我校8个非通用语种专业获批成立",2016年3月2日,https://news.bfsu.edu.cn/archives/253759。

"格鲁吉亚前总统'老谢'与中国的那些事儿",澎湃新闻,2014年7月7日,https://www.thepaper.cn/newsDetail_forward_1254682。

观察者网,"中文成格鲁吉亚第二必修外语",2019年2月23日,https://www.guancha.cn/internation/2019_02_23_491150.shtml。

---

① 中华人民共和国驻格鲁吉亚大使馆,"驻格鲁吉亚大使李岩在格主流媒体发表署名文章《2019年中国经济继续稳步前行,注重高质量发展》",2019年12月20日,https://www.mfa.gov.cn/ce/cege/chn/xwdt/t1726426.htm。

玛琳娜·吉布拉泽：《格鲁吉亚汉学发展与汉语教学》，《世界汉语教学》2004 年第 4 期。

南京魅力校园，"交流互动 共促发展——南京市第五高级中学开展外事接待活动"，2019 年 12 月 6 日，https：//baijiahao.baidu.com/s? id = 1652144081922952918&wfr = spider&for = pc。

山东理工大学网，"格鲁吉亚国家科学院两院士受聘学校名誉教授"，2018 年 11 月 29 日，https：//www.sdut.edu.cn/2018/1130/c4264a254539/page.htm。

搜狐网，"中国涉外教育集团在格鲁吉亚建校 引起该国国会议长和驻华大使的高度关注"，2020 年 1 月 13 日，https：//www.sohu.com/a/366439914_100195858。

天津在线，"中国学者岳晓光当选格鲁吉亚自然科学院外籍院士"，2020 年 12 月 4 日，https：//baijiahao.baidu.com/s? id = 1685119974941838459&wfr = spider&for = pc。

"王毅部长访问格鲁吉亚，格酒助力'一带一路'"，2019 年 6 月 14 日，https：//www.winesou.com/news/china_news/140413.html。

西安交通大学网，丝绸之路大学联盟，2018 年 12 月 28 日，http：//www.xjtu.edu.cn/gjjl/sczldxlm.htm。

新华网，"建设'一带一路'挖掘合作潜力——访格鲁吉亚驻华大使大卫·阿普恰乌利"，2016 年 5 月 16 日，http：//www.xinhuanet.com/world/2016 - 05/16/c_128984637.htm。

新浪网，"47 所中外高校达成《敦煌共识》成立'一带一路'高校联盟"，2015 年 10 月 17 日，http：//news.sina.com.cn/c/2015 - 10 - 17/doc - ifxivsee8519127.shtml。

杨恕：《格鲁吉亚教育科技现状》，《东欧中亚研究》1997 年第 5 期。

"中国电建格鲁吉亚代表处举行第比利斯盲校捐赠活动"，2019 年 12 月 16 日，http：//www.sinohydro.com/index.php/shzr/1400.html。

中国教育信息化网，http：//www.ict.edu.cn/news/gddt/jydt/n20191204_63997.shtml。

中国新闻网，"格鲁吉亚科大中学校长师生爱上'汉字的故事'"，

2012 年 5 月 17 日，https：//www.chinanews.com.cn/hwjy/2012/05-17/3896797.shtml。

中国一带一路网，"格鲁吉亚第比利斯开放大学孔子学院正式挂牌"，2019 年 12 月 22 日，https：//www.yidaiyilu.gov.cn/xwzx/hwxw/113409.htm。

中国一带一路网，"已同中国签订共建'一带一路'合作文件的国家一览"，https：//www.yidaiyilu.gov.cn/xwzx/roll/77298.htm。

中国一带一路网，"中国与格鲁吉亚签署共建'丝绸之路经济带'合作文件"，2015 年 3 月 10 日，https：//www.yidaiyilu.gov.cn/xwzx/hwxw/77005.htm。

中华人民共和国外交部，https：//www.fmprc.gov.cn/mfa_eng/wjb_663304/zzjg_663340/dozys_664276/gjlb_664280/3170_664312/。

中华人民共和国中央人民政府网，"格鲁吉亚总统访华前夕表示非常重视同中国的关系"，2006 年 4 月 9 日，http：//www.gov.cn/zwjw/2006-04/09/content_249291.htm。

中华人民共和国驻奥地利共和国大使馆，"张高丽访问格鲁吉亚"，2016 年 6 月 3 日，https：//www.mfa.gov.cn/ce/ceat//chn/zgyw/t1371387.htm。

中华人民共和国驻格鲁吉亚大使馆，"驻格鲁吉亚大使李岩会见格教育、科学、文化、体育部长"，2020 年 1 月 14 日，https：//www.mfa.gov.cn/ce/cege//chn/whjl/t1732201.htm。

中华人民共和国驻格鲁吉亚大使馆，"驻格鲁吉亚大使李岩在格主流媒体发表署名文章《2019 年中国经济继续稳步前行，注重高质量发展》"，2019 年 12 月 20 日，https：//www.mfa.gov.cn/ce/cege//chn/xwdt/t1726426.htm。

中华人民共和国驻格鲁吉亚大使馆，"驻格鲁吉亚大使岳斌赴第比利斯中学授课"，2014 年 2 月 12 日，https：//www.fmprc.gov.cn/ce/cege/chn/kxjy/t1127842.htm。

兰州大学格鲁吉亚研究中心（简介），2018 年 8 月 19 日，http：//grc.lzu.edu.cn/jianjie/info-5000.shtml。

Bureau of International Labor Affairs, U. S. Department of Labor, *Findings on the Worst Forms of Child Labor* (*2001*), 2002.

"一带一路"倡议：深化中格经济合作

Tamar Patashuri*

格鲁吉亚与中国的经济关系在过去几年中特别活跃，包括两国之间的直接贸易关系，以及中国对格鲁吉亚经济的直接投资。格鲁吉亚地处"一带一路"倡议下的中亚—西亚经济走廊内，该走廊为格鲁吉亚的经济发展创造了新的重要途径。格鲁吉亚可以在丝绸之路经济带（SREB）项目中发挥经济枢纽的作用，因为它已分别与欧盟和中国签订了自由贸易协定。中国明确表达了扩大其国际经济合作的意向，包括与格鲁吉亚的联系。

一 "一带一路"倡议和格鲁吉亚的角色

2013年，中国国家主席习近平提出了"一带一路"倡议①，这可以说是迄今为止，一个最雄心勃勃的外交政策举措。"一带一路"倡议将影响亚非欧等地区的60多个国家和40多亿人口。② 根据中国的官方声明，"一带一路"是参与国家实现相互理解和相互信任，从而实现双赢合作、

---

* Tamar Patashuri，格鲁吉亚国立大学讲师。
① 为避免混淆，尽管在其他文献中该倡议被表述为"新丝绸之路"（NSR）或"一带一路"（OBOR），本文将使用其最常见的称法"'一带一路'倡议"（BRI）。
② Swaine, M. D., "Chinese Views and Commentary on the 'One Belt, One Road'", China Leadership Monitor, Hoover Institution, 2015, No. 47.

繁荣、和平和友好的途径。①

中国国家主席习近平在 2013 年提出的"一带一路"倡议包括两部分："丝绸之路经济带"和"21 世纪海上丝绸之路"。丝绸之路经济带有三条连接中国的线路：经中亚到达欧洲，经西亚到达波斯湾和地中海，以及经南亚到达印度洋，而 21 世纪海上丝绸之路旨在建立地区水道之间的连接。

丝绸之路经济带是一个由公路、铁路和管道组成的陆上网络，与古老的丝绸之路贸易路线大致重叠，并通过欧亚大陆桥将中国东海岸与欧洲连接起来。② 丝绸之路经济带将从欧亚大陆桥分支出 5 条区域走廊：中蒙俄经济走廊、中亚—西亚经济走廊、中南半岛经济走廊、中巴经济走廊以及孟中印缅经济走廊。③ 应该指出的是，格鲁吉亚走廊（以及阿塞拜疆走廊）位于中亚—西亚经济走廊内。④

随着战略职能的不断扩大，格鲁吉亚正成为一个具有巨大潜力的通往欧洲和亚洲的门户。

"一带一路"倡议与其说是一系列定义明确的项目，倒不如说是一种愿景。一些学者认为，"一带一路"倡议显示了中国日益增长的在全球舞台重新自我定位的雄心，并认为这是中国"走出去"政策的延续。"一带一路"倡议包括两个部分："一带"，也被称为"丝绸之路经济带"（SREB），该经济带旨在建设通过中亚、俄罗斯和南高加索把中国和欧洲相连的铁路和公路基础设施；以及"一路"，即"21 世纪海上丝绸之路"，它从中国开始，一路经过东南亚、印度洋、波斯湾和地中海到达非

---

① National Development and Reform Commission, Vision and Actions on Jointly Building Silk Road Economic Belt and 21st – Century Maritime Silk Road, 2015, http://en.ndrc.gov.cn/newsrelease/201503/t20150330_669367.html.

② National Development and Reform Commission, Vision and Actions on Jointly Building the Silk Road Economic Belt and 21st Century Maritime Silk Road, 2015, http://www.fmprc.gov.cn/mfa_eng/zxxx_662805/t1249618.shtml.

③ Su G., "The Belt and Road Initiative in Global Perspectives", *China International Studies*, 2016, No. 57.

④ Van Dijk M. P., Martens P., The Silk Road and Chinese Interests in Central Asia and the Caucasus: The Case of Georgia, Maastricht School of Management Working Paper, 2016, August, https://www.msm.nl/resources/uploads/2016/09/MSM – WP2016 – 12 – 1.pdf.

洲，并最终到达欧洲。"一带一路"倡议最初被视为一项国内发展战略，旨在改善互联互通并促进中国西部欠发达省份的发展。①

"一带一路"倡议逐渐得到了全球认可，并成为21世纪最具全球影响的倡议之一。该倡议不仅仅局限于解决中国的国内挑战，还有望重塑全球贸易格局，并将重心从西方转移至东方。②

"一带一路"共有6条贸易走廊，其中一些已经开始运行，一些仍在建造之中，所以还无法列出所有可能的路线。所预期的"中国—中亚—西亚"贸易走廊覆盖多个国家，可能包括连接中国、哈萨克斯坦、阿塞拜疆、格鲁吉亚和土耳其，以及最终到达欧洲的欧洲—高加索—亚洲国际运输走廊（TRACECA）。该走廊为格鲁吉亚提供了大量的充分利用其战略位置和友好商业环境的机会。格鲁吉亚已经表达了希望成为"一带一路"沿线有价值的参与者的愿望，并在2015年主办了由中国政府共同发起的以丝绸之路经济带为主题的第比利斯丝绸之路论坛，这意味着格鲁吉亚正在成为"一带一路"倡议的重要合作伙伴。③ 作为连接亚洲和欧洲的关键节点，南高加索地区对中国越来越有吸引力，这体现中国在该地区日益频繁的经济活动。例如，截至2017年，中国已成为格鲁吉亚第三大贸易伙伴，双边贸易总额超过4亿美元，而在2002年，这一数字仅为1000万美元。此外，在同一年，中国还与格鲁吉亚签订了一项自由贸易协定（FTA），以进一步刺激双边贸易。在2015年成功举办第比利斯丝绸之路论坛的基础上，格鲁吉亚于2017年11月举办了第二届以"一带一路"倡议为主题的重大活动——第比利斯"一带一路"论坛。

尽管中格双方都有加强"一带一路"合作的政治意愿和共同期望，但双方仍面临一些障碍。除需进行硬基础设施现代化建设外，软基础设施工具的缺乏也带来了一系列挑战。例如，在检验从中国新疆维吾尔自治区一路穿越哈萨克斯坦和阿塞拜疆到达格鲁吉亚波蒂港的铁路的有效

---

① Szczudlik‑Tatar, J., "China's New Silk Road Diplomacy", Policy Paper, 2013.

② Frankopan, P., The silk roads: a new history of the world, Bloomsbury, London Oxford New York New Delhi Sydney, 2015.

③ Pantucci, R., Lain, S., "Silk Road: China's Project Could Transfrom Eurasia", EU Observer, 2015, https://euobserver.com/eu‑china/130762.

性时，发现于 2015 年 1 月 29 日在中国装载的货物抵达格鲁吉亚的时间为 2015 年 2 月 6 日。分析显示，约有三分之一的运输时间浪费在繁文缛节的手续方面。① 此外，穿越格鲁吉亚的走廊（TRACECA）也面临来自其他将中国腹地与欧洲相连的主要走廊（横贯西伯利亚和中哈萨克斯坦）的竞争。新开通的巴库—第比利斯—卡尔斯铁路可被看作是 TRACECA 的一个增值方面，但为了使其更好地发挥作用，还需要进行大量的工作，特别是在开发软基础设施工具方面。此外，安纳克利亚深海港口目前正处于建设的早期阶段，这意味着格鲁吉亚和走廊总体上能为市场上主要承运商提供的服务很少。②

令人鼓舞的是，格鲁吉亚有非常友好的商业环境，且在经商和经济自由方面，一直受到世界领先的国际组织的好评。该国具有稳定、友好的商业环境，腐败率低，且有着以增长为导向的税收体系和自由贸易政策。因此，格鲁吉亚可以利用这些优势来吸引更多的外国投资，同时在国内创造更多的附加价值。

格鲁吉亚最初并不是"一带一路"的成员，但后来逐渐成为中国宝贵的、值得信赖的合作伙伴。尽管格鲁吉亚的经济规模小，自然资源匮乏，但在改善商业环境方面，已取得了令人惊叹的进展，并被视为廉洁的投资目的地和"一带一路"倡议的战略要地。因此对中国来说，格鲁吉亚是一个有吸引力的合作伙伴。③

此外，作为提高国家整体竞争力的努力的一部分，格鲁吉亚还制定了一项关于改善落后基础设施和加强知识和技术转让以提高人力资本的计划。④

在世界银行 2020 年营商环境排名中，格鲁吉亚在 190 个国家中排名

---

① Grey, E., "Can the Trans - Caspian Route deliver the next freight revolution?" Features, 2015.
② M. Zabakhidze, R. Beradze, Georgia as a Transit Hub and its Increasing Potential in the Implementation of the Belt and Road Initiative, 2017.
③ Georgian National Investment Agency, Investment Climate and Opportunities in Georgia, Tbilisi, 2016.
④ Government of Georgia, Social-economic Development Strategy of Georgia "GEORGIA 2020", 2013.

第七位。

格鲁吉亚经济部长 Natia Turnava 表示，83.7 分是格鲁吉亚的"历史最高分"。她说，"格鲁吉亚在营商环境方面仍然处于区域领先地位，在欧洲和中亚 23 个国家中排名第一"。《营商环境报告》涵盖了 2018 年 5 月至 2019 年 5 月期间实施的 294 项监管体制改革。世界银行表示，全球有 115 个经济体为营商提供了更友好的环境。世界银行提出，《营商环境报告》提供了"客观衡量 190 个经济体以及选定的地方级和区域级城市的商业条例及其执行情况的标准"。

营商环境排名始于 2002 年，以国内中小企业为对象，主要衡量在其生命周期内所适用的商业条例。

二 产业政策/投资激励

格鲁吉亚政府已制定了多项工具，来支持对该国经济的投资。JSC 合伙基金是一项国有投资基金，成立于 2011 年。该基金的成员为格鲁吉亚交通、能源和基础设施领域的最大国有企业。该基金的主要目标是通过为处于发展初期的项目提供联合融资（股权、夹层融资等），来促进格鲁吉亚的国内外投资，特别是对旅游业、制造业、能源和农业的投资。

2013 年，政府成立了格鲁吉亚共同投资基金（GCF），来促进国内外投资。据政府称，GCF 是一项私募投资基金，资产为 60 亿美元，旨在通过私募股权结构，为投资者提供投资格鲁吉亚发展最快的行业和部门的独特机会。

"在格鲁吉亚生产"项目是政府为外国投资提供联合融资的另一个渠道，以鼓励投资者在格鲁吉亚建立有限责任公司。该项目旨在发展和支持创业，鼓励创建新企业，以及增强该国的出口潜力和吸引外商投资。在经济和可持续发展部创业发展局、国家财产局和格鲁吉亚技术和创新局的协调下，该项目为创业者提供融资和房地产以及技术援助。

国家财产局负责实体基础设施转让，即根据一定的投资义务条款将政府拥有的房地产免费转让给创业者。

低廉的劳动力成本是格鲁吉亚吸引外国投资的原因之一。格鲁吉亚作为连接亚洲和欧洲的区域交通枢纽的地位也越来越得到认可。格鲁吉亚的自由贸易制度为公司向国外市场出口在格鲁吉亚生产的产品提供了便利。在某些情况下，外国投资者可通过生产针对这些市场的产品而从这些协定中获益。

2018年10月，格鲁吉亚总理引入了电子居住证的概念，从而允许在格鲁吉亚没有实体居住的34个国家的公民以电子方式注册公司并开设银行账户。

（一）外贸区/自由港/贸易便利化

2007年6月，格鲁吉亚议会通过了《自由工业区法》，对自由工业区/经济区的形式和功能进行了规定。这些区域内的金融业务可以以任何一种货币进行。自由工业区内的外国公司可免缴利润税、财产税和增值税。目前，格鲁吉亚有四个自由工业区。

波蒂自由工业区（FIZ）：这是高加索地区的第一个自由工业区，成立于2008年。该工业区最初由总部位于阿联酋的RAK投资局（Rakia）开发，但在2017年，中国华信能源有限公司购买了其75%的股份，剩余25%的股份由格鲁吉亚政府持有。波蒂自由工业区占地300公顷，因靠近波蒂海港而受益。

埃及Fresh Electric公司位于库塔伊西，占地27公顷。该公司在2009年建造了一家厨房电器工厂。该公司已承诺在该区内建造十几家纺织、陶瓷和家电工厂，并宣布其计划投资20多亿美元。

2015年，总部位于中国乌鲁木齐的中国民营企业"华凌集团"在库塔伊西开发了另一个自由工业区。该工业区占地36公顷，主要经营木材、家具、石材、建材、药品、汽车零部件、电动汽车和饮料等。

位于第比利斯的第比利斯自由工业区占地17公顷，并被分成28个地块。该工业区可通往主要货物运输公路、第比利斯国际机场（30公里）和第比利斯市中心（17公里）。

（二）腐败

格鲁吉亚制定有惩治腐败的法律、法规和惩罚措施。根据《刑法》

第332—342条，格鲁吉亚将贿赂定为刑事犯罪。高级政府官员必须提交财务披露表（可在网上查找到该表格）。格鲁吉亚法律规定，如果政府官员被指控犯有腐败相关罪行，其未登记资产将被民事没收。收受贿赂的刑罚最低为6年监禁，并可视具体情况，延长至15年。对行贿的处罚包括罚款和/或至少两年监禁。情节严重的，如为实施违法行为而行贿，将处以4年以上7年以下监禁。根据《刑法》第332条和第333条，公务员滥用职权和越权属于犯罪行为，最高可判处8年监禁。公职人员的定义包括外国公职人员以及国际组织和法院的雇员。贿赂等白领犯罪属于检察官办公室的调查权限范围。

格鲁吉亚不是经合组织的《禁止在国际商业交易中贿赂外国公职人员公约》的签署国，但格鲁吉亚已经正式签署了《联合国反腐败公约》。格鲁吉亚与国家反腐败集团（GRECO）和经合组织的转型经济体反腐败网络（ACN）开展合作。

在2016年6月对格鲁吉亚进行评估后，经合组织于2016年9月发布了一份报告，提出格鲁吉亚在消除公共行政领域的小腐败方面取得了显著进展，现在应重点打击高层和复杂腐败行为。报告赞扬了格鲁吉亚的反腐败战略和行动计划执行监测和评估机制，并赞扬了其在这一进程中充分发挥民间团体的作用。报告还对格鲁吉亚通过一项新的《公务员制度法》表示欢迎，并建议其尽快通过其他立法，来推动公务员制度改革。报告指出，应加强对公务员事务局和国家实体中人力资源单位的管理，以确保实施所需的改革。报告强调，格鲁吉亚在调查腐败犯罪和使用现代手段没收犯罪收益方面有着不俗的表现。报告建议格鲁吉亚加强公司责任的履行以及对外国贿赂的调查，以纠正地方政府官员对腐败的错误认知。自2003年以来，格鲁吉亚在透明国际（TI）的腐败感知指数（CPI）报告中的排名显著提高。

在透明国际2019年腐败感知指数报告中，格鲁吉亚在180个国家中排名第44位（与哥斯达黎加、捷克共和国和拉脱维亚并列）。

虽然格鲁吉亚成功地打击了可见的、低级别的腐败，但仍然很容易发生透明国际所称的"精英"腐败：高级官员利用法律漏洞来牟取个人财富、地位或报偿。尽管此类证据大多是道听途说，但此种形式的腐败，或对其存在的看法，有可能会削弱公众和投资者对格鲁吉亚机构和投资环境的信心。因缺少明确的法律和道德标准，仍有可能在政府采购过程、公共行政实践和司法系统中存在腐败问题。①

（三）发展战略

目前，格鲁吉亚根据两份指导性战略文件来应对经济挑战。一份是2012年宣布的一项社会经济发展战略——"格鲁吉亚2020"，该文件为大多数经济部门在2020年之前实现长期增长提供了重要指引。该文件重点关注三个主要领域：提高私营部门的竞争力、开发人力资本和改善融资渠道。最近，在2016年，格鲁吉亚宣布了一项"四点计划"，该计划重点关注四个支柱，其中之一是经济发展。这两份文件都强调，必须进行基础设施现代化，这是格鲁吉亚成为交通枢纽和开启贸易机会的一个主要先决条件。此外，两份文件都提出，建设阿纳卡利亚深海港、发展东—西运输公路和巴库—第比利斯—卡尔斯铁路是实现这些目标的关键项目。格鲁吉亚是一个开放的经济体，并已签署了多项重要的贸易协定，包括最近与中国签署的自贸协定。此外，格鲁吉亚正在实施深度综合自由贸易区（DCFTA），以促进格鲁吉亚产品进入欧盟统一市场，从而实现出口多元化。然而，这是一个长期的过程，这些协定所产生的成果不会在短期内全部实现。

根据格鲁吉亚国家统计局2021年的数据，除欧盟外，中国是格鲁吉亚的第三大出口目的地，占格鲁吉亚出口总额的10.9%。中国也是格鲁吉亚的第三大投资国。据报道，中国的投资对象主要为农业、银行、电信、基础设施、酒店和轻工业。自2007年以来，中国华凌集团已在格鲁吉亚投资约5亿美元，其中一半资金用于投资自由经济区。②

根据格鲁吉亚国家统计局于1月20日发布的初步数据，在2020年，格鲁吉亚外贸总额为113亿美元，同比下降14.8%。

格鲁吉亚出口总额同比下降12%至33亿美元；进口总额同比下降

---

① STOPfake. gov, 2019, https：//www. stopfakes. gov/article？id = Georgia – Corruption.
② Tskhovrebova, A., Silk Road of Chinese Investment, 2016, pp. 60 – 65.

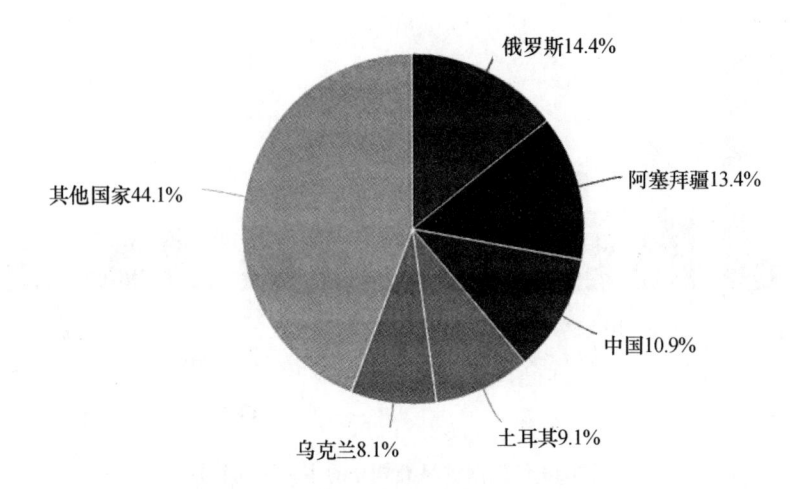

图 1　主要贸易伙伴在 2021 年 1—2 月总出口贸易额中所占的比重

资料来源：National Statistics Office of Georgia, https://www.geostat.ge/en/modules/categories/637/export.

15.9%至 80 亿美元。贸易逆差为 47 亿美元。

格鲁吉亚对欧盟成员国的出口占总出口额的 21.5%，即 7.185 亿美元，同比下降 13%。从欧盟的进口为 19 亿美元，占全年进口总额的 24.0%，较 2019 年下降了 17.2%。

格鲁吉亚对独联体国家的出口同比下降 24.5%至 15 亿美元（占出口总额的 45.2%），进口同比下降 1.8%至 23 亿美元（占进口总额的 29.9%）。①

中国以 4.763 亿美元的出口额位居格鲁吉亚第一大贸易伙伴，其次是阿塞拜疆、俄罗斯、保加利亚和乌克兰，出口额分别为 4.413 亿美元、4.41 亿美元、3.124 亿美元和 2.174 亿美元。

在进口方面，土耳其、俄罗斯、中国、美国和阿塞拜疆是格鲁吉亚最大的贸易伙伴，进口额分别为 14 亿美元、8.872 亿美元、7.087 亿美元、5.409 亿美元和 4.932 亿美元。

---

① Georgia's Foreign Trade in 2020, https://civil.ge/archives/391924.

(百万美元)

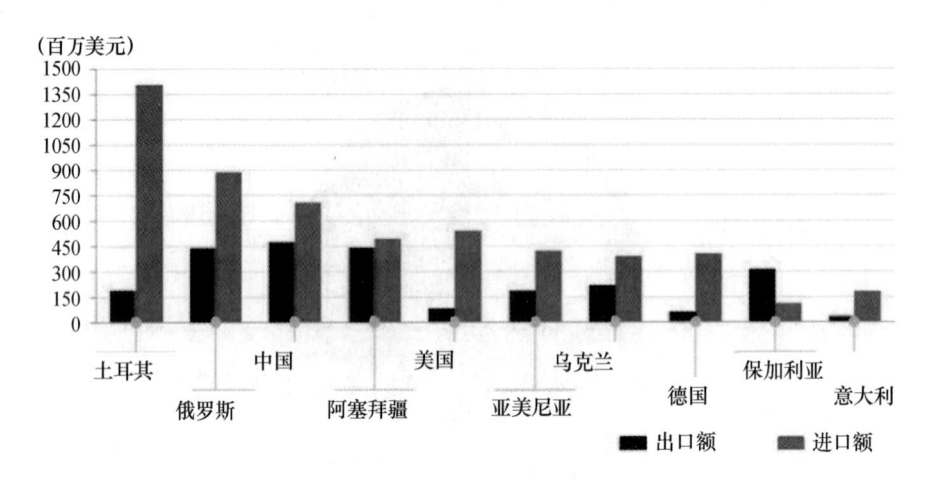

图2　2020年根据贸易额划分的主要贸易伙伴

资料来源：Georgia's Foreign Trade in 2020, https://civil.ge/Archives/391924.

在格鲁吉亚的外贸出口商品中，铜矿石和精矿排名第一，总额为7.294亿美元，其次是汽车转口——4.041亿美元；铁合金——2.473亿美元；葡萄酒——2.103亿美元；烈酒——1.322亿美元；矿泉水——1.166亿美元；药品——9910万美元；黄金——9760万美元；坚果——9400万美元；贵金属矿石及精矿——9000万美元；其他商品——11亿美元。

在格鲁吉亚的外贸进口商品中，汽车位列首位，总额为7.595亿美元，其次是铜矿和精矿——5.335亿美元；石油和石油油料——4.985亿美元；药品——3.271亿美元；石油天然气——2.946亿美元；手机——1.647亿美元；小麦——1.08亿美元；香烟——8890万美元；贵金属矿石及精矿——7710万美元；运输货物的机动车辆——7200万美元；其他商品——51亿美元。

(四) 参与"一带一路"倡议

在2015年，发生了两件令人瞩目的大事，这两件大事将格鲁吉亚和中国之间的合作提升到一个新的水平。首先，格鲁吉亚成为亚投行的第45个成员国，并主办了亚投行第六次首席谈判代表会议，从而奠定了其作为亚投行成员的地位。其次，在同年晚些时候，第比利斯主办了丝绸之路论坛。格鲁吉亚总理在2015年的论坛上提出要在"一带一路"倡议下建立4个项目：

1. 在黑海安纳克利亚新建一个深水港，该港口应能每年处理1亿吨货物，并能够接收大型巴拿马型船舶。

2. 改善格鲁吉亚的铁路网，以提高铁路速度，并使运输能力增至三倍。

3. 建设巴库—第比利斯—卡尔斯铁路（分别在阿塞拜疆、格鲁吉亚和土耳其），使从亚洲到欧洲的集装箱、货物和旅客运输速度提高45%。

4. 通过与世界银行、亚洲开发银行和其他捐助方合作，扩建格鲁吉亚的主要公路运输路线——东—西高速公路。

巴库—第比利斯—卡尔斯铁路已于2017年10月通车，其他项目正在建设之中。

2017年11月，第比利斯举办了"第比利斯'一带一路'论坛"。该论坛的官方网站称，论坛"旨在为政府和私营部门高层提供进行两年一次对话的平台"。来自50多个国家的约2000名代表参加了该论坛，包括摩尔多瓦和乌克兰两国的总理、中国商务部副部长和国际金融机构代表等。在为期两天的密集小组讨论中，格鲁吉亚表达了更强烈的成为连接欧洲和中国的交通枢纽的意向。在此次活动中，格鲁吉亚与中国签署了多项重要协定，如两国间关于发展经济区和创业能力的谅解备忘。JSC伙伴基金也签订了多份谅解备忘录，包括为协助推动工业化进程而与中国赛鼎工程有限公司签署的一份谅解备忘录。2017年5月14日在北京举行的"一带一路"国际合作高峰论坛上，中国华信能源有限公司与格鲁吉亚政府签署了两项重要的合作协议：《关于共同设立格鲁吉亚开发银行的谅解备忘录》和《关于共同设立格鲁吉亚国家建设基金的战略合作框架协议》。这些文件由格鲁吉亚第一副总理兼经济和可持续发展部部长Dimitri Kumsishvili和JSC伙伴基金首席执行官David Saganelidze签署。这些协议的总体目标是进一步推进中国华信与格鲁吉亚的战略合作，并推进"丝绸之路共同市场区"的建设，从而加快"一带一路"创新贸易模式的发展。此外，这些协议还表明，中国华信将与格鲁吉亚政府共同设立格鲁吉亚开发银行。该银行将由中国华信控股和经营，且为促进双边经济金融合作，业务重点将放在以人民币计价的金融服务和跨境人民币结算服务上。

三　中国与欧盟之间的贸易

中国崛起最显著的经济特征是其巨大的贸易额，特别是自 2000 年以来对全球市场的商品出口额。中国出口的成功已对欧盟产生了重大影响。随着中国技术水平的提高，并开始向欧盟提供更先进的产品，从而与欧盟公司展开竞争，这种影响变得更加显著。

自 20 世纪 70 年代中欧外交关系正常化以来，中国积极加强与欧盟的贸易关系。早在中国于 2001 年加入世界贸易组织（WTO）之前，中国与欧盟国家的贸易就已出现大幅增长。例如，在 1980 年，德国从中国进口的商品总额仅为 19 亿美元，但在随后的 20 年中，进口总额迅速增长至 169 亿美元。

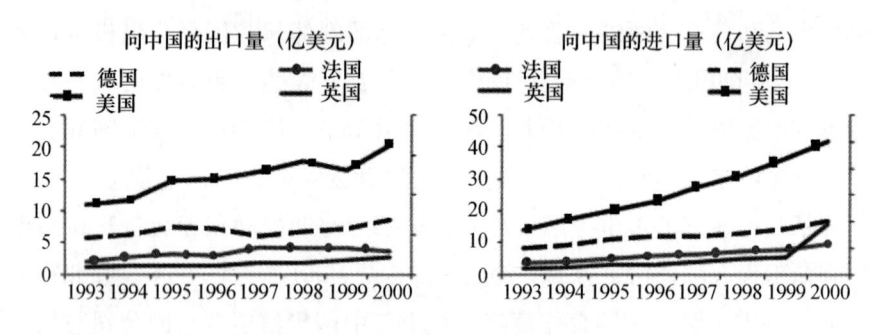

图 3　中国与欧盟国家的贸易情况

资料来源：法国外贸银行，联合国商品贸易统计数据库。

中国在 20 世纪 90 年代的发展有着非常重要的意义，因为它表明了中国在 20 世纪末融入全球经济的决心。虽然这一时期早于中国加入 WTO 的时间，且曾在是否授予中国 WTO 成员国地位方面存在争议，但 20 世纪 90 年代的全球经济环境具有包容性。在每年进行报批的前提下，欧盟和美国都已给予中国最惠国关税税率。

因此,加入WTO给中国带来了一个更加确定的国际环境。关税不确定性的降低,增强了中国制造企业的信心,使他们能够扩大国际合作并提高出口能力。此后,中国商品在欧盟国内市场的份额有了显著增长。2018年,欧盟对中国的贸易总额(出口加进口)约占欧盟对外贸易总额的15%。[1]

四 格鲁吉亚经济的前景

在过去10年中,中国和格鲁吉亚经济联系进一步加强,两国贸易关系进一步深化,且中国对格鲁吉亚经济进行了大量的直接投资。

现在,"一带一路"倡议为格鲁吉亚这个中国和欧洲之间的潜在交通枢纽提供了进一步加强中欧关系的机会。穿越格鲁吉亚的贸易走廊可促进中国和欧洲之间通过铁路进行的贸易,从而为格鲁吉亚带来利益,但如果格鲁吉亚分别与中国和欧洲建立贸易关系,则可以获得更多利益。简而言之,格鲁吉亚不仅仅充当一个过境国家的角色。

在此方面,格鲁吉亚具有以下四个对"一带一路"有吸引力的特点:(1)良好的营商环境——经济增长快,腐败率低,增长友好型税收政策;(2)自由跨境贸易——已与中国签订了自由贸易协定,并与欧盟签订了深度综合自由贸易区协定等;(3)地理位置优越——黑海、陆路与土耳其相连;(4)年轻、技术熟练、价格有竞争力的劳动力。

因此,格鲁吉亚可为中国提供一个更有效的与欧洲开展贸易的平台。然而,要使这个平台具有竞争力,还需要解决一些错综复杂的问题。格鲁吉亚在此方面的成功将在很大程度上取决于其是否可实现硬软基础设施的协调发展,以及是否可充分利用连接土耳其和安纳克利亚深海港的巴库—第比利斯—卡尔斯铁路。因此,"一带一路"倡议与格鲁吉亚经济

---

[1] EU – China trade and investment relations in challenging times, Trade between China and the European Union, https://www.europarl.europa.eu/RegData/etudes/STUD/2020/603492/EXPO_STU (2020) 603492_EN.pdf.

发展轨迹的融合与基础设施建设密切相关。与此同时，格鲁吉亚可利用其贸易协定和商业环境的优势，发展为南高加索地区和全世界的重要交通枢纽。

尽管前景令人鼓舞，但在过去十年中，格鲁吉亚过境量大幅下降，这对格鲁吉亚想要成为区域枢纽来说是一项重大挑战。在2017年1月至8月期间，格鲁吉亚的过境量较2016年同期减少了80万吨。自2012年以来，过境量每年都呈下降趋势。过境运输量下降的一个重要因素是穿越该国的TRACECA走廊的竞争力较低。虽然阿塞拜疆和土耳其正在改善其基础设施，并成为其各自区域内的交通枢纽，但经由格鲁吉亚的运输量仍在不断下降。这意味着仅仅升级硬基础设施并不能将格鲁吉亚转变为一个交通枢纽。①

然而，从积极的一面来看，哈萨克斯坦副总理Erbolat Dossaev在与世界银行总部举办的"'一带一路'倡议：建立亚洲、欧洲和全世界的联系专题讨论会"上的演讲中谈到了从中国到欧洲的"最短路径"，并指出了巴库—第比利斯—卡尔斯项目的重要性，同时声称该项目为到达地中海开辟了新的可能性。这条全长826公里的铁路项目被称为"丝绸铁路"。该项目于2017年10月正式开通，年客运能力为100万人次，货运能力为650万吨。至2034年，其年客运能力有望达到300万人次，货运能力有望达到1700万吨。②

虽然巴库—第比利斯—卡尔斯铁路已投入运营，且其重要性受到广泛认可，但TRACECA所遇到的常见问题也将会影响这条新开通的铁路路线。

从长远来看，安纳克利亚深海港可以提升格鲁吉亚作为运输枢纽的整体竞争力。据安纳克利亚开发财团称，第一阶段的建设将于2017年12月20日开始。在完成整个项目后，该海港将可容纳90万个集装箱，并可

---

① Commersant. ge, Georgia has not Become a Transit Hub for the Region, 2017.
② Turp, C., "Azerbaijan, Georgia, Turkey launch new 'Silk Rail' link", Outlook on Georgia, 2017.

运输150万吨散装货。① 但安纳克利亚深海港将面临来自该地区其他几个主要港口的竞争。这些港口包括土耳其的梅尔辛港、伊朗南部的本德阿巴斯港和乌克兰的敖德萨港。而伊朗和乌克兰的政治局势可能会使纳卡利亚成为一个较优选择。与此同时，梅尔辛港的吸引力将在很大程度上取决于巴库—第比利斯—卡尔斯铁路，该铁路的影响仍有待观察。

尽管评估与"一带一路"倡议相关的基础设施建设对格鲁吉亚成功转型为交通枢纽的潜在影响尚为时过早，但现有证据表明，该倡议为格鲁吉亚的基础设施现代化建设提供了明确的机会。如要充分发挥作为新连通枢纽的潜力，格鲁吉亚必须对老旧基础设施进行现代化改造。此外，还需要制定软基础设施工具。格鲁吉亚已在此方面取得了令人惊叹的进展。《营商环境报告》显示，在该地区内，格鲁吉亚的海关手续最简单，这有利于在未来提高该走廊的竞争力。

"一带一路"倡议既要从区域互联互通的角度构思，也要从促进国民经济发展的角度进行探索。如上文所述，格鲁吉亚经济经历了不平衡增长。一项经济政策研究表明，为解决这一问题，格鲁吉亚应利用该国的比较优势以及升级潜力在未来生产更多增值商品，同时重点关注具有高增长潜力的部门。② 基于对相对较低的工资和缺乏高技能劳动力的考虑，确定了两个优先行业，其中之一是劳动密集型轻工业，包括食品加工和纺织等子行业。由于中国的目标是将其劳动密集型产业转移至海外，而格鲁吉亚具有良好的商业环境和越来越多的自由工业区，两国可开展更广泛的合作。

根据格鲁吉亚国家统计局（Geostat）的初步数据，在2020年，从出口额方面来看，中国是格鲁吉亚最大的贸易伙伴。格鲁吉亚对中国的出口额达4.763亿美元，占该国出口总额的14.3%，较2019年增长了113.4%。在出口额方面，格鲁吉亚的第二和第三大贸易伙伴分别为阿塞拜疆（4.413亿美元）和俄罗斯（4.411亿美元）。总体而言，在2020年，前

---

① Gugunishvili, N., Anaklia Deep Sea Port Land Construction Works to start in December, 2017.

② Saha, D., Giucci, R., Towards strong and balanced growth: Georgia's economic policy priorities in 2017-2020 (Policy Studies Series No. PS/01/17), German Economic Team Georgia / ISET Policy Institute, Berlin / Tbilisi, 2017.

十大贸易伙伴占格鲁吉亚对外贸易总额的70.4%。最大的贸易伙伴为土耳其（15.9亿美元）、俄罗斯（13.2亿美元）和中国（11.8亿美元）。

格鲁吉亚的前三个出口项目分别为：（1）铜矿石和精矿——7.294亿美元，占出口总额的21.8%；（2）汽车——4.041亿美元，占出口总额的12.1%；（3）铁合金——2.473亿美元，占出口总额的7.4%。

2020年的主要进口商品为：（1）汽车——7.595亿美元，占进口总额的9.5%；（2）铜矿石和精矿——5.335亿美元，占进口总额的6.7%；（3）石油和石油油料——4.985亿美元，占进口总额的6.2%。

2020年，格鲁吉亚对外贸易总额为113.4亿美元，比去年下降了14.8%。其中，出口额为33.4亿美元，下降了12%；进口额为80亿美元，下降了15.9%。贸易赤字（衡量一个国家进口超过出口的贸易逆差的经济指标）为46.6亿美元，占贸易总额的41.1%。在2020年的最后一个月，出口额为3.257亿美元，进口额为7.99亿美元。在2020年12月，总贸易额为11.2亿美元，贸易差额为-4.733亿美元。①

2020年1月至6月，铜矿石和精矿重新占据出口排行榜首位，出口额为3.324亿美元，占出口总额的22.1%。汽车出口额为1.841亿美元，占出口总额的12.2%。铁合金出口额为1.176亿美元，占总出口额的7.8%，排名第三。

在格鲁吉亚，能源、交通、房地产和建筑以及加工业是吸引外国直接投资最多的行业。

在中国对格鲁吉亚的投资清单中，可以看到多个与建筑业相关的大型项目，如第比利斯海奥林匹克综合体。该项目由华凌集团投资，投资金额高达2亿美元，用于举办2015年青年奥林匹克节。华凌集团还投资了其他领域，如建筑、酒店、医疗、木材加工、水泥生产、保税区、飞机运输和银行业等。

对外直接投资不仅对当地市场和消费者有利，还对平衡对外贸易起到积极作用。格鲁吉亚的合资公司和外资公司在出口总额中的占比正在

---

① "2020 data: China is Georgia's top trading partner by exports", Agenda. ge, January 20, 2021.

(百万美元)

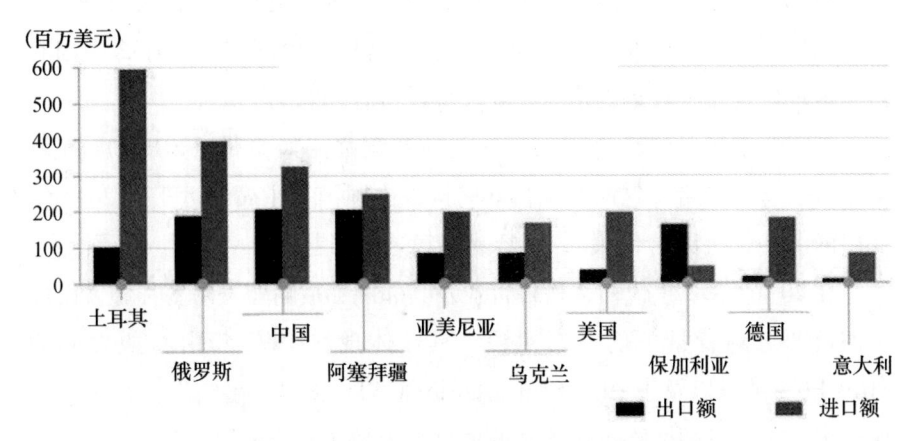

图4　以贸易额划分的格鲁吉亚主要贸易伙伴（2020年1—6月）

资料来源：格鲁吉亚国家统计局，https：//www.geostat.ge/media/32565/External-Merchandise-Trade-of-Georgia-in-January-June-2020.pdf。

逐年增长。

这里还应提到，中国计划在格鲁吉亚实施多个重要项目，这些项目有望取得重大成功。具体包括：第一，中国华信能源有限公司和欧亚投资有限责任公司于2018年投资10亿美元成立格鲁吉亚开发银行。[①] 从战略角度看，该银行将成为吸引中国投资者到格鲁吉亚投资的新磁石。

第二，格鲁吉亚茶产业的发展。[②]

第三，计划在格鲁吉亚伙伴基金和中国华商金融中心的支持下设立用于复兴格鲁吉亚的格鲁吉亚—中国基金，该基金将为格鲁吉亚的初创企业提供5,000万美元的预算（51%的资金由中国分担，41%的资金由格鲁吉亚分担）。[③]

---

① CBW, "One Billion USD Capital Chinese Bank to Launch in Georgia", *Caucasus Business Week*, May 15, 2017, http：//cbw.ge/banking/chinese-bank-one-billion-usd-capital-launch-georgia/.

② Hualing Group, "Georgian Tea Complex Project MOU Signing Ceremony", 2017, http：//hualing.ge/language/en/georgian-tea-complex-project-mou-signing-ceremony/.

③ Jorjoliani L., "Georgian Government upbeat on Chinese Trade", *Investor.ge*, Issue 4, August-September, 2017, http：//investor.ge/article.php? art=5.

第四，建立丝绸之路共同市场区，以促进创新贸易模式的发展。①

中格之间活跃的经济关系自然会引发这样一个问题：为什么中国有意与地理位置相距较远的格鲁吉亚发展经济合作？

基于北京提出的新全球项目，包括丝绸之路经济带（SREB）和 21 世纪海上丝绸之路（这两个项目共同构成中国国家主席习近平于 2013 年提出的"一带一路"倡议），很容易回答这个问题。

在 20 世纪 90 年代初，格鲁吉亚及其邻国和战略盟友阿塞拜疆就已成为旧丝绸之路背景下的考虑对象，具体体现在 1993 年由欧盟发起的 TRACECA 项目以及于 1996 年开始的 INOGATE 项目。事实上，几乎所有所设想的关于丝绸之路运输走廊的项目今天都在成功运行。

将格鲁吉亚纳入丝绸之路经济带项目是受到了已实施的丝绸之路运输走廊（SRTC）项目的推动。

此外，如果我们把 SRTC 或 TRACECA 项目与丝绸之路经济带的中亚—西亚经济走廊项目相比较，我们会发现差异至少体现在两个方面：首先，第一个项目是由西方（更具体地说是欧盟）发起的；而第二个项目是由东方（更具体地说是在中国）发起的。其次（我们认为这点非常重要），很显然，第一个项目主要是一个运输项目，而第二个项目要复杂得多，因为它是一个经济项目（这意味着除运输外，它还包括其他经济领域）。应该指出的是，如在 2002 年所提出的，格鲁吉亚运输走廊将在未来变成一个复杂的经济项目，因为它将促进不同经济领域的发展。②

五 格鲁吉亚：从能源运输枢纽转变为经济枢纽

中国和欧盟正在积极讨论建立自由贸易制度，这对格鲁吉亚来说有

---

① CEFC, "China Signs Two Cooperation Agreements with the Government of Georgia to Help Develop an Innovative Trade Model in the 'Silk Road Common Market Zone'", *CEFC China*, May 14, 2017, http://en.cefc.co/detail/news/749?lang=cn.

② Papava V., "On the Special Features of Georgia's International Economic Function", *Central Asia and the Caucasus*, 2002, No. 2 (14).

着非常重要的意义。① 在此方面，丝绸之路经济带开创了中国与欧盟之间经济合作的新局面。②

中国和格鲁吉亚都是世界贸易组织的成员。两国已经签署了自由贸易协定③，这对发展贸易关系非常重要。格鲁吉亚还与欧盟签署了深度综合自由贸易区（DCFTA）协定，并与欧洲自由贸易协会（EFTA）签署了自由贸易协定。因此，欧盟和中国之间贸易的扩展将使格鲁吉亚成为一个连接中国与欧洲的物流中心（巴库—第比利斯—卡尔斯铁路和安纳克利亚黑海深水港项目将发挥至关重要的作用），同时将提升格鲁吉亚的安全水平。④

需要进一步指出的是，在将里海的石油和天然气运输到土耳其方面，格鲁吉亚已经发挥了能源运输枢纽的作用。⑤

对格鲁吉亚来说，丝绸之路经济带项目为其提供了一个从能源运输枢纽转变为区域经济枢纽的机会。在此方面，应该指出，根据欧盟与格鲁吉亚签署的 DCFTA 协定，格鲁吉亚出口到欧盟的产品必须是在格鲁吉亚生产的。⑥ 因此，格鲁吉亚吸引了所有未与欧盟签订自由贸易协定的国家到格鲁吉亚投资，同时把所生产的产品出口至欧盟市场，这也包括已经在格鲁吉亚投资的中国。⑦

---

① Haver Z., "Rebalancing EU – China Relations: The Case for an EU – China FTA", *Global Policy*, February 9, 2017, http：//www.globalpolicyjournal.com/blog/09/02/2017/rebalancing – eu – china – relations – case – eu – china – fta.

② Gogolashvili K., "New Silk Road: A Stage for EU and China to Cooperate", Expert Opinion, 2017, No. 86. Tbilisi, Georgian Foundation for Strategic and International Studies, https：//www.gfsis.org/files/library/opinion – papers/86 – expert – opinion – eng.pdf.

③ "China, Georgia Sign FTA", *The State Council the People's Republic of China*, May 15, 2017, http：//english.gov.cn/news/international_exchanges/2017/05/15/content_281475656216746.htm.

④ Ajeganov B., "EU – China Trade to Bolster Security in the South Caucasus", *The CACI Analyst*, January 23, 2017, https：//www.cacianalyst.org/publications/analytical – articles/item/13423 – eu%E2%80%93china – trade – to – bolster – security – in – the – south – caucasus.html.

⑤ "Opening of Caspian Basin Pipeline", *U.S. Department of State*, May 25, 2005, https：//2001 – 2009.state.gov/r/pa/prs/ps/2005/46745.htm.

⑥ "Rules of Origin. Free Trade with the EU", *Ministry of Economy and Sustainable Development of Georgia*, 2017, http：//www.dcfta.gov.ge/en/dcfta – for – business/Rules – of – Origin –.

⑦ V. Charaia, V. Papava, "Belt and Road Initiative: Implications for Georgia and China – Georgia Economic Relations", *China International Studies*, November 2017.

因此，格鲁吉亚实际上可以成为该地区的经济中心，这与穿越格鲁吉亚的中亚—西亚经济走廊项目的内容完全一致。

六 结论

中国提出的新全球项目，如"一带一路"倡议包括的"丝绸之路经济带"和"21世纪海上丝绸之路"，为发展世界经济创造了新机遇。格鲁吉亚地处丝绸之路经济带项目中的中亚—西亚经济走廊内，该走廊主要为格鲁吉亚的经济发展创造了新的途径。格鲁吉亚与邻国阿塞拜疆一同积极参与丝绸之路运输走廊（SRTC）的创建和开发，目前该走廊已成功运作。可以说，丝绸之路经济带是对SRTC的进一步开发，因为该运输走廊正在转变为一个更加复杂的经济走廊。

中国对格鲁吉亚经济的投资日益增长，而且会随着丝绸之路经济带项目的实施，出现不可逆转的趋势。与中国这样一个具有巨大经济实力的国家建立紧密的经济关系绝对符合格鲁吉亚的利益，有利于其实现出口市场的多样化和吸引外国投资。

参考文献：

"2020 data: China is Georgia's top trading partner by exports", Agenda. ge, January 20, 2021.

Ajeganov B., "EU – China Trade to Bolster Security in the South Caucasus", *The CACI Analyst*, January 23, 2017, https://www.cacianalyst.org/publications/analytical – articles/item/13423 – eu%E2%80%93china – trade – to – bolster – security – in – the – south – caucasus. html.

CBW, "One Billion USD Capital Chinese Bank to Launch in Georgia", *Caucasus Business Week*, May 15, 2017, http://cbw.ge/banking/chinese – bank – one – billion – usd – capital – launch – georgia/.

CEFC, "China Signs Two Cooperation Agreements with the Government of Georgia to Help Develop an Innovative Trade Model in the 'Silk Road Common Market Zone'", *CEFC China*, May 14, 2017, http://en.cefc.co/detail/

news/749? lang = cn.

"China, Georgia Sign FTA", *The State Council the People's Republic of China*, May 15, 2017, http: //english. gov. cn/news/international _ exchanges/2017/05/15/content_281475656216746. htm.

Commersant. ge, Georgia has not Become a Transit Hub for the Region, 2017.

EU – China trade and investment relations in challenging times, Trade between China and the European Union, https: //www. europarl. europa. eu/RegData/etudes/STUD/2020/603492/EXPO_STU (2020) 603492_EN. pdf.

Frankopan, P. , The silk roads: a new history of the world, Bloomsbury, London Oxford New York New Delhi Sydney, 2015.

Georgia 2019 Crime & Safety Report, https: //www. osac. gov/Content/Report/8abe6b1a – 88fe – 411b – 860f – 15f4aead3a9a#: ~ : text = Per%20Georgian%20law%2C%20it%20is, via%20Abkhazia%20or%20South%20Ossetia.

Georgian National Investment Agency, Investment Climate and Opportunities in Georgia, Tbilisi, 2016.

Georgia's Foreign Trade in 2020, https: //civil. ge/archives/391924.

Gogolashvili K. , "New Silk Road: A Stage for EU and China to Cooperate", Expert Opinion, 2017, No. 86. Tbilisi, Georgian Foundation for Strategic and International Studies, https: //www. gfsis. org/files/library/opinion – papers/86 – expert – opinion – eng. pdf.

Government of Georgia, Social – economic Development Strategy of Georgia "GEORGIA 2020", 2013.

Grey, E. , "Can the Trans – Caspian Route deliver the next freight revolution?" Features, 2015.

Gugunishvili, N. , Anaklia Deep Sea Port Land Construction Works to start in December, 2017.

Haver Z. , "Rebalancing EU – China Relations: The Case for an EU – China FTA", *Global Policy*, February 9, 2017, http: //www. globalpolicyjournal. com/blog/09/02/2017/rebalancing – eu – china – relations – case – eu

- china - fta.

Hualing Group, "Georgian Tea Complex Project MOU Signing Ceremony", 2017, http: //hualing. ge/language/en/georgian - tea - complex - project - mou - signing - ceremony/.

Jorjoliani L. , "Georgian Government upbeat on Chinese Trade", *Investor. ge*, Issue 4, August - September, 2017, http: //investor. ge/article. php? art = 5.

M. Zabakhidze, R. Beradze, Georgia as a Transit Hub and its Increasing Potential in the Implementation of the Belt and Road Initiative, 2017.

National Development and Reform Commission, Vision and Actions on Jointly Building Silk Road Economic Belt and 21st - Century Maritime Silk Road, 2015, http: //en. ndrc. gov. cn/newsrelease/201503/t20150330 _ 669367. html.

National Development and Reform Commission, Vision and Actions on Jointly Building the Silk Road Economic Belt and 21st Century Maritime Silk Road, 2015, http: //www. fmprc. gov. cn/mfa_eng/zxxx_662805/t1249618. shtml.

"Opening of Caspian Basin Pipeline", *U. S. Department of State*, May 25, 2005, https: //2001 - 2009. state. gov/r/pa/prs/ps/2005/46745. htm.

Pantucci, R. , Lain, S. , "Silk Road: China's Project Could Transfrom Eurasia", EU Observer, 2015, https: //euobserver. com/eu - china/130762.

Papava V. , "On the Special Features of Georgia's International Economic Function", *Central Asia and the Caucasus*, 2002, No. 2 (14) .

"Rules of Origin. Free Trade with the EU", *Ministry of Economy and Sustainable Development of Georgia*, 2017, http: //www. dcfta. gov. ge/en/dcfta - for - businsess/Rules - of - Origin - .

Saha, D. , Giucci, R. , Towards strong and balanced growth: Georgia's economic policy priorities in 2017 - 2020 (Policy Studies Series No. PS/01/17), German Economic Team Georgia / ISET Policy Institute, Berlin / Tbilisi, 2017.

STOPfake, gov, 2019; https: //www. stopfakes. gov/article? id = Georgia - Corruption.

Su G. , "The Belt and Road Initiative in Global Perspectives", *China International Studies*, 2016, No. 57.

Swaine, M. D. , "Chinese Views and Commentary on the 'One Belt, One Road'", China Leadership Monitor, Hoover Institution, 2015, No. 47.

Szczudlik – Tatar, J. , "China's New Silk Road Diplomacy", Policy Paper, 2013.

Tskhovrebova, A. , Silk Road of Chinese Investment, 2016, pp. 60 – 65.

Turp, C. , "Azerbaijan, Georgia, Turkey launch new 'Silk Rail' link", Outlook on Georgia, 2017.

Van Dijk M. P. , Martens P. , The Silk Road and Chinese Interests in Central Asia and the Caucasus: The Case of Georgia, Maastricht School of Management Working Paper, 2016, August, https://www.msm.nl/resources/uploads/2016/09/MSM – WP2016 – 12 – 1. pdf.

V. Charaia, V. Papava, "Belt and Road Initiative: Implications for Georgia and China – Georgia Economic Relations", *China International Studies*, November 2017.

Chapter 1　China's Social Development Experience

Community Transformation and Improvement of Community Governance Efficiency from the Perspective of Building a Moderately Prosperous Society in All Respects[*]

Zhang Yi[**]

The process of building a moderately prosperous society in all respects involves the transformation of China from a settled society to a migratory society, from acquaintance communities to stranger communities, as well as from danwei-run society to residents' committee-run society. The physical structure and governance structure of communities also underwent significant changes. While the government adopts a top-down approach to foster the "ideal type" communities on the supply side through organizational building, community residents also construct the "ideal type" communities through "democratic consultation" on the demand side. Through interaction with the environment, the community forms its own interest structure with the residents' committee as the mainstay. The diachronic dynamics of various forces puts the community in the process of building from a "realistic type" to an "ideal type", manifesting characteristics of a bu-

---

[*] This article was originally published on *Sociological Studies* (No. 6, 2020), and the content has slightly changed.

[**] Zhang Yi, Professor, Director of National Institute of Social Development, CASS.

reaucratic governance structure, diversified community genres, heterogenous community residents, the financialization of governance funds, etc. This process results in the co-presence of "strong heteronomy" and "weak autonomy". To meet the needs of all interest groups, eliminate conflicts and stimulate vitality, it is necessary to balance the forces of "heteronomy" and "autonomy", and cultivate legal channels for the society to participate in governance, build a governance pattern of the community-run society and establish a governance system based on collaboration, participation and common interests in line with the new development stage at an earlier date.

As the basic unit of human life, communities are being constructed by theory and practice. To Tönnies, communities are the product of agricultural society. They are groups of people sharing similar social psychology, living in a certain geographical area, subject to influence of the same culture and norms (religion) and closely connected with certain production and socializing models.[1] Their characteristics become more prominent in comparison with the society in the industrialization process. In a settled society, residents will develop, through long term interactions, interpersonal relationships regulated by emotion and moral norms and a strong sense of identity and be obedient to traditional authority. Society is the product of industrialization and commercialization. The interpersonal relationships formed in it are phased, rational and contract-based, and are subject to legal contracts, with formal organizations as groups.

The Chicago School of the US sociology, led by Parker, expanded the scope of research from communities in an agricultural society to those in an industrial society, improved the community theory from the perspective of urbanization, differentiated the spatial distribution characteristics of different communities, and conducted studies on the complex relationship among urban structure, spatial dis-

---

[1] In a pre-agricultural society, namely, a hunting or herding society, human beings lived by water and grass, and were in a state of constant migration, so it was difficult for them to form communities. It was also impossible to delimit the boundaries between communities.

tance, racial discrimination, cultural assimilation, social isolation and regional ecological formation.

Wu made intensive research into communities in China. The students of Wu, including Fei, translated the English term "community" in Parker's paper into the Chinese term "社区" for the first time. This concept may refer to, in a general sense, industrial communities, agricultural communities and commercial communities, or village communities in particular. Although it has a locality connotation, clear or vague, it reflects different ways of production and life, and shapes the community identity of residents. Therefore, a community, that is originally from the academic research, is a social community bonded by acquaintance and kinship, characterized by mutual assistance based on both locality and blood ties[1]. Of course, one of the main reasons why Fei is so concerned about communities is that communities provide the most ideal and appropriate way to understand Chinese society[2].

Since the reform and opening up, and due to the restoration and reconstruction of sociology, the communities, as an academic concept in the theoretical research, have gradually transformed into a grassroots autonomous organization under the "guidance" of the district government or sub-district office of the city, replacing the residential areas in the period of planned economy. This resulted in transformation of the residents' committee into the community residents' committee, whose bureaucratic characteristics in terms of management and service provision enabled closer combination with communities.[3] A community is further divided into numerous grids based on roads, streets, alleys and buildings for grid-based management or

---

[1] Fei, "China's Modernization: Rethought on Urban Community Building", *Jiangsu Social Sciences*, 2001, Issue 1.

[2] Zhang, "From 'Cherishing One's Own Value' to Cherishing the Values of Others—Fei Xiaotong's Views on Liang Shuming's Rural Construction Proposition", *Sociological Studies*, 2019, Issue 5.

[3] In community research, some scholars ever raised the concept of community "disembedding", believing that communities formed in a certain locality and with cultural or value identity were uncommon in history, and the only ones that existed have disappeared under the influence of industrialization.

grid-based governance.① As a result, the community, as an administrative area or an area governed by the community residents' committee has dual attributes in the community building process: it has the classic meaning defined in sociology, and at the same time it is subject to administrative management. So in the process of autonomy capacity building, communities are also subject to heteronomy based on their clear boundary. ② In Fei's words, "the administrative system for urban community management is completely of Chinese style"③.

Therefore, the governance of urban grassroots society is increasingly dependent upon the community residents' committee.④ During the process of "building a

---

① Although in academic research, the identity is classified into locality-based community identity and relational community identity, the two are often intertwined with each other. Locality serves as the boundary of a community, while the relationship focuses on the interaction structure formed based on the locality.

② The "community" mentioned by Tönnies is more like "gemeinschaft", so many people translated the term directly into "gemeinschaft", referring to a group of people combined organically based on kinship, neighborhood and friendship in a certain locality, and regulated by social memory, habits, family system and norms. The "community" in academic sense is the acquaintance society and gemeinschaft as mentioned by Fei. There are still this kind of communities, such as the residential quarters for employees of enterprises, Party and government organizations and public institutions. However, in a "community" formed by commercial housing or houses from housing reform, such characteristics partly disappeared, and the society defined by Tönnies is transformed into the community in the real society, and the mechanic solidarity community as described by Durkheim is transformed into organic solidarity community. Therefore, the traditional communities are being transformed through industrialization into market-based, administrative communities. And even the structure of those typical residential quarters for employees of government organizations and enterprises was disassembled under the influence of marketization that resulted in embedding of a stranger society in an acquaintance society through housing sale and leasing.

③ Fei, "China's Modernization: Rethought on Urban Community Building", *Jiangsu Social Sciences*, 2001, Issue 1.

④ "Grassroots society governance" and "grassroots social governance" are two different concepts. Although scholars tend to interpret them indiscriminately in many cases, "grassroots society" is still under theoretical construction, while "grassroots social governance" has a clearly defined meaning. Since the 17th National Congress of the CPC, "the system of grassroots autonomy" has become a basic political system in China. The autonomy mainly refers to autonomy by administrative village residents and community residents. Therefore, the "grassroots social governance" refers to the "social governance at the grassroots level", and includes autonomy, rule of law, and rule of virtue. The "decision" of "building a new pattern of grassroots social governance" as made at the fourth Plenary Session of the 19th CPC Central Committee also refers to "building a new pattern of social governance at the grassroots level", rather than "building a new pattern of grassroots society governance", because the term "autonomy" can only be used at the administrative village and urban community level.

moderately prosperous society in all respects" and success in building a moderately prosperous society in all respects, and during the process of social management's gradually transforming into social governance, in order to keep in line with the structural changes of the grassroots society, community management is accordingly transformed into community governance, to play the dual functions of regularization and service supply at the grassroots level. The community in Chinese urban society is a kind of residential area, which is significantly different from the one formed and evolved in the west. In this case, the traditional community theory in the academic field cannot be applied directly to guide the community building in the administrative sense. Instead, the modernization of urban residential areas should proceed based on social development and changes, with community residents given legal channels to participate in community autonomy.

An important experience learned from the COVID-19 pandemic prevention and control is that the community organizations can effectively prevent and control the virus by monitoring the population flow, blocking the contagion source, isolating the suspected cases and providing psychological counseling, so as to reduce losses, and enable a quick return to normal life and reopening of businesses and schools, demonstrating the great strength of Chinese style community governance in case of emergency. And at the same time, concrete efforts should be made to improve the modern social governance system for the benefits of people, move ahead with the institutional innovation in urban social governance and top-level design in the new journey following success of building a moderately prosperous society in all respects, and continue to shift the focus of social governance and service to the grassroots levels, to make community an important basis for national and social governance. Only in this way can the governance efficiency be improved during the 14th Five-Year Plan period, and can the modernization level of community governance be constantly enhanced.

I. Shift from Danwei-run Society to Community-run Society: Transformation of the "Traditional Community" into the "Social Community"

During the whole process of building a moderately prosperous society in all respects since the reform and opening up, and along with the transformation of China from a planned economy to a market economy, the settled society based on the household registration system has also been rapidly transformed into a relocated society. This makes the population flow become the norm and calls for formation of a long-term resident governance model in the new urbanization process. During this change, communities, the structure of urban grassroots society, also underwent significant changes, which are reflected in the following aspects.

First, the grassroots social organizations are transformed from neighborhood and residential quarters for employees under Danwei system to "community system", and Danwei-run society is shifted into community-run society. In China, the grassroots governance body has been the sub-district office, the residents' committee since the early 1950s, and has changed into the sub-district office-communities since the 1990s. The community residents' committee, as a grassroots autonomous organization, is also a heteronomous organization, reflecting the will of the government and the sub-district office. The resident groups and the buildings under the residents' committee are the basic units of urban life. During the process of disintegration of the Danwei-system and the restructuring of state-owned enterprises, Danwei-run society is gradually giving way to the market. Accordingly Danwei people have become into "social people" and "market people". And due to the lack of similar organizations in the market, a new entity fully undertaking the functions of Danwei-run society is in urgent need. In the process of reform, the sub-district office and the residents' committee gradually exercise the duties of Danwei-run society within their administration, and become multi-functional organizations integrating management and service provision. Community-run society comes into being at the grassroots level with Chinese characteristics. [1] During the unbalanced development of urban society, residents have different requirements for service provided by the community due to different levels of income, different residential environments, and different expectations for life quality. Accordingly, different communities established in response to the needs of residents are also different in terms of management methods and capacity. Even in the same community, there are significant differences in the service quality and capacity between different residential quarters. In the meantime, some cities abolished the sub-district office, a dispatched organ of the government, so the work of the community is directly under the guidance by the district government. And during the process of Party building in some cities, the community development and governance functions were directly assigned to the Party committees at various levels, which established a special "community development governance committee" to respond to the ever-changing requirements for community governance. In this sense, the autonomy and heteronomy of communities have been increasingly strengthened. Behind community-run society stand government-run society or and Party committee-run society. Without personnel and financial support from the government and the Party committee, it is difficult for the community to take many of the major duties[2]. To support the government in conducting social management, the communities in many cities established a one-stop business hall bringing together 20 – 60 organizations according to the requirements of different departments to perform tasks under the leadership of the director or Party branch

---

[1] After state-owned enterprises no longer undertake community affairs following the restructuring and stripping of non-profit functions, which resulted in lay-off of a large number of workers, flow of migrant workers to cities, rise of non-public economy, reconstruction of residential areas and expansion of urban real estate development to surrounding areas, a new entity undertaking community affairs is in urgent need.

[2] Zhang, "Social Transformation and Innovation of Social Governance Pattern", *Evaluation of Chinese Social Science*, 2019, Issue 1.

secretary of the residents' committee. Bureaucratization of the community and its affiliates is required to improve the work efficiency. Some sub-district offices choose to give an administrative rank to the secretary of the Party branch/Party committee of the community or the director of the residents' committee or persons in charge of other service agencies, so that they could "legitimately" guide the work of community-run society. Although there have been many spontaneous social organizations registered with the community, they are unable to play the due role in governance due to the lack of financial support and mature management experience. The weaker the social organizations, the stronger the role the residents' committee has to play in community-run society. The "sub-district office" is a government agency, while the community residents' committee is more like extension of the government at grassroots level. [1]The bureaucratization of the residents' committee is mainly reflected in its administerization[2]. It is why Fei said that "being relied by the sub-district office for conducting work, the residents' committee is an autonomous mass organization in law, but in practice, it executes the specific tasks assigned by the sub-district office. The residents' committee is generally called a semi-official mass organization"[3].

Second, with the diversification of community types, the residents within the communities are also transforming from homogeneity to heterogeneity. In the process of urban expansion, a community is composed of the original residents' committee, the residents' committee of newly established residential quarters,

---

[1] The bureaucratic and administrative nature of the community is determined by the basic principle based on which it is formed. According to the *Organic Law of the Urban Residents' Committees of the People's Republic of China*, " The people's government of a city not divided into districts or a municipal district or its agency shall provided guidance, support and help for the residents' committee in its work. And the residents' committee shall assist the people's government of a city not divided into districts or a municipal district or its agency in conducting its work".

[2] Li, "Real Life of Grassroots Community Organizations: Preliminary Understanding of Shanghai Kangjian Community based on Field Survey", *Sociological Studies*, 2002, Issue 4.

[3] Fei, "China's Modernization: Rethought on Urban Community Building", *Jiangsu Social Sciences*, 2001, Issue 1.

the residential quarters for employees of government organizations and public institutions, the residential quarters for employees of big enterprises, urban villages and rural-urban continuum①. Thus, communities can be divided into urban communities, industrial and mining communities, rural communities and rural-urban continuum communities. ②With the diversification of community types, the composition of residents within a community is also increasingly diversified. Due to the fragmental land development, housing commercialization and differential land rent in the housing market, residents with different payment capacity would choose different residential quarters, which are divided into high-end residential quarters, general commercial residential quarters, industrial and mining residential quarters and old residential quarters. Residents are also classified into different social classes based on their consumption levels. The social classes are clearly labeled and regionalized. The walls between residential quarters make isolation within a community, which is not only the result of market allocation, but also the choice made by residents in different residential quarters. The greater the gap in social classes within the community, the stronger the need of residents in the higher grade residential quarters for walls out of safety concerns. The stronger the need of the higher grade residential quarters for isolation from the middle and low grade residential quarters, the harder it will be to achieve integration of residents of different residential quarters within the community. Thus, the community sees the change of original homogeneous residents to inter-bedding of heterogeneous residents.③ Meanwhile, in terms of household registration, due to the population

---

① Li, "Revocation of Shanty Areas and Building of New Communities—A Comparative Study on the Residence of Four Types of Low-income Earners", *Sociological Research*, 2019, Issue 5.

② The great changes in China's rural areas also led to deconstruction of the structure of the original rural community. The non-agriculturalization resulted in expanded regional boundary of communities and change of the way of work and interaction of residents, while the entry of agricultural enterprises changed the homogeneous composition of rural residents.

③ The rural communities are also becoming increasingly heterogeneous in the process of industrialization, and the agriculture, industry and commence coexist in rural China as described by Fei in his book *Jiangcun Economy*. For details, see Fei, 2007.

flow, registered residents and non-registered residents co-live in the community. Residents are no longer acquaintances or relatives, but strangers to each other. The frequent face-to-face, friendly interpersonal interactions in the traditional communities are changed to less frequent interactions based on the market relationship—service buyer and seller. To a large extent, the contractual relationship has replaced the ethical relationship as an important basis for governance, and the community, as an administrative area, has more characteristics of the "society" as described by Tönnies.① In the process of community administerization, due to the path dependence of villagers, some urban villages prefer the "one community and two governance models", and members of the same family are allowed to choose different identity, either as urban residents or rural residents. In the process of land urbanization, residents choosing to become urban residents will be managed by the community residents' committee, while those choosing to keep their rural hukou will still be managed by the villagers' committee. To save the governance costs, some urban villages adopted the organizational system of "one administrative group with two titles", some adopted two paralleling organizational systems, and some developed two governance bodies—the "residents' committee", responsible for managing the floating population, and the "economic organization", responsible for managing residents of the village or of the residents' committee. In terms of choice of interest preferences, the municipal government designed structured and integrated channels to encourage individuals and families to make choices in conformity with the government, the society and the market. Therefore, the process of transformation of the "community" into the "society" coincided with the shift of community-run-society from danwei-run society.

Third, the homogeneous community life becomes more and more diversified and individualized. Urbanization led to an increase in the number of long-term ur-

---

① Li once pointed out that "the urban grassroots communities are more and more like a society", for details, see Li, "Real Life of Grassroots Community Organizations: Preliminary Understanding of Shanghai Kangjian Community based on Field Survey", *Sociological Studies*, 2002, Issue 4.

ban residents in communities. These residents belong to different social classes, and have diversified cultural needs, religious beliefs and lifestyles. In daily life, residents rely much more on the market than on the residents' committee and the property management company stationed in the residential quarter. The market demand and service provision requires removal of the boundary between residential quarters, while in order to maintain the environment, order and ensure the safety of collective properties such as kindergarten and sports facilities, the property management company is strengthening isolation of residential quarters for closed-off management. The Internet, big data and face recognition are not used to break the walls between residential quarters, but to provide a powerful "panoramic" technical support for the identity management of residential quarters. The interactions among property owners within the residential quarter are mostly interest-based. With more neighbors being strangers, residents have a stronger identity to the residential quarter than to the community. Against the backdrop of classification of high-grade, middle-grade and low-grade residential quarters, and strengthened closed-off management, the community staff can only enter the residential quarters with the power granted by the government. There is some tension between the closure of the residential quarters and the accessibility of the community: even in the residential quarter developed by the same developer, commercial housing is often divided from relocated housing. Although there is only a wall between them, the social class and quality of property services residents received vary significantly.

Fourth, the right to profit in communities is possessed by both residents living in the place of household registration and those out. During the process of urbanization, the collective assets of the community or the remaining assets of the villagers' committee and the residents' committee following the restructuring of the collective ownership are transferred to the new economic organization(s) within the community, and the large part of the income generated from such assets is redistributable. The inappropriate distribution of such profit will compromise the commitment of residents to the community. As the residual claims formed based on household registration can only be passed down to residents of the original community, in order to ensure the continuation of residual claims, many urban grassroots communities and a majority of urban village communities formed as a result of expansion of urban land have established both the community economic organization(such as a company) and the community residents' committee. But the power and the financial strength of the economic organization are far greater than that of the residents' committee.

In the process of marketization, the community governance system established by the municipal government based on household registration can no longer meet the needs of a highly migratory society. In order to enable the functions of community-run society, a series of law-based reforms were conducted to transform the residents' committee into an autonomous and bureaucratic organization so as to meet the need for community governance. According to the *Organic Regulation on Urban Residents' Committees* (1954 – 1989) and the *Organic Law of Urban Residents' Committee of the People's Republic of China* (1990), the "residents' committee" or the "community residents' committee" is a grassroots autonomous organization, with its members(including the director, deputy director and members) elected by all the residents who have the right to vote or by representatives of each household in the residential area, to serve the term of one year(1954 – 1989), or three years (1990 – 2017) or five years(after 2018) and can be re-elected.① However, in practice, most of the members of the residents' committee are hired by the district gov-

---

① With regards to the organizational structure of the community residents' committee, it was clearly specified in the *Organic Law of the Urban Residents' Committees of the People's Republic of China* released in 1989 (the revised version was released in 2018), the *Notice of the General Office of the CPC Central Committee and the General Office of the State Council on the Forwarding of the Opinion of the Ministry of Civil Affairs on Promoting Urban Community Building Nationwide* dated November 2000, the *Opinion on Strengthening and Improving Urban Community Residents' Committees* issued by the General Office of the CPC Central Committee and the General Office of the State Council on November 2010 that, first, the government agencies, groups, troops, enterprises and institutions within the communities do not join the community residents' committee. Second, the director, deputy director and members of the community residents' committee shall be elected by all residents of the residential area who have the right to vote, or by representatives of each household. Third, one community shall in principle set up one community residents' committee.

ernment or the sub-district office (sometimes, the Party branch secretary or director of the residents' committee can become an officially budged employee as those of public institutions after working for some time through the prescribed procedures). The place of household registration of these workers is maybe within the city, but not within the community (the floating population is not edible for working as community workers in most regions). In many communities in megacities and megacity behemoths, floating residents far outnumber the locally registered residents, but they have no right to participate in community governance or to be hired as workers of the residents' committee. Therefore, the community governance turns out to be governance over a large number of non-local residents (floating population) by a small number of locally registered residents. This does not conform to the provisions of the *Organic Law of the Urban Residents' Committees of the People's Republic of China*. Contradictorily, a majority of workers of the property management companies are floating population, rather than locally registered residents. They are familiar neither with the community governance structure, nor with the composition of residents within the community. This is so called "governance by strangers". In a case reported during the COVID-19 outbreak, a security guard beat one property owner in the community. This was mainly caused by this governance model.

Authorities at higher levels are like thousands of threads and governments at the community level are the single needle that weaves. The social development tasks assigned by local government departments have to be implemented through the community residents' committee. In the process of transforming the "existing" structure towards the "ideal" structure under the guidance of the government, the community residents' committee is gradually transformed into a complex integrating the functions of administration, autonomy and market. It not only needs to complete the administrative tasks arranged by the Party committee and the government through the sub-district office, but also needs to meet the needs of residents in the communities. With the constant expansion of its administrative functions and service functions, there is a contradiction between the limited members and the unlimited tasks, thus giving rise to the need to divide the service functions from the administrative functions, with the administrative functions to be assumed by the community residents' committee and the service functions to be assumed by various service stations and centers, including the Party and mass service center(community service center), housekeeping service center, social work service station and community service station, and the need to establish the public activity center, family planning service center, day care center, elderly care and food service center, child care center, conflict mediation center among others through community standardization.① The expansion of community scale and increase of grids led to increased community governance costs, and the expanded administrative functions and service functions of the residents' committee led to bureaucratization of its internal organs.② At the same time, the residents' committee also purchases various basic public services from the market. To strengthen the management of community facilities, the secretary of the Party branch/Party committee in some communities concurrently serves as the director of the residents' committee through legal election. This will further centralize the power of the residents' committee, and achieve unity of the "heteronomy" subject of bureaucratic structure—the Party branch secretary, and the subject of "autonomy" selected by residents—the director, so that the will of the government and the service demand of residents can be combined in conducting multi-subject co-governance of communities led by Party building.

The reform designed to meet the diversified needs produced largely different results in the complicated reality, with each community having its own problems. One thing in common is the rising governance costs. The existence of various service agencies and activity centers, in addition to the community residents' committee, resulted in the need for more workers, higher costs of community building

---

① In the process of exploration and innovation, Shanghai municipality turned the community health service center, community cultural activity center, community affairs service center and other demonstrative centers into fully funded public institutions.

② In order to strengthen the functions of the residents' committee and its affiliates, the "ideal" type community designed by the government can only be developed through provision of people, money and work place.

or vitalization projects, higher daily operating costs, and consequently, heavier local financial burden. In the provincial capitals of all provinces (autonomous regions), the eastern coastal areas and areas with strong financial support, the residents' committee and its affiliates have a demonstrative effect in terms of sustainable development. However, in the central and western regions, remote areas and poor areas with low fiscal revenue, the community residents' committee has no much work to do. The number of residents in the community is smaller than that in a "standard" community, and the activity centers are poorly equipped, making the "joint action of communities, social organizations and social workers" a mere formality. In these communities, there is almost no involvement of professional social workers, so their development is unsustainable. Although the secretary of the community Party branch/Party committee is managed by the Party organization, the director of the residents' committee is guided by the department of civil affairs, the community grid members are dispatched by the administrative law-enforcement department, and workers of the office hall are hired through other channels, the activity funds and wages or living allowances of such personnel all come from fiscal budgets. The allowance to the building chiefs and unit chiefs in each residential quarter is also funded by the government. Without local financial support, the various community vitalization projects could hardly proceed. Therefore, in an economic upturn, it is easy to cover the community governance costs; while in an economic downturn, it is hard to cover such costs, making the quality of community governance compromised.

The process of building a moderately prosperous society in all respects boosted not only the transformation of the grand society, but also the transformation of the structure of grassroots society. This transformation process coincided with the disintegration of the danwei system and the formation of the post-danwei system. Under the arrangement of community-run society, the need for governing the social members who turned from "danwei persons" was partly addressed. This, to some extent, remedied the "loss of the original functions of the original structure" caused by the reform and achieved the following governance purposes. First, a new social stabilization mechanism was established through providing convenient services, which addressed the difficulty in accessing government services and other issues related to livelihood of residents, provided channels with Chinese characteristics for resolving grassroots social conflicts, and formed an organizational network centered on the community residents' committee. Second, as the residents' committee operates as a hand of the government at the grassroots level, it has established, through carrying out various projects, a mechanism for integration of government governance and social governance. Third, as the secretary of the community Party branch/Party committee concurrently serves as the director of the residents' committee and the person in charge of the collective economic organizations, the Party leadership was strengthened and a multi-subject leadership system was constructed at the grassroots level. Fourth, through the daily activities of the Party organization, the connection between Party members and residents was strengthened, and through the bureaucratic arrangements such as "grid chief", "building chief" and "unit chief", a communication channel from top to down was established. Moreover, a governance system based on joint actions with social groups and the police was established, to enhance the community governance capacity so as to contribute to building a moderately prosperous society in all respects and to China's reform, development and stability. But the transformation also gave rise to many less satisfactory structural negative functions.

II. "Strong Heteronomy" and "Weak Autonomy": Institutional Regulation and Weak Links in Governance

As mentioned above, in the process of building a moderately prosperous society in all respects, the structure of communities underwent significant changes. To match with the new structure, the functions of communities need to be upgraded, including "hardware" and "software" upgrading. This requires communities to shore up weak links as soon as possible as an overall planner and coordinator at the grassroots level, so as to address the problem of unbalanced and inadequate community building, and better meet the increasingly differentiated needs of residents.

First, as the main subject in community governance, the residents' committee acts more like an agent of the government, while other governing subjects, such as the community social organizations, are underdeveloped and have weak initiative and capacity for community governance. The capacity for community governance depends largely on the importance attached to by and support from the local Party committee or the government. However, the more importance attached by the Party and government leaders, the more likely the community residents' committee will act as an undertaker of community-run society, and the more difficult it will be to develop other main forces required for community autonomy, so the community residents' committee is more like an administrative body.① Among the three means of resource allocation—government, society and market, the potential of the "society" has not been fully tapped, which is typically represented by the alienation of the hypothesis of "governing the society" from the hypothesis of "using the society to achieve autonomy" in community governance. Although the *Organic Law of the Urban Residents' Committees of the People's Republic of China* defined the residents' committee as an autonomous organization, it also stated that "the people's government of a city not divided into districts or a municipal district or its agency shall provide guidance, support and help for the residents' committee in its work. And the residents' committee shall assist the people's government of a city not divided into districts or a municipal district or its agency in conducting its work". Therefore, the community residents' committee is obligated to complete the work assigned by the

---

① The issue of community "autonomy" and "heteronomy" has long been a topic of debate in the academic circle. However, scholars promoting autonomy do not completely deny government intervention, and those promoting heteronomy also talk about the importance of autonomous organizations often. Objectively, the ideal "pure autonomy" does not exist. In traditional Chinese society, although there were patriarchal clan rules and squires, the Baojia system had been maintained till the period of the Republic of China. Before the application of the Baojia system, the election of grassroots officials were all under the control of the government. Therefore, the saying that "the emperor's (state's) power does reach the counties where the patriarchal clan rules are applied" is only correct in a relative sense.

sub-district office or the district government if the sub-district office is abolished, just as the villagers' committee and village groups are obligated to complete the work assigned by the township government. Given the current situation, the communities should, while acknowledging heteronomy, improve the autonomy capacity [1]. Only by complementing administrative functions to autonomy functions, can the needs for healthy development and orderly governance of communities be met. In order to realize the effective allocation of resources among all parties through market competition, the government may purchase services through the market, and the society may participate in multi-subject co-governance of communities through the residents' committee. Only in this way, can the "constructive interactions among the government, the society and residents" be established, and can the principle of "governance based on collaboration, participation and common interests" be observed. When social forces are too weak to govern, it is necessary to encourage social organizations, social enterprises, social work agencies and residents to participate in governance. When there is no other governing subject in the community except the residents' committee, it is unilateral governance rather than multi-subject co-governance, so it is difficult to conduct "constructive interactions". Therefore, the focus of community building or community revitalization should be placed on the construction of infrastructure and organizational institutions. And at the same time, importance should be attached to cultivation of autonomous organizations and improvement of their capacity in autonomy.

Second, the community residents' committee is not in a harmonious relationship with the property management company and the homeowners' committee. The relocated long-term residents and residents living outside their place of household registration cannot participate in community governance. For residents, it is the residential quarter they are living in that they frequently interact with. And the service provider on behalf of the residential quarter is the property management compa-

---

[1] Tian, "Construction of Urban Community Pandemic Response System from the Perspective of Governance", *Social Science Journal*, 2020, Issue 1.

ny. The homeowners' committee meets the demand for daily services through the property management company selected from the market. Formally, the goods and services within the residential quarter are essentially "private goods" or "quasi-private goods" purchased by homeowners, and the homeowners' committee is responsible for purchasing and supervising such goods and services. Therefore, even at the grassroots level, the community is still at the middle position, with the "residential quarters" under it to manage and serve. In residential quarters with less residents living outside their place of household registration, it is easier to set up a homeowners' committee. In residential quarters with more residents living outside their place of household registration, it is difficult to set up a homeowners' committee, or the homeowners' committee is largely superfluous. In other words, under the current situation, it is difficult for homeowners to supervise the property management company in accordance with the law. They have no power to bargain the price of services they purchase or to participate in negotiation with the property management company to ensure the service quality. When there is no major conflict, residents will pay the property fees based on the rate previously set with the property management company, and accept the corresponding services. The problem, however, is that only property owners have the right to join the homeowners' committee, and the tenants can only sit on the sidelines. The tenants, as residents living in the community, have neither the right to vote or to be voted in the election of members of the community residents' committee, nor the right to participate in community governance. They can only offer suggestions through the lessor—the property owner. Similarly, from the perspective of actual right of residence, the property owners living outside their place of household registration have not established a regular relationship in governance with the residential quarter and the community. The community residents' committee has no role to play in intervening or settling the dispute between residents and the property management company. This would erode the sense of community of residents. However, a majority of contradictions within a community originate from the conflicts between the property owner(s) and the property management company, either due to long-delayed payment of the property fee by the property owners, or failure of the property management company to provide contracted services or encroachment of the public benefits by a few.

Third, the community residents' committees vary in capacity of providing supplementary services. As a grassroots autonomous organization, the community residents' committee should focus on maintaining social order and providing supplementary public services that the property community cannot provide, so as to meet the diversified demands of residents from the supply side. However, in some old residential quarters, due to the difficulty in collecting the property fees and lack of autonomous body—the homeowners' committee, it is impossible to buy the services from professional property management companies, so the living environment there is dirty, disorderly and bad. In small communities with 100 – 200 households, it is easy to address this problem. In medium-sized communities with 1000 – 2000 households or large communities with 3000 – 5000 households and more, the joint efforts of all departments concerned are needed to maintain a normally functioning community ecosystem.① Moreover, in case of any social risk that requires emergent governance, it is difficult for the resident's committee that has only 7 – 10 members to fulfill the task. If the residents' committee is incompetent in regular governance, it will be difficult to mobilize residents of the whole residential quarter to enhance the governance efficiency. In the absence of a property management company, some community residents' committees cannot even address random wastewater discharge and garbage pilling that seriously affected the normal life of residents.

Fourth, the community workers have lower pay packages. Except the secretary of community Party branch/Party committee and the director of the residents' committee who are likely to become officially budged employees as those of public institutions, other workers can hardly be long committed to their work, and most of them have a lower academic degree, and are middle-aged and old women or retired per-

---

① Communities in the US are of small scale, typically designed for 2, 500 – 8, 000 people.

sonnel. ① The turnover rate of the grid-based workers is high. Furthermore, many of the recruited workers are not residents of the community, so they are not familiar with the situation of the community. In case of emergency, the local government has to "channel down" officials to the community level, which in turn strengthens the "heteronomy" attribute of the community. For a long time, the residents' committee has worked in a way similar to that of the government. The members of the residents' committee are increasingly eager to become officially budgeted employees as those of public institutions or public servants. At present, is it possible to turn them into officially budgeted employees? What is the staffing quota? Who shall be considered first? The answers to these questions determine, to a large extent, the stability of the community residents' committee and its work performance. These have become the main object over which the community residents' committee bargains with the sub-district office or any other Party and government agency. In other words, the community workers are in the hope that the community residents' committee will be turned to the "grassroots government", with themselves being "civil servants" or officially budged employees as those of public institutions and thus having the top-down "administrative power". They don't want the community residents' committee to become an autonomous organization, and don't want themselves to be community service providers for long.

In terms of community governance, autonomy refers to co-governance by multiple subjects. However, under the current situation, the residents' committee mainly acts as an agent of the government in community governance, which is known as "strong heteronomy" model, but cannot fully mobilize the participation enthusiasm of residents. Due to the "weak autonomy", the role of "social coordination" and "public participation" cannot be fully played, which reduces the significance of social identity in the governance process. Following the Fourth Plenary Session of the

---

① In 2011, the General Office of the State Council issued the *Community Service System Construction Plan(2011 -2015)*, pointing out that active efforts should be made to promote the professionalization of community service personnel by implementing the policy of "one college student in one community", through the community service program involving 500, 000 college students.

19th CPC Central Committee that called for provision of "scientific and technological support" to community governance, many cities have added "smart community" elements in community governance to respond to the call of construction of "smart cities". However, the rapidly improved governance technologies still cannot unleash the power of "democratic consultation" in the new times. The designer of community governance attaches more importance to the bureaucratic construction of the residents' committee and the monitoring function of technologies, than to the value reconstruction in the sense of harmonious relationship among people.

In fact, in modern urban society, it is difficult for the residents' committee to govern the increasingly complex and large population on its own, either for regular governance or emergency governance. The involvement of regional modern social organizations and voluntary services can not only reduce the governance costs, but also help resolve conflicts. Both social organizations and voluntary groups need to be familiar with community affairs and service needs, in order to turn campaign-style governance or ritual or demonstrative governance into governance that is closely combined with diversified needs of residents. With the improvement of social class and income structure, residents have an increased need for participation in governance, which requires communities to establish a daily governance interface with social organizations and voluntary groups, so as to form a governance community based on collaboration, participation and common interests. Given the limited strength of communities, the quality of participation of social organizations and voluntary services determines to some extent the quality of community governance. However, neither a quality voluntary service interface, nor a link between the supply and demand of voluntary services has been established. Although localized management of social organizations and voluntary services has been achieved through institution building, the purpose of institution design has not been achieved in reality.

Furthermore, without effective integration of the residents' committee and residents in the community, residents tend to develop a sense of community identity that is too "fragmented" to form collective consciousness in the collective memory. Residents are inclined to form an identity structure in a differential pattern of "household", "floor", "unit", "building", "residential quarter" and "surrounding political and business environment", with themselves at the center. The structure may be further expanded to "school", "hospital", "park", "supermarket", "barber shop", "restaurant" and "police station and neighborhood police", to form a network of relationships. Guided by this cognitive orientation, residents even pay close attention to the nearby bicycle repair stores and locksmith, because they are closely related to such basic public services. But only a few residents know who the director of the residents' committee is and what the residents' committee is doing all day. Therefore, if the daily activities of the community residents' committee are not closely related to the daily life of residents, its existence is meaningful only to the government, not to residents. As the government is mainly concerned with the community zoning as part of urban planning, community bureaucratic structure, community resources, and how many and how well the tasks are fulfilled by the community. Therefore, scholars in community research often raise such questions as whose community it is, who are in the community, who is managing the community, who is building the community, who is sharing the results, who is evaluating the results, and who should be liable for the fall of the community. So the greater the gap in the sense of community and the resident's committee identity, the more difficult it is to share the results of community building.

In short, in the process of community transformation, with the upgrading of the residents' demand structure, the governance structure solely relying on the "residents' committee" to undertake community affairs can fulfill the task of service provision in the process of building a moderately prosperous society in all respects, but can hardly meet the requirements for governing a modern, pluralistic society.

III. Shift of Community-run Society from the Residents' Committee-run Society: Improve Governance Efficiency in Autonomy and Co-governance

In a community, the residents' committee is only one of the governing subjects. Only by building a collaborative governance system and a democratic consultation mechanism, can the answers to "whom to rely on" and "whom to serve" be found, and can a transition from the stage of "governing for the residents" to the stage of "governing by the residents" be achieved. Under the current governance pattern, only by maintaining "strong heteronomy" while fostering social organizations as the foundation for "autonomy", can a "strong autonomy" system be formed in "co-governance", so as to gradually transform from the "strong heteronomy" model to the "strong autonomy" model. However, due to the path dependence, the residents' committee is currently the only undertaker of community affairs. By the end of 2019, the number of registered social organizations in China was only 866,000, and their growth has been on the decline.[①] Given the less-developed social organizations, the assumption that the community governance capacity may be improved through participation of social organizations within the community is only valid in some areas. Therefore, in order to facilitate the shift of community-run society from the residents' committee-run society, it is necessary to conduct new top-level design in the new development stage, and to elevate the community governance innovation in grassroots society from the practical level to

---

[①] The Ministry of Civil Affairs, Statistics Communique of the Civilian Affairs 2019, http://www.mca.gov.cn/article/sj/tjgb/.

the theoretical level. ①

First, efforts are needed to improve the community governance system led by Party building, to straighten out the administrative, autonomous and market functions of the community, and to improve the institutional design for new communities pursuant to different governance needs and the development trend. According to the *Organic Law of the Urban Residents' Committees of the People's Republic of China* revised in 2018, a governance structure with one leadership and multiple subjects (one leadership refers to the leadership of the Party; multiple subjects include the local government, social organizations, volunteer service groups, resident autonomous organizations and local enterprises) and systems for regular governance and emergency governance should be established. Therefore, the focus should be placed on addressing the shortage of social organizations and social enterprises, cultivating the strength of residents for autonomy, and stimulating the social vitality. Without participation of residents, community governance will not be widely recognized, and is thus hard to achieve the purpose of society regularization. Given the fact that "social coordination" is weak at present, the "strong heteronomy" model supported by administrative bureaucracy is necessary, but the "weak capacity in autonomy" needs to

---

① In the sense of social governance, or in the "autonomy" logic of relying on the society for social governance, the residents' committee, as a governing subject, plays its role as an organization. In the process of promoting social development, various governing subjects within the community, namely social organizations, social enterprises, community governance foundations or community development foundations, property management companies, the homeowners' committee, voluntary groups and residents' representatives, should all play a governance role in the "community council" or similar platforms. The "community-run society" referred to in this paper is a governance model constructed to diversify the governing subjects, governance fund sources and governance needs, and to remove the management functions. The fundamental assumptions include "the community is an open system, rather than a closed system", "the residents' committee only has limited responsibilities in governance, rather than unlimited responsibilities", "the residents' committee undertakes governance functions rather than management functions", "the governance results are shared by residents but the governance process is not necessarily subject to approval by all residents", "the governance force is gradually shifting from the residents' committee to social organizations", "the governance fund source is gradually shifting from fiscal appropriation to the community foundations", and "voluntary organizations are a necessary complementary force to service supply".

be improved gradually. Without the intervention of "strong heteronomy", the funds required by the residents' committee to undertake community affairs cannot be guaranteed. But in the "strong autonomy" model, efforts are needed to prevent the unlimited expansion of responsibilities of the residents' committee in community governance or unlimited increase of governance costs, and to prevent the residents' committee from becoming a "government organ" or "government agency", and more importantly, to improve the capacity of social organizations in "social coordination".

Second, the focus of social governance should be shifted to communities, and the focus of community governance should be shifted to residential quarters. The governance reform of residential quarters should be oriented towards permitting non-local population(including the floating population) to participate in governance, and permitting tenants to participate in the whole process of democratic consultation, so as to prevent social isolation. The essence of a migratory society is that the labor force is in constant mobility. The vast majority of residents do not live in a fixed community for their entire life, but move from one city to another city or from one community to another community within the city. Therefore, the residential quarters should be included in the community organizational structures by strengthening the management functions of the homeowners' committee and empowering the actual users of property to participate in discussion of community affairs, so that the long-term residents may participate in grassroots autonomy and be entitled to the membership of the residents' committee, and the purpose of getting all residents in the community involved in governance can be achieved. ① Therefore, in making institutional arrangements, the residents should not be simply divided into registered residents and non-registered residents. The right to vote and to be voted in the selection of members of

---

① In some countries, the length of time residents live in the community serves as the basis for determining their right to governance and their access to basic public services. In fact, the policy of "enrolling pupils from designated areas" as implemented in the vast majority of cities in China also reflects this principle.

the residents' committee should not be determined based on the place of household registration, but be allocated proportionally based on the property ownership and right of long-term residents as tenants of the property. In the context of new-type urbanization, the original management system should be reformed on an urgent basis to adapt to the requirements of the new era. The rationality of community governance and service designed based on the household registration system is built on the theoretical assumption of closure of traditional communities. In the greater context of modernization which witnessed the gradually increasing marketization degree of communities, it is an irreversible trend and a practical need to get the floating population living in the community involved in community governance, since isolation within the community would prejudice the unity of residents. If the foundation of social solidarity is shaken due to disagreement among people, it is hard to maintain the order of the community, and to protect the interests of locally registered residents within the community. Landlords and tenants are communities of interests, and the population and social organizations within the community are in dynamic change. Only by establishing an "open", "dynamic" governance system on the basis of long-term residents, can the needs for social mobility led by modernization be met.

Third, efforts are needed to promote equal access to basic public services in communities to support balanced development of all types of communities. According to the financial strength and plan, relevant departments should conduct renovation of old residential quarters, strengthen building of communities on the outskirts and of newly built residential quarters, and improve the comprehensive coordination and governance capacity of residential quarters for employees of government organizations and enterprises. As the population size of communities is expanding, the communities have to depend on each residential quarter within to improve their governance system and capacity. The local financial(competent) department should provide support to communities and residential quarters with weaker governance capacity or incomplete governance systems or troubled with problems left over by history. By purchasing social services, it may help residential quarters improve governance capacity to form a solid foundation for grassroots governance and help build a coordination mechanism and a cost sharing mechanism among the communities, the regional Party and government organizations, enterprises and institutions. In order to cap the community governance costs, it is also necessary to mobilize the homeowners' committee to offset the imbalance with the property management company. At the same time, an interface for participation of local social organizations and voluntary service organizations in community governance should be established to achieve "collaborative" situation, professional and law-based governance, so as to reduce the dependence on fiscal funds for community operation. A platform for resolving the conflicts between the homeowners' committee and the property management company should be established by taking into account the tasks and requirements for "heteronomy" and for improving the "autonomy" system, to meet the needs of communities for service provision through the supply-side structural reform and to avoid the division of residents in competition for resources within the communities. Of course, for some urban communities directly transformed from rural communities in the process of urbanization, support should be given to the residential quarters within such communities to increase their strength in autonomy. The higher the degree of social modernization, the higher the requirement of the community residents on the quality of organized services. And higher social differentiation of community residents would lead to stronger heterogeneity and more stringent requirements of them for differentiated services.

Fourth, a stable, regular and professional community work team should be established, with the payment of members determined in light of the urban economic growth rate and price fluctuations, and their number determined based on the actual size of residents. It should be noted that in the central and western regions and northeast China, the income of community workers is very low, leading to a high turnover rate. In these places, even those with a bachelor's or master's degree in social work are unwilling to work in the community. To realize community autonomy, it is necessary to build a working team and to constantly improve the service level and professional capacity of team members. The small and medium-sized communities may have fewer community workers, while the oversized communities with more than 5,000 households may expand the workforce correspondingly. Less desired or redundant services arranged by the sub-district office should be cutback based on the resident survey, to use the limited manpower to provide basic public services such as livelihood guarantee and community regularization. Meanwhile, the status of the community as an independent legal entity should be improved. The secretary of the community Party branch/Party committee who is recommended to concurrently serve as the director of the community residents' committee and the person in charge of the community economic organizations should actively integrate the community resources, improve the accounting rules in terms of community governance to form a transparent, open financial system, standardize the financial management practices, and clarify the relationship between services purchased by the government, community autonomy services and services from market players, as well as effectively resolve conflicts among the homeowners' committee, the property management company and tenants of houses. Where conditions permit, support should also be given to community development foundations to help absorb social funds for community governance. Only by developing and expanding the community development foundations, can the communities have a strong economic foundation for autonomy, so as to reduce the dependence on local finance.

Fifth, a community service evaluation system led by a third party should be established, involving the community, the homeowners' committee, the property management company, tenants' representatives and voluntary groups, among others, to improve the supervision mechanism. In particular, an institutional and autonomous supervision system should be established to evaluate how well the frequently complained problems concerning the quality of services provided by the property management company or of the community public services are addressed. To avoid repetitive campaign-style rectifications, a blacklisting system should be established to strengthen market supervision and phase out property management companies incapable of conducting modern management or of improving their service quality, thus enabling communities to realize self-management, self-service and self-development amid the constructive interactions among the government, the market and the society.

In a word, following the completion of building a moderately prosperous society in all respects, China will have a higher urbanization level and a more complex urban structure. The unbalanced development of communities in cities will become more prominent, together with aging and migration issues of residents, and more problems concerning adaptability between governance structure and function will come out during the constant transformation of the society.

In this case, with the advance of modernization in the new development stage, the cask effect displayed by flaws in community governance will be amplified by media, so the communities will face new governance challenges in the future. In the governance model of the residents' committee-run society, with the increase of the resident's consumption level and their rising appeal for governance quality upgrading, the residents' committee, as a government agent will continue to seek to expand the service scope, increase the number of workers, apply for additional benefits and living allowance, turn workers to officially budgeted employees as those of public institutions or seek to build an administrative operation mechanism transforming community workers to civil servants. Guided by the assumption of "unlimited responsibility", how well the residents' committee can do in undertaking community affairs is largely dependent on the financial support received. The growth of residents' demand for community governance is rigid, while the fiscal growth entirely hinges on the economic growth. In the theoretical judgment that the economic growth has been slowing down, the sustainability of community governance by the residents' committee assigned with unlimited responsibilities is challenged. Therefore, in the process of building a moderately prosperous society in all respects, to upgrade the governance model from danwei-run society to residents' committee-run society is not only necessary but also innovative in the sense of path dependence. However, in the new journey following the completion of building a moderately prosperous society in all respects, it is also necessary to further upgrade the model community-run society, in order to utilize the social forces within and outside the community to build a "multi-subject co-governance model".

The maturity of social organizations within and outside the community determines the capacity of the "community-run society". Both the theoretical assumption of "undertaking community affairs by social forces" and the assumption of "undertaking community affairs by the government" are practically rational. Indeed, when social organizations grow bigger and stronger, the power of the residents' committee is sometimes challenged, and differences in governance orientation among different social organizations may also arise. However, in the context of social class diversification, in order to prevent residents from blaming the governance behind the residents' committee for the conflicts, the opinions of different social organizations must be respected during "democratic consultation". By establishing a council platform, the opinion leaders may seek consensus within the platform, so as to prevent the residents' committee from being singlehandedly blamed for governance failure. The more residents participating in social organizations, the easier it is to utilize the multi-subject consultation and balancing mechanism among social organizations to resolve disputes, and the more likely it is to resolve conflicts with community identity.

Therefore, a systematic summary of all existing problems must be conducted, to shore up the weak lines, establish a governance system based on collaboration, participation and common interests, improve the community autonomy, rule of virtue and rule of law, unleash social vitality, expand legal channels for residents to participate in democratic consultation and reduce the increasingly rising governance costs through autonomy and co-governance. This will supply quality services to residents and enhance the residents' sense of happiness, gain and security.

References

Fei, "China's Modernization: Rethought on Urban Community Building", *Jiangsu Social Sciences*, 2001, Issue 1.

Li, "Real Life of Grassroots Community Organizations: Preliminary Understanding of Shanghai Kangjian Community based on Field Survey", *Sociological Studies*, 2002, Issue 4.

Li, "Revocation of Shanty Areas and Building of New Communities—A Comparative Study on the Residence of Four Types of Low – income Earners", *Sociological Research*, 2019, Issue 5.

The Ministry of Civil Affairs, Statistics Communique of the Civilian Affairs 2019, http://www.mca.gov.cn/article/sj/tjgb/.

Tian, "Construction of Urban Community Pandemic Response System from the Perspective of Governance", *Social Science Journal*, 2020, Issue 1.

Zhang, "From 'Cherishing One's Own Value' to Cherishing the Values of Others—Fei Xiaotong's Views on Liang Shuming's Rural Construction Proposition", *Sociological Studies*, 2019, Issue 5.

Zhang, "Social Transformation and Innovation of Social Governance Pattern", *Evaluation of Chinese Social Science*, 2019, Issue 1.

Evolution of Development Concepts and Social Changes in China

Ouyang Xiangying[*]

The year 2021 marks the centenary of the Communist Party of China (CPC). The last 100 years have witnessed the earth-shaking changes in Chinese society, from a gradually disintegrating semi-colonial and semi-feudal society to the one in a new era of socialism with Chinese characteristics featuring prosperity and strength. The Chinese nation has achieved dramatic transformation from standing up and growing prosperous to becoming strong. China has made great strides in social development, although the process is not plain sailing. Since its birth, CPC has been exploring the way to liberate and develop China by putting forward different development concepts and measures according to the changes of main contradictions and different levels of productivity in different periods, and adjusting them at certain stages when problems were found. Today, China has become the world's second-largest economy. While admiring China's achievements, many countries are unaware of the difficulties as well as twists and turns in its development process. At the centenary of the CPC, it is necessary to systematically review its exploration and achievements in development concept, which can also serve as a reference for ruling parties in other developing countries.

---

[*] Ouyang Xiangying, Professor, Head of the Marxist International Political Economy Institute of World Economics and Politics, CASS.

I. Issues Raised

Theoretically, the answer to the question of whether social development is a "natural historical process" or a process guided by "rationality" or "absolute spirit" differs from thinker to thinker. Marx agrees with the former but Hegel agrees with the latter. However, Marx emphasizes the historical process of "humanized nature", without excluding human factors and conceptual factors. In Marx's view, history often leaps ahead. There are two key factors in achieving "leapfrog development". One is people and their practices. Historical choices are made by people. The other is science and technology, which develops and progresses by relying on people. This suggests that there is no pure nature excluding human factors, and that society as a collection of people must be guided by some ideas. The question is how the subjective is reflected in the objective, i.e., the process of people's understanding and exploration of the laws of social development.

Realistically, take China's Belt and Road Initiative (BRI) as an example, some underdeveloped countries and regions want to introduce high technology from China to develop their digital economy, but they lack plans to transform their existing agriculture, livestock, mining and processing industries. For one thing, local governments want China's support for high technology and digital economy, but they give less consideration to their supporting infrastructure and industry environment, resulting in the failure to negotiate projects or implement them after negotiation. For another, some Chinese companies are interested in competitive industries of BRI countries and regions such as mining and energy development. However, their governments consider such industries as their strategic materials and do not grant licenses to Chinese companies, leading to the failure of those companies to run normally.

The aspirations and concerns of some countries along Belt and Road are understandable. However, when dealing with real issues, both sides should align their actions to the same level to promote cooperation, and this presupposes a consensus. China's practical experience shows that its development is not achieved overnight, as can be seen from many rounds of adjustments in development concepts and industry policies. Patterns, priorities and modes of development need to be decided on the basis of actual conditions, with firm goals and flexible adjustments. For example, as the world's largest energy importer, China became the world's largest importer of crude oil in 2017 and the world's largest importer of natural gas in 2018. Many people are not aware that China was also a major petroleum exporter in the 1970s and 1980s. In 1985, China exported 36 million tons of petroleum, which reached a record high for China's petroleum exports and brought USD 6.7 billion in foreign exchange, accounting for 24.5% of the gross foreign export value that year. This is China's strategy of "petroleum for foreign exchange", in order to buy back equipment and materials needed for its development. With its continuous and rapid economic growth after 1985, China witnessed a gradual decline in its exports and a gradual increase in its imports (see Table 1). China imported 542 million tons of crude oil in 2020, with a value of RMB 1.22 trillion. Obviously, the development track of the industry has its own logic and serves the overall situation of national development.

Table 1   China's Crude Oil Production and Petroleum Import and Export in 1972 – 1993

Year	Crude Oil Output/ Million Tons	Annual Growth (%)	Petroleum Import/ Million Tons	Petroleum Export/ Million Tons	Net Import(+) or Net Export(-)
1972	45.672	15.87	0.652	0.806	-0.154
1973	53.614	17.39	0.138	1.819	-1.681
1974	64.850	20.96	0.113	5.180	-5.067
1975	77.059	18.83	0.203	10.579	-10.376
1976	87.156	13.10	0.201	9.300	-9.097
1977	93.638	7.44	0.301	10.691	-10.390

Continued

Year	Crude Oil Output/ Million Tons	Annual Growth (%)	Petroleum Import/ Million Tons	Petroleum Export/ Million Tons	Net Import(+) or Net Export(-)
1978	104.049	11.22	0.001	11.333	-11.332
1979	106.149	2.02	—	—	—
1980	105.942	-0.20	0.827	18.062	-17.235
1981	101.219	-4.46	0.710	18.842	-18.132
1982	102.205	0.97	1.572	20.897	-19.325
1983	106.066	3.78	1.349	20.926	-19.577
1984	114.601	8.05	1.125	28.687	-27.562
1985	124.887	8.89	0.900	36.304	-35.404
1986	130.670	4.63	3.501	34.620	-31.119
1987	134.125	2.64	3.234	32.938	-29.704
1988	137.028	2.16	5.084	31.423	-26.339
1989	137.651	0.45	10.651	31.064	-20.413
1990	138.284	0.46	7.556	31.104	-23.548
1991	139.791	1.09	12.495	29.307	-16.812
1992	142.037	1.61	21.247	28.956	-7.709
1993	144.004	1.38	32.960	23.150	+9.810

Source: Li Xin, "The Evolution of Petroleum Import-Export Status of China Since 1949", *Journal of Southwest Petroleum University (Social Science Edition)*, 2014, Issue 1, p. 4.

II. China's Development Concepts and Achievements over the Past Century

Looking back on its development over the past century, China has always been pursuing development and modernization. "Modernization has been the goal of all countries in the world, especially developing countries, since recent times. China's great success has opened up the way for developing countries to move towards modernization, provided a brand-new option for countries and nations which want to develop faster while preserving their independence, and contributed to new solutions to problems common to mankind. "①

From 1840, China was gradually reduced to a semi-colonial and semi-feudal society, so anti-imperialism and anti-feudalism became a fundamental task of the modern Chinese revolution. The failure of the Self-Strengthening Movement and the Hundred Days' Reform proved the failure of the reform movement within the landlord class. The theft of achievements of the 1911 Revolution by Yuan Shikai and the subsequent tangled warfare of the Northern Warlords(1912 – 1927) proved the unsuccessful trials of the Chinese bourgeoisie. The outbreak of the "October Revolution" in 1917 brought Marxism to China, which led to the birth of the CPC in Shanghai in 1921. The "New Culture Movement" laid the ideological foundation for the founding of the CPC and mainly advocated democracy and science. However, the push for modernization was controversial at the time. "In recent years the crude sericulture industry in China has been squeezed out by cheap production in the large modern factories, so women often go to these factories for short jobs. " ② This is quoted from Zhang Tailei's report to the Comintern on June 10, 1921, in which the Chinese communist also mentioned the term "modernization" for the first time. By the mid – 1920s, the concept of "modernization" was widely known to Chinese communists. Qu Qiubai's translation, published in *New Youth* No. 5 in 1926, refuted the hypocrisy of social democrats and reformist trade union leaders who claimed that China should be "economically modernized". The term "modernization" here refers to the capitalist way of doing business, with a critical connotation. Since the *New Youth* had already been reprinted as an official theoretical journal of the CPC Central Committee at that time, it can be assumed that in the early days, the Chinese communists were generally skeptical and critical of "modernization". Remarkably, in the early days, Chinese communists recognized that realization of so-

---

① The Theory Bureau of the Propaganda Department of the CPC Central Committee, *Face to Face with the Development of People's Republic of China*, Learning Publishing House & People's Publishing House, 2019, pp. 17 – 18.

② *Zhang Tailei Anthology*, People's Publishing House, 2013, p. 21.

cialism in the future in China would be a combination of commonalities and individuality. The ideal of socialism "varies from place to place and from time to time, so to realize this ideal, it is necessary to consider different places and times, and thus a new system that combines commonalities (or universality) and individuality (or particularity) is born. The Chinese ideal of socialism is necessarily different from that of Britain, Germany and Soviet Union"①.

When the Manchurian Incident broke out in 1931, the Japanese brazenly invaded China, shocking the whole country. Faced with the nation-wide enemy, the Chinese people changed their understanding of "modernization". In the autumn of 1931, when discussing the "Cultural Revolution in the Soviet Union", Qu Qubai advocated a new writing revolution until the realization of "Roman-style China's modernization"②. In 1933, *Shun Pao Monthly* organized a discussion on "China's modernization". In 1937, when Xie Juezai was stationed at the Lanzhou Office of the Eighth Route Army as a representative of the CPC Central Committee, he wrote several times to He Yaozu, director of the Northwest Office of Kuomintang, proposing that "buying and learning to use modern weapons is extremely important for the Northwest base"③. In 1938, Mao Zedong first used the word "modernization", saying, "The military cannot be reformed without modernization"④. Zhou Enlai also mentioned "modernization" several times in "How to Conduct a Protracted War". At this point, the Chinese communists had clearly given "modernization" a positive connotation.

From 1931 to 1945, the Japanese invasion brought great harm to China. From April 23 to June 11, 1945, the CPC held its Seventh National Congress in Yan'an, proposing a political line to defeat the Japanese invaders and establish a new democratic China. At that time, the CPC was not yet the ruling

---

① Li Dazhao, "Socialism and Social Movements" (Sept. 1923 – Apr. 1924), *in Collected Writings of Li Dazhao*, Vol. 4, People's Publishing House, 2013, p. 248.
② *Qu Qiubai Anthology*, Vol. 7, People's Publishing House, 2013, p. 229.
③ *Xie Juezai's Diary*, Vol. 1, People's Publishing House, 1984, p. 189.
④ *Selected Works of Mao Zedong*, Vol. 2, People's Publishing House, 1991, p. 511.

party, but it already possessed anti-Japanese bases in Shaanxi-Gansu-Ningxia area, Shanxi-Chahar-Hebei area, Shanxi-Hebei-Shandong-Henan area, Shanxi-Suiyuan area and Shandong, and its work in the Kuomintang-ruled areas was in full swing. As social productivity was greatly damaged, it was clearly proposed in the reports of the Seventh CPC National Congress and the Second Plenary Session of the Seventh CPC Central Committee that China should achieve "industrialization and modernization of agriculture" and "steadily develop itself from an agricultural country into an industrial country". In other words, although modernization was the vision and goal of development of the People's Republic of China under the leadership of the CPC, the first step to be achieved was preliminary modernization when overall productivity still lagged behind. In October 1949, the Chinese People's Political Consultative Conference(CPPCC) adopted *The Common Program of the People's Republic of China* (*Common Program* for short), which served as a provisional constitution for a period of time. In particular, on economic development, the *Common Program* stipulates that the state should "regulate state operated economy, co-operative economy, individual economy of peasants and handicraftsmen, private capitalist economy and state-capitalist economy in many ways, so that all aforementioned economic sectors, under the leadership of state operated economy, can cooperate with one another and play their respective roles and ultimately promote the economic development of society as a whole"[①]. This also fully reflected the nature of the new democracy in the transitional period, where China was not eager to move quickly into socialist modernization.

At the early stage of the founding of the People's Republic of China, people were rejuvenated with the enthusiasm of being the masters of the country and the national economy was fully restored. In 1952, the gross output value of industry

---

[①] Party History Research Center of the CPC Central Committee: *The 90 Years of the Communist Party of China*, History of Chinese Communist Party Publishing House, Party Building Books Publishing House, 2016, p. 344.

and agriculture reached RMB 81 billion, an increase of 77.6% over 1949. Of this gross, industrial output rose by 145.1% over 1949, and agricultural output by 48.4%, a solid step towards the goal of transforming from an agricultural country into an industrial one. ① At the First National People's Congress (NPC) in 1954, the need to modernize industry, agriculture, transportation and national defense was clearly proposed for the first time. However, a doubt exists whether modernization is the construction of tall buildings and the nation's access to electric lights and telephones or another model. In 1956, Mao Zedong made a speech on the Ten Major Relations at the expanded meeting of the Political Bureau of the CPC Central Committee. He pointed out that "we should learn from strengths of all nationalities and other countries", ② and that China should explore its own path based on its own realities when pursuing socialism, instead of following the path of Soviet Union in all respects. At the Third NPC in 1964, Zhou Enlai made a report on the work of the government, dividing modernization into modern agriculture, modern industry, modern national defense and modern science and technology. ③ Specifically, China adopted a "two-step strategy", with the goal of establishing an independent and relatively complete industrial system and national economic system in 15 years and fully realizing modernization in aforementioned four aspects by the end of the 20th century. By the end of 1965, the task of restructuring the national economy was fully completed. Consequently, the gross output value of industry and agriculture topped all previous records. The proportion of agriculture, light industry and heavy industry improved. The proportion between accumulation and consumption

---

① Party History Research Center of the CPC Central Committee: *The 90 Years of the Communist Party of China*, History of Chinese Communist Party Publishing House, Party Building Books Publishing House, 2016, p. 414.

② *Selected Works of Mao Zedong*, Vol. 2, People's Publishing House, 1986, p. 740.

③ Party History Research Center of the CPC Central Committee: *The 90 Years of the Communist Party of China*, History of Chinese Communist Party Publishing House, Party Building Books Publishing House, 2016, p. 536.

was basically restored to normal. This restructuring also brought about a balance of financial revenues and expenditures, a stable market and improved people's living standards. However, for many reasons, the unprecedented "Cultural Revolution" broke out in May 1966, causing social unrest. Overall, China was far cry from developed countries and its major neighboring countries (including regions) in the world despite a number of important achievements in food production, industry, transportation, capital construction, science and technology, and even diplomacy. From 1965 to 1975, China's GDP grew at an average annual rate of 4.7%, compared with 8.0% in Japan, 11.6% in South Korea and 9.1% in Taiwan of China. It also demonstrated the need for modernization in economic and social fields as well as in political and ideological fields.

In the days prior to the reform and opening-up policy, China was a relatively backward developing country in terms of total GDP and GDP per capita. In 1978, the per capita net income of rural households was only RMB 133.6, and their Engel coefficient was 67.7%, while the per capita net income of urban residents was RMB 343.4, and their Engel coefficient was 57.5%.① In 1979, during a meeting with Japanese Prime Minister Masayoshi Ohira, Deng Xiaoping proposed quantifying the "Four Modernizations" (modernization in agriculture, industry, national defense, and science and technology) as achieving a well-off level of USD 1,000 per capita gross national product by the end of the 20th century.② To that end, China adopted the reform and opening-up policy by setting up special economic zones firstly to explore a path of socialism with Chinese characteristics. From special economic zones to the opening of coastal areas and then that of inland areas, China attracted increasing foreign investment, and the advanced technology and management experience that came with it changed the way people think, rapidly expanding the private economy and injecting vitality into the na-

---

① Zeng & Hu: "An Analysis of Changes in the Income Gap between Urban and Rural Residents in China Since the Late 1970s and Its Impact on the Consumption Levels of Urban and Rural Residents", *Economic Review*, 2008, Issue 1.

② *Selected Works of Deng Xiaoping*, Vol. 2, People's Publishing House, 1994, p. 237.

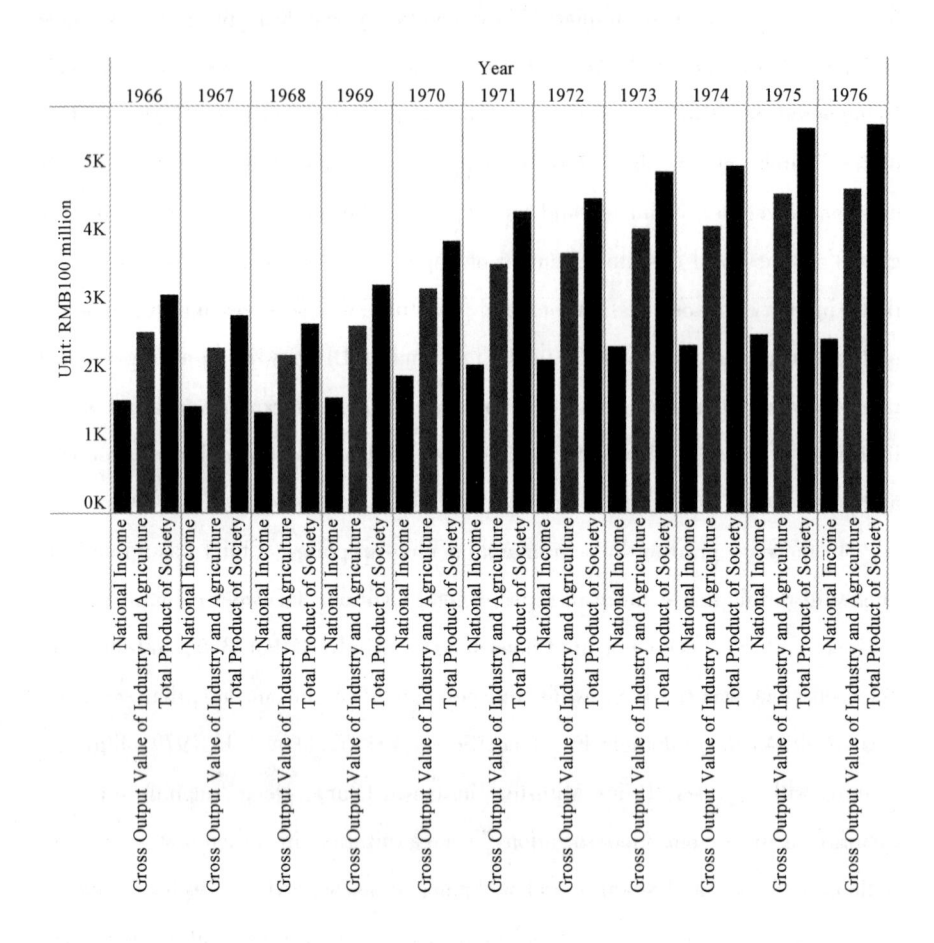

Figure 1 Total Product of Society, Gross Output Value of Industry and Agriculture and National Income in 1966 – 1976

Source: National Bureau of Statistics, *Statistical Yearbook of China* (*1984*), China Statistics Press, 1984, pp. 20 – 21.

tional economy.

The 13th CPC National Congress called for a "Three-Step Development Strategy" to develop China's economy. First, people were guaranteed adequate food and clothing, and this task was basically realized. Second, people were guaranteed to enjoy a moderately prosperous life by the end of the 20th century. Third, per capita GDP was expected to reach the level of a moderately developed country by the mid −21st century, further improving the people's wellbeing. ① This strategy was proposed in 1987, when the first step of economic development goal was still to guarantee people adequate food and clothing, which could be said to be realistic. After the successful completion of the Seventh Five-Year Plan, in December 1990, it was proposed at the Seventh Plenary Session of the 13th CPC Central Committee that in the next ten years, China would achieve the second strategic goal of modernization, raising the overall quality of the national economy to a new level. ② The report of the plenary session outlined the basic theory and practice of socialism with Chinese characteristics and summarized 12 principles, marking a further deepening of the Party's understanding of the road to socialism with Chinese characteristics. Deng Xiaoping pointed out in 1992 in the Southern Talks,"the essence of socialism is liberation and development of productivity, elimination of exploitation and polarization, and the ultimate achievement of prosperity for all. "③ If China wants socialism to achieve superiority over capitalism, it should not hesitate to draw on the achievements of all cultures and to learn from all advanced business practices and management methods of developed capitalist countries that reflect the laws of modern socialized production.

In the 1990s, the CPC Central Committee carried out a comprehensive package of reforms to the economic system, involving fiscal and taxation, finance, foreign trade, investment, planning, pricing, housing allotment, and state-owned enterprises, creating favorable conditions for ensuring economic development. In 1993, China's economy exceeded RMB 3 trillion for the first time. Excluding price

---

① Party History Research Center of the CPC Central Committee: *The 90 Years of the Communist Party of China*, History of Chinese Communist Party Publishing House, Party Building Books Publishing House, 2016, p. 745.

② Party History Research Center of the CPC Central Committee: *The 90 Years of the Communist Party of China*, History of Chinese Communist Party Publishing House, Party Building Books Publishing House, 2016, p. 785.

③ *Selected Works of Deng Xiaoping*, Vol. 3, People's Publishing House, 1993, p. 373.

increases, the per capita disposable income of urban residents nationwide increased by 9.5% over 1992, while that of rural residents grew by 3.2%. The total deposits of urban and rural residents reached RMB 1,520.4 billion at the end of 1993, an increase of 29% over 1992. Facing the complex and severe international environment, the CPC unwaveringly adheres to the basic state policy of opening up to the outside world and promotes the formation of a new pattern of multi-level, multi-channel and all-round opening to the outside world. On December 11, 2001, China officially joined the World Trade Organization (WTO) and became its 143rd member. The extensive growth brought about by the accelerated economic development led to the increasingly acute contradiction in the coordination of population, resources and environment. The Decision of the Central Committee of the Communist Party of China on Some Issues concerning the Improvement of the Socialist Market Economy was adopted at the Third Plenary Session of the 16th CPC Central Committee in October 2003. This was the first time that the CPC put forward the Scientific Outlook on Development completely in its official document, which stipulates that "China should uphold the principle of 'man first' and form the concept of overall, coordinated and sustainable development so as to promote the overall economic, social and human development" and that "China should, in accordance with the requirements of coordinating the development of urban and rural areas, of different regions, of economic and social sectors and of man and nature, and of coordinating the national development and the opening-up to the outside world", promote the development and progress of various undertakings.[①] From 2003 to 2007, China's GDP growth rate reached or exceeded 10% for five consecutive years, much higher than the average of the world economy during the same period, with the total economic aggregate rising from sixth to fourth place and the total import-export volume rising from sixth to third place in

---

① Party History Research Center of the CPC Central Committee: *The 90 Years of the Communist Party of China*, History of Chinese Communist Party Publishing House, Party Building Books Publishing House, 2016, p. 898.

the world. The 17th CPC National Congress emphasized the need to adhere to the Chinese-style path of carrying out industrialization in a new way, leading to particularly rapid development of electronic information industry. By 2011 China had become the world's first major electronic information manufacturer.

Xi Jinping was elected as General Secretary of the CPC Central Committee at the 18th CPC National Congress. A new development concept of innovation, coordination, green, openness and sharing was established at the Fifth Plenary Session of the 18th CPC National Congress in 2015. General Secretary Xi Jinping pointed out in his report at the 19th CPC National Congress in 2017 that "socialism with Chinese characteristics enters new era", marking a new historical position of China's development. With the aim of securing a decisive victory in building a moderately prosperous society in all respects and embarking on a new journey to fully build a modern socialist country in the new era, China has fully made a five-sphere integrated plan for promoting economic, political, cultural, social, and ecological progress and has implemented some top-level design programs such as the Belt and Road Initiative, establishment of Asian Infrastructure Investment Bank and New Development Bank, and Regional Comprehensive Economic Partnership. Western developed countries feel "threatened" by China's rapid development. Therefore, in 2018, the US provoked economic frictions and tech "decoupling" against China, making China face a more severe external situation.

The "Two Centenary Goals" were proposed for the first time in the report of the 15th CPC National Congress. By the time of celebrating the CPC's centenary, China would have a more developed national economy and better systems. By the time of celebrating the centenary of the People's Republic of China, it would be built into a modern socialist country that is prosperous, strong, democratic, culturally advanced. In the report of the 19th CPC National Congress, the timetable and roadmap for building a great modern socialist country were clearly defined, i. e. , China would achieve its first centenary goal of building a moderately prosperous society in all respects in 2020 and basically realize socialist modernization by 2035, and achieve its second centenary goal of building itself into a modern

.... Efficiency   — · — Structure   - - - - - Stability

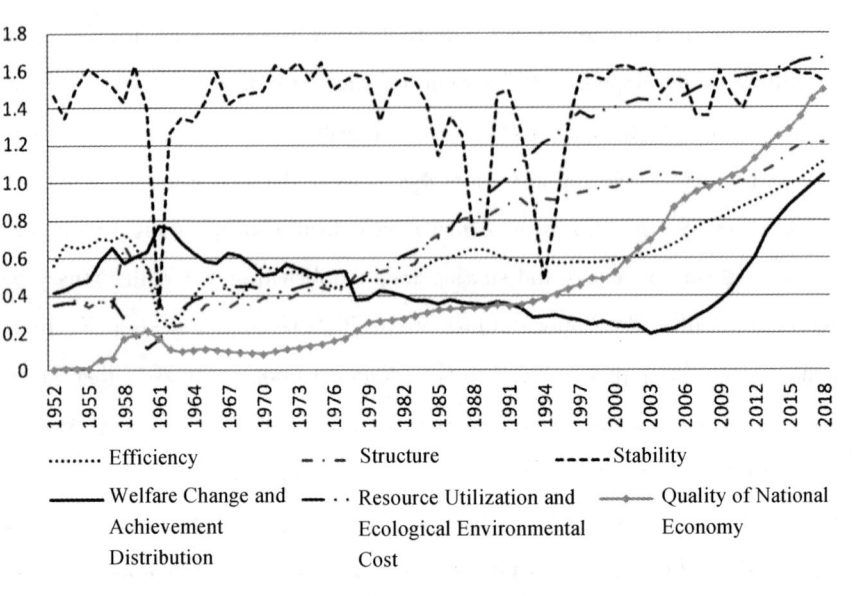

——— Welfare Change and   — · · Resource Utilization and   —•— Quality of National
Achievement   Ecological Environmental   Economy
Distribution   Cost

**Figure 2   The Index Changes of Quality of China's Economic
Growth in Six Dimensions in 1952 – 2018**

Source: Ren & Liu, "Historical Evolution and Evaluation of the Quality of Economic Growth Since the Founding of the People's Republic of China", *Seeker*, 2020, Issue 5, pp. 170 – 179.

socialist country that is prosperous, strong, democratic, culturally advanced, harmonious and beautiful by the middle of this century. Special mention needs to be made of the year 2020. This is the year when China became the only major economy in the world to achieve positive growth while fully responding with the COVID – 19 pandemic, with its total economic output reaching a new level of 100 trillion RMB. The primary reason for this hard-won success is the CPC Central Committee's insistence on putting people's lives and health first. Its timely and centralized leadership provided a guarantee for the victory in the COVID – 19 response and steady turnaround in economic development. On May 14, 2020, the meeting of the Standing Committee of the Political Bureau of the CPC Central Committee first proposed "deepening supply-side structural reform and maximizing advantages of China as a super-large market and its potential in domestic demand to build a new development pattern in which domestic and foreign markets boost each other"①. Since then, General Secretary Xi Jinping has repeatedly stressed the need to "gradually create a new development pattern where domestic and foreign markets can boost each other, with domestic market as the mainstay"②, in a bid to reshape China's new advantages in international cooperation and competition. In 2021, when the CPC celebrated its centenary birthday, the CPC Central Committee officially declared that China has completed a moderately prosperous society in all respects after conducting a systematic review of the achievement. With its commitment to the right path and innovation, the 100 - year-old CPC is in its prime. It will further reform and opening-up from a higher starting point and lead China to a new victory.

III. Conclusion

The history of China's development over the past century tells us that a strong CPC leadership is the key to the success of China's revolution and development. What is the source of the CPC's strength? One is the right theoretical guidance. In the course of the Chinese people's arduous exploration of the road to independence and development, the CPC took the lead in finding Marxism-Leninism and Mao Zedong Thought, enabling China to defeat imperialism, feudalism and bureaucrat capitalism, as well as wrong lines of "left" and "right" deviations, and ultimately guiding the Chinese revolution to victory. The second is practical exploration. There is no mature model of socialism, so developing such a large and poor country cannot rely on books alone. CPC has been combi-

---

① The Meeting of the Standing Committee of the Political Bureau of the CPC Central Committee Presided Over by Xi Jinping, people. cn, May 15, 2020.
② The CPC Central Committee's Proposals for Formulating the 14th Five-Year Plan(2021 - 2025) for National Economic and Social Development and the Long-Range Objectives Through the Year 2035, Website of State Council, http://www. gov. cn/zhengce/2020 - 11/03/content_5556991. htm, November 3, 2020.

ning theory and practice since its inception to explore the development path with Chinese characteristics. After the Third Plenary Session of the 11th CPC Central Committee, the Chinese communists gradually established Deng Xiaoping Theory, the Theory of Three Represents and the Scientific Outlook on Development as guiding ideologies that CPC must adhere to in the long run, while Xi Jinping Thought on Socialism with Chinese Characteristics for a New Era, as the latest achievement of localization of Marxism in China, serves as a guiding principle for China to realize its "Two Centenary Goals". The third is the masses. The CPC sticks to follow the mass line in its work, doing everything for the masses, relying on them in every task, and carrying out the principle of "from the masses, to the masses". People run the country is an essential feature and core of socialist democracy. General Secretary Xi Jinping evaluated the democracy and effectiveness of a country's political system with eight criteria in his speech, including: an orderly change of a country's leadership according to law; the management of state and social affairs, economic and cultural undertakings by all the people in accordance with the law; the unimpeded expression of the people's interests; the effective participation of all sectors of society in the political life of a country; rationality and democracy of a country's decision-making; the entry of talented people from all sectors into the state leadership and management system through fair competition; the leadership of the ruling party in state affairs in accordance with the Constitution; and the effective restraint and supervision of the use of power.[①] Facts have proven that as long as the CPC keeps the original aspiration of pursuing happiness for the Chinese people, rejuvenation for the Chinese nation, and the common good for the world, it will coordinate both domestic and international dynamics, give equal importance to development and security, and promote national development and world peace.

[①] Cui & Chen, Xi Jinping Evaluates the Democracy and Effectiveness of a Country's Political System based on Eight Criteria, people.cn, http://politics.people.com.cn/n/2014/0909/c1001 - 25622836.html, June 30, 2021.

A national development strategy is a strategy to plan and guide the development of a country's strength and potential to achieve national development goals. An economic development strategy serves the national development strategy. As it is related to the institutional makers' understanding of national conditions, development path and future vision, the economic development strategy should vary according to time and stage of development. Most of the time, China has formulated development strategies that are realistic and close to its national conditions, although some hasty and impetuous actions have brought losses to the cause of the Party and the country. Looking back on its development, the CPC has gone through a process of exploration on what modernization is and how it should be carried out. The CPC was suspicious of modernization when it was founded, but that changed when the War of Resistance against Japanese Aggression broke out. After the founding of the People's Republic of China, modernization was at first focused mainly on industrialization, and later specified in four areas, including industry, agriculture, transportation and national defense. At the 18th CPC National Congress, the all-round modernization strategy was put forward. At the Third Plenary Session of the 18th CPC Central Committee, the overall goal of comprehensively deepening reform was defined, namely modernizing China's governance system and capacity. At the 19th CPC National Congress, modernization guided by the new development concept was put forward, and the road map for modernization featuring the "two-step strategy" was further put forward, promoting the theoretical innovation of modernization. Only practice can make theory stand the test.

Looking back on the past 100 years, China has experienced the exploration process of learning from western countries, learning from the Soviet Union, learning from all the achievements of advanced civilization and taking its own path. Seeking truth from facts is an evidence-based summary of the CPC's experience. At the same time, the CPC also attaches great importance to innovation in theory and practice. China has had its share of detours and setbacks, but eventually overcame them and moved on. Other developing countries may be inspired by the evolution of China's development concept when formulating their own development strategies. China should not only be good at grasping the social principal contradiction and reforming all systems inconsistent with the development of productivity, but also embrace the world with an open mind. By doing so, China can learn from all the excellent achievements of mankind and ultimately follow its own path on the basis of combining selected achievements to promote its development and prosperity.

References

Cui & Chen, Xi Jinping Evaluates the Democracy and Effectiveness of a Country's Political System based on Eight Criteria, people. cn, http: // politics. people. com. cn/n/2014/0909/c1001 -25622836. html, June 30, 2021.

Li Dazhao, "Socialism and Social Movements" (Sept. 1923 - Apr. 1924), in *Collected Writings of Li Dazhao*, Vol. 4, People's Publishing House, 2013.

Party History Research Center of the CPC Central Committee: *The 90 Years of the Communist Party of China*, History of Chinese Communist Party Publishing House, Party Building Books Publishing House, 2016.

Qu Qiubai Anthology, Vol. 7, People's Publishing House, 2013.

Selected Works of Deng Xiaoping, Vol. 2, People's Publishing House, 1994.

Selected Works of Mao Zedong, Vol. 2, People's Publishing House, 1986.

The CPC Central Committee's Proposals for Formulating the 14th Five-Year Plan(2021 - 2025) for National Economic and Social Development and the Long-Range Objectives Through the Year 2035, Website of State Council, http: //www. gov. cn/zhengce/2020 - 11/03/content_5556991. htm, November 3, 2020.

The Meeting of the Standing Committee of the Political Bureau of the CPC Central Committee Presided Over by Xi Jinping, people. cn, May 15, 2020.

The Theory Bureau of the Propaganda Department of the CPC Central Committee, *Face to Face with the Development of People's Republic of China*, Learning Publishing House & People's Publishing House, 2019.

Xie Juezai's Diary, Vol. 1, People's Publishing House, 1984.

Zeng & Hu: "An Analysis of Changes in the Income Gap between Urban and Rural Residents in China Since the Late 1970s and Its Impact on the Consumption Levels of Urban and Rural Residents", *Economic Review*, 2008, Issue 1.

Zhang Tailei Anthology, People's Publishing House, 2013.

The Influence of China's Home-Based Old-Age Care Service Supply on the Elderly's Satisfaction*

Sun Zhaoyang**

I. Origin of the Issue

Since entering the aging society in 2000, China has seen an accelerated development trend in aging, and a rapid increase in demand for old-age care services, thus facing tremendous pressure in this regard. As shown in Figure 1, in 2010, there were 119 million elderly people aged over 65 in China, which was 2.4 times that of 49.4 million in 1982, increasing from 4.9% to 8.9%, with an average annual increase of 0.14 percentage points. In 2020, the number of elderly people reached 191 million, rapidly increasing to 13.5%, with an average annual increase of 0.46 percentage points in the past ten years. Since the 18th National Congress of the Communist Party of China, as the CPC Central Committee with Comrade Xi Jinping as the core has adhered to the people-centered development philosophy, attached great importance to the issue of aging

---

* This article was originally published on *Journal of the CCPS(CAG)* (No.1, 2021), with the original title "Impacts of Home-based Care Service on Satisfaction of the Elderly: An Analysis on the Survey of 8 Provinces", and the content has slightly changed.

** Sun Zhaoyang, Associate Professor, University of Chinese Academy of Social Sciences.

and old-age care, and paid attention to improving the elderly's sense of happiness, gain and security, China's old-age care and services have developed rapidly, and the content and scope of old-age care services have expanded rapidly. However, there are few empirical studies on the change effect of the supply structure of old-age care services, and the degree of influence of rich service supply on the satisfaction of the elderly is still unclear. Therefore, this paper studies the influence of home-based old-age care services on the satisfaction of the elderly from the perspective of service supply.

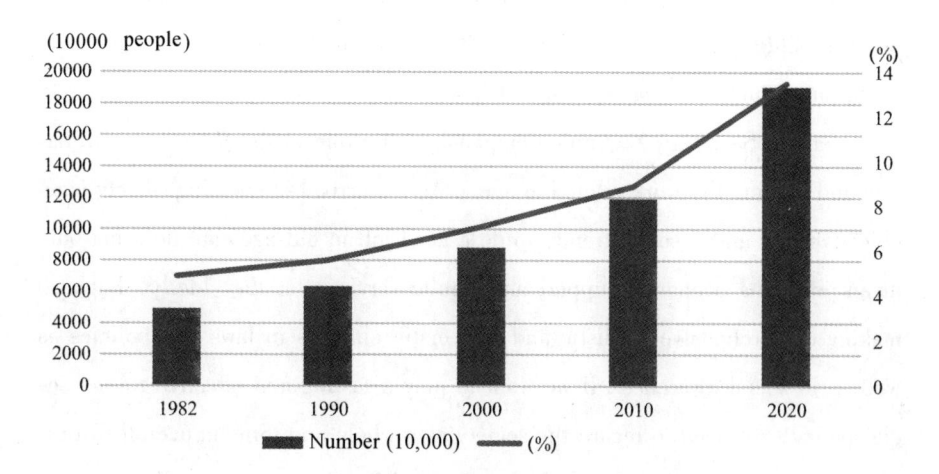

Figure 1   Number and Proportion of the Elderly Aged over 65 in China

Source: Website of National Bureau of Statistics of China(https://data.stats.gov.cn).

(i) Establishment of home-based old-age care system

General Secretary Xi Jinping has always accurately grasped the aging trend in China and the importance of aging work. In May, 2016, General Secretary Xi Jinping pointed out at the 32nd collective study of the Political Bureau of the Central Committee of the CPC that "China is one of the countries with a relatively high degree of population aging in the world, with the largest number of elderly people, the fastest aging speed and the heaviest task in dealing with population aging." ① By the end of 2019, China had about 176 million elderly people aged 65 and above, accounting for 12.6% of the total population, making it the country with most elderly people in the world. Further, influenced by the adjustment of the childbirth policy, China experienced a "baby boom" in the middle of 1960s and 1970s. Now most of these people, about 328 million, are between 45 and 59 years old, accounting for 23.5% of the total population, and will gradually reach the age for retirement in the next 15 years. It is estimated that the elderly population in China will reach 366 million by the middle of this century, accounting for 26.1% of the total population, and the dependency ratio of the elderly population will reach 43.7%, ② which will bring great pressure to the incomplete pension system in China.

General Secretary Xi Jinping emphasized the role of the Party in coordinating and leading the work related to aging. As the arrival of an aging society is an objective fact and a social trend, to do a good job in old-age care does not only mean providing economic support and public services for the elderly, but also making comprehensive, holistic and systematic changes in laws and policies as well as in social awareness. If we want to play a lasting and effective role of social policy, we need to regard the society as a whole and form an overall institutional framework to promote and coordinate different systems in playing their roles together, instead of relying only on a certain project, a certain department or a certain social system to assume responsibility ③. For this reason, General Secretary Xi Jinping emphasized that it is necessary to adhere to the combination of Party Committee's leadership, government's implementation, social participa-

---

① "Xi Jinping emphasized during the 32nd collective study of the Political Bureau of the CPC Central Committee: with the leadership of party committee and government, participation of the society and the action of people, promoting the comprehensive, coordinated and sustainable development of the cause of aging", *People's Daily*, May 29, 2016, page 1.

② Department of Economic and Social Affairs, Population Division, "World Population Prospects 2019, Volume II: Demographic Profiles – China", New York: United Nations, 2019.

③ Zhang Xiulan, Xu Yuebin, "Constructing China's Developmental Family Policy", *Social Sciences in China*, 2003, No. 6.

tion and all the people's action, the combination of coping with population aging and promoting economic and social development, and the combination of meeting the needs of the elderly and solving the problem of population aging, and put forward the strategic direction from the aspects of strengthening the active ideology in aging, improving the aging policy system, developing the old-age care service industry and aging industry, giving full play to the active role of the elderly, and improving the systems and mechanisms in aging work [1]. The Standing Committee of the National People's Congress revised the *Law on Protection of the Rights and Interests of the Elderly* twice, and the State Council successively promulgated a series of important documents such as *Several Opinions on Accelerating the Old-Age Care Service* and *Opinions on Promoting the Development of Old-Age Care Service*. The Ministry of Finance, the Ministry of Civil Affairs, the National Development and Reform Commission and other national ministries and commissions provide supporting policy support for the development of the old-age care cause in many aspects such as laws and regulations, financial support, market construction, system and personnel training, which constitute main pillars of the policy system for old-age care with Chinese characteristics.

General Secretary Xi Jinping put forward and established the strategic layout of home-based old-age care system. On the basis of emphasizing the active response to the aging of the population, the construction of the old-age care service system has been included in the outline of the national economic and social development plan in the 13th Five-Year Plan, thus realizing the overall planning of the old-age care strategy at the national level. General Secretary Xi Jinping pointed out in the report of the 19th National Congress of the Communist Party of China that "as we respond proactively to population aging, we will adopt policies and foster a social environment in which senior citizens are

---

[1] "Xi Jinping emphasized during the 32nd collective study of the Political Bureau of the CPC Central Committee: with the leadership of party committee and government, participation of the society and the action of people, promoting the comprehensive, coordinated and sustainable development of the cause of aging", *People's Daily*, May 29, 2016, page 1.

respected, cared for, and live happily in their later years. We will provide integrated elderly care and medical services, and accelerate the development of old-age programs and industries." ① The strategic goal of the old-age care work was further clarified in the Fourth Plenary Session of the 19th CPC Central Committee that "we will actively respond to the aging of the population, and accelerate the construction of an old-age care system that integrates home, communities and healthcare facilities". ② General Secretary Xi Jinping's strategic exposition has pointed out the direction for promoting the construction of multi-level old-age security system, ensuring people's old-age security, and developing the cause of old-age care with Chinese characteristics in the new era. China has built the world's largest social security network with a per capita GDP of only US $ 10, 000, which fully embodies the CPC Central Committee's people-centered development philosophy. Thanks to the efforts of the central and local governments, China has basically established an old-age service system based on home, supported by community, supplemented by institutions and combined with medical care. The preferential treatment programs for the elderly are richer and much further expanded. The social atmosphere of respecting and helping the elderly is increasingly strong, and diversified old-age service supply is initially formed.

(ii) Old-age services and satisfaction of the elderly

With the official establishment of the national policy to build a home-based old-age care system, some studies have begun to pay attention to its influence on the satisfaction of the elderly. One of these studies has analyzed the elderly's sat-

---

① Xi Jinping, *Secure a Decisive Victory in Building a Moderately Prosperous Society in All Respects and Strive for the Great Success of Socialism with Chinese Characteristics for a New Era*: Report at the 19th National Congress of the Communist Party of China, People's Publishing House, 2017, pp. 48, 46.

② Xi Jinping, *Secure a Decisive Victory in Building a Moderately Prosperous Society in All Respects and Strive for the Great Success of Socialism with Chinese Characteristics for a New Era*: Report at the 19th National Congress of the Communist Party of China, People's Publishing House, 2017, pp. 48, 46.

isfaction with the environment construction of different communities, and the influence of these subjective feelings on their overall life satisfaction [1]. Another study has evaluated the quality of community-based old-age services in Shanghai from five dimensions, such as reliability and responsiveness [2]. For rural areas, personal family factors such as family income, health status, old-age insurance and medical insurance, children's marriage expenses, children's filial piety and intergenerational cooperation, as well as external factors such as policy support, government and social concern and public opinion have a strong positive influence on the elderly's satisfaction in old-age care [3]. For urban areas, economic independence degree, service accessibility, health status, living comfort, community service, children's visit, housing conditions, living environment and other factors have a strong positive effect on improving the elderly's satisfaction with home care [4]. For the situation across China, elderly people who are women, live in rural areas, have spouses, are at advanced ages, are in good health, have more social participation, enjoy more children's visits or have higher income

---

[1] Qian Xuefei, Status Quo of Social Environment Construction of Community-Based Old-Age Services Influencing Life Satisfaction of Urban and Rural Elderly: Based on 1,440 questionnaires", *Northwest Population Journal*, No. 3, 2011.

[2] Zhang Xiaoyi, Liu Bangcheng, "Model Research on the Service Quality of Community Home-Based Old-Age Care: A Case Study of Shanghai'', *Chinese Journal of Population Science*, No. 3, 2011.

[3] Hu Shiyong, Li Yang, "Analysis of Influencing Factors of Rural Elderly's Satisfaction with Family-Based Old-Age Care", *Chinese Rural Economy*, No. 12, 2012; Wang Yanfang, Wang Xutao, "Multi-Factor Analysis of Influencing Rural Elderly's Life Satisfaction and Choice of Old-Age Care Mode", *China Economic Studies*, No. 5, 2014.

[4] Yan Bingqiu, Gao Xiaolu, "Influencing Factors and Community Differences of Urban Elderly's Satisfaction with Home-Based Old-Age Care", *Geographical Research*, No. 7, 2013; Yu Jie, Mark Rosenberg, Cheng Yang, "A Study on Satisfaction with Home-Based Old-Age Care and Institutions' Willingness of Operating Old-Age Care Business in Beijing", *Progress in Geography*, No. 12, 2015; Tang Di, Yu Yunjiang, Sun Xu, Gao Xiangdong, "A Study on Satisfaction of Government Purchased Community-Based Old-Age Services: An Empirical Analysis based on Data of A Survey in Shanghai", *Northwest Population Journal*, No. 3, 2017.

have higher life satisfaction ①.

On the whole, despite the different names and calibers of variables used in different studies on the factors influencing the elderly's life satisfaction, they mainly include three factors: individual, family and community. There are two problems in the above studies: First, they mostly use local or regional data, and the data were collected early (mostly before 2013), so they can no longer used to analyze the new changes of old-age care work after the 18th National Congress. Second, they mainly pay attention to the influence of individual and family factors, and lacks the analysis of the effect of old-age service supply, which is the main feature of old-age care work since the 18th National Congress. In view of this, this paper, by using the community-elderly matching survey data in eight provinces or cities in China in 2019, mainly analyzes the influence of the old-age care service supply on the satisfaction of the elderly under the construction of home-based old-age care system.

II. Research Hypothesis

To solve the problems of "low-level equilibrium trap"② and imbalance between supply and demand of old-age care services③, since the 18th National Congress of the Communist Party of China, an important measure for the construction of home-based old-age care system in China is to encourage diversified supply of old-age care services, that is, to give full play to the main suppliers of

---

① Liu Ji, "A Study on Life Satisfaction of the Elderly in China and Its Influencing Factors: Based on the Analysis of National Baseline Data of 'China Health and Retirement Longitudinal Study' (CHARLS) in 2011", *Scientific Research on Aging*, No. 1, 2015.

② Lin Bao, "'Low-Level Equilibrium Trap' and Policy Support in Old-Age Care Service Industry", *Journal of Xinjiang Normal University (Philosophy and Social Sciences Edition)*, No. 1, 2017.

③ Ni Dongsheng, Zhang Yanfang, "Research on Chinese government's Policy of Purchasing Old-Age Care Services under the Background of Supply-Demand Imbalance of Old-Age Care Services", *Journal of Central University of Finance and Economics*, No. 11, 2015.

government, community and family①, and to encourage enterprises, volunteers, social organizations and other market and social forces to fully and deeply participate in service supply ②, so as to expand the content and scope of the old-age care service supply, and better meet the needs of the elderly. Then, does the construction of home-based aged care service system and the enrichment of aged care service supply improve the elderly's satisfaction with aged care?

Satisfaction, as a kind of psychological state, is a subjective evaluation on objective things. Old-age care satisfaction is the evaluation of elderly people's own living conditions.

If the old-age service supply has an impact on the satisfaction of old-age work, then the elderly's satisfaction can be regarded as a function of the old-age service supply. Because the old-age service provided by the market and society has a substitution effect on the function of family-based old-age care, the more services provided in the market, the more it can make up for the needs of the elderly in the lack of family-based old-age care function, and make the elderly's life happier, thus making them more satisfied with old-age care. Hence, the article puts forward the following hypotheses.

Hypothesis 1: Incremental effect hypothesis, that is, the more old-age care services provided within the reach of the elderly, the higher the elderly's satisfaction.

According to the existing research experience ③, this paper uses the ordered logistic regression method for verification. Hypothesis 1 takes the number of old-age services as the independent variable of the elderly's satisfaction, and

---

① Tong Chunfen, Wang Lianjie, "Construction of Government Responsibility System for China's Home-Based Old-Age Care Services from the Perspective of Welfare Pluralism", *Northwest Population Journal*, No. 1, 2015.

② Peng Huamin, Welfare Triangle: A Paradigm of Social Policy Analysis", *Sociological Studies*, No. 4, 2006.

③ Zhang Miao, "An Analysis of Old-Age Care Status and Satisfaction of China's Rural Elderly", *The World of Survey and Research*, No. 6, 2016.

the model is as follows:

$$Y_i^* = \beta N_i + \gamma X_i + \varepsilon_i \qquad (1)$$

In it, N_i refers to the number of old-age care services provided near the home of the elderly, which is a continuous variable; X_i indicates the control variables that influence satisfaction; ε_i is an error term and obeys logical distribution; i represents the observed value. Y_i^* is a continuous latent variable that cannot be observed, but an orderly discrete variable Y_i that can be observed is the elderly's satisfaction. The relationship between them is as follows:

$$Y_i = j(j = 1,2,3) , \text{ if } c_{j-1} < Y_i^* \leq c_j \qquad (2)$$

In it, c_0, c_1, c_2 and c_3 are thresholds and parameters to be estimated, and $c_0 = -\infty, c_3 = +\infty$.

At the same time, this paper argues that elderly people with different demographic characteristics and family conditions have different demands for old-age care services. Under such conditions, the service supply can also be different to the elderly's satisfaction, which means that the impact of old-age care services on the elderly's satisfaction is heterogeneous. For this reason, this paper puts forward:

Hypothesis 2: Heterogeneous effect hypothesis, that is, there are differences in the effect of old-age care service projects on the elderly's satisfaction. Some services can improve their satisfaction, while others cannot.

According to formula(1), the hypothesis model is set as follows:

$$Y_i^* = \beta S_i + \gamma X_i + \varepsilon_i \qquad (3)$$

In it, S_i represents the old-age care services provided nearby, that is, the main explanatory variables; X_i refers to the control variables that affect satisfaction; ε_i is an error term and obeys logical distribution; i represents the observed value. Y_i^* and Y_i satisfy the setting of formula(2).

III. Data Sources and Variable Selection

(i) Data

To deeply study the construction of China's old-age care service system and the elderly's old-age care needs, the Institute of Social Development Strategy of the Chinese Academy of Social Sciences conducted a survey on China's aging and old-age care work from May to July in 2019. In this survey, 10 – 15 elderly people of each community in 800 communities of 80 counties from 8 provinces were selected by multi-stage and multi-level probability sampling method proportional to population size. These eight provinces are Liaoning, Hebei, Shandong, Shanghai, Henan, Guangdong, Sichuan and Shaanxi, representing the six geographical regions of Northeast China, North China, East China, South China, Southwest China and Northwest China respectively. 693 valid community questionnaires and 7,261 elderly questionnaires were actually received, with the recovery rates of 86.6% and 90.8%.

(ii) **Variable selection**

The dependent variable of this paper is the elderly's satisfaction, consisting of two parts. First, the elderly's satisfaction with the community-based old-age services, including the quality of medical and health services, provision of life assistance for the elderly, infrastructure and living environment; second, life satisfaction, including senses of happiness, gain and security, and it is obtained from the questions "Generally speaking, I am a happy person", "Compared with five years ago, how you feel about your living conditions" and "Even if life started all over again, I had nothing to change". The option values are: unsatisfied = 1, so-so = 2, satisfied = 3. Although these dimensions can't cover all aspects of the elderly's satisfaction, the contents involved are the key issues that the elderly care about in the building the home-based old-age care system, and are also the main aspects to measure the practical effect of the elderly's home-based old-age care work.

See Table 1 for the overall and classified satisfaction of the elderly.

Table 1   Survey of the Elderly's Life Satisfaction   (%)

	Urban and rural regionalization		Age group			Gender		Total
	Rural area	Urban area	60–69	70–79	Over 80	Male	Female	
Medical and health service quality	58.2	48.6	50.3	54.3	55.9	54.1	50.2	52.1
Providing help for the elderly's life	59.4	60	59	60.5	62.1	60.6	59	59.8
Infrastructure and living environment	62.5	61.8	61.8	62.6	62.1	62.5	61.7	62.1
Sense of happiness	63.5	65.9	64.9	64.6	66.8	64.9	65.2	65.1
Sense of gain	85.5	75.3	79	78.2	80.7	79.8	78.3	79
Sense of security	49.8	49.6	48.7	50.2	53.6	50.6	48.8	49.7

Source: According to the author's calculation. It has been weighted.

The independent variable in this paper is old-age care service supply. According to the experience of the existing research [1], this paper divides the old-age care services into four aspects: Life assistance, including food delivery service, helping to take a bath, and household cleaning; health care, including on-site medical treatment, community care, and purchase/lease of elderly products; cultural life, including lectures on disease prevention, psychological consultation/chat, and recreational activities; and rights protection, which means legal rights protection service. This variable operation is "Is there such a service nearby?" yes = 1 and no = 0. At the same time, according to the result of the elderly's choice, we can know that the number of nearby old-age care

---

[1] Zhang Xiaoyi, Liu Bangcheng, "Model Research on the Service Quality of Community Home-Based Old-Age Care: A Case Study of Shanghai", *Chinese Journal of Population Science*, No. 3, 2011; Ding Zhihong, Wang Lili, "Research on Equalization of China's Community Home-Based Old-Age Care Services", *Population Journal*, No. 5, 2011; Wang Qiong, "Demand for Home-Based Old-Age Care Services in Urban Communities and Its Influencing Factors: Based on National Survey Data of Urban Elderly People", *Population Research*, No. 1, 2016.

service supply. If there is no, the result will be 0, and if there are all of them, the result will be 10. This is a continuous variable. The supply and demand of old-age care services near the elderly are shown in Table 2.

Table 2　　　　　Supply and Demand of Old-age Care
　　　　　　　　　Services Near the Elderly　　　　　　(%)

	Supply	Demand	Supply gap
Food delivery service	28.5	10.5	18.0
Help with taking a bath	12.8	9.1	3.7
Household cleaning	24.0	15.3	8.7
On-site medical treatment	49.7	40.4	9.3
Community care	22.6	20.1	2.5
Purchase/lease of old-age products	19.0	18.0	1.0
Lecture on disease prevention	41.4	54.2	-12.8
Psychological consultation/chat	21.4	31.2	-9.8
Recreational activities	64.6	61.5	3.1
Legal rights protection service	41.2	41.6	-0.4

Note: Supply gap = supply-demand.
Source: According to the author's calculation.

In this paper, the control variables are divided into three categories: personal characteristics, family support, and community-based old-age service environment. Personal characteristic variables include: gender, age, education level, monthly income, self-rated health, disability, and household registration type. Family support variables include: spouse, number of surviving children, and maintenance. Community-based old-age service environment: area classification, free use of activity places, community health service center, day care center/old-age care center, and province. Statistical characteristics of variables are shown in Table 3.

Table 3　　　　　　　　Statistical Description of Variables

Variable	Variable definition	Quantity	Average value	Standard deviation
Gender	Female = 1, male = 0	7, 261	0.334	0.472
Age	Age of the elderly	7, 261	71.502	8.109
Degree of education	Never attended school = 1, primary school (private school) = 2, junior high school = 3, senior high school/technical secondary school/vocational high school = 4, university and above = 5	7, 248	2.362	0.981
Monthly income	Total monthly income	7, 261	1387.005	1776.246
Health condition	Healthy = 1, unhealthy = 0	7, 229	0.368	0.482
Disability situation	Disability = 1, self-care = 0	7, 261	0.122	0.328
Household registration	Non-agriculture = 1, agriculture = 0	7, 240	0.243	0.429
Have a spouse	Yes = 1, no = 0	7, 261	0.797	0.402
Number of children	Number of surviving children	7, 261	2.76	1.534
Maintenance situation	Supported by sons = 1, supported by daughters = 2, supported by sons and daughters in turn = 3, not supported by children = 4	7, 215	2.526	1.312
Regional classification	Urban = 1, rural = 0	7, 261	0.374	0.484
Free place for activities	Yes = 1, no = 0	7, 231	0.801	0.399
Community health service center	Yes = 1, no = 0	7, 220	0.881	0.324
Day Care Center/Old-age care center	Yes = 1, no = 0	7, 246	0.271	0.444
Province	Administrative division code	7, 261	35.164	13.539
Medical and health service quality	Dissatisfied = 1, so-so = 2, satisfied = 3	7, 236	2.477	0.597

Continued

Variable	Variable definition	Quantity	Average value	Standard deviation
Provision of life assistance for the elderly	Dissatisfied =1, so-so =2, satisfied =3	7,227	2.527	0.604
Infrastructure and living environment	Dissatisfied =1, so-so =2, satisfied =3	7,246	2.561	0.577
Sense of happiness	Dissatisfied =1, so-so =2, satisfied =3	7,236	2.613	0.56
Sense of gain	Dissatisfied =1, so-so =2, satisfied =3	7,171	2.774	0.477
Sense of security	Dissatisfied =1, so-so =2, satisfied =3	7,212	2.47	0.631
Number of services	Total number of old-age care services	7,125	3.089	2.755
Food delivery service	Yes =1, no =0	7,229	0.223	0.416
Help with taking a bath	Yes =1, no =0	7,221	0.112	0.316
Household cleaning	Yes =1, no =0	7,224	0.193	0.394
On-site medical treatment	Yes =1, no =0	7,245	0.552	0.497
Community care	Yes =1, no =0	7,209	0.204	0.403
Purchase/lease of old-age products	Yes =1, no =0	7,215	0.173	0.378
Lecture on disease prevention	Yes =1, no =0	7,229	0.403	0.491
Legal rights protection service	Yes =1, no =0	7,211	0.41	0.492
Psychological consultation/chat	Yes =1, no =0	7,210	0.204	0.403
Recreational activities	Yes =1, no =0	7,234	0.625	0.484

Source: According to the author's calculation.

IV. Findings

Home-based old-age care refers to the old-age care service system in which the elderly live at home, mainly obtaining old-age care service from the community. The community is the operation platform of old-age care service supply, the enterprises and social organizations provide the service content, old-age care institutions provide the service supplement for the disabled elderly, and the government provides the support for the disadvantaged elderly groups. Under the home-based old-age care system, the elderly get most of the old-age care services from the community, which can be a service provider and even more of a service platform organizer. If the old-age service can meet the needs of the elderly and make their life more comfortable, the more service projects near the elderly, the higher their satisfaction should be. According to formula(1), the regression results are summarized in models(1) - (6) in Tab. 4. On the whole, the number of old-age care services has a strong positive impact on all categories of the elderly's satisfaction, and the significance is above 1%. This shows that increasing old-age care services can effectively improve the elderly's satisfaction. Hypothesis 1 is verified. In terms of the degree of influence, the effect of old-age care service on the elderly's environment satisfaction is higher than that of life satisfaction, especially on the community infrastructure and living environment; in life satisfaction, it has the greatest effect on the elderly's sense of happiness, but has no significant effect on their sense of security. This shows that old-age care service supply can improve the elderly's satisfaction as a whole, but it has different effects on the satisfaction of the elderly in different aspects. Therefore, when developing the old-age care service industry, we should focus on promoting projects that can improve the elderly's satisfaction according to the needs and satisfaction characteristics of the local elderly.

Old-age care service projects meet the elderly's needs from different angles. With different degrees of demand, there are different satisfaction degrees to the service projects, and the influence effect on their satisfaction is also different. According to formula(3), the regression results are reported in models (7) - (12) in Table 2. The results show that life assistance services have the least impact on the improvement of the elderly's satisfaction. They have no significant positive impact on all categories of satisfaction, even most of them have negative impact, and some of them are significant above 5%, indicating that this kind of service is not the elderly's main demand, and that project supply in this regard has little influence on the elderly. Health care, cultural life and protection of rights have a positive impact on the improvement of elderly's satisfaction, with most of the significance of above 1%. The influence on the satisfaction of community-based old-age service environment is significantly higher than life satisfaction, among which it has the greatest impact on providing life assistance for the elderly and the least impact on the elderly's sense of security. On-site medical treatment in health care has a significant positive impact on all satisfaction, and lectures on disease prevention in cultural life also have a positive impact, almost all of which are significant at 1%. Among them, community care and recreational activities only have a significant positive impact on environmental satisfaction. There are differences in the direction, scope and significance of different types and projects of old-age care services on the elderly's satisfaction, which shows that old-age care services have significant heterogeneity. Hypothesis 2 is tested.

Table 4　　　　Regression Results of the Influence of Old-age Care Service Supply on the Elderly's Satisfaction

Dependent variable	Environmental satisfaction			Life satisfaction		
	Medical and health service quality	Provision of life assistance for the elderly	Community infrastructure and living environment	Sense of happiness	Sense of gain	Sense of security
	(1)	(2)	(3)	(4)	(5)	(6)
Number of old-age care services	0.138 ***	0.148 ***	0.163 ***	0.102 ***	0.068 ***	0.023
	(0.018)	(0.019)	(0.018)	(0.017)	(0.015)	(0.016)
Control variable	Yes	Yes	Yes	Yes	Yes	Yes
Observed value	6,746	6,739	6,756	6,747	6,689	6,737
Pseudo R^2	0.0728	0.0627	0.0674	0.0671	0.0730	0.0315

Continued

Dependent variable		Environmental satisfaction			Life satisfaction		
		Medical and health service quality	Provision of life assistance for the elderly	Community infrastructure and living environment	Sense of happiness	Sense of gain	Sense of security
		(7)	(8)	(9)	(10)	(11)	(12)
Life assistance	Food delivery service	-0.409 ***	-0.208 ***	-0.037	-0.238 ***	-0.258 ***	-0.292 ***
		(0.078)	(0.080)	(0.081)	(0.083)	(0.094)	(0.075)
	Help with taking a bath	-0.082	-0.235 **	-0.047	0.008	-0.108	0.231 **
		(0.103)	(0.109)	(0.107)	(0.113)	(0.120)	(0.100)
	Household cleaning	-0.230 ***	-0.130	-0.092	-0.135	-0.053	-0.012
		(0.088)	(0.093)	(0.094)	(0.096)	(0.109)	(0.083)
Health care	On-site medical treatment	0.444 ***	0.213 ***	0.261 ***	0.168 **	0.215 ***	0.027
		(0.067)	(0.068)	(0.069)	(0.069)	(0.083)	(0.062)
	Community care	0.373 ***	0.506 ***	0.404 ***	-0.060	0.003	0.056
		(0.086)	(0.092)	(0.091)	(0.089)	(0.108)	(0.085)
	Purchase/lease of old-age products	0.294 ***	0.163 *	0.175 *	0.352 ***	0.126	0.190 **
		(0.086)	(0.095)	(0.093)	(0.095)	(0.106)	(0.087)
Cultural life	Lecture on disease prevention	0.351 ***	0.239 ***	0.038	0.326 ***	0.296 ***	0.273 ***
		(0.075)	(0.078)	(0.079)	(0.083)	(0.099)	(0.073)
	Psychological consultation/chat	0.339 ***	0.484 ***	0.399 ***	0.139	-0.299 ***	0.189 **
		(0.089)	(0.098)	(0.094)	(0.094)	(0.112)	(0.080)
	Recreational activities	0.269 ***	0.352 ***	0.449 ***	-0.001	-0.012	-0.056
		(0.070)	(0.069)	(0.069)	(0.071)	(0.089)	(0.065)

Continued

Dependent variable		Environmental satisfaction			Life satisfaction		
		Medical and health service quality	Provision of life assistance for the elderly	Community infrastructure and living environment	Sense of happiness	Sense of gain	Sense of security
		(7)	(8)	(9)	(10)	(11)	(12)
Rights protection	Legal rights protection service	0.006	0.227 ***	0.128 *	0.204 ***	0.401 ***	-0.055
		(0.074)	(0.075)	(0.074)	(0.077)	(0.090)	(0.069)
	Control variable	Yes	Yes	Yes	Yes	Yes	Yes
	Observed value	6,746	6,739	6,756	6,747	6,689	6,737
	Pseudo R^2	0.0970	0.0844	0.0769	0.0669	0.0883	0.0355

Note: In parentheses is the standard error of robustness; ***, **, and * mean being significant at 1%, 5%, and 10%, respectively. Due to the limited length of this paper, the regression results of all variables are not shown. If you need them, you can ask the author for them.

Source: According to the author's calculation.

Why do different service items have different effects on the elderly's satisfaction? This is mainly due to the age structure and service demand preference of the elderly. Life assistance services have long been provided by family members, and path dependence and traditional habits are easy to form in the understanding of the elderly and society. Moreover, the average monthly income of the elderly people in the survey is 1,387 yuan, so they are unwilling to pay for such services for a long time when their family members can provide such services. Although the survey shows that the empty-nest elderly has reached 57.4%, China's elderly people still mainly belong to low-age elderly people. By the end of 2019, the elderly aged 60 - 69 accounted for 60%. Since they have good health and self-care ability, they have relatively low demand for such services. This kind of service belongs to the elderly's daily needs. If the price is set too high, it is difficult for the elderly to buy it. If the service price is too low, the enterprise has no profit and cannot develop continuously. Such service is not the elderly's main demand at present, so it does not have the base for wide-ranging demand in the short term, and needs long-term market construction. However, due to their limited self-care ability and conditions, advanced aged or disabled elderly people have very limited elasticity of such demand. To meet their needs and improve their quality of life, the government should strengthen special subsidies for such elderly people, or reduce rent and tax for service enterprises, so as to fully mobilize the power of the market.

Health care, cultural life and rights protection services require high professional knowledge and skills, which cannot be provided by family members under the traditional old-age care mode, but need specialized institutions and professionals to provide them. In particular, for on-site medical treatment, lectures on disease prevention, and legal rights protection service, professional doctors, nurses, lawyers, judges and other professionals are needed. For the elderly, these services are necessary and irreplaceable, so the supply of these services can best improve the elderly's satisfaction. With China entering a moderately prosperous society in all respects, the elderly also put forward higher requirements for life quality. In 2018, the average life expectancy in China reached 77 years old ①. Health has become the most important need of the elderly. Without healthy physiological and psychological conditions, the elderly cannot enjoy a happy and comfortable old age. On-site medical treatment and health knowledge can not only meet the needs of the elderly for treating diseases, but also reduce the consumption of time and energy such as transportation and waiting for medical treatment, and strengthen the prevention of diseases. These services are even more important for the elderly with chronic diseases or limited physical function. In recent years, infringement cases involving property, support, marriage, fraud and illegal fund-raising of the elderly have occurred from time to time,

---

① National Health and Wellness Commission, *China Health Statistical Yearbook 2019*, Peking Union Medical College Press, 2020.

and the property, physical and psychological security of the elderly are threatened. Therefore, this service supply can meet their urgent needs and improve their satisfaction. In the case of high price of professional services, we can encourage employees or college students of related majors to provide voluntary services, so as to improve the diversified social old-age care service supply.

The construction of home-based old-age care system and the development of old-age care service industry in China should be transformed, from a way of "helping the weak" to a way of "popularization", and from a "supplementing" type to an "improving" type. At the initial stage of the construction of home-based old-age care services, old-age care service supply focused on the elderly who were advanced aged, disabled, living alone or empty nesters. Therefore, it focused on the development of living auxiliary services such as helping with having meals, cleaning, walking and bathing, which had obvious characteristics of "helping the weak". However, the number of such elderly people is small, and the vast majority of low-aged elderly people with strong self-care ability are not willing to pay for such services. Therefore, the "dining table for the elderly" and "dining hall for the elderly", which were popular in previous years, have encountered difficulties in sustainable operation recently. Therefore, it has little impact on the elderly's overall satisfaction. Therefore, in terms of service objects, the construction of home-based old-age care system in China should be transformed from a way of "helping the weak" to a way of "popularization", that is, paying more attention to the needs of the majority of elderly people while focusing on the particularly difficult groups. In terms of service content, it should be changed from a "supplementing" type to an "improving" type, that is, from home services such as helping with having meals, cleaning and bathing to the services that can improve the elderly's life quality such as on-site medical treatment, health knowledge, psychological counseling and legal consultation. Due to the limitation of the current medical and health system and the lack of medical staff in China, it is difficult to realize completely free on-site medical and nursing services for the elderly, so the functions of "Internet plus medical care" and intelligent old-age care are even more important. However, this survey shows that only 38.2% of the communities provide free Internet access, only 21.5% of the elderly use mobile phones or computers to access the Internet, and only 29.7% of the elderly are willing to purchase old-age care services through the Internet. These infrastructures and services need to be further strengthened.

V. Conclusion

Based on the data of a "Survey of China's Aging and Old-Age Care Work" in 2019, using the sequential logistic regression method, this paper, from the aspect of old-age care service supply, analyzes the influence of the construction of home-based old-age care system on the elderly's satisfaction from six aspects: community medical and health services, living assistance, basic environment, sense of happiness, sense of gain and sense of security in two categories of environmental satisfaction and life satisfaction. The results show that since the 18th National Congress of the Communist Party of China, the CPC Central Committee with Comrade Xi Jinping as the core has attached great importance to the old-age care work, and gradually established and promoted the construction of home-based old-age care system. The old-age care service industry has developed rapidly, and the content and scope of old-age care services have grown rapidly, showing a strong incremental effect, that is, the more old-age care services, the higher the elderly's satisfaction; there is heterogeneous effect, that is, old-age care services have different degrees of influence on the elderly: health care has the greatest influence, cultural life and rights protection have a great influence, and life assistance has no significant positive impact.

Therefore, with the accelerated aging, China should continue to strengthen the construction of home-based old-age care system during the 14th Five-Year Plan period to meet the elderly's diversified needs and improve their satisfaction with old-age care. In the direction of development, we should pay attention to the transformation from a way of "helping the weak" to a way of "popularization" and from a "supplementing" type to an "improving" type. While ensuring life assistance services for a few elderly people with special difficulties, we should develop health assistance, cultural life and rights protection services to a greater extent, so as to improve the physical and mental health of the elderly and ensure that their legitimate rights and interests are not infringed. In the way of development, it is necessary to promote the use of "Internet plus medical care", smart old-age care, artificial intelligence and big data, and combine online services with offline smart equipment, so as to better improve the elderly's life quality with precise medical care and services. On service provider, we should encourage the diversification of service providers. While giving full play to traditional providers such as government, community and family, we need to mobilize enterprises and social organizations, and encourage doctors, lawyers and students of related majors to volunteer in the community, so as to make up for the shortage of government and market supply, meet the elderly's needs for health, law and culture, and improve their satisfaction with old-age care.

References

Ding Zhihong, Wang Lili, "Research on Equalization of China's Community Home-Based Old-Age Care Services", *Population Journal*, No. 5, 2011.

Hu Shiyong, Li Yang, "Analysis of Influencing Factors of Rural Elderly's Satisfaction with Family-Based Old-Age Care", *Chinese Rural Economy*, No. 12, 2012.

Lin Bao, " 'Low-Level Equilibrium Trap' and Policy Support in Old-Age Care Service Industry", *Journal of Xinjiang Normal University (Philosophy and Social Sciences Edition)*, No. 1, 2017.

Liu Ji, "A Study on Life Satisfaction of the Elderly in China and Its Influencing Factors: Based on the Analysis of National Baseline Data of 'China Health and Retirement Longitudinal Study' (CHARLS) in 2011", *Scientific Research on Aging*, No. 1, 2015.

National Health and Wellness Commission, *China Health Statistical Year-*

book 2019, Peking Union Medical College Press, 2020.

Ni Dongsheng, ZhangYanfang, "Research on Chinese government's Policy of Purchasing Old-Age Care Services under the Background of Supply-Demand Imbalance of Old-Age Care Services", *Journal of Central University of Finance and Economics*, No. 11, 2015.

Peng Huamin, "Welfare Triangle: A Paradigm of Social Policy Analysis", *Sociological Studies*, No. 4, 2006.

Qian Xuefei, "Status Quo of Social Environment Construction of Community-Based Old-Age Services Influencing Life Satisfaction of Urban and Rural Elderly: Based on 1,440 questionnaires", *Northwest Population Journal*, No. 3, 2011.

Tang Di, Yu Yunjiang, Sun Xu, Gao Xiangdong, "A Study on Satisfaction of Government Purchased Community-Based Old-Age Services: An Empirical Analysis based on Data of A Survey in Shanghai", *Northwest Population Journal*, No. 3, 2017.

Tong Chunfen, Wang Lianjie, "Construction of Government Responsibility System for China's Home-Based Old-Age Care Services from the Perspective of Welfare Pluralism", *Northwest Population Journal*, No. 1, 2015.

Wang Qiong, "Demand for Home-Based Old-Age Care Services in Urban Communities and Its Influencing Factors: Based on National Survey Data of Urban Elderly People", *Population Research*, No. 1, 2016.

Wang Yanfang, Wang Xutao, "Multi-Factor Analysis of Influencing Rural Elderly's Life Satisfaction and Choice of Old-Age Care Mode", *China Economic Studies*, No. 5, 2014.

Xi Jinping, *Secure a Decisive Victory in Building a Moderately Prosperous Society in All Respects and Strive for the Great Success of Socialism with Chinese Characteristics for a New Era: Report at the 19th National Congress of the Communist Party of China*, People's Publishing House, 2017.

"Xi Jinping emphasized during the 32nd collective study of the Political Bureau of the CPC Central Committee: with the leadership of party committee and government, participation of the society and the action of people, promoting the comprehensive, coordinated and sustainable development of the cause of aging", *People's Daily*, May 29, 2016, page 1.

Yan Bingqiu, Gao Xiaolu, "Influencing Factors and Community Differences of Urban Elderly's Satisfaction with Home-Based Old-Age Care", *Geographical Research*, No. 7, 2013.

Yu Jie, Mark Rosenberg, Cheng Yang, "A Study on Satisfaction with Home-Based Old-Age Care and Institutions' Willingness of Operating Old-Age Care Business in Beijing", *Progress in Geography*, No. 12, 2015.

Zhang Miao, "An Analysis of Old-Age Care Status and Satisfaction of China's Rural Elderly", *The World of Survey and Research*, No. 6, 2016.

Zhang Xiaoyi, Liu Bangcheng, "Model Research on the Service Quality of Community Home-Based Old-Age Care: A Case Study of Shanghai'", *Chinese Journal of Population Science*, No. 3, 2011.

Zhang Xiulan, Xu Yuebin, "Constructing China's Developmental Family Policy", *Social Sciences in China*, 2003, No. 6.

Chinese Youth's Social Integration and Social Participation During the 14th Five-Year Plan Period

Ma Feng[*]

During the 14th Five-Year Plan period, China has entered a new stage of development and embarked on a new journey of building a modern socialist country in an all-round way. The long-term prosperity and stability provide a new choice for youth development, and the breadth and depth of youth's social involvement in China will undergo fundamental changes. At the same time, China is facing profound changes in its development environment. In a new stage of development, a safer, higher-quality and more sustainable environment for young people to participate in society that meets the requirements of the development needs to be created so as to provide the motive force for the development of young people.

I. Introduction

"Young people are the new force and backbone of a country's economic and social development. To develop the cause of the Party and the country, we

---

[*] Ma Feng, Associate Professor, National Institute of Social Development, CASS.

must put young people at the heart of development."① To promote youth development and build a stage for youth development, the Central Committee of the Chinese Communist Party (CPC) has successively issued the "Medium-and Long-term Youth Development Plan (2016 – 2025)" (hereinafter referred to as the "Plan") and "Opinions on Promoting the System and Mechanism Reform for Social Mobility of Labor Force and Talented People" (hereinafter referred to as "Opinions"). The promulgation of the "Plan" and "Opinions" reflects that China strives to create a comprehensive and systematic institutional environment for the development of young people from institutional perspective of top-level design and comprehensive deepening of reforms, based on the overall strategy of the great rejuvenation of the Chinese nation, the actual needs of youth growth and development, and the staged characteristics of contemporary China's economic and social development. "All of us in the Party should care about young people and set the stage for them to excel."②

There is an interactive relationship between youth development and social development, and good social development can better promote youth development. Similarly, good youth development will also provide inexhaustible vitality and dividends for social development and the continuous optimization of the social environment. The world today is undergoing profound changes unseen in a century. The COVID – 19 pandemic of the century has accelerated the evolution of this change. The domestic and international environment is undergoing profound changes. Changes and new grounds are appearing alternately, which has profoundly affected China's social development. "China is facing profound and complex changes in its development environment. China's development is still in an

---

① Medium-and Long-term Youth Development Plan (2016 – 2025), http://www.gov.cn/zhengce/2017 – 04/13/content_5185555.htm#1.

② Xi Jinping, "Secure a Decisive Victory in Building a Moderately Prosperous Society in All Respects and Strive for the Great Success of Socialism with Chinese Characteristics for a New Era-Report Delivered at the 19th National Congress of the Communist Party of China", *Guangming Daily*, October 28, 2017, page 1.

important period of strategic opportunity, but opportunities and challenges have undergone new developments."①

China will enter a new development stage in the 14th Five-Year Plan period, in which social development will inevitably have a profound impact on youth development. Therefore, in view of the characteristics of changes in the environment and conditions that have occurred in the new development stage, while implementing the Plan and the Guidelines, "awareness must be raised about the new features and requirements brought about by the changing major contradictions in Chinese society, the new contradictions and challenges brought by the complex international environment"②. It is necessary to judge the new dynamics and new characteristics of youth development in a timely and targeted manner, and to keep up with the times to promote young people's social participation. At the same time, in response to the request of the times for building a modern socialist country in all aspects in the new development stage, based on the overall strategy of the great rejuvenation of the Chinese nation, we should create an environment that is compatible with the requirements of the new development stage for youth development.

II. Breadth and Depth of Youth's Social Participation in China have Undergone Fundamental Changes

The 13th Five-Year Plan period has witnessed the 40th anniversary of reform and opening up and the 70th anniversary of the founding of the People's Republic of China. From the historical perspective of the 40th anniversary of re-

---

① The CPC Central Committee's proposals for formulating the 14th Five-Year Plan (2021–2025) for National Economic and Social Development and the Long-Range Objectives Through the Year 2035, *People's Daily*, November 4, 2020, page 1.

② The CPC Central Committee's proposals for formulating the 14th Five-Year Plan (2021–2025) for National Economic and Social Development and the Long-Range Objectives Through the Year 2035, *People's Daily*, November 4, 2020, page 1.

form and opening up and the 70th anniversary of the founding of New China, tremendous changes have taken place in China and people's lives. China's economic might, scientific and technological capabilities, and overall national strength have reached new heights. "It is estimated that China's GDP will exceed 100 trillion yuan in 2020. China has made remarkable progress in poverty relief, with 55.75 million rural residents lifted out of poverty; China's annual grain output remained above 65 million kilograms for five years in a row; greater efforts have been made on pollution prevention and control and the ecological environment was significantly improved; China continued to open its door wider to the world; the joint pursuit of the Belt and Road Initiative yielded solid outcomes; the living standards of our people rose significantly. Higher education has entered the stage of popularization. Over 60 million urban jobs were added, and the world's largest social security system was established, with basic medical insurance covering more than 1.3 billion people and basic pension insurance covering nearly 1 billion people."① The historic achievements of China's social development today provide the best environment in history for the growth of young people in the new era. Compared with the young generation a hundred years ago, today's young people are in the best period of development in history.

First, educational development provides a starting platform for youth to participate in social development.

Xi Jinping, general secretary of the CPC Central Committee, has pointed out, "Education is fundamental to eradicate poverty in China. We need to ensure that all children from poor families can receive fair and quality education and learn at least one useful skill. Don't let the kids lose at the starting line, and try our best to stop poverty being passed on between generations."② China's e-

---

① The CPC Central Committee's proposals for formulating the 14th Five-Year Plan (2021 – 2025) for National Economic and Social Development and the Long-Range Objectives Through the Year 2035, *People's Daily*, November 4, 2020, page 1.

② *Excerpts from Xi Jinping's Discourse on the Construction of Socialist Society*, Beijing: Central Party Literature Press, 2017, p. 52.

conomic and social development reached new heights during the 13th Five-Year Plan period. The rich life also provides a stable family living conditions for the growth of young people, so that the family can provide a more stable material basis for the growth and development of children, thus enable children to become more diversified, more personalized, and better reveal their personality traits. The quality and level of development are higher than in other historical periods. From the perspective of children's education, which families have the highest expectation on, education plays an irreplaceable role in youth development, enabling young people to gain a foothold in society, have an equal start and chance. It is more conducive to shaping a social environment for young people to make progress and a social atmosphere for young people to be successful in life.

Table 1   Trends in the Number of Students Enrolled in Various Schools Nationwide (2010 – 2019)

Year	Number of students enrolled in secondary vocational schools (institutions) (10,000 people)	Enrollment of higher education institutions (10,000 people)	Number of undergraduate higher education institutions (10,000 people)	Enrollment of junior college students in higher education institutions (10,000 people)	Number of students enrolled in ordinary high schools (10,000 people)
2010	711.3957	661.8	351.2563	310.5	836.2
2011	649.9626	681.5	356.6411	324.9	850.8
2012	597.0785	688.8	374.0574	314.8	844.6
2013	541.2624	699.8	381.4331	318.4	822.7
2014	495.3553	721.4	383.4152	338	796.6
2015	479.8174	737.8	389.4184	348.4	796.6

Continued

Year	Number of students enrolled in secondary vocational schools (institutions) (10,000 people)	Enrollment of higher education institutions (10,000 people)	Number of undergraduate higher education institutions (10,000 people)	Enrollment of junior college students in higher education institutions (10,000 people)	Number of students enrolled in ordinary high schools (10,000 people)
2016	466.1428	748.6	405.4007	343.2	802.9
2017	451.5235	761.5	410.7534	350.7	800.1
2018	428.5024	790.9931	422.159	368.8341	792.7063
2019	600.4	914.9026	431.3	483.6146	839.4949

Source: National Bureau of Statistics.

Judging from the trends in Table 1, secondary vocational education and higher education gather the main youth groups in China. During the 13th Five-Year Plan period, the number of students enrolled in secondary vocational schools and higher education institutions at all levels and types has shown a general upward trend, but there are also differences in the levels of different academic qualifications. The number and size of undergraduate and junior college enrollment in institutions of higher education are basically stable, the enrollment of secondary vocational colleges (institutions) has fallen sharply, and the enrollment of regular senior secondary schools has been basically stable. Regular senior secondary schools and institutions of higher learning are still the "big producer" of enrollment, which shows that the students' inclination, destination, and concept of education are obvious affected by their family. Parents have a strong desire for their children to receive better education. The changes in the social environment also provide a solid material basis for young people to receive better education. From the data in 2018, compared with the previous data, the five indicators shown in Table 1 have shown a turning point. In 2019, the enrollment of higher education institutions exceeded 9.149 million. Similarly, the enrollment of secondary vocational schools (institutions) showed a sharp rebound following several years of decline, exceeding 6.004 million. Young people have more and more opportunities to receive education, especially higher education. In the context of high-quality economic development and transformation, vocational education has also become an important "lever" and "turning point" for some young people to change their life. "In 2019, the national pre-school gross enrollment rate reached 83.4%, an increase of 37 percentage points over 2000; the nine-year compulsory education consolidation rate was 94.8%; the gross enrollment rate for senior secondary school was 89.5%, twice that of 2000; the gross enrollment rate of higher education sector was 51.6%, four times that of 2000, entering the stage of popularization of education. In 2019, the average number of years of education for the newly added labor force was 13.7 years, an increase of 1.29 years over 2010, and the proportion of those who received higher education reached 50.9%."[1]

Second, employment development provides broad space for young people's participation in society.

"I noticed that in the past year, most people who enrolled in college when the entrance exam resumed in 1977 have retired. And a large number of people born after 2000 have entered university. More than 100 million people from our rural areas are gradually becoming permanent residents in our cities. 13 million have found jobs, and construction has begun on 5.8 million new homes for those people living in dilapidated houses. Many have already moved into their new warm homes", General Secretary Xi Jinping said in the 2019 New Year Speech.[2] Most people who enrolled in colleges when the entrance exam re-

---

[1] Wan Donghua, "Building a moderately prosperous society in all respects in the light of social development", *People's Daily*, August 4, 2020, page 11.

[2] "2019 New Year Speech by President Xi Jinping", *Guangming Daily*, January 1, 2019, page 1.

sumed in 1977 have retired, and they enjoy their old age in peace after having experienced the changes in the social environment of more than 40 years of reform and opening up. A new generation of college students born after 2000 have entered campus after "00" and are enjoying their youth. The development of generations of youth constitutes the main tone of the country's development. As shown in Table 2, as of 2019, the number of graduates from higher education institutions in China had reached 7.585298 million, which was a leapfrog development compared with the number ten years ago and the beginning of reform and opening up.

Table 2   Number of National Labor Force and the Number of Graduates from Higher Education Institutions and Secondary Vocational Schools (Institutions) in China

Year	Labor force (10,000 people)	Number of graduates from higher education institutions (10,000 people)	Number of graduates from secondary vocational schools (institutions) (10,000 people)
2010	78388	575.4	543.6524
2011	78579	608.2	541.1252
2012	78894	624.7	554.384
2013	79300	638.7	557.5587
2014	79690	659.4	516.1519
2015	80091	680.9	473.2654
2016	80694	704.2	440.5572
2017	80686	735.8	406.3981
2018	80567	753.3087	396.977
2019	89640	758.5298	493.4

Source: National Bureau of Statistics.

Youth development is an important part of social development. Our society is stable and orderly, and full of vitality. It is necessary to actively promote young people to get involved in the changes of social environment, and then drive the social creation. "The key to preventing consolidating the social structure is to deepen reform and promote equal opportunities. In fact, when a person is able to succeed in a society by his own efforts, it proves that the we live a very mobile society with fair opportunities. "① Young people are at the beginning of their lives, and they should be given resources for development when they need them most, and a platform for development when they need support most. The fairness of opportunity, the continuous social mobility environment and the sustainable improvement channel are important aspects related to youth development. After the Third Plenary Session of the 11th Central Committee of the CPC, the spatial distribution of China's population has undergone drastic changes. Flowing from villages to cities, from interior to coastal regions, from the west to the east, the spatial flow of China's population has developed with the deepening of the reform and opening up policy and the development of industrialization and urbanization, forming a large-scale flow of population. During this period, whether young people of the older generation or grow up today, they have participated in such a tide, accepted the changes of social environment, and in turn promote a more profound social change. During the 13th Five-Year Plan period, this change is even more obvious. In fact, "No one can be separated from the development of the times. The multiple factors of the development of the times prompt people to complete the process of socialization, and then exert an influence on the development of the society". ②

"China has more than 100 million market players and more than 170 million talents with higher education or various professional skills, and more than

---

① Ma Feng, "Stimulate social vitality by comprehensively deepening reform and correctly view social mobility issues", *People's Daily*, July 20, 2017, page 7.

② Li Chunling, Ma Feng, "Empty-nest youth: A group that wanders between 'survival' and 'dream'", *People's Forum*, 2017, No. 4.

400 million in middle-income groups. "① A mobile China embodies the strength of youth. Since the reform and opening up, the change of population mobility in China has been synchronized with the development and change of China, and has also brought about the improvement of people's life and further changes of social mobility.

"Employment is an important guarantee for social stability. A person cannot be integrated into society if he is out of work, and it is difficult to strengthen his identification with the country and society. If there are more unemployed people, social stability is in great danger. "② From the perspective of employment development, the economy was depressed at the beginning of the founding of the People's Republic of China. Since the reform and opening up, the continuous employment growth and the profound changes from the scale of employment to the employment structure have not only increased employment opportunities for young people, but also increased the possibilities and choices of employment. Employment is the foundation of people's livelihood. It is also the first step for young people to enter the society and settle down. It also involves human dignity. "A healthy and progressive nation should encourage people to work, get a job, and support their families through their own efforts, so as to serve the society and contribute to the country. "③ The realization of full employment and the development of high-quality employment provide a broader space for the growth and development of young people in our country. Comprehensively deepening reform has removed institutional barriers with greater courage, and played a key role in expanding and enlarging the middle-income group and unlocking promo-

---

① President Xi Jinping stressed analyzing China's economic situation from a comprehensive, dialectical and long-term perspective, and explore new opportunities and break new ground amid crises and changes when visited CPPCC National Committee members from the economic sector attending the third session of the 13th National Committee of the CPPCC, *People's Daily*, May 24, 2020, page 1.

② *Xi Jinping on the Construction of Socialist Society*, Beijing: Central Party Literature Press, 2017, p. 68.

③ *Xi Jinping on the Construction of Socialist Society*, Beijing: Central Party Literature Press, 2017, p. 68.

tion channels for young people. "Today, the majority of college students are around the age of 20; and they will be under the age of 30 by 2020, when we complete the building of a moderately prosperous society in all respects. They will be around 60 by the mid-21st century, when we basically realize our country's modernization." [1] Therefore, "We should accelerate the reform in an all-round way, create a fair and just social environment, promote social mobility and inspire the vigor and creativity of young people". [2] Education and employment are important aspects of youth development. Education represents a fair starting point, while employment represents a fair opportunity. It is also an important way and a medium for achieving the leap of social class and promoting the vertical mobility of young people.

III. Analysis of Youth's Social Participation in the New Development Stage

General Secretary Xi Jinping made a speech at the Symposium of Experts in Economic and Social Fields, saying that "the period of the 14th Five-Year Plan marks the realization of forming a well-off society in an all-round way, and the fruition of our first centennial objective. It marks the full-on start of a new journey, of building a modernized socialist country. This is the first Five-Year Plan toward our next centennial goal in which China will adapt to a new phase of development". [3] In the new phase of development, people's longing for a better life should be satisfied, and a development of higher quality, more efficient, fairer, more sustainable, and safer should be achieved.

---

[1] Young People Should Practice the Core Socialist Values—President Xi Jinping's Speech at a Symposium with the Faculty and Students of Peking University, *Guangming Daily*, May 5, 2014, page 2.

[2] Young People Should Practice the Core Socialist Values—President Xi Jinping's Speech at a Symposium with the Faculty and Students of Peking University, *Guangming Daily*, May 5, 2014, page 2.

[3] Xi Jinping's Speech at the Symposium of Experts in Economic and Social Fields, *Guangming Daily*, August 25, 2020, page 2.

At present, "the domestic development environment is also undergoing profound changes. Our country has entered a stage of high-quality development. What we now face is the contradiction between unbalanced and inadequate development and the people's ever-growing needs for a better life. The per capita GDP has reached US $10, 000, the urbanization rate has exceeded 60%, and the middle-income group has exceeded 400 million people. The people's requirements for a better life are constantly increasing". ① In the face of great changes in the world and the new development pattern in China, it is necessary to closely integrate the participation of young people in social development with the development requirements of the new development stage, further expand the development space of young people, expand the channels of social mobility, and constantly meet the development needs of young people for a better life.

The people's needs for a better life are increasingly extensive. They not only put forward higher demands for material and cultural life, but also have growing demands for democracy, rule of law, fairness, justice, security and the environment. These are also areas of great concern to young people, each of which involves their vital interests, growth interests and development interests.

A long-term forecast study shows: "In the next forty years, China's economy will continue to maintain a rapid growth trend; by 2052, China's economic aggregate will reach five times that of 2012, which is equivalent to an average annual growth rate of 3.5%."② "By 2052, China's total GDP will be equivalent to the sum of the GDP of all 33 OECD countries."③ In the new stage of development, we need to take into account the overall strategy of the great rejuvenation of the Chinese nation and the major changes unseen in the world in a

---

① Xi Jinping's Speech at the Symposium of Experts in Economic and Social Fields, *Guangming Daily*, August 25, 2020, page 2.

② Jorgen Randers, *2052: A Global Forecast for the Next Forty Years*, Translated by Qin Xuezheng, Tan Jing, Ye Shuo, Nanjing: Yilin Publishing House, 2019, p. 261.

③ Jorgen Randers, *2052: A Global Forecast for the Next Forty Years*, Translated by Qin Xuezheng, Tan Jing, Ye Shuo, Nanjing: Yilin Publishing House, 2019, p. 261.

century, strive to promote the integrated development of young people and their participation in social development, enhance their motivation, and create an environment for young people that meets the requirements of the new phase of development.

First, promote the participation of young people in society and create a safer environment for youth development.

Firstly, we need to establish a social development environment that is compatible with the new development pattern. The transformation of the pattern is overall and comprehensive, and the transfer of the principal contradiction has an impact on all aspects. We should establish a pattern of social development that is compatible with the new pattern of development. On the one hand, it is necessary to improve the ability and the level of social governance, focusing on the development goals and steps of the modernization. The transformation of the new development pattern and the new social development pattern should be integrated into the track of modernizing national governance system and governance capacity, and the modernization of governance should lead the transformation of the pattern, so as to form an operational mechanism for the participation of young people in social development and the sharing of the development achievements, which more reflects the synchronicity of development. On the other hand, we should promote more adequate and high-quality employment and transfer of young people, improve a comprehensive and sustainable social security system, strengthen the public health and disease control system, realize the coordination of economic and social development in a wider range of areas, and expand the breadth and depth of social mobility of young people.

Secondly, we should comprehensively deepen reform to eliminate the imbalance and inadequacy of young people's participation in society. In terms of income distribution, social mobility, social security, prevention and resolution of social risks, and adjustment of the pattern of social interests, consensus on social development needs to be built to the greatest extent possible, which must be resolved and solved in the process of comprehensively deepening reform. On the one hand, the ways and channels for youth groups to participate in the modernization of grassroots governance form a new mechanism for shared development of public interests and youth development. On the other hand, we should further improve the structure of income distribution, make the middle-income earners larger, and stronger, and intensify efforts to address the issue of relative poverty. Therefore, "people will lead a better life, and more notable and substantial progress will be achieved in promoting well-rounded human development and achieving common prosperity for everyone". [1]

Thirdly, efforts shall be made to achieve balanced development, narrow the digital divide and intelligence divide, and enhance the resources sharing of young people's participation in social development. Vocational education should be a breakthrough to motivate the potential and ability of unemployed young people, and improve their competitiveness in the labor market, help young people integrate into the overall situation of social development and become sharers and co-builders of social development.

Second, enhance motivation of young people and create a higher quality environment for youth development.

Firstly, we should ensure that young people can participate in the "four tasks" of social development. "From the perspective of youth development in the world: on the one hand, we should pay attention to the deep-seated social development issues such as economic growth, social mobility, income distribution, social security and others that affect youth development; on the other hand, we should pay attention to the needs of young people concerning the "four tasks"[2], namely, employment, study, property purchasing, and entrepreneurship related to personal development in the future. Social development

---

[1] The CPC Central Committee's proposals for formulating the 14th Five-Year Plan (2021 – 2025) for National Economic and Social Development and the Long-Range Objectives Through the Year 2035, *People's Daily*, November 4, 2020, page 1.

[2] The "four tasks" mainly include: study, employment, property purchasing and entrepreneurship. Study concerns a fair starting point, and employment involves a fair opportunity.

and the needs of youth development constitute two parts of a whole. We should not only constantly solve the deep-seated social development problems affecting youth development, create a good environment for economic and social development, but also guide young people to integrate into and participate in social development, so that they can promote social development through participation and sharing."① We should consolidate the foundation for young people to participate in social development. We will do a good job in the work involving young people's "four tasks". The "four tasks" are the main approach and route for young people to participate in social development, which should not only be ensured smooth, but also a stronger institutional environment should be provided.

Secondly, based on the new stage of development, we should open up channels for the mobility of young people and promote high-quality development of education and employment. In the new stage of development, efforts should be made to improve the quality of people's lives and raise the level of social development. In light of the new characteristics of the new stage of development, we should, on the one hand, pay more attention to the formation of a higher-quality employment structure, make the personnel training and education and the demand for jobs better matched, intensify supply side reform of employment, improve the structural problems in the supply of employment, and smooth the employment circulation system. On the other hand, efforts should be made to improve the spatial distribution of education, achieve balanced development of quality education, and draw a bottom line for fairness in education. Through education, we should equip young people with skills, hope, and motivation for self-development. We should strive to create a more sustainable environment for education and employment development, promote the modernization of social construction, and provide a higher level of environment for young people to in-

---

① Ma Feng, "A Study on the Values of South African Youth Participation in Social Development—Based on the Analysis of Values in the Dual Context of Risk Society and Cultural Transition", *Journal of Southwest University for Nationalities*, No. 10, 2019, pp. 45 –52.

tegrate into national development and social construction.

Thirdly, we should fully implement the "Medium-and Long-term Youth Development Plan (2016 – 2025)". The vitality of the system lies in its execution, and the key to planning is its execution. We should further improve the implementation of plans and support policies, improve the policy system for supporting youth development, give full play to the mechanism of joint conferences on youth employment from the central government to the county level, study youth development issues, assess the progress of the implementation of the plan, and solve problems that are troubling youth development in a timely manner. The link between the "Medium-and Long-term Youth Development Plan (2016 – 2025)" and the 14th Five-Year Plan should be realized to jointly play an role of policies, so as to release more stable and predictable policy signals for the growth and development of youth, improve the co-construction mechanism of policy support and the stage for youth development, make youth development more equitable, bring more benefits to all types of youth groups, and make basic public services accessible and equal to all types of youth groups.

Third, strengthen the institutional construction of youth participation in society and create a more sustainable environment for youth development.

We will use institutional systems to generate institutional dividends for the integration of youth into social development and social construction. Over the past century, young people have devoted themselves to national rejuvenation and prosperity, and the dividends they have generated are the source of strength for the cause of the Party and the people. In the new era, to succeed in the long march of national rejuvenation and cope with various difficulties and obstacles, we need to give full play to the role of the youth as the main force and unleash the "youth dividend".

We should give full play to the innovative nature of young people and promote their innovative and creative development in all walks of life. Young people are born with spirit of innovation and creativity. When they are at an age when it is natural to engage in innovation and creativity, they will surely make great achievements. The innovative and creative activities of young people are the vanguard and trend of social innovation activities. We should speed up the youth innovation and creativity support plan and give full play to the good experience and practices of Qianhai's innovation and creativity. On the one hand, we should create a modern business environment, encourage unicorn and other innovative and creative enterprises to compete with each other, and promote higher-quality development of the society, higher-quality development of industries, and the advancement of medium-high and high technology by innovation and creativity. On the other hand, we should increase the support for all types of youth groups by solving the problem with relative poverty. We should assist young people to become rich and successful, and guide young people to grow up and make progress, and develop a comprehensive and systematic auxiliary system covering finance, education, skill training and vocational training. In the central and western regions, we will speed up the establishment of auxiliary service centers for youth innovation and creativity, and create a new pattern in which young people are integrated into social development and social construction in an all-round and balanced way through microcredit, project support, targeted training, coordinated development of youth in the east and west, and mutual progress between urban and rural young people.

The development of the youth goes hand in hand with the development of the economy and society. If the country is stable and the society is progressive, young people will be progressive. Today's young people, while enjoying the best development opportunities in history, have also assumed the new mission and development responsibility entrusted by history. The future of young people depends on the future of the country and the nation. General Secretary Xi Jinping has fully affirmed the responsibilities and achievements of today's young people and said that "in the fight against COVID – 19, young people worked together with the vast number of front-line epidemic prevention and control workers, made heroic efforts, fought at the barricades and risked their lives, demonstrating the vigorous power of youth and delivering qualified answers. Our young people have proved through their actions that Chinese young people are capable of shouldering great responsibilities in the new era". ①

The general Secretary's affirmation is the best encouragement to the younger generation of the new era. At the National Commendation Conference for Fighting COVID – 19, the General Secretary once again gave full recognition and praise to young people in the new era. "The younger generation is the hope of the nation, and their devotions were touching and heartwarming", ② said General Secretary Xi Jinping. "The younger generation shows no fear confronting hardships, and they have carried daunting responsibilities on their shoulders with great passion. They have proved that they are the hope of the nation. Let's give them the thumbs up!"③ In the changing social environment of the new era, we should coordinate and promote the integration of young people in the new era into the social development, so that young people who make sacrifices and fight for future in the new era can share the joy of creation and the fruits of development, and build a broader stage and career platform for the growth and progress of young people in the new era.

References

"2019 New Year Speech by President Xi Jinping", *Guangming Daily*, January 1, 2019, page 1.

Excerpts from Xi Jinping's Discourse on the Construction of Socialist Society, Beijing: Central Party Literature Press, 2017.

General Secretary Xi Jinping's speech at National Commendation Conference for Fighting COVID – 19, *People's Daily*, September 9, 2020, page 2.

---

① President Xi replies to letter from Peking University post – 90s Party members fighting COVID – 19, *Hubei People's Daily*, March 17, 2020, page 1.
② General Secretary Xi Jinping's speech at National Commendation Conference for Fighting COVID – 19, *People's Daily*, September 9, 2020, page 2.
③ General Secretary Xi Jinping's speech at National Commendation Conference for Fighting COVID – 19, *People's Daily*, September 9, 2020, page 2.

Jorgen Randers, *2052: A Global Forecast for the Next Forty Years*, Translated by Qin Xuezheng, Tan Jing, Ye Shuo, Nanjing: Yilin Publishing House, 2019.

Ma Feng, "A Study on the Values of South African Youth Participation in Social Development—Based on the Analysis of Values in the Dual Context of Risk Society and Cultural Transition", *Journal of Southwest University for Nationalities*, No. 10, 2019.

Ma Feng, "Stimulate social vitality by comprehensively deepening reform and correctly view social mobility issues", *People's Daily*, July 20, 2017, page 7.

Medium-and Long-term Youth Development Plan (2016 – 2025), http://www.gov.cn/zhengce/2017 – 04/13/content_5185555.htm#1.

President Xi Jinping stressed analyzing China's economic situation from a comprehensive, dialectical and long-term perspective, and explore new opportunities and break new ground amid crises and changes when visited CPPCC National Committee members from the economic sector attending the third session of the 13th National Committee of the CPPCC, *People's Daily*, May 24, 2020, page 1.

President Xi replies to letter from Peking University post – 90s Party members fighting COVID – 19, *Hubei People's Daily*, March 17, 2020, page 1.

The CPC Central Committee's proposals for formulating the 14th Five-Year Plan (2021 – 2025) for National Economic and Social Development and the Long-Range Objectives Through the Year 2035, *People's Daily*, November 4, 2020, page 1.

Wan Donghua, "Building a moderately prosperous society in all respects in the light of social development", *People's Daily*, August 4, 2020, page 1.

Xi Jinping, "Secure a Decisive Victory in Building a Moderately Prosperous Society in All Respects and Strive for the Great Success of Socialism with Chinese Characteristics for a New Era-Report Delivered at the 19th National Congress of the Communist Party of China", *Guangming Daily*, October 28, 2017, page 1.

Xi Jinping on the Construction of Socialist Society, Beijing: Central Party Literature Press, 2017.

Xi Jinping's Speech at the Symposium of Experts in Economic and Social Fields, *Guangming Daily*, Nugust 25, 2020, page 2.

Young People Should Practice the Core Socialist Values-President Xi Jinping's Speech at a Symposium with the Faculty and Students of Peking University, *Guangming Daily*, May 5, 2014, page 2.

Chapter 2 China's Economic Development Experience

New Development Philosophy and China's Economic Growth

Lou Feng*

Since the reform and opening up, China's economy has developed rapidly and achieved world-renowned achievements: GDP reached 14.7 trillion U.S. dollars in 2020, accounting for 16.8% of the global share, ranking second in the world for twelve consecutive years; China's economy growth contribution rate (exchange rate method) has ranked first in the world for 15 consecutive years; international imports and exports have been ranked first in the world for 4 consecutive years. However, with the increase in economic aggregates and the continuous deepening of reform and opening up, the Chinese economy is also facing new challenges: the continuous reduction of new labor force, the increasingly prominent resource and environmental constraints, the rise of international trade protectionism, and the intensification of Sino-US trade frictions. At the same time, as a new round of scientific and technological revolution and industrial transformation is gestating and emerging, various disciplines are further cross-integrated, global scientific and technological competition and cooperation are extensive and deep, the cycle of scientific and technological innovation is shortening, and competition for scientific and technological dominance in the internation-

---

* Lou Feng, Professor, Head of Department of Economic Analysis and Forecasting, Institute of Quantitative and Technical Economics, CASS.

al society is becoming increasingly fierce.

Against such a complex international and domestic background, the Chinese government has clarified five new development concepts: innovation, coordination, green, openness and sharing. This is based on major judgments made based on changes in the international and domestic development environment and changes in China's economic development stages. It is to lead China's economic and social development with new development philosophy, solve major structural problems in China's economic development, and cultivate new drivers of economic development. The only way for healthy and sustainable economic development is of great practical significance for ensuring the steady and rapid growth of the Chinese economy in the medium and long term.

Based on the in-depth analysis of the essential connotation of the new development philosophy, this article will build a model of China's technology-energy-environment dynamic economic system, set high, medium, and low scenarios to predict and simulate China's mid-to long-term economic growth rate and maximum value from 2021 to 2040, then to analysis optimal industrial upgrading and structural transformation paths and international comparison of China's economic development, and finally put forward relevant policy recommendations.

I. The Essential Connotation of the New Development Philosophy

The new development philosophy contains very deep and rich meanings. It not only provides clear answers to the current development methods, mechanisms, and directions of the new era, but also integrates the direction, power, and other aspects of the development of the new era into a close organic system. The new development philosophy is the Chinese government's deeper and scientific understanding of the new situation of social development. It is also China's new concept of governing the country under the new trend. It is a theoretical weapon with great potential.

First, the innovative connotation of the new development philosophy. "Innovation is the soul of a nation's progress and an inexhaustible driving force for the prosperity of a country. If independent innovation capabilities cannot be improved, it will never be possible to get rid of technological backwardness by blindly relying on technology introduction. A nation without innovative capabilities can hardly stand in the forest of advanced nations."① Xi Jinping pointed out: "Innovation is the soul of a nation's progress and an inexhaustible source of a country's prosperity."② The Fifth Plenary Session of the 18th Central Committee of the CPC put forward five development concepts: innovation, coordination, greenness, openness, and sharing. Putting innovation in the first place and leading development with innovation highlights the extreme importance of innovation. Innovation is the first driving force for development. To insist on innovation and development, innovation must be placed at the core of the overall national development, and theoretical innovation must be continuously promoted. Institutional innovation, technological innovation, cultural innovation and other aspects of innovation, let innovation run through all the work of the party and the country, and let innovation become common practice in the whole society. The more than 40 years of China's reform and opening up have also been a systematic process of innovation in culture, science and technology, systems, and theories. It is also the source and driving force of China's economic development. The competition between countries is the competition of innovation; only by strengthening innovation and mastering the core key technologies can we ensure that China's industrial chain and supply chain are not controlled by others, and can continuously improve product quality in the increasingly competitive international market. China seeks room for development in order to promote China's modernization process.

Second, the coordinated connotation of the new development philoso-

---

① Wang Weiguang ed., *The Study on the Important Thought of Three Represents*, People's Publishing House, 2002, p. 547.

② Xi Jinping, "Speech During the Discussion with Outstanding Youth Representatives from All Walks of Life", *People's Daily*, May 5, 2013, page 2.

phy. Since the economy is a complete organic system, economic variables such as production, consumption, investment, trade, savings, distribution, population, energy, environment, currency, finance, and finance are interconnected, affect each other, and touch the whole body. To solve any specific problem, it is not just a single problem, but must be considered in conjunction with other problems. According to the barrel law in economics, the lowest limiting factors often determine the height of the development of things; therefore, it should use a coordinated method to solve the unbalanced contradictions accumulated in the development process. Only by coordinating together can we truly promote the coordinated and balanced development of Chinese society and realize the overall development and progress of the Chinese economy.

Third, the green connotation of the new development philosophy. The relationship between man and nature is symbiotic and economic growth is important. However, excessive consumption of natural resources and serious damage to the ecological environment to achieve this goal will be counterproductive. When analyzing the correlation between economic development and environmental protection, General Secretary Xi Jinping clearly stated that "we want green waters and green mountains, but also golden mountains and silver mountains. We prefer green waters and green mountains instead of golden mountains and silver mountains, and green waters and green mountains are golden mountains and silver mountains", "it is necessary to correctly handle the relationship between economic development and ecological environmental protection, and firmly establish the concept that protecting the ecological environment is to protect productivity, and to improve the ecological environment is to develop productivity".[1] "China's ecological environment contradictions have a historical accumulation process. It's getting worse, but it can't become worse and worse in

---

[1] Publicity Department of the Communist Party of China ed., *Important Speeches of General Secretary Xi Jinping*, People's Publishing House & Xue Xi Publishing House, 2014, pp. 120, 137.

our hands. The Communists should have such a mind and will."① On the one hand, it outlines the essential relationship between the environment and the economy; on the other hand, it also shows the attention and coordination. The symbiotic relationship between man and nature focuses on protecting the ecological environment and must not promote economic development at the expense of environmental damage.

Fourth, the open connotation of the new development philosophy. With the rapid development of economic globalization and industrial chain integration and the continuous improvement of world openness and diversity, international cooperation and competition are also facing an increasingly complex situation. The comparison and game of international forces have reached an unprecedented level. Opening up, development and win-win cooperation are one of the basic experiences of China's reform and opening up; It is also an inevitable requirement for China to move towards the future and the human community. "We will further promote high-level institutional opening-up and create new advantages in international cooperation and competition. Opening to the outside world is China's basic national policy and cannot be shaken at any time. In today's era, any idea of building behind closed doors, any practice of refusing people thousands of miles away, and any attempt to be egoistic and winner take all are moving against the trend of history! At present, economic globalization has encountered some back waves, but the world will never return to a state of mutual isolation and division. Opening up and cooperation is still a historical trend, and mutual benefit and win-win results are still the aspiration of the people. We should open the door and welcome all countries to share China's development opportunities and actively participate in global economic governance. We should actively conduct cooperation with all countries, regions and enterprises willing to cooperate with us"

---

① *Carry the Reform Through to the End*, People's Publishing House & Xue Xi Publishing House, 2017, p. 115.

①China's policy clearly puts forward that in the future, China must find methods and strategies to effectively deal with internal and external linkage relations, effectively improve the quality of China's opening to the outside world, form a deeply integrated development pattern, and improve China's voice and influence in the international market.

Fifth, the shared connotation of the new development philosophy. "Insist on shared development, we must insist on developing for the people, relying on the people for development, and sharing the fruits of development by the people, and make more effective institutional arrangements, so that all people can have more sense of gain in joint construction and shared development, strengthen development motivation, and enhance people's unity, moving forward steadily in the direction of common prosperity." The expression in the Proposal of the 13th Five-Year Plan (hereinafter referred to as the "Proposal") concisely pointed out the connotation and goals of shared development. This is one of the development goals pursued by the Chinese people. Only when common prosperity is achieved on the premise of achieving fairness and justice, the people's creativity, initiative and enthusiasm as the main body of practice will be promoted, and the sense of happiness and sense of gain will also be strengthened. Only then will it provide more impetus for social development and lay a solid foundation for the realization of a better life.

II. Scenario Prediction of China's Economic Growth Potential from 2021 to 2040

On the basis of the essential connotation of the above-mentioned new development philosophy, this article constructs China's technology-energy-environment dynamic economic system model based on relevant economics principles. The

---

① Xi Jinping, *Speech at the 30th Anniversary of the Development and Opening-up of Shanghai's Pudong*, People's Publishing House, 2020, pp. 8 – 9.

model includes nine modules: production module, trade module, residents' income and demand module, enterprise module, government revenue and expenditure module, equilibrium closed module, social welfare module, environment module and dynamic module, add up to 3762 equations. Based on this model system, three scenario predictions of high, medium and low are set up and simulated to calculate China's medium and long-term economic growth rate and the optimal path for industrial upgrading and structural transformation from 2021 to 2040. The main conclusions are as follows.

First, in the baseline scenario, the average annual GDP growth rates for the five periods of 2021 – 2025, 2026 – 2030, 2031 – 2035, and 2036 – 2040 are 6.2%, 4.8%, 4.3%, and 3.8%, respectively. In the rapid growth scenario, if China steadily promotes urbanization, promotes the transformation and upgrading of manufacturing, enhances the international competitiveness of products, and further increases the proportion of fiscal education funds in GDP, improves the quality of workers, and strengthens R&D investment, increases the added value of products and comprehensively deepens market-oriented reforms, in the five periods of 2021 – 2025, 2026 – 2030, 2031 – 2035 and 2036 – 2040, China may maintain a faster growth rate with an annual average of 6.8%, 5.4%, 4.9% and 4.4%. In the slower growth scenario, the average annual GDP growth rates for the five periods of 2021 – 2025, 2026 – 2030, 2031 – 2035, and 2036 – 2040 are 5.7%, 4.3%, 3.4%, and 2.8%, respectively (As shown in Table 1).

Table 1 Forecast of China's Potential Economic Growth Rate from 2021 to 2040 Unit:%

	Benchmark scenario	Rapid growth scenario	Slow growth scenario
2021	9.0	10.4	7.9
2022	5.7	6.1	5.4
2023	5.6	6.0	5.2
2024	5.5	5.9	5.0
2025	5.2	5.7	4.9

Continued

	Benchmark scenario	Rapid growth scenario	Slow growth scenario
Average in the 14th Five-Year Plan	6.2	6.8	5.7
2026	5.1	5.6	4.6
2027	4.9	5.5	4.4
2028	4.8	5.4	4.2
2029	4.7	5.2	4.1
2030	4.6	5.1	3.9
Average in the 15th Five-Year Plan	4.8	5.4	4.3
2031	4.4	5.0	3.8
2032	4.4	5.0	3.5
2033	4.3	4.9	3.4
2034	4.3	4.7	3.3
2035	4.2	4.7	3.2
Average in the 16th Five-Year Plan	4.3	4.9	3.4
2036	4.1	4.6	3.0
2037	3.9	4.5	2.9
2038	3.8	4.4	2.8
2039	3.7	4.3	2.7
2040	3.6	4.2	2.6
Average in the 17th Five-Year Plan	3.8	4.4	2.8

Figure 1 shows the growth trend of China's GDP under different scenarios from 2021 to 2040. The main reason for the sharp rise and fall of China's GDP growth in 2020 and 2021 is the impact of the COVID-19 epidemic, which makes China's GDP growth in 2020 significantly lower than its potential growth. The sharp recovery of GDP growth in 2021 is due to the base of the previous year, and the average growth rate in the past two years is still within a reasonable range. On the one hand, it shows that the COVID - 19 epidemic has been quickly and effectively controlled in China, and it failed to have a substantial impact on China's potential economic growth. However, it is worth noting that for the faster scenario and the slower scenario, the gap between them becomes larger and larger over time. By 2040, the GDP growth in the slower scenario will be 1.6 percentage points lower than that in the faster scenario. This also shows the importance and necessity of comprehensively deepening market-oriented reform in China.

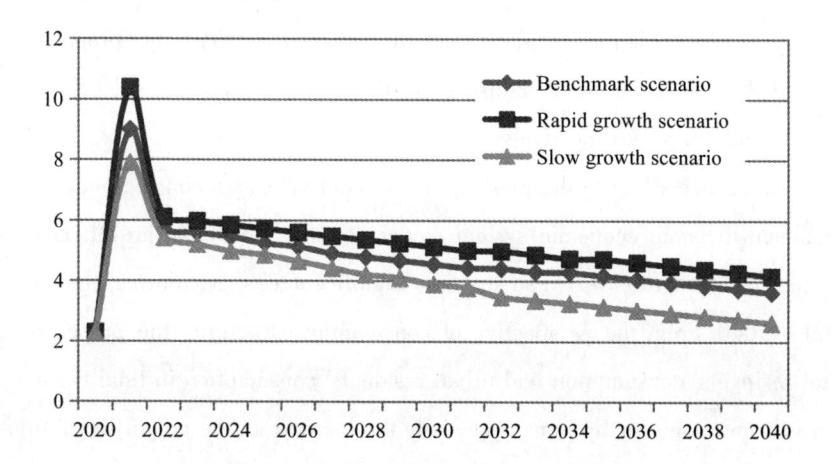

Figure 1 China's GDP growth trend under different scenarios from 2020 to 2040 (%)

Second, according to forecasts, under the baseline scenario, China's GDP at constant prices in 2040 will be 13.59 times that of 2010, 5.38 times in 2015, and 2.66 times in 2020. In the period 2021 -2040, the growth of the national economy will not only be reflected in the rapid increase in total volume, but will also cause major changes in the economic structure. This is due to the different growth rates of the three industries and the result of long-term accumulation from quantitative changes to qualitative changes. In the next 20 years, the changing trends of the three industries are roughly explained as follows: (1) From the perspective of industrial structure, the proportion of the three industries in the total economy has shown a steady development trend. Among them, the proportions of the primary industry and the secondary industry are declining year by year. The proportion of the tertiary industry has increased year by year; (2) During the period 2021 – 2040, the proportion of the primary industry will be basically stable, with a decline of only about 1.8%; while the proportion of the added value of the secondary industry in GDP will drop by nearly 10%. The tertiary industry has always maintained its largest share in the national economy, and will account for more than 60% in 2029, and its absolute dominance in the national economy will be further consolidated and strengthened. In 2040, the proportion of the added value of the three industries in the national economy will be 7.0%, 27.2% and 65.8% respectively.

Third, according to the prediction results of China's technology-energy-environment dynamic economic system model, China's economic growth momentum and its structure will also undergo significant changes during the period 2021 – 2040. From the perspective of consumption structure, the proportion of rural residents' consumption and urban residents' consumption in final consumption will increase year by year, especially the increase in the proportion of urban residents' consumption, while the proportion of government consumption in total consumption decreases year by year. On the one hand, it is related to China's strategic decision to strengthen urbanization. With the vigorous development of China, the urban population will continue to expand, and the income and social welfare of urban residents will also be further improved. On the other hand, it is also related to the long-term policy of "diligence and frugality" and "control public funds" by the Chinese government, and the proportion of government consumption declines. The main reason is that its consumption growth rate is smaller than that of urban residents, so its relative proportion is gradually decreasing. From the perspective of economic growth momentum, since 2012, the proportion of final consumption has exceeded the proportion of capital formation rate, and consumption has been and continues to be the main driving force of China's economic growth; in the next 20 years, investment-driven economic growth will gradually change to a new stage of development dominated by consumer demand; consumption growth (especially household consumption growth) will become the main driving force for China's economic growth and development in the future; investment growth will depend more on market demand and economic development. This will undoubtedly help improve the investment structure and improve investment efficiency.

Fourth, the prediction results show that the development speed and changes of each department are different. Agriculture has been developing at a relatively stable low speed, and its growth rate will slow down from 3.1% in 2019 to about 2.3% in 2040. Coal, mining and other industries and raw material processing industries corresponding to these departments, such as building materials smelting and other industries, show a similar situation. Petroleum, chemical and electric power industries played an important role in the national economy before 2020, and then began to decline. Although the speed of food, light textile and other light industries has been lower than GDP, they are very stable and basically keep pace with GDP. Machinery industry and electronic instrument industry will play an important role in the national economy in the future due to the high concentration of capital and technology. The development speed of these industries will always be faster than the growth of GDP; As the tertiary industry, transportation, post and telecommunications, commercial services, finance and insurance industries play a leading role in the future economy. The rapid and low development of these industries plays a very important role in driving the improvement of the quantity and quality of the national economy and promoting the adjustment of economic structure. Due to the different growth rates of various departments, their position in the national economy has also changed. With the gradual completion of industrialization and the rise of the tertiary industry, some industries with a high proportion in the national economy, such as agriculture, food, textile, building materials and chemical industry, have gradually decreased their share in the national economy. Instead, a number of new industries with highly intensive capital and technology, such as transportation equipment manufacturing, electronic and communication equipment manufacturing, finance and insurance, etc will have a high proportion in the national economy.

III. Research Conclusions and Policy Recommendations

The history of world economic development proves that when an economy reaches a certain level of rapid and sustained development, the economic growth rate will inevitably undergo a turning point and enter a phase of gradual slowing down. Similar to the development experience of many developed countries in the West, China is entering a stage of gradual decline in potential economic growth. However, while we are frankly accepting this objective development law, we still need to actively work to slow down the falling range of the potential economic growth rate from both the demand and supply factors. Because China is still in the ranks of developing countries, China's technological progress and innovation still have a lot of room for improvement, the dividends of institutional reforms have further potential for release, and there is huge demand for escalating consumer consumption. The specific recommendations are as follows.

First, strengthen independent innovation capabilities and promote technological innovation. Core technology is the basis of modern enterprise competition. Full attention must be paid to scientific research and technological innovation, with key common technologies, cutting-edge leading technologies, and disruptive technological innovations as breakthrough points, and strive to achieve independent control of key core technologies, and improve the stability and safety of China's advanced manufacturing industry chain and supply chain. At present, China's economic development is in a critical period of industrial restructuring and upgrading, and there is an urgent need to strengthen and rely on technological innovation. On the one hand, taking new development philosophy and "supply-side structural reforms" as development opportunities, formulate and improve relevant plans and industrial policies to promote independent innovation, independent capability and independent willingness of enterprises. In addition, the Chinese government should establish and improve the innovation of venture capital mechanisms, promote the development of venture capital institutions, ensure the tax reform and optimization of the enterprise technology research and development management system, encourage and guide enterprises to strengthen R&D investment, and enhance their innovation awareness; realize the importance of independent innovation of science and technology policies and the restructuring of investment and financing systems. Strengthen the protection of intellectual property rights, improve scientific and technological achievements and industrial support systems, technical service systems, and technical property rights trading systems, establish an external environmental protection system for corporate intellectual property rights, and ensure the sustainable development of corporate intellectual property rights increase independent innovation of enterprise economic and social benefits.

Second, China should replace quantity with quality and efficiency to increase capital utilization and labor productivity. While intensifying scientific and technological innovation and striving to increase total factor productivity, we should implement the essential connotation of the new development philosophy and improve the efficiency and quality of the supply of traditional production resources. First of all, reform is the source of power for social and economic development. We should further liberalize market access for high-end manufacturing and modern service industries, promote administrative approval and reform of monopoly industries, promote investment in areas with insufficient supply and high rates of return, and accelerate the progress of the investment negative list, trade facilitation, financial reforms and the internationalization of the RMB, and in and afterwards supervision, etc., to promote reform through opening up. Secondly, to meet the needs of modern economic development, it is necessary to increase investment in human capital, optimize labor allocation, and reduce labor costs and free flow will promote the orderly flow of labor between urban and rural areas, enterprises, universities, scientific research institutions, and technical sports, extend the retirement age to the aging population, and promote long-term balanced population development.

Third, innovate investment and financing models. Focus on introducing long-term equity social capital, and promote sustainable infrastructure and new urbanization. In the short term, we believe that investment is still one of the most important factors to promote China's economic growth. This is because, although China's population structure has been moving in a direction that is not conducive to economic growth, China's labor supply is still relatively abundant for a long time. At the same time, China has been a country with a high savings rate for a long time. This high savings will not change for a long time. High savings provides a possibility for high investment, but it is worth noting that we must have a good grasp of investment efficiency and direction. Among them, the key is to promote investment in research and development, high-end manufacturing, modern service industry, ecological and environmental protection, infrastructure and other fields, and optimize the investment structure.

The history of world urbanization shows that the development of urbanization has obvious phased characteristics. The urbanization rate is between 30% – 70%, which is the medium-term stage of urbanization and develops rapidly. At present, China's urbanization construction is in the stage of rapid development, and the proportion of urban population will increase from 17.9% in 1978 to 63.89% in 2020. From international experience, the urbanization process of a region will stabilize only when the urbanization rate reaches about 70%. Urbanization construction is not only a problem of improving the "urbanization rate", but also should pay attention to the "urban-rural integration" in the construction of "new urbanization". With the continuous improvement of urbanization level, large, medium and small city construction will need to build railway, highway and other transport facilities, as well as power, gas, tap water and sewage treatment infrastructure. It is necessary to provide old-age security, education, medical system, housing security, etc., and the acceleration of urbanization of household population will bring huge investment demand.

In the process of new urbanization, both transportation and other infrastructure construction and equalization of public services need a huge amount of capital investment. However, at present, there is no diversified investment and financing mechanism to meet the capital needs of urbanization. The financing mode is still dominated by bank loans, and the final repayment source is still land income. With the decrease of local government revenue, the difficulty of bank lending and the prominence of local debt, the huge capital gap has become the most direct problem faced by the new urbanization. Facing the huge capital demand, if the financing mechanism is not innovated, the construction of infrastructure and new urbanization will be unbearable and unsustainable. In view of the fact that China's high savings rate will remain for a period of time, it is necessary to categorize according to transportation and other infrastructure and new urbanization construction projects, and in-depth promote the reform of investment and financing systems and mechanisms, and focus on the introduction of long-term equity social capital, transportation and other infrastructure and new types of towns. The huge potential of chemical construction can be transformed into an important driving force for sustainable economic growth.

Fourth, break monopoly, loosen access, actively develop mixed ownership economy, and vigorously develop modern service industry and high-end manufacturing with high added value.

At present, some industries and fields in China have formed relatively serious monopolies. Although domestically relying on monopoly status to earn higher profits, problems such as serious waste and poor service quality are prominent, which severely restrict the development of modern service industries and some monopolistic industries of competitive business in China. Breaking monopolies, relaxing the barriers to entry for private capital, and actively developing a mixed-ownership economy are not only the requirements for improving the international competitiveness and service quality of Chinese enterprises, but also an important growth point for increasing the potential growth level in the future. From the perspective of changes in industrial structure, although China's tertiary industry's added value in GDP accounted for the first time in 2013, China's tertiary industry was still underdeveloped, especially the modern service industry with high added value.

In the next two decades, comprehensively deepening reforms will become the main theme of the times. The 2021 Government Work Report pointed out that it is necessary to enhance the economic vitality of various ownership systems and formulate measures for non-state capital to participate in investment projects of central enterprises. In the seven major fields of finance, oil, power, railways, telecommunications, resource development, and public utilities, launch a batch of investment projects to non-state-owned capital. Formulate specific measures for non-public enterprises to enter the franchise field, activate the growth potential of private investment, and stabilize the growth of private investment. Implement railway investment and financing system reforms, liberalize competitive businesses in more areas, and provide new impetus for economic growth. In addition to breaking monopolies and relaxing access, we should also increase fiscal interest discounts and targeted financial support, and vigorously support and guide market entities to develop energy conservation and environmental protection, a new generation of information technology, biology, high-end equipment manufacturing, new energy, integrated circuits, new materials and other high-end manufacturing industries, and promote the development of modern service industries such as finance, insurance, modern information and logistics, the Internet of Things, cultural creativity, education and training, and medical care, etc.

References

Carry the Reform Through to the End, People's Publishing House & Xue Xi Publishing House, 2017.

Gu Hailiang, "Discussion on Marxist Political Economy of New Development Concept", *Marxism and Reality*, Issue 1, 2016.

Liu Wei, "Adhere to the New Development Concept to Promote the Construction of a Modern Economic System", *Managing the World*, Issue 12, 2017.

Liu Wei, "The Internal Logic of Xi Jinping's Economic Thoughts on Socialism with Chinese Characteristics in the New Era", *Economic Research*, Issue 5, 2018.

Publicity Department of the Communist Party of China ed., *Important Speeches of General Secretary Xi Jinping*, People's Publishing House & Xue Xi Publishing House, 2014.

Qiu Haiping, "The Significant Theoretical and Practical Value of the New Development Concept", *Review of Political Economy*, Volume 10, Issue 6, 2019.

Ren Lixuan, "In-depth Implementation of the New Development Concept", *People's Daily*, May 11, 2021, Version 15.

Research Group of the Macroeconomic Research Center of the Chinese Academy of Social Sciences, "Research on China's Economic Growth Potential in the Next 15 Years and the Main Goals and Indicators of Economic and Social Development During the '14th Five-Year Plan' Period", *China Industrial Economy*, Issue 4, 2020.

Wang Weiguang ed., *The Study on the Important Thought of Three Represents*, People's Publishing House, 2002.

Xi Jinping, *Speech at the 30th Anniversary of the Development and Opening-up of Shanghai's Pudong*, People's Publishing House, 2020.

Xi Jinping, "Speech During the Discussion with Outstanding Youth Representatives from All Walks of Life", *People's Daily*, May 5, 2013, page 2.

Xiang Jiuyu, "New Development Concept and Cultural Confidence", *Chinese Social Sciences*, Issue 6, 2018.

Yang Jiayi, Li Jiaxiang, "Grasp, Adapt and Lead the New Normal of Economic Development with the 'Five Development Concepts'", *Economic Aspects*, Issue 4, 2016.

Zhang Xingmao, Li Baomin, "On the Five New Concepts of Economic and Social Development", *Marxist Studies*, Issue 12, 2015.

The Economic Benefits, Constraints and Promoting Strategies of China's Digital Trade Development[*]

Liu Hongkui[**]

In recent years, with the accelerated development of new generation of information and communications technology (ICT) and digital technology, the digital trade supported by digital economy has developed rapidly. According to the relevant report of the United Nations Conference on Trade and Development (UNCTAD), the scale of global e-commerce in 2017 has reached 29 trillion US dollars, and about 1.3 billion people shopped online [①]. It was also predicted in the report of the World Trade Organization (WTO) in 2018 that by 2030, digital technology is expected to help to increase the scale of global trade by 34% [②]. In addition, it is predicted in certain studies that by 2020, the sales of the global cross-border B2C commerce will reach 1 trillion US dollars [③], and there will

---

[*] This article was originally published on *Reform* (No. 3, 2020), with the original title "The Economic Effect and Development Strategy of Digital Trade", and the content has slightly changed.

[**] Liu Hongkui, Associate Professor, Institute of Economics, CASS.

[①] UNCTAD, "Global e-commerce sales surged to $29 trillion", March 29, 2019, https://unctad.org/en/pages/newsdetails.aspx?OriginalVersionID=2034.

[②] WTO, *World Trade Report 2018: The Future of World Trade: How Digital Technologies Are Transforming Global Commerce*, World Trade Organization publication, 2018.

[③] McKinsey Global Institute (MGI), "Globalization in Transition: The Future of Trade and Value Chains", 2019.

be devices worth about 50 billion US dollars connected to the Internet [1]. China's digital economy and digital trade are also developing rapidly. According to the data cited from relevant reports, the number of Internet users in China has increased rapidly from 21.5 million in 2000 to 829 million in 2019. Moreover, the number of Internet users in China now accounts for only 58% of the total population, which is expected to continue to increase in the future. China's Internet retail sales in 2018 reached 1.1 trillion US dollars, ranking first in the world, and about twice that of the United States [2]. It was predicted by E-marketer that China's e-commerce retail sales in 2019 would exceed 1.99 trillion US dollars, accounting for 35.3% of China's total volume of retail sales and 55.8% of global online sales [3].

The fourth industrial revolution is mainly characterized by digitization. Digital technology has spawned digital trade and greatly reduced the trade costs and time, and by making new trade products emerge constantly and changing the trade mode and trade scale of almost all industries, finally becomes a new driving force for the development of international trade. However, the new characteristics of digital trade have made the system of international trade rules no longer applicable, thus facing many constraints. In particular, the multilateral trade rules in the WTO framework have lagged behind the development of digital trade and cannot support its development needs. In view of this, all countries are negotiating and formulating digital trade rules in bilateral or regional trade agreements so as to explore a new international trade rule system.

---

[1] CISCO, "The Internet of Things, At - A - Glance", https://www.cisco.com/c/dam/en_us/solutions/trends/iot/docs/iot-aag.pdf.

[2] Congressional Research Service, "Digital Trade and U.S. Trade Policy", May 21, 2019, https://crsreports.congress.gov.

[3] E-Marketer, "2019: China to Surpass US in Total Retail Sales", January 23, 2019, https://www.emarketer.com/newsroom/index.php/2019-china-to-surpass-us-in-total-retail-sales/.

I. Definition of Digital Trade and Comparison with Traditional Trade

Digital trade is a new trade mode born out of digital economy. It is the product of economic globalization, ICT and digital technology developed to a certain stage with many new connotations. It gets rid of the constraints such as transportation and storage needed by the exchange of tangible products, greatly expands the boundary of tradable products, and has great development potential. Moreover, from the perspective of the development history of exchange economy or trade economy in human society, digital trade is significantly different from traditional trade in terms of exchange medium and mode. It represents a brand-new mode of production, exchange and consumption as well as the direction of future trade development, so it has significant theoretical value economically.

(i) Definition of digital trade

As a new trade mode, digital trade is rarely separated from the traditional trade for statistics and research. Although many countries, organizations and scholars have defined digital trade from different angles, a standard definition has not yet been formed at home and abroad. Digital trade originated in the United States. As a result, compared with other countries, American scholars and governmental agencies have done more relevant research and interpreted the concept of digital trade more comprehensively. In July 2013, the United States International Trade Commission (USITC) concluded in "Digital Trade in the U. S. and Global Economies, Part I" that digital trade refers to the exchange of products and services through network transmission, and includes four aspects: first, digital delivery content, such as digital music, games, videos and books; second, social media, such as social networking sites, websites for user evaluation, etc. ; third, search engines, such as general search engines and specialized search engines; fourth, other digitalized products and services, such as applications, data and computing services provided through cloud computing, and communication services transmitted through the Internet ①. However, the definition highlights the fact that digital trade products and services have to be delivered through the Internet, and excludes most physical products that could be traded through the Internet. Subsequently, USITC enriched the connotations of digital trade in the report "Digital Trade in the U. S. and Global Economies, Part II" released in 2014. According to the report, "digital trade includes both services and goods, in which the Internet and Internet-based technology play an important role in product ordering, production and delivery" . This definition focuses more on the supporting role of Internet technology based digital trade in finance, insurance, manufacturing and other industries ②. The Office of the United States Trade Representative (USTR) also pointed out in the "Key Barriers to Digital Trade" released in 2017 that digital trade was a relatively broad concept, which included both the sales of products online and provision of online services, and dataflow that helped to realize the global value chain (GVC) and services that helped to realize the intelligent manufacturing. Nowadays, almost all business activities are more or less driven by data or maintain international competitiveness by virtue of data ③. After that, Deardorff (2017) proposed in the study of comparative advantages in digital trade that international digital trade was a kind of trade activity involving many countries, in which some trade products themselves were digital products or any step or procedure in the ordering, delivery, payment or service concerning trade products was realized through Internet technology or digital technology ④.

Of course, other international organizations have also studied and defined digital trade from different perspectives. OECD has published a series of research re-

---

① U. S. International Trade Commission, "Digital Trade in the U. S. and Global Economies, Part I", July 2013.

② U. S. International Trade Commission, "Digital Trade in the U. S. and Global Economies, Part II", August 2014.

③ The Office of the U. S. Trade Representative, Key Barriers to Digital Trade, March 2017, https://ustr. gov/about − us/policy − offices/press − office/fact − sheets/2017/march/key − barriers − digital − trade.

④ Deardorff A. V. , "Comparative Advantage in Digital Trade", Working Papers 664, Research Seminar in International Economics, University of Michigan, 2017.

ports, indicating there is no generally accepted standard definition of digital trade. However, academia and research institutions agree that digital trade includes not only goods and services traded through the Internet and online platforms, but also digital products and services directly provided through the network[①]. Domestically, Xiong Li et al. (2011) studied digital trade earlier, believing that digital trade referred to an innovative business model providing digitized electronic information required by exchanges for the two sides of supply and demand on the Internet platform by virtue of digital technology [②]. Ma Shuzhong et al. (2018a, 2018b) systematically reviewed the connotations of digital trade, and defined it as a new trade activity conducive to promoting the transformation of consumer-oriented Internet to industrial Internet and finally achieving the intelligent manufacturing by realizing the efficient exchange of traditional tangible goods, new digital products and services, as well as digital knowledge and information through the effective application of ICT, and an expansion and extension of traditional trade in the era of digital economy [③]. This definition connects the Internet, digital technology, industrial transformation and trade together, which is more in line with the development trend of global trade in the era of Industry 4.0. From a broad perspective, Ivan Sarafanov et al. (2018) believed that digital trade included four core factors, namely the transaction of ICT products and services, digital products and services, personnel flow and data transmission [④].

---

① López González J, Jouanjeanm, "Digital Trade: Developing a Framework for Analysis", OECD Trade Policy Papers, No. 205, 2017, OECD Publishing; López González J, Ferencz J. , "Digital Trade and Market Openness", OECD Trade Policy Papers, No. 217, 2018, OECD Publishing.

② Xiong Li, Liu Hui, Liu Hualing, *Digital and Business*: *Collected Papers of the* 2010 *Global Digital Trade and Mobile Commerce Symposium*, Shanghai Academy of Social Sciences Press, 2010.

③ Ma Shuzhong, Fang Chao, Guo Jiwen, et al. , "Blue Paper on the Development of Digital Trade of the World and China", September 2018.

④ Ivan Sarafanov, Bai Shuqiang, "Research on the Cooperative Mechanism of Trade in Digital Products from the Perspective of WTO-On the Basis of the Development Status of and Barriers to Digital Trade", *Journal of International Trade*, No. 2, 2018.

From the above analysis, it is not difficult to conclude that the concept and economic connotations of digital trade have been constantly improved in its development process. Digital products and services were emphasized and other tangible goods were excluded in the early research on digital trade, which was relatively narrow and limited, and inconsistent with the actual economic development. In contrast, all products and services are included in the scope of digital trade in recent studies, and only the application of digital technologies in trade such as Internet, ICT, etc. is emphasized, which has greatly widened the boundary of digital trade and made its connotations increasingly perfect and realistic. But at present, the theoretical research on digital trade is still in the initial stage at home and abroad. With the development of digital trade, its concept will still be evolving. However, most scholars believe that digital trade is a new generation of trade mode which is significantly different from the traditional one.

(ii) Comparison between digital trade and traditional trade

From the perspective of long history, the author believes that the international trade has experienced three major stages of development, namely, traditional final product trade, GVC trade and digital trade [1]. The priorities of the trade mode, trade products, driving forces of development and trade policies vary from stage to stage. The first was the stage of final product trade before the 1970s characterized by unprecedented development of the final product trade between countries due to the progress of international transportation technology and the decrease of transportation cost. The second was the stage of GVC trade since the 1970s characterized by the production of the same product in many countries due to the decrease of costs on division of labor of cross-border production. The corresponding trade of intermediate products and parts has dominated the market, making the global trade volume and growth rate far higher than the global

---

[1] López González J, Jouanjeanm, "Digital Trade: Developing a Framework for Analysis", OECD Trade Policy Papers, No. 205, 2017, OECD Publishing.

GDP. The third will be the stage of digital trade in the future characterized by the continuous emergence of digital products and services such as cloud computing, 3D printing, online payment, social media, network platform, digital music, and e-books, etc. due to the progress of digital technology. The realization of tangible product trade also relies increasingly on e-commerce. Products are becoming smaller, individualized, and digitized, and the boundaries between products and services are increasingly blurred.

More specifically, the author summarized and compared the similarities and differences between digital trade and traditional trade economically by looking up and sorting out the existing literature (see Table 1). At present, digital trade and traditional trade have basically similar trade essence, trade objectives and economic theoretical support, but they are significantly different in the historical background, trade participants, trade objects, trade modes, trade timeliness and regulatory policies toward trade, etc. For example, digital trade promotes the trade of other products and services; besides, many digital products themselves are tradable. Another example is that in the era of digital trade, many new forms of trade barriers have emerged besides tariffs, a kind of dominant trade barrier before. In particular, data and their free flow will become the key factor affecting digital trade. Accordingly, priorities of trade policies have also changed. Besides traditional trade policies such as market access and non-discriminatory treatment, more attention has been paid to the data flow and storage policy, privacy protection and intellectual property protection, making them priorities of negotiations among countries. Of course, with the development of digital trade and the insightful exploration of economics theories, it is expected to form a new economics theory to systematically study digital trade in the future.

Table 1 Comparison between Digital Trade and Traditional Trade

		Traditional Trade	Digital Trade
Differences	Historical Background	· The first industrial revolution represented by steam engine, the second industrial revolution represented by electric power technology and the third industrial revolution represented by computer and information technology (IT)	· The third industrial revolution and the fourth industrial revolution represented by artificial intelligence (AI), industrial robots, Internet of Things, quantum communication, virtual reality and biotechnology
	Trade Participants	· Large multinational enterprises dominated. Small and medium-sized enterprises traded indirectly through agents, retailers and wholesalers. The suppliers and demanders usually did not directly negotiate transactions	· Internet platform enterprises are becoming increasingly prominent. Small and medium-sized enterprises become the main force. The emergence of platform enterprises and the access to the Internet and digital technology make it possible for suppliers and demanders to trade directly
	Trade Objects	· Tangible goods and essential productive factors dominated, while trade in services accounted for a relatively small proportion	· It includes not only digital products and services, but also traditional goods traded by platform enterprises. The proportion of trade in services will continue to rise
	Modes of Trade Transportation	· Transport goods mainly by land and sea. More physical documents (such as supporting materials, paper documents, etc.) were required for customs clearance	· Tangible goods are mainly sent by post and express, while digital products and services are delivered by digitalized means. Paper-free and electronic trade is realized
	Trade Timeliness	· A complete transaction took a long time, had many uncertain factors and high trade costs, and was easily restricted by spatial factors	· The emergence of platform enterprises and the application of ICT shorten the trade cycle, reduce trade uncertainties and transaction costs, and greatly weaken the constraints of geographical factors, etc.

Continued

		Traditional Trade	Digital Trade
Differences	Regulatory Policies toward Trade	· International organizations such as WTO were key regulatory agencies. Trade policies of various countries, as well as bilateral and regional trade agreements constituted the primary legal norms of global trade supervision	· It not only includes the regulatory agencies and regulatory laws and regulations under the traditional trade, but also emphasizes the data supervision and privacy protection in digital trade. However, the international regulatory policies of digital trade are still under drafting
Similarities	Trade Essence	· The two trade modes are essentially the flow and transfer of goods, services and essential productive factors between different economic entities	
	Trade Objectives	· They are all for the pursuit of trade welfare, the development of the national economy, the protection of national economic interests	
	Economic Theoretical Support	· Classical international trade theories: Theory of Comparative Advantage, Theory of Absolute Advantage, etc.	

Source: López González & Jouanjean (2017), *Blue Paper on the Development of Digital Trade of the World and China* (2018), etc.

II. Economic Benefits of Digital Trade Development

Mutual exchange of needed products is conducive to increasing the welfare of all participants, which has long been proved by Guan Zi in the Spring and Autumn Period of Ancient China, Adam Smith's Theory of Absolute Advantage and Ricardo's Theory of Comparative Advantage. Digital trade helps to reduce transaction costs and enrich the types of trade products, which is naturally of significant economic value. Specifically, from the perspectives such as micro subjects of economics, market efficiency and driving force of global trade development, digital trade has produced direct positive externalities (as shown in Table 2).

(i) **Perspective of consumers: increased types of trade products and improved consumer welfare**

Firstly, digital trade helps increase the variety and quantity of trade products directly, thus improving consumer welfare.

According to microeconomics, consumers prefer diversified consumption of products; it is also pointed out in the international trade theory that trade helps improve consumer welfare by enriching the variety of products in a country. Digital trade is conducive to making consumers increasingly convenient to learn more about products and services, and directly increasing the types and quantity of tradable goods, so as to improve consumer welfare. First, digital products can be traded, thus increasing the types of tradable products. Under the traditional trade mode, tradable products were dominated by tangible products and essential productive factors. However, the emergence and development of digital trade will give birth to more digital consumer goods (such as social networking games, videos, mobile applications, online education, e-books, online healthcare, etc.), [1] which will continue to be involved in international trade. On the basis of the original traditional tradable products, the previously non-tradable products became tradable, thus increasing the types of tradable products. With the accelerated development of digital economy such as 5G communication technology, virtual reality, cloud computing and AI [2], it is expected to further enrich the types of digital products and services and produce new benefits to consumers. Even in the near future, the trade volume of virtual reality products will exceed that of tangible products. Second, digital trade helps promote the transformation and upgrading of traditional trade products, thus updating and enriching the types of tradable products. As the Internet and digital technology continue to integrate with various industries such as finance, insurance, entertainment, education, medical care and retailing, digital trade has actually penetrated many sectors of almost all industries and enriched the types of trade products by promoting the transformation and upgrading of most traditional trade products. For example,

---

[1] Xia Jiechang, Xiao Yu, "Development Trend and Future Orientation of Digital Entertainment Consumption", *Reform*, No. 12, 2019.

[2] Li Xiaohua, "New Features of Digital Economy and the Formation Mechanism of New Driving Force of Digital Economy", *Reform*, No. 11, 2019.

in traditional trade, audio & video products, software and books need to be transmitted and moved in kind. However, in digital trade, these products can be transformed into virtual products and delivered online in the form of data packets. The upgrading of traditional trade products provides consumers with increasing diversified choices and improves consumer welfare.

Table 2   Direct Benefits of Digital Trade to Consumers, Producers and Markets

Economic Entity	Benefits of Digital Trade	Examples
Consumers	· Better access to and understanding of products · More product choices · Service delivery through additional channels	· Consumers prefer diversified channels, and adopt the traditional way, online and mobile channels to obtain information concerning products and services · Online search and comment make it easier for consumers to discover and understand products, compare prices, and conduct a transaction
Producers	· Improved logistics management · More efficient management of supply chain · Reduced operating costs · More effective business management · More market access	· Internet based logistics services help to improve the efficiency of global supply chain and increase scale of e-commerce · Cloud computing enables enterprises to outsource computer hardware and software services, and enables enterprises to work on their core business operations · Cloud computing helps to reduce costs in data intensive and transaction intensive industries · Networked enterprises create more efficient service delivery · Machine-to-Machine (M2M) communication and data analysis make resource management increasingly efficient

Continued

Economic Entity	Benefits of Digital Trade	Examples
Markets	· Increased market information and efficiency · There will be more and better interaction in the market	· Producers collect feedback from consumers and conduct market research with the help of social media · Data analysis can help producers customize products according to customer preferences and fix a price in an increasingly efficient manner

Source: VSITC, *Global Digital Trade 1—Market Opportunities and Key Foreign Trade Restrictions.*

Secondly, digital trade helps to reduce transaction costs and indirectly enrich the types of trade products, thus improving consumer welfare.

First, the reduction of transaction costs is conducive to the enrichment of tradable products. The emergence and wide application of new digital technologies such as online trading platform, big data and cloud computing have greatly reduced the cost of collecting and obtaining information for trade participants, thus increasing the probability of successful matching between demand and supply; besides, it is more convenient for trade participants to negotiate prices, thus making transaction decisions and behaviors increasingly efficient. In addition, the application of new technologies will make the tracking, supervision, customer evaluation and after-sales service of the entire transaction process become more efficient, transparent and faster, thus greatly reducing the cost of supervision. The reduction of a series of transaction costs makes some non-tradable costly products and services inaccessible to trade activities tradable.

Second, the reduction of transaction costs is conducive to the development of new products for trading enterprises. For the producers involved in the trade, the reduction of transaction costs will produce two benefits: on the one hand, low transaction costs will intensify the competition among producers, and then encourage producers who seek to be different from competitors to innovate continuously, so as to alleviate the pressure of market competition; on the other hand, the reduction of transaction costs makes enterprises invest more human and financial resources in the development of new products. In particular, low transaction costs help to expand the market scale, lead to digital technology innovation, and promote the continuous increase of the types of digital products.

Third, the reduction of transaction costs will help to lower the price of trade products. The total trade costs will be effectively reduced due to the reduction of transaction costs, which will further lower the price of trade goods and benefit consumers. On the one hand, from the perspective of demand theory, the reduction of transaction costs will reduce a part of trade costs directly transferred from producers to consumers in trade, through which the price of trade products drops; on the other hand, from the perspective of market competition, reducing trade costs will attract more enterprises to get access to the international trade market and participate in global competition, making the international trade market increasingly effective. For the same kind of tradable products, the greater the number of enterprises participating in the trade market is, the fiercer the trade competition and the lower the price of commodities will be.

(ii) Perspective of producers: providing new impetus for the development of GVC

After nearly 40 years of development, the global division of labor in production of tangible products has matured, which is characterized by increasingly long GVC, the increasingly high coordination costs, and the greater cost of division of labor than the benefits of division of labor. This is also an important reason for the slowdown of global division of labor in production in recent years. The wide application of digital technology and digital trade can not only reduce the costs on the organization and coordination of GVC of the existing products, but also provide a series of new tradable products and their GVC. Therefore, from the perspective of production, digital trade is expected to provide new impetus to GVC and promote the reconstruction of a new GVC system. First, the application of digital technologies (such as big data, cloud computing, Internet of Things) in all aspects of global division of labor in production will make the organization and coordination of GVC increasingly efficient and cost-effective. As a result, the depth and breadth of GVC division of labor will be further extended, thus promoting the new development of existing GVC. Second, from the perspective of development path of value chain, digital trade will promote the formation of a new GVC and a new development path. The continuous emergence of new digital products and services with the attributes of global production and consumption from the beginning will undoubtedly promote the emergence of GVC division of labor modes of a series of digital products, and such division of labor and exchange modes will be different from the GVC modes of traditional products. Third, from the perspective of form of value chain development, digital trade will promote the transformation of GVC to an advanced level. Digital trade will help to lower the transaction costs of GVC division of labor. Coupled with the continuous increase of the types of digital products and expansion of services, the length of GVC will be further extended. The decentralized and unbounded development of digital trade will attract more countries to participate in the global division of labor in production, and boost the transformation and upgrading of GVC. Fourth, from the perspective of value chain governance, the construction of the system of digital trade rules will provide guarantee for the transformation and development of GVC. Although there is no complete system of legal rules dedicated to digital trade worldwide, the primary trade issues under discussion concerning GVC are included in the issues concerning policies toward digital trade, thus becoming one of the topics of trade negotiations among countries. Therefore, the global system of digital trade rules will also be applicable to and serve the development of GVC.

(iii) Perspective of market efficiency: reducing trade barriers and degree of information asymmetry

From the perspective of market efficiency, the direct effect of the development of digital trade and the wide application of digital technology is enriching market information and making market information more sufficient, as well as promoting the interaction between market entities and improving market efficiency. The intensive, unbounded and platform-based development trend of digital trade will promote the closer ties between the trade participants and effectively reduce the degree of information asymmetry, thus realizing the efficient allocation of essential productive factors worldwide. First, reduce the degree of information asymmetry between the producers and consumers involved in trade. Under the traditional trade mode, restricted by time, space and distance, the suppliers and demanders of trade products had limited access to information, resulting in serious information asymmetry and low market efficiency. In the context of digital trade, however, the data regarding consumption and supply can be inquired and traced, and the information concerning purchase and comments of consumers is also recorded by network platform enterprises. Therefore, consumers can easily obtain the multi-dimensional information such as price, quality, quantity, model, nature and service of the products provided by producers; producers can also grasp consumer demand information more comprehensively and accurately by utilizing such information as types, quantities, preferences and comments of consumer goods provided on social media or trading platforms. Second, reduce trade barriers to enable more micro, small and medium-sized enterprises to widely participate in global trade. In the context of the traditional trade, restricted by many factors such as trade costs and information asymmetry, micro, small and medium-sized enterprises could not effectively participate in the global trade activities, resulting in the situation of multinational enterprises monopolizing the international trade market. However, the emergence of digital trade has greatly reduced the cost and threshold of trade participation, and built a new platform for micro, small and medium-sized enterprises to participate in global trade activities. In addition, with the help of digital trading platform, micro, small and medium-sized enterprises can not only understand the demand preference of customers, but also master the product information, market share and development status of competitors, so as to maintain market competitiveness by achieving differentiated production of products. Third, reduce the degree of information asymmetry among the trade participating enterprises and in the entire trade procedure. In the context of digital trade, the application of the real-time tracking system of supply chain and the product tracking system will significantly improve the transparency of the entire supply chain process, so that enterprises will have more information about upstream and downstream products, thus improving the efficiency of market-oriented production.

(iv) Perspective of new driving force of trade development: boosting the rapid development of global trade in services

The essence of digital trade is the exchange of services and the realization of its value, which is embodied not only in the direct digital trade products, but also in the services of e-commerce and platform enterprises. In view of this, it will become a new driving force for the development of trade in services. According to the data, more than 50% of the global trade in services has been digitized, and more than 12% of the merchandise trade has been carried out through the digital platforms provided by Internet enterprises [1]. The emergence and application of new technologies such as 5G communication technology, virtual reality, cloud computing, big data, AI and 3D printing, as well as the emergence of new economic models such as digital economy, Internet economy and platform enterprises have greatly enriched the types of trade in services and provided new impetus for the development and change of trade in services. According to statistics from McKinsey, driven by digital technology and digital trade, the growth rate of cross-border services is 60% higher than that of

---

[1] DHgate. com, "Seize the Opportunity of Digital Trade to Help Small and Medium-sized Enterprises Go Global-Partner Project of DHgate. com Vigorously Promotes Small and Medium-sized Cross-border E-commerce Enterprises to Explore Overseas Markets", January 10, 2020, https://seller. dhgate. com/news/media/i258602. html#cms_ Seize the Opportunity of Digital Trade to Help Small and Medium-sized Enterprises Go Global-List-1.

merchandise trade, and the economic value thus generated is far beyond the scope of statistics involved in traditional trade. If the economic value created by the three indicators of added value of export commodities, intangible assets sent to overseas subsidiaries by enterprises and free digital services for global users is included, the proportion of trade in services in global trade will rise from 23% to over 50% [1]. In the future, digital technology will not only be more deeply integrated with various professional services such as finance, education, health care, design and consulting, but also generate more new digital consumer goods and jointly promote the formation of Digital Global Value Chains, thus leading to the constantly rising proportion of trade in services in international trade.

III. Constraints on Digital Trade Development

The production and exchange attributes of digital trade also lead to many regulatory constraints on its development. Firstly, digital trade makes the boundary between tangible goods and intangible services increasingly blurred, so the classification and definition of digital trade products are not clear and unified under the traditional international trade rules (such as GATS of WTO). Secondly, digital trade relies heavily on the free dataflow. Due to different laws and regulations, cultural customs and historical traditions, countries have different requirements on data privacy protection, so it is difficult to reach an agreement on data privacy protection. Thirdly, the development of digital trade varies greatly among countries, making the policy objectives of digital trade vary from country to country, so the regulatory rules and priorities are also different. In this case, there is a serious lack of the system of legal rules in the production, transaction, payment, use and other aspects of digital trade products. So far, a set of perfect international rule systems of digital trade has not yet been formulated in

---

[1] McKinsey Global Institute (MGI), "Globalization in Transition: The Future of Trade and Value Chains", 2019.

the international community to guide and supervise it.

Although a series of rules related to the trade in goods, trade in services, protection of intellectual property rights, IT agreements and other fields are included in the framework of WTO, there is no package of solutions for digital products. Most importantly, the key barriers to digital trade in such aspect as dataflow have not been included in the relevant WTO agreements. In 2017, 71 member states of WTO negotiated on digital trade products, covering market access, data flow, data privacy protection, national treatment, intellectual property protection, etc., and jointly released the e-commerce initiative in 2019. However, due to the great differences in digital trade policies among large economies such as the United States, the European Union (EU) and China, it is still very difficult to reach an agreement in the short term [1].

Moreover, in order to resist the impact of liberalization of digital trade on their own development, many countries have adopted a series of non-tariff trade barriers specifically for digital trade on the grounds of protecting national security, information and individual privacy, including measures regarding digital trade localization, data privacy protection, intellectual property protection, Internet censorship and technical barriers, etc. The essence of these measures is whether to allow the cross-border free flow of data and information, which is the key to the development of digital trade. In addition, market access and foreign investment measures related to digital trade also restrict the development of digital trade to a certain extent, such as the access restrictions on electronic payment and the requirement that the hardware and software of digital products meet the specific national technical standards. The imperfection of international rules of digital trade and the resulting trade barriers restrict its development to a certain extent.

---

[1] WTO, "Work Programme on Electronic Commerce", December 13, 2017, https://www.wto.org/english/tratop_e/ecom_e/wkprog_e.htm; WTO, "Joint Statement on Electronic Commerce", January 25, 2019, https://trade.ec.europa.eu/doclib/docs/2019/january/tradoc_157643.pdf.

(i) Common measures regarding digital trade localization worldwide

Measures regarding digital trade localization mainly include the requirements for use of local digital product software and hardware, specific partners to be local enterprises, and transnational restrictions on transfer of technology, etc. ① Generally speaking, measures regarding digital trade localization are very common all over the world. In recent years, many countries have been introducing new measures regarding digital trade localization, with a distinct acceleration in such introduction since the international financial crisis in 2008 (as shown in Figure 1). There are also various ways in which countries implement digital trade localization (as shown in Table 3). Some countries required all digital trading enterprises to accept the provisions of data storage and data server localization. For example, countries like Brazil and Canada required enterprises to use some specified localized data while enforcing the law and conducting supervision. Countries and regions such as EU, South Korea, Russia, Indonesia, Vietnam, Brazil, and India required data localization for the sake of protecting information security and individual privacy. For example, Brazil once discussed whether to store all the data of domestic and foreign enterprises related to its citizens in the country; EU introduced new regulations to implement data localization measures in a broader field; according to the "Commercial Code" of Germany, domestic enterprises were required to store accounting data and files in the country, and another new requirement on local data storage of telecommunications sector was issued in 2017 in Germany; in order to meet the requirements of EU, American companies established cloud computing centers in EU; in 2015, the Department of Telecommunications of India released relevant policies, proposing the implementation of data localization measures, and requiring M2M (Machine-to-Machine) service providers of the telecommunications sector

---

① Congressional Research Service, "Digital Trade and U. S. Trade Policy", May 21, 2019, https://crsreports.congress.gov.

to store all Indian customer data in India [1].

The reason for introducing digital trade localization measures worldwide lies in the fact that compared with the trade in tangible goods, tariffs cannot be levied on intangible digital trade products that are more difficult to be identified and supervised, thus getting more risk factors involved. However, the measures regarding digital trade localization will not only burden domestic enterprises, but also hinder foreign investors from investing nationwide, and may even lead to conflicts of interest among countries, thus undermining the development of cross-border digital trade. In particular, the requirements of data localization restrict the development of various trades in service relying on dataflow (such as cloud computing, big data, financial services), and also increase the cost of data storage for enterprises, which results in diseconomies of scale, and is especially disadvantageous to small and medium-sized enterprises and not conducive to the development of GVC definitely.

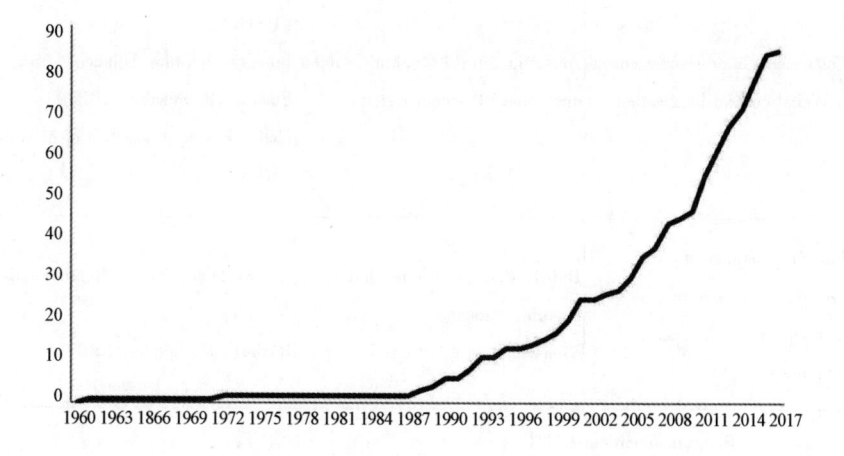

Figure 1 Number of Data Localization Measures Worldwide (1960 – 2017)

Note: The database contains data localization measures for 65 countries around the world.

Source: Digital Trade Assessment Database of the European Centre for International Political Economy (ECIPE).

---

[1] United States International Trade Commission, "Global Digital Trade 1—Market Opportunities and Key Foreign Trade Restrictions", August 2017.

It is difficult to be properly solved in the short term as many reasons are involved in the data localization measures, such as economic factors, ethics, morality, culture, and customs, etc. Therefore, it is crucial for the development of digital trade to seek a balance point among the free flow of data, privacy protection and national security and find an appropriate degree of data localization.

Table 3　　　　　　　Examples of Measures regarding Digital Trade Localization

Classification	Country	Source
Requirement on local data storage	Argentina, Australia, Canada, China, Greece, Indonesia, Venezuela, etc.	Business Software Alliance (BSA) Business Roundtable (BRT) Citibank (Citi)
Enforcement of or encouragement to digital content localization	Australia, Brazil, China, India and some EU member states	United States Trade Representative (USTR) Business Software Alliance (BSA) Business Roundtable (BRT) Motion Picture Association of America (MPAA)
Provide procurement preferences of governments and support localization enterprises	Brazil, Canada, China, India, Nigeria, Paraguay, Venezuela, etc.	United States Trade Representative (USTR) Business Roundtable (BRT)

Source: Relevant reports of USITC.

(ii) Big differences of data privacy protection among countries

Countries have taken a series of data privacy protection measures on the grounds of protecting national security and preventing the disclosure of sensitive individual and enterprise data. For example, according to the "General Data Protection Regulation" (GDPR) issued by the EU that came into force in

2018, enterprises in the EU were required to protect their individual data privacy in accordance with the regulations. Russia, Indonesia and some other countries also adopted EU regulatory standards. The Asia Pacific countries such as the United States adopted APEC data privacy standards, namely "Cross-Border Privacy Rules" (CBPR). However, there are differences in the regulatory systems for the collection, disclosure, and protection of data privacy-related information in different countries, the standards and cultures for data privacy protection also vary from country to country, and a unified standard has not yet been formulated in the international community. All these factors result in great differences in data privacy protection among countries and hinder the development of global digital trade. For example, the EU has not yet accepted the provisions on cross-border dataflow in its TISA negotiations with the United States, nor has the EU added the provisions on cross-border dataflow in its FTA with Japan, only promising to reconsider the issue within three years [1].

By virtue of its advantages in IT, the United States advocates more free cross-border dataflow and pays less attention to privacy protection. However, most countries represented by the EU generally believe that free cross-border dataflow is not conducive to data privacy protection and will pose a threat to individual privacy. Although the United States and the EU reached the "Safe Harbor Privacy Principles" in 2000 and realized free cross-border dataflow within in the framework of the Safe Harbor, the Safe Harbor eventually failed due to the abuse of European customer data by American enterprises. In 2016, in order to realize data transmission and sharing, the United States and the EU reached once again a new data sharing agreement, namely "EU-US Privacy Shield", which makes new provisions for individual privacy protection in data transmission between the United States and the EU. The new agreement clearly defines the premise for the United States to obtain EU related data, and emphasizes the

---

[1] Meltzer J P., "Cybersecurity and Digital Trade: What Role for International Trade Rules?", Working Paper 132, Global Economy and Development Brookings Institution.

EU's data sovereignty. As a result, the United States undertook more obligations, while the EU enjoyed more rights. Although the United States and the EU negotiated smoothly on certain aspects of free cross-border dataflow and data privacy protection and reached some consensus, fundamentally speaking, the differences between the United States and the EU still exist and have not been completely eliminated.

Excessive data privacy protection hinders the development of both enterprises and digital trade. For enterprises, the existence of digital trade barriers has brought a heavier cost burden to enterprises; for digital trade itself, trade barriers caused by data privacy protection have seriously hindered the development of digital trade toward transparency and efficiency. It was pointed out in "Digital Trade in the U. S. and Global Economies, Part I" that different implementation methods of "EU Data Protection Directive" by different EU member states would cause uncertainties and increase costs for American and EU enterprises. It was estimated by the European Commission that the cost of different regulatory methods for EU enterprises was about 3 billion US dollars per year [1]. In addition, it was estimated in some studies that the differences in data privacy protection mechanisms between the United States and the EU have reduced bilateral trade flows by 650 billion US dollars annually [2]. Therefore, countries around the world should strengthen negotiation and cooperation, find common ground in data privacy and protection mechanisms, and reform the existing regulatory measures so as to form a new privacy protection measures and framework conducive to the development of digital trade.

---

[1] U. S. International Trade Commission, "Digital Trade in the U. S. and Global Economies, Part I ", July 2013.

[2] U. S. International Trade Commission, "Digital Trade in the U. S. and Global Economies, Part I ", July 2013.

(iii) Great disputes about the intellectual property protection of digital products in various countries

A digital product is a kind of knowledge-intensive product which is easy to be copied and pirated. Therefore, compared with tangible goods, a digital product needs more intellectual property protection. The EU introduced a new copyright law in 2019 to meet the new needs of digital economy and digital trade, and more countries may follow suit in the future. However, the intellectual property protection system related to digital trade is still not perfect among countries, and there are great differences in the standards of intellectual property protection of digital products in different countries with no consensus reached yet. These problems have become one of the key barriers to the development of digital trade. For example, piracy of digital content is a major disadvantage in the development of digital trade. According to relevant reports, the trade volume of counterfeit and pirated goods reached 360 billion US dollars in 2008 and rose to 960 billion US dollars by 2015. Among them, the trade value of pirated digital music, films and software in various countries increased from 30 - 75 billion US dollars in 2008 to 80 - 240 billion US dollars in 2015 [1].

In addition, with the increasing types of online products arising from the development of digital trade, the related disputes over intellectual property have emerged one after another. However, the traditional intellectual property protection laws were not applicable to the disputes over the intellectual property protection of digital products. Therefore, within the framework of WTO, the United States, the EU and other member states have conducted a discussion on the issue of "intellectual property protection". Although they have reached an agreement on certain issues, there are still great disputes over many issues. The bills of different countries represent their own interests, which is likely to form digital trade barriers among countries. In this regard, the intellectual property protec-

---

[1] Congressional Research Service, "Digital Trade and U. S. Trade Policy", May 2017, https://crsreports.congress.gov.

tion in digital trade should be included in international negotiations. In the meantime, all countries should improve their laws and regulations of intellectual property protection, unify standards and strengthen cooperation.

(iv) Existence of Internet censorship in all countries for the sake of network security

In consideration of factors such as good order, public interest and national security, all countries have developed various censorship measures for Internet content and websites. For example, Japan has formulated national security censorship requirements on information and web services; India has also enacted relevant laws to prevent foreign network information that may threaten its national sovereignty and national defense and disturb the public order; According to the Electronic Transmission Act of Indonesia, the government has been empowered to screen and filter network information; Thailand has set up the Computer Data Filtering Committee to filter the information that is against the public interest and order; Russia has artificially filtered out thousands of foreign websites[①].

Worse still, different countries may have different censorship measures and standards for the same content. Such kind of differentiated Internet censorship standards can easily lead to invisible market access barriers and restrict enterprises from participating in global digital trade activities, because the transmission of digital products and services involved in digital trade activities has to be achieved on the Internet, and the Internet censorship standards directly determine whether digital products and services can get access to a country. Currently, in the global scope, Brazil, India, Indonesia and Russia have relatively more requirements on censorship. In addition, in order to protect and support the development of domestic digital trade sector and enterprises, the governments of various countries have adopted Internet censorship and cyber law

---

① United States International Trade Commission, "Global Digital Trade 1—Market Opportunities and Key Foreign Trade Restrictions", August 2017.

enforcement measures to examine foreign digital trade enterprises based on the ground of network security, thus restricting the development of cross-border digital trade.

IV. Strategies for Promoting Digital Trade Development in China

It is not difficult to conclude from the above that digital trade has many characteristics different from those of traditional trade, and is even expected to boost international trade to a new stage. The development of digital trade will also create new opportunities for micro market players, improve market efficiency and create new impetus for international trade development, thus producing significant economic benefits. In view of this, China needs to raise the strategic position of digital trade at the national level, while scholars, policy makers and relevant departments should speed up the research and formation of new ideas, rules and policies for the development of digital trade.

(i) Raising the strategic position of digital trade at the national level

With the continuous improvement of digital technologies such as 5G communication technology, 3D printing, cloud computing, Internet of Things and virtual reality, digital trade is expected to achieve a breakthrough in the near future, and have a profound impact on the future trade mode, trade rules, trade products and trade participants. Moreover, the development of trade in goods has hit a bottleneck. In the future, the priority of the international trade development will be given to trade in services, and certain trade in goods will also be service-oriented, all of which also depend on the development of digital trade. In view of the possible significant impact of digital trade, many countries have incorporated digital trade into their own development strategies, promulgated corresponding laws, regulations and policies to promote the development of digital trade, and actively participated in the global negotiations on digital trade rules. In fact, as early as 1998, the release of the report titled "Emerging Digital Economy" by the U. S. Department of Commerce officially opened the prelude to the development of global digital economy. In the 21st century, France took the lead in proposing the development strategies of digital trade in 2008. Subsequently, Japan, the United Kingdom and other countries and regions also successively issued strategic reports on digital economy and digital trade [1]. For example, the U. S. Congressional Research Service released "Digital Trade and U. S. Trade Policies" in 2017, emphasizing that the status and role of digital trade in global trade and economic development would be increasingly prominent, and the United States should play a leading role in shaping global digital trade policies [2]. In 2017, the EU also issued the report titled "Digital Trade Strategies".

In recent years, China has also actively responded to the development trend of digital trade and issued a number of policy documents such as the "E-commerce Law" in 2018. Chinese scholars and policy makers should learn from the practices of USITC and USTR to conduct a more systematic study of digital trade. Specifically, relevant ministries and commissions can take the lead to set up a joint research team composed of scholars and policy makers, so as to integrate theory with practice, and systematically study the status quo and characteristics of China's digital trade development, the future development direction of global digital trade, and possible systemic impact, thus providing theoretical guidance for formulating strategies for digital trade development at the national level. Moreover, all provinces and cities are encouraged to determine more specific development direction and key fields according to the national strategies for digital trade development and in combination with the regional comparative advantages, so as to form a regional development pattern with different emphasis that is both competitive and complementary.

---

[1] Ma Shuzhong, Fang Chao, Guo Jiwen, et al., "Blue Paper on the Development of Digital Trade of the World and China", September 2018.

[2] López González J, Jouanjeanm, "Digital Trade: Developing a Framework for Analysis", OECD Trade Policy Papers, No. 205, 2017, OECD Publishing.

(ii) **Exploring the development concept and regulatory idea of digital trade**

It can be concluded from the above that digital trade produces new economic benefits different from those of traditional trade, and also faces new trade barriers. Therefore, it is necessary to explore and form a new development concept and regulatory idea. First, generally speaking, digital trade has an important impact on almost all industries, and will integrate data, goods and services into trade products, thus invalidating the policies emphasizing only on a certain sector or a certain dimension of trade products. Therefore, as for the development concept and regulatory idea of digital trade, more attention should be paid to the overall vision, a systematic mode of thinking should be established, and a comprehensive approach should be adopted. Second, in the context of digital trade, the role of platform enterprises is increasingly prominent. Therefore, ways to encourage the development of various platform enterprises should be taken into consideration in policy making. At the same time, relevant laws and regulations should be enacted to prevent efficiency loss caused by monopoly of platform enterprises. Third, the formulation of digital trade policies should highlight inclusiveness, ensure wide access to information, prevent the emergence of a digital divide and avoid new inequalities. In particular, it is necessary to ensure that the vast number of micro, small and medium-sized enterprises and ordinary consumers enjoy the dividend of digital trade. Fourth, the international rules on digital trade are being developed. China should accelerate the absorption and learning of the international common rules and standards on digital trade, especially the new rules in regional trade agreements such as the "Transatlantic Trade and Investment Partnership" (TTIP), "Trade in Service Agreement" (TISA) and the "United States-Mexico-Canada Agreement" (USMCA); besides, it should boldly carry out the pilot projects by imitating good practices in accordance with China's situation, so as to take the initiative in future rule-making. For example, China can first pilot and implement the internationally accepted digital trade rules in all pilot free trade zones and Hainan Free Trade Port, so as to accumulate relevant regulatory experience. Fifth, under the "Trade Facilitation Agreement" of WTO, China should further improve the degree of trade facilitation of goods and services related to digital trade, so as to improve the international competitiveness of digital trade. Sixth, as for regulatory policies toward digital trade, a balance should be kept among the free cross-border dataflow, national security, domestic economic development and privacy protection. In general, such regulatory policies should ensure the efficient cross-border dataflow so as to guarantee the international competitiveness of China's digital trade, avoid major security incidents such as data leakage, theft and loss that threaten the national security, be conducive to the development of domestic digital sector, and ensure the proper protection of individual privacy.

(iii) Promoting the improvement of international digital trade rules in the framework of WTO

The continuous development of digital trade is bound to change the existing international trade rules, and effective multilateral international trade rules are of great significance to the healthy development of global and China's digital trade. Looking back on the history, China has benefited a lot after its accession to the WTO. Therefore, promoting the improvement of digital trade rules in the WTO framework plays an important and positive role in China's economic and trade development. However, there is no system of digital trade rules in WTO nowadays, and relevant negotiations are stagnant. So far, the WTO has only temporarily exempted tariffs on electronic transmission, while the tariffs on certain ICT products closely related to digital trade have been exempted according to the "Information Technology Agreement" (ITA). Moreover, no consensus has been reached on whether to permanently exempt the tariffs on electronic transmission, and non-tariff trade barriers cannot be dealt with by referring to ITA. Most importantly, key digital trade barriers such as cross-border dataflow have not been included in the relevant WTO agreements, and the access rules stipulated in the "General Agreement on Trade in Services" (GATS) are mainly "positive list", making it unable to solve the emerging access problems about digital products, since many emerging digital products have not been included in the existing "positive list" and no clause regarding intellectual property protection specifically for digital trade is available in the "Agreement on Trade-Related Aspects of Intellectual Property Rights" (TRIPS).

In this case, China should actively promote the formulation of international digital trade rules in the framework of WTO, and strive to make it conducive to the development of digital trade in China. First, China can promote the addition of some digital trade rules under the existing WTO agreements. For example, the classification system of trade products can be reformed in the agreements such as GATS, ITA, TRIPS, and the "Trade Facilitation Agreement", and the provisions related to digital trade such as cross-border dataflow, privacy protection, transfer of technology and intellectual property protection can be included. Second, China should promote the formation of a standing working group to discuss international digital trade rules under the multilateral framework of WTO. The working group can draft articles accepted by all countries in the WTO framework by referring to the widely applied and accepted digital trade rules and provisions in various kinds of FTA and RTA, especially the above-mentioned regional trade agreements, and submit them to the WTO for discussion. Third, China could also try to promote the formulation of a special agreement to solve digital trade issues in the framework of WTO.

(iv) Strengthening negotiations on digital trade rules in bilateral and regional trade agreements

Although it is the optimal goal for China to reach a digital trade agreementin the framework of WTO, it may be a long and tortuous process since there are so many difficulties ahead. Just because of this, all countries are trying to incorporate digital trade clauses into bilateral and regional trade agreements for the purpose of gradually solving barriers to digital trade development. In fact, there are many insightful rules on digital trade in bilateral or regional trade agreements at present. Among them, the clauses concerning digital trade in "Trans-Pacific Partnership Agreement" (TPP), TTIP, TiSA and USMCA represent the latest development and possible direction of digital trade rules. TPP eventually failed because of the withdrawal of the United States, but some of its rules on digital trade are still of valuable reference. For example, the prohibitions of tariffs on digital trade, cross-border dataflow, digital localization, mandatory source code disclosure and transfer of technology [1] in TPP are all embodied to some extent in USMCA, which, as the first formal agreement that includes perfect new digital trade rules, may become the standard of digital trade rules in future RTA negotiations. TTIP is the largest cooperation platform between the United States and EU on cross-border digital trade rules. As a typical agreement, TiSA has 23 member states currently including major developed countries such as the United States, the EU and Australia, and its trade volume in services accounts for about 70% of the global total. Both TTIP and TiSA aim to solve digital trade barriers in such fields as cross-border dataflow, digital localization and intellectual property protection. Among them, TTIP has made good progress in digital trade issues such as network openness, recognition of electronic authentication services, online consumer protection and cooperation in regulation.

In this context, China should also strengthen the negotiationon digital trade rules in bilateral and regional trade agreements. In fact, China has signed dozens of bilateral and regional agreements with other countries worldwide, and has been negotiating with relevant countries on more agreements. Therefore, China may consider conducting negotiations on digital trade and constructing rules in these bilateral and regional trade agreements to gather experience. First, China should intensively study the advanced and reasonable practices regarding digital trade in USMCA, TPP, TIPP, TiSA, etc., and study the possibility of their implementation in China. Appropriate measures could be applied in China's bilater-

---

[1] Congressional Research Service, "Digital Trade and U. S. Trade Policy", May 21, 2019, https://crsreports.congress.gov.

al and regional trade agreements to be signed in the future. Second, in the future bilateral and regional trade negotiations, bolder commitments can be made on such issues as the classification of digital trade products, cross-border dataflow and cooperation in regulation. Third, based on the development characteristics of digital trade in China, some guiding digital trade rules could be put forward.

(ⅴ) Accelerating the improvement of digital infrastructure construction

Just as trade in goods depends on the progress of transportation technology, digital trade is highly dependent on the perfection of digital infrastructure. Therefore, countries in the world are speeding up the improvement of digital infrastructure construction, in a bid to occupy favorable position in the future digital trade competitiveness. China is no exception. First, as a relatively new concept, digital infrastructure will play an increasingly important role in the era of digital economy. Therefore, it is necessary to define the scope and boundary of digital infrastructure more scientifically, and find out its deficiencies of China and solve them properly. Second, China should speed up the construction of new generation of ICT hardware infrastructure, especially the construction of 5G communication network. Meanwhile, attention should also be paid to the construction of digital infrastructure in central and western regions to prevent the emergence of new infrastructure gaps. Third, China should promote and improve the construction of network platform enterprises, and develop a number of world-class platform enterprises with international competitiveness. Although platform enterprises are profit-oriented, they also have the nature of quasi-public goods and can be included in the category of digital infrastructure on the premise of making them more inclusive and public, so as to help Chinese micro, small and medium-sized enterprises to carry out digital trade. Of course, a number of non-profit platform enterprises can also be established appropriately. Fourth, China should actively participate in the construction of overseas digital infrastructure by taking advantage of its competitive edge in the field of digital infrastructure, and appropriately promote China's IT related standards to become international general standards, so as to occupy a favorable position in the digital trade competition.

(vi) Exploring the establishment of a new product classification system in the context of digital trade

In the context of digital trade, the boundary between tangible goods and intangible services is becoming increasingly blurred, and the traditional "dichotomy" product classification system is becoming increasingly inapplicable and even hindering the development of digital trade. In particular, the WTO's method of classifying trade products into goods and services is no longer applicable in the era of digital trade. For example, as for 3D printing, it can be included in trade in services as design service on the one hand; on the other hand, it can also be included in trade in goods because the printing products can be printed into tangible goods by the buyer. In fact, many kinds of trade in goods are becoming increasingly service-oriented, and goods and services are interrelated and interwoven. Therefore, it is necessary to explore and construct a new product classification system in the context of digital trade. First, China should comprehensively summarize the new characteristics of digital trade products, reform its existing classification system of goods and services, explore and develop new product classification methods. Such methods should focus more on the using function of products instead of only distinguishing between goods and services. Second, it is necessary to conduct a prospective study on the new products, new formats and new modes that may appear in the future digital trade, and explore the ways of applying the new product classification system to emerging products. Therefore, the new product classification system should be more flexible and inclusive. Third, China should make it possible to regulate digital trade more reasonably under the new product classification system, and ensure that such a new classification system is conducive to determining the future tariff standards and their impact, so as to evaluate the positive and negative effects of digital trade on economic development.

References

CISCO, "The Internet of Things, At - A - Glance", https://www.cisco.com/c/dam/en_us/solutions/trends/iot/docs/iot - aag.pdf.

Congressional Research Service, "Digital Trade and U. S. Trade Policy", May 21, 2019, https://crsreports.congress.gov.

Deardorff A. V., "Comparative Advantage in Digital Trade", Working Papers 664, Research Seminar in International Economics, University of Michigan, 2017.

DHgate.com, "Seize the Opportunity of Digital Trade to Help Small and Medium-sized Enterprises Go Global-Partner Project of DHgate.com Vigorously Promotes Small and Medium-sized Cross-border E-commerce Enterprises to Explore Overseas Markets", January 10, 2020, https://seller.dhgate.com/news/media/i258602.html#cms_ Seize the Opportunity of Digital Trade to Help Small and Medium-sized Enterprises Go Global-List-1.

E - Marketer, "2019: China to Surpass US in Total Retail Sales", January 23, 2019, https://www.emarketer.com/newsroom/index.php/2019 - china - to - surpass - us - in - total - retail - sales/.

Ivan Sarafanov, Bai Shuqiang, "Research on the Cooperative Mechanism of Trade in Digital Products from the Perspective of WTO-On the Basis of the Development Status of and Barriers to Digital Trade", *Journal of International Trade*, No. 2, 2018.

Liu Hongkui, Associate professor, Institute of Economics, CASS.

Li Xiaohua, "New Features of Digital Economy and the Formation Mechanism of New Driving Force of Digital Economy", *Reform*, No. 11, 2019.

López González J, Ferencz J., "Digital Trade and Market Openness", OECD Trade Policy Papers, No. 217, 2018, OECD Publishing.

López González J, Jouanjeanm, "Digital Trade: Developing a Framework for Analysis", OECD Trade Policy Papers, No. 205, 2017, OECD Publishing.

Ma Shuzhong, Fang Chao, Guo Jiwen, et al., "Blue Paper on the Development of Digital Trade of the World and China", September 2018.

McKinsey Global Institute (MGI), "Globalization in Transition: The Future of Trade and Value Chains", 2019.

Meltzer J P., "Cybersecurity and Digital Trade: What Role for International Trade Rules?", Working Paper 132, Global Economy and Development Brookings Institution.

The Office of the U. S. Trade Representative, Key Barriers to Digital Trade, March 2017, https: //ustr. gov/about - us/policy - offices/press - office/fact - sheets/2017/march/key - barriers - digital - trade.

UNCTAD, "Global e - commerce sales surged to $29 trillion", March 29, 2019, https: //unctad. org/en/pages/newsdetails. aspx? OriginalVersionID = 2034.

United States International Trade Commission, "Global Digital Trade 1—Market Opportunities and Key Foreign Trade Restrictions", August 2017.

U. S. International Trade Commission, "Digital Trade in the U. S. and Global Economies, Part I ", July 2013.

U. S. International Trade Commission, "Digital Trade in the U. S. and Global Economies, Part II ", August 2014.

WTO, "Work Programme on Electronic Commerce", December 13, 2017, https: //www. wto. org/english/tratop_e/ecom_e/wkprog_e. htm.

WTO, "Joint Statement on Electronic Commerce", January 25, 2019, https: //trade. ec. europa. eu/doclib/docs/2019/january/tradoc_157643. pdf.

WTO, *World Trade Report 2018: The Future of World Trade: How Digital Technologies Are Transforming Global Commerce*, World Trade Organization publication, 2018.

Xia Jiechang, Xiao Yu, "Development Trend and Future Orientation of Digital Entertainment Consumption", *Reform*, No. 12, 2019.

Xiong Li, Liu Hui, Liu Hualing, *Digital and Business: Collected Papers of the 2010 Global Digital Trade and Mobile Commerce Symposium*, Shanghai Academy of Social Sciences Press, 2010.

Study on Sustainable Development of the Medical and Health Care Insurance Fund under the Background of China's Population Aging[*]

Ge Yanxia[**]

The medical security system is a major institutional arrangement to alleviate people's health care cost burdens, improve people's well-being and maintain social harmony and stability. Its design needs to be constantly adjusted in light of social development, changes in disease structure and degree of population aging. Over the past decades, China featured a relatively youthful populace, rapid economic growth and well-run basic medical and health care insurance fund, and had reaped the benefits of reform during the reform period. In the next 15 years, however, with accelerated population aging and normal economic development, China's medical and health care insurance fund will probably face unprecedented risks and challenges in maintaining a balanced budget.

Population aging is developing rapidly in China. The transitional changes in

---

[*] This article was originally published on *China Health Insurance* (No. 2, 2021), with the original title "Risk Analysis of Sustainable Development of Medical Insurance Funds under the Background of Population Aging", and the content has slightly changed.

[**] Ge Yanxia, Associate Professor, Deputy Director of Social Governance Research Office, National Institute of Social Development, CASS.

population age structure, employment structure and urban-rural structure will have profound impact on the future income and payment of the medical and health care insurance fund. In terms of the income of the medical and health care insurance fund, firstly, the growth of number of employees paying for medical insurance contributors has slowed down due to decline in working age population and employment rate; secondly, affected by the urban-rural structure of the population, the rural population has decreased, and the number of urban and rural residents participating in basic medical insurance program has decreased. Generally speaking, affected by the population structure changes and economic downward pressure, it is expected that during the 14th Five-Year Plan period, the growth rate of number of people enrolled in the medical insurance program and the income of medical and health care insurance fund will slow down. As for the payment of the medical and health care insurance fund, currently, the accelerated population structure aging in China has an increasing impact on the payment of the medical and health care insurance fund. Theoretically, population aging has two major impacts on the payment of the medical and health care insurance fund: firstly, the rise in the number and proportion of the elderly drives up the overall illness frequency and treatments (medical treatment and hospitalization) of residents; secondly, the treatment costs of the elderly are high due to long duration of illness and multiple complications. Both of them contribute to the high payment of the medical and health care insurance fund arising from population aging. Generally speaking, the acceleration of population aging will bring unprecedented challenges to the sustainable development of the medical and health care insurance fund.

Reasonable financing and steady operation can basically guarantee the sustainability of the medical insurance system. In order to effectively prevent risks and sustain the fund, the *Outline of the Healthy China 2030 Plan* in 2016 clearly proposed to improve the adjustment mechanism for stable and sustainable medical insurance financing and treatment to realize the medium and long-term actuarial balance of the fund.① The *Opinions of the CPC Central Committee and the State Council on Deepening the Medical Security System Reform* ("Opinions") issued in February 2020 further proposed to "establish a medical and health care insurance fund financing mechanism that adapts to the basic national conditions at the primary stage of socialism, matches the affordability of all parties, and aligns the basic healthcare needs, practically strengthen the fund operation management and fund risk warning and prevention, and resolutely forestall systemic risks".②

The academic circles discussed a lot about the medium and long-term actuarial balance of the medical and health care insurance fund and approaches to achieve it. Among them, Li Zijun, Feng Jin and Wang Zhen are of the opinion that raises the retirement age can improve the financial position of the employee medical and health care insurance fund.③ Deng Dasong and Yang Hongyan, Shi Ruoding and Wang Bingtao think otherwise that the reform scheme of raising the contribution rate may be more effective.④ Li Yaqing, Shen Shuguang and Wen Yuhui proposed to have retirees contribute to the medical insurance to alleviate the imbalance of the income and payment of the employee medical and health

---

① CPC Central Committee and the State Council, Outline of Healthy China 2030, 2016.

② CPC Central Committee and the State Council, Opinion on Deepening the Medical Security System Reform, 2020.

③ Li Zijun, "Forecast of the Income and Payment of Urban Employee Medicare fund and Comparative Analysis—from the Perspective of Different Policy Combinations and with Hubei Province as an Example", *Journal of Hunan Agricultural University (Social Science)*, 2019, 20 (03), pp. 83 – 89; Feng Jin, Wang Zhen, "Effect of Raising Retirement Age on Balance of the Urban Employee Medicare fund—a Study based on Policy Simulation", *Chinese Social Security Review*, 2019, 3 (02), pp. 109 – 121.

④ Deng Dasong, Yang Hongyan, "Estimation of the Basic Medicare Financing Rate under the Aging Trend", *Journal of Finance and Economics*, 2003 (12), pp. 39 – 44; Shi Ruoding, Wang Bingtao, "Analysis on the Impact of Demographic aging on Urban Basic Medicare Fund", *Reform & Opening*, 2011 (21), pp. 22 – 23.

care insurance fund. ① Chen Youhua, Wang Jinying and Ge Yanxia proposed to optimize the birth policies and enhance the inclusiveness of the birth policies to alleviate population aging and related problems brought thereby. ② Generally speaking, existing studies mainly focus on the effect of the retirement age policy and involvement of retirees in the contribution, but many factors influence the sustainable development of the medical and health care insurance fund. As the population aging picks up, the decline in the proportion of contributors and increasing demand for medical treatment will have a profound impact on the sustainable development of the medical and health care insurance fund. The author of this paper, on the basis of the 2019 basic medical insurance system and various core factors, builds the dynamic income and payment balance prediction model of China's medical and health care insurance fund, predicts the income and payment of China's medical and health care insurance fund from 2020 to 2035 in light of the future population size and structure, population health trend and medical insurance demand, wages and changes in insurance burden structure, analyzes the main factors influencing the sustainable development of the medical and health care insurance fund, and puts forward suggestions on accelerating the medical and health care insurance fund system reform and improving the sustainability of the fund.

---

① Li Yaqing, Shen Shuguang, "Policy of Contribution Free for Retirees and Payment Risk of Medicare fund—Evidence from Guangdong Province", *Population & Economics*, 2011 (03), pp. 70 – 77; Wen Yuhui, "A Study on Appropriate Contribution by Retirees to the Urban Employee Basic Medicare", *Modern Management Science*, 2015 (10), pp. 91 – 93.

② Chen Youhua, "Universality of Regional Experience in Application of the Two-child Policy and Related Problems—Evaluation of the "Study on China's Birth Policy in the 21st Century," *Population and Development*, 2009, 15 (01), pp. 9 – 22; Wang Jinying, Ge Yanxia, "China's Demographic Development Trend under the Comprehensive Implementation of the Two-child Policy", *Population Research*, 2016, 40 (06), pp. 3 – 21.

I. Estimation of the Income and Payment of China's Medical and Health Care Insurance Fund

The current basic medical insurance system of China is composed of the employee medical insurance and resident medical insurance. As for the fund-raising mechanism, the employee medical insurance is funded by the insured and employers according to the statutory contribution base and proportion, while the resident medical insurance is funded by the insured and governments at various levels. The basic medical insurance is generally spent on the reimbursement of hospitalization and outpatient. The two kinds of reimbursement payments have their respective payment threshold and reimbursement proportion. The employee medical insurance and resident medical insurance have their respective payment threshold and reimbursement proportion. The population size and structure changes also determine the income-payment balance of the medical and health care insurance fund, and in particular, have a significant impact on the income-payment balance of the medical and health care insurance fund during the current population transition period. On the one hand, changes in size and structure of China's labor force will significantly influence the contribution income of the medical and health care insurance fund; on the other hand, with the development of the population aging, the size and proportion of the elderly will grow continuously, the overall medical needs of the insured will increase year after year, and payment of the medical and health care insurance fund will up accordingly.

Therefore, under the current medical insurance system, the contribution income of the medical insurance can be computed as follows:

$$I_n = I_n^z (Z * \bar{W}_n * \omega_n^1 + Z * \bar{W}_n * \omega_n^2) \\ + I_n^j (C * a_n + C * b_n) \tag{1}$$

Where, I_n represents the contribution income of the medical insurance in

Year n; $I_n^z(Z * \bar{W}_n * \omega_n^1 + Z * \bar{W}_n * \omega_n^2)$ is the function representing the contribution income of the employee medical insurance in Year n; Z represents the number of employee medical insurance participants in a year; $\bar{W}_n$ represents the per capita contribution base of the employee medical insurance; ω_n^1 represents the contribution proportion of employees; ω_n^2 represents the contribution proportion of employers; $I_n^j(C * a_n + C * b_n)$ is the function representing the contribution income of the resident medical insurance in Year n; C represents the number of resident medical insurance participants in a year; a_n represents the per capita contribution amount of residents; b_n represents the per capita amount contributed by governments at various levels.

The reimbursement payment of the medical insurance can be computed as follows:

$$P_n = P_n^z \left(\sum_{i=15}^{60} x_i * X_i * \alpha_i + \sum_{i=15}^{60} y_i * Y_i * \beta_i \right)$$
$$+ P_n^j \left(\sum_{k=0}^{100} x_k * X_k * \mu_k + \sum_{k=0}^{100} y_k * Y_k * \vartheta_k \right) \quad (2)$$

Where, P_n represents the reimbursement payment of the medical insurance in Year n. $P_n^z \left(\sum_{i=15}^{60} x_i * X_i * \alpha_i + \sum_{i=15}^{60} y_i * Y_i * \beta_i \right)$ is the function representing the reimbursement payment of the employee medical insurance in Year n; x_i represents the number of hospitalization of employee medical insurance participants aged i; X_i represents the hospitalization costs/ time of population aged i; α_i represents the reimbursement proportion of the hospitalization costs; y_i represents the outpatient times of employee medical insurance participants aged i; Y_i represents the outpatient costs of the insured aged i; and β_i represents the reimbursement proportion of the outpatient costs.

$P_n^j \left(\sum_{k=0}^{100} x_k * X_k * \mu_k + \sum_{k=0}^{100} y_k * Y_k * \vartheta_k \right)$ is the function representing the reimbursement payment of the resident medical insurance in Year n; x_k represents the hospitalization times of resident medical insurance participants aged k; X_k represents hospitalization costs per time; μ_k represents the reimbursement proportion of the hospitalization costs; y_k represents the outpatient times of resident medical insurance participants aged k; Y_k represents the outpatient costs per time; ϑ_k represents the reimbursement proportion of the outpatient costs.

Further, t_n, the balance of the medical and health care insurance fund in Year n can be expressed as follows:

$$t_n = I_n - P_n$$

T_n, the cumulative balance of the medical and health care insurance fund can be expressed as follows:

$$T_n = T_{n-1} + t_n$$

The income and payment data of the medical and health care insurance fund can be obtained by bringing relevant parameters and basic data to the above formulas. It should be noted that the population data by age and sex (2020 – 2035) used in this paper come from the author's previous population prediction results. See the *Population Development Trend in China under the Comprehensive Implementation of the Two-child Policy* for details. Besides, all prediction models are based on certain assumptions. This paper, based on the data available, follows the change law of various factors and sets assumptions as reasonable as possible. The author assumes that the visit rate and hospitalization rate of the insured by age and sex during the assumption period will follow the trend showed in the National Health Services Survey 2013 – 2018; the average outpatient costs per time, average hospitalization costs per time and employees' wages adopt the average growth rate (2010 – 2019). Moreover, due to data limitations, the employee medical and health care insurance fund herein does not cover the maternity insurance.

II. Income and Payment of China's Medical and Health Care Insurance Fund in the Next 15 Years

Under the current medical insurance system and the above assumptions, the prediction results show that China's medical and health care insurance fund cannot make both ends meet in the long run. It is estimated that the year 2026 will see a gap in the current year balance of the medical and health care insurance fund for the first time, and the year 2034 will see a gap in its cumulative balance for the first time. The medical and health care insurance fund of regions with considerable outflow of labor force and rapid population aging will face more severe payment (see Figure 1).

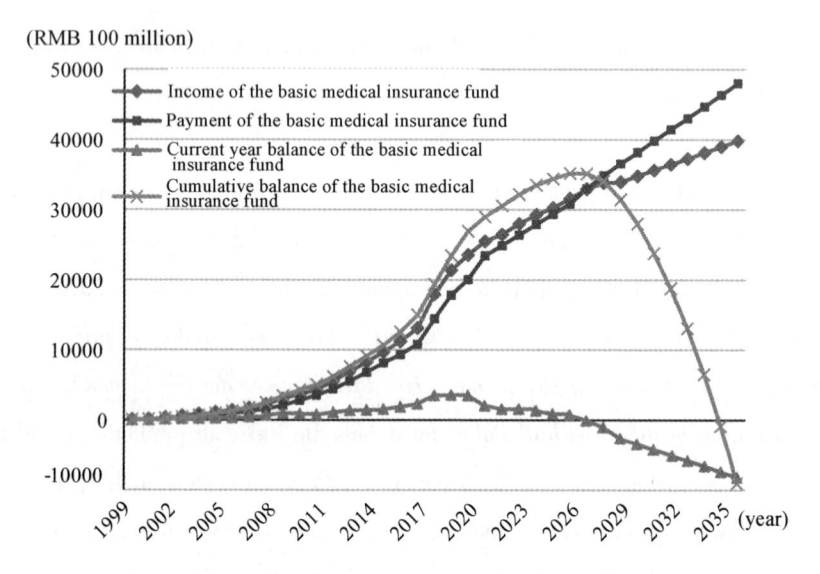

Figure 1 Changes in income and payment of China's basic medical and health care insurance fund

We can see the seriousness of the problem more clearly after forecasting the income and payment of the employee medical insurance and urban and rural resident medical insurance. Since the resident medical insurance participants age faster, the resident medical and health care insurance fund will run a deficit earlier. The prediction results show that under the current system, the year 2021 and 2023 will probably see a gap in the current year balance and cumulative balance of the resident medical and health care insurance fund for the first time (see Figure 2); as for the employee medical insurance, despite the considerable balance of the employee medical and health care insurance fund so far, under the current system, the gap in the current year balance of the employee medical and health care insurance fund will be seen ten years later, namely 2030, and the gap in the cumulative balance will be viewed around 2039 (see Figure 3).

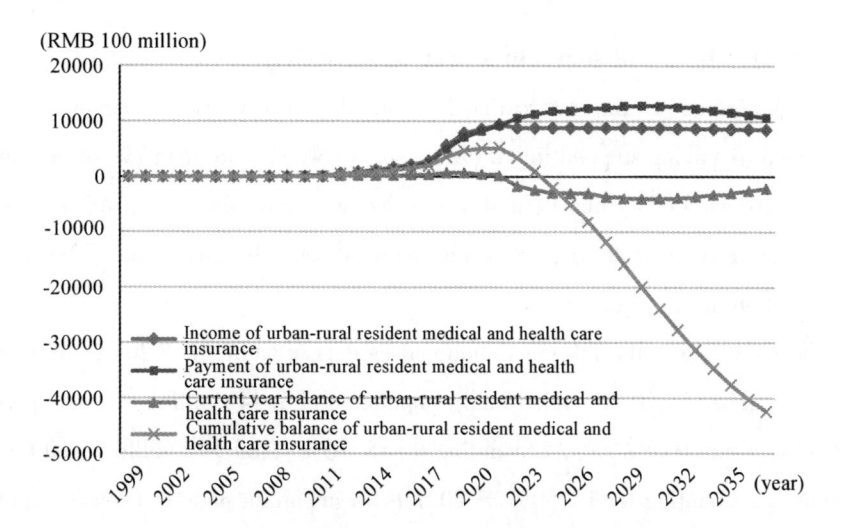

Figure 2   Changes in income and payment of the resident medical and health care insurance fund

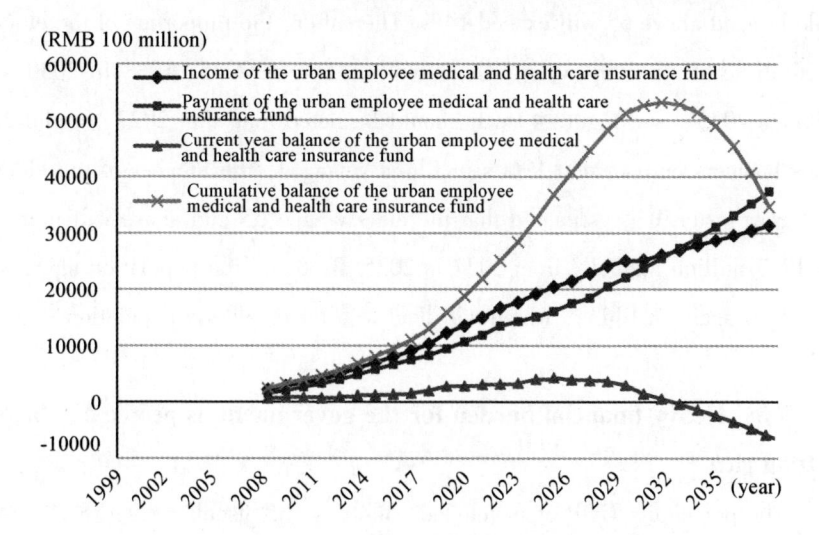

Figure 3   Changes in income and payment of the employee medical and health care insurance fund

III. Main Factors Influencing the Sustainability of China's Medical and Health Care Insurance Fund

(i) China will step into a deep aging society

According to the international standards, a country or region can be deemed as having stepped into an aging society when more than 7% of its population are aged 65 or above, and a deep aging society when 14% of its population are aged 65 or above, and super aging society when more than 20% of its population are aged 65 or above.

According to the 7th population census data of China in 2020, as of 0: 00 on November 1, 2020, China had a population of 1.443 billion, including 264 million aged 60 or above, accounting for 18.70%, and 191 million aged 65 or above, accounting for 13.50%.[①] 2021 is an important node in China's population aging process. The population forecast data showed that China will step from an aging society into a deep aging society after 2021 when the proportion of the elderly aged above 65 will exceed 14%. Thereafter, the proportion of the elderly aged above 65 in China will further grow to 15% in 2025, 19% in 2030 and 23% in 2035 (see Figure 4). It should be noted that after 2027, as the 2nd baby boomers born in mid 1960s in China get aged, the number of the elderly will grow faster. It is estimated that the elderly aged 65 and above will increase by 12.7 million annually from 2027 to 2035. By then, the population aging will speed up again in China, which will lead to a larger elderly population.

(ii) Heavy financial burden for the government as people age before getting rich

The per capita GDP of developed countries will usually reach $10,000

[①] National Bureau of Statistics, *Communique of the Seventh National Population Census*, May 11, 2021.

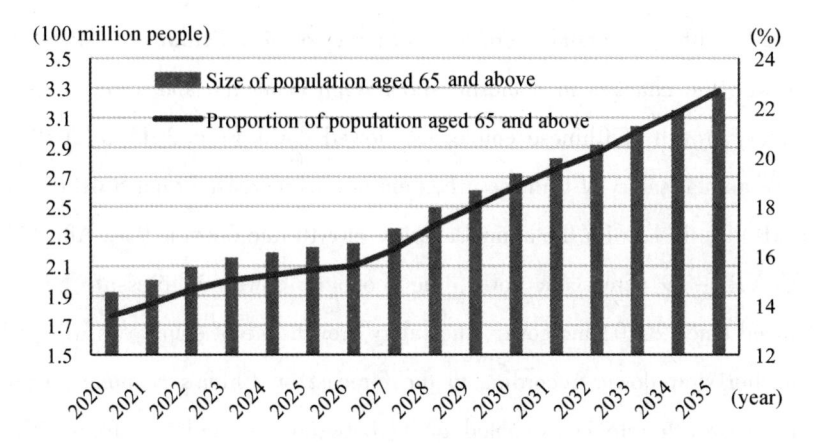

```
(100 million people)                                          (%)
 3.5 ┬─────────────────────────────────────────────────┬ 24
 3.3 │    ▬▬ Size of population aged 65 and above      │
 3.1 │    ── Proportion of population aged 65 and above│ 22
 2.9 │                                                 │
 2.7 │                                                 │ 20
 2.5 │                                                 │
 2.3 │                                                 │ 18
 2.1 │                                                 │ 16
 1.9 │                                                 │
 1.7 │                                                 │ 14
 1.5 └─────────────────────────────────────────────────┘ 12
      2020 ... 2035                              (year)
```

Figure 4 Changes in elderly population 2020 – 2035

when entering the aging society and averagely $20, 000 when entering the deep aging society, and usually $40, 000 when entering the super aging society (mainly refer to Germany and Japan). However, the per capita GDP of China was only $800 when entering the aging society in 2000, and slightly above $10, 000 when entering the deep aging society in 2021. Most developed countries were overburdened by medical costs in the face of the increasingly serious population aging, while China's financial reserves are far less than those of developed countries when in the same stage of population aging, which means that the contradiction between China's population aging and the government's financial payment ability will be more prominent, and the medical insurance system will also face greater challenges and pressure.

(ⅲ) Slow growth of salary income and medical and health care insurance fund income

When the contribution ratio is certain, the growth rate of employees' salary income will largely determine the growth rate of the medical and health care insurance fund income. During the 15 years from 2000 to 2015, both China's economy and employees' salary have grown rapidly; moreover, the average annual salary of urban employees has increased from RMB 9,333 to RMB 62,029, with the annual average growth rate of 38%. However, after 2015, along with the changes in domestic and foreign economic and social situation, the salary growth of Chinese employees slowed down. From 2015 to 2019, the average annual salary of Chinese urban employees increased from RMB 62,029 to RMB 90,134, with the annual average growth rate down to 9%. Affected by the COVID-19 across the world, the economic downward pressure has been enhanced since 2020; moreover, the salary growth rate of employees will probably further slow down. According to the forecast on China's economy, China's economic growth rate is estimated to be between 3% and 5% from 2020 to 2035[1]. Assume that the salary growth rate of urban employees aligns with the economic growth rate during this period, then the average annual salary growth from 2020 to 2035 will be around 4%, and the salary will rise from RMB 96,720 to RMB 161,010 (see Figure 5). For the coming period, the salary growth rate of employees will obviously slow down, which will largely lead to slowdown of the growth rate of the medical and health care insurance fund income.

(ⅳ) Continuous decline in the proportion of contributors in the insured

Along with the decline in working age population, the proportion of medical insurance contributors in the insured will drop continuously, and contribution burden will get increasingly heavy. According to the forecast on China's working

---

[1] See Huang Qunhui, "China will cross the middle-income trap if it maintains the 5% economic growth rate to 2035", SOHU Think Tank, https://www.sohu.com/a/416892247_100160903, sept. 7, 2020; Vice President of Renmin University: Cautious Expectation on the 3.17% Potential Economic Growth of China 2020 - 2035, WWW.CHINANEWS.COM, https://www.chinanews.com/cj/2020/11 -22/9344776.shtml, November 22, 2020; Yang Weimin, "China Needs to Maintain the Average Annual Growth of 4.73% to Double the Economic Output or Per Capita Income by 2035", WWW.CHINANEWS.COM, https://www.chinanews.com/cj/2020/11 - 28/9349651.shtml, November 28, 2020.

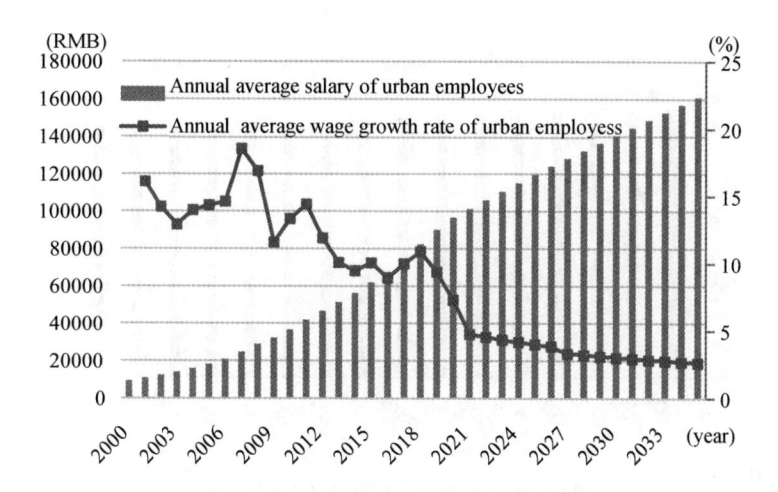

Figure 5 Changes in wage of urban employees

age population and insurance rate by age and sex and the number of retirees from 2020 to 2035, the proportion of medical insurance contributors to the insured across the country will drop from 94% in 2020 to 93% in 2025, 92% in 2030 and 90% in 2035. Among others, the proportion of the contributors to the employee medical insurance will drop faster from 75% in 2020, to 72% in 2025, 70% in 2030 and 68% in 2035 (see Figure 6).

If the ratio of the insured to contributors is defined as the contribution burden coefficient of medical and health care insurance fund, from 2020 to 2035, the coefficient will increase year after year, and is expected to rise from 1.07 in 2020 to 1.08 in 2025, to 1.09 in 2030 and 1.11 in 2035; among them, the contribution burden coefficient of the employee medical insurance will increase more obviously, and is expected to rise from 1.34 in 2020 to 1.38 in 2025, and to 1.43 and 1.47 in 2030 and 2035, respectively.

(v) Mounting demand for medical services

As the Chinese people's health awareness improves, the people's demand for medical services has mounted. First, the demand for inpatient service has in-

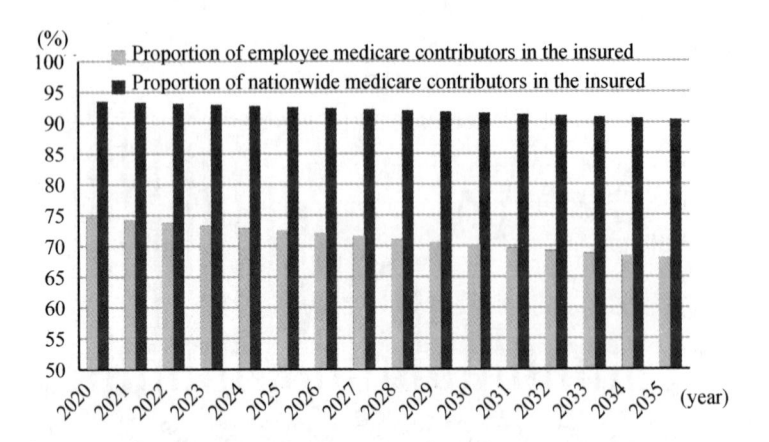

Figure 6   Changes in the proportion of medical insurance contributors

creased significantly. The data of the National Health Services Survey showed that the hospitalization rate of the Chinese residents was about 18% in 2018, which is 14 percentage points above that in 1993; the annual average per capita inpatients were 0.18, 0.14 above that in 1993 (see Figure 7). Second, the demand for medical services has increased remarkably. According to the data of the National Health Services Survey, the 2-week visit rate of the Chinese residents was about 23% in 2018, 6 percentage points above that in 1993; the annual per capita visits were about 6, 1.6 times above those in 1993 (see Figure 8).

(vi) Rapid increase in per capita health expenditure

The progress of medical devices and diagnosis technology not only leads to high treatment and medication costs, but also drives up the medical expenses and personal health expenditure. It is estimated according to data of the National Bureau of Statistics that from 2014 to 2019, the per capita health expenses grew annually by 12.45% in China, and the average annual growth rate of the per capita disposable income was 9.02%. The growth rate of the per capital health expenses is obviously higher than that of the per capita disposable income (see

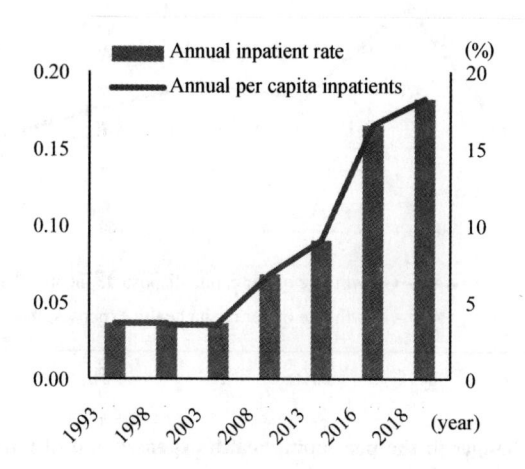

Figure 7 Changes in demand for inpatient services

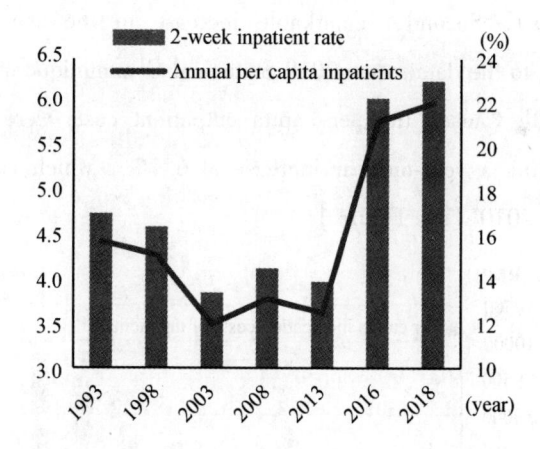

Figure 8 Changes in visits and per capita visits

Figure 9), which indicates that the residents' health expense burden is mounting.

The growth of per capita health expenditure is attributable to the continuous growth of the average medical expenses, which is mainly reflected in two aspects. First, remarkable increase in the average inpatient costs. According to the data in the 2019 Statistical Communique on Development of China's Health

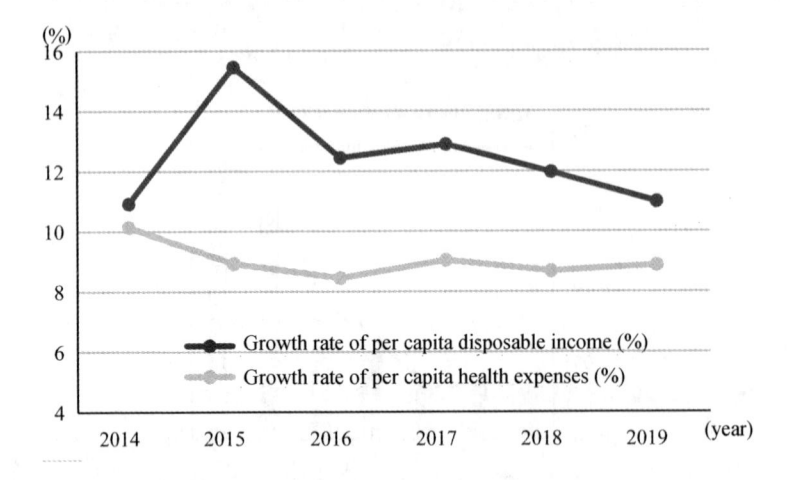

Figure 9   Changes in the per capita health expenses and disposable income

Cause, the per capita inpatient costs were RMB 9,848 in 2019, representing a year-on-year increase of 6.0%, which is 1.6 times as much as that in 2010 (see Figure 10). Second, remarkable increase in the average outpatient costs. According to the data in the 2019 Statistical Communique on Development of China's Health Cause, the per capita outpatient costs were RMB 291 in 2019, representing a year-on-year increase of 6.1%, which is 1.7 times as much as that in 2010 (see Figure 11).

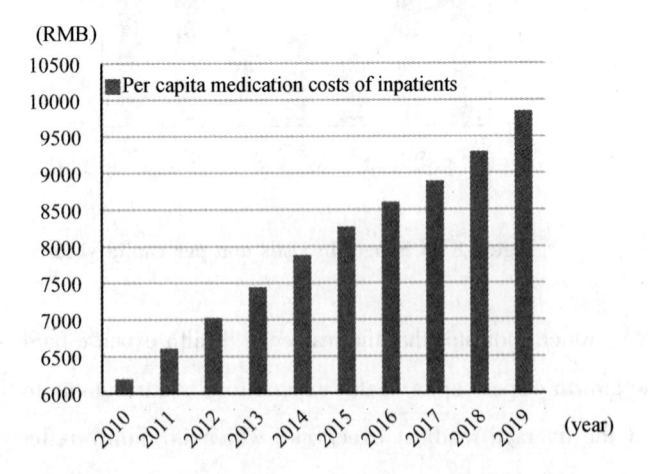

Figure 10   Growth trend of average inpatient costs

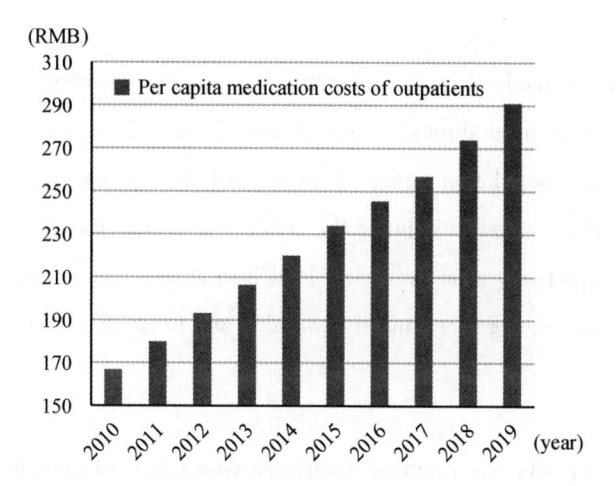

Figure 11　Growth trend of average outpatient costs

IV. Summary and Suggestions

Population aging is developing rapidly in China. The turning changes in population age structure, employment structure and urban-rural structure will have profound impact on the future income and payment of the medical and health care insurance fund. Under the current medical insurance system, the author builds the dynamic income and payment balance prediction model to simulate the income and payment balance of China's medical and health care insurance fund (2020 – 2035) according to the data regarding the population size and structure, population health and medical treatment, wages and contribution to the medical insurance. The results show that under the current system, the medical and health care insurance fund is not sustainable. It is estimated that the year 2026 will see a gap in the current year balance of the medical and health care insurance fund for the first time, and the year 2034 will see a gap in its cumulative balance for the first time. Among others, the gap in the cumulative balance of the employee medical and health care insurance fund and resident medical and health care insurance fund will appear around 2039 and 2023, respectively.

The basic medical insurance system can sustain provided that the fund can make both ends meet through scientific and reasonable management. Under the background of population aging, it is suggested to firmly grasp the key 14th Five-Year Plan period to improve the stable and sustainable financing operation mechanism, actively promote the medical insurance payment reform, strengthen fund operation management and risk warning and prevention, and firmly forestall systematic risks.

(i) Improve the medical insurance financing mechanism and expand the medical and health care insurance funding sources

Resolutely implement the requirements of the *Opinions* on perfecting the stable and sustainable financing operation mechanism. First, gradually raise the medical insurance contribution base in light of the economic and social development to guarantee stable and sustainable source of the basic medical and health care insurance fund. In July 2018, the General Office of the CPC Central Committee and the General Office of the State Council issued the *State Tax and Local Tax Collection System Reform Scheme*, which clearly stipulates that the tax authority shall be responsible for collecting the social insurance premiums as of January 1, 2019, including the basic medical insurance. Compared with the social security authority, the tax authority has the pay data of employees. Therefore, collection of the social security payments by the tax authority is conducive to solving the perennial problem of false contribution base and effectively protecting the rights and interest of the insured and guaranteeing sustainable development of the fund. Though the central government has officially issued corresponding documents, the employee medical insurance contribution base of a considerable number of enterprises is still based on the basic salary. Therefore, it is suggested to determine the contribution base according to the actual salary as soon as possible to guarantee that the income growth of the medical and health care insurance fund aligns with the economic and social development pace. Second, perfect the financing sharing and adjustment mechanism to balance the financing and contribution responsibilities of individuals, employers and the government. China may learn from the experience of developed countries, and perfect the financing sharing and adjustment mechanism by gradually increasing individuals' contribution proportion to cope with the increasing payment stress of the medical and health care insurance fund. Third, increase financial subsidies, especially the investment in resident medical insurance. It is suggested to further raise the taxes on sectors influencing residents' health, such as tobacco and alcohol, and use some of the taxes collected to make up the gap of the medical and health care insurance fund. Fourth, consolidate and raise the overall planning level, comprehensively carry out the basic medical insurance planning at the municipal and prefectural level, encourage provincial planning, expand and strengthen the fund pool, and enhance the risk resistance capacity of the fund.

(ii) Reform the medical insurance payment mechanism and optimize the medical insurance payment structure to improve the efficiency of the medical and health care insurance fund

Establish an effective and efficient medical insurance payment mechanism and optimize the payment structure of the medical and health care insurance fund to improve the efficiency of the medical and health care insurance fund. First, reform the medical insurance payment mechanism. Gradually and moderately raise demanders' sharing proportion and individuals' contribution proportion, and increase the medical services afforded by individuals to avoid excessive medical risks. Second, optimize the medical insurance payment structure. On the one hand, appropriately expand the reimbursement scope of outpatient expenses and raise the reimbursement proportion, and fundamentally reduce the risk of major diseases by strengthening the treatment and management of indisposition and chronic diseases; on the other hand, optimize the structure of drugs covered by the medical insurance, highlight the basic medication needs of common diseases, chronic disease, major diseases and public health, and pay attention to the medication of children and other special groups. In addition, accelerate the implementation of the *Guidelines for Establishing and Improving the Outpatient Joint Security Mechanism for Employee Basic Medical Insurance*, reform the personal account of the employee medical insurance, establish and perfect the outpatient joint security mechanism, raise the efficiency of the medical and health care insurance fund, and gradually alleviate the medical burden of the insured to make the system fairer and sustainable. Third, explore the way to separate the payment for medical service and drugs and devices, and weaken the economic relations between hospitals, doctors and drugs and devices from system and mechanism to reduce excessive prescription, control overgrowth of medical expenses and unreasonable medical insurance payment.

(iii) Strengthen research on sustainable development of the medical and health care insurance fund

In the next 10 – 20 years, with the acceleration of population aging and normal economic development, China's medical and health care insurance fund will face unprecedented risks and challenges to make both ends meet. Therefore, it is urgent to strengthen fund risk warning and prevention. First, strengthen the research on sustainability of the medical and health care insurance fund, fully consider the core factors affecting the income and payment of the medical and health care insurance fund, and establish a normalized monitoring, prediction and analysis mechanism. In view of the accelerated population aging, it is necessary to strengthen the analysis and research on factors related to the medical insurance payment, such as residents' medical service demand structure and medical service price. Second, scientifically budget the income and payment of the medical and health care insurance fund, strengthen the budget implementation and supervision, comprehensively implement the budget performance management to realize medium and long-term actuarial balance of the fund, and improve the fund operation risk assessment and warning mechanism to guarantee the steady and sustainable operation of the fund. Budget the income and payment of the medical and health care insurance fund by the planning level, and summarize by level; meanwhile, embody the budget of the medical and health care insurance fund into the government budget performance management system, which is of great significance to promote the actuarial balance of the medical and health care insurance fund and guarantee the long-term and sustainable operation of the fund.

References

Huang Qunhui, "China will cross the middle-income trap if it maintains the 5% economic growth rate to 2035", SOHU Think Tank, https://www.sohu.com/a/416892247_100160903, sept. 7, 2020.

National Bureau of Statistics, *Communique of the Seventh National Population Census*, May 11, 2021.

Vice President of Renmin University: Cautious Expectation on the 3.17% Potential Economic Growth of China 2020 – 2035, WWW.CHINANEWS.COM, https://www.chinanews.com/cj/2020/11 – 22/9344776.shtml, November 22, 2020.

Yang Weimin, "China Needs to Maintain the Average Annual Growth of 4.73% to Double the Economic Output or Per Capita Income by 2035", WWW.CHINANEWS.COM, https://www.chinanews.com/cj/2020/11 – 28/9349651.shtml, November 28, 2020.

Chapter 3 Understanding China's Social Development

Insurance and Social Changes in China

Sergii Rudenko *,
Svitlana Glovatska **, Olga Shukovilova ***

The development of China's insurance market is an indicator of social changes in the country and one of the tools for eliminating poverty and building a moderately prosperous society.

China's insurance market is the most promising and fastest-growing among the markets of developing countries, and its success benefits from the government-led reforms and a stable economy.

According to the British Center for Economics & Business Research (BCEBR), China is now the world's second largest economy by GDP, and will become the world's leading economy in 2028—five years ahead of schedule. The stable economy enables China to subsidize insurance and develop this industry[1].

Also, China is currently the second largest insurance market in the world and is seen as a key driver of global insurance growth in the next decade.

Until 1986, the People's Insurance Company of China (PICC) was the only

---

　* Sergii Rudenko, Professor, DSc. Ukrainian President of CASS-ONMU: Center of China Studies, Rector of Odessa National Maritime University.

　** Svitlana Glovatska, Ukrainian Director of CASS-ONMU: Center of China Studies.

　*** Olga Shukovilova, Student of Odessa National Maritime University.

　[1] Катаргин. С. Как устроен страховой рынок в Китае, www.if24.ru/strahovoj-rynok-v-kitae/.

company in the insurance market in China. The lack of competition led to stagnation of the industry—it began to develop actively only after the monopoly was broken.

(100 million yuan)

Year	Total Assets	Property Insurance Companies	Life Insurance Companies	Reinsurance Companies	Domestic Funded Insurance Companies	Foreign-funded Insurance Companies
2002	6320.00	948.00	5161.00	211.00		
2003	9088.00	1176.00	7657.00	255.00		
2004	11953.68	1411.38	8352.90	262.37	11540.63	413.05
2005	15286.44	1718.81	13458.27	292.70	14630.97	665.64
2006	19704.19	2340.45	17446.26	311.31	18862.60	862.66
2007	28912.78	3880.51	23249.16	877.26	27656.26	1256.51
2008	33418.83	4687.03	27138.45	994.45	31893.93	1524.91
2009	40634.75	4892.62	33655.05	1162.01	38582.37	2052.39
2010	50481.61	5833.52	42642.66	1151.79	47860.49	2621.12
2011	59828.94	7919.95	49798.19	1579.11	56822.12	3006.83
2012	73545.73	9477.47	60991.22	1845.25	70080.33	3465.40
2013	82886.95	10941.45	68250.07	2103.93	78551.67	4335.28
2014	101591.47	14061.48	82487.20	3513.56	94950.98	6640.49
2015	123597.76	18481.13	99324.83	5187.38	115057.96	6539.80
2016	153764.66	23849.82	126557.51	2765.61	144646.59	9118.07
2017	169377.32	24901.04	131885.05	3150.32	158956.86	10420.46
2018	183305.24	23502.73	146032.48	3633.48	171695.83	11609.41

Figure 1 Assets of Chinese insurance companies for 2002 – 2018

Source: Statista Research Department.

The modern Chinese insurance market is represented by two systems: the compulsory social insurance system and the commercial insurance system.

Insurance Law of the People's Republic of China was promulgated in 1995 with the purpose of regulating commercial insurance activities, protecting the legitimate rights and interests of the parties involved, strengthening supervision and regulation of the insurance industry and promoting its healthy development. The adoption of this law and the establishment of a regulator led to the stabilization of the country's insurance market. After joining the WTO in 2001, the Chinese market became open to foreign insurance companies, which brought it closer to the global insurance market.

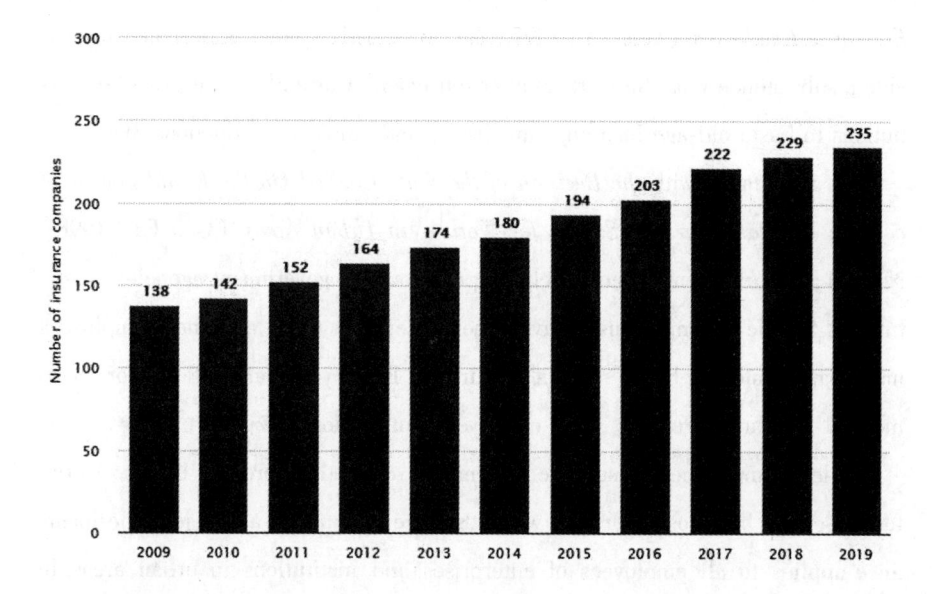

Figure 2 The number of insurance companies in the PRC for 2009 – 2019
Source: Statista.

The Social Insurance Law of the People's Republic of China was adopted in 2010 for the purposes of regulating social insurance relationships, securing citizens' legitimate rights and interests to participate in a social insurance system and receive social insurance benefits.

The social insurance system follows the principle of wide coverage, modest benefits, multi-tiered programmes and a sustainable system. The level of the social insurance system shall correspond to that of economic and social development.

The government creates a system of compulsory social insurance in strict accordance with law, with the aim of protecting citizens in case of old age, illness, occupational injury or childbirth. These insurances include: basic old-age insurance, basic medical insurance, work injury insurance, unemployment insurance, maternity insurance.

The basic old-age insurance system was established according to *the Decision of the State Council on Creation of a Unified Basic Old-age Insurance System for Enterprise Employees* (Guo Fa [1997] No. 26). This system is designed to provide a subsistence wage for workers after retirement. Currently, enterprises' contributions to basic old-age insurance are 20%, and employee deductions 8%.

In accordance with *the Decision of the State Council On the Establishment of a Basic Medical Insurance System for Workers in Urban Areas* (Guo Fa [1998] No. 44), all urban employers, including enterprises, government agencies, institutions, public organizations, private non-enterprise units and their employees must participate in basic medical insurance. Employer contributions for basic medical insurance are 10%, and employee contributions 2%.

The unemployment insurance system was created to provide living security for those who have lost their jobs while they are looking for a new job. The insurance applies to all employees of enterprises and institutions in urban areas. In Beijing, unemployment insurance contributions from enterprises are 1%, and employee contributions 0.2% at present.

Contributions go to the unemployment insurance fund, which pays unemployment benefits, medical benefits, and benefits for professional retraining during the period of receiving unemployment benefits.

The rights to receive unemployment benefits apply to the following employees: (1) those who were not firedon their own free will; (2) those who were registered as unemployed and applying for employment; (3) those who have participated in unemployment insurance for at least 1 year.

The maximum period for receiving unemployment benefits is from 12 to 24 months, depending on the length of service of the employee at the previous place of work.

Work injury insurance is used to provide medical care and benefits to employees who have been injured at work or fallen ill as a consequence of professional activities. The main document governing work injury insurance is *Regulation on Work-Related Injury Insurances* promulgated on December 20, 2010.

The average level of deductions for insurance against occupational injuries should be about 0.75%, while for enterprises with a fairly low level of danger is 0.5%, for enterprises with an average level of danger—1% and for enterprises with a sufficiently high level of danger—1.5%. Employees do not contribute to work injury insurance.

Maternity insurance is used to provide medical care and material benefits during the period of maternity leave. The insurance system applies to workers in urban areas. Deductions are made from the funds of the enterprise and should not exceed 0.5% of the wage.

Contributions go to the maternity insurance fund and are spent on medical care, maternity benefits (i.e. wages during maternity leave), and maternity allowances for their spouses, etc.

The Housing provident fund collects contributions that are used for housing construction and mortgage loans for employees.

Contributions to the accumulation fund are paid by government organizations, state-owned enterprises, collectively owned enterprises in urban areas, foreign-funded enterprises, private enterprises in urban areas, as well as other enterprises, institutions, organizations in urban areas and their employees.

Contributions made to the housing provident fund are the property of employees. These contributions can be used by the employees for acquisition, construction, reconstruction or capital repairs of living quarters. In addition, contributions can be collected in case of retirement, disability, going abroad or used to pay interest on a mortgage loan or to pay rent if it exceeds the size of the household's wages.

In accordance with *the Regulation on the Administration of Housing Provident Fund* released on March 24, 2019, the amount of employee and employer contributions must be at least 5% of the employee's average monthly salary of the previous year.

At present, contributions to housing provident fund are 12% each from an enterprise and an employee in Beijing ①.

The Chinese government, given the difficult financial situation of Chinese enterprises, which are faced with an increase in labor and raw materials costs, lowered contribution rates on unemployment insurance, work injury insurance and maternity insurance. In the context of a slowdown in economy, these measures are intended to reduce the burden on businesses and stimulate economic growth. According to the estimates of the Chinese State Council, the current contribution cuts will save 27 billion yuan for Chinese enterprises. The released funds can be used to modernize production, for example, to fulfill the "Made in China 2025" plan for the development of high-tech products with high added value ②.

It should be noted that these types of insurance exist in most of the developed countries of the world.

Table 1　　　　　　　　　Social insurance of the PRC

Item		aggregate Data				Index (%) (2018 as Percentage of the Following Years)			Average Annual Growth Rate (%)	
		1978	2000	2017	2018	1978	2000	2017	1979-2018	2001-2018
Welfare and Social Insurance										
Revenue of Social Insurance Fund	(100 million yuan)		2644.9	67154.5	79254.8		2996.5	118.0		20.8
Expenses of Social Insurance Fund	(100 million yuan)		2385.6	57145.6	67792.7		2841.7	118.6		20.4
Contributors in Basic Pension Insurance	(10 000 persons)		13617.4	91548.3	94293.3		692.4	103.0		11.3
Number of Employees Joining Unemployment Insurance	(10 000 persons)		10408.4	18784.2	19643.5		188.7	104.6		3.6
Contributors in Basic Medical Care Insurance	(10 000 persons)		3786.9	117681.4	134458.6		3550.6	114.3		21.9

Source: Statista Research Department.

In 2019, the *Resolution of the CPC Central Committee and State Council on Opening up the Chinese Insurance Market* was adopted, and a number of reforms were announced, aiming at facilitating the access of foreign insurers to Chinese insurance market, which served as an additional incentive for the devel-

---

　① Обязательные отчисления на социальное страхование в КНР, www.chinawindow.ru/china/legal-information-china/business-faq/social-security-prc/.

　② Снижение отчислений в фонды социального страхования, www.chinawindow.ru/china/legal-information-china/business-faq/social-security-decrease/.

opment of insurance in China and allowed foreign insurance companies and foreign financial institutions to become shareholders of Chinese insurance companies. According to Xinhua News Agency, by the end of 2020, foreign insurers created 64 foreign-funded insurance companies, 124 offices and 18 insurance agencies throughout the country with a total asset of 1.46 trillion yuan, and the total assets of insurers in 2020 increased by 13.3% and reached 23.3 trillion yuan.

In addition, further easing of foreign insurers' access to Chinese insurance market was confirmed in China's 14th Five-Year Plan and in "The Two Sessions" for 2021.

However, according to analysts at RBC Capital Markets, foreign insurers will not reach the scale and market share of large Chinese insurers, but rather will contribute to the development of the national market, since the Chinese government welcomes the inflow of foreign capital. According to the Swiss Re Institute, foreign insurance companies occupy only about 2% of the Chinese insurance market, and the five largest Chinese state-owned insurance companies cover more than 70% of the market (see Figure 3) [1].

Domestic total	766 380.8	98.04%
Foreign/JV total	15 306.5	1.96%
Grand total	781 687.3	
Top five market share		73.50%
Top ten market share		85.05%

Figure 3 The ratio of Chinese and foreign insurance companies

The Swiss Re Institute estimates that insurance companies in emerging markets will be hit the most by COVID-19, because premium income will decline by 3.6% in 2020 and 2021. However, the Chinese insurance market is an ex-

---

[1] Swiss Re Institute, "The Chinese Insurance Market", Switzerland, 2018, p.39.

ception—with an average premium income growth of 7% from 2020 to 2021. This growth is supported by the rapid recovery of economy, support of public policies, increased risk awareness and active customer engagement on the part of insurers. Obviously it is this growth that will be the main driver of the shift of global insurance opportunities to emerging Asia, especially China [1].

According to China Banking and Insurance Regulatory Commission, as of the end of the fourth quarter of 2020, insurance companies recorded a basic premium income of 4.5 trillion yuan, an increase of 6.1% year on year. Payments on insurance compensation reached 1.4 trillion yuan, up 7.9% over the last year. The volume of insurance policies grew at a steady pace: as of the end of the fourth quarter of 2020, the number of new insurance policies totaled 52.6 billion, an increase of 6.3% year on year. By the end of the third quarter of 2020, the average ratio of composite solvency of the surveyed insurance companies was 242.5% while the average ratio of basic solvency is 230.5%. For the comprehensive risk rating, 98 insurance companies were assigned to class A, 73 to class B, five to class C and one to class D [2].

China and Asia will become even stronger than before due to today's crisis, as higher risk awareness and awakening demand for social protection will spur growth in the coming years, with China at the top, analysts said.

Over the next few years, analysts expected a double-digit increase in premiums in China. China's insurance premiums will grow by 777 billion euros by 2030, which is comparable to the total market size of Great Britain, France, Germany and Italy [3].

The Fourth Industrial Revolution will give new impetus to the development

---

[1] Swiss Re Institute, "The Chinese Insurance Market", Switzerland, 2018, p. 39.

[2] China Banking and Insurance Regulatory Commission, "Supervisory Statistics of the Banking and Insurance Sectors - - 2020 Q4", Feburary 9, 2021, www.cbirc.gov.cn/en/view/pages/ItemDetail.html?docId=967412&itemId=983.

[3] Allianz представил прогноз развития страхового рынка Азии и Китая до 2030 года, https://forinsurer.com/news/20/07/13/38229.

of the insurance industry, create and expand new needs for risk management and provide technical support to it, which will convert challenges into opportunities for the insurance industry.

References

Allianz представил прогноз развития страхового рынка Азии и Китая до 2030 года, https://forinsurer.com/news/20/07/13/38229.

Катаргин. С. Как устроен страховой рынок в Китае, www.if24.ru/strahovoj-rynok-v-kitae/.

China Banking and Insurance Regulatory Commission, "Supervisory Statistics of the Banking and Insurance Sectors - - 2020 Q4", Feburary 9, 2021, www.cbirc.gov.cn/en/view/pages/ItemDetail.html? docId = 967412&itemId = 983.

Снижение отчислений в фонды социального страхования, www.chinawindow.ru/china/legal-information-china/business-faq/social-security-decrease/.

Обязательные отчисления на социальное страхование в КНР, www.chinawindow.ru/china/legal-information-china/business-faq/social-security-prc/.

Swiss Re Institute, "The Chinese Insurance Market", Switzerland, 2018, p. 39.

Milestones of China's Social Change: Massification and Internationalization of Higher Education

Dzmitry Smaliakou [*]

In the last 30 years, mass and internationalized university has become an important priority for the development of national higher education systems. At the same time, the development of these areas has acquired the status of not only a valuable criterion for the success of the national higher education, but also national state, and the lag in mentioned areas indicates the social lag of the entire state. In this light, the development of mass and internationalized higher education may be observed in aspect of modernization, and be recognized as an element of the national ability to update social, governmental, and economic structure. In the socio-philosophical sense, this is the ability of society to respond to the changing challenges of the historical moment, or in other words, to reply the demands of time.

The focus on modernization opens up another important socio-philosophical perspective—national subjectness, that is frequently correspondent with state ability to act as independent subject, which is considered by international partners as equal part of international dialogue. In this regard, massification and in-

---

[*] Dzmitry Smaliakou, Senior Research Fellow of Sino-Belarusian Research Center of Philosophy and Culture of the Institute of Philosophy of National Academy of Science of Belarus.

ternationalization of higher education may indicate the ability of a national subject to be a party of international negotiations, as the subject who is able to establish and save an agreement in modern world's circumstances. This understanding also includes assumption that there is no other powerful patron, who first necessary provides the preliminary permission for any father agreement, as well as no metropolises, that are imposing and guard subject's opinion. In this context, mass and internationalized higher education is seen as one of the most important condition for the "maturation" of the nation, an element of its subjectness.

Moreover, in modern circumstances, the knowledge economy offers more effective and less traumatic mechanisms for transforming society and its main activities. Scientific and technological progress has significantly simplified socio-economic modernization, but at the same time, it has imposed high demands on national subjects regarding intellectual and creative abilities, as well as developed social and educational infrastructure. In this regard, it is possible to say that globalization and knowledge-based economy have caused dramatic changes in the character and functions of higher education, but also important to understand that higher education is also having deep influence on global communication and cooperation. This influence is not only recognized as economic competition or influence competition between stakeholders, but a valuable part of "tidal wave of the public sector reform around the world"[1]. Social and economic innovation provide the transition from one historical epoch to another.

China is one of the most striking examples of the successful massification and internationalization of higher education in hard condition of social and economic transformations of developing country. The rapid development of higher education has affected not only to rebuild Chinese economic, recently signifi-

---

[1] Mok, K. H., "Restructuring in Hong Kong, Taiwan and Mainland China", *Higher Education Research & Development*, 2003, Vol. 22, Iss. 2, pp. 117 – 129.

cantly increased by GDP, but also completely eradicate poverty①. In this regard, it is relevant to focus on the Chinese experience of the massification and internationalization of higher education, that could assist for better structure and scale understanding of social changes, that China has undergone over the past 30 years. The results of this study will be useful for better understanding the essence of modern social processes, the structure of modern modernization, and therefore will assist to grasp the meaning of social changes that indicate a change in the epochs of socio-economic development.

I. Methodological Framework

Scientific literature consists of a number socio-philosophical hypotheses describing the genesis of the internationalisation of higher education. Most of these hypotheses are based on macro-factors, such as globalization. Particularly, H. De Wit② and J. Knight③ pointed their researches to the dialectical nature of internationalisation as a form of opposition to globalization. The presented approach often acts as a common point in modern theoretical models, while the geopolitical agenda, including those presented in the form of problems of changing economic patterns, is somehow linked to the phenomenon of globalization. Other researchers such as J. Stier④ also start from the concept of globalization, considering internationalization as a continuous communication between developed and developing countries. Developed countries in this communication provide their

---

① Textor, C., "Ratio of residents living below the extreme poverty line in China 2000 – 2020", https://www.statista.com/statistics/1086836/china-poverty-ratio/

② De Wit, H., "The history of internationalization of higher education", in D. Deardorff et al., eds., *The SAGE handbook of international higher education*, California, 2012, pp. 43 – 60.

③ Knight, J., "Internationalization remodeled: definition, approaches, and rationales", *Journal of Studies in International Education*, 1997, Vol. 1, No. 8, pp. 5 – 31.

④ Stier, J., "Taking a critical stance toward internationalization ideologies in higher education: idealism, instrumentalism and educationalism", *Globalisation, Societies and Education*, 2004, Vol. 2, iss. 1, pp. 83 – 97.

technologies and innovations, in other hand, developing countries—the experience of working and interacting in emerging markets.

The internationalisation and massification of higher education has deep connections inside problem of quality. Particularly worth mentioning are the articles of M. Tight[1]、M. Giannakis、N. Bullivant[2], as well as Y. Yang[3], which describe how the higher education formed the request for improving the quality of education in the conditions of a mass university. Regarding the social development, there particularly shows the connection between mass higher education and class liberalization and emancipation of society[4]. In general, the connection between mass higher education, the problem of education quality and socio-economic development has been found not only in framework of developing countries, but also traced on developed examples. Particularly, P. J. Gumport conducted a broad study of mass higher education in the USA and formation of postmass higher education[5].

The author's model also proceeds from macro-factors, but not particularly globalization. The key point of change is observed in the disintegration of the imperialist universe, which completed by the end of the 20th century, and still af-

---

[1] Tight M., "Mass Higher Education and Massification", *High Education Policy*, 2019, No. 32, pp. 93 – 108.

[2] Giannakis M., Bullivant N., "The Massification of Higher Education in the UK: aspects of service quality", *Journal of Further and Higher Education*, 2016, Vol. 40, No. 5, pp. 630 – 648.

[3] Yang Y., "Higher Education in China: Massification, Accessibility, and Quality Issues", in Collins C., Lee M., Hawkins J., Neubauer D. eds., *The Palgrave Handbook of Asia Pacific Higher Education*, New York: Palgrave Macmillan, 2016, pp. 315 – 330.

[4] Hornsby D. J., Osman R., "Massification in higher education: large classes and student learning", *High Education*, 2014, No. 67, pp. 711 – 719; Dias D., "Has Massification of Higher Education led to more Equity? Clues to a reflection on Portu – guese education arena", *International Journal of Inclusive Education*, 2015, Vol. 19, No. 2, pp. 103 – 120; Mok K. H., Wu A., "Higher Education, Changing Labour Market and Social Mobility in the Era of Massification in China", *Journal of Education and Work*, 2016, Vol. 29, No. 1, pp. 77 – 97.

[5] Gumport P. J., "The United States Country Report: Trends in Higher Education from Massification to Post – Massification", 1997, http: //course. napla. coplacdigital. org/wp – content/uploads/2016/09/Trends – in – Higher – Education – from – Massification – to – Post – Massification. pdf.

fects global world in form of postimperialism and neoimperialist manifestations. The dissemination of world imperialism formed the socio-political conditions for the development of the internationalisation of higher education, which contributes to the national stability of the interacting subjects[1]. The focus on respecting national peculiarities became an important trend not only in education, but also in international cooperation and economic interaction, essentially changing the old concept of globalization as a purposeful and universalizing improvement of numerous imperfect particulars. In this regard, internationalisation of higher education is understood as the process, formed at the intersection of vectors between international integration and improvement of the quality of higher education, where each direction contributes to mutual acceleration of development[2].

In this conception, the mass higher education is an internal factor for the formation of academic demand for internationalisation by forming the need to improve the quality of education, and by acting as an institutional tool for the implementation of the integration agenda. In this sense, a mass university is both a tool for implementing integration, and one of the requirements for its implementation. Together, the massification and internationalization of higher education act as a mean of local decolonization, allowing the national state to develop its own subjectness, as well as the solution to the classic problems of Marxism associated with alienated labor and monopoly on the means of production[3].

In general, the massification and internationalisation of higher education are the elements of the qualitative restructuring of the national state. Assisting in formation of national subjectness mass and internationalized university is making postcolonial subject to be recognized as negotiating side. In terms of domestic pol-

---

[1] Smaliakou D. A., "The genesis of higher education internationalisation", *The Education and Science Journal*, 2019, Vol. 8, No. 20, pp. 9–28.

[2] Smaliakou D. A., "Internationalization of higher education: socio–philosophical aspect", *Doklady of the National Academy of Sciences of Belarus*, 2020, Vol. 3, No. 64, pp. 371–378.

[3] Smaliakou D. A., "Institutional conditions of internationalisation of higher education: Mass higher school", *The Education and Science Journal*, 2021, Vol. 23, No. 5, pp. 11–37.

icy, massification and internationalization of higher education are an opportunity to use external resources to modernize and stabilize social development. Together, both processes provide a qualitative restructuring of the social and economic life of society, allowing the national subject to integrate into the structure of international interaction, thereby strengthening national stability, significantly improving the quality of work in the field of knowledge[1]. Under these conditions, some states successfully massify and internationalize higher education, while others lag behind for various (mostly colonial) reasons[2]. Thus, the ability to mass and internationalize higher education is the ability to social and economic modernization, and hence to the rapid socio-economic development of the national subject.

II. Scientific Hypothesis

From the socio-philosophical point of view, the massification of higher education is acting as a mechanism for the qualitative restructuring of public life, affecting both the change in economic and socio-cultural interactions. Institutionally, the massification of higher education became possible by public-private partnerships that provide both sufficient funding and flexibility in relation to the labor market and the demand for competencies.

China is a successful example of the effective implementation of the massification and internationalization of higher education. The parallel development of the higher education system and the economic system of China has allowed it to significantly modernize both the economy and social relations within society, ensuring dynamic economic growth, including the development of infrastructure and welfare.

---

[1] Smaliakou, D. A., *Internationalisation of Higher Education: theory, practice, prospects*, Minsk: Belarusian Science, 2020, p. 223.

[2] Smaliakou, D. A., "Internationalisation of Higher Education in light of national development problems, Proceedings of the National Academy of Sciences of Belarus", *Humanitarian Series*, 2021, Vol. 2, No. 66, pp. 135–141.

III. Scientific Literature and Statistical Material

The author's personal attempts to analyze the process of massification and internationalization of higher education in China were made by two monographs *Belarusian and Chinese Cooperation in Sphere of Higher Education*①, *Internationalisation of Higher Education: theory, practice, prospects*②, and a series of articles: "Improving higher education in Belarus taking into account the Chinese experience"③, "Institutional Conditions of Internationalization of Higher Education: Mass Higher School"④. On the basis of this material, this paper builds a theoretical model of the mass higher school of China and its internationalisation, determines the main stages of the implementation of these processes, and outlines the main results.

In framework of presented article specialized analytical and statistical materials were used for better understanding the processes in China. ⑤

---

① Smaliakou, D. A. , "Belarusian and Chinese cooperation in sphere of Higher Education", Minsk: Institute of Philosophy National Academy of Science of Belarus, 2017, p. 149.

② Smaliakou, D. A. , *Internationalisation of Higher Education: theory, practice, prospects*, Minsk: Belarusian Science, 2020, p. 223.

③ Smaliakou, D. A. , "Improving higher education in Belarus taking into account the Chinese experience", Herald of the Belarusian State Economic University, *Journal of Science*, 2019, No. 1, pp. 19 – 28.

④ Smaliakou D. A. , "Institutional conditions of internationalisation of higher education: Mass higher school", *The Education and Science Journal*, 2021, Vol. 23, No. 5, pp. 11 – 37.

⑤ The following works were used as analytical lifferature. Pan M. , Luo D. , "A comparative analysis on models of higher education massification", Front, 2008, No. 3, pp. 64 – 78; Gao Y. , "Massification of Higher Education in China: Problems and Solutions", in Wu A. , Haw – kins J. eds. , *Massification of Higher Education in Asia: Quality, Excel – lence and Governance*, Singapore: Springer, 2018. pp. 9 – 19; Wu A. , Hawkins J. , *Massification of Higher Education in Asia*, Singapore: Springer, 2018, p. 147; Mok K. H. , Chan S. J. , "After Massification and Response to Internationalization: Quality Assurance of Higher Education in Taiwan and Hong Kong", in Collins C. , Lee M. , Hawkins J. , Neubauer D. eds. , *The Palgrave Handbook of Asia Pacific Higher Education*, New York: Palgrave Macmillan, 2016, pp. 423 – 438; Mok K. , Jiang J. , "Massification of higher education and challenges for graduate employment and social mobility: East Asian experiences and sociological reflections", *International Journal of Educational Development*, 2018, pp. 44 – 51; Reddy K. S. , Xie E. , Tang Q. , "Higher education, high – impact research, and world university rankings: A case of India and comparison with China", *Pacific Science Review B: Humanities and Social Sciences*, 2016, Vol. 1, No. 2, pp. 1 – 21; Ding, X. , China's Higher Education Market, DIFID WB Collaboration on Knowledge and Skills in the New Economy, 2004, January, https://siteresources.worldbank.org/EDUCATION/Resources/2782001126210664195/16369711126210694253/China_Higher_Education.pdf.

IV. Research Results and Discussion

The massification of higher education is a term that was finally established in the scientific literature by the 1960s and denoted a dynamic increase in both the number of institutions of higher education and the students studying there[①]. Mass higher education originated in the United States, where subsidizing veterans, fighting racism and fighting for women's rights. Through the support of other vulnerable groups, there was an extensive increase of the number of students studying in the universities. In this regard, mass higher education in America became possible by state funding for the education of those who were previously excluded from higher education. The growth in the number of students required a corresponding number of teachers, which in turn contributed to an increase in the total number of universities.

Continued: Statistics are from: https://www.statista.com/; https://tradingeconomics.com/; Roser M., Ortiz – Ospina E., Tertiary Education, 2013, https://ourworldindata.org/tertiary – education; Reports and data from the UNESCO Institute for Statistics: Research facilities in science and technology in Asia, Unesco, 1968, https://gospin.unesco.org/files/his_pdfs/Research_facilities_in_S – T_in_Asia_China_en.pdf; World Science report, Unesco, 1988, https://gospin.unesco.org/files/his_pdfs/WSR1998_China_EN.pdf; World Science report, Unesco, 2015, https://gospin.unesco.org/files/his_pdfs/USR2015_China_RU.pdf; Facts and figures: Business and innovation from the UNESCO Science Report, Towards 2030, Unesco, https://en.unesco.org/node/252281; World Inequality Database on Education, https://www.education – inequalities.org/; and especially statistics from these articles: Calderon, A. J., Analytics & Insights, Massification of higher education revisited, Rmit University, 2018, http://cdn02.pucp.education/academico/2018/08/23165810/na_mass_revis_230818.pdf; Fu – tao Huang, A Comparative Study of Massification of Higher Education in China and Japan, https://www.researchgate.net/publication/44835451_A_Comparative_study_of_massification_of_higher_education_in_China_and_Japan? enrichId = rgreq – dadf04403177d6a39e365ac7f649f324 – XXX&enrichSource = Y292ZXJQYWdlOzQ0ODM1NDUxO0FT OjI4MTA5NzI2Mzk2MDA2NEAxNDQ0MDMwMjE4MjIy&el = 1_x_2&_esc = publicationCoverPdf.

① Gumport P. J., "The United States Country Report: Trends in Higher Education from Massification to Post – Massification", 1997, p. 50, http://course.napla.coplacdigital.org/wp – content/uploads/2016/09/Trends – in – Higher – Education – from – Massification – to – Post – Massification.pdf.

Similar processes occurred in Southeast Asia. South Korea, Japan, and other countries radically increased investment in higher education, thereby contributing to the intensive modernization of society and the economy. In the early 1980s, these trends reached China, where the mass higher education became one of the priorities of the country's modernization as part of the reform and opening up.

It is important to note that China already has had experience in the field of modernization of higher education through international cooperation. In particular, it is worth mentioning the Chinese educational mission in 1872 – 1881 (Chinese children went to study in the United States in search of the latest Western knowledge, primarily in the field of engineering sciences). Here is the international origin of the first Chinese university, Imperial University of Peking. It was established in 1898 according to the Western model and was later transformed into Peking University. Peking Pedagogical University, Tsinghua University, established as part of the Roosevelt Scholarship Program, allowed more than 1, 300 Chinese students to study in the United States from 1909 to 1929. In the same context, there was also the experience of educational cooperation between China and USSR in the middle of the twentieth century. However, previous modernization had limited effect and did not show large-scale consequences for the country. Until the end of the 20th century China still lagged behind in social, economic and technological development from Europe and America. The employment picture did not change significantly.

By the beginning of the reform and opening up, higher education in China was fully funded from the state budget. There were not so many students studied in China, and they received a small scholarship. Since the mid-1980s, China established paid education at universities, that in the face of rising incomes of society has contributed to an increase in the number of students. Since 1989, paid tuition has become ubiquitous, but students with higher grades could qualify for certain discounts. Old practices were also preserved in such disciplines as agriculture and forestry, pedagogy. Students were not only exempt from tuition fees, but also received a scholarship from the government. Since 1997, free higher education in the China was totally reduced.

The possibility of paid tuition for all categories of students opened the door to mass higher education, which was an important economic and political breakthrough in China. Previously, the state budget was the only financial source for the Chinese universities to support elite higher education, but in the context of a rapid increase in the number of applicants, such a mechanism was ineffective. As a result of the reform, the coverage of the population with higher education has significantly increased.

Meanwhile, the growth in the number of students led to a change in the ratio to the number of teaching staff, reaching a ratio of 18 to 1, and in less successful universities 30 to 1. There were needed particular steps to improve the quality of teaching and learning. These steps were: to eliminate distance education, to increase the number of Chinese students studying abroad, to attract foreign partners to prepare and implement joint educational programs, to invest financial and intellectual resources into a limited number of advanced universities.

Since the early 1980s, Chinese citizens have received the right to travel abroad for higher education (already in 1983, 7, 000 people left China mainly to the United States and Japan). At the same time, state programs were being launched for the targeted direction of studying abroad. In total, more than 2 million Chinese students went to study abroad between 1978 and 2011, making China a leader in academic mobility by 2010. This was necessary in order to attract advanced experiences and technologies to China, including in the field of higher education to make possible the full modernization of the country and the integration of its economy into the world system of labor distribution. Nowadays, China sends around 1 million students abroad (around 18% of global mobility), and most of them study in America (333, 935 students), Australia

(143, 323 students) and United Kingdom (107, 813 students)[1].

Graduates of leading Chinese universities are extremely in demand among local employers. In this regard, the best applicants do not go abroad, but enter advanced Chinese universities. The achievement of a number of world-class Chinese universities was ensured by the implementation of important state programs: "Project 211" and "Project 985", which aimed at strengthening the overall institutional capacity, developing key disciplinary areas, as well as the public service system. In the result, some Chinese universities became able to compete with the world centers of higher education. At the same time, China has made more significant steps towards foreign partners by creating joint training programs.

Currently, the number of students within China continues to increase. In 2015, an increase of 40% was recorded by 2012, and by 2019, an increase of another 50%. Over the fisrt 30 years of implementing the reform and opening up, China has doubled its own value of the Education Level Index (from 0.362 in 1980 to 0.614 in 2014), and the educational level of the Chinese population only increased by 10% in the period 2000 – 2010, and the number of Chinese citizens with higher education were expected to exceed 200 million people by 2020.

Such a rapid development of mass education has allowed China to make significant progress in the field of science and innovation. By 2013, the number of researchers in China reached 1, 484 thousand people. While in 2003 China generated only 5% of scientific publications in the world, by 2013 this proportion increased to 20%. As a result, by the end of the 2010s, China had evolved from a backward country leading a subsistence economy into a state with huge human resources, and a nation of higher education.

Modern science tends to interpret the difference in development between

---

[1] Global Flow of Tertiary – Level Students, Unesco, http://uis.unesco.org/en/uis-student-flow#slideoutmenu.

China and India. If China succeeded in mass higher education, India has left with an elite university system. At the same time, from roughly the same size of GDP and population in a 20 - year time period, China's nominal GDP became 6 times that of India. Innovation not only has contributed to this state of affairs, but also expanded the social base of educated employee, primarily at the expense of women and the poor people.

For the period from 2000 to 2020, China ranked first in the world in terms of GDP at purchasing power parity, with a 40% increase in the number of students in the country in 2015 compared to 2012, and a 50% increase in university students by 2019. The growth of students in China from 1994 to 2003 was quit moderate (6% of high school graduates in 1994 to 17% in 2003)①, but nowadays, this numbers quit scientifically increased to 32% (average level)②.

The average level of higher education is impressive for country with middle level of development, but the social picture of higher education is much more important. First of all, it is important to note that China provide higher education for 38% of female high school graduates and 26% male, 31% of the richest class, 33% middle class and 33% for the poorest, 38% urban and 26% of rural. If we compare these numbers with 2010, we could find that social changes were significant (at that time, the poorest students accounted for 10%, Yural 10%, female 16%)③.

To compere the mass higher education and GDP growth, we could find that the most frequent growth of students is simultaneous to GDP growth. If from 1990 to 1998 GDP growth only doubled, then in era of frequent massification of high-

---

① Fu‐tao Huang, "A Comparative Study of Massification of Higher Education in China and Japan", https://www.researchgate.net/publication/44835451_A_Comparative_study_of_massification_of _higher_education_in_China_and_Japan? enrichId = rgreq - dadf04403177d6a39e365ac7f649f324 - XXX&enrichSource = Y292ZXJQYWdlOzQ0ODM1NDUxO0FTOjI4MTA5NzI2Mzk2MDA2NEAxNDQ0MD MwMjE4MjIy&el = 1_x_2&_esc = publicationCoverPdf.
② World Inequality Database on Education, https://www.education-inequalities.org/.
③ World Inequality Database on Education, https://www.education-inequalities.org/.

er education (1998 – nowadays) GDP doubled every 4 years, and in total numbers the economic growth of 1998 looks even more notable①.

V. Future Problems

Future problems of higher education in China are also the problems of social development, which could be described into the three following statements.

First, this "success" (mass higher education in China) is, however, at the expense of equity in terms of institutions' operating conditions. There is a widening gap between institutions at difference tiers in the hierarchy and concomitant differences in students' learning experiences②.

Second, college graduates, especially those who do not have efficient social capital, may seriously suffer from the difficulties in finding jobs amid massification of higher education③.

Third, China has invested considerably in education since the 2000s and had moved from having a ratio of under 10% in 2000 to attain a 48.4% the education proportion by 2016. It is highly likely that China will attain a ratio of 60% within the next five years and 70% within the next 10 years④.

The first statement is a remark on quality of education, that means the quality in different Chinese universities is so much variable, and the value of diploma is also not same. One can say, that nowadays it is not so important as long as economic and society have a lot of space for development and all graduates could find appropriate jobs. As long as this space will be eliminated, higher ed-

---

① China GDP, tradingeconomics. com, https://tradingeconomics. com/china/gdp#stats.

② Qiang Zha, "CHINA: Massification has increased inequalities", University world news, 2011, https://www. universityworldnews. com/post. php? story = 20110708162827633.

③ Mok, K. H., "Restructuring in Hong Kong, Taiwan and Mainland China", Higher Education Research & Development, 2003, Vol. 22, Iss. 2, pp. 117 – 129.

④ Calderon, A. J., "Analytics & Insights. Massification of higher education revisited", Rmit University, 2018, http://cdn02. pucp. education/academico/2018/08/23165810/na _ mass _ revis _ 230818. pdf.

ucation system will need more and more quality. In this regard, international affairs are the most important instrument for quality assessment. That's why it is so important for universities to develop international relations even now, when the problems with student enrolment and finding job for graduates are not so huge.

The second statement also appeals to the quality of education and the value of higher education. Sometimes for future career, graduates need help of parents or affiliated people, and in this regard the quality of education is not so important. Moreover, at the moment, the most important issue for China is to make higher education be attractive for vulnerable classes, such as poor people, or women. In this regard, China demonstrates social success that favorably distinguishes China from other developing countries in Asia, Africa or Latin America. However, in the future this problem could be more important and be a barrier for further social development of China.

The third statement provides the optimistic view on future development that will be much more difficult to achieve than previous results. To make the number of higher education attendance of more than 50% needs deep changes in social picture of country and to provide new technological and social instruments for life and work. In this regard, further massification and internationalization of Chinese university need to pay more attention to international relations and faster changing into innovating areas. Belt and Road Initiative could really be effective in this case, but universities need to make their education more qualified, otherwise the future growth of students will be not so effective as before and could become an instrument for hidden unemployment.

VI. Conclusions

Reform and opening up totally changed Chinese economic and life. Massification and internationalized higher education could be recognized as a key factor for social development and change of labor market in China. Due to the mutual (public and private) financing of higher education, higher education charging-system provided condition for rapid development of universities. Moreover, academic mobility also made a great achievement into the raised number of educated people in China.

Further development of higher education' quality and the goal that the number of attendance of higher education reaches 50% will demand more active position for Chinese university in international cooperation. In this regard, time will tell if China could reach the level of wealth countries or will stay on the level of developing countries. The key point is innovative economic that demand for more and more qualified and creative workers. This is a new challenge for Chinese higher education that will effect on further social development of China.

References

Calderon, A. J. , "Analytics & Insights. Massification of higher education revisited", Rmit University, 2018, http: //cdn02. pucp. education/academico/2018/08/23165810/na_mass_revis_230818. pdf.

China GDP, tradingeconomics. com, https: //tradingeconomics. com/china/gdp#stats.

De Wit, H. , "The history of internationalization of higher education", in D. Deardorff et al. , eds. , *The SAGE handbook of international higher education*, California, 2012, pp. 43 – 60.

Dias D. , "Has Massification of Higher Education led to more Equity? Clues to a reflection on Portu – guese education arena", *International Journal of Inclusive Education*, 2015, Vol. 19, No. 2, pp. 103 – 120.

Fu – tao Huang, "A Comparative Study of Massification of Higher Education in China and Japan", https: //www. researchgate. net/publication/44835451_A_Comparative_study_of_massification_of_higher_education_in_China_and_Japan? enrichId = rgreq – dadf04403177d6a39e365ac7f649f324 – XXX&enrichSource = Y292ZXJQYWdlOzQ0ODM1NDUxO0FTOjI4MTA5NzI2M zk2MDA2NEAxNDQ0MDMwMjE4MjIy&el = 1 _ x _ 2& _ esc = publicationCover Pdf.

Giannakis M., Bullivant N., "The Massification of Higher Education in the UK: aspects of service quality", *Journal of Further and Higher Education*, 2016, Vol. 40, No. 5, pp. 630 - 648.

Global Flow of Tertiary - Level Students, Unesco, http://uis.unesco.org/en/uis - student - flow#slideoutmenu.

Gumport P. J., "The United States Country Report: Trends in Higher Education from Massification to Post - Massification", 1997, http://course.napla.coplacdigital.org/wp - content/uploads/2016/09/Trends - in - Higher - Education - from - Massification - to - Post - Massification.pdf.

Gumport P. J., "The United States Country Report: Trends in Higher Education from Massification to Post - Massification", 1997, p. 50, http://course.napla.coplacdigital.org/wp - content/uploads/2016/09/Trends - in - Higher - Education - from - Massification - to - Post - Massification.pdf.

Hornsby D. J., Osman R., "Massification in higher education: large classes and student learning", *High Education*, 2014, No. 67.

Knight, J., "Internationalization remodeled: definition, approaches, and rationales", *Journal of Studies in International Education*, 1997, Vol. 1, No. 8.

Mok, K. H., "Restructuring in Hong Kong, Taiwan and Mainland China", *Higher Education Research & Development*, 2003, Vol. 22, Iss. 2.

Mok K. H., Wu A., "Higher Education, Changing Labour Market and Social Mobility in the Era of Massification in China", *Journal of Education and Work*, 2016, Vol. 29, No. 1.

Qiang Zha, "CHINA: Massification has increased inequalities", University world news, 2011, https://www.universityworldnews.com/post.php?story = 20110708162827633.

Smaliakou, D. A., "Belarusian and Chinese cooperation in sphere of Higher Education", Minsk: Institute of Philosophy National Academy of Science of Belarus, 2017.

Smaliakou, D. A., *Internationalisation of Higher Education: theory, practice, prospects*, Minsk: Belarusian Science, 2020.

Smaliakou, D. A. , "Internationalisation of Higher Education in light of national development problems, Proceedings of the National Academy of Sciences of Belarus", *Humanitarian Series*, 2021, Vol. 2, No. 66.

Smaliakou, D. A. "Improving higher education in Belarus taking into account the Chinese experience", Herald of the Belarusian State Economic University, *Journal of Science*, 2019, No 1.

Smaliakou D. , "Institutional conditions of internationalisation of higher education: Mass higher school", *The Education and Science Journal*, 2021, Vol. 23, No. 5.

Smaliakou D. A. , "The genesis of higher education internationalisation", *The Education and Science Journal*, 2019, Vol. 8, No. 20.

Smaliakou D. A. , "Internationalization of higher education: socio – philosophical aspect", *Doklady of the National Academy of Sciences of Belarus*, 2020, Vol. 3, No. 64.

Smaliakou D. "Institutional conditions of internationalisation of higher education: Mass higher school", *The Education and Science Journal*, 2021, Vol. 23, No. 5.

Stier, J. , "Taking a critical stance toward internationalization ideologies in higher education: idealism, instrumentalism and educationalism", *Globalisation, Societies and Education*, 2004, Vol. 2, iss. 1.

Textor, C. , "Ratio of residents living below the extreme poverty line in China 2000 – 2020", https://www.statista.com/statistics/1086836/china – poverty – ratio/.

Tight M. , "Mass Higher Education and Massification", 2019, No. 32.

World Inequality Database on Education, https://www.education – inequalities.org/.

Yang Y. , "Higher Education in China: Massification, Accessibility, and Quality Issues", in Collins C. , Lee M. , Hawkins J. , Neubauer D. eds. , *The Palgrave Handbook of Asia Pacific Higher Education*, New York: Palgrave Macmillan, 2016.

Middle-Class Development in China and Its Influence for Sustainable Development

Ivan Semenist [*]

The current development of the world economy is determined by the growth of the middle class with the corresponding level of income, as evidenced by the increase in consumer spending in 2020 up to $ 41 trillion. The spending of the middle class in China is 17.8% of the world level with a population of about 20% of the total population of the earth. In the 1950s, over 90% of the global middle class resided in Europe and North America. Today, over 20% live in China. China is experiencing the fastest expansion of the middle class the world has ever seen, during a period when the global middle class is already expanding at a historically unprecedented rate thanks in part to some of its neighbors like India. By 2027, we estimate that 1.2 billion Chinese will be in the middle class, making up one quarter of the world total. China already makes up the largest middle-class consumption market segment in the world and is a priority market for major multinational firms. Chinese middle-class consumption initially followed the growth path of the Western middle class, with increasing consumer demand for higher quality products, large investments in home ownership, and

---

[*] Ivan Semenist, Associate Professor, Doctor, Head of Oriental Department, Borys Grinchenko Kyiv University.

vehicle purchases. It is now setting its own middle-class trends. Chinese fintech and e-commerce platforms are changing the way consumers and sellers interact, and they are exporting this knowledge to other developing countries. [1]

Table 1　　　Top 10 Countries by Total Middle-class Expenditures in 2020

(Unit: trillion USD, 2011 PPP)

Country	Middle-class consumption
China	7.3
United States	4.7
India	2.9
Japan	2.0
Russian Federation	1.6
Germany	1.5
Indonesia	1.2
United Kingdom	1.1
Brazil	1.1
France	1.0

Source: Authors' calculations, based on methodology in Kharas (2010) and using International Monetary Fund June 2020 GDP estimates.

A positive aspect of the study of the formation and development of the middle class and its influence on key economic indicators is its interdisciplinarity. Research by social scientists allows us to form a "profile" of the middle class. Economists will determine its relationship with economic stability in the country, while political scientists substantiate the influence of the middle class on managerial decision-making and the formation of state policy priorities. Sociologists tend to classify the middle class according to professional char-

---

[1] Homi Kharas & Meagan Dooley, "China's Influence on the Global Middle Class", https://www.brookings.edu/wp-content/uploads/2020/10/FP_20201012_china_middle_class_kharas_dooley.pdf.

acteristics or job status, as well as related indicators. The middle class is mainly engaged in mental work or physical work on a technical basis. As a rule, it is well educated, has professional knowledge and significant professional skills. These characteristics of the middle class make it possible to achieve higher indicators of human development, have an appropriate level and quality of life, career growth, and plan the future. Note that such signs of the middle class are very important for the formation of future generations and the progressive development of society, because representatives of the middle class strive for a high level of education for their children, form the intellectual capital of the nation, and they are a prerequisite for China's prosperity and competitiveness at the world level. The economic strength of the state is formed primarily due to human capital and its effective use, which provides an appropriate level of not only income but also education and health. Modern discussions about the Chinese middle class and the criteria for its allocation made it possible to single out two main features: the level of per capita income and the availability of durable goods at the disposal of the family. China's transition to a middle-class country is not yet complete. It will continue adding significant numbers until 2027 when an estimated 1.2 billion Chinese will be in the middle class, one-quarter of the global total.

Let us emphasize that the representatives of the Chinese middle class do not assess the level of income as finite and constant, but perceive it as the middle of the path to achieving wealth. This indicates strategic thinking, a tendency to plan for future development, and a gradual transition from the lowest stage to the highest stage of individual development. Let us note the interdisciplinarity of research on the development of the middle class in China. A significant number of scientific works on life, behavioral features are studied in sociology, economics, politics, and other areas. Studying the characteristics of the behavior of representatives of the middle class in China in international relations and foreign policy, scientists have come to the conclusion that this particular group of the population is more liberal than representatives of other strata of society.[1] That is, the presence and number of the middle class in the country can significantly affect the flexibility of the formation and development of international relations, and determine the country's economic course for the future. There are different points of view on assessing the level of income and expenditure of the middle class. In the works of Li Peilin, the standard of income of the middle class and the reasonable rate of income of one of three criteria for distinguishing the middle class are covered. According to the author, the other two indicators are profession and education. That is, it is possible to identify a group of the population as the middle class, provided that the standard of income is observed, as well as the conformity of the profession, and the level of education. The results of calculating this standard of income are presented in the works of Li Peilin and Zhang Yi "The scale and identity of the Chinese middle class", and also tested at the annual conference of the Chinese Sociological Society "International Forum for Comparison of the Middle Class". The socio-economic development of the middle class in China over the past 20 years has achieved stable growth in Chinese society. Regardless of the criterion for distinguishing the middle class, its role and significance are not in doubt. However, the difference in methods of assessment shows that the above-mentioned tricriteria system (income standard, profession, and education) as one of the scientific concepts about the middle class and the image of the middle class in society (the middle class based on indicators of income or consumption) affects the assessment of the growth rate of the number of representatives of the middle class in China. Among scholars, the question of differentiating the middle class by profession is debatable. It is argued that we should also compare working conditions, the level of income of employees of government agencies, directors, heads of departments, general clerks, and others. According to a survey conduc-

---

[1] Johnston, A. I., "Chinese middle class attitudes towards international affairs: Nascent liberalization?", *The China Quarterly*, 2004, No. 179, pp. 603 – 628, http://search.proquest.com/docview/229505762/fulltextPDF/131603BE30756FCFAF8/6? accountid = 35419.

ted by the Urban Research Group of the National Bureau of Statistics, the current income standards for urban residents in China are distributed. There is a saying that the 10 richest people in modern Chinese society are categorized into: (1) private entrepreneurs and individuals; (2) business contractors or rented business personnel; (3) stock market players and winners; (4) chief specialists of enterprises financed from abroad; (5) patent personnel with technical inventions; (6) stars of show business and sports; (7) CEOs of the new economy; (8) experienced lawyers, brokers and advertising staff; (9) returnees; (10) leading scientists and experts. ①

This distribution is broadly consistent with a survey conducted by the Urban Research Group of the National Bureau of Statistics. The largest number of China's middle class comes from the above 10 groups of people. Among them, private business owners and senior employees of foreign-funded enterprises deserve special attention. In recent years, with the explosive development of private enterprises and the covert privatization of some state-owned enterprises, private enterprises have become the production machine for the middle class in China. Likewise, multinational companies such as Motorola have copied China's "scarce" middle class like an assembly line. Some conceptions of the development of the middle class may be characteristics of the initial stage of its formation. This is a consequence of rapid economic growth, rapid social change, and multidimensional differentiation of society. Consequently, it can be predicted that by 2030 further economic growth, an increase in social wealth, and an improvement in people's living standards will contribute to the deepening of the concept of the middle class, to meet the public's perception of the middle class.

There are many views about the future of the Chinese middle class. Merrill Lynch predicts that China's middle class will reach 350 million in the next 10 years. There is no doubt that China will need a larger middle-class population in

---

① Как живут люди в Китае-особенности и традиции Китайцев, https: //gruz – china. ru/blog/kak – zhivut – lyudi – v – kitae – osobennosti – i.

the future. In addition to the aforementioned 10 wealthy people and some national civil servants, professor Xiao Zhuoji of Peking University believes that in the future, China's middle class will mainly come from the following five types of highly qualified professionals. First, the research staff who can transform scientific and technological advances in the field. They place the results of their research in companies as technology stocks. If the company goes public, it can receive significant dividends and recognition. Second, middle and top managers in the financial securities industry. This does not apply to workers in the current system, but to workers in private and foreign enterprises. Third, the professionals of intermediary agencies such as lawyers, accountants, and appraisers. The income of these people significantly increased after China's accession to the WTO (World Trade Organization). Fourth, another component of the middle class is Chinese middle and upper-level personnel in overseas-funded enterprises. Fifth, some stock market shareholders may also become middle class. Niu Wenyuan, member of the National Committee of CPPCC and Chief Research Fellow of the Sustainable Development Strategy Group of the Chinese Academy of Social Sciences, proposed five criteria for assessing whether the country has sufficient conditions for the development of the middle class: (1) Has achieved an urbanization rate above 70%; (2) the volume of white-collar workers is large or at least equal to the level of blue-collar workers; (3) Engel's coefficient has decreased to an average of 0.3 or less; (4) the Gini coefficient between 0.25 and 0.30 is controlled and maintained; (5) the average duration of schooling years has reached 12 years or more per capita.

At the same time, there are certain differences in the conditions of the separation of the middle class, depending on the provinces and cities. For example, a Beijing resident needs to have an income of at least $ 1,000 per month in order to belong to the middle class, while a rural resident needs to have an income 10 times lower[1].

---

[1] Gruz – China, Kak zhivut lyudi v Kitaye – osobennosti i traditsii kitaytsev, 2019, https://gruz – china. ru/blog/kak – zhivut – lyudi – v – kitae – osobennosti – i.

Research by consulting firm McKinsey & Company shows that 76% of China's urban population will be middle-class by 2022. An expanded analysis of the results found that a middle-class urban family would have incomes between $9,000 and $34,000 per year. Although this range is significantly lower than in developed countries, taking into account market prices, it allows for the same standard of living for the middle class in China ①. As indicated in the "Rise of the Middle Class in China" report, prepared with the participation of the Asian Development Bank, the middle class includes those who spend between $2 and $20 per day ②. According to a study by Credit Suisse Bank, at the present stage of development, the middle class in China makes up 20% of the country's working-age population, that is, more than 100 million people. In this case, the key criterion is the level of income per year, which for the middle class ranges from 10 thousand to 100 thousand US dollars. Note that the middle class makes up half of the population in the United States and two-thirds of the population in South Korea③. At the present stage of economic development, practically in all countries of the world, there is an increase in the size of the middle class. The absolute number and percentage of the population is increasing, and in the next 15 – 20 years it will claim the status of the middle class. Even according to the pessimistic forecast, the growth of the total number of representatives of the middle class in the world can be 1 billion in 2019, and up to over 2 billion in the near future. According to the calculations of the inertial forecast, the middle class in the world will be 3 billion people. The fastest-growing middle class is forecast to be in Asia. At the same time, India will outstrip China for a long period. If China achieves its goals, then 75% of the country's population by 2030 will have a middle-class standard of living, and the level of poverty will be significantly reduced. Along with the growth of the mid-

---

① China today, Rivni zhyttya v Kytayi (serednij klas), 2019, https://prc.today.
② Svpressa, "Podem srednego klassa v Kitae", 2019, https://svpressa.ru/world/article/45629/.
③ Gruz – China, Kak zhivut lyudi v Kitaye – osobennosti i traditsii kitaytsev, 2019, https://gruz – china.ru/blog/kak – zhivut – lyudi – v – kitae – osobennosti – i.

dle class, the share of consumption is growing. Accordingly, the pace of economic development is increasing and the country's GDP is growing. In 2020, China became the leader in terms of consumption of the middle class, $ 7.3 billion. The second place in the ranking is occupied by the United States, and the third position belongs to India with a consumption volume of $ 4.7 billion and $ 2.9 billion, respectively.

The importance of the middle class for the development of the Chinese economy is growing rapidly. The continuous increase in this category is the main condition for the implementation of China's 2020 strategy of "internal circulation"①, which assumes the growth of domestic consumption at the expense of the middle class. The middle class is a significant beneficiary of economic reforms in China, which actively supports the economic reform policy, implemented by the government, and hopes that the policy will remain stable in order to ensure the country's stable growth and stable growth of its own income. At present, in order to increase the level of economic development of individual countries and the world as a whole, it becomes necessary to form and grow a middle class, which ensures a high level of domestic consumption and, accordingly, contributes to the socio-economic development of the national economy.

An analysis of the structure of spending by representatives of the middle class in China shows a significant share of funding for education and the upbringing of future generations, while less spending on entertainment and travel. The upbringing of children by middle class in China is special. The future generation is called the "generation of future emperors", who have much higher standards and consumption habits than the older generation. According to experts, the average Chinese family spends about 40% – 50% of their income on raising children. A significant part is spent on tuition fees in institutions with a

---

① Bin News, "Vnutrennyaya tsirkulyatsiya – novaya ekonomicheskaya strategiya Kitaya", 2019, https://bin.ua/news/foreign/world/254924 – vnutrennyaya – cirkulyaciya – novaya – yekonomicheskaya.html.

high reputation, classes with tutors and the purchase of computers. It is worth noting that even on weekends, children take foreign language courses or learn computer. At the same time, this generation is also characterized by an increase in demand for fast food. The estimated spending on the ready-to-eat food industry is $ 4 billion, while pocket money and gifts for children in China are $ 5 billion. Note that children under the age of 14 in China make up 25% of the population and are potential representatives of the middle class in the future [1]. Based on the above, we can draw a conclusion that China's middle class attaches great importance to education. China considers raising the level of education as a priority and a prerequisite for further economic development of the country as a whole. Investment in human capital today is the foundation of a country's competitiveness for the future.

In conclusion, the global middle class is evolving fast. It will be influenced by the preference of Chinese consumers and the preference for the type of politics that will best serve middle-class interests of stability and steady growth of economic opportunities for themselves and their families. It can be stated that China's domestic policy is aimed at constant support of the middle class in order to increase its size, because if the middle class is the majority in society, then there is stability and rationality. Under such conditions, the process of building and developing the country's economic system is greatly facilitated. In this regard, the role of the state and its importance in maintaining the middle class is increasing. It is not aimed at increasing the number of people with average incomes, but at improving the quality of life, and promoting the formation of a certain culture of consumption and the rational distribution of costs and the upbringing of future generations. The results of the study proved the need for the formation and development of a middle class to reduce poverty and increase economic growth. The country's overall progress is being achieved by increasing

---

[1] Maschtenko E. , "Malenkiy imperator kitayskoy semi", https: //zn. ua/SOCIUM/malenkiy_imperator_kitayskoy_semi. html.

consumption as a consequence of rising incomes. Representatives of the middle class in China not only have an appropriate level of material well-being, but are also characterized by a special distribution of expenses. The structure of expenditures indicates a significant level of investment in human capital, which indicates the formation of a person-centered economy. China views the middle class as a locomotive for the country's development in the future, which is subject to the implementation of the "circulation economy" strategy.

References

Bin News, "Vnutrennyaya tsirkulyatsiya – novaya ekonomicheskaya strategiya Kitaya", 2019, https://bin.ua/news/foreign/world/254924 – vnutrennyaya – cirkulyaciya – novaya – yekonomicheskaya.html.

China today, Rivni zhyttya v Kytayi (serednij klas), 2019, https://prc.today.

Gruz – China, Kak zhivut lyudi v Kitaye – osobennosti i traditsii kitaytsev, 2019, https://gruz – china.ru/blog/kak – zhivut – lyudi – v – kitae – osobennosti – i.

Homi Kharas & Meagan Dooley, "China's Influence on the Global Middle Class", https://www.brookings.edu/wp – content/uploads/2020/10/FP_20201012_china_middle_class_kharas_dooley.pdf.

Johnston, A. I., "Chinese middle class attitudes towards international affairs: Nascent liberalization?", *The China Quarterly*, 2004, No. 179, pp. 603 – 628, http://search.proquest.com/docview/229505762/fulltextPDF/131603BE30756FCFAF8/6?accountid=35419.

Maschtenko E., "Malenkiy imperator kitayskoy semi", https://zn.ua/SOCIUM/malenkiy_imperator_kitayskoy_semi.html.

Svpressa, "Podem srednego klassa v Kitae", 2019, https://svpressa.ru/world/article/45629/.

Как живут люди в Китае-особенности и традиции Китайцев, https://gruz – china.ru/blog/kak – zhivut – lyudi – v – kitae – osobennosti – i.

Social Development of China and the Significance of Intellectual Property

Svitlana Glovatska*, Alina Litvinenko, Viktoria Baderko**

The intellectual property system is the main economic and legal institution that contributes to the economic development of mankind, its social progress, scientific innovation and cultural flourishing. With the rapid development of world science and technology and the acceleration of the process of economic globalization, the role of intellectual property system in economic and social life is growing, and the issue about intellectual property protection is attracting wide attention of the world community.

China is an ancient civilized country with a history for thousands of years. Over the years, numerous eminent Chinese scientists, inventors, writers and artists—with their brilliant intellectual achievements—have made a huge contribution to the development and progress of all mankind.

Over the past more than 40 years in implementing the policy of reform and opening up, the Chinese government has attached great importance to intellectual property, which gave impetus to the rapid development of the country's economy and all-round progress of society.

---

* Svitlana Glovatska, PhD, Associate Professor of Ukrainian Director of CASS-ONMU: Center of China Studies.

** Alina Litvinenko, Viktoria Baderko, Students of Odessa National Ocean University.

Since 1979, China has become a party to the main international conventions in the field of intellectual property, as a result the rights to intellectual property objects in China in their modern sense were recognized and protected.

In 1980 China became a member of the World Intellectual Property Organization (WIPO) by joining the Convention Establishing the World Intellectual Property Organization. Further, on December 19, 1984, China joined the Paris Convention for the Protection of Industrial Property, which was adopted in 1883.

In 1989, China, having become a party to the Madrid Agreement Concerning the International Registration of Trademarks, entered the Madrid system, which allows the protection of trademarks in many countries by obtaining an international registration, and is valid in each of the designated contracting parties.

In 1992, China joined the adopted-in-1886 Berne Convention for the Protection of Literary and Artistic Works and the 1971 Geneva World Copyright Convention (formerly known as 1952 Universal Copyright Convention).

On October 1, 1993, China joined the Patent Cooperation Treaty (PCT), which allows soliciting a patent protection of an invention simultaneously in each of many countries by filing an "international" patent application. The application is filed through the Chinese Online Office for Submission and Management of WIPO Applications.

In 2001, China entered the World Trade Organization (WTO), and accordingly became a party-country to the Agreement on Trade-Related Aspects of Intellectual Property Rights (TRIPS).

Over the past several decades, China has made significant progresses in increasing the number of patent applications both domestically and abroad. This was facilitated by increased spending on the R&D sector, improved innovation capacity and strong government support.

Thus in 1999 the World Intellectual Property Organization received only 276 applications from China, but China had increased this number to a 200 times more by the year of 2019 and topped the three largest applicant-countries under the Patent Cooperation Treaty (PCT) with 58,990 applications, ahead of the United States (57,840) and Japan (52,660) and demonstrated an increase of 10.6%, while the United States achieved only 2.8%, and Japan 5.9% [1].

The creation of a unified intellectual property system in China began in 2008 with the issuance of *the Outline of the National Intellectual Property Strategy*, in which intellectual property is regarded as the main guarantee and incentive for innovation. The purpose for the adoption of the State Strategy was to tap the country's innovative potential and build an innovative country, enhance the market competitiveness of Chinese enterprises and the country's overall competitiveness, expand foreign contacts for mutual benefits, improve the system of socialist market economy, regulate the market structure and build a harmonious society.

In November, 2011, the Chinese government established the National Leading Group to Combat Intellectual Property Infringement and Counterfeiting under the leadership of the Vice Premier of the State Council, which consisted of the members from 29 national ministries and commissions and was responsible for adoption of administrative measures, exercising criminal justice power, maintaining public order and dealing with general legal and educational issues.

Two documents were presented to illustrate the best practices in coordination of intellectual property protection in China. One describes the experiences of such activities on a national level carried out by the National Leading Group to Combat Intellectual Property Infringement and Counterfeiting, and the other describes the experiences carried out at a local level by the Shanghai People's Municipal Government (SPMG) [2].

---

[1] WIPO Statistics Database, February 2021.

[2] Координация защиты интеллектуальной собственности на национальном и региональном уровне, wipo/ace/12/5 rev. 2, https://www.wipo.int/edocs/mdocs/enforcement/ru/wipo_ace_12/wipo_ace_12_5_rev_2.pdf.

In 2012, the newly elected General Secretary of the Communist Party of China Xi Jinping formulated a new "Chinese Dream of Great Rejuvenation of the Nation". The new "Chinese Dream" is based on two global projects: Belt and Road Initiative (BRI) and "Made in China 2025".

The Belt and Road Initiative is a Chinese mega-project designated at the highest level, which was officially announced in 2014 and initially included the Silk Road Economic Belt and the 21st Century Maritime Silk Road ①. Since 2017, while implementing the Belt and Road Initiative, the Polar Silk Road and Digital Silk Road projects have emerged to supplement the Initiative. In addition, the report released by the Office of the Leading Group for Promotion of BRI Construction for 2019 also mentioned the "Green Silk Road" ②.

Under the BRI, bilateral agreements on cooperation in intellectual property were signed between China and Ukraine and Kyrgyzstan. Then, more and more cooperation mechanisms in the field of intellectual property between China and Europe, America, Japan, South Korea and BRICS were established. Besides, a number of international conferences and other events on intellectual property were held, so as to establish an interactive mechanism in intellectual property protection within the framework of the Belt and Road Initiative ③.

The "Made in China 2025" strategy aims to strengthen the country's position as a global leader in high-tech industries. The Strategy, calculated for 10 years, is a comprehensive plan for the development of 10 core industries of the national economy (see Figure 1), covering all stages of production of goods—

---

① Аудит зовнішньої політики: Україна — Китай: Дискусійна записка, Інститут світової політики, 2016, http://iwp.org.ua/ukr/public/1842.html.

② Гловацька С. М. Пройктий потенціал ініціативи "Один пояс, один шлях" / Пройктний та логістичний менеджмент: нові знання на базі двох методологій. Том 3: монографія / [авт. кол.: С. В. Руденко, І. О. Лапкіна, Т. А. Ковтун та ін.]. – Одеса: Купрійнко СВ, 2020 – 235с.

③ Чжан Чжчэн. Государственная стратегия Китая в области интеллектуальной собственности: реализация и перспективы, Государственное управление по делам интеллектуальной собственности, https://rospatent.gov.ru/content/uploadfiles/presentations/VEFTchzendoklad.pdf.

from research and development to after-sales services. The achievement of the goals formulated in it is intended to ensure the smooth implementation of the 13th Five-Year Plan for China during the period of 2016 – 2020. The Strategy aims to develop the economy based on domestic innovation, and facilitate the shift of China from a country as imitator to the one as creator. Obviously, it is impossible to realize this strategy without the protection of intellectual property rights.

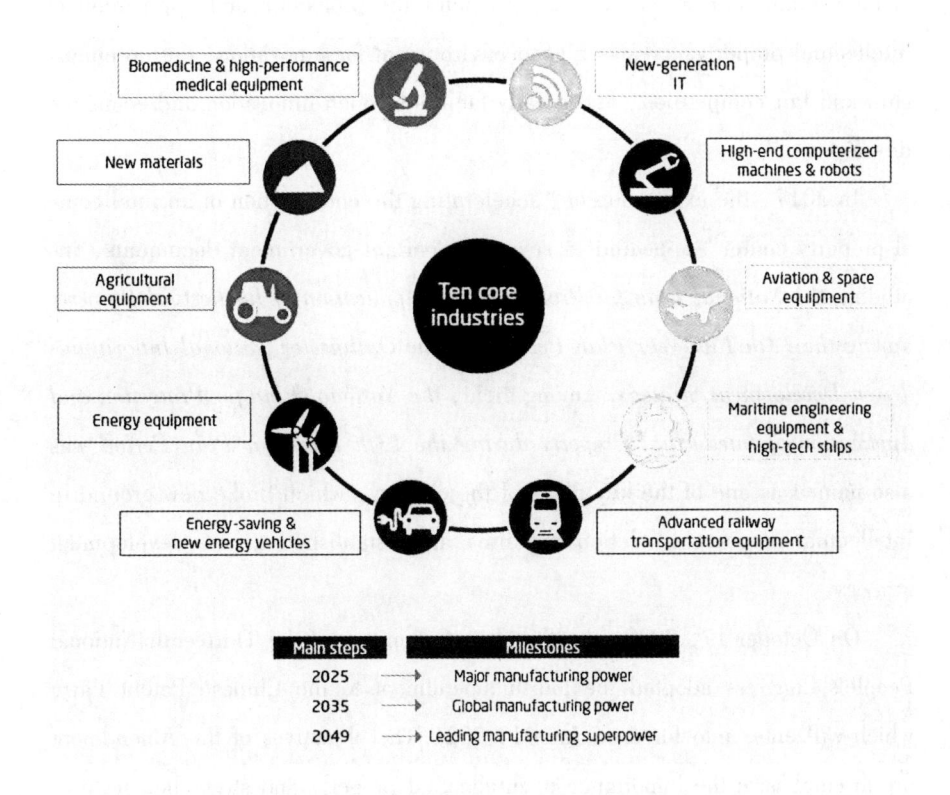

Figure 1 Ten core industries underpinning "MIC 2025"

Source: According to the data of the State Council.

In 2014, *the Action Plan for In-depth Implementation of the National Intellectual Property Strategy* (*2014 – 2022*) was adopted for further implementation of the State Strategy in the field of intellectual property for 2014 – 2020.

In 2015, the State council made several decisions on accelerating the development of China into a leading country in the field of intellectual property in the new context. In 2016, *the Outline for National Innovation-driven Development Strategy* was formulated, which clearly articulated the Strategy implemented in the field of intellectual property and the measures to accelerate the development of China into a leading country in the field of intellectual property. This document specifies the measures of deepening the reform in key areas of intellectual property protection, promotes the protection and application of intellectual property, creates a good environment for innovation, entrepreneurship and fair competition, and greatly facilitates open innovation and economic development[1].

In 2017, the expression of "accelerating the construction of an intellectual property center" appeared in several important government documents, including *the National Plan for Protection and Application of Intellectual Property during the 13th Five-year Plan Period* and *the Outline for National Innovation-driven Development Strategy*. Among them, *the National Plan for Protection and Application of Intellectual Property during the 13th Five-year Plan Period* was also named as one of the key plans of the country, which broke new ground in intellectual property protection in China and established a new development strategy.

On October 17, 2020, the Standing Committee of the Thirteenth National People's Congress adopted the fourth amendment to the Chinese Patent Law, which will enter into force on June 1, 2021. The objectives of the Amendment are to emphasize the importance of intellectual property and strengthen its protection, optimize the protection of patent rights, prevent infringement and promote the application of patents and commercialization of inventions, thus protec-

---

[1] Shen Changyu, "China – on course to become an IP powerhouse", WIPO Magazine, https://www.wipo.int/wipo_magazine/en/2016/si/article_0002.

ting and encouraging innovation ①.

President Xi Jinping stressed for many times the importance of accelerating innovation in science and technology during the 14th Five-Year Plan period (2021 – 2025), and called for establishing a powerful and effective legal system for intellectual property protection, so as to make innovation a key element for the country's future prosperity. The importance of technological progress and innovation for the country cannot be overemphasized. President Xi Jinping said China should foster an environment in which intellectual property is protected, knowledge and talents are respected and scientists are reasonably rewarded ②.

Since 2013, the Chinese government has successfully implemented more than 170 measures to suppress violations of intellectual property rights. Consequently, a total of 1.3 million cases of violations of intellectual property rights were investigated, and the perpetrators were brought to justice. ③

In January, 2019, the Chinese government established an intellectual property court as a division of the Supreme People's Court for patent and advanced technology appeals. By the end of 2020, the intellectual property court had handled over 4,000 cases. In addition to the intellectual property court, there are four intermediate courts that specialize in intellectual property protection in Beijing, Shanghai, Guangdong and Hainan.

The Chinese government pays great attention to the dissemination of the information about intellectual property and the education on intellectual property idea, and respects the work of intellectual property protection.

China is fully aware of the need to create a culture of respecting knowl-

---

① Liaoteng Wang & Dr. Jian Li & Qiang Lin & Shanqiang Xiao & Xiaobin Zong & Xiaodong Li & Lulin Gao, "The Long – Awaited Fourth Amendment to the Chinese Patent Law: An In – Depth Look", https://www.ipwatchdog.com/2020/12/15/long – awaited – fourth – amendment – chinese – patent – law – depth – look/id = 128185/.

② "Innovations in science and technology indispensable for quality development", China Daily, https://www.chinadaily.com.cn/a/202009/14/.

③ According to the Advisory Committee for Right Protection of the World Intellectual Property Organization.

edge, admiring innovation and abiding by laws, so as to establish a powerful intellectual property center and raise public awareness of intellectual property issues. In recent years, China has organized many events related to intellectual property, such as the IPR Protection Week, and the celebration of World Intellectual Property Day, and launched pilot demonstration education projects on intellectual property in primary and secondary schools. The Chinese government encourages higher educational institutions to establish majors and curricula related to intellectual property, build public education platforms, and arrange special training of personnel, and promotes the of interaction between intellectual property administrations and the media ①.

Through its actions, China is demonstrating a strong determination to enforce an effective intellectual property rights regime and to bring the national system in line with other developed systems in Europe and the US. In a relatively short period of time, China has covered a path that took developed countries tens and even hundreds of years to walk through.

It is safe to say that China is at the final stage of achieving the strategic goal set in 2008—achieving a high level in the field of creation, application, protection and management of intellectual property rights, and transformation from a country of "imitator" into a country of "creator". So far, China ranks first in the world in many key indicators in the field of intellectual property.

This is evidenced by the data from China, which in fact demonstrates a growing understanding of the global structure of intellectual property. Along with rising research funding, improved innovation capacity and strong political support, the number of patent applications inevitably increases in China.

Thus, in 2019, the Trademark Office of China National Intellectual Property Administration received 7.8 million trademark applications, while China Na-

---

① Чжан Чжчэн. Государственная стратегия Китая в области интеллектуальной собственности: реализация и перспективы, Государственное управление по делам интеллектуальной собственности, https://rospatent.gov.ru/content/uploadfiles/presentations/VEFTchzendoklad.pdf.

tional Intellectual Property Administration received about 4.3 million patent applications of all types.

Globally, China's number of applications under the Madrid Protocol is growing, and its number of applications under the Patent Cooperation Treaty (PCT) exceeded that of the United States for the first time.

According to the World Intellectual Property Organization, China has filed the most patent applications in the world since 2015. The scale of China's filing is astounding when viewed in relation to global totals.

In 2019, China topped the three countries of most patent applications under PCT with 58,990 applications. In terms of the number of applications filed in 2019, China accounted for more than 43% of the global volume (see Figure 2); in terms of the number of registered trademark applications—more than 51% (see Figure 3), and the amount of applications for industrial design—52% (see Figure 4) [1].

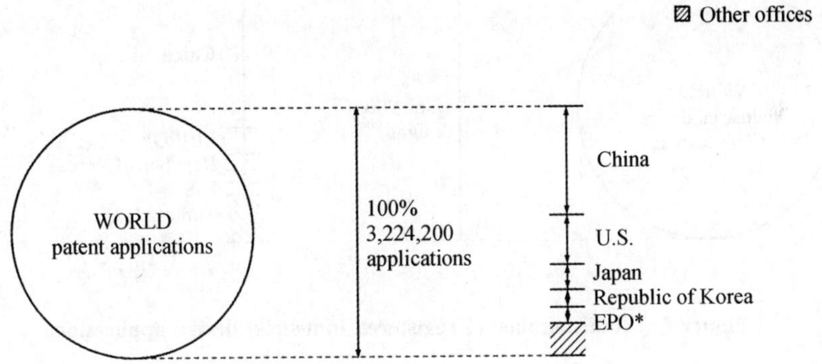

Figure 2　Total number of patent applications

In 2020, despite the COVID-19 pandemic, about 275,900 PCT international applications were filed by China, which is 4% more than that of 2019. China continued to maintain its leading position in the number of applica-

---

[1] WIPO Statistics Database, February 2021.

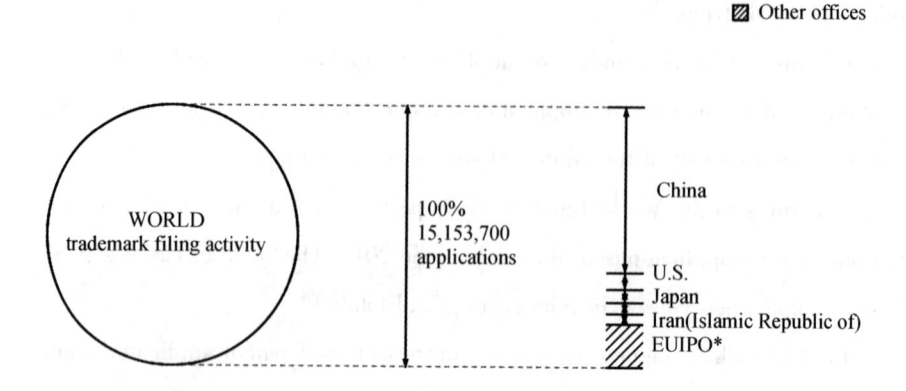

Figure 3   Total number of registered trademark applications

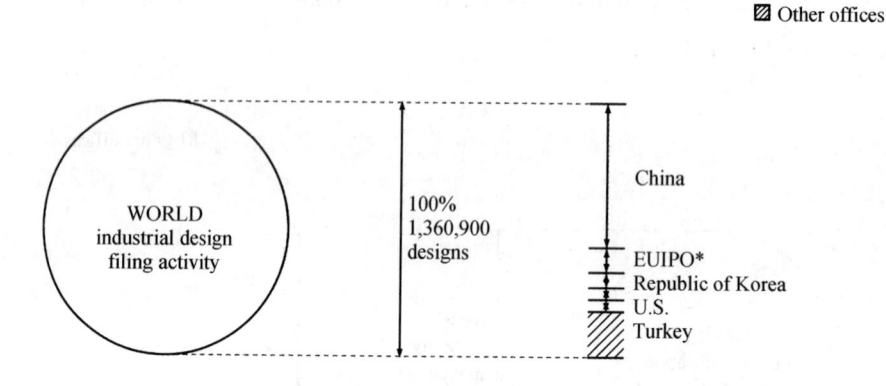

(WORLD trademark filing activity: 100% — 15,153,700 applications; China, U.S., Japan, Iran(Islamic Republic of), EUIPO*, Other offices)

Figure 4   Total number of registered industrial design applications

(WORLD industrial design filing activity: 100% — 1,360,900 designs; China, EUIPO*, Republic of Korea, U.S., Turkey, Other offices)

tions filed of 68,720, which is 16.1% more than that of 2019 (see Figure 5)①.

China has made significant progress in EPO's Patent Index 2020, ranking 4th after the US, Germany and Japan. At the same time, the number of applications submitted by China increased by 9.9% compared to that of 2019 and amounted to 13,432, which is the largest increase among the top 10 countries in

---

① WIPO Statistics Database, February 2021.

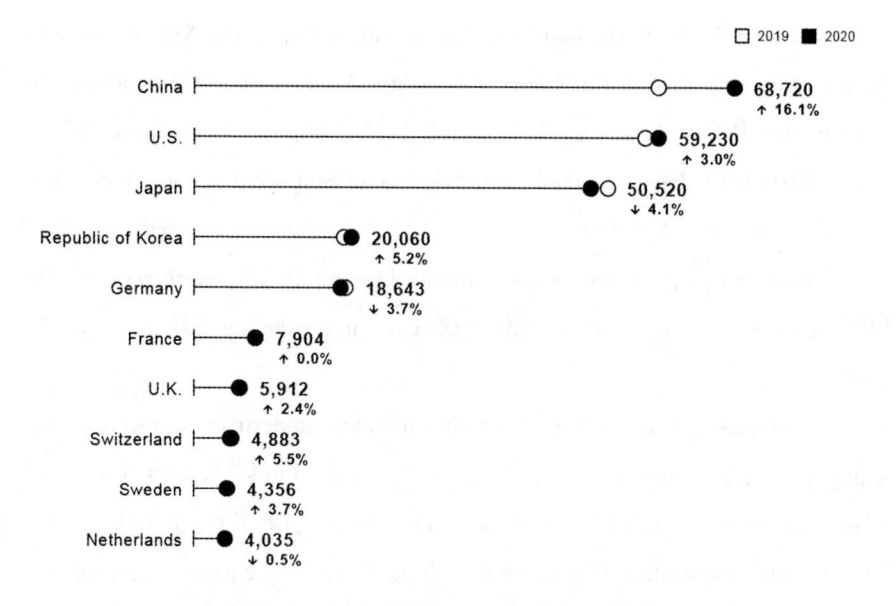

```
                                                    □ 2019  ■ 2020
        China  ├────────────────────────────○──● 68,720
                                                   ↑ 16.1%
         U.S.  ├──────────────────────────○● 59,230
                                              ↑ 3.0%
        Japan  ├───────────────────────●○ 50,520
                                           ↓ 4.1%
Republic of Korea ├─────────────○● 20,060
                                  ↑ 5.2%
      Germany  ├──────────────● 18,643
                                ↓ 3.7%
       France  ├──────● 7,904
                       ↑ 0.0%
         U.K.  ├────● 5,912
                     ↑ 2.4%
  Switzerland  ├──● 4,883
                   ↑ 5.5%
       Sweden  ├──● 4,356
                   ↑ 3.7%
  Netherlands  ├──● 4,035
                   ↓ 0.5%
```

Figure 5   Number of PCT applications filed in 2020

the 2020 index[①].

China's strong performance can be attributed to the efforts of the Chinese government to democratize and protect intellectual property rights.

Looking into the future, it can be predicted that the development of intellectual property in China will remain rapid and sustainable, and that China's intellectual property will further contribute to the development of the country itself and the global intellectual property system.

References

European Patent Office, https://www.epo.org/about-us/annual-reports-statistics/statistics.html.

Innovations in science and technology indispensable for quality development, CHINA DAILY, https://www.chinadaily.com.cn/a/202009/14/.

---

① European Patent Office, https://www.epo.org/about-us/annual-reports-statistics/statistics.html.

Liao teng Wang & Dr. Jian Li & Qiang Lin & Shanqiang Xiao & Xiaobin Zong & Xiaodong Li & Lulin Gao, The Long – Awaited Fourth Amendment to the Chinese Patent Law: An In – Depth Look, https://www.ipwatchdog.com/2020/12/15/long – awaited – fourth – amendment – chinese – patent – law – depth – look/id = 128185/.

Shen Changyu, "China – on course to become an IP powerhouse", WIPO Magazine, https://www.wipo.int/wipo_magazine/en/2016/ si/article _0002.

Координация защиты интеллектуальной собственности на национальном и региональном уровне // wipo/ace/12/5 rev.2, https://www.wipo.int/edocs/mdocs/enforcement/ru/wipo_ace_12/wipo_ace_12_5_rev_2.pdf.

Аудит зовнішньої політики: Україна — Китай: Дискусійна записка // Інститут світової політики, 2016. http://iwp.org.ua/ukr/public/1842.html.

Гловацька С. М. Проєктний потенціал ініціативи "Один пояс, один шлях" / Проєктний та логістичний менеджмент: нові знання на базі двох методологій. Том 3: монографія / [авт. кол.: С. В. Руденко, І. О. Лапкіна, Т. А. Ковтун та ін.]. – Одеса: Купрієнко СВ, 2020 – 235с.

Чжан Чжчэн. Государственная стратегия Китая в области интеллектуальной собственности: реализация и перспективы. // Государственное управление по делам интеллектуальной собственности. https://rospatent.gov.ru/content/uploadfiles/presentations/VEFTchzendoklad.pdf.

Chapter 4 Belt and Road Initiative and Global Development Initiatives

Global Development Initiatives: The Significance and Objectives of Social Modernization

Anatoly Lazarevich *

In recent years, the topic of modernization, its essence, tasks, ways of implementation, has come to the fore both in public discussion and in expert discussions. Philosophically speaking, there is every reason to classify modernization as one of those essential factors of social life that acquire relevance and have a real impact on sociocultural processes much more often than become the subject of widespread discussion. Social modernization, obviously, should not be understood simply as an isolated historical event or a series of events. Rather, it represents a particular quality or general purpose of these events. Modernization works, even when it is not spoken about directly; it can be regarded as an immanent sign of an ascending civilization process.

The implicit nature of modernization process means it is not always obvious, but constant present at the topic of modernization in philosophical-historical and socio-economic theory. The prerequisites of the modern concept of modernization were formed in a large number of social theories of the 19th-20th centuries, such as the theories of E. Durkheim, K. Marx, G. Main, A. Giddens,

---

* Anatoly Lazarevich, Professor, Doctor, Director of the Institute of Philosophy of National Academy of Sciences of Belarus.

W. Moore, A. Toffler, A. Touraine, R. Nisbet, J. Galbraith, J. Habermas, P. Sztompka, S. Huntington. A lot of literature on this issue has been prepared by modern Russian scientists, including V. L. Inozemtsev, S. N. Gavrov[①], V. S. Stepin, M. V. Ilyin, N. A. Krichesvsky, V. M. Mezhuev and many others. The number of dissertations and articles on this topic, published over the past 5 – 10 years, is estimated, without exaggeration, in hundreds.

Belarusian science did not stand aside from the discussion of the conceptual aspects of socio-economic modernization. First of all, I would like to name the collection of scientific works *Belarus and Russia in the European Context: Problems of State Management of the Modernization Process*, published as a result of the international scientific conference on this topic, which was organized by the Institute of Philosophy of the National Academy of Sciences of Belarus[②]. Later, a number of other scientific forums devoted to the problems of social modernization took place.

At the same time, the "intrascientific" conversation about social modernization often does not bring the theoretical result that one would like to get. As paradoxical as it may sound, the experts "understand each other too well" . While talking about the strategy of modernization, one can refer to a whole range of concepts that are the common property of socio-philosophical thought. However, when a topic that has been discussed for a long time in expert circles becomes a part of a wider public opinion, a certain conventionality of intrascientific agreements on the interpretation of certain concepts and the lack of public understanding of the specifics, goals and values of the process under discussion are

---

① Gavrov, S. N. , Modernization in the name of empire. Sociocultural aspects of modernization processes in Russia, Editorial URSS, 2010; Gavrov, S. N. , Modernization of Russia: post-imperial transit, МГУДТ, 2010.

② A. A. Lazarevich et al. , Belarus and Russia in the European context: the problems of the state management of the modernization process: Materials of the international scientific – practical conference, Minsk, October 20 – 21, 2011; National Academy of Sciences of Belarus, Institute of philosophy. – Minsk: Pravo I ekonomika, 2012, p. 381.

revealed. This fully applies to the concept and phenomenon of social modernization. They are interpreted in very different ways, and often confused with other concepts (in particular, with "innovative development", "transformation of society"). Or they are even devalued as an independent entity (according to the principle "nothing is new", or "any progressive development is modernization").

Of course, one should hardly take on faith that social modernization is imperative and not have any doubts about it. However, it is also true that doubts about the concept of modernization and the ways of its use, developed within the expert community, coming into the general public consciousness, give the effect of bewilderment and even rejection. Modernization, when it is declared as a slogan, should have a mobilizing function, and coordinate social forces to achieve clearly defined goals. However, when there is misunderstanding or misinterpretation, it is difficult to talk about mobilization. An alternative path is a public consensus on modernization, based on understanding of the necessity and inevitability of change. This kind of consensus is akin to the "pragmatic" idea, i. e. rationally accepted faith, which belongs to the American philosopher Charles Pierce. However, in this regard, the need for a broad dialogue on the goals and criteria of modernization is obvious, in which the state, science, education system, business, and public organizations should take part.

The problematic field of this dialogue is not formulated speculatively, but it comes from life itself. Several such problems will be outlined below, which may deserve a more detailed discussion.

I. Is Modernization an "Eternal Today"?

In his famous work "Modernity: an unfinished project", the German philosopher J. Habermas says that the value of "modern" is an antithesis to the "traditional" and "ancient". It was first articulated in the rhetoric of the Christian church of the 5th century AD. From that time, the idea of modernity contains two complementary meanings, which are "renewal", i. e. overcoming the old, and "modernizing", i. e. bringing in line with the urgent needs of today. ① One can talk about many separate facts of modernization: global modernization (such as the agricultural revolution and then industrial revolution at the entire Western world) and local modernization (like Peter's reforms in Russia); predominantly cosmetic modernization (such as the Meiji reforms in Japan in the 19th century) and deep modernization, which led to the formation of a new socio-economic structure (socialist revolution in the Russian Empire and a number of other states); successful modernization (industrial breakthrough of China and the states of Southeast Asia in the last quarter of the twentieth century) and unsuccessful modernization ("perestroika" and "acceleration" in the Soviet Union).

In the 1950s – 1960s, the Soviet Union laid the foundations for modern innovative potential in space exploration, aircraft construction, nuclear industry, rocket science, production of submarines, and many other types of weapons. The international resonance of these achievements was so great that in a number of advanced states of the world, they began to actively learn the Russian language awaiting the future "Soviet miracle".

In the early 1970s, Soviet science undertook a grandiose attempt to gather the best minds of the country and, relying on vast science, through brainstorming, find a way out on the base of scientific and technological progress (STP) to overcome stagnation. The work on the Comprehensive Program of STP for 20 years began. During the development of this program, a lot of analytical work was done, which helped to solve many interdisciplinary problems of scientific and technological development.

However, the main conclusion was disappointing. Due to insensitivity of the economic system existing at that time to the achievements of scientific and tech-

---

① Habermas, J., "Modernity: an unfinished project", Jurgen Habermas Political works, Praxis, 2005.

nological progress, due to the lack of competition between domestic producers in the domestic and world markets in conditions of deficit, the lag was inevitable. The country was slowly slipping into economic crisis, which first manifested itself in the second half of the 1980s in the form of a massive collapse of the utilization rate of production capacities in many technologically unrelated spheres of activity, which soon developed into the economic and political depression that ended with the collapse of the Soviet Union.

A common feature of all these and many other examples is that, firstly, the need for renewal is an objective prerequisite of any modernization; secondly, it is important to feel the rhythm of time ("spontaneously renewing relevance of the spirit of time", in accordance with the formula of the famous German philosopher J. Habermas), and purposefully form the need for renewal, based on self-awareness and responsibility of a person, leading social group or society as a whole as carriers of culture and values of the new era. In this regard, all modernizations, although they are based on different technological bases, have much in common in terms of their worldview, socio-psychological and organizational design.

II. The Trajectory of the Modernization Process: Straight or Wave

A certain difficulty with the "recognition" of the phenomenon of social modernization as an independent factor of the socio-historical process is caused by the fact that it is not always possible to distinguish it from the development of the material and technological base of society. For at least the latest three centuries, the productive forces of society have been developing almost continuously, with increasing intensity. Does this mean that humanity has lived and lives in conditions of permanent modernization? Probably, one can say so, but this "devalues" the idea of modernization as a special stage, a mobilizing factor of social development.

Another point of view not only recognizes, but even accentuates its socially transformative aspect in the process of modernization. The principles of modernization are fully implemented where and when the improvement of production processes and communications leads to a progressive change of the forms of social community, strengthening the dignity of the individual, expanding the possibilities of their self-fulfillment, and improving the quality of life in general.

It is clear that this "extra-material" component of modernization is assessed with slightly different criteria than the technological one. It is often possible to identify its significant changes only by looking back, keeping in sight the whole decades of the life of society. In this regard, although modernization can bring a relatively quick economic effect, its socio-cultural impact is measured with much longer periods. However, this does not mean that the sociocultural impact can be neglected.

Combining the linear trajectory of technological progress and the stepped trajectory of spiritual and cultural progress, with significant "horizontal" planes of stability, A. Toffler introduces the concept of civilizational waves. Having passed the "crest" of the agrarian and industrial wave, the thinker argues, humanity will soon pass the test of the post-industrial wave with its new technological dominants, new forms of organization of production and social relations, a new way of life and thinking. ①

One of the effects of contact with a new wave is, according to Toffler, "futuroshock", namely disorientation of a person in a rapidly changing socio-technological world. ② Futuroshock is not only characterized by the loss of the "organic connection" of the personality with spiritual tradition, but is also capable of provoking the rejection of progress, social rigidity, and anti-modernization behavioral attitudes. It seems that it is these attitudes, along with the technologi-

---

① Toffler, A. The third wave. – M. : AST, 2002.

② Toffler, A. Shock of the future: Translation from English — M. : LLC "AST Publishing house", 2002.

cal lag, lack of qualified personnel, lack of investment, etc. , are among the most important risks today of renewing the economic structure and the entire social space.

III. "Catching up" and "Outstripping" Modernization

Often (and especially in Russian-language literature) one can find such a definition of modernization, in which it is characterized as the process of improving objects of the technical nature (machinery, equipment, buildings, etc.), bringing them in line with new criteria, requirements, norms. Such a definition does not give the answer "where" these requirements and norms come from, why they remain "external" for the modernization process, and develop outside it. Social modernization, understood in this way, is "by definition" catching up, and its result with a high degree of probability bears the traits of the secondary nature (the task is to reproduce what has already become the standard in a technically more perfect environment, and possibly at the very moment, when new standards are already emerging there).

It is possible that in some cases there is no other way to overcome a deep technological lag. However, the stake on the catching-up type of social modernization itself contains the risk of "lagging behind forever". At some stage, it is necessary to arrange the accents of transformations in such a way as to move from the reproduction of known social and technological trends to their foresight. In other words, the quality and effectiveness of modernization processes directly depends on how much attention was paid to their strategic planning, on what ideological and methodological basis their "anticipatory reflection" was built.

Another example of the collapse of the catch-up modernization in our memory is, of course, the Soviet perestroika. It was started as a typical modernization project, the goals of which were formulated on the whole correctly, one might say, classically. At the April 1985 plenum of the CPSU Central Committee,

M. S. Gorbachev noted: "We need revolutionary shifts, transition to fundamentally new technological systems, to technology of the latest generations, which gives the highest effectiveness". ① Even now, after more than three decades, it is hardly possible to set any other requirements for technological modernization. At the same time, one of the main mistakes of this project has been repeatedly analyzed that its focus on the development of one leading sphere of industry, heavy engineering. Large investments in this area diverted funds, which, among other things, could be spent on scientific and innovative activities, growth of the production of consumer goods, and social expenditures. Together with a number of other external and internal factors, this quickly led to the increase of social tension and political disintegration of the state.

In this regard, one should pay attention to the fact that true modernization is not just the improvement of certain components of society, but its large-scale, mainly evolutionary, but dynamic transformation, which obeys the laws of consistency, interdependence and synergy of its subsystems. Therefore, an important scientific and practical task today is the creation of promising social and humanitarian technologies designed to provide a theoretical and methodological foundation of systemic modernization, to establish the connection between fundamental science and practice in such areas as strategic planning and prediction of socio-economic and cultural development; technological reorganization of all spheres of activity, education; spiritual and moral education; digital management. Of course, this is impossible without investment in the field of social and humanitarian science and education. In those areas, within the framework of which, before our eyes, the practical ways of using the potential of high technologies that are actively included in our everyday life, and the latest scientific and technical knowledge to improve the quality of life of a particular person, their

---

① M. S. Gorbachev, "On convocation of the next XXVII congress of CPSU and tasks connected with its preparation and holding", Report of the General Secretary of the CPSU Central Committee, http: //www.historyru.com/docs/rulers/gorbachev/gorbachev-doc-3.html#/overview.

intellectual, moral and psychological, social and communicative parameters are justified.

IV. "Eastern" and "Western" Modernization

In the aforementioned expert discussions in recent years, the question has often arisen of what is or should be the source of genuine modernization: the "grassroots" movement and self-organization of economic entities or the will of the state. The positions of the supporters of each of these approaches mark the principles of modernization of the Western and Eastern model.

The first one is connected, first of all, with the implementation of rational and pragmatic ideals of progress that are based on the phenomenon of effectiveness, which is maximally coupled with advances in science and technology. Bearing its economic fruits, it at the same time testifies to the growing de-traditionalization and atomization of the socio-cultural space. It is included in the system of direct and feedback links with the processes of formation of civil society and self-government, formation of mass consciousness and mass culture, being both generated by these phenomena and generating them.

The second one is widely based on tradition, established way of life, administrative and managerial potential, which can be accumulated, first of all, by the forces of the state apparatus. It can take place at the initiative of the state, outside the framework of socio-cultural reorganization according to the standards of the modern era, and, therefore, it is not necessarily the "reverse side" of de-traditionalization.

The images of the subject of modernization transformations in the first and second cases are fundamentally different. In the liberal model, this is, first of all, a bearer of private initiative, an entrepreneur; in the conservative model, it is a social community, a group, many employees of one enterprise, and is united by informal relationships and connections, which leads to characterize this community as a "collective subject".

What does the above have to do with the socio-economic development of the Republic of Belarus? Being located at the historical border of the cultural areas of the West and the East of the European continent, Belarus, obviously, cannot but face the situation of competition between two paradigms in the matter of choosing the modernization strategy. Any planning in this area should be based on a balanced analysis of the ratio of these alternatives, on not always accurately predicted social effects from the fact that these alternatives will be combined in one way or another in the course of any modernization process.

V. Modernization and Tasks of Innovative Development

Today it is quite obvious that public understanding of the tasks and meaning of modernization is not developing as easily as one would like. One of the difficulties was that the polemic about modernization interfered with the discussion of the strategy, methodology, and goals of innovative development that had begun several years earlier. And now, even competent interlocutors can say that "modernization" and "innovation" are words, if not completely devoid of meaningful significance, then at least denoting the same process, and the difference between them lies in plane of rhetoric.

This position is not a purely Belarusian phenomenon. Let's take the collection of scientific papers "Forcing to innovations: strategy for Russia" as an example, which is published in 2009 under the editorship of one of the prominent theorists of post-industrial development V. L. Inozemtsev. We will see the following: among the most significant problems posed by the authors is the question of "theoretical confusion in the understanding... of modernization and innovation".[1] The authors of the collection note that "in this case, pluralism is inappropriate that modernization in theoretical terms and practical implementation is

---

[1] V. L. Inozemtsev ed., *Forcing to innovations: strategy for Russia*, Collection of articles and materials, Center of research of postindustrial society, 2009.

not equal to innovation". The ingrained interpretation of modernization and innovation as practically synonymous words significantly complicates the practical implementation of modernization tasks.

The concept of "innovation" today is most often interpreted in accordance with the "Frascati guide", the document adopted by the Organization for Economic Cooperation and Development (OECD) in 1993 at the Italian city of the same name and defining innovation as "final result of innovation, embodied in the form of a new or improved product introduced in the market, a new or improved technological process used in practice, or in a new approach to social services". Such an interpretation allows and even welcomes that innovation be interpreted as a result of the transformation of idea into a market product or technology, a new form of social service and communication. At the same time, as noted by the Russian expert V. M. Kudrov, the "result" of the introduction of innovation in a broad sense can be a new production, managerial, and organizational process, new production management and even a new (that is, "modernized") person, both a manufacturer and a consumer of a new product. [1]

Innovative development of society as its strategic reference point assumes that it is the scientific and technological potential that becomes the factor that determines the rate and quality level of socio-economic processes, social welfare, and competitiveness in the world. In this regard, innovation can be called the most "mature" manifestation of modernization, but modernization itself is not always innovative in nature. Moreover, if the modernization process can be "launched" by a volitional decision, carried out in the project format, as mentioned above, then innovative reorganization is always a delicate self-regulating process associated not only with the organizational conditions of innovation, but also with the innovative culture of thinking. In other words, this process is associated with a gradual increase of the "degree" of creativity and innovative responsiveness at various levels of the economy and social structure, and this, of

---

[1] Kudrov, V. M., "Innovative economy-imperative of time", *Modern Europe*, No. 2, 2009.

course, cannot be achieved through the directive way.

What has been said allows one to more clearly define the understanding of social modernization. If we talk about Belarus, then it is, of course, not the first in history, and does not pretend to be a "revelation". However, it still differs from the previous ones in the fact that from the very beginning, from the stage of setting strategic goals, the idea about its innovative nature is formed, about focusing on informatization processes and building the society based on knowledge.

Of course, to state this does not mean to achieve it in practice. Modern social modernization faces a particularly ambitious task: to find a way to synthesize the effectiveness of the management vertical and cultivation of grassroots initiative, formal criteria of socio-economic progress and stochastics of innovative creativity, "dry numbers" of target indicators and freedom of entrepreneurial activity, and a number of other features. This is a very difficult task, and the higher the responsibility for its implementation.

VI. Modernization Mechanisms: Technological, Social, Cultural

It has already been indicated above that the tasks of modernization according to the innovative model should meet the special requirements for the subject of these processes, the "modernized person". That is why, along with the technological component of modernization, its socio-organizational and cultural component deserves the closest attention.

The generation that will take responsibility for the long-term effect of modernization, for its productivity that this generation needs to be purposefully educated today. The systematic preparation of young people for life in a high-tech and information society is one of the most important tasks of the education system, and its worldview, theoretical and methodological support "lies on the shoulders" of Belarusian science, primarily humanitarian one. Citizens should understand the practical value of science in general and its "Belarusian component" in particular, see in it new horizons for their professional activities and personal development, so as to be able to accumulate scientific information, possess the skills of critical analysis of exponentially growing information flows. So the meaning of implementation of the innovative potential of humanitarian knowledge is, first of all, in the formation of innovative readiness of citizens, innovative competence of specialists and managers.

For several years now, the issues of socialization of innovations, psychology of the innovation process have been developed under the auspices of the Institute of philosophy of the National Academy of Sciences of Belarus. A training method has been created for increasing the creative and innovative competence of management and engineering and technical staff, with the help of which the training seminars are held at the enterprises of the real sector of the economy. The Institute has created a special scientific and practical unit, the Center of Management of Knowledge and Competence, and the specialists of which solve theoretical and methodological tasks of making the search and creative environment at enterprises, issues of prospective management of the professional development of their employees, setting the forecasting cycle, and continuous improvement of management and production processes.

I would like to emphasize one more socio-cultural aspect of modernization. Practice shows that well-implemented modernization measures, no matter what parameters their effectiveness is assessed with, one way or another, always turn out to be the "test of strength" for existing organizational and management schemes. And this is their undoubted plus. It is obvious that only those institutions, regulations, administrative algorithms that pass the "stress test" of modernization can claim a place in the socio-cultural system of tomorrow.

VII. So What, After All, is Social Modernization?

Is it possible to give an unambiguous definition of this phenomenon? It was no accident that I violated the academic canon by bringing the question of definition to the concluding part of the article instead of the beginning. The aspects of the problem field of modernization considered above give us different approaches to answering this question. Perhaps, one should go along the path of not defining, but classifying the types of modernization, highlighting, first of all, the endogenous ("self-motivated", arising from the logic of development of local civilization and culture) and exogenous ("catching up", focused on foreign cultural samples) forms and their varieties. However, one can choose another way, trying to conceptually consolidate the "framework" understanding of the process of social modernization through enumeration of its criterion features.

Modernization in modern society is a complex socio-cultural process unfolding in the plane of scientific, industrial-technological and socio-economic development, evolution of the forms of social communication and solidarity, personal worldview and social consciousness. The core element of this process is the renewal of the technological base of the social structure, including production, management, social, humanitarian technologies, norms of behavior, ways of life. The content of this process is the consistent (not instantaneous) consolidation of the spiritual and creative forces of society around the tasks of creating, organizational and personnel support and reinforcement of the "technological core".

In other words, social modernization is a complex program for the renewal of all structural components of society, involving systemic qualitative changes in scientific, technical, cultural, and educational policy, in the organization of production and the management system, in public consciousness and the way of life of people. Two factors are of particular importance, which are creativity (innovations) and the mechanism of demand and socialization of its results. Therefore, it is extremely important to form a creative environment in society, using the energy of young people and the experience of the older generation, the knowledge of specialists, the potential of science, education and culture.

Social modernization should not be reduced to a chaotic transformation of separate objects and even sectors of the economy. This is a comprehensive program for the future, taking into account the prospects of development of the world economic system, trends of regional and global cooperation, the progress of science and technology, the tasks of preserving nature, human, and humanitarian values. In other words, modernization is directly related to the global civilizational process, the main ideologemes of which are aimed at a radical transformation of the industrial development model and the construction of innovative information-digital society or a society based on knowledge, professional competencies and humanitarian values.

In the implementation of this modernization strategy, the new scientific knowledge will have the key importance, which in a special way actualizes the role of fundamental science. The world of the future is a high-tech world. It will be impossible to build any modernization program in this high-tech world without an appropriate scientific, humanitarian and cultural base.

References

A. A. Lazarevich et al., Belarus and Russia in the European context: the problems of the state management of the modernization process: Materials of the international scientific – practical conference, Minsk, October 20 – 21, 2011.

Gavrov, S. N., Modernization in the name of empire. Sociocultural aspects of modernization processes in Russia, Editorial URSS, 2010.

Gavrov, S. N., Modernization of Russia: post – imperial transit, МГУДТ, 2010.

Habermas, J., "Modern – an unfinished project", Jurgen Habermas, Political works, Praxis, 2005.

Kudrov, V. M., "Innovative economy – imperative of time", *Modern Europe*, 2009, No. 2.

M. S. Gorbachev, "On convocation of the next XXVII congress of CPSU and tasks connected with its preparation and holding", Report of the General

Secretary of the CPSU Central Committee, http://www.historyru.com/docs/rulers/gorbachev/gorbachev-doc-3.html#/overview.

National Academy of Sciences of Belarus, Institute of philosophy. – Minsk: Pravo I ekonomika, 2012.

Toffler, A., *Shock of the future: Translation from English*, LLC "AST Publishing house", 2002.

Toffler, A., *The third wave*, AST, 2002.

V. L. Inozemtsev ed., *Forcing to innovations: strategy for Russia, Collection of articles and materials*, Center of research of postindustrial society, 2009.

Cooperation Between Belt and Road Initiative and Eurasian Economic Union

Gao Yuan*

Chinese President Xi Jinping clearly pointed out, developing and deepening Sino-Russian relations is the strategic choice of the two countries. (Both countries) must strengthen strategic cooperation and jointly promote the sustained and stable growth of the world economy, promote the peaceful resolution of international and regional hotspot issues, improve the global governance system, and inject more positive energy into world peace and stability.① In a sense, the Sino-Russian relationship is becoming an indispensable positive factor for maintaining international strategic balance and world peace and stability.

2021 is the 20th anniversary of the signing of the "China-Russia Treaty of Good-Neighborliness and Friendly Cooperation". President Xi Jinping pointed out that China and Russia "will advance bilateral relations at a higher level, in a broader field, and at a deeper level. In the face of the COVID – 19 pandemic as well as the profound change unseen in a century, China and Russia have firmly supported each other and cooperated closely and effectively, which is a

---

* Gao Yuan, Associate professor, Institute of Information Studies, Chinese Academy of Social Sciences.

① "Xi Jinping Meets with Russian President Putin", Xinhua News Agency, May 14, 2017, http://www.xinhuanet.com/world/2017 – 05/14/c_1120969876.htm.

vivid demonstration of the China-Russia comprehensive strategic partnership of coordination for a new era."① The two countries "support each other on issues of core interests. They are important partners on the road of development and revitalization, play a mainstay role in international affairs, and promote greater development of Sino-Russian relations in the new era to better benefit both countries and the rest of the world".②

I. The Docking of SREB with EEU Opens a New Phase of China-Russia Comprehensive Strategic Cooperation

The world is facing major changes unseen in a century, and the world is entering an unprecedented period of major development, changes and adjustments. In the face of a series of new situations and new problems, such as the increasingly prominent phenomenon of anti-globalization and the increasing uncertainty of international politics and economy, whether or not targeted countermeasures and plans can be put forward in a timely manner is undoubtedly a new test of the wisdom and ability of the entire world, especially the major powers. Since 2013, the Communist Party of China Central Committee with Comrade Xi Jinping at its core has put forward a major initiative to jointly build the Belt and Road with countries along the route on the basis of coordinating domestic development and international trends. Its core content is to "promote infrastructure construction and interconnection, link national policies and development

---

① "Xi Jinping and the President of Russia jointly witness the commencement ceremony of the Sino-Russian nuclear energy cooperation project", China Broadcasting Network, May 20, 2021, http://china.cnr.cn/news/20210520/t20210520_525490833.shtml.

② "The Ministry of Foreign Affairs talks about the outcome of the China-Russia Foreign Ministers' Meeting: Both sides will continue to support each other on issues of core interests", International Online, March 23, 2021, http://news.cri.cn/20210323/df34b8eb-7469-753c-2358-d6e456622c19.html.

strategies, deepen pragmatic cooperation, promote coordinated and linked development, and achieve common prosperity". ①

Since the establishment of a strategic cooperative partnership between China and Russia in 2001, China and Russia have always maintained the spirit of equality, mutual benefit and sincere cooperation in bilateral relations and international affairs, and can adopt the same or similar positions on major international issues to oppose hegemonism, advocate a multi-polar world and actively maintain the stability of the international social order. As permanent members of the UN Security Council, both China and Russia are very concerned about the evolution of the international order. On the 60th anniversary of the end of World War II, China and Russia issued the "Joint Statement on the International Order in the 21st Century", jointly expressing their views on the future international order. At the same time, the two countries also support each other's development goals and carry out extensive cooperation at the strategic level. In February 2014, Chinese President Xi Jinping attended the opening ceremony of the Sochi Winter Olympics. The leaders of China and Russia reached an agreement on jointly promoting the Belt and Road Initiative. In 2015, Russia joined the Asian Infrastructure Investment Bank (AIIB), becoming the third largest shareholder after China and India. In May 2015, China and Russia issued the "Joint Statement between the People's Republic of China and the Russian Federation on Cooperation in Coordinating Development of the Silk Road Economic Belt and the Eurasian Economic Union", which formally established the SREB and EEU cooperation mode. ② The cooperation between the two countries has not only effec-

---

① Xi Jinping, "Opening a New Starting Point for Cooperation and Seeking New Driving Forces for Development-Opening Speech at the Roundtable Summit of the 'Belt and Road' International Cooperation Summit Forum", *People's Daily*, May 16, 2017, http://politics.people.com.cn/n1/2017/0516/c1001-29277113.html.

② "Joint Statement of the People's Republic of China and the Russian Federation on Docking and Cooperation between the Construction of the Silk Road Economic Belt and the Eurasian Economic Union", Xinhua News Agency, May 9, 2015, http://www.xinhuanet.com//world/2015-05/09/c_127780866.htm.

tively maintained the stability of the international order, but also laid the foundation for the further improvement of bilateral relations. In 2016, the two heads of state jointly issued the "Joint Statement on Strengthening Global Strategic Stability", aimed at responding to the growing challenge of negative forces in international affairs. In 2017, the signing of the "Joint Statement on Further Deepening the China-Russia Comprehensive Strategic Partnership of Coordination" has further pointed out the development direction for China-Russia comprehensive strategic cooperation in the new era from five aspects including political mutual trust, pragmatic cooperation, security cooperation, people-to-people and cultural exchanges, and international cooperation.

On October 25, 2019, Premier Li Keqiang of the State Council and the Prime Ministers of the member states of the Eurasian Economic Union jointly issued the "Joint Statement on the Effectiveness of the 'Economic and Trade Cooperation Agreement between the People's Republic of China and the Eurasian Economic Union' signed on May 17, 2018". The "Joint Statement" reaffirmed the traditional friendship and strong economic and trade relations between the People's Republic of China and the member states of the Eurasian Economic Union (the Republic of Armenia, the Republic of Belarus, the Republic of Kazakhstan, the Republic of Kyrgyz, and the Russian Federation). The "Joint Statement" announced that "Economic and Trade Cooperation Agreement between the People's Republic of China and the Eurasian Economic Union" formally came into effect. Both sides believe that the entry into force of the Agreement is an important measure for building a common economic development space, and realizing the docking of the Belt and Road Initiative with the Eurasian Economic Union, and the coordinated development of the Belt and Road Initiative and the Greater Eurasian Partnership. The two sides believe that the signing of the Agreement will help to carry out mutually beneficial cooperation and constructive dialogue in the economic and trade field. It is necessary to start the implementation of the provisions of the Agreement to promote bilateral trade and cooperation as soon as possible, and ensure the due role of cooperation mechanisms including the Joint Committee of the Agreement. ① With this as a sign, the Belt and Road Initiative and the Eurasian Economic Union have entered a new stage of simultaneous advancement of pragmatic cooperation and institutional construction.

Since 2020, despite the spread of the COVID - 19 pandemic in the world, the Belt and Road cooperation projects have been generally stable without extensive delays, showing its strong resilience. ② As a century-long cause across Eurasia, the smooth advancement of the Belt and Road, especially the Silk Road Economic Belt construction, is inseparable from the deepening of the strategic cooperation between China and Russia. Russia is an important cooperative partner of China in building the Belt and Road, and China is also a strategic partner of the Eurasian Economic Union. The two sides firmly support each other on issues involving each other's core interests, and actively promote the coordination of development strategies including the docking of the SREB and EEU, which not only conforms to the objective requirements of the adjustment of the current international political and economic new order, but is also conducive to continuously consolidating and deepening the existing partnership between the two countries, thus opening up a new situation in the construction of China-Russia comprehensive strategic cooperation in the new era. ③

With the continuous advancement of the Belt and Road Initiative, the docking of SREB and EEU has become a new starting point for China-Russia com-

---

① "Joint Statement on the Effectiveness of the 'Economic and Trade Cooperation Agreement between the People's Republic of China and the Eurasian Economic Union' signed on May 17, 2018", Xinhua News Agency, October 25, 2019, http: //www. gov. cn/xinwen/2019 - 10/25/content _ 5445095. htm.

② "The Belt and Road Initiative is Resilient (Expert interpretation)", People's Daily Overseas Edition, March 16, 2020, http: //paper. people. com. cn/rmrbhwb/html/2020 - 03/16/content _ 1976481. htm.

③ Xi Jinping: "Promote China-Russia Comprehensive Strategic Partnership to Reach the Peak", People's Daily Overseas Edition, September 12, 2018, http: //paper. people. com. cn/rmrbhwb/html/ 2018 - 09/12/content_1880724. htm.

prehensive strategic cooperation. China and Russia jointly agreed that they "will continue to give play to their respective advantages, based on the principles of mutual benefit and mutual understanding, centering on the alignment of China-Russia development strategies and the integration of the construction of the Belt and Road with the Eurasian Economic Union, and are committed to deepening practical cooperation in various fields to consolidate the material foundation for the sustainable development of Sino-Russian relations". [1] China and Russia will take the docking of the SREB and EEU as an opportunity to continue to comprehensively deepen strategic and pragmatic cooperation in various fields.

On the one hand, the continuous promotion of the Belt and Road Initiative ideas and the continuous implementation of pragmatic policies are conducive to exploring the huge potential and space for cooperation between China and Russia, thereby laying a solid material foundation for the comprehensive strategic cooperation between China and Russia in the new era. Both China and Russia belong to the Eurasian continent. They are connected by mountains and rivers and their peoples live next to each other. They have broad space for deepening all-round cooperation. In July 2017, President Xi Jinping pointed out before his visit to Russia that major strategic projects are the cornerstone of economic and trade cooperation between the two countries. Their comprehensive benefits and strategic effects cannot simply be reflected and measured by numbers. The two sides need to carry out more cooperation in joint research and development, joint production, and promotion and application. [2] In recent years, within the framework of the docking of SREB and EEU, China and Russia have made great efforts to promote the integration of upstream and downstream cooperation in the energy field in terms of bilateral major projects. At the level of interconnection,

---

[1] "Joint Statement of the People's Republic of China and the Russian Federation on Further Deepening the Comprehensive Strategic Partnership of Cooperation", Xinhua News Agency, June 6, 2019, http://www.xinhuanet.com/2019-06/06/c_1124588552.htm.

[2] "Xi Jinping Accepts Interview by Russian Media", People's Daily Online, July 4, 2017, http://cpc.people.com.cn/big5/n1/2017/0704/c64094-29380500.html.

China has actively participated in Russia's proposal for joint development and construction of the coastal international transport corridor, which ultimately facilitated the smooth progress of major cross-border infrastructure construction projects such as the Tongjiang Railway Bridge and the Heihe Highway Bridge which will soon be completed. With the assistance of Russia, the China-Europe Express can become a reality. Russia is also actively inviting China to jointly develop and utilize sea passages, especially the construction of the Arctic waterway and the creation of the "Polar Silk Road". With the help of the docking of SREB and EEU, China and Russia have shown a new situation and good development prospects for comprehensive and pragmatic cooperation in a series of fields such as energy, transportation, investment, and major projects.

On the other hand, the docking of the SREB and EEU will also help China and Russia continue to play a constructive role in the formation of a new international political and economic order. At the same time, the reality of international political and economic development in the post-financial crisis era also fully demonstrates that the "economic imperialism, liberal hegemonism, democratic fundamentalism, and international financial oligarchy" led by Western powers have become the head of evil and the source of crisis in today's world. ① Facing the collective rise of emerging market countries, the revolution of the old world order has entered a countdown. The multiple coexistence of a community with a shared future for mankind and the future of a multi-polar world provide a development direction for the advent of the new international order. However, a few Western powers are unwilling to voluntarily give up their monopoly advantage over the world's political and economic order. They still try their best to create exclusive international economic and trade organizations and corresponding rules, and continue to use them to safeguard the monopoly interests of major international capital.

---

① Zhang Shuhua, "Sino-Russian Cooperation Breaks the Dilemma of World Governance", *Global Times*, September 27, 2016, https://opinion.huanqiu.com/article/9CaKrnJXO6U.

The openness and inclusiveness of the Belt and Road Initiative provides valuable practical experience for the coming of the future international order. As President Xi Jinping said in his speech at the opening ceremony of the Boao Forum for Asia in April 2018 that "the BRI originated in China, but the opportunities and benefits it creates belong to the world. China has no geopolitical calculations, seeks no exclusionary blocs and imposes no business deals on others". ① China's Belt and Road Initiative is not the kind of strategic thinking of Western countries that seeks to achieve quick victory under fierce competition; this initiative is different from zero-sum. The logic of the game is to cater to all actors who can accept it and enrich it with their own vision, experience and resources. ②

In 2019, relying on the SREB and EEU connection, China and Russia are accelerating the drawing of a future-oriented "Eurasia Development Roadmap". It is based on the coordinated development of the Silk Road Economic Belt and the Eurasian Economic Union, and based on the basic principles of extensive consultation, joint contribution and shared benefits and the basic spirit of openness and inclusiveness, to achieve a higher degree of interconnection and win-win sharing of development results in the Eurasian countries along the Belt and Road and related countries outside the region. Therefore, to a certain extent, the efforts and corresponding plans to build a new international political and economic order centered on China and Russia have gradually taken shape. The Belt and Road Initiative proposed by China and the Eurasian Economic Union of Russia have successively been comprehensive. The countries involved have gone far beyond the geographic boundaries of the Eurasian continent, and have evolved into one of the most constructive public products in the reconstruction of

---

① Xi Jinping, "Openness for Greater Prosperity, Innovation for a Better Future—Keynote Speech at the Opening Ceremony of the Boao Forum for Asia 2018 Annual Conference", *People's Daily*, April 11, 2018.

② De Yevremenko, "China-Russia Strategic Partnership and the Construction of Greater Eurasia", *Foreign Social Sciences*, Issue 4, 2017.

the international political and economic map.

II. The Docking of SREB with EEU Helps Expand the Economic Space of the Eurasian Continent

New progress has been made continuously in the docking of the SREB and EEU, which has injected new impetus into the development of Sino-Russian relations in the new era. Under the macro background of the docking of the SREB and EEU, China and Russia will usher in a series of new opportunities in economic cooperation and expansion of economic space in the new era.

Restricted by multiple factors such as different geopolitical patterns, economic development priorities, domestic development status and objective conditions, China-Russia economic relations have been significantly lagging behind the expansion of cooperation in other areas. However, the continuous advancement of the Belt and Road Initiative, especially the launch of the docking of SREB and EEU process, provides an excellent opportunity for China and Russia to make up for the "shortcomings" in the field of economic cooperation.

On the one hand, economic cooperation has increasingly become the area with the greatest growth potential and development space in the relationship between the two countries. In recent years, the continuous and in-depth advancement of the Belt and Road construction, has provided an excellent opportunity for China and Russia to make up for the "shortcomings" in the field of economic cooperation. According to the latest official data released by the Ministry of Commerce, in 2018, the trade volume between China and Russia broke through the 100 billion U.S. dollar mark for the first time, reaching 107.8 billion U.S. dollars. China has maintained its position as Russia's largest trading partner for ten consecutive years. In 2017, at the first Belt and Road International Cooperation Summit Forum, China reached a series of cooperation consensus, important measures and practical results with other countries' governments, localities, and enterprises. The scope covers five categories, including policy coordination, connectivity of infrastructure and facilities, unimpeded trade, financial integration, and people-to-people bonds, with a total of 76 major items and more than 270 specific results. Among them, the progress of China-Russia cooperation in the field of investment is particularly outstanding. The National Development and Reform Commission of China announced the establishment of a Sino-Russian Regional Cooperation Development Investment Fund with a total scale of 100 billion yuan and the first phase of 10 billion yuan to promote development cooperation between Northeast China and the Russian Far East. [1] It can be said that under the promotion of the Belt and Road Initiative, China and Russia have begun to gradually break the relative stagnation in the field of economic cooperation over the years. In the future, with the in-depth development of pragmatic cooperation between the two countries under the framework of the Belt and Road, economic cooperation is expected to become one of the most important areas of development potential and room for growth in the future development of bilateral relations.

On the other hand, China's Belt and Road Initiative and the Eurasian Economic Union continue to make important progress. In 2014, one year after the Chinese government put forward the Belt and Road Initiative, Russia subsequently initiated and established the Eurasian Economic Union strategy aimed at seeking the economic integration of the Eurasian region. However, as mutually beneficial and win-win effect of China's BRI continues to increase its attractiveness in the Eurasian continent, and Russia and other Eurasian countries have their own strong will to accelerate their development, China and Russia finally made a major strategic decision to end the "parallel operation" between the Belt and Road and the Eurasian Economic Union, and actively promote the docking of the two.

---

[1] "List of Outcomes of the Belt and Road International Cooperation Summit Forum", the official website of the Ministry of Foreign Affairs of China, May 16, 2017, http://www.fmprc.gov.cn/web/zyxw/t1461873.shtm.

In May 2015, China and Russia signed the "Joint Statement on Cooperation in Coordinating Development of the Silk Road Economic Belt and the Eurasian Economic Union". The statement emphasized that China will "support Russia to actively promote the integration process within the framework of the Eurasian Economic Union". At the same time, China and Russia will also "start negotiations on economic and trade cooperation with the Eurasian Economic Union. The two sides will jointly negotiate to ensure sustained and stable growth of the regional economy, strengthen regional economic integration, and maintain regional peace and development". [1] In recent years, while continuing to commit to the goal of Eurasian regional integration, Russia has gradually chosen to proceed from reality, and while actively responding to the Belt and Road Initiative, it has continued to attach importance to its rational connection with the Eurasian Economic Union. Regarding the importance of the Belt and Road Initiative to promote the integration of Eurasia, Russian President Putin emphasized that it not only "provided a creative method for promoting the integrated development of energy, infrastructure, transportation, industry, and humanities cooperation", but also "created conditions for the Eurasian continent to discuss its future development in a wider range". [2]

In October 2017, China and the Eurasian Economic Commission signed the "Joint Statement on Substantively Concluding the Negotiations on the Economic and Trade Cooperation Agreement between China and the Eurasian Economic Union", marking that the institutionalization of the economic and trade cooperation between China and the Eurasian Economic Union has achieved substantial

---

[1] "Joint Statement between the People's Republic of China and the Russian Federation on the Docking and Cooperation between the Construction of the Silk Road Economic Belt and the Eurasian Economic Union", May 9, 2015, http://www.xinhuanet.com/world/2015-05/09/c_127780866.htm.

[2] Vladimir Putin, "Speech at the opening ceremony of the Belt and Road International Cooperation Summit Forum", *China Investment*, Issue 11, 2017, pp. 33 – 34.

progress.① At the same time, the cooperation agreement between the Eurasian Economic Union and China's Silk Road Economic Belt reached by the leaders of China and Russia has taken an important step towards institutionalization. ② The negotiations have yielded fruitful results, and the most important of which is the signing of economic and trade agreements between the two parties. The Agreement covers 13 chapters including customs cooperation, trade facilitation, intellectual property rights, departmental cooperation, and government procurement, and includes relevant provisions such as e-commerce and market competition. According to the agreement, China and Russia agreed to further simplify customs clearance procedures and reduce the cost of trade in goods by strengthening cooperation, information exchange, and experience exchange. The Agreement aims to further reduce non-tariff trade barriers, improve trade facilitation, create a good environment for industrial development, promote the in-depth development of economic and trade relations between China and the Eurasian Economic Union and its member states, bring benefits to enterprises and people, and provide institutional guarantee for bilateral economic and trade cooperation. ③ Of course, it is also necessary to objectively recognize that in terms of content, the current agreement is still a framework document. Although it stipulates the direction of future negotiations between China and the Eurasian Economic Union and its member states, it does not involve substantive content such as tariff reduction or exemption, simplification of customs declaration procedures, and unification of customs standards. The main reason for this is that the member states of the

---

① "China and the Eurasian Economic Union have substantively concluded negotiations on an economic and trade cooperation agreement", Xinhua News Agency, October 1, 2017, http: // www. xinhuanet. com/2017 - 10/01/c_1121756577. htm.

② "China and the Eurasian Economic Union have substantively concluded negotiations on an economic and trade cooperation agreement", Xinhua News Agency, October 1, 2017, http: // www. xinhuanet. com/2017 - 10/01/c_1121756577. htm.

③ "China and the Eurasian Economic Union formally sign an economic and trade cooperation agreement", Ministry of Commerce of the People's Republic of China, May 17, 2018, http: // www. mofcom. gov. cn/article/ae/ai/201805/20180502745041. shtml.

Eurasian Economic Union and China still have important issues that need to be resolved in terms of the arrangement of interests in many areas. Currently, they are not ready to remove tariff barriers and open their domestic markets for Chinese goods and services. In the short term, China and the Eurasian Economic Union are still facing great difficulties in signing a comprehensive Free Trade Area Agreement (FTA). The root cause is the poor economic resilience of the Eurasian Economic Union and the internal structural problems that have not been effectively resolved. ① In the future, the liberalization of trade relations between the Eurasian Economic Union and China still needs to overcome difficulties and continue to advance.

The docking of the SREB and EEU has also promoted the integration of international economic cooperation systems in the Eurasian region, and promoted the coordination of various mechanisms to promote the development of the region. Through the Belt and Road Initiative, China and Eurasian countries have gradually established strong bilateral relations, such as the completion of the docking of the Belt and Road Initiative and Kazakhstan's "Bright Road" plan, and the establishment of the "Great Stone" Special Economic Zone in Belarus which are inseparable from the smooth advancement of the SREB and EEU docking. Through the SREB and EEU docking, China and Russia effectively avoided vicious competition in the Eurasian region; they coordinated with each other on the basis of not changing the regional economic cooperation plans and mechanisms of the two sides. At the same time, small and medium-sized countries in the Eurasian region can participate to the greatest extent in the regional cooperation plan advocated by the two countries and maximize their benefits. Through the docking and cooperation of the two major countries at the regional level, a wealth of bilateral and multilateral actions can be carried out quickly and a bet-

---

① Cong Xiaonan, "The Economic Obstacles and Realistic Choices of China-Eurasian Economic Union FTA—Based on Computable General Equilibrium GMR-CGE", *Russian Studies*, Issue 1, 2018, p. 106.

ter synergy effect can be formed.

From the end of 2019 to the beginning of 2020, under the influence of the COVID – 19 pandemic, China's foreign trade has shown a downward trend. However, in the first quarter of 2020, China-Russia trade volume reached US $25.35 billion, a year-on-year increase of 3.4%, and the growth rate ranked second among China's major trading partners. Specially, China's exports to Russia were US $9.15 billion, a year-on-year decrease of 14.6%; imports from Russia were US $16.2 billion, a year-on-year increase of 17.3%, and the growth rate of imports ranked first among China's major trading partners. [1] The fact that the Sino-Russian economic and trade relations can withstand the impact of the pandemic and have risen against the trend is mainly due to the continuous advancement of Sino-Russian practical cooperation in recent years, which has improved the quality of economic and trade cooperation between the two countries and the degree of interdependence between the two countries' economies, making the Sino-Russian economy and trade resilient towards the impact of changes in the external environment. At the same time, normalized epidemic prevention and control has created new momentum for the economic development of the two countries and created more opportunities for regional economic and trade cooperation. While China and Russia are mutually beneficial and win-win, they also provide new growth points for the recovery of the world economy.

It can be said that the porous and multi-choice development brought about by the docking of SREB and EEU not only promoted the improvement of Sino-Russian bilateral relations, but also consolidated the status of the two countries as coordinators in the multi-level political and economic process. China and Russia continue to promote the evolution of the economic and political order in the Eurasian region by jointly advocating the establishment and jointly promoting the regional cooperation framework, which will help to form a new Eurasian regional

---

[1] Data source: official website of the General Administration of Customs of China, http://43.248.49.97/.

order and a new path of integration based on the principle of sovereignty and taking into account the development of all countries.

III. The Docking of SREB with EEU Promotes the Establishment of a Community of Shared Future for Asia and Europe

The docking between the Silk Road Economic Belt and the Eurasian Economic Union is the largest regional cooperation project in the Eurasian space. It can not only change the economic landscape of the Eurasian region, but may even pave the way for the reconstruction of the Eurasian space. The docking of the SREB and EEU is an opportunity created for the Eurasian Economic Union countries on the one hand, and on the other hand, it is also a special test for the Eurasian elites in terms of policy implementation and political maturity. And the result of the advancement of the SREB and EEU docking process is also of great significance to the construction of "a community with a shared future" in the wider space of Asia and Europe.

In March 2013, when Xi Jinping delivered a speech at the Moscow Institute of International Relations, he formally put forward the concept of "a community with a shared future". Later, he explained this concept on multiple occasions. At the Boao Forum for Asia Annual Conference, the Indonesian National Assembly, the UNESCO Headquarters in Paris, the "Asia-African Leaders' Meeting" in Indonesia, the 70th General Debate of the UN General Assembly, the opening ceremony of the Paris Climate Conference, the opening ceremony of the 2016 G20 Business Summit, the High-level Meeting on "Consulting and Building a Community with a Shared Future for Mankind" at the Palais des Nations, Geneva, Switzerland, and the Global Party Congress, he repeatedly explained the concept and meaning of a community with a shared future for mankind.

In the report of the 19th Congress of the Communist Party of China, General Secretary Xi Jinping made a clear summary of the connotation of a community with a shared future for mankind, that is, "creating an open, inclusive, clean and beautiful world that enjoys lasting peace, universal security, and common prosperity". ① The idea of building a community with a shared future draws on precious ideas from human history. It not only inherits the traditional Chinese cultural ideas that "the world is the public, the world is unified, and the unity of nature and man", it is also the contemporary crystallization of Marx's "community of free people". Contrary to the principle of self-identification in the Western geopolitical system, the theoretical basis of this system is the principle of self-discrimination and the principle of coordination, which incorporates the "relationship" categories in traditional Chinese cultural concepts such as "mysterious tongs" and "mixing". ②

Russia's conception of the integration of the Eurasian region is concentratedly reflected in the concept of "Greater Eurasia". In fact, the concept of "Greater Eurasia" has gradually formed a broader connotation under the interpretation of countries in the region. In addition to the Greater Eurasian Partnership promoted by Russia, Nazarbayev, the first President of Kazakhstan, also called for the establishment of a Eurasian community with a shared future in 2019. ③ The continuous enrichment and expansion of the concept of "Greater Eurasia" not only echoes the concept of "a community with a shared future" from the side, but also has an inherent consistency with the logic of the SREB and EEU docking. The gradual interpretation of the concept of "Greater Eura-

---

① "Xi Jinping's Report at the 19th National Congress of the Communist Party of China", People's Daily Online, January 3, 2018, http://cpc.people.com.cn/n1/2017/1028/c64094-29613660.html.

② Ma Liangwen, "Russia and China are the two pillars of the Eurasian Consortium", *Russian Studies*, Issue 5, 2018, p. 28.

③ "Nazarbayev Calls for the Building of a Community with a Shared Future for Europe and Asia", China News Network, November 13, 2019, http://www.chinanews.com/gj/2019/11-13/9006106.shtml.

sia" reflects the objective process of increasing connectivity in the Eurasian region, and at the same time promotes the macro-regional construction based on ideas and identity.

On the one hand, transportation first is an important breakthrough for the Belt and Road Initiative. The important tasks of the Belt and Road nitiative are interconnection, and the development of transportation and corresponding infrastructure in Eurasia to ensure reliable supply of resources and China's economic export capacity. This is the primary task of the process of connecting the Silk Road Economic Belt and the Eurasian Economic Union, and it is also the basic condition for the implementation of the "Greater Eurasian" concept. Only by fundamentally transforming the transportation infrastructure and ensuring the substantive connection of the Eurasian Continental Bridge, can the huge markets of Europe, Asia, China, and the European Union be reliably connected. The economic and trade agreement between the Eurasian Economic Union and China will create better conditions for infrastructure construction and investment; mechanisms such as the Asian Infrastructure Investment Bank and the BRICS New Development Bank are the institutional guarantee for China's participation in the construction of transportation infrastructure in Eurasian countries.

China strives to ensure the diversification of transportation routes, and the long delay in major transportation and logistics infrastructure projects in Russia has prompted China to seek alternative directions. But this does not mean that the Silk Road Economic Belt will weaken Russia's role as a major transit country in Eurasia. Currently, the China-Europe Express trains that have been opened all have considerable distances within Russia. Driven by the China-Europe train, Russia's role as a logistics hub for the east and west ends of the Eurasian continent will be further strengthened.

Of course, it is still too early to assert that Eurasia has made breakthroughs in the construction of modern logistics and transportation infrastructure. There are many situations and factors that hinder the rapid start of such large-scale infrastructure projects. At present, not only at the level of cooperation between countries in the Eurasian region, but even in Russia, there is no unified and systematic cargo transportation regulation organization, but low-level railway, waterway, and road transportation combined transportation or collaborative management systems. As a result, the so-called "bottlenecks" and "stuck necks" have become chronic diseases that Russia's unified transportation system has never been able to effectively solve, often causing a large amount of cargo to accumulate in seaports. If these problems are not resolved, the launch of large-scale Eurasian transportation and logistics infrastructure projects will be destined to face economic inefficiency at the beginning, which may eventually make existing transportation system more fragmented. Therefore, in the process of constructing the transportation corridor of the Silk Road Economic Belt within the Eurasian Economic Union countries, we must first solve the economic interconnection of the macro-region. It is necessary to realize the modernization of the unified transportation system management mechanism, meanwhile some countries and the Eurasian Economic Union's integrated institutions must implement corresponding regional, industrial, investment and trade policies. All in all, the transportation corridor of the Silk Road Economic Belt should also become a transportation corridor connecting the economic space of Europe and Asia.

On the other hand, the docking of the SREB and EEU not only has material connotations, but also has important significance in the "docking" of ideas and concepts. The continuous extension of the connotation of the concept of "Greater Eurasia" has theoretically provided more favorable conditions for the construction of an Asia-Europe community with a shared future, while the SREB and EEU docking has given impetus to the development of new Eurasian regionalism. The "Greater Eurasian" concept expands the Eurasian region into the Greater Eurasian region, expands the connotation of SREB and EEU multilateral cooperation, and enhances the level of trust in cooperation. This kind of trust will inevitably promote the smooth docking and efficient cooperation of the SREB and EEU. It's harmonious development conforms to the interests of China, Russia, and other countries of the Eurasian Economic Union, as well as the broader regional actors in Eurasia.

The docking of SREB and EEU is a process not only of promoting regional development, but also of promoting the construction of regional rules. After obtaining the early harvest of specific projects, it becomes very important to use multilateral cooperation platforms to formulate common rules and standards. Use the SREB and EEU docking framework to form general rules in the broad Eurasian space, and use the signing of relevant rules and agreements to form predictable institutional arrangements. The specific design of the common system helps to summarize and improve the regional cooperation model. This is also in line with the spirit of the historic decision jointly made by President Xi Jinping and President Putin to dock the Silk Road Economic Belt and the Eurasian Economic Union.

Promoting the construction of a community with a shared future in such a grand geographic space will inevitably be interfered by various internal and external forces. Various traditional and non-traditional security threats within Eurasia, as well as the diverse characteristics of religion, culture, and society, will adversely affect the process. Some major powers outside the region have their hands on regional issues in many sub-regional spaces in Eurasian Inland. They can use political, economic and military means to obstruct, delay or even undermine regional cooperation.

IV. Summary: The Docking of SREB with EEU Shapes Sino-Russian Relations in the Post-Pandemic Era

After more than 70 years of development, Sino-Russian relations are at the best period in history. The two countries have solid political mutual trust and firmly support each other on issues involving each other's core interests and major concerns. The two sides have established a complete mechanism for high-level exchanges and cooperation in various fields, and have carried out multi-field and all-round cooperation with rich content and strategic significance.

At present, the COVID-19 pandemic is still raging, and countries around the world are still fighting the pandemic. Especially affected by the pandemic, normal international economic and trade relations have not been restored. Anti-globalization and unilateralism have intensified trends and behaviors. In order to shake off the pandemic crisis and maintain their country's hegemony, some Western countries have tried their best to promote unilateralism and isolationism, and they will tear up agreements and harm the interests of other countries. The global order has been challenged like never before.

In the face of changes, it is the right choice for all countries in the world to work together and cooperate for a win-win situation. President Xi Jinping pointed out that international cooperation is inseparable from sincere mutual trust and like-minded partners. ① Russia is China's largest neighbor and an important priority partner for cooperation in various fields. The two sides uphold the concept of sustainable development, actively carry out cooperation in clean energy such as natural gas, take scientific and technological innovation, digital economy, and online e-commerce as new cooperation growth points, and carry out effective cooperation on the utilization and protection of cross-border resources and the construction of cross-border nature reserves. The joint construction of the Belt and Road and the "Greater Eurasian Partnership" share the same concept. The two major initiatives support and promote each other, and they are not incompatible. This will strongly promote regional economic integration and help achieve common sustainable development. With the consolidation of the comprehensive strategic partnership between China and Russia in the new era, the spillover effect brought about by the docking of the two major initiatives has gradually become prominent. Small and medium-sized countries in the Eurasian region gain economic benefits, and the peace and development of the entire region can be

---

① Xi Jinping, "Speech at the Plenary Session of the 23rd St. Petersburg International Economic Forum", China Government Network, June 7, 2019, http://www.gov.cn/gongbao/content/2019/content_5401339.htm.

maintained and continued. As the speed of the transformation of the international landscape continues to accelerate, this docking will also facilitate the establishment of a fair and reasonable new international political and economic order, and lay the foundation for the creation of an Asia-Europe community with a shared future.

References

"China and the Eurasian Economic Union formally sign an economic and trade cooperation agreement", Ministry of Commerce of the People's Republic of China, May 17, 2018, http://www.mofcom.gov.cn/article/ae/ai/201805/20180502745041.shtml.

"China and the Eurasian Economic Union have substantively concluded negotiations on an economic and trade cooperation agreement", Xinhua News Agency, October 1, 2017, http://www.xinhuanet.com/2017-10/01/c_1121756577.htm.

Cong Xiaonan: "The Economic Obstacles and Realistic Choices of China-Eurasian Economic Union FTA—Based on Computable General Equilibrium GMR-CGE", Russian Studies, Issue 1, 2018.

De Yevremenko: "China-Russia Strategic Partnership and the Construction of Greater Eurasia", Foreign Social Sciences, Issue 4, 2017.

"Joint Statement between the People's Republic of China and the Russian Federation on the Docking and Cooperation between the Construction of the Silk Road Economic Belt and the Eurasian Economic Union", May 9, 2015, http://www.xinhuanet.com/world/2015-05/09/c_127780866.htm.

"Joint Statement of the People's Republic of China and the Russian Federation on Docking and Cooperation between the Construction of the Silk Road Economic Belt and the Eurasian Economic Union", Xinhua News Agency, May 9, 2015, http://www.xinhuanet.com//world/2015-05/09/c_127780866.htm.

"Joint Statement of the People's Republic of China and the Russian Federation on Further Deepening the Comprehensive Strategic Partnership of Cooperation", Xinhua News Agency, June 6, 2019, http://www.xinhuanet.com/2019-06/06/c_1124588552.htm.

"Joint Statement on the Effectiveness of the 'Economic and Trade Cooperation Agreement between the People's Republic of China and the Eurasian Economic Union' signed on May 17, 2018", Xinhua News Agency, October 25, 2019, http://www.gov.cn/xinwen/2019-10/25/content_5445095.htm.

"List of Outcomes of the 'Belt and Road' International Cooperation Summit Forum", the official website of the Ministry of Foreign Affairs of China, May 16, 2017, http://www.fmprc.gov.cn/web/zyxw/t1461873.shtm.

Ma Liangwen: "Russia and China are the two pillars of the Eurasian Consortium", Russian Studies, Issue 5, 2018, p. 28.

"Nazarbayev Calls for the Building of a Community with a Shared Future for Europe and Asia", China News Network, November 13, 2019, http://www.chinanews.com/gj/2019/11-13/9006106.shtml.

"The Belt and Road Initiative is Resilient (Expert interpretation)", People's Daily Overseas Edition, March 16, 2020, http://paper.people.com.cn/rmrbhwb/html/2020-03/16/content_1976481.htm.

"The Ministry of Foreign Affairs talks about the outcome of the China-Russia Foreign Ministers' Meeting: Both sides will continue to support each other on issues of core interests", International Online, March 23, 2021, http://news.cri.cn/20210323/df34b8eb-7469-753c-2358-d6e456622c19.html.

Vladimir Putin: Speech at the opening ceremony of the "Belt and Road" International Cooperation Summit Forum, China Investment, Issue 11, 2017, pp. 33-34.

Xi Jinping, "Opening a New Starting Point for Cooperation and Seeking New Driving Forces for Development-Opening Speech at the Roundtable Summit of the 'Belt and Road' International Cooperation Summit Forum", *People's Daily*, May 16, 2017, http://politics.people.com.cn/n1/2017/0516/c1001-29277113.html.

Xi Jinping: "Openness for Greater Prosperity, Innovation for a Better Future—Keynote Speech at the Opening Ceremony of the Boao Forum for Asia 2018 Annual Conference", People's Daily, April 11, 2018.

Xi Jinping: "Promote China-Russia Comprehensive Strategic Partnership to Reach the Peak", People's Daily Overseas Edition, September 12, 2018, http://paper.people.com.cn/rmrbhwb/html/2018-09/12/content_1880724.htm.

Xi Jinping: "Speech at the Plenary Session of the 23rd St. Petersburg International Economic Forum", China Government Network, June 7, 2019, http://www.gov.cn/gongbao/content/2019/content_5401339.htm.

"Xi Jinping Accepts Interview by Russian Media", People's Daily Online, July 4, 2017, http://cpc.people.com.cn/big5/n1/2017/0704/c64094-29380500.html.

"Xi Jinping and the President of Russia jointly witness the commencement ceremony of the Sino-Russian nuclear energy cooperation project", China Broadcasting Network, May 20, 2021, http://china.cnr.cn/news/20210520/t20210520_525490833.shtml.

"Xi Jinping Meets with Russian President Putin", Xinhua News Agency, May 14, 2017, http://www.xinhuanet.com/world/2017-05/14/c_1120969876.htm.

"Xi Jinping's Report at the 19th National Congress of the Communist Party of China", People's Daily Online, January 3, 2018, http://cpc.people.com.cn/n1/2017/1028/c64094-29613660.html.

Zhang Shuhua: "Sino-Russian Cooperation Breaks the Dilemma of World Governance", Global Times, September 27, 2016, https://opinion.huanqiu.com/article/9CaKrnJXO6U.

Belt and Road Initiative and Humanistic Exchange Between China and Ukraine

Olena Shypotilova[*], Svitlana Glovatska[**]

The article analyzes the humanitarian communication and cooperation between China and Ukraine within the concept of Belt and Road. The authors emphasize that this area of cooperation involves intellectual exchange between students, university professors, and enrichment of Ukrainian and Chinese culture. For Ukraine, the project provides an opportunity to use investments, modernize the education sector, and create a platform for the unification of European and Asian civilizations.

Belt and Road Initiative is the largest development project in the history of humankind, aimed at creating and strengthening multinational ties, and strengthening the intensity of economic, cultural and political exchanges. This Chinese initiative remains the largest macroeconomic project in the world. About $ 350 billion is planned by China for specific projects under the 2022 initiative. Completion of the project Belt and Road is scheduled for 2049 (to the 100th anniversary of the establishment of the People's Republic of China), which should lead to the consolidation of 65 countries in vast Euro-Asian space and part of Africa.

---

[*] Olena Shypotilova, PhD, Associate Professor, Odessa National Maritime University.
[**] Svitlana Glovatska, PhD, Associate Professor, Ukrainian Director of CASS-ONMU: Center of China Studies.

Ukraine, as part of Eastern Europe, is located at the crossroads of "paths" and the interests of different countries. For Ukraine, China's new European policy is a certain amount of opportunities. The Belt and Road Initiative can potentially help the Ukrainian economy emerge from the crisis by diversifying opportunities and development ways.

It is important for Ukraine to take into account the strategic nature of European-Chinese relations and to build its relations with China. China's development of economic and infrastructure projects in Central Asia means that in the future on the Europe-China route traffic will grow. It is important for Ukraine to support China's development of the Trans-Caspian route, which connects Europe with Kazakhstan and China through the Caucasus and the Caspian Sea. This route has already allowed Ukraine to send goods through the Black Sea, Georgia and Azerbaijan. In 2016, Georgia signed a Free Trade Agreement with China, and Belarus received observer status in the "16 + 1" format. All this indicates that Belt and Road has great potential for market development, prosperity and strengthening stability throughout the Euro-Asian territory.

Ukraine can use the economic potential of the Belt and Road both for the development of its own national economy and for the successful implementation of European integration. Ukraine must also be prepared for fierce competition in the Belt and Road project, especially for large players (for example, global carriers DHL and UPS). This determines the need to form alliances and build effective relationships with Chinese partners to compete with global companies. However, despite the mention in the press of discussing the possibility of Ukraine's accession to the "16 + 1" format, no official accession talks were actually held, and participation in the Belt and Road project is determined by the relevant roadmap[①].

[①] Kiktenko V. O., "Ukraine in the 'One Belt, One Road project': regional and global dimension", 2018, https://sinologist.com.ua/kiktenko-v-o-ukrayina-v-proekti-odyn-poyas-odyn-shlyah-regionalnyj-ta-globalnyj-vymir/.

V. Kiktenko, Head of the Far East Department of the A. Yu. Krymsky Institute of Oriental Studies of the National Academy of Sciences of Ukraine, President of the Ukrainian Association of Chinese Studies, emphasizes that it is planning Ukrainian-Chinese cooperation and Ukraine's participation in the Belt and Road project and interaction formats. Although there are still differences among European politicians on the Belt and Road Initiative, the economic benefits of this initiative are due to mutual interest and will certainly contribute to the development of transregional cooperation. China's powerful social-economic rise has given rise to the Belt and Road Initiative, which should become an important tool for cooperation between the participating countries. If at first Beijing's initiative was virtually unnoticed in the EU, today the European Parliament and European governments recognize the achievements and prospects of economic cooperation in the framework of Belt and Road. ①

The are many historical studies on this issue. ②The aim of the study is to analyze the achievements and prospects of humanitarian cooperation between Ukraine and China within the concept Belt and Road.

The field of cultural and humanitarian relations is always a special area of

---

① Kiktenko V. O., "Ukraine in the 'One Belt, One Road project': regional and global dimension", 2018, https://sinologist.com.ua/kiktenko-v-o-ukrayina-v-proekti-odyn-poyas-odyn-shlyah-regionalnyj-ta-globalnyj-vymir/.

② Bilorus O. H., "Globalization and security of development", Kyiv: KNEU, 2001; Honcharuk A., "Ukrainian-Chinese strategic partnership at the present stage", 2014, https://sinologist.com.ua/ukrayinsko-kitajske-strategichne-pa; Glovatska S. M., "Ukraine in the global megaproject 'One Belt, One Road'", China-Ukraine: prospects for academic and business cooperation: materials International. scientific-practical conf, Odessa, Phoenix, 2019, pp. 28-31; Kiktenko V. O., "Reforms and openness as a basis for building socialism with Chinese characteristics", Ukraine-China, 2018, No. 14, pp. 28-31; Onishchenko A. V., "Ukraine and China: new realities and prospects of foreign economic cooperation in the XXI century", Scientific Bulletin of Uzhgorod University, Editors: V. P. Mikloda (ed.), M. I. Pityulych, N. M. Gapak and others, Uzhhorod: Uzhhorod National University Publishing House, 2011, Special issue. 33, Part 2, pp. 205-207; Popkov V. V., "China: the new format of globalization", China-Ukraine: prospects for academic and business cooperation: materials International, scientific-practical conf, Odessa, May 27-28, 2019, pp. 18-23; Liui Yenchzhao, Pekna T. V., SunVei, "The Direct investments of Chinese enterprises in Ukraine", Current economic problems, 2012. No. 8 (134), pp. 413-418.

international cooperation. The value of the potential of the humanitarian vector is noted in all large-scale international initiatives and concepts. The Chinese side has announced and launched a major educational project aimed at promoting student exchanges within the countries along Silk Road Economic Belt. The Chinese government annually allocates 10,000 grants for students from countries involved in the construction of the Silk Road Economic Belt, some of which are successfully implemented under the project of the University of Shanghai Cooperation Organization (SCO) ①.

The main directions of the humanitarian vector of the SREB are holding joint Years of Culture, including holding film and television festivals; organizing book fairs; submitting joint applications for registration of world objects UNESCO heritage; increasing tourism exchanges; developing exchanges in the field of sports; expanding cooperation in the medical field; strengthening scientific cooperation, intensification of efforts to protect the environment and conserve biological diversity; using Internet platforms and new media to create a friendly cultural environment and positive public opinion.

In 2010, Ukraine's relations with China were further intensified, as evidenced by a series of official visits by the two countries' leaders in 2010 – 2013, during which the parties signed a number of important documents on deepening cooperation between Kyiv and Beijing, including "Joint Declaration on the Establishment and Development of Strategic Partnership Relations between Ukraine and China", "Treaty on Friendship and Cooperation between Ukraine and China", "Joint Declaration of Ukraine and China on Further Deepening Strategic Partnership" and "Joint Statement On Developing Strategic Partnership between Ukraine and China for 2014 – 2018".

In the following years, a series of visits took place at the level of foreign

---

① Kulyntsev Yu. V., "The Strategy of Development and Silk Road Economic Belt Concept: Integration Potential of Cultural and Humanitarian Cooperation", China in world and regional politics. History and modernity, Issue XXIV: annual edition / comp., Resp. ed. E. I. Safronova, Moscow, pp. 131 – 144.

ministers, parliaments, and public organizations. The central topics for the dialogue of Ukrainian-Chinese relations in 2016 – 2019 were the discussion of cooperation between countries in international organizations, dialogue on cooperation in the forum of the Belt and Road Initiative and others. Moreover, a series of talks was held at the level of business structures on expanding cooperation and attracting investment, primarily for the development of the high-tech sector of the Ukrainian space economy, infrastructure, energy saving and the IT sector.

The strategic task for Ukraine is to intensify the attraction of Chinese investments to increase exports of goods with high added value, as well as to expand cooperation in the industrial-innovative and scientific spheres. No less important issue for Ukraine is the creation of technology parks and technological development zones with the participation of Chinese capital. It is also important for Ukraine to finance large infrastructure facilities and agricultural projects in China, in connection with which China plans to allocate 10 billion dollars. An equally important task is for Ukraine to obtain cheap loans from China to stabilize the Ukrainian economy in the face of hybrid Russian aggression and the spread of the COVID – 19 epidemic. Under the current circumstances, Chinese banks may become an additional source of external loans, and even alternatives to IMF credit revenues for Ukraine.

An important area of the Ukrainian-Chinese strategic partnership is relations in the humanitarian and cultural spheres. It is known that the works of classics of Ukrainian literature were published during the Ukrainian Soviet Socialist Republic. Already in 1992, the first special research center on Ukraine (now the Center for Ukrainian Studies) was established at Wuhan University. In 2002, the Days of Ukrainian Culture were held in China for the first time, which contributed to a deeper understanding of Ukrainian culture by the Chinese people. The international conference "Ukraine-China: Ways to Cooperation" took place in Kiev. Currently, the Joint Ukrainian-Chinese Commission in the field of culture is actively coordinating and planning cultural cooperation between Ukraine and China. At the same time, about 2,000 Chinese students study in Ukrainian universities. Ukrainian-Chinese relations in the field of science and aerospace are developing dynamically. The Ukrainian-Chinese Belt and Road Forum is being actively held, relations are developing at the level of the Academy of Sciences of the two countries, and the Confucius Institute is active in Kiev. Ukraine should intensify research on the study of Chinese history, philosophy, language and culture, as the country still has an acute shortage of sinologists.

According to the report of the Minister of Education of Ukraine D. Tabachnyk on June 20, 2011, about 1,000 foreign students from Ukraine studied in China and about 6,000 Chinese students studied in Ukraine. According to the UNESCO report, Ukrainian universities have become especially popular with Chinese students. The Ministry of Education and Science of Ukraine reported that about 10% of foreign students in Ukraine are Chinese citizens[①].

In 2016, the Chinese-Ukrainian cultural program was extremely diverse. The most important was the opening of Taras Shevchenko's exhibition at the Beijing Art Museum in Daxing District on September 23. The museum has become a platform for various exhibitions featuring works by contemporary Chinese and Ukrainian artists, sculptors and photographers. Over the past few years, more than 100 Sino-Ukrainian cultural events have been held, as well as more than 3,800 different commercial exhibitions and exchanges. In recent years, Ukraine has been experiencing a cultural and linguistic "fever of China" and the unique Ukrainian culture is of great interest to the Chinese people.

In autumn 2016, a Ukrainian delegation led by the Minister of Culture of Ukraine E. Nyschuk visited China. During the talks between E. Nyschuk and Chinese Minister of Culture Luo Shugang, the establishment of a Ukrainian cul-

---

① Liu Xiangzhong, "Social – cultural exchange between China and Ukraine: history and present", 2018, https://sinologist.com.ua/lyu – syanchzhun – sotsialno – kulturnyj – obmin – mizh – kytayem – ta – ukrayinoyu – istoriya – ta – suchasnist/.

tural center in China, as well as the promotion of folk crafts and cultural events by both countries were discussed. The Chinese side also paid great attention to material and technical assistance to Ukraine in the field of education. 23, 500 new computers were purchased for Ukrainian secondary schools and three linguistic facilities for the Kyiv Gymnasium of Oriental Languages, where about 600 children study Chinese.

The International Trade Organization "Silk Road" has allocated $ 200, 000 to Ukraine for educational programs for students of secondary schools with special needs.

After Ukraine's independence, as the largest country in Europe, Chinese scholars became interested in studying and translating Ukrainian history and realities from Ukraine's point of view. According to incomplete statistics, the following works on the history of Ukraine have been published: the translation of the *History of Ukraine* by Western scholar Paul Robert Magochi (Chinese Encyclopedia Publishing House, 2009), *Slavic Culture* edited by Liu Zuxi (Zhejiang People's Publishing House, 1993) contains special section on Ukrainian culture; Zhao Yunzhong's *Ukraine: Difficult Historical Paths* (published by East China Normal University Press, 2005), Li Yan's *Don't Forget about the Past and Face the Future: A Study of the Holodomor of the Soviet Union from 1932 to 1933 and Relations between Ukraine and Russia* (Social Sciences Academic Press, 2014), Wen Yi's *Ukraine: Janus in Smoke* (CITIC Press Group, 2016).

Works on Ukrainian politics, economics and diplomacy were published: translation of Kuchma's *Ukraine: Politics, Economics and Diplomacy* (Eastern Publishing House, 2001), Song Dongfang's *Ukrainian Travels* (Nanjing University Press, 2016), Shen Lihua's *Studies on the Relationship between Russia and Ukraine after the Collapse of the Soviet Union* (Heilongjiang University Press, 2017), Ren Fei's *Ukrainian History and Modern Political Economy* (Economic Science Press, 2017), Gu Zhihong's *Very Neighboring Countries: Ukraine and Russia* (University of National Defense Press, 2000), translation of Pavlov's

Chapter 4   Belt and Road Initiative and Global Development Initiatives   515

Transitional Macroeconomics: *Ukrainian Reform* (Democracy and Construction Press, 2001), Zhang Hong's *Conflict and Cooperation*: *Interpretation of Economic Relations between Ukraine and Russia (1991 – 2008)* (Intellectual Property Publishing House, 2010), Zhang Hong's *Study of Political Stability in Transition Countries*: *Theoretical Reflections on the Ukrainian Crisis* (Social Sciences Academic Press, 2016) . In addition, Huang Yuezhao of the Institute of Russian, Eastern European and Central Asian Studies of the Chinese Academy of Social Sciences published the *New Ukrainian-Chinese Dictionary* (The Commercial Press, 2013), which is larger than the 1990 dictionary. ①

On September 25 – 27, 2018, the Days of Ukrainian Culture in China took place in Beijing and Dunhuang. The decision to hold these events was made by the Governments of Ukraine and China following the fourth meeting of the Ukrainian-Chinese Subcommittee on Cultural Cooperation and the Third Meeting of the Commission on Cooperation between the Government of Ukraine and the Government of the People's Republic of China②.

On September 25, in Beijing, Minister of Culture of Ukraine Ye. Nyschuk and Minister of Culture and Tourism of the People's Republic of China Luo Shugang officially opened the Days of Ukrainian Culture in China. The events within the framework of the "Days of Culture" began with the grand opening of the exhibition of cultural monuments and decorative and applied arts from the museums of Ukraine "Colorful Rose in a Golden Wreath" in the architectural and artistic museum complex of the Palace Museum of China. Visitors were able to get acquainted with Ukrainian jewelry and antiquities, 10 – 12 centuries of amber, which from ancient times to the present is used for the manufacture of jewelry, that from the time of Trypillia (one of the oldest agricultural civilizations),

---

① Liu Xiangzhong, "Social-cultural exchange between China and Ukraine: history and present", 2018, https: //sinologist. com. ua/lyu – syanchzhun – sotsialno – kulturnyj – obmin – mizh – kytayem – ta – ukrayinoyu – istoriya – ta – suchasnist/.

② "Days of Ukrainian Culture in the People's Republic of China", https: //sinologist. com. ua/dni – kultury – ukrayiny – u – kytajskij – narodnij – respublitsi/.

Scythians to the era of KyivanRus (the greatest flowering of Ukrainian statehood in the Middle Ages).

"I can't help but be proud that Ukrainian relics are presented in the largest palace complex in the world, the Palace Museum, which has sincerely opened its doors for the presentation of Ukrainian culture", said Minister of Culture of Ukraine E. Nyschuk. "I am confident that in the future friendship and mutual understanding between our countries will deepen, contribute to the expansion of the artistic space, and serve to increase the interest of ordinary citizens in the creative achievements of artists of Ukrainian and Chinese cultures. I sincerely wish success to the Days of Ukrainian Culture in China and I hope that Ukrainian culture will leave an unforgettable impression in the hearts of the Chinese people" [①].

During the Days of Culture there were performances of the National Honored Academic Folk Choir of Ukraine named after G. G. Veryovka, an exhibition of works by the famous Ukrainian photographer V. Kozyuk, as well as master classes of Petrykivka painting. As part of the Days of Culture, the Ukrainian delegation took part in the International Cultural EXPO "Silk Road" (Dunhuang, September 27 – 28, 2018), where Ukraine was represented as the main guest country.

Cooperation with the regions of Ukraine did not escape China's interest. For example, in Odessa, international scientific conferences were held within the project Belt and Road on the basis of Odessa National Maritime University. Rector of ONMU, Professor S. V. Rudenko stressed that Odessa National Maritime University works under direct agreements with Tianjin University, Northwestern Polytechnical University (Shanghai), Shanghai Maritime University (Shanghai), Chinese University of Geosciences (Wuhan), Wuhan University of Science and Technology (Wuhan), Dalian University of Technology

---

① "Days of Ukrainian Culture in the People's Republic of China", https://sinologist.com.ua/dni-kultury-ukrayiny-u-kytajskij-narodnij-respublitsi/.

(Dalian) and the Institute of Sociology of the Chinese Academy of Sciences (Beijing) [1].

The history of cooperation between Odessa National Maritime University and the Institute of Sociology of the Chinese Academy of Social Sciences began in 2016 with the signing of the Agreement on Cooperation and Organization of the First International Scientific Conference "Social Transformations: Family, Marriage, Youth, Middle Class and Innovation Management of Countries along the New Silk Road" on September 14 – 18, 2016.

From April 24 to 26, 2017, with the support of the Consulate General in Odessa and the Southern Research Center of the Transport Academy of Sciences of Ukraine, Odessa National Maritime University together with the Institute of Sociology of the Chinese Academy of Social Sciences held II International Scientific Conference "Social Transformations: Family, Marriage , Youth, Transport and Innovation Management of Countries along the New Silk Road" .

On April 25, 2017, at a solemn meeting of the Academic Council of ONMU, an agreement was signed between ONMU and the Institute of Sociology of the Chinese Academy of Social Sciences on the establishment of the Science Center for Social Development Studies of the Belt and Road. The grand opening ceremony of the Science Center was attended by representatives of the Institute of Sociology of the Chinese Academy of Social Sciences, led by the Deputy Director of the Institute of Sociology, Mr. Zhao Kebin and Consul General of the People's Republic of China in Odessa, Ms. Zhao Xiangong[2].

On October 30, 2018, within the framework of the Third Scientific Confer-

---

[1] Shypotilova O. P, Kozhanov A. V. , "Pages of the history of cooperation of Odessa National Maritime University with the People's Republic of China", Chinese civilization: traditions and modernity: materials of the XIV International Scientific Conference, November 5, 2020, Kyiv: Helvetica Publishing House, pp. 136 – 139.

[2] Shypotilova O. P, Kozhanov A. V. , "Pages of the history of cooperation of Odessa National Maritime University with the People's Republic of China", Chinese civilization: traditions and modernity: materials of the XIV International Scientific Conference, November 5, 2020, Kyiv: Helvetica Publishing House, pp. 136 – 139.

ence "Social Development of Countries along the Belt and Road: Development of the New Silk Road in Ukraine", the University opened an office of the Belt and Road Research Center for Social Development Studies. Classes are held here with the participation of scientists from the two countries, and there is Chinese literature on the history, economy, traditions and development strategy of China.

On December 5 – 8, 2017, the Science Center for Social Development Studies of the Belt and Road (CASS-ONMU) organized the First Sino-Ukrainian Scientific and Academic Dialogue "Chinese Opportunities for Ukraine" in Beijing (China). The delegation of ONMU consisting of eight people was headed by the rector of the university prof. S. V. Rudenko. Each participant in the dialogue made a report and made proposals for expanding cooperation between ONMU and CASS.

In 2019, a photo exhibition dedicated to the 70th anniversary of the establishment of the People's Republic of China was opened at Odessa National Maritime University. This exhibition allowed students, scholars and anyone interested to learn more about the history of China's development and success. The exhibition is dedicated to the achievements of China, which was held at ONMU together with the Consulate General of the People's Republic of China in Odessa and the Chinese Academy of Social Sciences. In March 2019, ONMU hosted an exhibition dedicated to the 40th anniversary of the policy of reforms and opening up of China.

On October 16, 2019, the students of ONMU, who won the competition of student works on Chinese research, dedicated to the 70th anniversary of the establishment of the People's Republic of China, were awarded. The winners of the competition were awarded diplomas of ONMU and KASN. The diplomas of the winners were presented by the rector of ONMU, prof. S. V. Rudenko; Director of the Bureau of International Cooperation of the Chinese Academy of Social Sciences, Prof. Wang Lei; Director of the Institute of Social Development of the Chinese Academy of Social Sciences, Prof. Zhang Yi.

Thus, in the framework of humanitarian cooperation within the framework of the concept of the Belt and Road between the People's Republic of China and Ukraine, fruitful cooperation has been established, which has its achievements and future prospects. The activities include exchanges between students, internships for teachers, holding scientific forums, seminars and conferences, Days of Culture, art exhibitions. Bridges of unity of the Ukrainian and Chinese nations were created, which allowed to ensure intercultural communication and deepening of globalization processes.

References

Bilorus O. H. , "Globalization and security of development", 2001, Kyiv: KNEU.

"Days of Ukrainian Culture in the People's Republic of China", https: // sinologist. com. ua/dni – kultury – ukrayiny – u – kytajskij – narodnij – respublitsi/.

Glovatska S. M. , "Ukraine in the global megaproject 'One Belt, One Road'", China – Ukraine: prospects for academic and business cooperation: materials International, scientific – practical conf, (Odessa, May 27 – 28, 2019), Odessa, Phoenix, 2019.

Honcharuk A. , "Ukrainian – Chinese strategic partnership at the present stage", 2014, https: //sinologist. com. ua/ukrayinsko – kitajske – strategichne – pa.

Kiktenko V. O. , "Reforms and openness as a basis for building socialism with Chinese characteristics", Ukraine – China, 2018, No. 14.

Kiktenko V. O. , "Ukraine in the "One Belt, One Road project": regional and global dimension", 2018, https: //sinologist. com. ua/kiktenko – v – o – ukrayina – v – proekti – odyn – poyas – odyn – shlyah – regionalnyj – ta – globalnyj – vymir/.

Kulyntsev Yu. V. , "The Strategy of Development and Silk Road Economic Belt Concept: Integration Potential of Cultural and Humanitarian Cooperation",

China in world and regional politics, History and modernity, Issue XXIV: annual edition / comp., Resp. ed. E. I. Safronova, Moscow.

Liui Yenchzhao, Pekna T. V., SunVei., "The Direct investments of Chinese enterprises in Ukraine", *Current economic problems*, 2012, No. 8.

Liu Xiangzhong., "Social – cultural exchange between China and Ukraine: history and present", 2018, https://sinologist.com.ua/lyu – syanchzhun – sotsialno – kulturnyj – obmin – mizh – kytayem – ta – ukrayinoyu – istoriya – ta – suchasnist/.

Onishchenko A. V., "Ukraine and China: new realities and prospects of foreign economic cooperation in the XXI century", Scientific Bulletin of Uzhgorod University: Series: Economics, Editors: V. P. Mikloda (ed.), M. I. Pityulych, N. M. Gapak and others, Uzhhorod: Uzhhorod National University Publishing House, 2011, Special issue. 33. Part 2.

Popkov V. V., "China: the new format of globalization", China – Ukraine: prospects for academic and business cooperation: materials International, scientific – practical conf (Odessa, May 27 – 28, 2019), Odessa, Phoenix, 2019.

Shypotilova O. P, Kozhanov A. V., "Pages of the history of cooperation of Odessa National Maritime University with the People's Republic of China", Chinese civilization: traditions and modernity: materials of the XIV International Scientific Conference, November 5, 2020, Kyiv: Helvetica Publishing House.

"The G7 will announce an infrastructure project as opposed to China", 2021, https://www.ukrinform.ua/rubric – world/3263705 – g7 – ogolosit – pro – infrastrukturnij – proekt – na – protivagu – kitau – zmi.html.

Belt and Road Initiative: The Retrospect of the Past 30 Years and Deepening of Education Cooperation Between China and Georgia

Lu Yujing[*]

Both being countries with a long history and attaching great importance to education, China and Georgia have great potential for cooperation in the field of education. The Chinese language education in Georgia has gone through a course of nearly 30 years. Chinese language learning has brought scholarships, opportunities to study in China's universities and employment opportunities to Georgian youth. In particular, the establishment and functioning of Confucius Institute has served as a platform for educational exchanges. The introduction of Chinese language into the education system of Georgia has provided primary and middle school students with the opportunity to choose Chinese as a second foreign language, which is the expectation for cooperation in education, culture, science and other aspects of the senior leaders of the two countries. Education in the Georgian language and Georgian studies in China have also been developing. Future educational exchanges and cooperation should be further deepened.

---

[*] Lu Yujing, Professor, Lanzhou University, Director of Confucius Institute of Tbilisi Open Teaching University.

Georgia as a small country has a long history and well-established culture. Like China, the government and people of Georgia also regard education as vital, and the proportion of the population in Georgia receiving education is very high. Government investment in education is also high. For example, in 2016, the budget of the Ministry of Education and Science in Georgia was 905 million-lari ($410.4 million). And, "education in Georgia is free from age 6 to age 18. Free of charge for education is a constitutional requirement. The state provides related expenses, including textbooks and laptops, for free."[①] After the independence of Georgia in 1992, the development of education, science and technology was seriously interfered by the political and economic situation and was in a very difficult situation. However, the process of reform was relatively fast. Russia's influence in Georgia's science and education sector is shrinking, while the role of the West is expanding. [②]Many people in Georgia can speak multiple languages. In addition to English being the first foreign language, Russian, Turkish, German and some other languages go into the category of the second foreign language courses in public schools. What's more, in early 2019, Chinese was planned to be incorporated into the primary and secondary education system. The students are in the same school from kindergarten to high school. The rate of college degree holders among the people in professions like waiters and taxi drivers being very high is a proof that all Georgian people has university education background.

Since the establishment of diplomatic ties between China and Georgia in 1992, exchanges in the field of education and culture have grown increasingly frequent from scratch. But so far, the most significant part of educational exchanges has been in language education, especially Chinese language teaching in Georgia, as well as various free courses and scholarships provided to Georgian

---

① Bureau of International Labor Affairs, U. S. Department of Labor, *Findings on the Worst Forms of Child Labor (2001)*, 2002.

② Yang Shu, "The present state of Georgia Education and Science", *Eastern and Central Asian Studies*, No. 5, 1997.

students by non-profit organizations such as Confucius Institutes. Other cooperation is just beginning to emerge, and there is great potential to be tapped in this cooperation.

I. Three Stages of Chinese Education in Georgia

The educational exchanges between China and Georgia are based on the premise of the establishment of friendly relations between the two countries and the continuous exploration and deepening of cooperation.

In March 2011, the then Chinese Ambassador to Georgia Chen Jianfu called on the then Georgian President Shevardnadze, who recalled the good relations between Georgia and China after the collapse of the Soviet Union, who, while in power, actively promoted plans to revive the ancient Silk Road. Under the plan, roads linking Asian and the European continent would pass through Central Asia and the Caucasus, greatly reducing the time it takes to travel by land between the Eurasian continents[①]. It is precisely because of such bilateral relations and the needs of economic development that the two countries have frequent political, economic and cultural exchanges, which need the support of language.

The Georgian government has always supported Chinese language teaching. In April 2006, at the invitation of the then Chinese President Hu Jintao, the then Georgian President Mikheil Saakashvili visited China and said, Chinese youth are the future of China. They are smart, outstanding and educated patriots. Chinese is the language of the 21st century, and he hopes that more young Georgians will learn Chinese and strengthen exchanges with China[②].

[①] "Former Georgian President 'LaoXie' and China", *The Paper*, July 7, 2014, https://www.thepaper.cn/newsDetail_ forward_ 1254682.

[②] The State Council of the People's Republic of China, "On the eve of Georgian President's visit to China, he expresses great importance to relations with China", April 9, 2006, http://www.gov.cn/zwjw/2006 - 04/09/content_ 249291. htm.

The educational exchanges between China and Georgia started from Chinese language teaching in Georgia, which is around the turn of the century. After more than 20 years, it has trained a group of talents who understand Chinese language and Chinese culture and are active in different industries such as education, tourism and commerce in Georgia, contributing to the culture and economy of the two countries.

Chinese teaching in Georgia has gone through three stages: the beginning of Chinese education in Georgia; the establishment of Confucius Institutes which expanded the scope of Chinese language education; the new development of Chinese language after entering Georgian education system in public schools.

(i) Department of Chinese, School of Oriental and African Studies: the beginning of Chinese education and research (1992 – 2007)

Tbilisi Institute of Asia and Africa was the first institution to teach Chinese and do Chinese studies in Georgia. In 1992, Tbilisi Institute of Asia and Africa set up its Chinese Department, which enrolls 60 – 70 students every year. It was taught by Liu Guangwen, a Chinese lived in Georgia, and most of the later Sinologists were being taught by from her[①]. From the very beginning, the Chinese Embassy in Georgia helped the Chinese language teaching in the school. The embassy contacted universities in China to send oral language teachers to School of Oriental and African Studies every year. Since 1995, many Chinese majors have opportunity to study in China for one year, while some excellent learners get funded to study for a master's or doctor's degree in China. These students become the backbone in Georgia to do Chinese teaching and Chinese culture study. The once a Chinese learner, then took to the stage of Chinese teaching. Some of these learners are engaged in jobs related to the Chinese language and Chinese people, like being in enterprises, government departments, or tourism.

---

① Marine Jibladze, "Sinoligy and Chinese Language Teaching in Georgia", *Chinese Teaching in the World*, No. 4, 2004.

(ii) **The establishment of Confucius Institutes: promoting language and culture exchange (2008 – 2018)**

From 2008 to 2010, with the support of the Confucius Institute Headquarters, Lanzhou University and Tbilisi Free University cooperated to establish a Confucius Institute at Free University, and Chinese education in Georgia entered a new stage. The Confucius Institute has started Chinese language courses in many universities and public and private schools in Tbilisi to meet students' demand for Chinese language learning. As time goes by, more and more students join the team of Chinese learning.

In November 2017, the Confucius Classroom at Tbilisi Open University was opened. As always, the Confucius Classroom is committed to helping students who want to learn Chinese and learn about Chinese culture. By the time it was upgraded to a Confucius Institute in December 2019[①], it was teaching Chinese in 30 schools and 4 universities.

In addition to Chinese language teaching, the Confucius Institute helped the Georgian people to understand China and Chinese culture through various cultural activities. The annual Confucius Institute Spring Festival Gala, cultural activities such as on Mid-Autumn Festival and Dragon Boat Festival, the "Meet us on Saturdays", and the "Meeting Chinese Culture on Campus" held from time to time in different schools provide the Georgian people chance of close contact with different aspects of Chinese culture.

The two Confucius Institutes, each with its own strengths, have brought convenience to local people of all ages and different walks of life who are interested in learning Chinese and learning about Chinese culture.

In June 2020, Xinjiang Medical University and Kutaisi University jointly build the third Confucius Institute. It is believed that, like the first two, it will

---

① Belt and Road Portal, "Confucius Institute of the Open University of Tbilisi in Georgia was officially inaugurated", December 22, 2019, https://www.yidaiyilu.gov.cn/xwzx/hwxw/113409.htm.

play crucial role in the cultural exchange between the two countries.

In addition to participating in teaching and cultural activities, Confucius Institutes' volunteers and teachers have conducted some research related to Chinese teaching in Georgia, such as "Investigation and Research on Chinese Teaching in Georgia", "A Study on the Motivation of Georgian Middle School Students in Chinese Learning", "Case Study of Chinese Classroom Management in Georgian Schools". These attempts on the one hand can provide an in-depth understanding of the education situation in Georgia, and on the other hand, provide reference content for Chinese teaching there, so as to promote education through research.

Similarly, Georgian students who have the opportunity to study in China through Scholarships of China for the Georgian Citizens also focus on a certain aspect of bilateral relations. The doctoral thesis "Analysis of the Status Quo and Future Prospects of China – Georgia Relations" written by Nino Tetunashvili, then an overseas student in East China Normal University in 2016 is a case in point.

(iii) Chinese language included in Georgian education system: new opportunities and challenges (2019 –)

In February 2019, Chinese was introduced into the Georgian education system. "The Ministry of Education of Georgia announced that from the beginning of the new school year, Chinese will become a compulsory second foreign language in all primary and secondary schools in Georgia. Parents can now choose between Chinese and Russian. English is now the first foreign language in Georgia. Russian is the second foreign language spoken in this former Soviet republic. After Russian, some Georgian schools have chosen to teach Italian, French and German. Local pupils are required to learn English from the first grade. Starting from the fifth grade, they begin to choose to learn a second foreign language. Parents often choose Russian, a non-European language, as their second foreign language. But in recent years, Chinese language has become increasingly popular in Georgia. More and more parents called for opening Chinese lessons in school①. "Confucius Institutes have been operating in Georgia for a long time. People used to be able to get Chinese education through Confucius Institutes. Some universities in Georgia also offer courses on Orientalism in the study of China", said Chitadze, a scholar of politics. Prior than that, Georgia's Minister of Education and Science, Bakiashvili and the Chinese ambassador to Georgia signed a memorandum in Tbilisi, which mentioned that in the field of Chinese education, China will provide assistance to Georgia, including training Chinese language teachers for Georgia.

There is still much to be done after the Chinese language has entered the education system, and there is still a long way to go. Some of the Georgian people and a small number of those engaged in higher or secondary education, hold opposite opinion to Chinese teaching and learning. They only see the surface of the problem, and apparently they do not understand that Chinese people are meant to help them.

In January 2020, the opening ceremony and ribbon-cutting ceremony of the China Institute of Foreign Education (Georgia) under the banner of China Foreign Education Group were held②. Guangzhou Institute for Foreign Studies has sent Chinese language teachers to work in China Institute of Foreign Education. The establishment and operation of this institute marks another mode of educational cooperation besides Confucius Institutes.

Under the new situation, when Chinese becomes a compulsory course and being taught in more campuses, a set of local textbooks is in great need. In December 2020, The Georgian-Chinese language textbook *Learning Chinese with Ease*, compiled by teachers of the Confucius Institute at Tbilisi Open University,

---

① Www. guancha. cn, "Chinese becomes a required second language in Georgia", February 23, 2019, https: //www. guancha. cn/internation/2019_ 02_ 23_ 491150. shtml.

② Sohu. com, "The establishment of a school by the China foreign education group in Georgia has attracted the attention of the country's parliamentary speaker and the ambassador to China", January 13, 2020, https: //www. sohu. com/a/366439914_ 100195858.

was published, bringing convenience to the majority of school students as well as those who are beginning to learn Chinese. It is possible to unify the teaching materials and the teaching progress. This textbook makes the life of school students who only know Georgian and some Georgian teachers in schools join the ranks of learning Chinese easily.

II. Georgian Language Teaching and Georgian Studies in China

Compared with Chinese education in Georgia, Georgian language education and Georgian studies in China started a few years later. It started gradually under the background of the Belt and Road Initiative and the cooperation agreement between China and Georgia.

During the visits to Central and Southeast Asian countries in September and October 2013, Chinese President Xi Jinping put forward the major initiatives of jointly building the Silk Road Economic Belt and the 21st Century Maritime Silk Road, which have drawn high attention from the international community. A series of international summits, forums, seminars and expos with the theme of "Belt and Road" have been successfully held in various localities, which have played an important role in enhancing understanding, building consensus and deepening cooperation. As of January 30, 2021, China has signed 205 cooperation documents with 171 countries and international organizations on jointly building Belt and Road. ①China and Georgia signed a memorandum of cooperation relatively early.

On March 9, 2015, the Ministry of Commerce of China and the Ministry of Economy and Sustainable Development of Georgia signed a Joint Statement on the Launch of China-Georgia Free Trade Agreement Negotiation Feasibility Study

---

① Belt and Road Portal, "List of countries that have signed cooperation documents with China to jointly build the Belt and Road", https://www.yidaiyilu.gov.cn/xwzx/roll/77298.htm.

in Beijing, agreeing to set up a joint expert group as soon as possible and launch the project. The two sides also signed a memorandum of understanding on strengthening cooperation in building the Silk Road Economic Belt. The two sides expressed willingness to, within the above-stated framework, jointly promote economic and trade cooperation and comprehensively upgrade the level of trade, investment, economic and technological cooperation and infrastructure connectivity[1].

It is worth mentioning that the New Silk Road University Alliance was founded. On May 22, 2015, nearly 100 universities from 22 countries and regions joined the New Silk Road University Alliance, which was initiated by Xi'an Jiaotong University. The Alliance is a non-governmental, non-profit, open, international higher education cooperation platform established by universities at home and abroad with the theme of "jointly building an education cooperation platform to promote regional openness and development" . Promote exchanges and cooperation among universities of countries and regions along the "New Silk Road Economic Belt" in such fields as inter-college exchange, personnel training, scientific research cooperation, cultural communication, policy research, and medical services, so as to enhance understanding and friendship among young people and cultivate high-quality and versatile talents with an international perspective. It serves the development and construction along the "New Silk Road Economic Belt" and the Eurasian region. By the end of 2018, 151 universities from 38 countries and regions had become members of the New Silk Road University Alliance, forming a platform for higher education cooperation covering five continents and carrying out diversified exchanges and cooperation[2].

The Silk Road (Dunhuang) International Cultural Expo held in October, 2015 is another example of cooperation in education. Fudan University, Beijing

---

[1] Belt and Road Portal, "China and Georgia sign cooperation document on joint construction of Silk Road Economic Belt", March 10, 2015, https://www.yidaiyilu.gov.cn/xwzx/hwxw/77005.htm.

[2] Xi' an Jiaotong University, "Silk Road University Alliance", December 28, 2018, http://www.xjtu.edu.cn/gjjl/sczldxlm.htm.

Normal University, Lanzhou University, and Russia's Ural State University of Economics, South Korea's Pukyong National University and other 41 Chinese and foreign universities founded the strategic alliance, to explore transnational cultivation and cross-border flow of talent training mechanism, cultivating high-quality talents with international vision. On the same day, 46 universities reached the Dunhuang Consensus and jointly established the think tank of the Belt and Road International Union of Colleges and Universities. The Alliance aimed at jointly build a Belt and Road higher education community, promote comprehensive exchanges and cooperation in education, science and technology, culture and other fields among universities of countries and regions along the Belt and Road, and serve the economic and social development of countries and regions along the Belt and Road[①].

In this context, the establishment of the Center for Georgian Studies and the preparation of the Georgian language program are well-reasoned. In June 2017, Lanzhou University established the Georgian Research Center, "forming an academic team of experts and scholars in the fields of education, economics, literature, culturology, linguistics, law and other disciplines"[②]. Researchers have published many papers on Georgian studies. Che Rushan and Xu Xu's "Foundation and Potential of China-Georgia Higher Education Cooperation" is one example.

In October 2019, "China Research Center" was set up in Georgian University of Science and Technology, which is dedicated to the study of all aspects of China. The Center has held two international conferences to discuss various issues in Sino-Georgian educational, cultural and economic exchanges.

Peking University offered Georgian language courses to Russian major

---

① Sina, "47 Chinese and foreign universities reached the 'Dunhuang Consensus' and established the Belt and Road University Alliance", October 17, 2015, http://news.sina.com.cn/c/2015-10-17/doc-ifxivsee8519127.shtml.

② "Georgia Research Center of Lanzhou University (Introduction)", August 19, 2018, http://grc.lzu.edu.cn/jianjie/info-5000.shtml.

students before 2016. Natalia Maisuradze's textbook *Crash Georgian* was published by Peking University in 2016, becoming the first textbook for Chinese people to learn Georgian. Prior to that, Georgian language major with 4 years of schooling was approved to be established in Beijing Foreign Studies University in 2015[1].

The establishment of the above institutions, professional preparation, and publication of textbooks have become a stepping stone for Georgian language learning and Georgian studies. It is quite hopeful to form a team of researchers who understand Georgian language, economy and culture gradually.

In addition, in the past few years after the establishment of the Confucius Institutes, teachers, volunteers and some employees of Chinese enterprises in Georgia started to learn Georgian language. They learned Georgian after their arrival in Tbilis in order to be able to use it in daily life. Some of those who left Georgia and returned to China still continued to learn it out of love.

But so far, in China only a few people know Georgia or understand Georgian culture. Communicating in English or Russian with each other, to some extent, restrictes or even hinders the depth of the exchange. Entry-level Georgian does not help education and cultural exchange. Enterprises is still in urgent need of available Chinese-Geogian language users, but relying on Georgia's Chinese student is always insufficient. After all, because of culture difference, mutual understanding is difficult. It is expected that in the near future, China's Georgian major students will be able to fill the gap.

III. Multiple Aspects of Sino-Georgian Educational Exchange

Educational exchanges between China and Georgia are manifested in multi-

---

[1] Beijing Foreign Studies University, "8 non-universal language majors in our school have been approved for establishment", March 2, 2016, https://news.bfsu.edu.cn/archives/253759.

ple levels and forms. High-level officials' talks on strengthening cooperation and that is a guide in language and cultural exchange; Cooperation between educational institutions, research institutions and cultural groups of the two countries is exploring a win-win mode of cooperation in education and culture; Language learners' going to the other country for further study as individuals is a result of educational cooperation.

(i) Leading role of ambassadors and high-level officials in educational exchanges

In May 2012, the "Stories of Chinese Characters" public course, sponsored by the Chinese Embassy in Georgia and co-sponsored by the Confucius Institute in Georgia, was officially launched to face the Ministry of Education of Georgia, the teachers and students of 2 universities and 17 public schools. About 100 people attended the event, including school leaders, teachers and students, as well as mainstream media from both China and Georgia[①].

"In 2013, China-Georgia relations grew steadily with sound momentum of cooperation and exchanges in various fields…Cultural and people-to-people exchanges between the two countries were very active. Confucius Institute at Tbilisi Free University was functioning well. In May, the 12th 'Chinese Bridge' Final Competition, Chinese Proficiency Competition for College Students in Georgia was successfully held. In June, an award ceremony was held in Georgia to essays on 'China in the eyes of Georgians'. In August, the activities of Georgian Culture Day were successfully held in China. China also held acrobatic performances and 'Sino-Georgian Martial Arts Exchange' and other activities in Georgia."[②] This description is an epitome of Sino-Georgian cultural exchanges

---

① ChinaNews, "Georgia University of Science and Technology Middle School Principal, Teachers and Students Fall in Love with 'The Story of Chinese Characters'", May 17, 2012, https://www.chinanews.com/hwjy/2012/05-17/3896797.shtml.

② Ministry of Foreign Affairs of People's Republic of China, https://www.fmprc.gov.cn/mfa_eng/wjb_663304/zzjg_663340/dozys_664276/gjlb_664280/3170_664312/.

in recent years, and the activities are becoming routines.

In February 2014, the then Chinese Ambassador Yue Bin was invited to Tbilisi Public School No. 98 to give a lecture on Chinese history and culture, to more than 40 students from Class 1, Grade 6. The principal of the school listened to the lecture together with around 10 teachers from the school. In a standard 45-minute session, ambassador Yue through the Chinese idiom "extensive and profound", told the story of ancient Chinese philosophy, poetry, literature, music, art, construction process, the four great inventions to introduce rich cultural heritage. He elaborated profoundly on the large scale, exquisite quality, rich connotation, inclusive characteristics of Chinese culture, and interpreted Chinese historical tradition and contemporary domestic and foreign policies. He introduced the concept of harmonious society and peaceful diplomacy that China advocates. He also introduced China's economic and social development in the past 35 years of reform and opening up, with detailed data, and expressed his vision of realizing the Chinese Dream of the great rejuvenation. On May 14 of the same year, Ambassador Yue visited Tbilisi Public School No. 98 at invitation to observe a public course on Chinese history and culture held by the school. "As the relationship between China and Georgia continues to deepen, Georgian students' learning of the Chinese language will be of great use", the ambassador said. He encouraged the students to increase their interest in Chinese history, culture and contemporary development, to learn Chinese well and become successors to the cause of China-Georgia friendship. [1]

In an interview with People's Daily in May 2016, David Apchauli, the then Georgian Ambassador to China, talked about the 25th anniversary of the establishment Sino-Georgian diplomatic ties in 2017. "Since the establishment of diplomatic ties, the political mutual trust between the two countries has been

---

[1] Embassy of the People's Republic of China in Georgia, "Ambassador to Georgia Yue Bin teaches at Tbilisi Middle School", February 12, 2014, https://www.fmprc.gov.cn/ce/cege/chn/kxjy/t1127842.htm.

strengthened and the cooperation in economy, trade, culture, education and other fields has been deepening", he said. "In order to better promote the implementation of the Belt & Road, he hoped that in the future, the two countries could continue to enhance mutual understanding and strengthen cultural and people-to-people exchanges, so as to provide support and guarantee for economic and trade cooperation. "①

In June 2016, the then Chinese Vice Premier Zhang Gaoli of the State Council met with Georgian President Giorgi Margvelashvili in Tbilisi. He talked about "the need to expand people-to-people and cultural exchanges, fully tap the potential of bilateral cooperation in tourism, culture, education, science and technology and other areas as well as at the local level, and consolidate the public support for China-Georgia friendship. We should continue to maintain close communication and cooperation in international and regional affairs". ②

China's State Councilor and Foreign Minister Wang Yi of the People's Republic of China visited Georgia in May 2019. Georgia's Prime Minister Bakhtadze said, "Georgia attaches great importance to the partnership with China, which is an important direction of Georgia's diplomacy. In recent years, the friendly cooperative relations between the two countries have been developing steadily." He is satisfied with the development of bilateral relations, especially after the signing of the free trade agreement between Georgia and China. The Georgia side is willing to vigorously promote the Chinese language in Georgia, to welcome more Chinese enterprises to invest and do business and more Chinese tourists to visit Georgia. ③

---

① Xinhuanet, "Building the Belt and Road to tap the potential of cooperation—Interview with Georgian Ambassador to China David Apchauli", May 16, 2016, http://www.xinhuanet.com/world/2016-05/16/c_128984637.htm.

② The Chinese Education Information Website, http://www.ict.edu.cn/news/gddt/jydt/n20191204_63997.shtml.

③ "Minister Wang Yi Visits Georgia, and Georgian Wine Helps Promote the Belt and Road Initiative", June 14, 2019, https://www.winesou.com/news/china_news/140413.html.

Archil Kalandia, the Georgian Ambassador to China, and his delegation visited Peking University in October 2019. Tian Gang, vice president of Peking University, said, Peking University welcomes Georgian scholars and students to visit us. At present, our university has also opened Georgian language as a public elective course. More and more Chinese students are becoming interested in Georgia and its ancient language. He is looking forward to having more students of foreign language and culture, international relations, public policy and other related professional to go study in Georgia, and also hoping that more Georgian students and scholars come to visit Peking University, to further advance our wide communication with Georgia college. While Ambassador Kalandia said, "Both Georgia and China are countries with a long history and unique culture, and there are good prospects for cooperation in humanities, education and medical care. We hope to deepen the cooperation and exchanges between Georgia's top universities and Peking University, in an all-round way in the future." He is willing to provide opportunities for Peking University students to visit Georgia for exchange, which not only means learning language and culture, but also enhancing their understanding of policies and environment in China and Europe, so as to promote their all-round development. ①

Head of the Department of Education of Gansu Province Ms. Wang Haiyan visited Georgia in November 2019. She visited Tbilisi Public School No. 21 and Caucasus University, as well as the then Confucius Classroom at TOU. She encouraged Chinese teachers and volunteers of Confucius Classroom to devote to their teaching, try finding the beauty in life, cooperate to solve problems and do some translation in spare time, to polish skills in telling good Chinese story while also be good at telling Georgian stories, to realize it is better to communicate via combining education with entertainment. Since education is a two-way process, it is necessary to learn from the students while teaching. She asked the

---

① Peking University, "Georgian Ambassador to China visits Peking University", October 10, 2019, http://www.oir.pku.edu.cn/info/1035/4768.htm.

teachers to focus on cultivating and protecting students' enthusiasm for active communication, and to stimulate their interest in learning Chinese. ①

On the evening of February 19, the then Ambassador Ji Yanchi and his wife held a reception for Georgian Sinologists on the Lantern Festival in Tbilisi. Top officials in education filed like vice minister Aburadze of Ministry of Education, Science, Culture and Sports, President of the Chamber of Commerce and Industry Chikhwani, former education minister Nakashidze, chairman of the Friendship Group of Georgian Members of the Georgian Parliament, Danielia, chairman of the Silk Road cultural center Ms. Liu Guangwen, Sinologist Marine Jibladze, and personel from the government, parliament, education, media, altogether more than 300 people from all walks of life attended. This annual event becomes a tradition from several years ago and the latest reception before the outbreak of COVID - 19 is in January 2020 by ambassador Li Yan. The reception provided a very good opportunity for sinologists, Chinese language teachers and people related to Sino-Georgian friendship.

On January 13, 2020, the then Chinese Ambassador Li Yan met with the newly appointed Georgian Minister of Education, Science, Culture and Sports Chekhenceli in Chinese Embassy. They exchanged views on bilateral relations and cooperation in the fields of education, science, culture and sports. Ambassador Li said that China attaches great importance to the development of bilateral relations and is willing to maintain close communication and cooperation with Georgia to push bilateral cooperation in the fields of education, science, culture and sports to a new level. Chekhenceli spoke highly of the current cooperation achievements in education and humanities between Georgia and China, expressing willingness to continue to support the development and expansion of Chinese language teaching in Georgia and push the two countries to conduct in-depth mutual learning in education, science, culture and sports so as

---

① Embassy of the People's Republic of China in the Republic of Austria, "Zhang Gaoli visits Georgia", June 3, 2016, https://www.mfa.gov.cn/ce/ceat//chn/zgyw/t1371387.htm.

to add more achievements to bilateral development. ①

(ii) Exchange of teaching and research personnel between institutions

In recent years, the exchanges between educational institutions of China and Georgia have gradually increased.

On November 29, 2018, the president's office meeting of Shandong University of Technology agreed to appointed Prof. Giorgi Kveshetadze, academician and president of the National Academy of Sciences of Georgia, and Prof. Dinatin Sardunishvili, academician of the National Academy of Sciences of Georgia, as honorary professors②.

On the afternoon of December 5, 2019, with the strong support of the Foreign Affairs Office of Nanjing Municipal People's Government, Nanjing No. 5 Senior High School received a delegation of principals from Georgia. Secretary of the Party Committee of Nanjing No. 5 Senior High School, and representatives of department heads warmly welcomed the visiting guests. There is a friendly relationship between Tbilisi Public School No. 98 and Nanjing No. 5 Middle School③. Coooperation between universities is more frequent, such as of Tbilisi Open University and Lanzhou University, Tbilisi Free University and Zhengzhou University etc.

On December 1, 2020, Yue Xiaoguang, Chinese scholar, Assistant to the President of the European University of Cyprus, Fellow of the International As-

---

① Embassy of the People's Republic of China in Georgia, "Ambassador Li Yan meets Georgian Minister of Education, Science, Culture and Sports", January 14, 2020, http://ge.china-embassy.org/chn/whjl/t1732201.htm.

② Shandong University of Technology, "Two academicians of Georgian National Academy of Sciences are employed as honorary professors of the school", November 29, 2018, https://www.sdut.edu.cn/2018/1130/c4264a254539/page.htm.

③ Nanjing Charming Campus, "Communication and interaction to promote development together—Nanjing No. 5 Senior High School conducts foreign affairs reception activities", December 6, 2019, https://baijiahao.baidu.com/s?id=1652144081922952918&wfr=spider&for=pc.

sociation of Engineering Technology (IETI) and Academician of Pakistan Academy of Engineering, was approved by the majority vote after a one-day session of the conference agenda. On the evening of the same day, he received a congratulatory letter from Paata J. Kervalishvli, President of the Georgia Academy of Natural Sciences, congratulating him on his election as a Foreign Academician of the Department of Computer and Information Science of the Georgia Academy of Natural Sciences. [1]

(iii) Students exchange between the two countries, especially Georgian students, study in China with Chinese scholarships

All the time, the enthusiasm of Georgian students to learn Chinese is increasing. After learning Chinese for a period of time, their language ability reach a certain level, and parts of the students take part in the Chinese language test to know about their academic performance. Both Confucius Institutes in Tbilisi have Chinese language test centers, and hold several HSK, HSKK, YCT tests each year, with an average of 30 candidates taking each time. In addition to testing their Chinese language proficiency, most of the students also apply for Chinese (government, Chinese language teachers) scholarships.

In recent years, a variety of scholarships have been offered to help realize the dream of learning Chinese in China.

The number of Chinese government scholarships will be 10 per year before 2015 and 25 per year starting from 2016. In the past five years, nearly one hundred students have had the opportunity to study in Chinese universities.

The Confucius Institute Scholarship, which is renamed the Chinese Language Teacher Scholarship in 2020, welcomes large number of students. Only in the past four years, Confucius Institute at TOU has successfully recommended

---

[1] Tianjin Online, "Chinese scholar Yue Xiaoguang elected as foreign academician of Georgian Academy of Natural Sciences", December 4, 2020, https://baijiahao.baidu.com/s? id = 1685119974941838459&wfr = spider&for = pc.

40 students to study in Chinese universities.

There are also university president's scholarship, enterprise scholarship, etc., available for students to choose from.

Qualified students study at different universities in China, either for one year of Chinese language study, or to complete an undergraduate or graduate degree. Many students return from China and pursue careers related to China and the Chinese language. Whether they return to Georgia or stay in China temporarily, they serve as a bridge for cultural and educational exchanges between the two countries.

In addition to the above scholarship programs to help Georgian students, Chinese enterprises in Georgia are also supporting education of the local people.

In November 2019, China Chemical presented computers, printers, school bags and stationery to teachers and students of Tbilisi Public School No. 64. In December the same year, Power China Georgian volunteer service team visited Tbilisi Public School No. 202 for the Blind and held a donation and volunteer service activity. Representatives of the school, teachers and representatives of Black Sea Branch of the 16th Bureau of Hydropower Engineering attended the meeting. The volunteer service team brought teaching aids and toys for blind children to the school and had a sincere and friendly talk with the teachers and children. The donation was a follow-up to the previous volunteer activities, and is warmly welcomed by the school representatives and the children. He Peng, the representative of Power China in Georgia, said "Georgia is a country along the Belt and Road Initiative of China. Power China is willing to help the development of Georgia, bring warmth to the children through various forms of help to the best of our ability, and plant seeds of love and hope in the hearts of the children." [1] These two examples show the support of Chinese companies to Georgia's education and the love and care of the Chinese people for Georgian

---

[1] "PowerChina Georgia Representative Office Held a Donation Event for the Tbilisi School for the Blind", December 16, 2019, http://www.sinohydro.com/index.php/shzr/1400.html.

students.

From scholarships to study in China, to giving back to local by Chinese companies, China has provided help to Georgia's education, boosting people-to-people connection along the Belt and Road.

In addition to education visit and Chinese teaching, the exchanges of folk culture and education are also increasingly frequent. In 2019, the Erisoni Song and Dance Troupe toured China and staged the CCTV Mid-Autumn Festival Gala. The Chinese Huizhou opera Psycho (Jinghunji) was performed in four cities in Georgia, which further enhanced the mutual understanding and friendship between the two peoples. ①China looks forward to working with Georgia to further tap the potential of cooperation and bring more benefits to the two countries and two peoples.

IV. Conclusion

Over the past three decades, high-level officials of China and Georgia have made efforts to promote bilateral cooperation in education, science, culture and sports. In practice, China has made unremitting efforts for educational and cultural exchanges and provided great help to Georgia in terms of manpower, funds and policies (scholarships). At the same time, China actively established Georgian language major and formed Georgian research center in universities to conduct Georgian studies.

We look forward to expanding educational exchanges between the two countries in the next few years, strengthening cooperation between schools, discussing short-term (one semester or one year) exchange of teachers, and exploring the feasibility of student exchange programs, rather than relying solely on Chi-

---

① Embassy of the People's Republic of China in Georgia, "Chinese Ambassador to Georgia Li Yan published a signed article on mainstream media in Georgia 'China's Economy Continues to Advance Steadily in 2019, Focusing on High-Quality Development'", December 20, 2019, https://www.mfa.gov.cn/ce/cege//chn/xwdt/t1726426.htm.

nese scholarship programs. It is expected that learning from each other after the establishment of a relationship between universities or schools will surely bring harvest to each other. It is expected that the cooperation between disciplines and universities will bring practical results to both sides.

References

Beijing Foreign Studies University, "8 non-universal language majors in our school have been approved for establishment", March 2, 2016, https: // news. bfsu. edu. cn/archives/253759.

Belt and Road Portal, "China and Georgia sign cooperation document on joint construction of Silk Road Economic Belt", March 10, 2015, https: // www. yidaiyilu. gov. cn/xwzx/hwxw/77005. htm.

Belt and Road Portal, "Confucius Institute of the Open University of Tbilisi in Georgia was officially inaugurated", December 22, 2019, https: // www. yidaiyilu. gov. cn/xwzx/hwxw/113409. htm.

Belt and Road Portal, "List of countries that have signed cooperation documents with China to jointly build the Belt and Road", https: // www. yidaiyilu. gov. cn/xwzx/roll/77298. htm.

Bureau of International Labor Affairs, U. S. Department of Labor, *Findings on the Worst Forms of Child Labor (2001)*, 2002.

ChinaNews, "Georgia University of Science and Technology Middle School Principal, Teachers and Students Fall in Love with 'The Story of Chinese Characters'", May 17, 2012, https: //www. chinanews. com/hwjy/2012/05 – 17/3896797. shtml.

Embassy of the People's Republic of China in Georgia, "Ambassador Li Yan meets Georgian Minister of Education, Science, Culture and Sports", January 14, 2020, http: //ge. china-embassy. org/chn/whjl/t1732201. htm.

Embassy of the People's Republic of China in Georgia, "Ambassador to Georgia Yue Bin teaches at Tbilisi Middle School", February 12, 2014, https: //www. fmprc. gov. cn/ce/cege/chn/kxjy/t1127842. htm.

Embassy of the People's Republic of China in Georgia, "Chinese Ambassador to Georgia Li Yan published a signed article on mainstream media in Georgia 'China's Economy Continues to Advance Steadily in 2019, Focusing on High-Quality Development'", December 20, 2019, https://www.mfa.gov.cn/ce/cege//chn/xwdt/t1726426.htm.

Embassy of the People's Republic of China in the Republic of Austria, "Zhang Gaoli visits Georgia", June 3, 2016, https://www.mfa.gov.cn/ce/ceat//chn/zgyw/t1371387.htm.

"Former Georgian President 'LaoXie' and China", *The Paper*, July 7, 2014, https://www.thepaper.cn/newsDetail_ forward_ 1254682.

"Georgia Research Center of Lanzhou University (Introduction)", August 19, 2018, http://grc.lzu.edu.cn/jianjie/info – 5000.shtml.

Marine Jibladze, "Sinoligy and Chinese Language Teaching in Georgia", *Chinese Teaching in the World*, No. 4, 2004.

"Minister Wang Yi Visits Georgia, and Georgian Wine Helps Promote the Belt and Road Initiative", June 14, 2019, https://www.winesou.com/news/china_ news/140413.html.

Ministry of Foreign Affairs of People's Republic of China, https://www.fmprc.gov.cn/mfa_ eng/wjb_ 663304/zzjg_ 663340/dozys_ 664276/gjlb_ 664280/3170_ 664312/.

Nanjing Charming Campus, "Communication and interaction to promote development together—Nanjing No. 5 Senior High School conducts foreign affairs reception activities", December 6, 2019, https://baijiahao.baidu.com/s? id = 1652144081922952918&wfr = spider&for = pc.

Peking University, "Georgian Ambassador to China visits Peking University", October 10, 2019, http://www.oir.pku.edu.cn/info/1035/4768.htm.

"PowerChina Georgia Representative Office Held a Donation Event for the Tbilisi School for the Blind", December 16, 2019, http://www.sinohydro.com/index.php/shzr/1400.html.

Shandong University of Technology, "Two academicians of Georgian National Academy of Sciences are employed as honorary professors of the school", November 29, 2018, https: //www. sdut. edu. cn/2018/1130/c4264a254539/page. htm.

Sina, "47 Chinese and foreign universities reached the 'Dunhuang Consensus' and established the Belt and Road University Alliance", October 17, 2015, http: //news. sina. com. cn/c/2015 - 10 - 17/doc - ifxivsee8519127. shtml.

Sohu. com, "The establishment of a school by the China foreign education group in Georgia has attracted the attention of the country's parliamentary speaker and the ambassador to China", January 13, 2020, https: //www. sohu. com/a/366439914_ 100195858.

The State Council of the People's Republic of China, "On the eve of Georgian President's visit to China, he expresses great importance to relations with China", April 9, 2006, http: //www. gov. cn/zwjw/2006 - 04/09/content _ 249291. htm.

Tianjin Online, "Chinese scholar Yue Xiaoguang elected as foreign academician of Georgian Academy of Natural Sciences", December 4, 2020, https: //baijiahao. baidu. com/s? id = 1685119974941838459&wfr = spider&for = pc.

Www. guancha. cn, "Chinese becomes a required second language in Georgia", February 23, 2019, https: //www. guancha. cn/internation/2019_ 02_ 23_ 491150. shtml.

Xi' an Jiaotong University, "Silk Road University Alliance", December 28, 2018, http: //www. xjtu. edu. cn/gjjl/sczldxlm. htm.

Xinhuanet, "Building the Belt and Road to tap the potential of cooperation—Interview with Georgian Ambassador to China David Apchauli", May 16, 2016, http: //www. xinhuanet. com/world/2016 -05/16/c_ 128984637. htm.

Yang Shu, "The present state of Georgia Education and Science", *Eastern and Central Asian Studies*, No. 5, 1997.

Belt and Road Initiative: Deepening Economic Collaboration Between Georgia and China

Tamar Patashuri [*]

Georgia's economic relations with China have been especially activated in the past couple of years. This includes both direct trade relations between the two countries as well as Chinese direct investment in the Georgian economy. Georgia finds its place in one of the corridors of Belt and Road Initiative (BRI), the Central Asia-West Asia Economic Corridor which creates principally new ways for the development of its economy. Georgia can play the role of an economic hub in the SREB project as it already has free trade agreements in place with both the EU as well as China. China's interest to expand its international economic outreach is quite clear and that includes Georgia as well.

I. Belt and Road Initiative and the Role of Georgia

In 2013, President of China Xi Jinping launched the BRI[①], arguably the

---

[*] Tamar Patashuri, Lecturer, Georgian National University SEU.

[①] To avoid confusion, although in the literature the initiative has been referred as New Silk Road (NSR), or One Belt One Road (OBOR), this paper will use the most recent reference, Belt and Road Initiative (BRI).

most ambitious foreign policy move yet. The BRI promises to have an impact upon more than 4 billion people in over 60 countries across Asia, Europe, Africa and beyond①. According to official Chinese statements, the BRI has been defined as a way towards win-win cooperation, prosperity, peace and friendship by enabling mutual understanding and trust among the participant countries②.

The Silk Road Economic Belt and the 21st Century Maritime Silk Road (MSR), both of which together create the Belt and Road Initiative (BRI), launched by the Chinese president Xi Jinping in 2013. The SREB has three routes connecting China to Europe through Central Asia, the Persian Gulf, the Mediterranean via West Asia, and the Indian Ocean through South Asia, and the MSR has been planned to create connections among regional waterways.

The SREB composes an overland network of road, rail and pipelines roughly following the old Silk Road trading routes to connect China's east coast with Europe via the Eurasian land bridge③. Five regional corridors will then branch off this land bridge: the China-Mongolia-Russia Economic Corridor, the Central Asia-West Asia Economic Corridor, the Indo-China Peninsula Economic Corridor, the China-Pakistan Economic Corridor and the Bangladesh-China-India-Myanmar Economic Corridor ④. It should be pointed out that the Georgian Corridor (as well as that of Azerbaijan) is located in the Central Asia-West Asia E-

---

① Swaine, M. D., "Chinese Views and Commentary on the 'One Belt, One Road'", China Leadership Monitor, Hoover Institution, 2015, No. 47.

② National Development and Reform Commission, Vision and Actions on Jointly Building Silk Road Economic Belt and 21st - Century Maritime Silk Road, 2015, http://en.ndrc.gov.cn/newsrelease/201503/t20150330_669367.html.

③ National Development and Reform Commission, Vision and Actions on Jointly Building the Silk Road Economic Belt and 21st Century Maritime Silk Road, 2015, http://www.fmprc.gov.cn/mfa_eng/zxxx_662805/t1249618.shtml.

④ Su G., "The Belt and Road Initiative in Global Perspectives", China International Studies, 2016, No. 57.

conomic Corridor [1].

While its strategic functions are expanding, Georgia is becoming a gateway to Europe and Asia with great potential.

The BRI is more of a vision than a set of well-defined projects. Some scholars argue that the BRI showcases China's growing ambition to reposition itself globally and perceive it as a continuation of China's "Going Out" policy. The BRI incorporates two parts: the "Belt", also referred to as the concept of the "Silk Road Economic Belt" which aims to build railway and road infrastructure linking China to Europe though Central Asia, Russia and the South Caucasus; and the "Road", or the "Maritime Silk Road of the 21st century" which connects China to Africa and ultimately Europe through Southeast Asia, the Indian Ocean, the Persian Gulf and the Mediterranean Sea. Initially, the BRI was seen as a domestic development strategy to improve connectivity and to boost China's underdeveloped western provinces. [2]

Gradually, the BRI has gained global recognition and it is now regarded as one of the most significant initiative with global implications of the 21st century. Its scope goes beyond addressing China's domestic challenges and it is expected to re-shape global trade patterns and shift the centre of gravity from West to East [3].

The Belt and Road collectively account for six trade corridors, some of which are already functioning and some of which are still under construction. It is not yet possible to exhaustively list all possible routes. One of the anticipated trade corridors, "China – Central Asia West Asia", covers several countries and could encompass the TRACECA connecting China, Kazakhstan, Azerbai-

---

[1] Van Dijk M. P., Martens P., The Silk Road and Chinese Interests in Central Asia and the Caucasus: The Case of Georgia, Maastricht School of Management Working Paper, 2016, August, https://www.msm.nl/resources/uploads/2016/09/MSM – WP2016 – 12 – 1.pdf.

[2] Szczudlik – Tatar, J., "China's New Silk Road Diplomacy", Policy Paper, 2013.

[3] Frankopan, P., The silk roads: a new history of the world, Bloomsbury, London Oxford New York New Delhi Sydney, 2015.

jan, Georgia and Turkey, and ultimately Europe. This corridor presents numerous opportunities for Georgia to utilize its strategic location and business-friendly environment. Georgia has voiced its desire to position itself as a valuable player along the Belt and Road and in 2015 hosted the Tbilisi Silk Road Forum, dedicated to the SREB, co-sponsored by the Chinese government, implying that Georgia was becoming an important partner in the BRI[1]. The growing interest of China in the South Caucasus region as a key intersection between Asia and Europe has been reflected in enhanced economic activities. For instance, as of 2017, China has become Georgia's third largest trading partner with a total trade turnover of more than US $400 million, compared to just US $10 million in 2002. In addition, in the same year, China has signed a free trade agreement (FTA) with Georgia to further stimulate bilateral trade and, most recently, building upon the success of the Tbilisi Silk Road Forum of two years earlier, in November 2017 Georgia hosted the second another major event, Tbilisi Belt and Road Forum focused on the BRI.

However, despite the political will and mutual desire of both sides to enhance cooperation under the BRI, there are a number of obstacles faced by China and Georgia. Apart from the need to modernize and develop hard infrastructure, a range of challenges derive from a lack of soft infrastructure tools. For instance, while examining the efficacy of the connection between Xinjiang province in China to the port of Poti in Georgia, going through Kazakhstan and Azerbaijan, it was revealed that railway cargo loaded in China on 29th January 2015, arrived in Georgia on 6th February 2015. The analysis showed that almost a third of the transit time was spent undergoing bureaucratic procedures[2]. Moreover, the corridor passing through Georgia (TRACECA) is facing competition from other major corridors connecting China's hinterland with Europe (Trans Si-

---

[1] Pantucci, R., Lain, S., "Silk Road: China's Project Could Transfrom Eurasia", EU Observer, 2015, https://euobserver.com/eu-china/130762.

[2] Grey, E., "Can the Trans-Caspian Route deliver the next freight revolution?" Features, 2015.

beria and Central Kazakhstan). The newly launched Baku-Tbilisi-Kars railway could be regarded as a value-added aspect to TRACECA, nonetheless in order to make it functional more work is needed especially towards the development of soft infrastructure tools. In addition, Anaklia Deep Sea port being at the early stages of construction means that Georgia and the corridor as a whole has a little to offer to the major carriers operating on the market[①].

Encouragingly, Georgia has a welcoming business environment and is consistently ranked high by leading international organizations in the areas of doing business and economic freedom. The country offers a stable and welcoming environment for business, with low rates of corruption, a growth-oriented tax system and liberal trade policy. Thus, Georgia can build upon these advantages to attract more foreign investment and to create more added value within the country.

Initially, Georgia was not part of the BRI, but it has gradually become a valuable and reliable partner for China. Although Georgia has a small economy and lacks natural resources, it is an attractive partner for China as it has made impressive progress towards improving its business environment and is considered a corruption-free investment destination and a strategic location for the BRI[②].

Moreover, Georgia has set out a plan for the improvement of poor infrastructure coupled with increasing knowledge and technology transfer to enhance human capital as an integral part of boosting the overall competitiveness of the country[③].

Georgia is the 7th among 190 states in the World Bank Doing Business 2020 ranking.

---

① M. Zabakhidze, R. Beradze, Georgia as a Transit Hub and its Increasing Potential in the Implementation of the Belt and Road Initiative, 2017.

② Georgian National Investment Agency, Investment Climate and Opportunities in Georgia, Tbilisi, 2016.

③ Government of Georgia, Social-economic Development Strategy of Georgia "GEORGIA 2020", 2013.

Georgian Economy Minister Natia Turnava says that the 83.7 score is the "historic maximum" for Georgia. Georgia remains to be the regional leader for doing business, the first amongst the 23 countries of Europe and Central Asia," she said. Doing Business has captured 294 regulatory reforms carried out between May 2018 and May 2019. Worldwide, 115 economies made it easier to do business, the World Bank said. The World Bank says that its Doing Business project provides "objective measures of business regulations and their enforcement across 190 economies and selected cities at the subnational and regional level".

Doing Business ranking was launched in 2002, looking at domestic small and medium-size companies and measuring the regulations applying to them through their life cycle.

II. Industrial Policies/ Investment Incentives

The Georgian government has created several tools to support investment in the country's economy. The JSC Partnership Fund is a state-owned investment fund, established in 2011. The fund owns the largest Georgian state-owned enterprises operating in the transportation, energy, and infrastructure sectors. The Fund's main objective is to promote domestic and foreign investment in Georgia by providing co-financing (equity, mezzanine, etc.) in projects at their initial stage of development, with a focus on tourism, manufacturing, energy, and agriculture.

In 2013, the government launched the Georgian Co-Investment Fund (GCF) to promote foreign and domestic investments. According to the government, the GCF is a six billion USD private investment fund with a mandate of providing investors with unique access, through a private equity structure, to opportunities in Georgia's fastest growing industries and sectors.

The government's "Produce in Georgia" program is another tool for jointly financing foreign investment under which investors establish limited liability companies in Georgia. The program aims to develop and support entrepreneurship, encourage creation of new enterprises, and increase export potential and investment in the country. Coordinated by the Ministry of Economy and Sustainable Development through its Entrepreneurship Development Agency, National Agency of State Property, and Technology and Innovation Agency of Georgia, the project provides access to finance, access to real property, and technical assistant to entrepreneurs.

The National Agency of State Property is in charge of the Physical Infrastructure Transfer Component, i. e., the free-of-charge transfer of government-owned real property to an entrepreneur under certain investment obligations.

Low labor costs contribute to the attractiveness of Georgia as a foreign investment destination. Georgia is also increasingly recognized as a regional transportation hub that links Asia and Europe. Georgia's free trade regimes provide easy access for companies to export goods produced in Georgia to foreign markets. In some cases, foreign investors can benefit from these agreements by producing goods that target these markets.

In October 2018, Georgia's Prime Minister introduced the concept of electronic residency, allowing citizens of 34 countries to register their companies electronically and open bank accounts in Georgia while not having a physical presence in the country.

(i) Foreign trade zones/free ports/trade facilitation

In June 2007, the Parliament of Georgia adopted the Law on Free Industrial Zones, which defines the form and function of free industrial/economic zones. Financial operations in such zones may be performed in any currency. Foreign companies operating in free industrial zones are exempt from taxes on profit, property, and VAT. Currently, there are four free industrial zones in Georgia:

Poti Free Industrial Zone (FIZ): This is the first free industrial zone in the Caucasus region, established in 2008. UAE-based RAK Investment Authority

(Rakia) initially developed the zone, but in 2017, CEFC China Energy Company Limited purchased 75 percent of shares, and the Georgian government holds the remaining 25 percent. Poti FIZ, a 300-hectare area, benefits from its close proximity to the Poti Sea Port.

A 27-hectare plot in Kutaisi is home to the Egyptian company Fresh Electric, which constructed a kitchen appliances factory in 2009. The company has committed to building about one dozen textile, ceramics, and home appliances factories in the zone, and announced its intention to invest over USD two billion.

Chinese private corporation "Hualing Group", based in Urumqi, China, developed another FIZ in Kutaisi in 2015. This FIZ is a 36-hectare area that houses businesses focused on sales of wood, furniture, stone, building materials, pharmaceuticals, auto spare parts, electric vehicles, and beverages.

The Tbilisi Free Zone (TFZ) in Tbilisi occupies 17 hectares divided into 28 plots. TFZ has access to the main cargo transportation highway, Tbilisi International Airport (30 km), and the Tbilisi city center (17 km).

(ii) **Corruption**

Georgia has laws, regulations, and penalties to combat corruption. Georgia criminalizes bribery under Articles 332-342 of the Criminal Code. Senior public officials must file financial disclosure forms, which are available online, and Georgian legislation provides for the civil forfeiture of undocumented assets of public officials who are charged with corruption-related offenses. Penalties for accepting a bribe start at six years in prison and can extend to 15 years, depending on the circumstances. Penalties for giving a bribe can include a fine, a minimum prison sentence of two years, or both. In aggravated circumstances, when a bribe is given to commit an illegal act, the penalty is from four to seven years. Abuse of authority and exceeding authority by public servants are criminal acts under Articles 332 and 333 of the criminal code and carry a maximum penalty of eight years imprisonment. The definition of a public official includes foreign public officials and employees of international organizations and courts. White collar crimes, such as bribery, fall under the investigative jurisdiction of the Prosecutor's Office.

Georgia is not a signatory to the OECD Convention on Combating Bribery of Foreign Public Officials in International Business Transactions. Georgia has, however, ratified the UN Convention against Corruption. Georgia cooperates with the Group of States against Corruption (GRECO) and the OECD's Anti-Corruption Network for Transition Economies (ACN).

Following its assessment of Georgia in June 2016, the OECD released a report in September 2016 that concluded Georgia had achieved remarkable progress in eliminating petty corruption in public administration and should now focus on combating high-level and complex corruption. The report commends Georgia's mechanism for monitoring and evaluating the implementation of its Anti-Corruption Strategy and Action Plan, as well as the role given to civil society in this process. It also welcomes the adoption of a new Law on Civil Service and recommends that the remaining legislation to implement civil service reforms is adopted without delay. The report notes that the Civil Service Bureau and Human Resources units in state entities should be strengthened to ensure the implementation of the required reforms. The report highlights Georgia's good track record in prosecuting corruption crimes and in using modern methods to confiscate criminal proceeds. It recommends that Georgia increase enforcement of corporate liability and the prosecution of foreign bribery to address the perception of corruption among local government officials. Since 2003, Georgia has significantly improved its ranking in Transparency International's (TI) Corruption Perceptions Index (CPI) report.

Transparency International ranked Georgia 44th out of 180 countries in the 2019 edition of its Corruption Perceptions Index (the same rank as Costa Rica, the Czech Republic, and Latvia).

While Georgia has been successful in fighting visible, low-level corruption, Georgia remains vulnerable to what Transparency International calls "elite" corruption: high-level officials exploiting legal loopholes for personal enrichment, status, or retribution. Although the evidence is mostly anecdotal, this form of corruption, or the perception of its existence, has the potential to erode public and investor confidence in Georgia's institutions and the investment environment. Corruption remains a potential problem in public procurement processes, public administration practices, and the judicial system due to unclear laws and ethical standards[1].

(iii) Development strategy

Currently, the government of Georgia uses two guiding strategy documents to tackle economic challenges. A social economic development strategy "Georgia 2020", announced in 2012, is a broad guiding document directed at long-term growth of most economic sectors beyond 2020. Boosting the private sector's competitiveness, development of human capital and improving access to finance are three main areas on which the document focuses. More recently, in 2016 the Georgian government announced a "4-point plan" focused on 4 pillars, one of which is economic development. Both documents emphasize the need to modernize infrastructure as a key pre-condition to position Georgia as a transit hub and to unlock trade opportunities. Furthermore, both documents mention Anaklia Deep Sea Port, the development of the East-West transport highway and the Baku-Tbilisi-Kars railway as pivotal projects towards achieving those goals. Georgia is an open economy and has signed several important trade agreements, most recently an FTA with China. Furthermore, Georgia is implementing the DCFTA to open access to the EU's single market for Georgian products and ultimately to support export diversification. Nonetheless, this is a long-term process and the results of these agreements will not be fully realized for some time.

According to the 2021 data of National Statistics Office of Georgia, excluding the EU, China is the third largest export destination for Georgia accounting for 10.9% of total exports. China is Georgia's third largest investor as well. Reportedly, Chinese investments target agriculture, banking, telecommuni-

---

[1] STOPfake.gov, 2019, https://www.stopfakes.gov/article?id=Georgia-Corruption.

cation, infrastructure, hospitality and light industry. Since 2007, Chinese company Hualing Group has made an approximate US $500 million investment in Georgia, half of which has been in Free Economic Zones[①].

Exports by countries

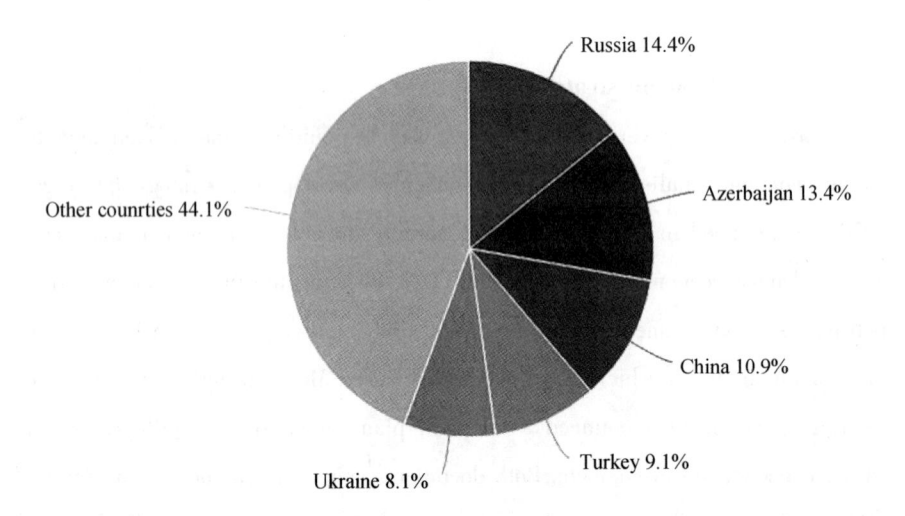

Figure 1 Share of the Top Trading Partners in Total Exports in January-February 2021

Source: National Statistics Office of Georgia, https://www.geostat.ge/en/modules/categories/637/export.

Georgia's foreign trade turnover decreased by 14.8% in 2020 year-on-year, equaling USD 11.3 billion, according to the preliminary figures released by the National Statistics Office of Georgia on January 20.

Exports from Georgia decreased by 12% year-on-year to USD 3.3 billion, while imports decreased by 15.9% year-on-year to USD 8 billion. The trade gap stood at USD 4.7 billion.

Exports from Georgia to European Union (EU) member states constituted

---

① Tskhovrebova, A., Silk Road of Chinese Investment, 2016, pp. 60 – 65.

21.5% of total exports, equaling USD 718.5 million, a 13% decrease year-on-year. Imports from EU amounted to USD 1.9 billion, 24.0% of total annual imports and a 17.2% decrease from 2019.

Georgia's exports to CIS countries were down by 24.5% year-on-year to USD 1.5 billion (45.2% of total exports), and imports were down by 1.8% to USD 2.3 billion (29.9% of total imports)[①].

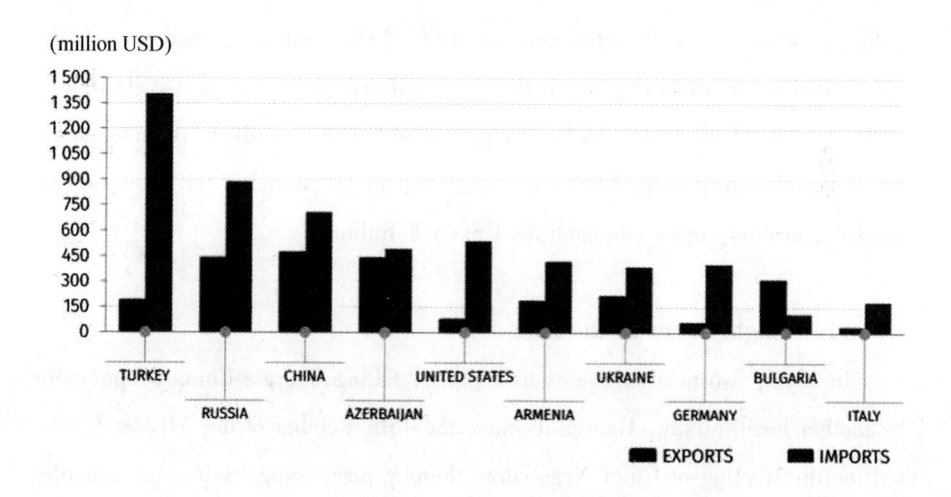

Figure 2   Top Trading Partners by Turnover in 2020
Source: Georgia's Foreign Trade in 2020, https://civil.ge/archives/391924.

China tops the list of largest trading partners by exports with USD 476.3 million, followed by Azerbaijan, Russia, Bulgaria and Ukraine with USD 441.3 million, USD 441 million, USD 312.4 million and USD 217.4 million, respectively.

Turkey, Russia, China, the U.S. and Azerbaijan are the top trading partners of Georgia in terms of imports with USD 1.4 billion, USD 887.2 million, USD 708.7 million, USD 540.9 million and USD 493.2 million, respectively.

Copper ores and concentrates top of the list of export commodities with USD

---

① Georgia's Foreign Trade in 2020, https://civil.ge/archives/391924.

729. 4 million, followed by re-export of cars with USD 404. 1 million; ferroalloys-USD 247. 3 million; wine – USD 210. 3 million; spirits-USD 132. 2 million; mineral waters-USD 116. 6 million; medicines-USD 99. 1 million; gold-USD 97. 6 million; nuts-USD 94 million; precious metal ores and concentrates-USD 90. 0 million; other commodities-USD 1. 1 billion.

Cars are on top of the list of import commodities in Georgia's foreign trade with USD 759. 5 million, followed by copper ores and concentrates-USD 533. 5 million; petroleum and petroleum oils-USD 498. 5 million; medicines-USD 327. 1 million; petroleum gases-USD 294. 6 million; mobile phones-USD 164. 7 million; wheat-USD 108. 0 million; cigarettes-USD 88. 9 million; precious metal ores and concentrates-USD 77. 1 million; motor vehicles for transport of goods-72 million; other commodities-USD 5. 1 billion.

(iv) Engagement in the BRI

In 2015, two notable events took place, taking Georgia-China cooperation to another level. Firstly, Georgia became the 45th member of the AIIB and hosted its 6th Meeting of Chief Negotiators thereby positioning itself as a valuable member of the group. Later that year, Tbilisi hosted the Silk Road Forum. The Prime Minister of Georgia outlined the following four anticipated projects under the BRI at the 2015 forum:

1. A new deep-water seaport in Anaklia, on the Black Sea, to handle 100 million tons of cargo per year, with the capacity to receive large Panamax-type vessels.

2. Improvement of Georgia's railway network to increase rail speed, leading to the tripling of transit capacity.

3. Constructing the Baku-Tbilisi-Kars railroad (in Azerbaijan, Georgia and Turkey, respectively) to allow 45% faster delivery of containers and freight and passengers from Asia to Europe.

4. Expanding the East-West Highway, Georgia's main road transport route, in cooperation with the World Bank, the ADB, and other donors.

The Baku-Tbilisi-Kars railway opened in October 2017, whereas the other initiatives listed above are in the process of implementation.

In November 2017, Tbilisi hosted the "Tbilisi Belt and Road Forum". The official website of the forum stated that it "aims to serve as a biennial platform for high-level government and private sector dialogues". The forum gathered around 2,000 delegates from more than 50 countries including the Prime Ministers of Moldova and Ukraine, the Deputy Minister of Commerce of China and representatives of international financial institutions. During two days of intensive panel discussions, Georgia reinforced its intention to become a transit hub connecting Europe and China. During this event Georgia has signed several important agreements with China, for instance an MoU on developing economic zones and entrepreneurial capacity between the countries. The JSC Partnership Fund has also established several MoUs including one with Chinese engineering company SEDIN Engineering Co to assist the industrialization process. At the Belt and Road Forum for International Cooperation held in Beijing on 14 May 2017, CEFC China Energy Company Limited signed two important cooperation agreements with the government of Georgia: a Memorandum of Understanding on the Joint Establishment of the Georgian Development Bank; and a Strategic Cooperation Framework Agreement on the Joint Establishment of the Georgian National Construction Fund. These documents were signed by Dimitri Kumsishvili, Georgia's First Deputy Prime Minister and Minister of Economy and Sustainable Development, and David Saganelidze, CEO of the JSC Partnership Fund. The overarching aim of these agreements is to further advance strategic cooperation between CEFC China and the government of Georgia as well as to build the planned "Silk Road Common Market Zone", which is intended to accelerate the development of an innovative Belt and Road trade model. Furthermore, these agreements state that CEFC China will work with the government of Georgia to set up the Georgian Development Bank. This bank will be controlled and operated by CEFC China and, in order to boost bilateral economic and financial cooperation, focus will be placed on RMB-denominated financial services and cross-border RMB settlement services.

III. Trade Between China and the European Union

The most prominent economic characteristic associated with China's rise is the massive amount of trade it does, notably exports of goods to the global market since the 2000s. The success of Chinese exports has had a significant impact on the EU. This impact has become even more significant as China has moved up the technology ladder and has started to offer more advanced goods to the EU, thus competing with EU companies.

Since the normalisation of China-EU diplomatic relations in the 1970s, China has actively strengthened its trade relationship with the EU. There was a massive increase in Chinese trade with EU countries even before China's accession to the World Trade Organisation in 2001. For example, Germany imported goods worth only USD 1.9 billion from China in 1980, but imports rapidly grew to USD 16.9 billion in the twenty subsequent years.

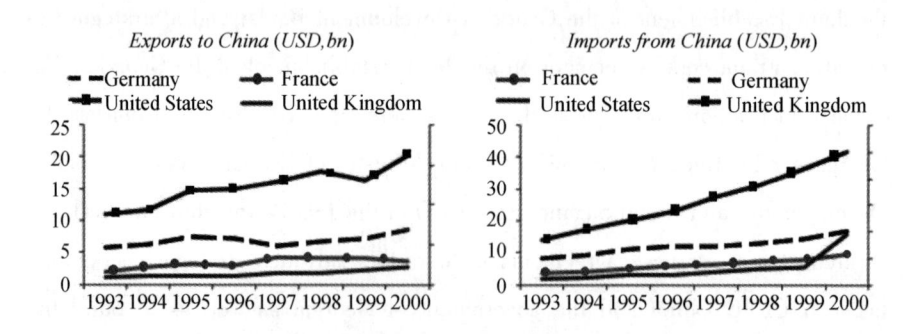

Figure 3   Trade Between China and the EU

Source: Natixis, UNComtrade

The developments in the 1990s were important, because they showed China's determination to integrate with the global economy in the late twentieth century. Although this period predated China's WTO membership, and there was a debate over whether or not to grant such a status to China, the global economic environment in the 1990s was accommodative. The EU and the US had both already given China the most-favoured nation (MFN) tariff rate, subject to annual approval.

Therefore, what WTO membership really offered China was a more certain international environment. Reduced uncertainty around tariffs made Chinese manufacturing companies more confident, enabling them to extend international cooperation and increase their exporting capacities. Since then, the EU has seen a more significant increase in Chinese goods in its domestic market share. In 2018, total EU trade (exports plus imports) with China made up nearly 15% of the EU's total extra-EU trade[①].

Ⅳ. Prospects of the Georgian Economy

China and Georgia have tightened their economic ties over the past decade, reflected in a deeper trade relationship and substantial Chinese direct investment into the Georgia economy.

Now, the BRI presents an opportunity for Georgia, as a potential transit hub between China and Europe, to further strengthen this relationship. The trade corridor passing through Georgia may bring Georgia the benefit of its share of increased trade between China and Europe via rail, but Georgia could gain even more by developing its trade relationships with China and Europe respectively. Briefly speaking, Georgia could be more than just a transit country.

In this regard, Georgia has four main characteristics that may be attractive for the BRI: 1. Business-friendly environment, namely fast growing economy, low corruption rates, growth-friendly tax policy. 2. Liberal cross-border trade –

---

① EU-China trade and investment relations in challenging times, Trade between China and the European Union, https://www.europarl.europa.eu/RegData/etudes/STUD/2020/603492/EXPO _ STU (2020) 603492_EN.pdf.

FTA with China and DCFTA with EU, among other agreements. 3. Strategic geographical location – Black Sea, overland links to Turkey. 4. Young, skilled and competitively priced labor force.

Thus, Georgia can offer a platform to China through which it can more efficiently trade with Europe. However, for this platform to become competitive, some complex and interrelated issues need to be addressed. Georgia's success in this regard will largely depend on the success of coordinated hard and soft infrastructure development and taking full advantage of the Baku-Tbilisi-Kars railway link to Turkey and Anaklia Deep Sea Port. In this vein, convergence between the BRI and Georgia's economic development trajectory is linked to infrastructure development. At the same time, Georgia can utilize the advantages of its trade agreements and business environment to become an important transit hub in the South Caucasus region and beyond.

However, despite some encouraging prospects, in the last decade there has been a significant drop in transit going through Georgia and this represents a major challenge if the country is to position itself as a regional hub. In January-August 2017, transit through Georgia declined by 800, 000 tons compared to the same period of 2016. This declining trend has been observed every year since 2012. One of the key factors in the declining transit volumes is the low competitiveness of the TRACECA corridor passing through the country. While Azerbaijan and Turkey are developing their infrastructure, and becoming transit hubs in their respective regions, the volume passing through Georgia is constantly declining. This implies that solely upgrading hard infrastructure would not automatically transform Georgia into a transit hub[①].

However, on a positive note, during his speech at the panel discussion entitled "Belt and Road Initiative: Building bonds across Asia, Europe and beyond" held at the World Bank Headquarters, Kazakhstan's Deputy Prime Minister Erbolat Dossaev spoke about "the shortest way" from China to Europe and

---

① Commersant. ge, Georgia has not Become a Transit Hub for the Region, 2017.

noted the importance of the Baku-Tbilisi-Kars project, claiming that it will also open up new possibilities toward the Mediterranean Sea. This 826km railway project, known as 'Silk Rail', was officially opened in October 2017 with the capacity to transport one million passengers and 6.5 million tons of freight per year, with potential to reach three million passengers and 17 million tons of freight by 2034①.

Although the Baku-Tbilisi-Kars railway is already operating and its significance has been widely acclaimed, the general problems that apply to TRACECA will also affect this newly launched railway route.

From a long-term perspective, Anaklia Deep Sea Port could boost the overall competitiveness of Georgia as a transit hub. According to the Anaklia Development Consortium, the first phase of construction will start on 20 December 2017, and once the entire project is finished it will make a capacity of 900,000 containers, and a 1.5 million bulk cargo transportation②. However, Anaklia Deep Sea Port is facing competition from several other major ports in the region. Such ports include Mersin Port in Turkey, Bender Abas in Southern Iran and Odessa in Ukraine. However, the political situations in Iran and Ukraine respectively may make Anaklia a more favorable choice in comparison. The attractiveness of Mersin Port, meanwhile, will depend largely on the Baku-Tbilisi-Kars railway, the impact of which remains to be seen.

Although it is too early to evaluate the impact of BRI-related infrastructure development on Georgia's potential transformation into a transit hub, current evidence suggests the existence of clear opportunities for Georgia to modernize its infrastructure. To ensure that the full potential of this new connectivity is achieved, old infrastructure needs to be modernized. In addition, soft infrastructure tools need to be put in place. Georgia has shown impressive progress in this

---

① Turp, C., "Azerbaijan, Georgia, Turkey launch new 'Silk Rail' link", Outlook on Georgia, 2017.

② Gugunishvili, N., Anaklia Deep Sea Port Land Construction Works to start in December, 2017.

direction. According to the Doing Business Report, Georgia has the simplest customs procedures in the region and this could be leveraged to improve the competitiveness of this corridor in the future.

As well as conceptualizing the initiative from a regional connectivity perspective, it is important to explore BRI to find ways to boost the national economy. As mentioned earlier, the Georgian economy has experienced unbalanced growth. To address this, according to a study on economic policy, Georgia should focus on sectors with high growth potential by drawing on comparative advantages of the country as well as its potential to upgrade towards producing more value-added goods in the future[①]. Given the relatively low wages and lack of a highly skilled workforce, one of the two priority sectors identified is labor-intensive light industry that incorporates sub-sectors such as food processing and textiles. As China aims to shift its labor-intensive industries overseas, the preferential business environment and further development of FIZs in Georgia could allow for greater cooperation.

China is Georgia's top trading partner by exports in 2020, according to the preliminary data from the National Statistics Office of Georgia (Geostat). Georgian exports amounted to $476.3 million to China which is 14.3% of the total exports of the country and an increase of 113.4% compared to 2019. After China, the top partners of Georgia by exports, were Azerbaijan ($441.3 million) and Russia ($441.1 million). Overall, the share of the top ten trading partners in the total external trade turnover of Georgia amounted to 70.4% in 2020. The top trading partners were Turkey ($1.59 billion), Russia ($1.32 billion) and China ($1.18 billion).

The top three export items were the following: (1) Copper ores and concentrates - $729.4 million, 21.8% of total exports; (2) Motor cars -

---

① Saha, D., Giucci, R., Towards strong and balanced growth: Georgia's economic policy priorities in 2017 - 2020 (Policy Studies Series No. PS/01/17), German Economic Team Georgia / ISET Policy Institute, Berlin / Tbilisi, 2017.

$404.1 million, 12.1% of total exports; (3) Ferroalloys – $247.3 million, 7.4% of the total exports.

The top import commodities in 2020 were as follows: (1) Motor cars – $759.5 million, 9.5% of the total imports; (2) Copper ores and concentrates – $533.5 million, 6.7% of total imports; (3) Petroleum and petroleum oils – $498.5 million, 6.2% of total imports.

The external trade turnover of Georgia amounted to $11.34 billion in 2020, which is a decrease of 14.8% compared to last year. The value of exports decreased 12% and amounted to $3.34 billion, while imports decreased 15.9%, amounting to $8 billion. The trade deficit (an economic measure of the negative balance of trade in which a country's imports exceed its exports) amounted to $4.66 billion and its share in trade turnover made for 41.1%. In the last month of 2020, exports amounted to $325.7 million, while imports amounted to $799 million. In December 2020, total turnover amounted to $1.12 billion, while the trade balance was – $473.3 million[①].

In January-June 2020, copper ores and concentrates reclaimed the first place in the list of top export items, equaling USD 332.4 million or 22.1 percent of total exports. The exports of motor cars totaled USD 184.1 million and their share in the total exports amounted to 12.2 percent. The ferroalloys exports occupied the third place standing at USD 117.6 million and constituting 7.8 percent of the total exports.

Sectors which attract the most foreign direct investments (FDIs) in Georgia are considered to be: energy, transport, real estate and construction, and processing industries.

Several large projects can be distinguished in the list of Chinese investment in Georgia connected with the construction sector, for example, the Tbilisi Sea Olympic Complex, an especially large investment, prepared for the 2015 Youth

---

① "2020 data: China is Georgia's top trading partner by exports", Agenda.ge, January 20, 2021.

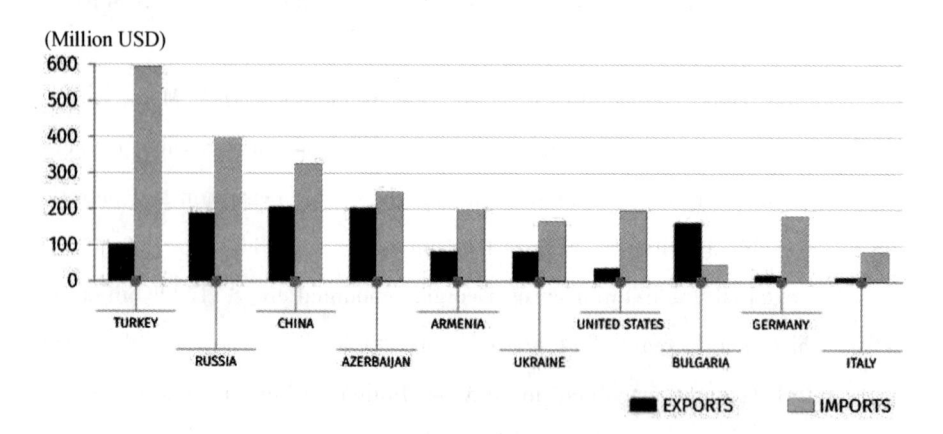

Figure 4 Top Trading Partners by Turnover in January – June 2020

Source: National Statistics Office of Georgia, https://www.geostat.ge/media/32565/External-Merchandise-Trade-of-Georgia-in- January-June – 2020. pdf.

Olympic Festival with USD 200 million in investment from the Hualing Group. The Hualing Group invested in such sectors as construction, hotels, medical care, wood processing, cement production, free trade zones, airplane transfers and the banking sector.

FDIs play an active role not only in favor of the local market and consumers but also in balancing the external trade. The share of companies created together with Georgian and foreign participation in the overall exports is growing year by year.

Several important projects that are already planned by the Chinese in Georgia and whose operation can reach significant success should also be mentioned here. These include 1. the creation of the Georgia Development Bank with USD 1 billion in capital from 2018 by the CEFC China Energy Company Limited and Eurasian Invest LLC [1]. In strategic terms, this bank will serve as a new magnet

---

[1] CBW, "One Billion USD Capital Chinese Bank to Launch in Georgia", *Caucasus Business Week*, May 15, 2017, http://cbw.ge/banking/chinese – bank – one – billion – usd – capital – launch – georgia/.

for attracting Chinese investors to Georgia.

2. Development of tea production in Georgia①.

3. Creation of the Georgian-Chinese Fund for the Regeneration of Georgia which will be implemented with the support of the Georgia Partnership Fund and Chinese CFC, and fund Georgian startups with its USD 50 million budget (51% of the money will be Chinese contribution while 41% will be Georgian) ②.

4. Creation of the Silk Road Common Market Zone which should facilitate the development of an innovative trade model③.

The activation of China-Georgia economic relations naturally begs the question about why China is interested in developing economic cooperation with a geographically remote Georgia.

Answering this question is not at all difficult based upon new global projects put forward by Beijing, including the Silk Road Economic Belt and the 21st Century Maritime Silk Road, both of which together create a Belt and Road Initiative (BRI), launched by the Chinese president Xi Jinping in 2013.

Georgia, together with its neighbor and strategic ally, Azerbaijan, has been considered in the context of the Ancient Silk Road right from the beginning of the 1990s. The practical implications of this idea have been the TRACECA project initiated by the EU in 1993, the INOGATE project starting in 1996. In fact, practically all projects envisaged in terms of the Silk Road transport corridor are functioning successfully today.

The inclusion of Georgia in the SREB project is facilitated by the already implemented Silk Road Transport Corridor (SRTC) project.

---

① Hualing Group, "Georgian Tea Complex Project MOU Signing Ceremony", 2017, http://hualing.ge/language/en/georgian-tea-complex-project-mou-signing-ceremony/.

② Jorjoliani L., "Georgian Government upbeat on Chinese Trade", *Investor. ge*, Issue 4, August-September, 2017, http://investor.ge/article.php?art=5.

③ CEFC, "China Signs Two Cooperation Agreements with the Government of Georgia to Help Develop an Innovative Trade Model in the 'Silk Road Common Market Zone'", *CEFC China*, May 14, 2017, http://en.cefc.co/detail/news/749?lang=cn.

If we compare the SRTC or TRACECA with the SREB's Central Asia-West Asia Economic Corridor projects, the differences, on the other hand, lie in at least two things: first of all, the first project was initiated by the West (more specifically, the EU) while the second one originated in the East (more specifically, in China) and secondly, (which, we believe is very important) the first project is clearly and primarily a transport project while the second one is much more complex as it is economic (which means that apart from transport it also includes other economic fields). It should be pointed out that the idea about the transport corridor for Georgia would, in the future, turn into a complex economic project as it would facilitate the development of different parts of the economy as was voiced back in 2002[1].

V. Georgia: From Energy Transportation Hub to Economic Hub

The fact that the institution of a free trade regime between China and the EU is under active discussion is very important for Georgia[2]. In this regard, the SREB creates a new stage in the economic cooperation between China and the EU[3].

China and Georgia are members of the World Trade Organization. The fact that a free trade agreement has been signed between the two countries[4] is very

---

[1] Papava V., "On the Special Features of Georgia's International Economic Function", *Central Asia and the Caucasus*, 2002, No. 2 (14).

[2] Haver Z., "Rebalancing EU – China Relations: The Case for an EU – China FTA", *Global Policy*, February 9, 2017, http://www.globalpolicyjournal.com/blog/09/02/2017/rebalancing – eu – china – relations – case – eu – china – fta.

[3] Gogolashvili K., "New Silk Road: A Stage for EU and China to Cooperate", Expert Opinion, 2017, No. 86. Tbilisi, Georgian Foundation for Strategic and International Studies, https://www.gfsis.org/files/library/opinion – papers/86 – expert – opinion – eng.pdf.

[4] "China, Georgia Sign FTA", *The State Council the People's Republic of China*, May 15, 2017, http://english.gov.cn/news/international_exchanges/2017/05/15/content_281475656216746.htm.

important in terms of the development of trade relations. Georgia also has the Deep and Comprehensive Free Trade Area (DCFTA) Agreement with the EU as well as a free trade agreement with the European Free Trade Association (EFTA). Hence, the expansion of trade between the EU and China will enable Georgia to become a logistical hub, connecting China with Europe (for which the Baku-Tbilisi-Kars railway and the implementation of the Anaklia Black Sea Deep Water Port project will have vital importance) and increase the level of its security at the same time [1].

Of further note is that due to the transportation of Caspian oil and gas to Turkey, Georgia already plays the role of an energy resources transportation hub[2].

For Georgia, the SREB project creates an opportunity to transform its role as an energy resources transportation hub to a regional economic hub in general. In this regard, it should be underlined that with the DCFTA agreement signed between the EU and Georgia, products exported from Georgia to the EU must be produced in Georgia[3]. This, therefore, makes Georgia attractive to all countries without free trade agreements with the EU to invest in Georgia and export the production manufactured here to the EU market. This includes China as well which is already investing in Georgia[4].

Consequently, Georgia can actually become an economic hub in the region which would be in full accordance with the content of the Central Asia-West Asia Economic Corridor project crossing Georgia.

---

[1] Ajeganov B., "EU – China Trade to Bolster Security in the South Caucasus", *The CACI Analyst*, January 23, 2017, https://www.cacianalyst.org/publications/analytical-articles/item/13423-eu%E2%80%93china-trade-to-bolster-security-in-the-south-caucasus.html.

[2] "Opening of Caspian Basin Pipeline", *U. S. Department of State*, May 25, 2005, https://2001-2009.state.gov/r/pa/prs/ps/2005/46745.htm.

[3] "Rules of Origin. Free Trade with the EU", *Ministry of Economy and Sustainable Development of Georgia*, 2017, http://www.dcfta.gov.ge/en/dcfta-for-businness/Rules-of-Origin-.

[4] V. Charaia, V. Papava, "Belt and Road Initiative: Implications for Georgia and China – Georgia Economic Relations", *China International Studies*, November 2017.

VI. Conclusion

The new global projects put forward by China such as the SREB and the 21st Century Maritime Silk Road, which combined make up the Belt and Road Initiative, create new opportunities for developing the world economy. Georgia finds its place in one of the corridors, the Central Asia-West Asia Economic Corridor of the SREB project, which creates principally new ways for the development of its economy. Together with neighboring Azerbaijan, Georgia has been actively participating in the creation and development of the SRTC, which is already successfully operating. It can be said that the SREB is the further development of the SRTC as the transport corridor is being transformed into a much more complex economic corridor.

The level of Chinese investment in the Georgian economy is growing practically day by day and this trend will have an irreversible character in terms of the implementation of the SREB project. Close economic ties with a country of tremendous economic capabilities are definitely in Georgia's interests in order to diversify export markets and attract foreign investment.

References

"2020 data: China is Georgia's top trading partner by exports", Agenda. ge, January 20, 2021.

Ajeganov B., "EU – China Trade to Bolster Security in the South Caucasus", *The CACI Analyst*, January 23, 2017, https://www.cacianalyst.org/publications/analytical-articles/item/13423-eu%E2%80%93china-trade-to-bolster-security-in-the-south-caucasus.html.

CBW, "One Billion USD Capital Chinese Bank to Launch in Georgia", *Caucasus Business Week*, May 15, 2017, http://cbw.ge/banking/chinese-bank-one-billion-usd-capital-launch-georgia/.

CEFC, "China Signs Two Cooperation Agreements with the Government of

Georgia to Help Develop an Innovative Trade Model in the 'Silk Road Common Market Zone'", *CEFC China*, May 14, 2017, http: //en. cefc. co/detail/news/749? lang = cn.

"China, Georgia Sign FTA", *The State Council the People's Republic of China*, May 15, 2017, http: //english. gov. cn/news/international _ exchanges/2017/05/15/content_281475656216746. htm.

Commersant. ge, Georgia has not Become a Transit Hub for the Region, 2017.

EU – China trade and investment relations in challenging times, Trade between China and the European Union, https: //www. europarl. europa. eu/RegData/etudes/STUD/2020/603492/EXPO_STU (2020) 603492_EN. pdf.

Frankopan, P., The silk roads: a new history of the world, Bloomsbury, London Oxford New York New Delhi Sydney, 2015.

Georgia 2019 Crime & Safety Report, https: //www. osac. gov/Content/Report/8abe6b1a – 88fe – 411b – 860f – 15f4aead3a9a#: ~ : text = Per%20Georgian%20law%2C%20it%20is, via%20Abkhazia%20or%20South%20Ossetia.

Georgian National Investment Agency, Investment Climate and Opportunities in Georgia, Tbilisi, 2016.

Georgia's Foreign Trade in 2020, https: //civil. ge/archives/391924.

Gogolashvili K., "New Silk Road: A Stage for EU and China to Cooperate", Expert Opinion, 2017, No. 86. Tbilisi, Georgian Foundation for Strategic and International Studies, https: //www. gfsis. org/files/library/opinion – papers/86 – expert – opinion – eng. pdf.

Government of Georgia, Social – economic Development Strategy of Georgia "GEORGIA 2020", 2013.

Grey, E., "Can the Trans – Caspian Route deliver the next freight revolution?" Features, 2015.

Gugunishvili, N., Anaklia Deep Sea Port Land Construction Works to start in December, 2017.

Haver Z., "Rebalancing EU – China Relations: The Case for an EU –

China FTA", *Global Policy*, February 9, 2017, http://www.globalpolicy-journal.com/blog/09/02/2017/rebalancing-eu-china-relations-case-eu-china-fta.

Hualing Group, "Georgian Tea Complex Project MOU Signing Ceremony", 2017, http://hualing.ge/language/en/georgian-tea-complex-project-mou-signing-ceremony/.

Jorjoliani L., "Georgian Government upbeat on Chinese Trade", *Investor.ge*, Issue 4, August-September, 2017, http://investor.ge/article.php?art=5.

M. Zabakhidze, R. Beradze, Georgia as a Transit Hub and its Increasing Potential in the Implementation of the Belt and Road Initiative, 2017.

National Development and Reform Commission, Vision and Actions on Jointly Building Silk Road Economic Belt and 21st-Century Maritime Silk Road, 2015, http://en.ndrc.gov.cn/newsrelease/201503/t20150330_669367.html.

National Development and Reform Commission, Vision and Actions on Jointly Building the Silk Road Economic Belt and 21st Century Maritime Silk Road, 2015, http://www.fmprc.gov.cn/mfa_eng/zxxx_662805/t1249618.shtml.

"Opening of Caspian Basin Pipeline", *U.S. Department of State*, May 25, 2005, https://2001-2009.state.gov/r/pa/prs/ps/2005/46745.htm.

Pantucci, R., Lain, S., "Silk Road: China's Project Could Transfrom Eurasia", EU Observer, 2015, https://euobserver.com/eu-china/130762.

Papava V., "On the Special Features of Georgia's International Economic Function", *Central Asia and the Caucasus*, 2002, No. 2 (14).

"Rules of Origin. Free Trade with the EU", *Ministry of Economy and Sustainable Development of Georgia*, 2017, http://www.dcfta.gov.ge/en/dcfta-for-businness/Rules-of-Origin-.

Saha, D., Giucci, R., Towards strong and balanced growth: Georgia's economic policy priorities in 2017-2020 (Policy Studies Series No. PS/01/17), German Economic Team Georgia / ISET Policy Institute, Berlin / Tbilisi, 2017.

STOPfake, gov, 2019; https: //www. stopfakes. gov/article? id = Georgia – Corruption.

Su G. , "The Belt and Road Initiative in Global Perspectives", *China International Studies*, 2016, No. 57.

Swaine, M. D. , "Chinese Views and Commentary on the 'One Belt, One Road'", China Leadership Monitor, Hoover Institution, 2015, No. 47.

Szczudlik – Tatar, J. , "China's New Silk Road Diplomacy", Policy Paper, 2013.

Tskhovrebova, A. , Silk Road of Chinese Investment, 2016, pp. 60 – 65.

Turp, C. , "Azerbaijan, Georgia, Turkey launch new 'Silk Rail' link", Outlook on Georgia, 2017.

Van Dijk M. P. , Martens P. , The Silk Road and Chinese Interests in Central Asia and the Caucasus: The Case of Georgia, Maastricht School of Management Working Paper, 2016, August, https: //www. msm. nl/resources/uploads/2016/09/MSM – WP2016 – 12 – 1. pdf.

V. Charaia, V. Papava, "Belt and Road Initiative: Implications for Georgia and China – Georgia Economic Relations", *China International Studies*, November 2017.